Communications
in Computer and Information Science    189

T0092615

Vaclav Snasel   Jan Platos
Eyas El-Qawasmeh (Eds.)

# Digital Information Processing and Communications

International Conference, ICDIPC 2011
Ostrava, Czech Republic, July 7-9, 2011
Proceedings, Part II

 Springer

Volume Editors

Vaclav Snasel
Jan Platos
VŠB-Technical University of Ostrava
Faculty of Electrical Engineering and Computer Science
17. listopadu 15, 708 33 Ostrava-Poruba, Czech Republic
E-mail: {vaclav.snasel, jan.platos}@vsb.cz

Eyas El-Qawasmeh
King Saud University
Information Systems Department
Riyadh 11543, Saudi Arabia
E-mail: eyasa@usa.net

ISSN 1865-0929                           e-ISSN 1865-0937
ISBN 978-3-642-22409-6                    e-ISBN 978-3-642-22410-2
DOI 10.1007/978-3-642-22410-2
Springer Heidelberg Dordrecht London New York

Library of Congress Control Number: 2011930951

CR Subject Classification (1998): I.2, H.4, H.3, C.2, D.2, H.5

*Typesetting:* Camera-ready by author, data conversion by Scientific Publishing Services, Chennai, India

Printed on acid-free paper

Springer is part of Springer Science+Business Media (www.springer.com)

# Message from the Chairs

The International Conference on Digital Information Processing and Communications (ICDIPC 2011) co-sponsored by Springer was organized and hosted by the VSB Technical University of Ostrava, Czech Republic, during July 7–9, 2011, in association with the Society of Digital Information and Wireless Communications. ICDIPC a major event in the area of digital information and communications, and serves as a forum for scientists and engineers to meet and present their latest research results, ideas, and papers in the diverse areas of networking, data processing, digital information, computer science, and other related topics in this area.

ICDIPC 2011 included guest lectures and 94 research papers for presentation in the technical session. This meeting was a great opportunity for participants to exchange knowledge and experience. The attendees joined us from around the world to discuss new ideas in the areas of software requirements, development, testing, and other applications related to software engineering. We are grateful to the VSB Technical University of Ostrava, Czech Republic, for hosting this conference. We use this occasion to express our thanks to the Technical Committee and to all the external reviewers. We are grateful to Springer for co-sponsoring the event. Finally, we would like to thank all the participants and sponsors.

Vaclav Snasel
Yoshiro Imai
Jan Platos
Renata Wachowiak-Smolikova

# Preface

On behalf of the ICDIPC 2011 conference, the Program Committee and the VSB Technical University of Ostrava, Czech Republic, we welcome you to the proceedings of The International Conference on Digital Information Processing and Communications (ICDIPC 2011) held at the VSB-Technical University of Ostrava.

The ICDIPC 2011 conference explored new advances in software engineering including software requirements, development, testing, computer systems, and digital information and data communications technologies. It brought together researchers from various areas of software engineering, information sciences, and data communications to address both theoretical and applied aspects of software engineering and computer systems. We hope that the discussions and exchange of ideas will contribute to advancements in the technology in the near future.

The conference received 235 papers, out of which 91 were accepted, resulting in an acceptance rate of 39%. The accepted papers are authored by researchers from 27 countries covering many significant areas of digital information and data communications. Each paper was evaluated by a minimum of two reviewers.

Finally, we believe that the proceedings document the best research in the studied areas. We express our thanks to the VSB Technical University of Ostrava, Czech Republic, Springer, the authors and the organizers of the conference.

Jan Martinovič

# Organization

## General Chairs

Vaclav Snasel                     VSB Technical University of Ostrava,
                                     Czech Republic
Yoshiro Imai                      Kagawa University, Japan

## Program Chairs

Jan Platos                        VSB Technical University of Ostrava,
                                     Czech Republic
Renata Wachowiak-Smolikova        Nipissing University, Canada

## Program Co-chair

Noraziah Ahmad                    Universiti Malaysia Pahang, Malaysia

## Proceedings Chair

Jan Martinovič                    VŠB TU Ostrava, Czech Republic

## Publicity Chairs

Ezendu Ariwa                      London Metropolitan University, UK
Eyas El-Qawasmeh                  King Saud University, Saudi Arabia

# Table of Contents – Part II

## Software Engineering

## Data Compression

## Networks

# Computer Security

# Hardware and Systems

# Multimedia

# Ad Hoc Network

# Artificial Intelligence

# Signal Processing

# Cloud Computing

# Forensics

# Security

# Software and Systems

# Mobile Networking

# Miscellaneous Topics in Digital Information and Communications

# Table of Contents – Part I

# Neural Networks

# Distributed and Parallel Processing

# Biometrics Technologies

# E-Learning

# Information Ethics

# Image Processing

# Information and Data Management

# Comparison of System Dynamics and BPM for Software Process Simulation

Jan Kožusznik, Svatopluk Štolfa, David Ježek, and Štěpán Kuchař

Department of Computer Science
VŠB - Technical University of Ostrava, Faculty of Electrical Engineering
and Computer Science
708 33, Ostrava - Poruba, Czech Republic
{jan.kozusznik,svatopluk.stolfa,david.jezek,
stepan.kuchar}@vsb.cz

**Abstract.** Modeling and simulation of a software process is one way a company can decide which software process and/or its adjustment is the best solution for its current project. Since there are many different approaches to modeling and simulation and all of them have pros and cons, the very first task is the selection of the appropriate and useful model and simulation approach for the current domain and selected conditions. In this paper we focus on applying a discrete event based modeling and simulation approach and system dynamics modeling and simulation approach to the real case study of the software process. The issue is the comparison of the approaches that should answer the questions: what type of information can we get from the simulation results and how can we use it for decisions about the software process.

## 1 Introduction

*Business processes* represent the core of company behaviour. They define activities which companies (i.e. their employees) perform to satisfy their customers. For a definition of the term *business process*, we use the definition from [1]: "*Business process* is a set of one or more linked procedures or *activities* which collectively realize a business objective or policy goal, normally within the structure defining functional roles and relationships." A process of IS development is called *the software process*. *The software process* is also a kind of business process but it has its specific aspects[2].

Software engineering is a discipline that is involved in software process development and maintenance [3]. The main purpose is risk and cost reduction during software development.

A process development could be divided into activities of different kinds as is defined by the process life-cycle engineering [4]. The process life cycle spiral includes these activities: M*eta-modeling*; *Modeling, Analysis; Simulation; Redesign; Visualization*; *Prototyping, walk-through and performance support; Administration; Integration; Environment generation*; *Instantiation and enactment; Monitoring, recording and auditing; History capture and replay; Articulation; Evolution*; *Process asset management*. Description of every activity is provided in [4].

V. Snasel, J. Platos, and E. El-Qawasmeh (Eds.): ICDIPC 2011, Part II, CCIS 189, pp. 1–15, 2011.

Since we are cooperating with local software development companies on the development of the best practices for the software development, our intention was to use modeling and simulation tools for the examination of software processes in companies. Although we know, that there are many approaches and tools [5], at the very beginning we just wanted to use our own business modeling tool called BPStudio [6,7]. BPStudio is a discrete event based modeling and simulation tool that was primarily developed for the modeling and simulation of classic business processes. We have created some models in that tool and soon realized, that the software process is actually very specific. The use of our tool was limited to some extent of getting some of the desired information from the simulation. We have realized that the discrete event based simulation cannot really fulfill all our expectations and we decided to involve some other approaches.

In this paper we are going to describe an application of a discrete event based modeling and simulation approach and a system dynamics modeling and simulation approach to the real case study of the software process. The goal is a comparison of the approaches that should answer the questions: what type of information can we get from the simulation results and how can we use it for decisions about the software process.

This paper is organized as follows: section 2 describes the ways of software process modeling and simulation; section 3 presents our tool and method for discrete event based modeling and simulation; section 4 summarizes the system dynamics approach for modeling and simulation of software processes. In section 5 we present the case study of the software process, its modeling and simulation using both approaches and we discuss result. Section 6 concludes and discusses the future work.

## 2  Software Process Modeling and Simulation

There exist many modeling techniques for process modeling as is mentioned in [8]. On the other hand, the software process is quite specific [9] and it has been characterized as "the most complex endeavor humankind has ever attempted" [10]. However, software process could be modeled formally [11].

The main objectives and goals for software process modeling are defined in [11]:

- facilitate human understanding and communication
- support process improvement
- support process management
- automated guidance in performing process
- automated execution support
- simulation

A simulation is a specific objective for the modeling and it has been used in the last two decades for the software process [12]. For a planned project, it enables calculating or predicting: cost (effort), duration, or its schedule. More specific, main reasons why to simulate is defined in [5]:

- strategic management [13,14]
- planning [14]
- control and operational management [14]

- process improvement and technology adoption [14]
- understanding, [14] and
- training and learning [14]

Generally, simulation helps to achieve the optimal balance among quality, budget and duration [15]. Simulation helps forecast and quantify process trajectories in respect to their actual performance [16].

Here are the leading paradigms used for software process simulation [5]:

- discrete event simulation [17] – controlled by discrete events occurrence, useful for modeling activity orchestration
- continuous simulation System Dynamics [17,18] – controlled by continuous time and change of parameters in process is modeled as system of differential equations
- state-based simulation – not widely used
- hybrid model [19,15] – combines approach of discrete event approach and continuous simulation system dynamics
- knowledge-based simulation[16] - textual and primarily used for process understanding and educational purposes
- agent-based simulation [20] - just starting to be applied to system and software development
- qualitative [21].

## 3 Process Modeling Based on Petri Nets and BPM Method

Petri Nets are one of the formal mechanisms used for the description, verification and simulation of processes. The classical Petri Nets were founded by Carl Adam Petri [22] as a basic tool to describe chemical processes, but since then they have evolved into a very strong process modeling technique that supports temporal aspects of the process, stochastic behavior, hierarchisation of the models and even description of process resources and data (High-Level Petri Nets [23]). Properties of Petri Nets have been studied for over 40 years and this research makes Petri Nets a very well defined mechanism for verification and simulation of processes.

Petri Nets describe the process as a set of transitions (activities, tasks) that are connected with places. A place in the Petri Net can contain any number of tokens that represent available resources or occurrences of appropriate events. Whenever all the places preceding any transition are active (i.e. they contain at least one token), the transition can be performed. By firing the transition one token from each preceding place is taken away and at the same time one token is generated to every following place. This changes the state of the process that is described by the number of tokens in each place. Simulation in Petri Nets is a sequence of these atomic state changes and thus corresponds to the discrete event type of simulation.

Modeling and simulation of software processes and business processes in general presents some specific problems which lead to the creation of specialized modeling methods. The BPM Method [7] is one of these methods based on the Petri Nets approach and is used in the case study presented in this paper. The BPM Method looks at the three elemental views of the process – architecture of the process, objects and resources utilized in the process and the behavior of the process. Each of these aspects is described by one of the models included in the BPM Method.

We had to extend this basic BPM Method by a number of new mechanism that were needed for performing more relevant and more accurate simulations needed for software process assessment and improvement. These extensions are all supported by various types of Petri Nets and their properties and so they don't disturb the formal nature of the method.

The first extension was the addition of stochastic parameters to activities in the coordination model. Stochastic properties were added to the time duration of activities, their waiting time duration and their scenario probability. These parameters and their conversion to the Petri Nets properties were described in our last paper[24]. We also introduced a very important mechanic for running automatic simulations for modeled processes to test their performance for multiple concurrently running projects, sharing limited human and artificial resources in the process, etc. The last extension that we added to the coordination model is the notion of weighted arcs. Arcs in the Petri Net can be weighted by any natural number and this defines how many tokens are consumed from the input place or produced to the output place when the transition is fired. The BPM Method didn't have this property but it is very useful for describing the software processes.

## 4 System Dynamics

System dynamics model software process as a closed-loop version of a system (Fig. 1). Input represents requirements, specifications and resources; otherwise output represents artifacts. The input is transformed to output and the operation is influenced by a controller that changes the behavior of the system.

System dynamic simulation approach was developed by Jay Wright Forrester – published in [25]. It was adopted for the software process modeling purpose by Tarek Abdel-Hamid [12]. This approach is also named continuous system modeling because the model is computed in respect to continuous time. It is the main difference from discrete-event modeling.

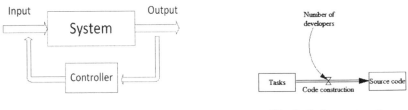

**Fig. 1.** Closed-loop system          **Fig. 2.** Code construction

System dynamics model is composed from these elements (adopted from [26]):

| Element | Notation | Description |
|---|---|---|
| Level | Tasks | It represents an accumulation over time – also called a stock or state variable. |
| Source/Sink |  | It indicates that flows come from or go to somewhere external to the process. |
| Rate |  | It is also called flow and it effect changes in levels. |
| Auxiliary | Only label | It is converter of input to outputs, it helps elaborate the detail of level and rate structures. |
| Information Links |  | It is used to represent the information flow that could influence value of some auxiliary or rate element. |

The system is modeled as a structure of levels connected by flows and information links. Flows between levels represent process entities that are conserved within flow chains. Information links only provide data from auxiliary, flow or level to another auxiliary or flow (Fig. 2). Individual events are not tracked; tasks are modeled by levels and the system could be described by system differential equations.

It has a very simple parallel to the physical system of water basins (level) connected with valued pipes (rates). Pipes could be controlled based on the level of other water basins or other computed factors (auxiliary). Information about control is represented by an information link. The amount of level in a specific time T is equal to:

$$\int_0^T \left( \sum_{i \in Input} f_i(t) + \sum_{o \in Output} f_o(t) \right) dt$$

Functions $f_i(t)$ represent input flows to a level, while $f_o(t)$ represents output flows.

The system dynamics approach to software process modeling represents artifacts (requirements, design, source code, documents, errors, tasks) as value of levels – it set this apart from Petri net approach because it does not distinguish any particular artifact. Transformation or artifact production is modeled by flows where time of duration or productivity is expressed by rate of flow.

## 5 Simulation Example of Software Process

The model of the process consists of eight sub-processes: Requirement analysis, Architectural design, Design, Construction, Testing, Deployment, and Incident management (Fig. 3).

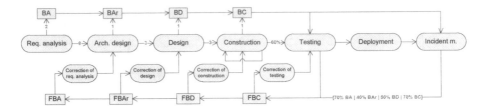

**Fig. 3.** Scheme of the process example

The sub-process, "Requirement analysis," contains two main activities: "Make Analysis document" and "Customer review of an Analysis document". The first activity creates eight software features in one step that are the input to the next activity. The second one creates two analysis faults (BA) in one step that simulates the fault rate of this sub-process.

The next sub-process, "Architectural design," consists of one main activity that is executed for each input feature that is generated in "Requirement analysis." Each execution generates one fault in architectural analysis (BAr) and 3 system architecture blocks that are passed to "Design" sub-process.

Each system architecture block from the previous sub-process is processed in the sub-process "Software design". In that sub-process, three programmers' tasks and one design fault (BD) are generated for each input system architecture block.

Sub-process, "Software construction", is one of the most complicated processes in the model. Basically, the software construction processes all programmers' tasks and the result, the source code, is reviewed by the designer. The activity that represents the revision has two scenarios: one for the successful review which has a probability of 60% and one for the unsuccessful revision with a probability of 40%. Successful revision generates a source code for the sub-process "Testing" and one fault (BC) that was not found in the revision. The unsuccessful revision returns the task to programmer and the task has to be processed again.

The main purpose of the sub-process "Testing" in the model is decreasing the number of faults. This sub-process is separated into two steps represented by two activities. The first activity is testing and has two scenarios, both of them with a probability of 50 percent: one for failure during the testing and one for the test without any failures. If there is a failure, the activity "Select type of fault" is executed. This activity contains four scenarios, each for one type of fault: fault in requirement analysis (FBA), fault in architectural design (FBAr), fault in design (FBD) and fault in the source code (FBC). Each scenario has a different probability (20%, 10%, 10%, 50%).

The sub-process, "Deployment," contains the activity build module. The input to this activity is the tested source code. The weight of this input is 20-∞, which means the module is built if and only if there exists at least 20 tested source codes or more.

Incident management models and simulates developed software operation during usage of the system. Faults could be identified by the customer – identified fault is named "failure" – and they are reported and fixed. Every kind of fault has a specified probability of identification (BA – 70%, BAr – 40%, BD – 50%, BC – 70%). Every fault is identified as failure (terminology for "bugs" classification is specified in [27]) or it becomes a hidden fault (it is the abstraction that is used for simple simulation of the end of the software project).

The BPM method with our extensions described in chapter 3 contains support for many aspects of software process modeling. Decision branching of the process is realized by scenarios of activities. Each scenario of the activity can have a different duration time interval and different probability of execution. Output arcs of the activity are assigned to different scenarios, so tokens are placed in different places based on the selected scenario.

Since the duration of the activity has no exact value in the software process, the BPM method allows for defining minimum and maximum time for the duration of the activity. The random value from this interval is generated for each execution of the activity.

A simulation experiment with the BPM examines one pass through the process. A dependency between a number of work products (tokens in given places) and time is demonstrated in Fig. 4. These artifacts are inspected: Task (for programmers), Faults (not processed), Failures (discovered fault), Hidden faults (these faults have no chance for discovering), and   Built software (every finished build).

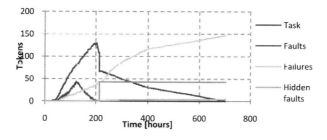

**Fig. 4.** BPM simulation results

A different kind of information is expressed – about a schedule and quality. Three main milestones can be defined in graph – **programmers have started to implement** (50 h) - requirement analysis is finished and a number of tasks starts increasing, when **implementation phase is finished** (210 h) – a number of task stops increasing and keeps near to zero value, because customer operates software and incidents are fixed, and when **software operation is stabilized** (810 h) - number of software builds stops increasing and no other fault could be identified.

BPM simulation use stochastic generator for scenario selection and activity duration, that's make each run of simulation unique. For 500 runs **software operation is stabilized** in range 557h – 1005h with mean in 768h and the total number of failures on end of simulation is in range 110 – 180 with mean in 147.

Software quality is expressed by number of hidden and discovered failures.

The BPM Method is also able to describe human resource utilization in the process thanks to the shared resources extensions we added to the method. It is therefore possible to simulate the process with varying number of available human resources and choose the best balance between the number of resources and their utilization.

This resource utilization is measured by simple counting up the time when the resource is performing any activity.

Utilization is an interesting result of the simulation but it isn't very useful in optimizing the performance of the process. When optimizing the number of resources in the process we aren't interested in answering how long one resource was doing something in the process, but rather how long did we have to wait for the resource when we needed it to perform another activity. One resource can't perform two activities at the same time but processes run concurrently and they very often need the same resource to be able to continue their run (e.g. one developer is needed to implement a new feature to one system and at the same time needs to repair a fault in another system). When this happens the resource somehow has to perform these tasks sequentially:

- finish the first task and then start the second one, or
- pause the first task and return to it after finishing the second one, or
- switch back and forth between these tasks.

In either way one task will have to wait for the completion of the other (or partial completion in the case of the third option). It is therefore important to be able to simulate and measure these waiting times. The BPM Method can easily model this, but is able to model only the first sequentializing option (i.e. finish the first task and then start the second one). Whenever an activity is enabled but the resource isn't available, the BPM Method counts and notes the time needed for the resource to become available to perform the activity. Total waiting time for one resource is then just a sum of these noted times for this appropriate resource.

To show an example of the utilization and waiting time we made a simulation experiment on the modeled software process. The simulation was set to two customer entries and the second entry came to the process a week after the first. The implementation team consisted of one change manager, three developers, two designers, one project manager, one analyst and one tester. The result of this simulation is shown in Fig. 5.

These results show that the most utilized resources are the developers and designers (two designers combined are more utilized than one tester). At the same time, the waiting time shows that this team could profit by hiring another developer because the process had to wait the most for the availability of these resources.

But how much would the process benefit if additional resources were hired? This question can be answered by running simulations with varying number of resources and comparing the utilization results. A following experiment was performed with the same parameters as the former, only the number of developer resources were changed to find the right balance between the number of developers and their utilization. Results of this experiment are shown in Fig. 6.

The utilizations and waiting times of each resource in one role are very similar as seen in Fig. 5, so we used the average value to visualize the graph. This similarity is caused by the fact that all resources have the same properties in the BPM Method. But in reality every human resource is different with diverse sets of abilities and skills and this could be integrated into models and simulations.

Results depicted in Fig. 6 show that the process is highly parallel for a small number of developers, because the utilization of developers is only a bit lower than

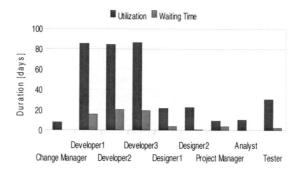

**Fig. 5.** Utilization and Waiting time of human resources

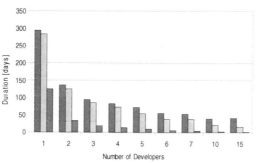

**Fig. 6.** Process performance related to the number of developer resources

the total duration of the process. This property starts to degrade at approximately 5 developers in the team. The next indicator could be the rate of total duration reduction that starts to stagnate at about 6 developers. If we wanted to minimize the waiting time, the ideal number would be 15 developers, but at this point the developers are highly underutilized.

Example implementation with system dynamics is different to the previous due to the mentioned differences. Modeling of specific construction will follow. In advance, system dynamics don't use stochastic parameters. This condition is fulfilled by the substitution of stochastic parameters with their means – activity duration and number of generated artifacts.

The number of artifacts is modeled with levels: Required_features, System_architecture_blocks, Tasks, Revised_source_code etc. Activities transforming input artifacts to output ones are represented by two co-flows (p. 165 in [26]) connected to specific level variables. There is an example of an activity named Design in Fig. 7. This activity represents the creation of the detailed design based on designed system blocks. The detailed design is represented directly by the artifact Task that is processed in the activity Code_construction. The first flow represents processing of input artifacts (System_architecture_blocks created in

Architecture_design activity) and is influenced by the mean value of activity duration and the number of participating employees:

$$Design = \frac{employee}{duration}$$

The second flow means the production of a new artifact (Tasks) and its rate depends on rate of the first one and artifact productivity - number of output artifacts created from one input artifact:

$$Design\_production = Design \cdot productivity$$

In advance, the rate of first flow should be controlled to ensure the nonnegative values of the input level:

$$Design = \begin{cases} 0 \dots if\ System\_architecture\_blocks\ \leq 0 \\ \dfrac{employee}{duration} \dots other\ wise \end{cases}$$

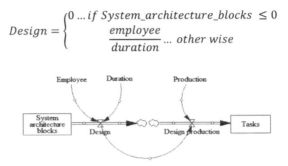

**Fig. 7.** Design

A very similar concept is applied to the fault generation. There exists one flow for every kind of fault. These flows depend on production of a specific artifact. Productivity means in that case how many faults are produced during the production of output tasks. Faults are aggregated by specific level variables – see Fig. 8.

Different scenarios are modeled by a different flow (situation named split flow process on p. 165 in [26]). The probability of every scenario defines the coefficient that is used for representing flow. There is an example of two scenarios during code revision in Fig.9.

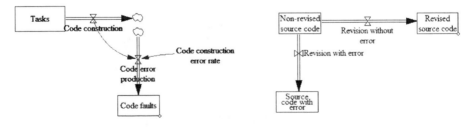
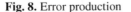

**Fig. 8.** Error production                    **Fig. 9.** Code revision - split flow process

Each scenario has its own separate flow. Code revision without error has a probability of 60% ($p_1$) and code revision with error has a probability of 40% ($p_2$). For simplicity, we consider the same duration for both scenarios. The flow rate is defined for each scenario:

$$code\_revision\_without\_fault = \begin{cases} 0 \dots if\ non\_revised\_code \leq 0 \\ \dfrac{1}{duration} \cdot p_1 \dots other\ wise \end{cases}$$

$$code\_revision\_with\_fault = \begin{cases} 0 \dots if\ non\_revised\_code \leq 0 \\ \dfrac{1}{duration} \cdot p_2 \dots other\ wise \end{cases}$$

In the case of a different duration of scenarios ($t_1$ for scenario without error, $t_2$ for scenario with error), instead of *duration*, the parameter *average_duration* is used, expressing average duration of one element of production:

$$average\_duration = p_1 \cdot t_1 + p_2 \cdot t_2$$

The scenario for code revision without faults has a duration of 0.375 hours and the probability of occurrence is 60% while a scenario with a bug has 0.292 hours and a probability of 40%. The Nominal_duration is equal to

$$p_1 \cdot t_1 + p_2 \cdot t_2 = 0.6 \cdot 0.375 + 0.4 \cdot 0.292 = 0.3418$$

It leads to flow rates:

$$code\_revision\_without\_fault = \begin{cases} 0 \dots if\ non_{revised_{code}} \leq 0 \\ \dfrac{1}{0.3418} \cdot 0.6 \dots other\ wise \end{cases}$$

$$code\_revision\_with\_fault = \begin{cases} 0 \dots if\ non\_revised\_code \leq 0 \\ \dfrac{1}{0.3418} \cdot 0.4 \dots other\ wise \end{cases}$$

There is an allocation of resources in the presented system dynamics model. The reason is modeling of this mechanism is not easy in the system dynamics and we suppose that it does not have a noticeable influence on the presented model.

The main benefit of system dynamics use for simulation is the continuous change of simulation parameters. For demonstration purposes, we identify the productivity of developers during code construction as a changing parameter based on their skills. A course of productivity curve is often named a learning curve and is traditionally defined in terms of unit costs of production. The flow rate for the code construction activity is defined:

$$code\_construction = \frac{employee}{duration \cdot productivity}$$

The most widely used representation for learning curves is called the log-linear learning curve, expressed as (mentioned on page 230 in [26]):

$$productivity = a \cdot x^n$$

An attribute $a$ is the cost of the first unit, $x$ is cumulative output, and $n$ is the learning curve slope. The slope is related to the learning rate expressed in a percentage (value from interval <0, 1>) and it defines that cost scales by $p\%$ for every doubling of accumulative output. After it, for slope is true:

$$n = \log_2 p$$

Cumulative output is equal to the number of produced units of source code increased by one (cumulative output express the number of already produced units).

We will construct a graph with results for similar artifacts as was mentioned previously. The constructed graph is in Fig. 10. The results are very similar to the BPM. The main difference is in the progression of the amount of faults and failures, and at the time the implementation ends (the BPM simulation provides 200 while the SD provides 230). The progression of the amount of faults ranges from 0 to 210 hours because the BPM model counts all faults and after the first build of software deployed to the customer (after 210h), some of the faults are categorized as hidden. From this point, the progression of the SD is similar. The SD provides continuous modeling and the amount of build software is greater than zero (float number) much earlier than in the BPM simulation because the BPM uses an integer number and the number of the build software is increased from 0 to 1 after 216 hours. The amount of build software is an important value because a value greater than 0 is a condition for incident management to produce incidents from customers. Reported incidents increase the number failures and the number of tasks.

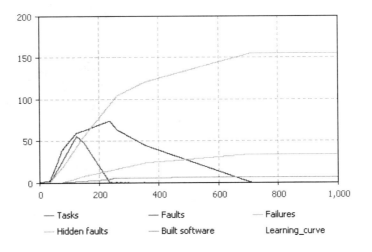

**Fig. 10.** System dynamics result

Different results are displayed when the model of the learning curve is enabled (Fig. 11). The implementation phase is finished after 170 hours but the software operation is stabilized in almost the same time as in the previous model. It indicates that the productivity of programmers only has an influence on the implementation phase, while it is not bottleneck according to the duration of the whole project.

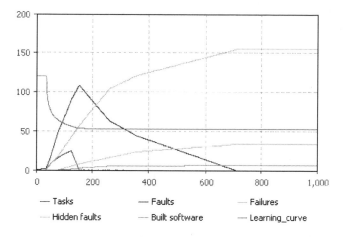

**Fig. 11.** Simulation with learning curve

## 6 Conclusion

In this paper we described and compared two different approaches to software process simulation – the BPM Method as a representative of discrete event simulation and system dynamics for continuous simulations. Even though both approaches can be very effectively used for simulating software processes, they vary in difficulty of modeling and they serve different purposes due to their inherent advantages.

Models of the BPM Method describe the real sequence of activities performed in the process exactly and can be easily fine grained by hierarchisation. However, this detailed specification can backfire because the processes tend to be very complex and every activity is important. This is particularly relevant for simulations, because the model has to be very detailed to acquire accurate results. This can lead to a generation of an enormous number of diagrams that are hard to read and manage. On the other hand, the BPM Method is very useful in its management of specific resources in the process and their utilization. Each resource and customer request in the process can have different properties and abilities and this can be used to control the flow in the process and the possibility of choosing the right resource for the job. This advantage could even be utilized to support the company's management choices by the suggestion that skills are lacking in the process. Human resources in the process could then be trained to use these skills and thus raise the effectiveness of the process. We are planning to focus on this problem in our future research.

On the other hand, system dynamics can be used on a more abstract level than the BPM Method and does not need to be so specific. This is made possible by their continuous approach to everything in the process. System dynamics is very useful for its feedback options that can influence various related parameters of the process like learning and improvement during the process, communication overhead, error rates and even increasing experience of human resources. Modeling these parameters by the discrete event methods is difficult and confuses the complex models even more. Another important difference is modeling the continuous production of some artifact. An activity consuming this artifact could start execution even if this artifact is not fully finished.

# 7 Future Work

The previous comparison has some weaknesses. The System dynamics model was practically identical to the BPM model, to ensure comparable results. However, modeling possibilities are quite different – every parameter (delay, error rate, productivity) could change during simulation. This possibility was presented by the addition of a learning curve to the example. In our opinion, this possibility probably better reflects the reality; therefore, we would like to compare these two approaches with real company values and use every possible feature for precise representation of the reality during the creation of each model.

**Acknowledgements.** This research has been supported by the internal grant agency of VSB-TU of Ostrava - SP2011/56 Knowledge approach to the modeling, simulation and visualization of software processes.

# References

1. Workflow Management Coalition: Workflow Management Coalition Terminology & Glossary (Document No. WFMC-TC-1011). Workflow Management Coalition Specification (1999)
2. Štolfa, S., Kožusznik, J., Košinár, M., Duží, M., Číhalová, M., Vondrák, I.: Building Process Definition with Ontology Background. Paper presented at the CISIM 2010, Krakow, Poland (2010)
3. Humphrey, W.S.: A Discipline for Software Engineering. Addison-Wesley Professional, Reading (1995)
4. Scacchi, W., Mi, P.: Process Life Cycle Engineering: A Knowledge-Based Approach and Environment. Intelligent Systems in Accounting, Finance, and Management 6, 83–107 (1997)
5. Raffo, D.M., Wakeland, W.: Moving Up the CMMI Capability and Maturity Levels Using Simulation (trans: Institute SE) (2008)
6. Vondrák, I.: Business Process Studio, version 3.0. VŠB – Technical University of Ostrava (2000)
7. Vondrák, I., Szturc, R., Kružel, M.: Company Driven by Process Models. Paper presented at the European Concurrent Engineering Conference ECEC 1999, Erlangen-Nuremberg, Germany (1999)
8. Vergidis, K., Tiwari, A., Majeed, B.: Business Process Analysis and Optimization: Beyond Reengineering. IEEE Transactions on Systems, Man, and Cybernetics, Part C: Applications and Reviews 38(1), 69–82 (2008)

9. Raffo, D.M.: Modeling software processes quantitatively and assessing the impact of potential process changes on process performance. Ph.D. thesis, Carnegie Mellon University (1996)
10. Brooks, F.P.: No Silver Bullet - Essence and Accidents of Software Engineering (reprinted form information processing 1986). Computer 20(4), 10–19 (1987)
11. Curtis, B., Kellner, M.I., Over, J.: Process modeling. Commun. ACM 35(9), 75–90 (1992)
12. Abdel-Hamid, T., Madnick, S.: Software Project Dynamics: An Integrated Approach. Prentice Hall, Englewood Cliffs (1991)
13. Raffo, D., Wernick, P.: Software process simulation modelling. Journal of Systems and Software 59(3), 223–225 (2001)
14. Raffo, D.M., Kellner, M.I.: Empirical analysis in software process simulation modeling. Journal of Systems and Software 53(1), 31–41 (2000)
15. Rus, I., Collofello, J., Lakey, P.: Software process simulation for reliability management. Journal of Systems and Software 46(2-3), 173–182 (1999)
16. Scacchi, W.: Experience with software process simulation and modeling. Journal of Systems and Software 46(2-3), 183–192 (1999)
17. Raffo, D.M., Vandeville, J.V., Martin, R.H.: Software process simulation to achieve higher CMM levels. Journal of Systems and Software 46(2-3), 163–172 (1999)
18. Ruiz, M., Ramos, I., Toro, M.: Using dynamic modeling and simulation to improve the COTS software process. In: Bomarius, F., Iida, H. (eds.) PROFES 2004. LNCS, vol. 3009, pp. 568–581. Springer, Heidelberg (2004)
19. Donzelli, P., Iazeolla, G.: Hybrid simulation modelling of the software process. Journal of Systems and Software 59(3), 227–235 (2001)
20. David, N., Sichman, J.S., Coelho, H.: Towards an emergence-driven software process for agent-based simulation. In: Sichman, J.S., Bousquet, F., Davidsson, P. (eds.) MABS 2002. LNCS (LNAI), vol. 2581, pp. 89–104. Springer, Heidelberg (2003)
21. Zhang, H., Huo, M., Kitchenham, B., Jeffery, R.: Qualitative simulation model for software engineering process. In: Proceedings of Australian Software Engineering Conference (2006)
22. Petri, C.A.: Kommunikation mit Automaten. PhD thesis, Institut für instrumentelle Mathematik, Bonn (1962)
23. van der Aalst, W.M.P.: Putting high-level Petri nets to work in industry. Computers in Industry 25(1), 45–54 (1994), doi:10.1016/0166-3615(94)90031-0
24. Kuchař, Š., Kožusznik, J.: BPM Method Extension for Automatic Process Simulation. In: Lencse, G. (ed.) 8th Industrial Simulation Conference 2010, Budapest, Hungary, Ghent, Belgium, June 7 - 9 (2010)
25. Forrester, J.W.: Industrial Dynamics. Pegasus Communications (1961)
26. Madachy, R.J.: Software Process Dynamics, 2nd edn. Wiley-IEEE Press (2008)
27. IEEE Std 610.12-1990: IEEE Standard Glossary of Software Engineering Terminology. IEEE Standards Board (1990)

# Knowledge Based Approach to Software Development Process Modeling

Jan Kožusznik and Svatopluk Štolfa

Department of Computer Science
VŠB - Technical University of Ostrava,
Faculty of Electrical Engineering and Computer Science
708 33, Ostrava - Poruba, Czech Republic
{jan.kozusznik,svatopluk.stolfa}@vsb.cz

**Abstract.** Modeling a software process is one way a can company decide which software process and/or its adjustment is the best solution for the current project. Modeling is the way the process is presented or simulated. Since there are many different approaches to modeling and all of them have pros and cons, the very first task is the selection of an appropriate and useful modeling approach for the current goal and selected conditions. In this paper, we propose an approach based on ontologies.

**Keywords:** ontology, knowledge representation, modeling, simulation, software development process.

## 1 Introduction

Modeling the process is always driven by the specific goal. The goal has to be selected before the modeling is performed, because the modeling approach depends on the desired point of view and that point of view depends on the goal. Our intention is to develop a modeling approach that can be used, at least at the beginning of the modeling, without the knowledge of the real goal. We decided to use an ontology based approach that could fulfill some necessary properties: *iterativeness* – the model can be modeled from the abstract viewpoint and then refined; *transformation* between different types of model approaches; *integration of approaches* – avoiding duplicities when modeling by one approach and then switching to another.

The goal of this paper is to describe how to use ontologies for the creation of such software process models.

This paper is organized as follows: section 2 provides an introduction to the problem of the software development process, section 3 describes the most current software process modeling, section 4 presents our knowledge-based approach to software process modeling, section 5 discusses the properties of using an ontology and the OWL for process modeling, section 6 demonstrates the presented approach of the case study, section 7 concludes, and section 8 discusses our future work.

V. Snasel, J. Platos, and E. El-Qawasmeh (Eds.): ICDIPC 2011, Part II, CCIS 189, pp. 16–28, 2011.

## 2  Software Development Process

*Business processes* represent the core of company behaviour. They define activities which companies (their employees) perform to satisfy their customers. For a definition of the term business process, we use the definition from (WfMC, 1999): "Business process is a set of one or more linked procedures or *activities* which collectively realize a business objective or policy goal, normally within the structure defining functional roles and relationships." A process of IS development is called *the software process*. The software process is also a kind of business process but it has its specific aspects.

Software engineering is a discipline that is involved in software process development and maintenance [1]. The main purpose is risk and cost reduction during software development.

A process development could be divided into activities of different kind, as is defined by the process life-cycle engineering [2]. The process life cycle spiral includes these activities: M*eta-modeling*; *Modeling, Analysis; Simulation; Redesign; Visualization*; *Prototyping, walk-through and performance support; Administration; Integration; Environment generation*; *Instantiation and enactment; Monitoring, recording and auditing; History capture and replay; Articulation; Evolution*; *Process asset management*. A description of every activity is provided in [2].

## 3  Modeling Discipline

Modeling is often used in other disciplines and it is beneficial for the software development process. The term model means a representation of one system – modeled system – by another system. The modeled system often comes from reality or another artificial complex system and the model is its simplification – abstraction. Three functions of abstraction for modeling during database system development are defined [3,4] – see Fig. 1.

- — *Aggregation* – entity   containing other parts from modeled domain is represented by one entity in the model;
- — *Classification* – class of similar entities and their features is identified;
- — *Generalization* – different set class of entities are unified into one class with similar properties.

There exist many modeling techniques for process modeling as is mentioned in [5]. On the other hand, the software development process is quite specific [6] and it has been characterized as "the most complex endeavor humankind has ever attempted" [7]. Nonetheless, the software process could be modeled formally [8].

A knowledge-based approach to software process engineering has already been dealt with in [9-11]. The benefits of the knowledge-based  approach to modeling and simulation(KBS) compared to a Discrete-Event Simulation (DES - [6]) and System Dynamics (SD - [12]) are discussed in [13].

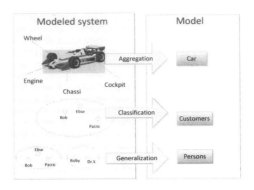

**Fig. 1.** Functions of abstraction

## 3.1 Knowledge Based Approach to Process Modeling

Summarising the comparison of the KBS approach to DES and SD approaches provided in [13], we now list the activities supported by particular models in Table 1. Explanation of items in Table 1:

— *S* – this activity is fully supported by given modeling approach;
— *SL* - this activity is supported by given modeling approach but different approach appears to be more appropriate;
— *LT* – this activity is not supported by given approach, but, in our opinion, this restriction is due to the framework used for the model development rather than due to the approach in general;
— *WS* – this activity seems that the given approach will most likely never be supported.

Based on the previous summary, the knowledge-based approach has been chosen also as primary tool for capturing and dealing with software process for SPI purposes.

The selected approach was mainly inspected as a tool for process simulation but it is strong enough to be used during the whole process lifecycle. It also deals with problems or goals defined in the introduction:

— iterativeness – mentioned by Redesign and Evolution;
— transformation – support in principle – defined by mappings between different domains;
— an integration of other methodologies –  mapping or transformation could be defined between different approaches.

## 3.2 State-of-the-Art of Knowledge Based Approach

A well-defined meta-model of a software process[1] for the knowledge-based approach is described in [11]. Authors defined *a unified resource model* (URM) for integrating types of objects appearing in models of the software process. Their URM consists of resource *classes* and *relations* between different types of resources. The type of

---

[1] Authors use term model of software development.

**Table 1.** Summary of comparison of different approaches

| | Knowledge-based | Discrete event | System dynamics |
|---|---|---|---|
| Meta-modeling | **S**(ontology can be easily managed) | **SL** | |
| Modeling | **S**(supports an incremental development of a model) | **SL** | |
| Analysis | **S** | **SL** (supported only by few implementations of DES) | |
| Simulation | **S** | **SL** (support only the monolithic simulation) | |
| Redesign | **S** (supports an automatic transformation) | **SL** | |
| Visualization | **LT** | **S** | |
| Prototyping, walk-through and performance support | **S** | **LT** | |
| Administration | **S** | | |
| Integration | | **LT** | |
| Environment generation | | **LT** | |
| Instantiation and enactment | | **LT** | |
| Monitoring, recording and auditing | **S** | | |
| History capture and replay | **S** | | |
| Articulation | **S** | **WS** | |
| Evolution | **S** (supports an automatic transformation) | **SL** | |
| Process asset management | **S** | **LT** | |

resource could be a *developed system*, a *document* (or more generally artifact), a development *tool*, a particular *software process²* and others. This meta-model defines the generic model that consists of tree objects: *resource, simple-resource, aggregate-resource*; and relations among these classes: *is-a-subclass; has-member-resource, has-neighbors, has-resource-specs*. This generic model is specialized into five specific models for *developed software-system, document, agent, tool* and *process*. In every model, object types are specified – *Resource* becomes *Tool, Simple-resource* becomes *Program* and *aggregate-resource* becomes *Toolkit* in the tool model. Additional relations among resources from different model have also been added.

However, the previous approach was based on the platform for AI and knowledge representation named Knowledgecraft. This platform had been developed by the Carnegie Group in the 80's and 90's [14]. At the present, this platform is not available any more. It was based on Common Lisp language and knowledge definition by frames.

## 4  Suggested Approach

The current mainstream for knowledge representation and its use is in the applications of semantic webs[15] and multi-agent systems.

There was already an applied concept of ontology based modeling on process modeling and simulations. A model represented by an ontology was transformed into a description for JSIM simulation system [16]. The ontology approach offers basic functions of abstraction for modeling. The generalization is represented by the relation "superclass" between sets. The conceptualization is represented by sets and individuals. The aggregation is not directly supported but it could be represented by object property.  To analyse, design and build the semantic annotation of a software process, we follow the W3C recommendations on OWL/DLW3C, see [17].

OWL is a language classified as a description logic-based language that is a subset of the first-order language. The language offers definitions of:

— sets (the term class will be used instead of set according to OWL terminology in the rest of the paper) and their individuals - classification,
— relations between sets – inheritance, disjunction, equivalence;
— various constraints of classes;
— possible relations between individuals – object properties.

Particular constructions used in the model of the software development process will be discussed later.

## 5  Specificities of a Modeling by a Ontology and OWL

The presented approach which uses OWL has some disadvantages – it lacks the possibility of defining that an individual represents a class again (this possibility is called the *multilevel classification* in the rest of the paper). This could be perceived as

---

² Authors use term development process.

a pointless issue but this possibility is advocated in [4]. Multilevel classification is also important during the use of meta-model based OMG specifications [18,19].

A meta-model represents classification abstraction of a modeled element – it defines basic concepts and their relations used during modeling (its conceptualization). It defines modeling language or modeling methodology. The term "meta" expresses that it is a conceptualization of elements used for modeling. Usability of multilevel classification for (meta)modeling is presented in Fig. 2. "Role" represents a class of individuals that stand for individual roles in the presented meta-model ("Project manager", "Analyst"). This relation is represented by a dashed line marked as "is item of". On the other hand, these particular individuals represent a set of other individuals (people): in the role "Project manager" – John; in the role "Designer" –Alice, Lilian (same individual as in class "Project manager"). Relations could be treated similarly. The link between "Role" and "WorkUnit" (named "carries out") defines the relation with the domain of specific classes. The link between "Project manager" and "Requirement analysis" is an item of the relation, but it defines another set of links between individuals from the specific classes – it defines a relation between the classes.

We are aware of this limitation and our initial approach will prevent the necessity of multilevel classification. This could be done by a different modeling approach. A relation named "contains" can be defined as expressing that a specific role contains a specific person. There is also a different approach in the manner of the meta-model definition. The class "Role" can be defined as a set of individuals that play some role. The subset "Designer" defines a set of persons in the role "Designer". The choice between defining by individuals and by class depends on the level of abstraction. Particular people will be defined during software development process modeling. Roles are quite abstract and unreal objects so they are expressed by class.

There is another specificity of OWL use for modeling. A link cannot be defined between a set and another set or individual. Only links between individuals (it is called an object property in OWL) can be defined.

The presented modeling process is based on a top-bottom approach to modeling. A meta-model that is based on previous studies ([19]) is used. It becomes more specific

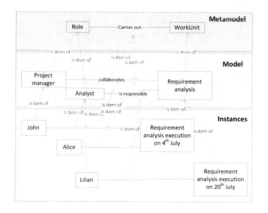

**Fig. 2.** Multilevel classification

during modeling. However, the opposite sequence is also possible. Individuals and their specialized sets are defined during modeling. Their structure could lead to a more general system of sets which defines a common meta-model.

# 6   Software Process Model Creation

Our presented example process is an easy development process that is followed in a middle-sized software company. The input to this process is "Customer Needs" and the output is a "Developed System". The role "Project manager" is responsible for the execution of this process (Fig. 3). The "Software Development Process (SDP)" consists of four sub-processes (Fig. 4): "Requirements Elicitation and Analysis (REA)", "Software Design (SD)", "Software Construction (SC)" and "System Testing (ST)". In this level of abstraction, new roles are present. The names of roles and their responsibilities are: "Analyst" that is responsible for REA, "Designer" is responsible for SD, "Programmer" is responsible for SC, and "Tester" is responsible for ST. Each sub-process consumes and produces some artifacts: "Customer Needs" is input to the REA. "Analysis Document" part "Requirements Specification" is created there and is passed to the SD. SD sub-process produces Design part of an analysis document. Design goes to the "Software Construction" and the "Developed system" is created there. In ST, several tests are performed and the output is a "Developed System" and "Test Report". If necessary, each sub-process can be refined to more detail as is shown in Fig. 5 and so on. Its activities are defined as responsible roles connected with solid lines, and cooperating roles connected with dashed lines.

## 6.1   Meta-model Creation

A creation of the software process meta-model is defined in [19]. This paper provides a clear overview of the problem. Different approaches and methodologies are considered - including the OMG business process definition meta-model (for more details see [20]). The authors suggested a simple mechanism for the integration of multiple meta-models into simple cores with possible flexible extension for the purpose of further modeling. 5 metamodels from different viewpoints are identified: *activity* (Fig. 6), *product, decision, context* and *strategy*; and from one integrating part- *process domain meta-model* (Fig. 7).These mentioned meta-models are defined

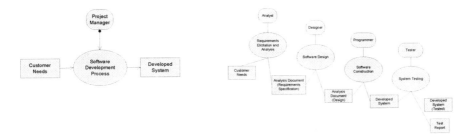

**Fig. 3.** Software development process      **Fig. 4.** Sub-processes of a Software Development Process

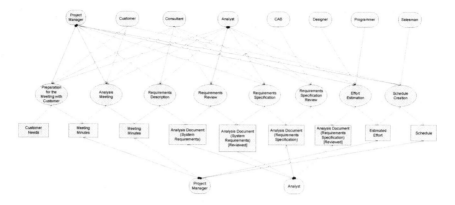

**Fig. 5.** Sub-process REA

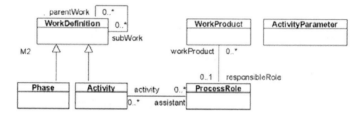

**Fig. 6.** Activity-oriented metamodel - [19]

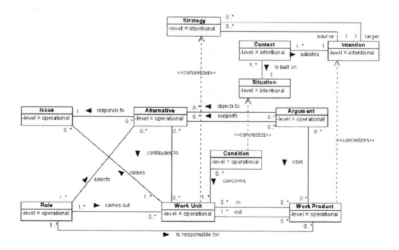

**Fig. 7.** Process domain metamodel - [19]

by MOF – Meta-Object Facility that is the language used for "meta-model" creation – MOF is defined in a "meta-metamodel" level). Activity and process domain metamodel are presented in (figures originate from [19]).

Before modeling, these metamodels are combined into one that contains selected subclasses of every part. The selection is based on the demands placed on the process.

We have created a separate ontology for every part of the meta-model. These ontologies are defined in OWL by the tool Protégé. Classes from particular parts of the meta-model are represented by ontology classes, while associations are represented by object properties and inheritance is represented by sub-classing. There are two types of associations, which differ:

— associations with a name where names of roles are omitted – e.g. association "raises" between classes "Work Unit" and "Issue" in a process domain meta-model,
— and associations where only names of roles are defined – association between "Activity" and "ProcessRole" with roles "activity" and "assistant" in the activity-oriented meta-model.

Associations with names are represented by one object property with the same name and one inverse object property where the name has the suffix "!". "Domains" and "Ranges" are selected according to a defined direction of the meaning of the association. Object property "raises" has defined domain as class "Work Unit" and range as class "Issue". There also exists the inverse object property "raises!" where the domain and the range are swapped.

Associations with two defined roles are represented by two object properties that are inverse. The name of every object property $– name(object\_property)$- is constructed by this pattern:

$$name(object\_property) = name(class) + "." + name(role) \qquad (1)$$

Value $name(class)$ represents name of class that defines "Domains". Value $name(role)$ represents name of role of class that defines "Ranges" of the relation. Association between "Activity" and "ProcessRole" with roles "activity" and "assistant" is represented by these object properties:

— $ProcessRole.activity$ with domain "ProcessRole" and with range "Activity"
— $Activity.assistant$ with domain "Activity" and with range "ProcessRole"

Every specialized meta-model ontology imports a core ontology that represents process domain meta-model – see Fig. 8. The import of ontologies is directly supported by OWL and it means that the importing ontology includes all elements from the imported ontology (also other imports). In a case when both ontologies contain two elements with the same name, the elements are distinguished by the namespace of its origin ontology. This situation is even eliminated in our presented approach because the same name for elements means the same things. On the other hand, there are classes that have different names in different ontologies but present the same class [19]. It is solved in the specific ontology that imports the core ontology – there is defined that a specific class is equivalent to the same class (but with a different name). Class "WorkDefinition" from an activity-oriented meta-model is defined as equivalent to "WorkUnit" from the process domain meta-model. It is defined in the ontology representing the activity-oriented metamodel.

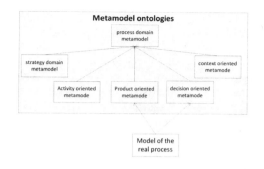

**Fig. 8.** Ontology import structure

## 6.2 Model Creation

Model creation of the example process starts from the meta-model that is defined in a previous section. The model is created as an ontology in the Protégé tool that imports necessary meta-model ontologies. Since we model the prescription of the process, the classes are modeled. When there is a need to model the particular execution of the process, modeling by the entities is used. This type of modeling is not described in this text.

At a high level of abstraction, our example process consists of three basic elements that are modeled as a specialization of three meta-model classes. The SDP process is a specialization of "Work Unit", "Project Manager" is a specialization of "Role", and "Customer Needs" and "Developed System" are specializations of "Work Product". "Project Manager" is responsible for the execution of the SPD. This is modeled as a restriction on the "Project Manager": "Project manager" can only carry out the SDP.

For the simplification of the modeling of the example, let us say that the responsibility and cooperation of the "Work Unit" is the same. Otherwise the solution would be the creation of the sub-property of the "carries_out" property from the meta-model and appropriate restrictions would be created.

The same principle of property restrictions is applied to the connections of the "Customer Needs" that is input to the SDP ("WorkProduct.in" property with domain "Work Product" and range "Work Unit") and "Developed System" that is output from the SDP ("WorkProduct.out" property with domain "Work product" and range "Work Unit").

When we want to model a more detailed description of the model (Fig. 5), we can use an aggregation function for the description of the connection between the SDP process and its sub-processes – REA, SD, SC, and ST that are defined as a specialization of the "Work_Unit". The aggregation is realized in the SDP "Work_Unit" by the property "subWork":

- SDP "subWork" only (REA, SD, SC, ST)
- SDP "subWork" some REA
- SDP "subWork" some SD
- SDP "subWork" some SC
- SDP "subWork" some ST

The same principle is used for the aggregation of "Requirements Specification" and "Design" into "Analysis Document". The responsibilities of the roles are modeled by the "carry_out" property and in/out "Work Product" for the new "Work Units" are defined by the "WorkProduct.in" and "Work.Product.out" properties.

One new situation has to be solved, "Customer Needs" is the input into the SDP and REA that is in fact part of the SDP. The solution is the restriction on the "Customer Needs" property "WorkProduct.in" only SDP or REA.

Then, when there is a need for another lower level abstraction, the same principles for modeling are used again: specialization and splitting-up into components as inverse procedures to the generalization and aggregation functions of abstraction.

This type of modeling can be used for the modeling of well-known domains, where the meta-models are already defined. Otherwise, the meta-models and models must be recognized and defined first; three functions of abstraction are used.

# 7  Conclusion

An approach of process modeling with ontologies (or formal knowledge) has many benefits, as was discussed in the beginning of this paper. Another valuable benefit is the possibility of combining more meta-model ontologies during modeling. A mechanism of ontology import is used for this purpose. One metamodel ontology could also extend (import) another ontology metamodel. Equivalence between semantically same classes with different names could be used. The structure of the ontology is simultaneously proved with an inference machine during model creation.

However, the great disadvantage is that fact that modeling itself is very troublesome. A huge model becomes unclear. On the other hand, it is only a limitation of the tool which is used – process modeling in OWL is similar to a PDF creation in a text editor. It is necessary to create a superstructure over it. The superstructure could provide a visual overview with a possibility of ontology creation. It will be discussed in the next chapter.

# 8  Future Works

The superstructure of the direct ontology definition will be created in the future. Our vision is to provide a graphical editor. The editor will provide a view of a selected part of the model. There is also a planned feature for the simple creation of typical model constructs.

Methodology creation is another important issue. A full overview of modeling construction or patterns will be arranged for the purpose of process modeling. For every construction, a corresponding implementation in OWL will be defined. The methodology will solve the problem of when to use individuals for modeling and when to use subclasses.

The created model is not the goal itself. It is necessary to utilize its possibilities. Model simulation is possible. The model needs to be enriched with information about the order of the particular activities. A mechanism of ontology extension will again be used. A transformation to a simulation model follows. Transformations for various simulation approaches will be defined. A process enactment is similar to the process simulation and it is planned to be developed. Apart from simulation or enactment, various analyses could also be used.

The modeling possibility of OWL is limited. For example, it does not support the multilevel classification. An examination of another language is our next work. A platform OpenCYC exists that is even available as an open source. The platform is declared as knowledgebase with inference machine. The language for knowledge formulation is used. This language is first order logic (FOL) with some constructions from second order logic.

**Acknowledgements.** This research has been supported by the internal grant agency of VSB-TU of Ostrava - SP2011/56 Knowledge approach to the modeling, simulation and visualization of software processes.

# References

1. Humphrey, W.S.: A Discipline for Software Engineering. Addison-Wesley Professional, Reading (1995)
2. Scacchi, W., Mi, P.: Process Life Cycle Engineering: A Knowledge-Based Approach and Environment. Intelligent Systems in Accounting, Finance, and Management 6, 83–107 (1997)
3. Smith, J.M., Smith, D.C.P.: Database abstractions: aggregation and generalization. ACM Trans. Database Syst. 2(2), 105–133 (1977), doi:10.1145/320544.320546
4. Machado, E.P., Traina Jr., C., Araujo, M.R.B.: Classification abstraction: An intrinsic element in database systems. In: Yakhno, T. (ed.) ADVIS 2000. LNCS, vol. 1909, p. 57. Springer, Heidelberg (2000)
5. Vergidis, K., Tiwari, A., Majeed, B.: Business Process Analysis and Optimization: Beyond Reengineering. IEEE Transactions on Systems, Man, and Cybernetics, Part C: Applications and Reviews 38(1), 69–82 (2008)
6. Raffo, D.M.: Modeling software processes quantitatively and assessing the impact of potential process changes on process performance. Ph.D. thesis, Carnegie Mellon University (1996)
7. Brooks, F.P.: No Silver Bullet - Essence and Accidents of Software Engineering (reprinted form information processing 86, 1986). Computer 20(4), 10–19 (1987)
8. Curtis, B., Kellner, M.I., Over, J.: Process modeling. Commun. ACM 35(9), 75–90 (1992)
9. Garg, P.K., Scacchi, W.: ISHYS: Designing an Intelligent oftware Hypertext System. IEEE Expert: Intelligent Systems and Their Applications 4(3), 52–63 (1989)
10. Mi, P., Scacchi, W.: A Knowledge-Based Environment for Modeling and Simulating Software Engineering Processes. IEEE Trans. on Knowl. and Data Eng. 2(3), 283–294 (1990), doi:10.1109/69.60792
11. Mi, P., Scacchi, W.: A meta-model for formulating knowledge-based models of software development. Decis. Support Syst 17(4), 313–330 (1996),
    http://dx.doi.org/10.1016/0167-92369600007-3
12. Madachy, R.J.: Software Process Dynamics, 2nd edn. Wiley-IEEE Press (2008)
13. Scacchi, W.: Experience with software process simulation and modeling. Journal of Systems and Software 46(2-3), 183–192 (1999)

14. Laurent, J.-P., Ayel, J., Thome, F., Ziebelin, D.: Comparative Evaluation of Three Expert System Development Tools: Kee, Knowledge Craft, Art. The Knowledge Engineering Review 1(04), 18–29 (1984), doi:10.1017/S0269888900000631
15. Allemang, D., Hendler, J.: Semantic Web for the Working Ontologist: Effective Modeling in RDFS and OWL. Morgan Kaufmann, San Francisco (2008)
16. Silver, G.A., Lacy, L.W., Miller, J.A.: Ontology based representations of simulation models following the process interaction world view. Paper Presented at the Proceedings of the 38th Conference on Winter Simulation, Monterey, California (2006)
17. W3C OWL 2 Web Ontology Language (2009),
    http://www.w3.org/TR/owl2-overview/
18. Object Management Group(OMG), OMG Unified Modeling Language(OMG UML), Infrastructure, Version 2.3 (2010)
19. Hug, C., Front, A., Rieu, D., Henderson-Sellers, B.: A method to build information systems engineering process metamodels. Journal of Systems and Software 82(10), 1730–1742 (2009), doi:10.1016/j.jss.2009.05.020
20. Object Management Group(OMG), Business Process Definition MetaModel (BPDM),Version 1.0 (2008)

# User Interfaces and Usability Issues Form Mobile Applications

Jakub Larysz, Martin Němec, and Radoslav Fasuga

VŠB-Technical University of Ostrava,
Faculty of Electrical Engineering and Computer Science,
17. Listopadu 15/2172, 708 33 Ostrava Poruba, Czech Republic
Jakub.Larysz@vsb.cz, Martin.Nemec@vsb.cz, Radoslav.Fasuga@vsb.cz

**Abstract.** The possibilities of using GUI in environment of the mobile communication technologies are dicussed in the present article regarding the capabilities of mobile operating system Android, Windows Phone 7 and iOS. The mobile platform controls are comparted to the applications programming possibilities in one programming language and to the development environment with the possibility of deploying applications to the multiple operating systems. Our results are summarized in the conclusion.

**Keywords:** Android, Windows Phone 7, iOS, Java, XML, C#, XAML, Objective-C, Xcode, Graphical User Interface (GUI).

## 1 Introduction

When looking into the history of mobile phones one can observe how fast the user interface has been changing, and transforming the hardware elements into the software form. Nearly forty years have passed since 1973when the first prototype of an analog mobile phone was presented passed. Typically of the modern technology the development moves forward quickly.

Nowadays, the electronics can be met at every step, the cell phones do not longer perform only the role of a communication device.Mobile phones are ideally to replace offices, livingrooms or tourist guides. Mobile technologies are still going forward and keep pace with the new information technologies.

Moreover, operating systems are installed in the current mobile devices, the performance of these systems is comparable to the desktop operating systems,thus a huge variety of the use of themobile communication technologies is offered. Every task to be performed with such device is influenced by their technical equipment (e.g. GPS modules, camera, Internet connection via WiFi, etc.) and by the applications that are installed.

With the rising popularity of smartphones and the opportunities offered by this device the requirements regarding mobile devices applications and user interface are increasing. This article focuses on the three most popular technologies, the possibilities ofcreating GUI [1] and the possibility of efficient application programming (for all platforms at once).

V. Snasel, J. Platos, and E. El-Qawasmeh (Eds.): ICDIPC 2011, Part II, CCIS 189, pp. 29–43, 2011.

## 2 State of the Art

Nowadays there is a large number of the operating systems and different versions of mobile communication technology. Moreover, the choice of OS tested is determined by its popularity among the users. As shown in the survey [2] the most popular mobile devices with increasing market share include the iPhone and Apple iPad, which operate on the iOS operating system.The second most populár one is a rapidly evolving Android by Google. The third platform to compare is the innovative Windows Phone 7 by Microsoft, which aborted the further development of the Windows Mobile operating system and set a new direction in the form of a Windows Phone 7 operating system. It should be noted that the operating system  Windows Phone 7 was officially launched on the European market not before October 21st 2010.

The division of the market at the end of 2010 is shown on Figure 1. The largest part of the chart includes other operating systems on the market at present, nevertheless they display a downward trend in their popularity. However, only the operating systems, with the increasing popularity and prevalence are discussed in the present paper

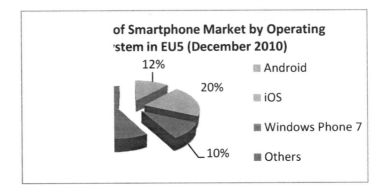

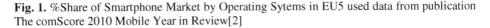

**Fig. 1.** %Share of Smartphone Market by Operating Sytems in EU5 used data from publication The comScore 2010 Mobile Year in Review[2]

It is expected that Windows Phone 7 is to be chosen due to its growing market share [3]. Although it may seem  that Microsoft is losing its as shown in the previous chart, it should be noted that its market share is increasing, its growth is only a little slower comparing to the rapidly spreading Android. Considering the prospects of the development of these mobile operating systems, we decided to compare and test the user interface iOS [4] operating system, Android [5] and Windows Phone [6].

## 3 Research Subject

The operating system chosen for mobile platforms are compared in the present paper, particularly the graphical user interface. Furthermore different platforms are compared from both the GUI point of view and the user point of view. Moreover, the development opportunities for the developers are taken into consideration. Additionally, the development environment for various operating systems is described and the diversity of options (GUI elements, controls, etc.) is compared.

## 4 Applications Programming Principle

The Programming applications for all the three operating systems discussed is based on the same principle, which is now used for encoding and web pages. In the case of the web site the content is separated from the design, as well as in the case of the mobile device applications where the user interface and the programming logic are programmed separately. Nevertheless, the opportunity of designing the user interface directly to the code can be taken as well, thus the advantage of dynamic programming languages and classes , which belong to the displayable user interface elements can be taken as well.

## 5 GUI of Operating Systems iOS, Android and Windows Phone 7

The developers for each of the operating systemsdiffer in their thinking and approach to the graphical user interface. Therefore, there are differences between the descriptions and names of UI elements, as well as the distribution of these elements into groups. The usability of the application can be greatly affected by its graphical user interface (GUI); therefore, it is necessary to test these applications regarding these effects and impacts [7].

### 5.1 Stricktness of iOS

 The standards of the iOS operating system are strictly set for the developers as well as the well-proven methods; this helps to create a user-friendly interface. These standards are forwarded using the tutorials and documentation to the developer sof the third party applications, resulting in a consistent user interface iOS and other applications. Thanks to this strictness regarding the standards, the users do not have to o get used to the new layout of standard components or application control [8].

### Application Controls

Apple is trying to remove the imaginary barrier between the user and the device. Although all devices that work with the aforementioned operating systems have a touch screen, Apple has modified the nomenclature of interaction the user performs with the application or device in general; Gestures are used to control the device, i.e. the movements or touches of one or more fingers are involved. Gestures, which can control e.g. the iPhone are described in Table 1 This terminology is further borrowed into other platforms such as Windows Phone 7.

**Table 1.** Gestures and Its Meaning

| Gesture | Action |
| --- | --- |
| Tap | To press or select a control or item (analogous to a single mouse click). |
| Drag | To scroll or pan (that is, move side to side). |
| Flick | To scroll or pan quickly. |
| Swipe | In a table-view row, to reveal the Delete button. |
| Double tap | To zoom in and center a block of content or an image. To zoom out (if already zoomed in). |
| Pinch open | To zoom in. |
| Pinch close | To zoom out. |
| Touch and hold | In editable text, to display a magnified view for cursor positioning. |
| Shake | To initiate an undo or redo action. |

The controls are divided into several groups, Bars, Content Views, Group Alerts, Action Sheets, Modal Views, and Controls System-Provided Buttons and Icons. Furthermore, these groups are subdivided into specific user interface elements.

## Bars

The status bar, navigation bar, tab bar and toolbar are UI elements that have a specifically defined appearance and behavior in the iOS applications in the; they are used mostly for navigation applications, browsing, or for application control . It is not essential that these panels are used in everyapplication but if they are included in the application, it is important that they are used correctly.

## Content Views

iOS provides a few views that are designed for displaying custom content applications. Each view has certain characteristics and behaviors that provides a specific view to be used for a particular type of information.

## Alerts, Action Sheets and Modal Views

Alerts, action sheets, and modal views are temporary views that appear when a user needs to be notified, or when there is another option to be used by the user , or if it is necessary to offer additional functions. However, users cannot work with the program until one of the following views is on the screen.

## Controls

Controls are user interface elements which the user interacts with in order to induce action or receive information from the view. iOS provides a large number of controls that can be used in the applications, e.g. the elements such as the Date and Time Picker, Search Bar, and Page Indicator.

**System-provided Buttons and Icons**

There is a large amount of system buttoms and icons provided for the developers in order to promote consistency with the iOS user interface. These buttoms and icons canfacilitate their work of creating the user interface and its significance.

It could be said that Apple's developers are most likely to reach the ideal mobile device that is operated intuitively. Moreover, they try to make the application to resembletangible things. This is achieved by using the above-mentioned principles of gestures and the user interface of the system.

## 5.2  Android 2.3

The controls in the Android are called widgets, and they are mostly visual the elements that can be used in the final application. The widgets are stored in the android.widget package. Moreover, there are also abstract classes next to the directly defined feature classes; these classes can be distinguished by the prefix Abs. The following phrases describe the various visual elements of the android.widget.package

**Android.view.View**

Android.view.Viev is the class that is a fundamental building block for the user interface components. The View occupies a rectangular space on the screen and is responsible for rendering and event operations. View is the base class for widgets that are used to create interactive user interface. ViewGroup is an expacting class of View and it is the base class for layout components; these are invisible containers including the other View or ViewGroup objcls. Furthcrmorc, ViewGroup defines their layout on the desktop. The classes that directly inherit properties and methods of the View class are following: AnalogClock, ImageView, KeyboardView, ProgressBar, SurfaceView, TextView, and ViewGroup ViewStub. These classes can branch forthand thus their characteristics can be inherited by their descendents.

**Android.view.ViewGroup**

Android.view.ViewGroup is a special case of class View, which can contain other objects like View - these objects are called children. ViewGroup is the base class for the container layout and the view. The class also defines the ViewGroup.LayoutParams class, which serves as a base class of properties. The classes that inherit directly from class ViewGroup are: AbsoluteLayout, FrameLayout, LinearLayout, RelativeLayout, SlidingDrawer.

As can be seenthere are two main groups of elements in Android, unlike in the case of iOS. While the Class View is extended by the features that the user normally works with in the application, the ViewGroup class contains mainly the key elements that divide the area of applications in which only the individual user interface elements are inserted. This group of elements can be compared to the Content Views group, although we would not be accurate if dealing only with this group of elements. ViewGroup contains other elements that are included in the iOS in the Controls group. These are elements such as DatePicker and TimePicker, which are represented by one indicator iOS Date and TimePicker, whose functions affect only specified constants.

As far as the android.view.View class is concerned, this class includes the remaining elements that are contained in groups of Bars, Alerts, Action Sheets and Modal Views and some elements of the Controls group. Here, in the importance of strictness and the logic elements of the division respecting the user as well as the importance of the iOS platform is seen . The divison of elements into two groups regarding Android is ether focused on the heredity of elements, namely the simple elements with a parent, the View class and the elements that can contain other elements, either inheriting from the class ViewGroup or class View.

By comparing the distribution pattern of GUI elements of the iOS operating system to Android, one draws tothe conclusion that the distribution of elements Android is based on class inheritance, not on a logical divison into groups, as it is in the case of iOS. In addition, there is the posibility for thedevelopers to modify each elements using the inheritance of abstract classes, and to create the individual graphical user interface elements.

### 5.3   Windows Phone 7 – the Youngest Mobile Operating System

The Windows Phone platform developers have based the application development on the Silverlight framework, which has also taken over the Silverlight controls with only minor changes, due to the limitations of the mobile devices. The developers of applications for Windows Mobile 7 got into their hands  a set of components that are designed to be easy to work with and which are universal so they can cover the whole range of applications.

The only elements which the other platforms lack are the elements of the Rectangle, Ellipse, and maps. Rectangle and Ellipse objects are used to draw rectangular and elliptical shape. The Map control has light Bing Maps API for Silverlight Control [9].

As already mentioned in the introduction this platform is very universal and therefore it can be used by application developers in any way. This approach is appropriate if the author of this application complies with the principles of graphical user interface and already has enough experience in creating the user-friendly applications [10].

## 6   Apple iOS, Windows Phone 7 and Android 2.3 GUI Comparison

Several applications were created to compare the options of each OS; these applications were used to verifythe basic options and comparisons of individual applications. One of the main applications used in almost all mobile phones is the Phone Directory test application. This application aims to simulate the phonebook enhanced for email addresses; a list of names appears after starting the application up where each name represents a contact person. After selecting a list item one can call a phone number stored or edit a contact.

### PhoneDirectory Application

The main screen of the Phone Directory is designed by elements which create a chart consisting of one column and a few rows. The main screen of the Phone Directory with its basic layout for the Android platform is shown in the Figure 2.a). LinearLayout is used in the main application area for the placement of the other control elements („Add Contact" button and TextView objects for contacts). Similar applications were developed to compare it with other graphical interfaces of Windows Phone and iOS operating systems.

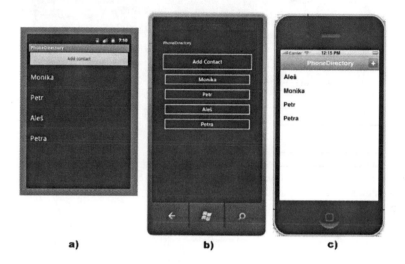

a)                          b)                          c)

**Fig. 2.** Application Phone Directory for compared platforms

Although these are identical applications, there are some differences present. Regarding the Windows Phone application the first difference is the graphic of different application components, which is not as crucial as buttons and other components because these can change their appearance. The crucial diference is the list of contacts. The use of one of the Android ListView components was replaced by a combination of StackPanel and Button (Fig. 2. b)).

iOS represents the 3rd optionhow to the design of themain screen application. In the iOS has been the main application layout using Table View, a view that sorts the data into rows in one column (Fig. 2. c)).

There is a button with the"Add Contact," text under the heading of the application the purpose of this button is to add a new contact to your list. In iOS application, Figure 2. c) is the „Add Contact" button replaced by the button with a sign „+" in the heading of the application.

The context menu is the next part of the testing application , it, pops up after a contact is selected. This menu contains three buttons and one text part, which is represented by different objects in each platform. It is TextView in Android, in Windows i tis the Phone TextBlock and in iOS it is the text part represented by Label, which is a part of the Alert View control.

The menu in Android is provided by the PopupWindow control, which draws separate XML file that defines the layout of this menu (Fig. 3. a)). After selecting a contact a dialog pops up and further steps can be taken.A contact can be called or

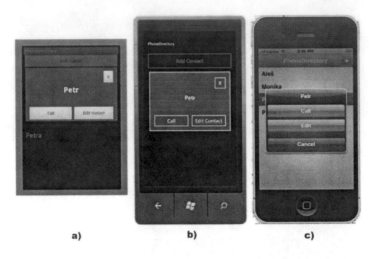

**Fig. 3.** Aplication Phone Directory with shown context menu by: a) popup.xml via PopupWindow control in Android, b) Popup control in Windows Phone 7 and c) Alert control in iOS.

edited. Dialling a number is done via the system,by  pressing the Edit button PopupWindow control with XML file appears ,which allows tto edit the contact.

In the Windows Phone the Popup element is used for the pop up menu editing and calling each contact and the menu to add a new contact element; Popup is the equivalent to PopupWindow in Android. Its function is the same, only the programming work differs. While Android needs XML file to display the PopupWindow, Windows Phone 7 can display directly the element of XAML file.

After one from the the contacts is select in the iOS application version GUI element Alert View pops up as shown in Fig 3. c). This makes it possibile to choose whether to call a contact or to edit it.

"Add contact" button can be seen in Android or Windows Phone.Nevertheless, it does not react while touching. This is caused by the PopupWindow in Android or Popup conrol in Windows Phone. Nevertheless, both Android and Windows Phone do not need to cover full-screen nor to overalay the applications. However, both of them disables features that are covered by this element. The Edit screen consists of four elements, TextView (Android, Fig. 4. a)) or four TextBlock objects (Windows Phone, Fig. 4. b)). These work as the labels for the text fields and the screen header. EditText (Android) or TextBlock (Windows Phone) occurs three times. Moreover, there are three EditText (Android) or TextBox (Windows Phone), which represent the text field.

If a contact is edited or selected in iOS the entire area getssuperimposed by the Modal View element (Fig. 4. c)), this element contains thedescriptions of fields that are represented by the element Label, input text field Text Field to complete or edit the information; Moreover it contains the Finish buttom or the Cancel button.

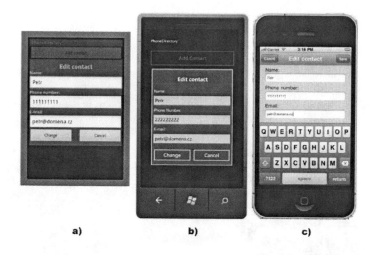

**Fig. 4.** Application Phone Directory with shown edit form.

Comparing the two applications, Android and Windows Phone 7 operating systems, we fond out that these platforms are equal from the graphical user interface point of view, there is a styling components option in Windows Phone 7 platform for the programmers applications. Therefore, the same appearance as in the case of Android applications can be achieved. From a programming point of view, the Android platform is not as flexible as the Windows Phone 7; E.g. in the case of working with a text via string.xml file.

It is already clear that iOS platform has simpler and clearer user interface, unlike the abovedescribed applications of Android and Windows Phone 7. The developer is limited by using predefined options for the development. Therefore, they have to comply with standards set by the GUI applications for the iOS operating system. This ensures that the components of Table View and Alert View have the same design in all applications system, which is a clear advantage for the users; as they are not forced to adapt to different functionality or appearance of the same elements of applications designed by the other developers.

## 7  Platform Differences

Despite the efforts of developers to develop applications usabe ideally for all the platforms, there still is a need to avoid the development of several versions of the program and to develop only one application that would be ideal for use on all platforms. The problem arises with the fact that there are also elements that contain only one platform. This can lead to differences in the appearance eventhough one tries to program the same application for different platforms. Nevertheless, the application logic can be maintained.

## 7.1   Examples of Different GUI Elements

### Date and Time Picker

The comparison of the Date and Time Picker elements and Android is offered in Figure 5, Android developers are working with two GUI components, while developers of iOS use a single one influencing its appearance by the setting of its display modes (Date and Time, Time, Date, Countdown Timer).

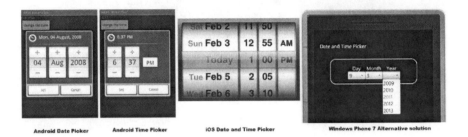

**Fig. 5.** Comparation of Date, Time Picker of Android Platform, Date and Time Picker of iOS and alternative solution of Date Picker in Windows Phone 7

There is no such component for Windows 7 Phone but one can programme such element due to the universality of these elements, Fig. 5. Using three ComboBox one can select values within days, months and years. It depends on what values are assigned to each ComboBox and how it can be named.

### Analog and Digital Clock

Clocks is another element that is not contained in every operating system as a GUI element. In the case of Android this element is defined separately, both in the analogue and digital form. Regarding the applications for the iOS system the clock is included as a part of an element status bar that shows the other system information related to the status of the iPhone. Alternatives have to be chosen in Windows Phone 7 such as using the TextBlock element. The comparison of Android features, iOS and Windows Phone 7 is shown in Figure 6.

**Fig. 6.** Comparison of Clock widgets from Android and Status Bar from iOS

### Tabs in applications

A bookmark can be a frequent feature of applications. Using them one can move in the application neatly and quickly. The comparison of the bookmarks solutions in each operating system can be seen in the following Figure 7.

**Android TabLayout**            **iOS Tab Bar**            **Windows Phone 7 Application Menu**

**Fig. 7.** Comparison of Tab application solutions. Windows Phone 7 does not contain any component for example like as Tab Bar in iOS However, thesystem component called Application Menu can be used. This menu is expansed in the picture showing the menu items. In collapsed mode only buttons can be seen.

The examples demonstratethat the same problems can be resolved using different solutions. Although Android and iOS contain complete solutions for the selection of date and timemaking the user interface transparent and clear, the Windows Phone 7 applications can deal with this lack usingan alternative of universal GUI components.

## 8  Applications Multiplatform Programming

Eventhough each platform has its own official developer methods and environments, it is equally inefficient to develop mobile applications for multiple platforms in their official environment and formal programming language. Consequently, these processes are very time demanding and expensive (one has to employ several programmers for a single application development for various platforms). This problem started to be discussed bysome developers and therefore various methods of creating applications that can then be run on different mobile platforms have emerged. The developer creates one application that can be transmitted to different platforms. However, as already noted above, there are some features that are not present in some platforms. Therefore, the solution is limited to some of these differences. GUI objects are generally described as the alternative development component, which the Windows Phone 7 platform [11] does not include.

### 8.1  Metismo Bedrock

Metismo Bedrock [11] is a commercial product that enables application development for a wide range of mobile devices, not only for mobile phones. It is an environment that includes a database of mobile devices, for which applications can be developed The development itself is unified by one programming language and J2ME.

Furthermore, the application is compiled into C ++, and eventually extended to all the selected mobile device platforms.

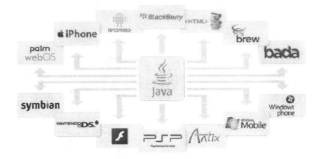

**Fig. 8.** Metismo Bedrock visualisation which platforms are supported.

Due to the fact that the application development is unified by one programming language, developers are not forced to install many development environments than that used to develop applications in J2ME. The Bedrock technology allows programmers to use the parameters of the code; therefore the source code for different mobile devices can simply be changed. This allows the programmer to manage only one project for multiple platforms.

Regarding the facilities that support J2ME applications, application development is exactly the same. The development application is the only additional step that takes Java code and translates it intoa human-readable form, Visual C ++ including all comments. Then the programmer can make changes in the code. This code is then compiled by the compiler, which belongs to a specific device or operating system (e. g.: Xcode for the iPhone). The code is also linked with a Bedrock specific platforms library of, which imitate the standard JSR libraries.

As a result of the abov mentioned processes there is an application written in J2ME, which can be quickly recompiled and run on any supported platform.

### 8.2  Nitobi PhoneGap

Nitobi PhoneGap [12] is an open source platform, which uses the implementation of web standards by which developers and companies can develop mobile applications for a free download, commercial purposes or a combination of these options. This application is based on the technologies of web pages design with HTML5, CSS3 and JavaScript. On this platform applications for the iOS operating system, Android, Blackberry, webOS SymbianWRT can be developed. As already mentioned above Windows Phone 7 is the latest operating system that does not have a sufficient support; however, it should be supported soon in this project. Currently,only the old Windows Mobile version is supported. Nevertheless, Microsoft abandoned it when the Windows Phone 7 was launched.

PhoneGap has not implemented its own development environment. For each platform the official development environment needs to be installed; this environment is then supplemented by PhoneGap plugin. The principle of the development of applications using this tool is in the programming of applications using Web standards. This is then processed by PhoneGap Framework, and finally it is expanded itto other operating systems.

### 8.3 Compromising between Native Development Environtment and Other Development Platforms

With the above platforms, the advantage of rapid spread of applications between different operating systems can be gained; however, the benefits of the original GUI elements, which contains a native development environment might be lost Nevertheless, there are exceptions, for example in game developing or some 3D applications. In this case iOS and Android platforms are generalized by OpenGL Framework; this feature enables to share the 3D applications between this platforms.

## 9   Operating Systems Features

In order to avoid the discuss taken only the platform programmer perspective, the user perspective is offered and compared with the programmer one. Users are already familiar with the iPhone and Android devices. Nevertheless, Windows Phone 7 is on the market very shortly. Therefore, they try to be visible and promote thein products to the potentional users.

Without any doubts Android offers the most available features, then goes iPhone and then Windows Phone 7. However, one should take into consideration thatthe first two mentioned operating systems have come througha few years of development unlike the new Windows Phone 7 operating system [13]. AlthoughWindows Phone has not at the same level as the other two platforms yet it brings new features. These are the "Live tiles" that create the main screen of the device calledthe Start screen. These are the hybrids of widgets and applications icons Fig. 9.

**Fig. 9.** Windows Phone 7 Live tiles overview. Tiles are spread to larger area than physical size of mobile phone screen. It should be interesting for users, from GUI side.

Live tiles refer to the application, but also show the latest information on the start screen. Windows Phone 7 also brings together the various functions of the operating system to a hub - the junction between the components and screens. Each Hub

(Marketplace, Office, People, Xbox Live and Zune) hasa tight integration with native applications and third-party applications. For example, in the Hub People one can see the status, comments, and a like of our contacts Fig. 10.

**Fig. 10.** People hub overview, hubs are much wider than hardware screen. User can scroll screen from side to side to view content of hub.

Regarding the Windows Phone 7 it can be said that  that Microsoft has created a new and advanced OS and although it is not clear whether this operating system will be  successfull enough to hold the interest ofa large number of users. However, it is clear that the developers  of Microsoft pioneered an area which might be interesting for the general public.

## 10   Conclusion

While the testing and comparing the iOS operating system, Android and Windows Phone 7, we concluded that the iOS operating systém provils the best graphical user interface. This is because the consistency with the user interface operating system and the application is maintained   , which is ensured through the GUI elements and their use description

The possibilities of GUI operating systems Android, Windows Phone 7 and iOS were tested and compared using the testing applications. Nevertheless, these operating systems contain different features and therefore, identical applications cannot be created. However, it was proved that it might be possible to create identical applications even for different operating systems,eventhough thein graphic differ.

As proved above, Metismo Bedrock, Nitobi PhoneGap etc. might be very helpful regarding these issues as they make it possible to use one application and distribute it to a wide range of mobile operating systems. As already mentioned, the differences in the features do not always allow to produce visuály and functionally similar application for all the operating systems.

Addressing the support of the ESF project - OP VK CZ.1.07/2.2.00/07.0339.

# References

1. Tidwell, J.: Designing Interfaces: Patterns for Effective Interaction Design. O'Reilly Media, Inc., USA (2006)
2. comScore, http://www.comscore.com
3. itbusiness, http://www.itbusiness.com
4. Apple, http://www.apple.com
5. Google Android, http://www.android.com
6. Microsoft Windows Phone 7,
   http://www.microsoft.com/windowsphone/enus/default.aspx
7. Hwang, S.-M., Chae, H.-C.: Desing & Implementation of Mobile UITesting Tool. In: Lee, G., Ahn, T.N., Howard, D., Slezak, D. (eds.) ICHIT 2008: Proceedings of International Conference on Convergence and Hybrid InformationTechnology, pp. 704–707 (2008)
8. Clark, J.: Tapworthy: Design Great iPhone Apps. O'Reilly Media, Inc., Canada (2010)
9. Bing Maps Silverlight Control for Windows Phone,
   http://msdn.microsoft.com/en-us/library/ff941096VS.92.aspx
10. Ballard, B.: Designing the Mobile User Experience. John Wiley & Sons Ltd., USA (2007)
11. Miguel, A., da Cruz, R., Faria, J.P.: A Metamodel-Based Approa hfor Automatic User Interface Generation. In: PT I. Petriu, D., Rouquette, N., Haugen, O. (eds.) Model Driven Engineering Languages and Systems, pp. 256–270 (2010)
12. Metismo Bedrock, http://www.metismo.com/developers.html
13. Nitobi PhoneGap, http://www.phonegap.com
14. pcworld.com, http://www.pcworld.com

# Capturing Supermarket Shopper Behavior
# Using SmartBasket

Ufuk Celikkan, Gizem Somun, Ulas Kutuk,
Irem Gamzeli, Elif Dicle Cinar, and Irem Atici

Faculty of Engineering and Computer Sciences
Izmir University of Economics
Sakarya Cad. No:156, Balcova, Izmir, Turkey
ufuk.celikkan@ieu.edu.tr,
{gizem.somun,ulas.kutuk,irem.gamzeli,
elif.cinar,irem.atici}@std.ieu.edu.tr

**Abstract.** Retail stores make marketing decisions using customer demographic
and sales data to determine which customer and product group combination best
contributes increased profit. Customer profile and sales data are of great help
but they alone do not portray the whole picture. Tracking the location of a customer in a store and analyzing the customer shopping path and marrying the result to customer profile and sales data is of high interest for marketing for the
purpose of streamlining store operations, maintaining customer royalty and increasing sales. In this paper, we propose a system for supermarkets that tracks
the path of a shopping cart associated with a customer profile to understand the
customer shopping behavior. The proposed system uses IR LED plates installed
on the carts which are monitored by small and inexpensive in-shelf networked
IP cameras. The shopping carts are equipped with a low cost input device that
has a monitor to gather customer profile information. The system is integrated
with the supermarket's web site to customize the overall shopping experience.
The data collected is mined to find out the relationships among product placement, customer profile and product purchase decisions. The system is designed
to monitor real time movements of the shopping cart.

**Keywords:** Customer Tracking, Shopping Behavior, Navigation Patterns, Image Processing.

## 1 Introduction

Offering the right product, at the right price, in the right place and at the right time to
customers is an elusive goal for retail owners. Detecting patterns in customer behavior
and understanding the thought process in purchasing decisions is very helpful in gaining competitive advantage. Store owners want to be knowledgeable about their customers' profiles, the relationship between customer profiles and customer shopping
habits and the products that the customers want to have in their stores. The amount of
time a customer spends in a particular aisle and in which order they visit the aisles are

V. Snasel, J. Platos, and E. El-Qawasmeh (Eds.): ICDIPC 2011, Part II, CCIS 189, pp. 44–53, 2011.

of particular interest to the owner. A supermarket owner is also keen on knowing if a product is drawing the attention of the customers or not. It is essential to separate a customer passing by a product group from a customer paying close attention to a product group, even though no purchasing activity has occurred in both. The former case is especially significant because the product simply goes unnoticed and maybe needing a relocation. In the latter, the customer has looked at the product group but chosen not to buy the product which may indicate that a product re-design or a price adjustment is due. Information of this kind is very valuable and cannot be obtained from cash register sales data. It requires tracking data.

Gaining an insight into customer behavior can be achieved by analyzing data from multiple sources. Our goal in this paper is to present a novel and cost effective solution to collect customer location data and combine this data with customer profile and purchase data to make inferences about customer behavior, hence to help the retail owner to develop effective marketing decisions and to determine future strategic direction. This provides a wholesome solution to supermarket business intelligence. The systems also improves the overall customer shopping experience by dynamically adapting customer services and offering individualized service based on customer profile.

Tracking data is collected using in-shelf IP cameras by detecting the IR LED plates installed on the cart. The system also includes a low cost electronic device with a touch monitor and an integrated barcode reader (similar to an entry level tablet PC). This device is also installed on the shopping cart to facilitate interaction with customers for creating their profiles and customizing their stay in the supermarket.

Smart Cart software is implemented using C# and .NET technologies. Processing of the frames is done using open source computer vision library OpenCV [1]. The System Architecture Section presents the architecture and implementation details of the proposed system.

## 2   Related Work

There are numerous techniques developed to track people and assets especially in inventory tracking and supply chain management [2]-[5]. Some of these are commercial products and some of them are still under development in research labs. One such commercial application from PLUS uses Ultrawide band technology to track people and assets in retail stores and grocery stores real time [6]. This technology can pinpoint the exact location of a customer but is very expensive. Shopper movement is tracked by a camera using face and eye detection in [7]. Computer vision based approaches do not require expensive hardware to implement but use advanced image processing algorithms. Therefore, these approaches do not easily lend themselves to real time monitoring as they require extensive back-end image processing. Their use in retail shops and grocery stores are not as widespread as in the case of RFID based deployments. RFID based solutions usually equip the carts and shelves with readers and store items with tags [8], [9]. The system described in [8] is a comprehensive proposal with rich features however, no real implementation exists. Its cost estimate is also high due to the readers installed both on the carts and in the shelves. Cost of RFID tags is negligible. However, the cost of the readers makes RFID based deployments an issue. It is also not possible to accurately determine if a shopping cart is facing one product group or another since the cart can be anywhere within the range of the reader. Increasing the number of readers do not solve the problem, since overlapping readers will register a reading simultaneously.

The analysis of tracking information in retail shops, grocery stores and supermarkets has not been explored much. However, there is plenty of work done on navigation patterns in e-commerce [10], [11]. Mining the traversals of on-line shopper using the web logs allows online retailers to get an insight into online purchasing behavior and enables the web designer to better design their web sites. The same approach is used in [9] to discover traversal patterns in retail stores. That study needs further work as it needs to use real data instead of a computer generated data set.

Our approach presented in this paper is similar to the one in [9] which tracks carts instead of people. This is in contrast to the system described in [7] which tracks people. On the other hand [7] uses a video based system similar to the system proposed in this paper whereas the system in [9] uses RFID. Our system strikes the right balance between cost effectiveness and overall system performance, furnished with many customer oriented features.

## 3   System Architecture

The proposed system uses IR LEDs and IP cameras to track the shopping cart. An infrared LED is a type of electronic device that produces light in the infrared part of the spectrum just below what the naked eye can see. Although invisible to human eye many cameras can see infrared light. IR LED plates are installed on the cart and are detected by low cost in-shelf cameras. Fig. 1 depicts a snapshot of a LED plate on the cart taken by an IP camera. Cart ID is encoded by using different LED configurations. The on or off status of a LED indicates the cart ID. For each product group within an aisle an in-shelf camera detects the presence of light emitted from the LED and after processing the captured image, determines the Cart ID. The IP cameras are wirelessly connected to a server that processes the captured images. The store server is the central hub for all data exchanges. Its primary job is to receive images captured and sent by the cameras, process those images and store the results to the database which is later used in path mining. Other hardware components of the system consist of a tablet PC like device with a touch screen monitor similar to the one shown in Fig. 2 and an integrated barcode reader. This device will be used to interact with customers for creating their profiles and personalizing the shopping experience. It communicates wirelessly with the server as well. Fig. 3 shows the overall architecture of the system.

The SmartBasket system consists of three software modules which are responsible for detecting the cart ID, customer interaction and transaction mining.

**Fig. 1.** Shopping cart installed with an IR LED plate

**Fig. 2.** Shopping cart equipped with an input device

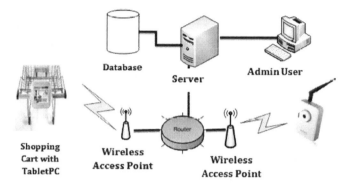

**Fig. 3.** SmartBasket architecture

*1)*  Shopping Cart Detection Module
*2)*  Shopping Cart Customer Application (for the customer)
*3)*  Transaction Mining Module (for the retail owner)

A customer, before begins shopping, interacts with the tablet PC using Cart Application installed on it which creates a customer profile using the customer's demographic information. The customer is also presented a voluntary pre-prepared survey to collect customer opinion about shopping experience. The Cart application associates the cart with a customer as shown in Fig 4. This module also offers personalized shopping experience by advising or warning about other products, offering promotions and directing the customer to product location.

Customer demographic information is stored in the database; therefore standard security measures are applied to protect the wireless network infrastructure, store server and the database against sniffing and unauthorized access.

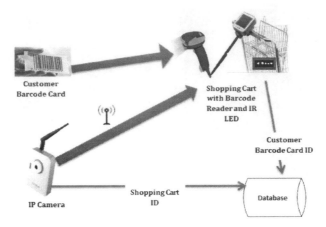

**Fig. 4.** Shopping cart and customer ID association

## 3.1 Shopping Cart Detection Module

Each shopping cart is equipped with an IR LED plate to identify carts. Each LED represents a bit. Therefore, with an 8-LED configuration it is possible to identify 255 carts. When parity checking is used 1 LED would be used for checksum, thus 127 carts would be identified. Fig. 5 demonstrates how an IR LED plate on a cart is translated into a cart ID. The camera is fully calibrated and strategically located so that an unconstructed view of the LED plate would be captured. The LED plates would be placed at two different locations on the cart. One plate is installed at the base of the cart on the right side and the other would be placed in the front. The image captured by the camera is transferred to the server for processing over the IP network one frame per second. Capturing frequency is configurable and depends on the resolution and color quality of the video frame. A time stamp is appended to every frame to allow the temporal ordering of the frames on the server. This enables the server to perform off-line or batch processing due to network delays. The processing of the images is computationally efficient therefore the system can be used real time.

The processing of the image starts with finding the squares on the image as the IR led plate is in the shape of a rectangle with a predefined width and height proportion. All the contours on the frame must be found in order to find the rectangles. The square detection algorithm extracts the region of interest corresponding to the LED plate by filtering out the noise surrounding the rectangle [1]. The area within the rectangle is applied a threshold to isolate the IR LEDs that are on. Then, the plate is divided into $n$ equal regions where $n$ is the number of LEDS on the plate. A blob detection algorithm is applied to each region. The presence and absence of blobs are mapped into a bit string and converted into a decimal shopping cart ID. After the cart ID is determined the detection module stores *(Cart ID, Camera IP, timestamp)* data into a database.

The next step is to determine the product group location where the shopping cart is positioned at. The IP camera is located such that it can monitor several product groups within an aisle, and therefore reducing the number of cameras used. The position of the LED plate rectangle in a frame indicates the exact location of the shopping cart as shown in Fig. 6. Once the location of the cart and the product group is determined, the detection module generates the quadruplet *(Customer ID, Cart ID, Location ID, time-stamp)* and stores it into the database. In reality, data is stored in the database in multiple tables. The quadruplet is computed after performing database joins.

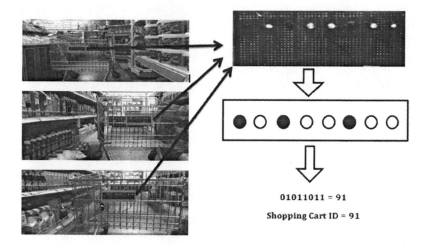

**Fig. 5.** Detecting cart ID

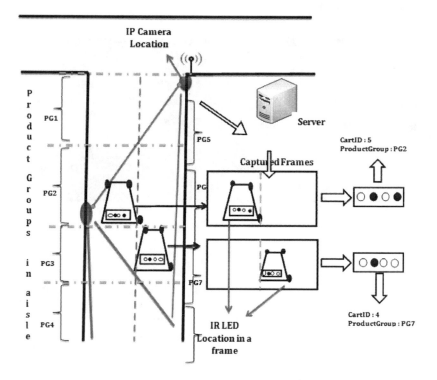

**Fig. 6.** Finding the location of a shopping cart from the captured frame

The location data stored into the database is verified for consistency. If a cart is not being used by any customer then detection of a traveling cart with that cart ID is erroneous and therefore should not be entered into the system database. In another scenario if a cart is detected in an aisle at time $t$, then it is impossible for that cart to be in a remote isle at time $t$ plus one second. These scenarios indicate that either the frame acquired by the camera does not show the LEDs properly or the processing module incorrectly processes the image. In certain cases error correction would be possible, however, it would not be as easy as detecting the error.

## 3.2 Shopping Cart Application

The carts is equipped with a low cost electronic device with a touch screen monitor that is capable of scanning product bar codes and wirelessly transmitting information to the central server. This device will be activated by the customer upon picking the cart after having their store issued shopping card scanned. This results in establishing an association between the cart and customer profile. Another purpose of this device is to provide a personal and customized shopping experience to the customer as the customer is now "known" to the store. The device will provide product information and promotions tailored to the customer and can even suggest the location of a related product. For instance, the location of the cream will be suggested for those who are planning to purchase coffee. The device will ask the customer short survey questions about the customer's shopping experience. This is voluntary however. Example user interfaces are shown in Fig 7.

**Fig. 7.** Sample Shopping Cart Application GUIs

## 3.3 Transaction Mining

There is a close parallelism between the navigation of a user at an electronic commerce site and a supermarket shopper navigating through the supermarket aisles or sections at a retail store. Web navigation patterns attempt to decipher customer purchasing behavior and reacts to the result by providing efficient access between highly correlated objects, better authoring design for web pages, putting advertisements in ideal places and better customer classification [5], [6]. The very same approach could also be used in supermarket tracking as well. Once a customer completes the shopping at the checkout counter, the transaction mining module will start generating the pair *(C, P)*. *C* is the customer record with attributes such as age, gender and salary and *P* is a set of ordered pairs denoting a path where *P = {(s,i) / s is the segment id housing the product group and i is the product purchased}*. *(s,-)* indicates that no product is purchased from that product group. An example pair would be *((age=30, sex=male)*, *((baby, diaper) (beverages, beer)))*. For example, if one finds a pattern like the one just given, it would be a savvy marketing decision to place a new beer product next to diapers for its promotion. We define *ΔP* as follows. *ΔP= {(s, i, t) / (s, i)    P and t is the time spent at segment s}*. Then the path *{(s1, i1, 5), (s2,-, 0), (s3,-, 0), (s4, i2, 3))* may indicate that segments *s2* and *s3* went unnoticed. This could be an expected shopping path. However, if product groups, *s2, s3* and *s4* contain related products then a close examination is due to understand the cause, as the products in *s2* and *s3* may be unblocked or not visible.

Based on the study done in [9] - [11], it possible to make various other inferences on the navigation pattern of a supermarket customer. The overall data flow of the system is shown in Fig. 8.

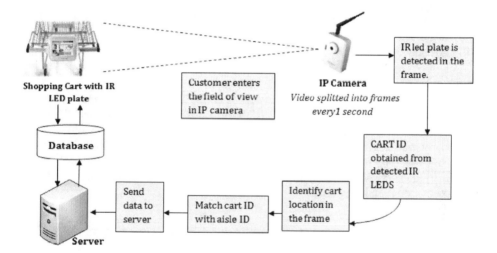

**Fig. 8.** System Data Flow

## 4   Conclusion

Customer purchasing habits is an important concern of the supermarket owners [12]. Getting insight into a customer decision making process would provide invaluable information to the owner to offer better and diverse products, provide better customer service and gain advantage over the competitor. In this paper we propose a system that collects tracking information of a supermarket shopping cart and associates location data with customer profile and purchase data to help the owner in marketing decisions and store operations. The proposed system is a video based system that detects IR LED plates installed on the shopping cart. The system is integrated with a tablet PC like device also installed on the cart to personalize the customer shopping experience and expedite the checkout process. The collected data is analyzed to provide analytics and statistics to the store owner for future merchandizing decisions.

Our system is a low cost solution to customer tracking. The cost of an IR LED plate and an IP camera used in the system is less than $70 combined. The item that increases the overall cost of the proposed system is the tablet PC on the cart which is not required for tracking but provides several advantages. It personalizes the shopping experience for customer by offering products of interest or sometimes by warning the customer about some products due to health and dietary restrictions. It provides shopping efficiency by directing the customer to the next product to be purchased. The use of bar code scanner speeds up the check-out time at the cash register and allows payment of the goods even before reaching the check-out counter.

The system's cart ID detection algorithm heavily relies on getting a high quality image with visible LEDs. The lighting conditions and blockage caused by other carts and shoppers may hinder the ability to collect data. This can be rectified by increasing the LED plates on a cart or positioning the camera for minimal interference by the other shoppers.

The cart detection and shopping cart application module is currently in system and integration test phase, as of writing of this paper. The transaction mining module is still under development.

**Acknowledgments.** The authors would like to thank Assoc. Prof. Dr. Yasar Sahin Guneri for conceiving the idea and for his continual support and Armağan Atik of Ozdilek shopping center for giving us insight into supermarket operations. The study is a part of a graduation project supervised by Assist.Prof.Dr. Ufuk Celikkan, and implementation has been done by Gizem Somun, Ulas Kutuk, Elif Dicle Cinar, Irem Atici and Irem Gamzeli. The system will be tested in a very small local supermarket owned by the family of one of the authors. We would like to thank the owners for their cooperation and support.

# References

1. Bradski, G., Kaehler, A.: Learning OpenCV: Computer Vision with the OpenCV Library. O'Reilly Media, Sebastopol (2008)
2. Liu, H., Darabi, H., Banerjee, P., Liu, J.: Survey of wireless indoor positioning techniques and systems. IEEE Transaction on Systems and Cybernetics Part C-Applications and Reviews 37(6), 1067–1080 (2007)
3. Chen, D., Tsai, S., Kim, K.H., Hsu, C.H., Singh, J.P., Girod, B.: Low-Cost Asset Tracking using Location-Aware Camera Phones. In: Proceedings of SPIE-The International Society for Optical Engineering, vol. 7798, p. 77980R (2010)
4. Francia, G.A.: An intelligent RFID based wireless tools and asset tracking system. In: Proceedings of the International Conference on Wireless Networks/International Conference on Pervasive Computing and Communications, vol. 1 & 2, pp. 651–657 (2004)
5. Michael, K., McCathie, L.: The pros and cons of RFID in supply chain management. In: International Conference on Mobile Business, pp. 623–629 (2005)
6. Plus Location Systems, http://www.plus-ls.com/ (accessed April 15, 2011)

7. Liu, X.M., Krahnstoever, N., Yu, T., Tu, P.: What are customers looking at? In: IEEE Conference on Advanced Video and Signal Based Surveillance, London, England (2007)
8. Hurjui, C., Graur, A., Turcu, C.D.: Monitoring the shopping activities from the supermarkets based on the intelligent basket by using the RFID technology. In: ELEKTRONIKA IR ELEKTROTECHNIKA, vol: 83(3), pp. 7–10 (2008)
9. Liao, I.E., Lin, W.C.: Shopping path analysis and transaction mining based on RFID technology. In: Proceedings of the 1st RFID Eurasia Conference, Istanbul, Turkey, pp. 292–296 (2007)
10. Lee, Y.S., Yen, S.J., Tu, G.H., Hsieh, M.C.: Mining traveling and purchasing behaviors of customers in electronic commerce environment. In: IEEE International Conference on e-Technology, e-Commerce and e-Service Proceeding, pp. 227–230 (2004)
11. Lee, Y.S., Yen, S.J.: Incremental and interactive mining of web traversal patterns. Information Sciences 178(2), 287–306 (2008)
12. Conversation with retail store Ozdilek located in Izmir, Turkey

# An Approach for Securing and Validating Business Processes Based on a Defined Enterprise Security Ontology Criteria

Ahmed A. Hussein[1,2], Ahmed Ghoneim[1], and Reiner R. Dumke[2]

[1] College of Computers and Information Sciences, King Saud University, Saudi Arabia
{ahussein,ghoneim}@ksu.edu.sa
[2] Faculty of Computer Science, University of Otto Magdeburg, Magdeburg, Germany
dumke@ics.cs.uni-mafdeburg.de

**Abstract.** The security ontology criteria are a vital de-facto in Service Oriented Architecture (SOA) which guarantees a secure orchestration of the organizational services to face the new security aspects. Quality of Service (QoS) is a set of standards and algorithms used to measure the performance of a service by monitoring quality affecting factors. In this paper we secure and validate the business processes by introducing a framework and a security tag. The security tag is used to represent certain infrastructure quality of service criteria within business processes of an enterprise. This is achieved by correlating the infrastructure security components performance and business process through an enterprise infrastructure-based security token presented in the BPEL file in newly introduced attributes. The framework then applies its developed algorithm to validate the enterprise security ontology criteria by using the provided enterprise WSS security and the calculated intervals for the (QoS) throughput coefficients of the enterprise infrastructure security components and outputs consistency value indicators for both the WSS and the token value provided in the BPEL. We tested the framework functionality through a real case study of a rich and secure banking environment.

**Keywords:** Security ontology, BPEL, SOA, QoS, Web Service, Business process.

## 1 Introduction

Today's; most of the enterprises are concerned to fully secure their internal business processes. Existing security ontology policies differ from one enterprise to another. Most of the current security ontology policies apply the infrastructure security; and common web services security (WSS) which defines SOAP extensions to implement client authentication, message integrity through XML signature and message confidentiality through XML encryption on the message level. Those policies provide the basic security functionalities, neglecting the relationships and details within the enterprise business processes.

The core representation of organizations is the business processes in which allows organizations to illustrate and implement their main services in an efficient secured

V. Snasel, J. Platos, and E. El-Qawasmeh (Eds.): ICDIPC 2011, Part II, CCIS 189, pp. 54–66, 2011.
© Springer-Verlag Berlin Heidelberg 2011

and maintainable manner. The Business processes schema is represented by a BPEL (Business Process Execution Language) that contains detailed descriptions of services carrying out processes as web services. As a standard XML schema, BPEL allows for defining new tags such as a new security and internal relationships tags. Web services are referenced inside the BPEL and presented in a WSDL form; it is an xml standard representation that illustrates functions' attributes and behaviors.

The main components of SOA are "Services" which correspond to a business modules or application functionalities. Services are programmed using standard (XML-based) languages and protocols, and implemented via a self-describing inter-face based on open standards [1, 2, and 3].

Web service composition allows the combination and invocation of existing Web services through the so-called service orchestration. To compose services as business processes, a BPM engine executes activities described by the Web Services Business Process Execution Language (WS-BPEL2.0) [7].

Our motivation; in addition to securing the web services; is to address the security of the business processes. In this paper we introduced a novel approach that provides a solution for the addressed issue. This is achieved by correlating the infrastructure security components performance within the BPEL file using a new security tag.

The remainder of this paper is as follow. In Section 2, the proposed framework, its components and its behavior are described. The applicability of the proposed framework using a real case study in a banking environment is described in Section 3. Section 4 illustrates the related works. Finally, In Section 5, conclusions and future work are discussed.

## 2  Proposed Framework

This section consists of three parts, the first one describes the required inputs to the framework, and the second one describes the developed validation algorithm, while the third one describes the framework's core components and illustrates their functionalities. The three parts are described as follows:

### a.  Inputs

The inputs to the framework consist of three main inputs; the first one is the *WSS policy* which reflects the standard WSS (Web Service Security); mentioned in the previous section; the enterprise applies. The second input is the interval values of the *Enterprise-based infrastructure security coefficients*, those coefficients are based on the security (QoS) provided by the enterprise infrastructure security components (Firewalls, Wireless security and Intrusion detection prevention system –IDP). The third input is the enterprise BPEL file and its related WSDL file that are needed to be validated. Table 1 illustrates sample of first input provided in a.csv (Comma delimited) format, the existence value could be *1* for an existing policy or *0* for inexistency. Table 2 illustrates the second input as an interval for each calculated (QoS) coefficient of the infrastructure security components. Finally, Figure 1 illustrates a snapshot of a business process *IssueOrderProces* BPEL file.

**Table 1.** WSS Policy example

| Item | Existence |
|---|---|
| Authentication | 1 |
| Message Integrity | 0 |
| Message Confidentiality | 1 |

```
<?xml version = "1.0" encoding = "ISO-8859-1" ?>
<process name="IssueOrderProcess"

targetNamespace="http://xmlns.oracle.com/FinancialWF_jws/Finan      /IssueOrderProcess"
        xmlns="http://schemas.xmlsoap.org/ws/2003/03/busin      ocess/
.....
.....
 <partnerLin name="issueorderprocess_client" p  nerLinkType="client:IssueOrderProcess"
myRole="IssueOrderProcessProvider" partnerRole="IssueOrderProcessRequester"/>
    <partnerLink name="getManagers"
partnerRole="WorkFlowRoutersPortType_Role"
partnerLinkType="ns1:WorkFlowRoutersPortType_PL"/>
.....
....
<sequence name="main">
    <!-- Receive input from requestor. -->
    <receive name="receiveInput" partnerLink="issueorderprocess_client"
portType="client:IssueOrderProcess" operation="process" variable="inputVariable"
createInstance="yes"/>

    <!-- Asynchronous callback to the requester -->
    <assign name="Assign_1">
      <copy>
        <from expression="'Test'"/>
        <to variable="Input_getAccountingAuditingDepartmentManager_InputVariable"
          part="parameters"
          query="/ns1:getAccountingAuditingDepartmentManager/ns1:dummy"/>
      </copy>
    </assign>
  <invoke name="getAccountingAuditingManager"

inputVariable="Input_getAccountingAuditingDepartmentManager_InputVariable"

outputVariable="Output_getAccountingAuditingDepartmentManager_OutputVariable"
        partnerLink="getManagers"
        portType="ns1:WorkFlowRoutersPortType"
        operation="getAccountingAuditingDepartmentManager"/>
 ..
..
```

*This maps to the invoking of "getAccountingAuditingManager"*

*This maps to the IssueOrderProcess. wsdl*

**Fig. 1.** Snapshot of the "IssueOrderProces" BPEL file

**Table 2.** Infrastructure Security components (QoS) coefficients

| QoS coefficient | Belongs to | Interval | |
|---|---|---|---|
| | | Lower | Upper |
| Q1 | Firewall | C1 | C2 |
| Q2 | Wireless Security | C3 | C4 |
| Q3 | IDP | C5 | C6 |

## b. Core Components

The proposed framework is composed of two core components as shown in Figure 2: Security Ontology engine and Validation engine. The security ontology engine performs two actions, a *normal action* in which it generates an *XML formatted policy script* from the *WSS policy*, and a *feedback action* fired by the validation engine that verifies the token value (*P*) existed in the BPEL file against a proposed formula (1) of the calculated lower and upper values of the *Enterprise-based infrastructure security (QoS) coefficients.*

$$P= \sum_{m=1}^{3} Q_{tp(m)} \tag{1}$$

Where

$$C_{2i-1} \leq Q_{tp(i)} \leq C_{2i} \ \forall \ i=\{1,2,3\}$$

The lower and upper values ($C_{2i-1}$ & $C_{2i}$ ) of the *Enterprise-based infrastructure security(QoS) coefficients* are grabbed by calculating the min. and the max. of the *(QoS) throughput* ($Q_{tp}$) for a given time interval *(Time$_g$)* provided by the equations,

$$Q_{tp}= \frac{Reqs}{Ts} \tag{2}$$

$$Time_g= n*T_s \quad n \geq 1 \tag{3}$$

Where Req$_s$ represents the total number of completed requests and the T$_s$ represents the unit time, and

$$Minimum[Q_{tp(i)}]=C_{(2i-1)} \ \& \ Maximum[Q_{tp(i)}]=C_{(2i)} \quad \forall \ i=\{1,2,3\}$$

This is achieved by sending complete system requests (i.e. Login requests) within a unit time ($T_s$); for a given time interval (Time$_g$); through the three main appliances of the infrastructure security (firewall, wireless security and IDP) in the enterprise. Existence of the appliances is determined based on the values of the coefficients, for instance if there is no IDP then the values of C5 and C6 will be zeros.

The Validation engine; as the second core component; performs three actions; the first one is to validate the WSDL file against the *formatted XML policy script (see table3)*, the second action is to validate the BPEL file attributes by matching the token value presented in the newly introduced attribute "wsTokenValue" within the <plnk: partnerLinkType> node, against the value presented in the newly introduced attribute "bpelTokenValue" within the <partnerLink> node. The third action is verifying the token value by calling the *feedback action* of the security ontology engine. The validation engine; therefore; generates either a validated BPEL or a rejected BPEL with a consistency value that provides a valuable indication of why the file has been rejected or accepted; for instance; a BPEL file could be rejected because it has a wrong provided token value due to incorrect interval values of one or more of the (QoS) coefficients, in which indicates that those coefficients values were not calculated for this enterprise infrastructure or the infrastructure security component performance at the time of calculating the token value is changing and needs revision by the network personnel.

The Consistency value is composed of two parts *{Part I. Part II}*:

a.   Part I:*{WSS_AuthenticationValue,WSS_MessageIntegrityValue,W SS_MessageConfidentialityValue}*
b.   Part II: *{ $Q_{tp(1)}$_IndicatorValue, $Q_{tp(2)}$_IndicatorValue, $Q_{tp(3)}$_IndicatorValue}*

As mentioned in section (2.1), the values contained in part one could be either 1 or 0, while the values contained in part II are shown in *table 5* below.

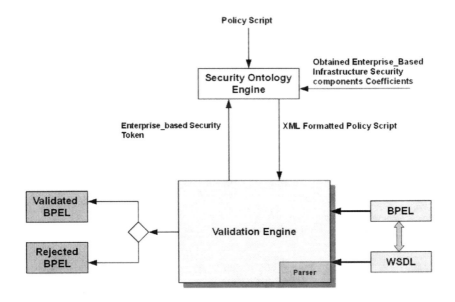

**Fig. 2.** The proposed framework

**Table 3.** XML Formatted Policy Script generated by Security Ontology Engine

```
<?xml version="1.0" encoding="ISO-8859-1"?>

<WSSPolicy>
  <item>
      <Type>Authentication</Type>
      <Value>1</Value>
  </item>
  <item>
      <Type>Message-Confidentiality</Type>
      <Value>0</Value>
  </item>
  <item>
      <Type>Message-Integrity</Type>
      <Value>1</Value>
  </item>
</WSSPolicy>
```

## c. The Validation Algorithm

The main function of the validation algorithm; *"ValidateToken"*; is to verify that the token value existing in the provided BPEL (that is needed to be validated) is within the correct intervals of the calculated token value($P$) generated from *equation 1* using the calculated (QoS) coefficients obtained from *equations 2 and 3*.

*Table 6* shows the Validation algorithm's structure which is composed of two sub-routines, "Verify(i,j,k)" and "Verifyold(i,j,k) ". Table 4 shows the abstract implementation of the two subroutines.

**Table 4.** An abstract view for validation algorithm

| # | B[3] = A | B[1] = B | B[2] = C |
|---|----------|----------|----------|
| 1 | $q_1,q_2 \rightarrow$ new($q_3$) | $q_2,q_3 \rightarrow$ new($q_1$) | $q_1,q_3 \rightarrow$ new($q_2$) |
| 2 | new($q_3$),$q_2 \rightarrow$ new($q_1$) | new($q_1$),$q_2 \rightarrow$ new($q_3$) | new($q_2$),$q_1 \rightarrow$ new($q_3$) |
| 3 | new($q_3$),$q_1 \rightarrow$ new($q_2$) | new($q_1$),$q_3 \rightarrow$ new($q_2$) | new($q_2$),$q_3 \rightarrow$ new($q_1$) |
| 4 | new($q_3$),new($q_2$) $\rightarrow$ new($q_1$) | new($q_1$),new($q_2$) $\rightarrow$new($q_3$) | new($q_2$),new($q_1$) $\rightarrow$new($q_3$) |
| 5 | new($q_3$),new($q_1$) $\rightarrow$ new($q_2$) | new($q_1$),new($q_3$) $\rightarrow$new($q_2$) | new($q_2$),new($q_3$) $\rightarrow$new($q_1$) |

**Table 5.** $Q_{tp(m)}$ value Indicators (Part II of consistency value)

| # | Expression | $Q_{tp(m)}$ value Indicator | feedback |
|---|---|---|---|
| 1 | A<>0, B<>0,C<>0 | Pv1,Pv2,Pv3 | Token value (P) is correct |
| 2 | A=0, B=0,C=0 | Pv4,Pv5,Pv6 | Token Value(p) is incorrect due to incorrect coefficients values for firewall, Wireless Security and IDP appliances |
| 3 | A=0,B<>0,C<>0 | Pv3 | Q3 correct |
| 4 | A<>0,B=0,C<>0 | Pv1 | Q1 correct |
| 5 | A<>0,B<>0,C=0 | Pv2 | Q2 correct |
| 6 | A=0,B=0,C<>0 | Pv5 | Q2 Wrong➔ Wireless Security coefficient values are not within given intervals |
| 7 | A=0,B<>0,C=0 | Pv4 | Q1 wrong➔ Firewall coefficients' values are not within given intervals |
| 8 | A<>0,B=0,C=0 | Pv6 | Q3 Wrong➔ IDP coefficients' values are not within given intervals |

**Table 6.** ValidateToken Algorithm Structure

```
INPUT 1    P #Token value
INPUT 2    q1.c1,q1.c2,q2.c3,q2.c4,q3.c5,q3.c6

BEGIN  #MAIN

       value[q(i)].maxoldcoef=value[q(i)].maxcoef  for i=1,2,3
       value[q(i)].minoldcoef=value[q(i)].mincoef  for i=1,2,3

       FOR each m in [i,j,k]
         {
           Call Verify(m,j,k)
           if b[m]<>0 { call verify(k,m,j)}
           if b[m]<>0 {call  verifyold(j,m,k)}
           if b[m]<>0   {call verify(j,m,k)}
           if b[m]<>0 {call verify(k,m,j)}
         }

       Switch (b[m]) for m=1,2,3
       #All co-officients are correct
       Case b[m]<> 0 , Accept Token Value
       #All co-officients are not correct
       Case b[m]= 0 , Reject Token Value
```

**Table 6.** (*continued*)

```
        # Coefficients of IDP appliance is valid
        Case b[3]=0 AND b[2]<>0 AND b[1]<>0
          {

             Call verifyold(2,1,3)
             if b=0
               {
                  Call verifyold(1,2,3)}
                  if b<>0
                    {
                          # Coefficients of Firewall appliance is valid
                          Q1 is wrong
                      ELSE
                          # Coefficients of Firewall, wireless security appliance is
valid
                          Q1 AND Q2 is wrong
                    }
               }
             ELSE
               # Coefficients of wireless security appliance is valid
               {   Q2 is Wrong }
          }

    .
    .
    .       # The remaining five cases shown in the table for B[1],B[2],B[3]
    .
    .


END  # MAIN


Verify(i,j,k) # Subroutine
 BEGIN
        q(i).max_newcoef=P-value[q(j)].mincoef-value[q(k)].mincoef
        q(i).min_newcoef=P-value[q(j)].maxcoef-value[q(k)].maxcoef

      # verifying new range of coef(i) against old coef(i)
          IF q(i).max_newcoef<value[q(i)].maxcoef AND
             q(i).min_newcoef<value[q(i)].mincoef
             {
                   value[q(i)].maxcoef=q(i).max_newcoef
                   value[q(i)].mincoef=q(i).min_newcoef
             }
          ELSE
                   {B=0}

END   #  verify Subroutine
```

**Table 6.** (*continued*)

```
Verifyold(i,j,k) # Verify Old Arguments Subroutine
BEGIN
        q(i).max_newcoef=P-value[q(j)].mincoef-value[q(k)].minoldcoef
        q(i).min_newcoef=P-value[q(j)].maxcoef-value[q(k)].maxoldcoef

        # verifying new range of coef(i) against old coef(i)
        IF  q(i).max_newcoef<value[q(i)].maxcoef AND
            q(i).min_newcoef<value[q(i)].mincoef
          {
            value[q(i)].maxcoef=q(i).max_newcoef
            value[q(i)].mincoef=q(i).min_newcoef
          }
      ELSE
            { B=0}
END  # Procedure verify Old Arguments
```

Following the structure of the *"ValidateToken"* algorithm, there is only one loop that iterates a maximum of 6 iterations with respect to the values of $Q_{tp(m)}$ being verified. Thus the time complexity of the *"ValidateToken"* algorithm is $O(1)$.

## 3   Case Study

We've implemented the framework in a banking environment that has its own automated business processes in BPEL format generated by oracle BPA Suite; its network has infrastructure security components which include a SRX 3600 Juniper firewall, a Wireless security component for Wireless access points Cisco1520, and a juniper IDP250 Intrusion Detection and Prevention Appliance. The implementation has been performed as follow:

1.  Obtaining the bank security ontology criteria, Policy Script.
2.  Obtaining the bank BPEL file that is needed to be validated.
3.  Creating different configurations from the original provided BPEL file to contain different token values and WSS security standards to trace the framework functionality.
4.  Obtaining the values for the (QoS) throughput coefficients, a snapshot of Firewall related values shown in *table 7* have been calculated using JMeter (a tool that can perform N requests per second and measures the percentage of completion) to send 40 requests per second for a unit time $(T_s)$ of 900 seconds and for a given time interval $(Time_g)$ of 14400 seconds. This step has been applied for the other infrastructure components existing in the banking environment (wireless security and IDP). The actual intervals calculated for all the appliances were:

$$1996 \leq Q_1 \leq 2342$$
$$1807 \leq Q_2 \leq 2113$$
$$1363 \leq Q_3 \leq 1765$$

5.  The above inputs are then fed into the framework to be processed through two different types of test cases, one type is to match the *WSS security* (No.1→No.8) and the other is to validate the token value (No.9→No.16). *Table 8* shows the results obtained from the framework for each configuration, and is composed of the following attributes

   a.  BPEL: BPEL version.
   b.  WSS security policy: The enterprise WSS security standard presented in WSDL file.
   c.  Token: Token value that appears in both the newly introduced "wsTokenValue" within the <plnk: partnerLinkType> node, and the newly introduced attribute "bpelTokenValue" within the <partnerLink> in the BPEL file.
   d.  Test Cases - Qtp(m): $Q_{tp(m)}$ values used to calculate the token value using *equation 1* for test cases purpose.
   e.  Consistency Value: resulted from the framework.
   f.  Expected Consistency Value: the expected value the framework should output.

**Table 7.** Snapshot of Firewall calculated QoS coefficients (40 RpS, $T_s$=900s, $Time_g$=14400s, $C_1$=1996, $C_2$=2342)

| $Q_{tp}$ | No. incomplete-Requests |
|---|---|
| 2342 | 58 |
| 2114 | 286 |
| 2210 | 190 |
| 2098 | 302 |
| .... | .... |
| 1996 | 404 |
| .... | ..... |

Reading through the results in table 8, and for the two types of the test cases used, the framework was capable to distinct between each configuration and provides a correct consistency value.

**Table 8.** The output results of test

| # | BPEL | Enterprise WSS Security Policy | Token $(Q_{pv1}+Q_{pv2}+Q_{pv3})$ | Test Cases - $Q_{pvint}$ | | | Consistency Value | Expected Consistency Value | Comment |
|---|---|---|---|---|---|---|---|---|---|
| | | | | $Q_{int1}$ | $Q_{int2}$ | $Q_{int3}$ | | | |
| 1 | Original | 0,0,0 | 6100 | 2300 | 2100 | 1700 | (0,0,0):{pv1,pv2,pv3} | (0,0,0):{pv1,pv2,pv3} | -WSS is matched<br>-Token value is within the given interval |
| 2 | Ver.1 | 0,0,1 | 6100 | 2300 | 2100 | 1700 | (0,0,1):{pv1,pv2,pv3} | (0,0,1):{pv1,pv2,pv3} | " |
| 3 | Ver.2 | 0,1,0 | 6100 | 2300 | 2100 | 1700 | (0,1,0):{pv1,pv2,pv3} | (0,1,0):{pv1,pv2,pv3} | " |
| 4 | Ver.3 | 0,1,1 | 6100 | 2300 | 2100 | 1700 | (0,1,1):{pv1,pv2,pv3} | (0,1,1):{pv1,pv2,pv3} | " |
| 5 | Ver.4 | 1,1,1 | 6100 | 2300 | 2100 | 1700 | (1,1,1):{pv1,pv2,pv3} | (1,1,1):{pv1,pv2,pv3} | " |
| 6 | Ver.5 | 1,0,0 | 6100 | 2300 | 2100 | 1700 | (1,0,0):{pv1,pv2,pv3} | (1,0,0):{pv1,pv2,pv3} | " |
| 7 | Ver.6 | 1,0,1 | 6100 | 2300 | 2100 | 1700 | (1,0,1):{pv1,pv2,pv3} | (1,0,1):{pv1,pv2,pv3} | " |
| 8 | Ver.7 | 1,1,0 | 6100 | 2300 | 2100 | 1700 | (1,1,0):{pv1,pv2,pv3} | (1,1,0):{pv1,pv2,pv3} | " |
| 9 | Ver.8 | 0,0,0 | 4200 | 2300 | 200 | 1700 | (0,0,0):{pv1,pv5,pv3} | (0,0,0):{pv1,pv5,pv3} | -WSS is matched<br>-Token value is not within interval due to Q2 is not within the given interval |
| 10 | Ver.9 | 0,0,1 | 3000 | 2000 | 700 | 300 | (0,0,1):{pv1,pv5,pv6} | (0,0,1):{pv1,pv5,pv6} | -WSS is matched<br>-Token value is not within interval due to Q2 & Q3 are not within the given intervals. |
| 11 | Ver.10 | 0,1,0 | 5432 | 2050 | 1900 | 1482 | (0,1,0):{pv1,pv2,pv3} | (0,1,0):{pv1,pv2,pv3} | -WSS is matched<br>-Token value is within the given interval |
| 12 | Ver.11 | 0,1,1 | 6032 | 2332 | 2113 | 1587 | (0,1,1):{pv1,pv2,pv3} | (0,1,1):{pv1,pv2,pv3} | -WSS is matched<br>-Token value is within the given interval |
| 13 | Ver.12 | 1,1,1 | 6000 | 2300 | 2050 | 1650 | (1,1,1):{pv1,pv2,pv3} | (1,1,1):{pv1,pv2,pv3} | -WSS is matched<br>-Token value is within the given interval |
| 14 | Ver.13 | 1,0,0 | 4000 | 1200 | 2200 | 600 | (1,0,0):{pv1,pv5,pv6} | (1,0,0):{pv1,pv5,pv6} | -WSS is matched<br>-Token value is not within interval due to Q1 & Q2 & Q3 are not within the given intervals. |
| 15 | Ver.14 | 1,0,1 | 6010 | 2290 | 2050 | 1670 | (1,0,1):{pv1,pv2,pv3} | (1,0,1):{pv1,pv2,pv3} | -WSS is matched<br>-Token value is within the given interval |
| 16 | Ver.15 | 1,1,0 | 5980 | 2280 | 2050 | 1650 | (1,1,0):{pv1,pv2,pv3} | (1,1,0):{pv1,pv2,pv3} | -WSS is matched<br>-Token value is within the given interval |

## 4 Related Works

Huang [4] proposed a new ontology that represents the security constraints as a policy and then built the framework that uses the proposed ontology. The framework illustrates the integration workflow between business rules and non-functional description into policy specification. A connectional security model presented in [5], which classified the security policies to the integration of dynamic selection of services provided by foreign organizations, and then the proposed model, determines an aggregation of security requirements in cross organizational service compositions.

In [6], a novel technique to translate WS-BPEL processes into non-Markovian stochastic petri nets is presented. The obtained model is helping software engineering to develop QoS-guaranteed software solution. A semantic Enterprise Services Bus (ESB) to implement a technical ontology-based matching and provide business and technological consistency is introduced in [8]. In [10] an approach is presented to improve end-to-end security by annotating service descriptions with security objectives between partners. A process model-driven transformation approach to concrete security implementations such as XACML or AXIS2 security configurations was introduced in [9]. In [11] a service improving is done through integrating industrial functional and non functional business and industrial properties in service registries.

The previous related works did not address the following concepts: securing the BPEL by introducing a new security tag, correlating the infrastructure security components performance with the BPEL through the new security Token tag, and finally measuring and tracing the inconsistency ;if exists; in the token value with respect to the calculated (QoS) coefficients of the existing infrastructure.

## 5 Conclusion and Future Work

In this paper, a framework that uses the (QoS) coefficients as a part for generating a secured enterprise business processes is introduced. It consists of two core components, the security ontology engine which generates the formatted enterprise *WSS policy script* and verifies the value of the *Enterprise-based infrastructure security Token* provided in the BPEL file against the calculated (QoS) coefficients. And the validation engine that parses and validates the provided WSDL against the enterprise *WSS policy script* and requests BPEL token value verification by the first component to generate a valid or rejected BPEL. Implementing the framework through a real case study in a banking environment that has its own infrastructure security components and its own automated Business processes (BPEL) allows us to provide validated or rejected banking BPEL file and to trace the functionality of the framework, by matching the resulted consistency value against the expected.

In a future work, we are planning to formalize the matching of the of the BPEL consistency using automata and modeling the internal behavior of the framework using Petri Net.

# References

1. Erl, T.: Service-Oriented Architecture (SOA): Concepts, Technology, and Design. Prentice Hall, Englewood Cliffs (2005)
2. Papazoglou, Mike, P.: Service-Oriented Computing: Concepts, Characteristics and Directions. In: Proceedings of the Fourth International Conference on Web Information Systems Engineering (WISE 2003), p. 3 (2003)
3. Diaz, F., Graciela, O., Salgado, René, S., Silvana, G.-A.: Web Services for Software evelopment: the Case of a Web Service that Composes Web Services. In: The Third International Conference on Software Engineering Advances, pp. 31–36 (October 2008)
4. Huang, D.: Semantic Descriptions of Web Services Security Constraints. In: SOSE 2006: Proceedings of the Second IEEE International Symposium on Service-Oriented System Engineering, pp. 81–84 (2006)
5. Menzel, M., Wolter, C., Meinel, C.: Towards the Aggregation of Security Requirements in Cross-Organisational Service Compositions. In: 11th International Conference, BIS 2008, Innsbruck, Austria, May 5-7. LNCS, pp. 297–308. Springer, Heidelberg (2008)
6. Bruneo, D., Distefano, S., Longo, F., Scarpa, M.: QoS Assesment of WS-BPEL Processes through non-Makrovian Stochastic Petri Nets. In: Proceeding of 2010 IEEE International Symposium on Parallel & Distributed Processing (IPDPS), Atlanta, USA, April 19-23 (2010); ISBN: 978-1-4244-6442-5
7. OASIS Web Services Business Process Execution Language (WSBPEL)TC. :Web Services Business Process Execution Language Version 2.0, OASIS (April 2007), http://docs.oasis-open.org/wsbpel/2.0/wsbpelv2.0.html
8. Zayati, Sidhom, L., Badr, Y., Biennier, F., Moalla, M.: Towards Business Ontologies Matching for Inter-Enterprise Collaboration Platform in a Lean Manufacturing Strategy. In: PRO-VE 2010, pp. 746–754 (2010)
9. Wolter, C., Menzel, M., Schaad, A., Miseldine, P., Meinel, C.: Model-driven Business Process Security Requirement Specification. Journal of Systems Architecture, Secure Service-Oriented Architectures (Special Issue on Secure SOA) 55(4), 211–223 (2009); ISSN 1383-7621
10. Badr, Y., Biennier, F., Tata, S.: The Integration of Corporate Security Strategies in Collaborative Business Processes. IEEE Transactions on Services Computing (99) (2010); ISSN: 1939-1374
11. Biennier, F., Aubry, R., Maranzana, M.: Integration of Business and Industrial Knowledge on Services to Set Trusted Business Communities of Organizations. In: PRO-VE 2010, pp. 420–426 (2010)

# A Dynamic Reconfigurable-Based Approach for Connectivity Mismatches of Web Services

Samir Elmougy[1,2] and Ahmed Ghoneim[1,3]

[1] College of Computer and Information Sciences, King Saud University,
Riyadh 11543, Saudi Arabia
[2] Faculty of Computer Sciences and Information Systems, Mansoura University,
Mansoura 35516, Egypt
[3] Faculty of Science, Menofia University, Shebin Elkom, Egypt
{mougy,ghoneim}@ksu.edu.sa

**Abstract.** Web services are the main stones of building and developing internal organization business workflow. If the connectivity of these web services is not well defined, companies that rely on them may face many problems especially when integration and composition are needed. Companies need a well-defined harmonic structure of the web service connectivity within their workflow. The most challenge of these companies is to keep their workflow structure harmonic by handling unexpected changes or new policies. In this paper, we face this problem by proposing a framework with supporting some dedicated dynamic reconfigurable algorithms to generate and develop an automatically efficient adaptor. This adapter is designed to work in the case of the behavioral and graph mismatches within the web services connectivity for business workflow. The proposed framework composes of two main engines namely pre-mismatch and post-mismatch detectors to detect the existing mismatches in both of the generated and the reconfigurable workflows with considering the possibility of existing mismatches within some composite web services. A real case study obtained from PayPal system is used to illustrate the proposed framework functionalities.

**Keywords:** Business model, web services connectivity, mismatches detector, mismatch composition, software adaptation, software reconfiguration.

## 1 Introduction

Nowadays, most of the web applications are suffering from the expensive cost, and different user's requirements such as increasing the reliability of the systems especially if there is a contiguous development of these applications. To reduce the cost and the complexity of building web applications to achieve a better and stable performance based on the user requirements in practice, different software components are assembled from previous versions or from previous products through plugging them into a stable compatible component together. Some problems can be appeared because of this process in which some components may not fit correctly in others, so adaptation plan is a good choice to eliminate any resulting mismatches.

V. Snasel, J. Platos, and E. El-Qawasmeh (Eds.): ICDIPC 2011, Part II, CCIS 189, pp. 67–81, 2011.
© Springer-Verlag Berlin Heidelberg 2011

Software adaptation has become one of the main technologies used in software industry. It is used to provide efficient techniques to arrange existing developed codes and slices of software components to be able to reuse them in developing new systems. It works by detecting mismatches that may be arising from the integration or composition of these components and guaranteeing that they will interact without failure.

Web service is one of the main and most choice used today for the purpose of development the Web applications. It communicates and interacts at the design time using a business workflow which specifies a sequence of message exchange supported by the service [1]. In Service Oriented Architecture (SOA), because different Web services can be assembled, composed, and integrated, it is hard to guarantee that any used software component is fitted perfectly. Adaptation process is an efficient solution to ensure and validate that the interoperation is failure free or failed among these Web services [2]. Adaption approaches can be classified into two main types based on the types of the mismatch: the interface mismatch which occurs in the development phase, and the behavioral mismatch which occurs in the running phase [2, 3].

The graph mismatch is the differences that occur when two services with interfaces $I_k$ and $I_r$ have operations that have the same functionality but differ in operation names, number, order, or type of input/output parameters. If two or more services have the same functionality of operations but with different operation names, order, number, or different parameters types of input/output.

In this work, a new framework and its main algorithms for developing efficient adaptors for web service in the case of the behavioral and graph mismatch within the web services connectivity for business workflow including the mismatches within composite web services is proposed. This proposed framework composes of two main engines namely the pre-mismatched and the post-mismatched engines. The pre-mismatch detector engine is used to detect the existing mismatch in the generated workflow. The post-mismatch detector engine is used to detect the mismatch of the reconfigurable workflow, if any exists. These detectors may be continuously repeated till reach a stable adaptable state that accepts the proposed reconfiguring. Also, the proposed framework can detect the mismatches within composite web services. A real case study derived from the PayPal system is discussed using Petri nets to illustrate the proposed framework.

The remainder of this paper is organized as follows. The main proposed framework and the required dynamic algorithms are shown and discussed in Section 2. A PayPal system as a real case study is presented in Section 3. Some recently related work is presented in Section 4. Conclusion and future work are discussed in Section 5.

## 2   The Proposed Framework

In this section, we introduce the proposed framework for checking the mismatching between the graphical representation of the core services of any organization and their corresponding operational behaviors through a continuous reconfiguring the generated graph and the operational behavior at each step till reach a stable adaptable state that accept the reconfiguring.

## 2.1 The Main Proposed Framework

The main proposed framework as shown in *Fig. 1* is composed of the following components. The input of the framework is *Org-Map-WSs* that represent the organizational services and workflow. The second component is *Org-Parser* that parses *Org-Map-WSs* to generate the graph representation and the operational behavior through a Graph-*Generator* and *Behavior-Generator* respectively. *Graph-Generator*, as shown in *Algorithm 1*, generates a graph $G = (\{V, V^*\}, E)$ *where V* is the set of single services, $V^*$ is the set of composite web services and *E* is the set of edges that represent the communications of these services.

**Algorithm 1.** Graph generator

//Graph_generator generates the extracted graph as abstract view for each organizational features
Graph _generator(WSs_BL,G)
BEGIN
    Graph _generator → WS_parser (WSs_BL)

    ∀ WS$_i$, Classify WS$_i$: simple WS$_i$ is classified into v$_i$ ‖ composite WS$_i$ is

    classified into v$^*_i$

    }

    // Detect the flow of output from WS$_a$ to be used as input to WS$_b$

    ∀ WS$_{i,}$,WS$_j$, $i \neq j$

        {
            If in(WS$_i$) ≅ out(*WS$_j$* ) *then* e$_{ij}$(WS$_i$ , WS$_j$)
        }
    // Generate the graph G

    $G=(\{V=\{v_i\}, V^*=\{v^*_i\}\}, E = \{e_{ij}\})$

END

## 2.2 Framework Behavior Algorithms

*Behavior-Generator*, as shown in *Algorithm 2*, is used to detect the operational behavior for both of the simple and composite web services within the parsed original BPEL. This algorithm calls the function *Detect_input_output* that presented in *Algorithm 2.1* to create different lists of WS inputs and outputs for both of simple WS and composite WS.

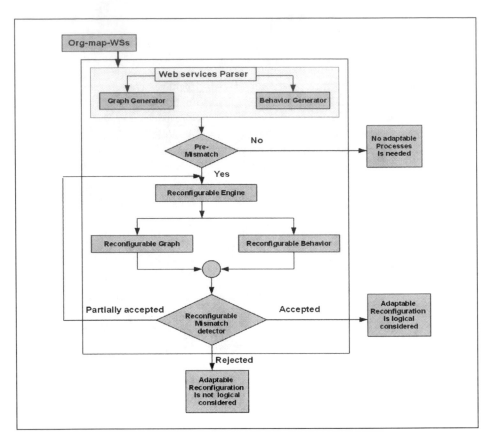

**Fig. 1.** The main proposed framework

**Algorithm 2.** Behavior generator

// Behavior generator generates all the sub-features as view of operational composite web services as well as the BL itself.
Behavior_generator (WSs_BL, G)
BEGIN
    BPEL_WS_parser_open =WS_parser (WSs_BL)

    G_parser_open =G_parser (G)

    // present how the simple or composite web services operational behave

    $\forall$ WS$_i$ do

        Detect_input_output(WS$_i$,WS$_i$-Input_List, WS$_i$-Input_List, WS$^*_i$-Input_List, WS$^*_i$-Output_List)
END

**Algorithm 2.1.** Detector procedure for behavior generator algorithm

```
// Detect procedure
Detect_input_output(WSᵢ,WSᵢ-Input_List, WSᵢ-Input_List, WS*ᵢ-Input_List, WS*ᵢ-
Output_List)
{
    If WSᵢ ∈ V then

    {

        Create WSᵢ-Input-List
        Repeat
            Extract WSᵢ-Input
            Add (WSᵢ-Input, WSᵢ-Input-List)
        Until end of input detected
        Create WSᵢ-Out-List
        Repeat
            Extract WSᵢ-Out
            Add (WSᵢ-Out,WSᵢ-Output-List)
        Until end of output detected
    }

    Else // the extracted WSᵢ is composite

    {

        Create WS*ᵢ-Input-List
        Repeat
            Extract WS*ᵢ-input
            Add (WS*ᵢ -Inout, WS*ᵢ-Input-List)
        Until end of input detected
        Create WSᵢ-Out-List
        Repeat
            Extract WS*ᵢ-Out
            Add (WS*ᵢ-Out,WS*ᵢ-Output-List)
        Until end of output detected
        Create WS*ᵢ-Internal-List
        Repeat
            Extract WSₖ from WS*ᵢ
            Add (WSₖ , WS*ᵢ-internal-List)
            Detect_input_output(WSₖ,WSₖ-Input_List,   WSₖ-Input_List,   WS*ₖ-
            Input_List, WS*ₖ-Output_List)
        Until end of internal service detected
    }

}
```

*Pre-Mismatch-Detector,* the third component, checks whether there is a mismatch in the generated graph and the operational behavior. The main processes of it are presented in *Algorithm 3* where it starts by using all WS input and output lists in addition to the internal list of each composite WS and the operation list of each WS. The core functionality of the *Pre_Mismatch* procedure is composed of three main stages. In the first stage, the pre-mismatch behavior for the input of each WS detects whether the WS input matches some of the WS operation input and adds the result to the pre-mismatch-behaviour_list[]. The same detection is applied for the output of each WS. At the graph level and for each composite WS, the pre-mismatch graph for the input of each composite WS detects whether the composite WS input matches one of the internal WS input and adds the result to the pre-mismatch-graph_list[]. Note that, the operation list of each WS is used as a parameter in the main *Pre-Mismatch-Detector* as shown in *Algorithm 3.1.* If at least one of the output mismatch behavior list or mismatch graph list is empty, no adaptable tool is needed; otherwise pass all mismatch lists to the *reconfigurable_engine.*

**Algorithm 3.** Pre-mismatch

---

Procedure Pre-Mismatch (WS$_i$-Input-List, WS$_i$-Output-List, WS$^*_i$-Input-List, WS$^*_i$-Output-List, WS$^*_i$-Internal-List, WS$_i$-Operation-List)
BEGIN
    Create Pre-Mismatch_Behaviour_in_List[], Pre-Mismatch_Behaviour_out_List[],

    Pre-Mismatch_graph_in_List[], Pre-Mismatch_graph_out_List[];

    // pre-Mismatch starts its process by checking the inputs to a composite web

    service WS$^*_I$ are represented as inputs for the simple web services within the

    composite

    For all Web services WS$_i$ do

        BEGIN
        If WS$_i$-Input-List < > [ ]
            For all WS$_i$-input in WS$_i$-Input-List do
                If   WS$_i$-input   does   not   match   any   of   WS$_i$-Operation-

                List.operation_input_list

                    // there is a Mismatch problem within the operation level for

                    WS$_i$

                    Add(Pre-Mismatch_Behaviour_in_List   (WS$_i$-input,   WS$_i$-

                    Input-List, WS$_i$-Operation-List);

---

//Then reconfigurable_engine_op(WS$_i$-input, WS$_i$-Input-List, WS$_i$-Simple-List)

For all WS$_i$-output in WS$_i$-output-List do
If WSi-output does not match any of WSi-Operation-List.operation_output_list

// there is a Mismatch problem within the operation level for WS$_i$

Add(Pre-Mismatch_Behaviour_out_List (WS$_i$-output, WS$_i$-Output-List, WS$_i$-Operation-List);

If WS$^*_i$-Input-List < > [ ]
For all WS$^*_i$-input in WS$^*_i$-Input-List do
For all WS$_k$ in WS$^*_i$-Internal-List do

If WS$^*_i$-input does not match one of WS$_k$-Input_List

// there is a Mismatch problem within the operation level for WS$_i$
Add(Pre-Mismatch_graph_in_List(WS$^*_i$-input, WS$_k$-Input_List);
If WS$^*_i$-Ouput-List < > [ ]

For all WS$^*_i$-output in WS$^*_i$-Input-List do
For all WS$_k$ in WS$^*_i$-Internal-List do

If WS$^*_i$-output does not match one of WS$_k$-out_List

// there is a Mismatch problem within the operation level for WS$_i$
Add([], Pre-Mismatch_graph_out_List (WS$^*_i$-output, WS$_k$-Output_List);
END

END PRE-MisMatch

**Algorithm 3.1.** Operation detection

```
Detect_operations(WSᵢ)
BEGIN
    Create WSᵢ-Operation-List

    Repeat

        Extract Operation
        Repeat
            If operation input_detected then
                Add(Operation_Input, operation_input_list[]);

            If operation input_detected then
                Add(Operation_output, operation_output_list[]);

        Until end of operation_input detected && operation_output detected
        Add({Operation,  operation_input_list[],  operation_output_list[]]}, WSᵢ-
        Operation-List)
    Until end of operation detected

END
```

The reconfigurable engine starts by using the graph and operational behavior generated from the parser to import the adaptable rules specifically designed for each mismatch. These rules are general for graph and its behaviors where the user is allowed to change or update the generated BPEL. The second stage is to apply the rules followed by changing both of the behavior and graph representatives. The main functionality of the reconfigurable engine is shown in *Algorithm 4*.

**Algorithm 4.** Reconfigurable engine

```
// reconfigurable_engine steps
Reconfigurable_engine(Pre-Mismatch_Behaviour_in_List[],                    Pre-
Mismatch_Behaviour_out_List[],        Pre-Mismatch_graph_in_List[],        Pre-
Mismatch_graph_out_List[])
BEGIN
    If Pre-Mismatch_Behaviour_in_List and Pre-Mismatch_Behaviour_out_List is

    not empty

            // behaviour level
            For all behavior mismatch event bmeᵢ do
                {
                    Import adaptable rules(bmeᵢ) ;
```

```
                    Reconfigure_apply(rules(bme_i))

            }

    If Pre-Mismatch_ graph _in_List and Pre-Mismatch_graph_out_List is not
    empty
            // graph level
            For all graph mismatch event sme_i do
            {
                    Import adaptable rules(sme_i) ;

                    Reconfigure_apply(rules(sme_i))

            }
END
```

The post mismatch detector component presented in *Algorithm 5* is used to check whether the reconfigurable graph and/or the reconfigurable behavior are considered acceptable, partially acceptable, or rejectable. In the case of rejecting, both of the reconfigurable planes of the graph and behavior contain a lot of mismatches. If either the reconfigurable graph or the reconfigurable behavior is matched, the reconfigurable plan is partially accepted. If reconfigurable plane is matched, it is fully accepted. These different cases are shown in *Table 1*.

**Algorithm 5.** Post-mismatch detector

```
PostMismatch-detector()
// Based on the reconfigurable plans:
BEGIN
  Graph_generator(reconfigured_WSs_BL,G);

  Behavior_generator (reconfigured_WSs_BL, G);

  Pre-Mismatch(WSi-Input-List, WSi-Output-List, WS*i-Input-List, WS*i-Output-

  List, WS*i-Internal-List, WSi-Operation-List);

  Pre-Mismatch_Behaviour_in_List[], Pre-Mismatch_Behaviour_out_List[], Pre-

  Mismatch_graph_in_List[], Pre-Mismatch_graph_out_List[])'

  If Pre-Mismatch_Behaviour_in_List[] and Pre-Mismatch_Behaviour_out_List[]

  are empty
```

```
{

        Reconfigurable plan for the behavior level :=True;
        IF  Pre-Mismatch_graph_in_List[]  and  Pre-Mismatch_graph_out_List[]
        are empty
                // Adaptation reconfiguration is logically accepted;
                Reconfigurable plan for the graph level = True;
        ELSE
        {
                // Adaptation reconfiguration is partially logically accepted;

                Reconfigurable_engine(Pre-Mismatch_Behaviour_in_List[], Pre-

                Mismatch_Behaviour_out_List[], Pre-Mismatch_graph_in_List[],

                Pre-Mismatch_graph_out_List[])


        }
    ELSE

    {

        Reconfigurable plan for the behavior level = FALSE;
        IF reconfigurable plan for the graph level = FLASE
                // Adaptation reconfiguration is logically rejected
                // No feedback to reconfigure engine
                EXIT();
        Else
        {
                //Adaptation reconfiguration is partially logically considered
                Reconfigurable_engine(Pre-Mismatch_Behaviour_in_List[],    Pre-
                Mismatch_Behaviour_out_List[], Pre-Mismatch_graph_in_List[], Pre-
                Mismatch_graph_out_List[])
        }
    }

END PostMismtach-detector
```

Reconfigurable engine for reconfiguring the generated graph and operational behaviors again using graph theory algorithms such as minimum cut, maximum flow
and quality of services, QoS, such as response time, availability, and throughput.
Repeated this processes until the reconfiguring generated graph and operational behaviors are accepted.

The general inputs are the organizational mapping web services in the separated
business logic each business logic describes one feature at the organization.

**Table 1.** Possible cases for the mismatch algorithms

| Reconfigurable behavior plan | Reconfigurable graph plan | Decision | Action |
|---|---|---|---|
| Matched | matched | accepted | success and terminate |
| Matched | miss-matched | partially accepted | feedback to reconfigurable engine |
| miss-matched | matched | partially accepted | feedback to reconfigurable engine |
| miss-matched | miss-matched | rejected | failure and terminate |

## 3  Case Study

To illustrate the proposed framework functionality, PayPal system is used as a case study. PayPal system provides both of sending and receiving money between different users. First, the user has to register for a new account with the PayPal system to establish new links with his banking account. When the system accepted the account, the user can send and request money. The following web services represent the architectural prospective of the PayPal system (please note we include only the web services that are related to our case study):

1.  Send_Money_To_Bank Account: sending money to user's bank account.
2.  Request_Money_From_Bank_Account: request money from user's bank account.

Also, the following web services represent the architectural prospective of the Banking Account Management System (also, we included only the web services that are related to our case study):

1.  Check_Account_Balance: checking user's banking account balance, the bank uses this service before it transfers money to PayPal
2.  Transfer_Money: transfer money to PayPal account.

*Fig. 2.a* shows the original graph representation for sending money to bank account. As shown in this figure, the following conditions are necessary:

1.  A sending money to user "A" event is triggered, PayPal checks an existing balance of the user's "B" PayPal account, if there is enough balance it sends money to users "B" banking account using (Send _Money_To_Bank_Account) web service.
2.  If there is no enough balance exists for user "B", money is requested from banking account event is triggered launching the (Request _Money_From_Bank_Account) web service.

When a request money event is received, the bank checks for existing balance for the user "B" using (Check_Account_Balance) web service. If his balance exists, a transfer money event is triggered launching the (Transfer_Money) web service to transfer the requested amount to the PayPal user account. If B's balance is not enough, the bank rejects the request with a notification message.

To apply the proposed framework to the original BPEL, we carry out the following two processes:

a) Parsing the original BPEL to generate a graph representative and its behavior as shown in *Fig. 2.a* using *Alg. 1* and *Alg. 2*.

b) Pre-mismatch detecting of the graph representation to ensure the connectivity between the web services within the logic (A→ B, B → C, B → D, A1 →  C1, A1 → B1, and C1→ B ) using a set of rules given in *Algorithm 3*.

c) The reconfigurable mismatch detector suggests a new adaptation as shown in *Fig. 2.b* to the existing BPEL as follows: (A→ B, B → C, B → D, and C→ C11, C → C2, D → D1, D → D2 and C → A1, A1 → C1, A1 → B1, and C1→ B) using a set of rules given in *Algorithm 4*.

d) Post-Mismatch detector parses the reconfigurable graph generated shown in *Fig. 2.b* to check the possibility of mismatch within the web services in the graph as given in *Algorithm 5*. If this detector detects a mismatch in C → A1, "partially accepted", it sends a feedback to the reconfigurable engine given above to provide a solution to this problem.

e) The reconfigurable mismatch detector works again to suggest a new adaptation to the generated BPEL as shown in *Fig. 3.c* as follows: (A→ B, B → C, B → D, and C→ C11, C → C2, D → D1, D → D2 and C2 → A1, A1 → C1, A1 → B1, and C1→ B). The means the engine removes (C → A1) and adds (C2 → A1).

f) Repeat starting from point (c) if it is partially accepted else the reconfigurable BPEL is accepted.

## 4  Related Work

Many researchers have been worked toward proposing and implementing efficient automatic adaptors to solve the problem of mismatch in web services components. Schmidt and Reussner [4] propose adaptors similar to the synchronous products for concurrent component. Dumas et al [5] apply the set of adaptation operations definitions to generate a behavioral interface adaption approach. They describe the transformations required for soling the adaptation problem by defining a trace-based algebra for it. Also, they describe the mapping between the components behavioral interfaces by presenting a suitable visual notation.

R. Mateescu et al [6] use process algebra to provide techniques for the adapter synthesis. Alfaro et al. [7, 8] apply game theory to obtain a behavioral adaptation. Canal et al. [2] proposed efficient model-based software for adaptation process with designing two different algorithms to deal with different and complex mismatch situations at the graph and behavior levels. Their first algorithm is based on the synchronous products of Labeled Transition Systems (LTS) and the second algorithm applies Petri net encoding.

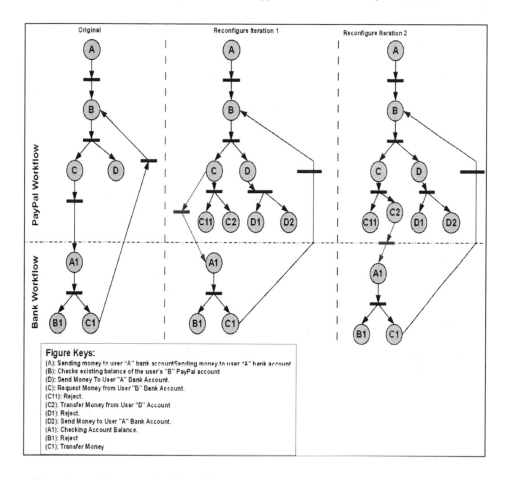

**Fig. 3.a.** The graph representative generated from parsing the original BPEL using *Alg. 1* and *Alg. 2*

**Fig. 3.b.** The suggested new adaptation for the existing BPEL in *Fig. 3.a* using the reconfigurable mismatch detector presented in *Alg. 4*

**Fig. 3.c.** The suggested adaptation for the previous reconfigurable BPEL shown in *Fig. 2.b* using the post mismatch detector presented in *Alg. 5*

In [9], Nezhad et al. apply different automatic tools to build a semi-automated adaptation. This system can only generate an adaptor in the absence case of deadlock by displaying a mismatch tree to allow the user to analyze it and identify whether the mismatch problem is solved or not. In [3], Bracciali et al. present another approach to describe service behavior for adapting process based on Pi calculus. In this approach, two main phases are used. First, the adapting specification is used to construct the mapping between the interfaces. Second, a proper automatic adaptor algorithm is constructed. Wu et al. [10] propose a service adaptation method based on applying a dependency graph to describe the service with Pi calculus

In [11], Foster et al. present a model-based method for verifying Web service compositions where Web service orchestration is represented using a finite state machine.

Borgi et al. [12] present an adaptation mythology for solving the behavioral mismatches between any BPEL processes using an intermediate workflow language to describe the interfaces of component behavioral. Their methodology can detect behavioral mismatches using some lock analysis techniques. Kongdenfha et al. [1] classify different mismatch patterns. They propose and implement adaptation templates using stand alone adaptor and Aspect-Oriented Approach (AOP).

Most of the previous related works were focused on the abstract level without addressing concurrent functions to derive the mismatches. Also, most of these works did not provide separated engines for the mismatch detectors. In this paper, ours focuses on overcoming the above problems by proposing a reconfigurable approach for detecting mismatch within the web services connectivity for business workflow.

# 5 Conclusion and Future Work

The proposed approach in this paper deals with the reconfiguration of the mismatch that may appear in either the behavioral level or in the graph level. The separated mismatch engine used in the proposed framework increases the total system performance and the used reconfigurable approach increases the consistency within the workflow or within the composite web services. Ours focuses on overcoming the abstract level with addressing concurrent functions to derive the mismatches and providing separated engines for the mismatch detectors.

Also, a real case study is derived from PayPal system and banking system to provide a rich mismatch problems when logically combined to illustrate the proposed framework.

Future work is directed into two main directions. First, LTS is planned to use to formalize the theoretical foundations. Second, implementing a tool for testing the mismatches problems within the graph and behavior representatives for any organizational workflow,

## References

1. Kongdenfha, W., Motahari-Nezhad, H.R., Benatallah, B., Casati, F., Saint-Paul, R.: Mismatch Patterns and Adaptation Aspects: A Foundation for Rapid Development of Web Service Adapters. IEEE Transactions on Service Computing 2(2), 94–107 (2009)
2. Canal, C., Poizat, P., Salaün, G.: Model-based Adaptation of Behavioral Mismatching Components. IEEE Transactions on Software Engineering 34(4), 546–563 (2008)
3. Bracciali, A., Brogi, A., Canal, C.: A Formal Approach to Component Adaptation. Elsevier Journal of Systems and Software 74(1), 45–48 (2005); Special Issue on Automated Component-Based Software Engineering
4. Schmidt, H.W., Reussner, R.H.: Generating Adapters for Concurrent Component Protocol Synchronization. In: 5th International Conference on Formal Methods for Open Object-Based Distributed Systems (IFIP TC6/WG6.1), pp. 213–229. Kluwer Academic Publishers, Dordrecht (2002)
5. Dumas, M., Spork, M., Wang, K.: Adapt or Perish: Algebra and Visual Notation for Service Interface Adaptation. In: Dustdar, S., Fiadeiro, J.L., Sheth, A.P. (eds.) BPM 2006. LNCS, vol. 4102, pp. 65–80. Springer, Heidelberg (2006)

6. Mateescu, R., Poizat, P., Salaun, G.: Behavioral Adaptation of Component Compositions Based on Process Algebra Encodings. In: Proc. of ASE, pp. 385–388 (2007)
7. de Alfaro, L., Stoelinga, M.: Interfaces: A Game-Theoretic Framework to Reason about Open Systems. In: 2nd International Workshop on Foundations of Coordination Languages and Software Architectures, FOCLASA (2003)
8. de Alfaro, L., Henzinger, T.A.: Interface Automata. In: 8th European Software Engineering Conference, Vienna, Austria, September 10-14 (2001)
9. Nezhad, H.R.M., Benatallah, B., Martens, A.: Francisco Curbera, and Fabio Casati: Semi-automated adaptation of service interactions. In: WWW, pp. 993–1002 (2007)
10. Wu, B., Deng, S., Wu, J., Li, Y., Kuang, L., Yin, J.: Service Behavioral Adaptation Based on Dependency Graph. In: The 2008 IEEE Asia-Pacific Services Computing Conference, December 09 -12 (2008)
11. Foster, H., Uchitel, S., Magee, J., Kramer, J.: Compatibility Verification for Web Service Choreography. I. In: EEE International Conference on Web Services (ICWS 2004), San Diego, CA (July 2004)
12. Brogi, A., Popescu, R.: Automated Generation of BPEL Adapters. In: Dan, A., Lamersdorf, W. (eds.) ICSOC 2006. LNCS, vol. 4294, pp. 27–39. Springer, Heidelberg (2006)

# Reducing Alphabet Using Genetic Algorithms

Jan Platos and Pavel Kromer

Department of Computer Science, FEECS,
VSB-Technical University of Ostrava
17. listopadu 15, 70833 Ostrava Poruba
Czech Republic
{jan.platos,pavel.kromer}@vsb.cz

**Abstract.** In the past, several approaches for data compression were developed. The base approach use characters as basic compression unit, but syllable-based and word based approaches were also developed. These approaches define strict borders between basic units. These borders are valid only for tested collections. Moreover, there may be words, which are not syllables, but it is useful to use them even in syllable based approach or in character based approach. Of course, testing of all possibilities is not realizable in finite time. Therefor, a optimization technique may be used as possible solution. This paper describes first steps in the way to optimal compression alphabet - designing the basic algorithms for alphabet reduction using genetic algorithms.

**Keywords:** genetic algorithms, data compression, alphabet reduction.

## 1 Introduction

Data compression is one of the mayor topic these days. Large amount of data must be stored in data warehouses and archives and lot of data must be transmitted through data lines. Data compression algorithms were usually designed for data processing symbol by symbol. The input symbols of these algorithms are usually taken from ASCII table, i.e. the size of the input alphabet is 256 symbols which are representable by 8-bit number. This approach has advantage, that there is not necessary to store the alphabet into compressed data, because it exists on every computer.

In last 20 years, this compression schema was modified in the area of text compression, but the similar improvements are applicable to other type of data. In this area a new approach for data compression was developed. In this approach, larger semantic elements than characters are used in data compression. At first, a problematics of large text files compression was studied. The experiments shown that using of words as basic symbols leads to the better compression [6,16,7,23]. Many standard compression algorithms were modified to support this approach. The second modification was using of syllables to text compression [11]. This approach is little bit more complicated than the word based approach, because it is necessary to select extract syllables from text according grammatical rules.

V. Snasel, J. Platos, and E. El-Qawasmeh (Eds.): ICDIPC 2011, Part II, CCIS 189, pp. 82–92, 2011.

Both approaches share an disadvantage, that the dictionary of the alphabet must stored to the data to enable decompression. This problem may be partially solved by the principle designed by Lansky in [13], where a subset of the most frequent syllables is created for each supported language and this syllable set is distributed with the compression/decompression algorithms and therefore, it is not necessary to store all syllable to the compressed data.

Three different approaches to text compression, based on the selection of input symbols, were defined - character-based, syllable-based, and word-based. The question is what type is the most suitable for defined texts. In [12], authors compared the single file parsing methods used on input text files of a size 1KB-5MB by means of the Burrows-Wheeler Transform for different languages (English, Czech, and German). They considered these input symbol types: letters, syllables, words, 3-grams, and 5-grams. Comparing letter-based, syllable-based, and word-based compression, they found out that character-based compression is the most suitable for small files (up to 200KB) and that syllable-based compression is the best for files of a size 200KB-5MB. Compression which uses natural text units such as words or syllables is 10-30% better than compression with 5-grams and 3-grams. For larger files, word-based compression methods will be the best.

The results mentioned in the previous paragraph are very interesting, but these experiments define some strict borders between these methods. These borders are valid only for the tested languages or only for tested collections. Moreover, there may be words, which are not syllables, but it is useful to use them even in syllable based approach or in character based approach. Of course, testing of all possibilities is not realizable in finite time. Therefor, a optimization technique may be used as possible solution.

This paper describes first steps in the way to optimal compression alphabet - designing the basic algorithms for alphabet reduction using genetic algorithms.

The rest of the paper is organized as follows. The Section 2 describes the basic of data compression and the Section 3 describe basic of the genetics algorithms. Section 4 is focused on the description of basic algorithm and Section 5 contain experimental result of the basic algorithm on several files. In the last Section, a conclusion of the first experiments and future work is defined.

## 2    Data Compression

The area of data compression is wide and complex and its origin dates back to the mid-20th century, when the theory of information was defined [20]. In information theory, information is represented as data. The amount of information contained in the data can be expressed as the Shannon entropy [20]. Entropy is measured in units such as bits and the same unit is used for the data. The rest of the data is redundant and may be eliminated. For example, in [21] Shannon experimentally discovers that the entropy for English is between 0.6 to 1.3 bits per character. The elimination of the redundancy is also called data compression. Therefore, the entropy may also be explained as a maximal limit for data compression.

Compression algorithms and compression transformations process data by symbols such as bytes (characters), pixels, or any other symbol. Almost all algorithms (transforms) are independent of the type or size of the symbol. In addition to that, these algorithms are not dependent on the type of data.

Many compression algorithms and transformations have been developed. Compression algorithms usually process data in their original form, but it is possible to use one or more transformations for the conversion of data into a more suitable form.

Compression algorithms may be divided into 3 main categories. The first category is statistical algorithm. Statistical methods use probability of the symbols for assigning shorter codes to more probable symbols and longer codes to least probable ones. Because of this, these methods use only necessary amount of bits to represent data and, therefore, they are able to eliminate all redundancy. The represent ants of this algorithms are Shannon-Fano encoding [20], Huffman Encoding [8], Arithmetic encoding [1,17,18] and Prediction by Partial Match algorithm [5,15].

The second category is Dictionary-based algorithms. Dictionary-based methods use a dictionary as a memory of processed data (sequence of symbols) and the actual processed data are encoded as pointers to the previous occurrence of the symbol sequence. The type of dictionary and representation of the pointers depend on the algorithms. Almost all algorithms in this category are based on the following two algorithms. LZ77 [24] represent the dictionary as a structure called a sliding window of a certain size. This window contains processed symbols (in their raw form) and the new data are encoded as a triplet describing a similar sequence found in the sliding window. The triplet contains the length of the sequence found, the position of the sequence, and the first different symbol after the sequence. The last part of the triplet solves the problem, when no sequence is found in the dictionary. The LZ78 [25] algorithm uses different approach. The dictionary is dynamically created from the data by phrases. These phrases are created from the phrases in the dictionary and the next symbol. The pointers are encoded as a doublet. The first part of the doublet is the number of the phrase in the dictionary and the second one is the first different symbol.

The third category is Transformation for data compression. These transformation are used as a preprocessors before one of the compression algorithm from the first or second category is used. The most well know transformation for data compression are Run-Length encoding [19], Move-To-Front transformation [3] and Burrows-Wheeler transformation [4].

More information about data compression may be found in [19].

## 3   Genetic Algorithms

Genetic algorithms are a popular variant of evolutionary algorithms. They are based on the programmatical implementation of genetic evolution and they emphasize selection and crossover as the most important operations in the whole evolutionary optimization process [9,14].

Genetic algorithms evolve a population of chromosomes representing potential problem solutions encoded into suitable data structures. The evolution is performed by genetic operators modifying the chromosomes, i.e. the encoded forms of problem solutions. Proper encoding is vital for the effectiveness of the evolutionary searches. It defines the genotype, the space of all encoded problem solutions, which is different from the phenotype, the space of all problem solutions. Genetic algorithms explore the genotype of the problem being investigated and the size and shape of the problem genotype define its fitness landscape.

Finding good encoding is a non-trivial and problem-dependent task affecting the performance and results of an evolutionary search in a given problem domain. The solutions might be encoded into binary strings, integer vectors or real vectors, or more complex, often tree-like, hierarchical structures. The encoding choice is based on the needs of a particular application area. The original (canonical) GA described by John Holland encoded problems as fixed-length binary strings.

**Algorithm 1.** A summary of genetic algorithm

| |
|---|
| 1 Define objective (fitness) function and problem encoding |
| 2 Encode initial population $P$ of possible solutions as fixed length strings |
| 3 Evaluate chromosomes in initial population using objective function |
| 4 **while** *Termination criteria not satisfied* **do** |
| 5     Apply selection operator to select parent chromosomes for reproduction: $sel(P_i) \rightarrow parent_1$, $sel(P_i) \rightarrow parent_2$ |
| 6     Apply crossover operator on parents with respect to crossover probability $P_C$ to produce new chromosomes: $cross(P_C, parent_1, parent_2) \rightarrow \{offspring_1, offspring_2\}$ |
| 7     Apply mutation operator on offspring chromosomes with respect to mutation probability $P_M$: $mut(P_M, offspring_1) \rightarrow offspring_1$, $mut(P_M, offspring_2) \rightarrow offspring_2$ |
| 8     Evaluate offspring chromosomes: $fit(offspring_1) \rightarrow offspring_1^{fit}$, $fit(offspring_2) \rightarrow offspring_2^{fit}$ |
| 9     Create new population from current population and offspring chromosomes: $migrate(offspring_1, offsprig_2, P_i) \rightarrow P_{i+1}$ |
| 10 **end** |

The iterative phase of an evolutionary search process starts with an initial population of individuals that can be generated randomly or seeded with potentially good solutions. Artificial evolution consists of the iterative application of genetic operators, introducing to the algorithm evolutionary principles such as inheritance, the survival of the fittest, and random perturbations. Iteratively, the current population of problem solutions is modified with the aim of forming a new and, it is hoped, better population to be used in the next generation. The evolution of problem solutions ends after specified termination criteria have been satisfied, and especially the criterion of finding an optimal solution. However, the decision as to whether a problem solution is the best one (i.e. a global optimum was reached) is impossible in many problem areas. After the termination of the search process, the evolution winner is decoded and presented as the most optimal solution found.

### 3.1   Genetic Operators

Genetic operators and termination criteria are the most influential parameters of every evolutionary algorithm. All the operators presented bellow have several implementations that perform differently in various application areas.

- A selection operator is used for selecting chromosomes from a population. Through this operator, selection pressure is applied to the population of solutions with the aim of picking promising solutions to form the following generation. The selected chromosomes are called parents.
- A crossover operator modifies the selected chromosomes from one population to the next by exchanging one or more of their subparts. Crossover is used for emulating the sexual reproduction of diploid organisms with the aim of passing on and increasing the good properties of parents for offspring chromosomes. The most commonly used implementations of the crossover operator are one-point crossover (see Figure 1a) and two point crossover Figure 1b. Both of them exchange one or more subparts of the parent chromosomes to create offspring chromosomes.
- A mutation operator introduces random perturbations into chromosome structure; it is used for changing chromosomes randomly and introducing new genetic material into the population. The usually used bit mutation, which changes each bit of the chromosome with certain probability, is illustrated in Figure 1c.

Besides genetic operators, termination criteria are another important factor affecting the search process. Widely used termination criteria include:

- reaching a globally optimal solution (which is often hard or impossible to recognize)
- passing a certain number of generations
- passing a certain number of generations without any significant improvement in the population

Many variants of the standard generational GA have been proposed. The main differences lie mostly in particular selection, crossover, mutation, and replacement strategies [14].

Genetic algorithms have been successfully used to solve non-trivial multimodal optimization problems. They inherit the robustness of emulated natural optimization processes and excel in browsing huge, potentially noisy problem domains. Their clear principles, ease of interpretation, intuitive and reusable practical use and significant results have made genetic algorithms the method of choice for industrial applications, while their carefully elaborated theoretical foundations attract the attention of academics.

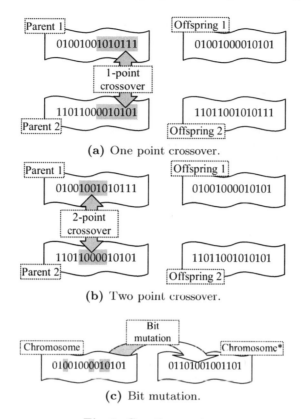

**Fig. 1.** Genetic operators

## 4    Reducing Alphabet

As was mentioned above, this paper is focused on first steps on the way toward efficient Alphabet evolving algorithm. The basic step is the selection of the used algorithms. From the previous section is obvious, that suggested algorithm is based on genetic algorithms. This decision was made, because the genetic algorithms are very efficient in searching for optimal set of items from the universum. The following section describes the previous work in this field.

### 4.1    Previous Work

The genetic algorithm were successfully used in data compression. In the area of text compression, one of the first algorithm were published by Üçoluk and Toroslu [22]. In this paper, Genetic algorithms are used for selection of the syllable subset of Turkish language to the improve of the data compression using Huffman encoding. This approach leads to the improvement up to 20% in compression ratio.

In [10] authors used genetic algorithm for determination of the characteristic syllables in Czech, English and German language. These characteristics syllables are stored into dictionary, which is part of the compression algorithm and it is not necessary to place them into compressed data. This leads to reduction of used space. The determined characteristic syllables lead to improvement up to 10% in compression ratio.

## 4.2  Proposed Algorithm

As was mentioned above, this paper is focused on the reduction of the needed alphabet using genetic algorithms. Moreover, it is focused on definition of right parameters, which lead into fast convergence of genetics algorithm with achievement of good results.

The setup of the algorithm was as follows. The chromosomes are represented as binary fixed length string. The length of the vector is set as the whole alphabet derived from ASCII table - 256 symbols. Each bit represent the presence of the symbol of the alphabet. The selection operator was defined as *semi-elitary*. This means the the one parent was select randomly and the second is selected according its fitness value. This leads into balance between convergence to local optimum and search of possible new areas of search space. The crossover operator was defined as *two-point crossover* and the mutation simply change the bit value according to defined probability.

The most difficult problem was to select the right *Fitness function*. The first designed fitness function was defined as follows:

1. Get the alphabet for current chromosome.
2. Try to parse input data according selected alphabet.
3. If the whole data may be parsed, then set the fitness value to the number of used symbols.
4. If the file cannot be parsed, set the fitness value to the very high value equal to the square of the maximum alphabet size.

This fitness function has very serious problems with the point 4. This point means, that any chromosome which alphabet does not have a necessary symbol is excluded from the further processing. This totalistic criterion leads to very bad behavior of whole optimization algorithm - the algorithm was not able to find any valid solution, even when total number of population size was large.

The solution to this problem was found with the following procedure. Each data file has a set of symbols which creates its minimal alphabet. It is clear, that the minimal alphabet of text files contain all used characters and some of white spaces. The minimal alphabet of binary file contain all used bytes. The new fitness function is defined as follows:

1. Get the minimal alphabet of the current data file (this step is done only once for on data file).
2. Get the alphabet for current chromosome.
3. Try to parse input data according selected alphabet.
4. If the whole data may be parsed, then set the fitness value to the number of used symbols.
5. If the file cannot be parsed, penalize each missing symbol from minimal alphabet by the size of the total alphabet.

This fitness function has much better results than the previous one and the solution may be found very quickly.

# 5 Experiments

The experiments for this task was set in the following way. The goal is to find out which parameters of GA are suitable for this type of problem. Because the parameters may differ for different data file, several data files were tested.

## 5.1 Testing Files

The testing files was selected according the number of symbols in them. The following files where selected: *aaa.txt*, *alphabet.txt* and *alice29.txt* from the Canterbury corpus [2], the DNA file *humdyst.chr* from the Historic DNA corpus and Executable files for Windows - the testing application itself. The files *aaa.txt* and *humdyst.chr* are representative of files with very small minimal alphabet - one and four symbols. The file *alphabet.txt* contains repetitions of the English alphabet of small letter, i.e. 26 different symbols. The file *alice29.txt* if an electronic version the the ALICE'S ADVENTURES IN WONDERLAND from Lewis Carroll and represents a typical text file. The last file called *exe* is a representative of the file with minimal alphabet equal to the whole ASCII table.

## 5.2 Parameters of the GA

The Genetic algorithms has several parameters which must be set according to solved problem. Moreover, it is usual to design an another genetic algorithm which evolve parameter to another GA algorithm. In our case, the parameters which must be set are the probability of the cross-over, probability of the mutation and size of the population. Other parameters were set as follows: the crossover type is two point, selection is semi-elitist, the GA looking for the minimal fitness value and the termination criteria is set to 100000 generations or achieving of the minimal alphabet size.

The probability of the crossover was set from 0.1 to 0.9 with the 0.1 step. The mutation probability was set to 0.001, 0.005, 0.01 and 0.05. The population size was set to 10 and 100. The experiments shows, that the size of the population has very small influence to the overall results, This is done by the selection operator which prefer better chromosomes. Therefore, the depicted results was achieved with population size of 100.

## 5.3 Results for the Files with Small Alphabet

The results achieved for the files *aaa.txt* and *humdyst.chr* are depicted in Table 1 and Table 2.

**Table 1.** Number of processed iteration for file *aaa.txt* with one symbol

| Mutation | Crossover 0.1 | 0.2 | 0.3 | 0.4 | 0.5 | 0.6 | 0.7 | 0.8 | 0.9 |
|---|---|---|---|---|---|---|---|---|---|
| 0.001 | 3744 | 2680 | 3472 | 2890 | 4570 | 2517 | 3179 | 2744 | 1624 |
| 0.005 | 1876 | 3583 | 2720 | 2877 | 3120 | 2654 | 2019 | 3111 | 2210 |
| 0.01 | 4361 | 4449 | 6537 | 5276 | 3529 | 6822 | 5106 | 3128 | 3183 |
| 0.05 | 100000 | 100000 | 100000 | 100000 | 100000 | 100000 | 100000 | 100000 | 100000 |

**Table 2.** Number of processed iteration for file *humdyst.chr* with 4 symbols

| Mutation | Crossover 0.1 | 0.2 | 0.3 | 0.4 | 0.5 | 0.6 | 0.7 | 0.8 | 0.9 |
|---|---|---|---|---|---|---|---|---|---|
| 0.001 | 4802 | 3839 | 5180 | 4313 | 4643 | 3062 | 4286 | 4011 | 4740 |
| 0.005 | 3078 | 1791 | 2999 | 3411 | 2780 | 2407 | 2428 | 3018 | 1882 |
| 0.01 | 4428 | 3497 | 4731 | 4919 | 6114 | 5181 | 2983 | 5602 | 4217 |
| 0.05 | 100000 | 100000 | 100000 | 100000 | 100000 | 100000 | 100000 | 100000 | 100000 |

As may be seen form the table, the best results were achieved with the mutation probability set to 0.005 and crossover probability set to 0.1 or 0.9. These two different probabilities of crossover leads to very similar behavior of the genetic algorithm. The best achieved results were around 1800 performed iteration until the optimal alphabet was found. As may be seen, when the mutation probability was set to 0.5, then it was not possible to find an alphabet. The algorithm ends on maximal number of generation terminating criterion.

### 5.4   Results for the Files with Medium-Sized Alphabet

The results achieved for the files *alphabet.txt* and *alice29.txt* are depicted in Table 3 and Table 4. As may be seen, the best results were achieved with mutation probability set to 0.005 and the worst with 0.5. The setting of crossover probability is less significant, but the best results were achieved with smaller numbers.

**Table 3.** Number of processed iteration for file *alphabet.txt*

| Mutation | Crossover 0.1 | 0.2 | 0.3 | 0.4 | 0.5 | 0.6 | 0.7 | 0.8 | 0.9 |
|---|---|---|---|---|---|---|---|---|---|
| 0.001 | 8946 | 6123 | 5305 | 6979 | 6075 | 7869 | 4841 | 5896 | 6042 |
| 0.005 | 3974 | 2249 | 3360 | 4762 | 3431 | 3338 | 3213 | 3547 | 3910 |
| 0.01 | 5233 | 6221 | 4609 | 5227 | 3447 | 5681 | 4894 | 4116 | 4782 |
| 0.05 | 100000 | 100000 | 100000 | 100000 | 100000 | 100000 | 100000 | 100000 | 100000 |

**Table 4.** Number of processed iteration for file *alice29.txt*

| Mutation | Crossover | | | | | | | | |
|---|---|---|---|---|---|---|---|---|---|
| | 0.1 | 0.2 | 0.3 | 0.4 | 0.5 | 0.6 | 0.7 | 0.8 | 0.9 |
| **0.001** | 6698 | 6768 | 6406 | 6886 | 9626 | 6412 | 8147 | 7286 | 7869 |
| **0.005** | 3213 | 3422 | 3531 | 3333 | 3169 | 4911 | 4820 | 5116 | 3996 |
| **0.01** | 3871 | 5067 | 5209 | 4295 | 4789 | 6964 | 5991 | 5510 | 5980 |
| **0.05** | 100000 | 100000 | 100000 | 100000 | 100000 | 100000 | 100000 | 100000 | 100000 |

## 5.5   Results for the Files with Large Alphabet

The results achieved for the file *exe* are depicted in Table 5. Once again, the best results were achieved with mutation probability set to 0.005 and crossover probability set to small numbers.

**Table 5.** Number of processed iteration for file *exe*

| Mutation | Crossover | | | | | | | | |
|---|---|---|---|---|---|---|---|---|---|
| | 0.1 | 0.2 | 0.3 | 0.4 | 0.5 | 0.6 | 0.7 | 0.8 | 0.9 |
| **0.001** | 6612 | 6587 | 6399 | 4781 | 6249 | 5837 | 6761 | 7108 | 6744 |
| **0.005** | 3241 | 2431 | 2926 | 3595 | 4021 | 4437 | 5048 | 4067 | 3605 |
| **0.01** | 4935 | 4143 | 6002 | 5880 | 5410 | 5127 | 4026 | 4811 | 5344 |
| **0.05** | 100000 | 100000 | 100000 | 100000 | 100000 | 100000 | 100000 | 100000 | 100000 |

# 6   Conclusion

The suggested algorithm works well for any type of files. The minimal alphabet was found in all cases in less than 300 iterations and in some cases in less than 200 iterations. The suggested fitness function works well. In the future, the next steps will be performed to achieve the final goal - definition of the optimal alphabet. The step two will be the algorithm for selection of the optimal alphabet from all possible 1-grams and 2-grams. This lead to optimization in space with size of more than 65535+256 symbols the right combination. Of course, usually in normal text files only few thousands of 2-grams is used.

**Acknowledgments.** This work was supported by the Grant Agency of the Czech Republic, under the grant no. P202/11/P142.

# References

1. Abramson, N.: Information Theory and Coding. McGraw-Hill, New York (1963)
2. Arnold, R., Bell, T.: A corpus for the evaluation of lossless compression algorithms. In: Storer, J.A., Cohn, M. (eds.) Proc. 1997 IEEE Data Compression Conference, pp. 201–210. IEEE Computer Society Press, Los Alamitos (1997)
3. Bentley, J.L., Sleator, D.D., Tarjan, R.E., Wei, V.K.: A locally adaptive data compression scheme. Commun. ACM 29(4), 320–330 (1986)

4. Burrows, M., Wheeler, D.J.: A block-sorting lossless data compression algorithm. Technical report, Digital SRC Research Report (1994)
5. Cleary, J.G., Ian, Witten, H.: Data compression using adaptive coding and partial string matching. IEEE Transactions on Communications 32, 396–402 (1984)
6. Dvorský, J., Pokorný, J., Snášel, V.: Word-based compression methods and indexing for text retrieval systems. In: Eder, J., Rozman, I., Welzer, T. (eds.) ADBIS 1999. LNCS, vol. 1691, pp. 75–84. Springer, Heidelberg (1999)
7. Horspool, R.N.: Constructing word-based text compression algorithms. In: Proc. IEEE Data Compression Conference, pp. 62–81. IEEE Computer Society Press, Los Alamitos (1992)
8. Huffman, D.A.: A method for the construction of minimum-redundancy codes. Institute of Radio Engineers 40(9), 1098–1101 (1952)
9. Koza, J.: Genetic programming: A paradigm for genetically breeding populations of computer programs to solve problems. Technical Report STAN-CS-90-1314, Dept. of Computer Science, Stanford University (1990)
10. Kuthan, T., Lansky, J.: Genetic algorithms in syllable-based text compression. In: Pokorný, J., Snásel, V., Richta, K. (eds.) CEUR Workshop Proceedings. DATESO, vol. 235 (2007), CEUR-WS.org
11. Lánský, J.: Slabiková komprese. Master's thesis, Charles University in Prague, in czech language (April 2005)
12. Lansky, J., Chernik, K., Vlickova, Z.: Comparison of text models for bwt. In: DCC 2007: Proceedings of the 2007 Data Compression Conference, p. 389. IEEE Computer Society, Washington, DC, USA (2007)
13. Lansky, J., Zemlicka, M.: Text compression: Syllables. In: Richta, K., Snásel, V., Pokorný, J. (eds.) CEUR Workshop Proceedings. DATESO, vol. 129, pp. 32–45 (2005), CEUR-WS.org
14. Mitchell, M.: An Introduction to Genetic Algorithms. MIT Press, Cambridge (1996)
15. Moffat, A.: Implementing the ppm data compression scheme. IEEE Transactions on Communications 38(11), 1917–1921 (1990)
16. Moffat, A., Isal, R.Y.K.: Word-based text compression using the burrows-wheeler transform. Inf. Process. Manage. 41(5), 1175–1192 (2005)
17. Rissanen, J.: Generalized kraft inequality and arithmetic coding. IBM Journal of Research and Development 20(3), 198–203 (1976)
18. Rissanen, J., Langgon Jr, G.G.: Arithmetic coding. IBM Journal of Research and Development 23(2), 149–162 (1979)
19. Salomon, D.: Data Compression - The Complete Reference, 4th edn. Springer, London (2007)
20. Shannon, C.E.: A mathematical theory of communication. Bell System Technical Journal 27, 379–423, 623–656 (1948)
21. Shannon, C.E.: Prediction and entropy of printed english. Bell Systems Technical Journal 30, 50–64 (1951)
22. Üçoluk, G., Toroslu, I.H.: A genetic algorithm approach for verification of the syllable-based text compression technique. Journal of Information Science 23(5), 365–372 (1997)
23. Witten, I., Moffat, A., Bell, T.: Managing Gigabytes: Compressing and Indexing Documents and Images. Van Nostrand Reinhold (1994)
24. Ziv, J., Lempel, A.: A universal algorithm for sequential data compression. IEEE Transactions on Information Theory IT-23(3), 337–343 (1977)
25. Ziv, J., Lempel, A.: Compression of individual sequences via variable-rate coding. IEEE Transactions on Information Theory IT-24(5), 530–536 (1978)

# On the Quality of Service Optimization
# for WiMAX Networks Using Multi-hop Relay Stations

Chutima Prommak and Chitapong Wechtaison

School of Telecommunication Engineering,
Suranaree University of Technology
Nakhon Ratchasima, Thailand
cprommak@sut.ac.th

**Abstract.** Network quality of services and the limitation of network installation budget are important concerns in the widespread deployment of mobile Wi-MAX access networks. This paper presents a novel quality of service optimization model for WiMAX networks utilizing multi-hop relay stations with special considerations of network budget limitation. The proposed model aims to optimize the network quality of services in term of the user access data rate guarantee and the radio service coverage to serve potential user traffic demand in the target service area by determining optimal locations to install base stations and relay stations in the multi-hop manner. The numerical results and analysis show that the proposed model can improve the user access data rate and enhance the network service coverage compared with other existing techniques.

**Keywords:** Network quality of services, Network optimization, WiMAX, Access networks, Network planning, Wireless networks.

## 1 Introduction

WiMAX (Wireless Interoperability for Microwave Access) network technology has become potential solutions to bring broadband internet access to people in the remote area where wired network infrastructures cannot reach [1], [2]. With the support of the IEEE 802.16j standard, one can deploy the network topology using multi-hop relay stations (RSs) to enhance services of the base stations. As illustrated in fig.1, RSs can provide coverage extension to the cell boundary area, the shadowing area and the coverage-hole area [1], [2]. To enable network operators to provide low cost coverage with the quality of services guarantee, there is a need for an efficient network design.

Several works have devoted to the studies of the performance improvement of wireless networks and the wireless network design problems. In [3], the authors proposed an adaptive cross-layer bandwidth scheduling strategies for the hierarchical cellular networks. [4] presented a study of the baseband transceiver for WIMAX IEEE802.16d. Research works in [5-16] dealt with the wireless network design problems. [5-7] presented the studies of the radio network planning for cellular networks. In [8-12], the authors considered WiMAX radio network planning and presented the practical network deployment with performance analysis and evaluation.

V. Snasel, J. Platos, and E. El-Qawasmeh (Eds.): ICDIPC 2011, Part II, CCIS 189, pp. 93–106, 2011.

Although the results gave insight of the real network performance, the mathematical model was not used to optimize the network installation. Later works in [13-15] proposed mathematical models for the base station (BS) placement problems. The objective was to minimize the network cost but the multi-hop relay topology was not considered.

In [16], the authors proposed an integer programming formulation dealing with the BS and RS placement problem for the WiMAX multi-hop relay networks. The objective was to determine the locations of BSs and RSs by minimizing the network cost and the normalized path losses between the user demand locations and BS/RS locations. While their contribution is significant, the proposed planning method could not provide quality of services guarantee. For this reason, efficient WiMAX network planning techniques are needed.

In our paper we propose a novel WiMAX network planning approach, accounting for the quality of services guarantee in the design process. Specifically, we aim to solve the BS and RS placement problem for the WiMAX networks that can maximize the network quality of services in term of the network service coverage and the access data rate to the target users by deploying not only the BSs but also the multiple hop RSs in the WiMAX networks.

The rest of the paper is organized as followed. Section 2 provides the problem definition and describes the problem formulation. Section 3 presents numerical experiments and comparisons. Section 4 demonstrates network planning experiments in real service scenarios. Finally, section 5 concludes the paper.

## 2   Quality of Service Optimization for WiMAX Networks

The problems of quality of service optimization for WiMAX networks are defined and mathematically formulated as follows:

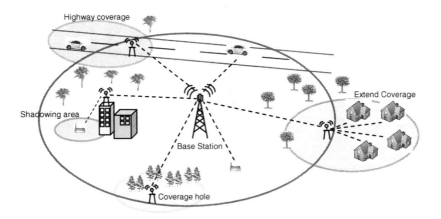

**Fig. 1.** Relay station deployment in WiMAX networks

## 2.1  Problem Definition

In the WiMAX network planning, we consider the problem of maximizing quality of services of the network by determining the optimal locations to install BSs and RSs. We denote the proposed problem as a MQoS problem which involves selecting locations to install the BSs and the RSs from candidate sites of BS and RS, respectively, so that the network quality of services in term of the user data rate guarantee and the radio service coverage are maximized for a given budget limitation. In particular, here the multiple-hop network configuration is formed in the way that the users can access the network directly through the BSs or indirectly via the RSs which connect to the BSs.

In the network planning model, we consider that BSs and RSs operate at the same transmitting power (a specified value). We consider that the user demand is modeled by Demand Points (DPs) which represent the geographic distribution of the expected user traffic in the service area and the target service area is represented by a set of discrete grid points called Signal Test Points (STPs) at which the received signal strength is tested. The network quality of services in term of the user access data rate and the network service coverage are incorporated in the model via the received sensitivity requirement at DPs and STPs, respectively. Such requirements in turn provide the user access rate guarantee.

## 2.2  Problem Formulation

The problem of network quality of service optimization for WiMAX networks is formulated as an integer linear programming model, denoted as MQoS model. Table 1 defines notations used in the model. The notations consist of sets, decision variables and parameters.

The proposed model aims to devise the optimal WiMAX network configuration deploying multi-hop relay stations and maximize the network quality of services in term of the service coverage availability and the user access data rate guarantee. These can be mathematically written as the objective function (1).

$$Maximize \ \sum_{h=1}^{t}(u_{hj}+v_{hi})+\sum_{g=1}^{d}(x_{gj}+y_{gi}) \tag{1}$$

The network design requirements, such as signal quality, user data rate and the user distribution characteristics, are incorporated into the mathematical model through four sets of constraints, denoted C1, C2, C3 and C4. C1 is a constraint that put a budget limitation on the network construction cost. C2 consists of constraints that ensure the signal strength level in the target service area. C3 is a set of constraints that specify the access data rate requirement to population of the target network users. The last set C4 consists of constraints that allow multi-hop connections between mobile users and base stations through intermediate relay stations.

**Table 1.** Notations

|  | Parameters | Definition |
|---|---|---|
| Sets: | $B$ | A set of candidate sites to install base stations (BSs) |
|  | $R$ | A set of candidate sites to install relay stations (RSs) |
|  | $D$ | A set of demand points (DPs) |
|  | $T$ | A set of best signal test points (STPs) |
| Decision variables: | $\beta_j$ | A binary {0, 1} variable that equals 1 if the BS is installed at site $j, j \in B$; 0 otherwise |
|  | $\gamma_i$ | A binary {0, 1} variable that equals 1 if the RS is installed at site $i, i \in R$; 0 otherwise |
|  | $u_{hj}$ | A binary {0, 1} variable that equals 1 if the STP $h$ is assigned to BS $j$, $h \in T$ and $j \in B$; 0 otherwise |
|  | $v_{hi}$ | A binary {0, 1} variable that equals 1 if the STP $h$ is assigned to RS $i$, $h \in T$ and $i \in R$; 0 otherwise |
|  | $x_{gj}$ | A binary {0, 1} variable that equals 1 if the DP $g$ is assigned to BS $j$, $g \in D$ and $j \in B$; 0 otherwise |
|  | $y_{gi}$ | A binary {0, 1} variable that equals 1 if the DP $g$ is assigned to RS $i$, $g \in D$ and $i \in R$; 0 otherwise |
|  | $w_{ij}$ | A binary {0, 1} variable that equals 1 if the RS $i$ is assigned to BS $j$, $i \in R$ and $j \in B$; 0 otherwise |
| Constant parameters: | $F_j$ | Cost to install base station $j, j \in B$ |
|  | $E_i$ | Cost to install relay station $i, i \in R$ |
|  | $C$ | Network installation budget |
|  | $P_t$ | The received signal strength threshold for STPs |
|  | $P_d$ | The received signal strength threshold for DPs |
|  | $P_r$ | The received signal strength threshold for RSs |
|  | $P_{hj}$ | The signal strength that a STP $h$ receives from BS $j$, $h \in T$ and $j \in B$ |
|  | $P_{hi}$ | The signal strength that a STP $h$ receives from RS $i$, $h \in T$ and $i \in R$ |
|  | $P_{gj}$ | The signal strength that a DP $g$ receives from BS $j$, $g \in D$ and $j \in B$ |
|  | $P_{gi}$ | The signal strength that a DP $g$ receives from RS $i$, $g \in D$ and $i \in R$ |

**C1: Budget limitation**

$$\sum_{\forall j \in B} F_j \beta_j + \sum_{\forall i \in R} E_i \gamma_i \leq C \tag{2}$$

Constraint (2) specifies budget limitation on the network cost, including the equipments and the construction cost of base stations and the relay stations required in the network.

**C2: Radio signal requirements**

$$\sum_{\forall j \in B} u_{hj} + \sum_{\forall i \in R} v_{hi} \leq 1 \qquad\qquad , \forall h \in T \tag{3}$$

$$u_{hj} \leq \beta_j \qquad\qquad , \forall h \in T, j \in B \qquad (4)$$

$$v_{hi} \leq \gamma_j \qquad\qquad , \forall h \in T, i \in R \qquad (5)$$

$$u_{hj}\left(P_{hj} - P_t\right) \geq 0 \qquad\qquad , \forall h \in T, j \in B \qquad (6)$$

$$v_{hi}\left(P_{hi} - P_t\right) \geq 0 \qquad\qquad , \forall h \in T, i \in R \qquad (7)$$

Constraints (3) – (7) specify the radio signal coverage of the network by assessing the signal strength at each STP $h$ and ensuring that the signal strength received at STP $h$ from BS $j$ or RS $i$ must be greater than the threshold $P_t$.

### C3: User access data rate requirements

$$\sum_{\forall j \in B} x_{gj} + \sum_{\forall i \in R} y_{gi} \leq 1 \qquad\qquad , \forall g \in D \qquad (8)$$

$$x_{gj} \leq \beta_j \qquad\qquad , \forall g \in D, j \in B \qquad (9)$$

$$y_{gi} \leq \gamma_j \qquad\qquad , \forall g \in D, i \in R \qquad (10)$$

$$x_{gj}\left(P_{gj} - P_d\right) \geq 0 \qquad\qquad , \forall g \in D, j \in B \qquad (11)$$

$$y_{gj}\left(P_{gj} - P_d\right) \geq 0 \qquad\qquad , \forall g \in D, i \in R \qquad (12)$$

Constraints (8) – (12) enforce the network to accommodate the target user traffic demand and guarantee the user access rate by specifying that the signal strength the user at DP $g$ receives from the BS $j$ or the RS $i$ is greater than the threshold $P_d$ so that the data transmission can operate at the required data rate.

### C4: Multi-hop connections

$$\sum_{\forall j \in B} w_{ij} = \gamma_i \qquad\qquad , \forall i \in R \qquad (13)$$

$$w_{ij} \leq \beta_j \qquad\qquad , \forall i \in R, j \in B \qquad (14)$$

$$w_{ij}\left(P_{ij} - P_r\right) \geq 0 \qquad\qquad j \in B, i \in R \qquad (15)$$

Constraints (13) – (15) allow the multi-hop connections from a user to BS via an intermediate RS. Constraint (13) specifies that the installed RS must be connected to one BS. Constraint (14) specifies that the selected BS must be installed. Finally, to ensure the radio connectivity, constraint (15) states that RS $i$ can connect to BS $j$ if the signal strength received at RS $i$ from BS $j$ is greater than the threshold $P_r$.

## 3   Numerical Experiments and Comparisons

This section demonstrates the numerical experiments of the WiMAX network planning using the proposed MQoS model. The network performance is evaluated in term of the percentage of the user data rate and the service coverage guarantee under the specified budget limitation.

### 3.1   Experiment Setup

In numerical experiments, we use the design scenarios of the service area of size 3km×3km as shown in fig.2. The number of candidate sites to install BSs and RSs are 20 and 60, respectively. There are 200 DPs and 256 STPs (grid size of 200m×200m). We consider cost of BS and RS are $120,000 and $40,000, respectively. These are approximate cost from typical suppliers [13]. We consider the WiMAX standards IEEE 802.16. Table 2 shows the parameters used in the numerical studies (see [13] for more details). Table 3 presents the minimum received signal strength (in dBm) to be able to achieve a certain physical data rate according to the choices of modulation techniques. The transmit power of each BS and RS used for the tests are 35 dBm which are typical values used in the WiMAX networks [6].

It is necessary to compute the received signal strength at DPs and STPs and input the obtained values in the MQoS model to find the optimal locations to install BSs and RSs. This computation can be done by using the propagation model. In this paper we use the Stanford University Interim (SUI) model which is recommended by the IEEE 802.16 to evaluate the path loss in WiMAX networks [14-15].

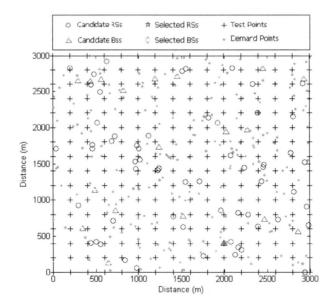

**Fig. 2.** Numerical experiment setup

**Table 2.** Parameters used in the network planning experiments

| Parameters | Value |
|---|---|
| Height of BSs and RSs | 60 m |
| Height of TPs | 2 m |
| Transmitted Power | 35 dBm |
| Transmitted antenna gain | 16 dBi |
| Received antenna gain | 2 dBi |
| Frequency | 2.5 GHz |
| Terrain type | C |
| Bandwidth | 3.5 MHz |
| Data rate requirement for DPs | 12.71 Mbps |
| Data rate requirement for STPs | 5.64 Mbps |
| Cost of each base station | 120,000 $ |
| Cost of each relay station | 48,000 $ |

**Table 3.** Receiver sensitivity threshold for physical data rate requirement (Alvarion Breeze-MAX at 3.5 MHz)

| Modulation tech-niques | Physical data rate (Mbps) | Receiver sensitivity threshold (dBm) |
|---|---|---|
| BPSK 1/2 | 1.41 | -100 |
| BPSK 3/4 | 2.12 | -98 |
| QPSK 1/2 | 2.82 | -97 |
| QPSK 3/4 | 4.23 | -94 |
| QAM 16 1/2 | 5.64 | -91 |
| QAM 16 3/4 | 8.47 | -88 |
| QAM 64 2/3 | 11.29 | -83 |
| QAM 64 3/4 | 12.71 | -82 |

### 3.2 Result Comparison and Analysis

The WiMAX network planning for the considered scenarios is solved by inputting the set of BS and RS candidate sites and other parameters to the MQoS model and implementing the MQoS model with the ILOG-OPL development studio. Then it is solved with CPLEX 5.2 optimization solver. Computations are performed on an Intel Centrino Core2 Duo Processor 2.0 GHz and 2GB of RAM.

We compare performances of the network obtained from the proposed model with those obtained from other techniques including the Uniform BS placement (UB) and the Estimating Approximation (EA) method. In UB, the BSs are simply distributed uniformly across the target service region whereas in EA the center of gravity technique is used to find the location of BSs for a set of specified DPs. The following shows numerical result analysis and comparisons.

Table 4 shows numerical results comparing the network planning using the MQoS model and that using the UB and EA method. The performance matrices used for the comparison included the budget limitation, the number of installed BSs and RSs, and the quality of services in term of the user data rate guarantee and the service coverage guarantee. The results show that the MQoS model results in better network performances in all cases of the budget limitation. Specifically, in the case where the budget limitation is of 800,000 US$, the MQoS model could yield the network configuration that guarantees 100% user access data rate requirement and provides 100% service coverage guarantee. Fig. 3 compares the network quality of services in term of the percentage of the user data rate and the service coverage guarantee.

To analyze the signal propagation characteristic across the service area, we apply the SUI path loss model [14-15] in the computation. Fig.4 shows the cumulative density function of the received signal strength at STPs and DPs for the case of budget limitation 800,000 US$. Different design techniques yield different signal propagation characteristics in the service area. We can see that the network configuration designed by the MQoS model yields better signal quality, i.e. stronger signal level, at STPs and DPs compared with those of the EA and UB method. This results in higher access data rates to end users.

**Table 4.** Numerical result comparisons

| Budget limitation (US$) | 400,000 | | | 800,000 | | |
|---|---|---|---|---|---|---|
| Techniques | MQoS | UB | EA | MQoS | UB | EA |
| Number of BSs used | 2 | 3 | 3 | 4 | 6 | 6 |
| Number of RSs used | 3 | 0 | 0 | 6 | 0 | 0 |
| Number of served DPs | 157 | 148 | 118 | 200 | 192 | 170 |
| Number of served STPs | 244 | 240 | 236 | 256 | 256 | 243 |
| Guarantee user access data rate | 78.50% | 74.00% | 59.00% | 100.00% | 96.00% | 85.00% |
| Guarantee radio service coverage | 95.31% | 93.75% | 92.19% | 100.00% | 100.00% | 94.92% |

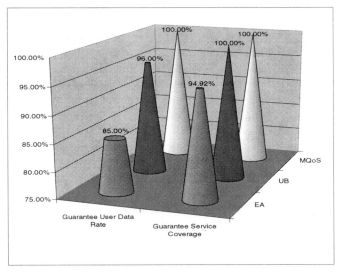

**Fig. 3.** Quality of service comparison

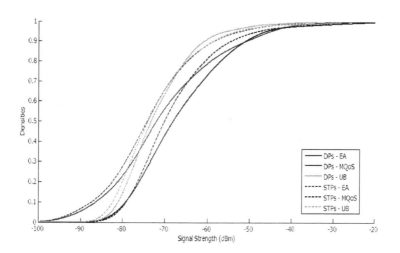

**Fig. 4.** CDF graph of signal propagation characteristic at DPs and STPs for the case of budget limitation 800,000 US$

# 4  Network Planning Experiments

This section demonstrates the network planning experiments of a real service scenario of downtown area in Nakhon Ratchasima province, Thailand. The service area considered here is of size 5km×8.5km as shown in fig.6. The candidate sites to install BSs and RSs are selected from a set of potential buildings and existing cellular BSs. The number of candidate sites to install BSs and RSs are 55 sites. There are 207 DPs and 770 STPs (grid size of 250m×250m). We consider the cost of each BS and RS are $120,000 and $40,000 which are an approximate cost from typical suppliers [13]. Table 5 shows the parameters used in these experiments (see [13] for more details).

**Table 5.** Parameters used in the network planning experiments

| Parameters | Value |
|---|---|
| Budget limitation (million US$) | {0.5, 1.0, 1.5, 2.0. 2.5} million US$ |
| Height of BSs and RSs | 30 m |
| Height of TPs | 2 m |
| Transmitted Power | 35 dBm |
| Transmitted antenna gain | 16 dBi |
| Received antenna gain | 2 dBi |
| Frequency | 2.5 GHz |
| Terrain type | A |
| Bandwidth | 3.5 MHz |
| Data rate requirement for DPs | 12.71 Mbps |
| Data rate requirement for STPs | 5.64 Mbps |
| Cost of each base station | 120,000 $ |
| Cost of each relay station | 48,000 $ |

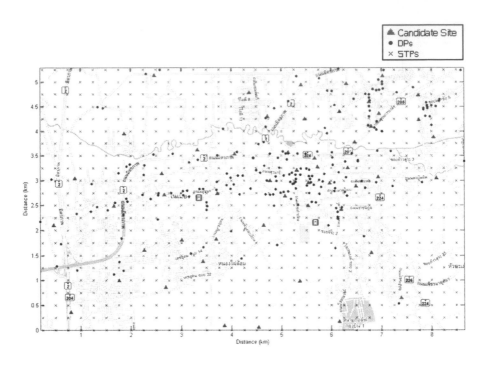

**Fig. 5.** Network planning scenario in downtown of Nakhon Ratchasima, Thailand

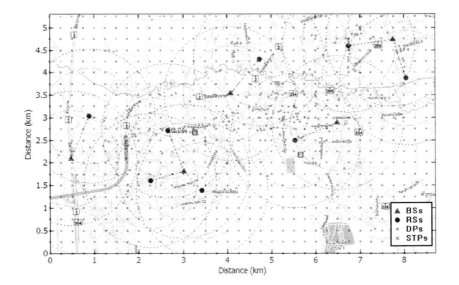

**Fig. 6.** WiMAX network layout shows selected BS and RS sites and the resulting service coverage when using MQoS2 with budget limitation of one million US$

## 4.1 Resulting Network Configurations

The WiMAX network planning for the considered scenarios is solved by inputting the set of BS and RS candidate sites and other parameters to the MQoS model and implementing the MQoS model with the ILOG-OPL development studio. Then it is solved with CPLEX 5.2 optimization solver. Computations are performed on an Intel Centrino Core2 Duo Processor 2.0 GHz and 2GB of RAM.

Fig.7 shows the resulting network configuration for the case that the budget limitation is one million US$. The figure depicts the selected sites to install BSs and RSs. The figure also presents the service coverage area in which five BSs and eight RSs are installed. We can achieve 100% service coverage in the target area and guarantee the required user data rate at all DPs in the coverage area.

## 4.2 Quality of Service Comparisons

Table 6 shows numerical results comparing the performances of networks designed with the MQoS models in which MQoS1 uses the objective function (1) whereas MQoS2 further modifies the objective function (1) by applying different weight factors to DPs and STPs. Particularly, we consider DPs are more important than STPs. The performance matrices used for the comparison included the network installation cost, the number of installed BSs and RSs, and the quality of services in term of the user access rate guarantee and the service coverage guarantee.

The results in Table 6 show that in the case of low budget installation cost (0.5 – 1.5 million US$), MQoS2 could result in better signal quality to the area where potential users/customers exist; as we can see that MQoS2 yields higher percentage of the user access data rate guarantee compared with those of MQoS1. In the case of high budget installation cost (2 – 2.5 million US$), both MQoS1 and MQoS2 could provide 100% guarantee on the user access data rate requirement and the radio service coverage.

**Table 6.** Network performance comparisons

| Budget limitation (million US$) | | 0.5 | 1.0 | 1.5 | 2.0 | 2.5 |
|---|---|---|---|---|---|---|
| Real installation cost (million US$) | MQoS1 | 0.480 | 0.984 | 1.488 | 1.944 | 2.472 |
| | MQoS2 | 0.480 | 0.984 | 1.464 | 1.992 | 2.472 |
| Number of BSs used | MQoS1 | 2 | 7 | 10 | 15 | 19 |
| | MQoS2 | 2 | 5 | 9 | 15 | 19 |
| Number of RSs used | MQoS1 | 5 | 3 | 6 | 3 | 4 |
| | MQoS2 | 5 | 8 | 8 | 4 | 4 |
| Number of served DPs | MQoS1 | 156 | 160 | 197 | 207 | 207 |
| | MQoS2 | 168 | 201 | 207 | 207 | 207 |
| Number of served STPs | MQoS1 | 418 | 699 | 768 | 770 | 770 |
| | MQoS2 | 361 | 578 | 728 | 770 | 770 |
| Guarantee user access data rate | MQoS1 | 75.36% | 77.29% | 95.17% | 100.00% | 100.00% |
| | MQoS2 | 81.16% | 97.10% | 100.00% | 100.00% | 100.00% |
| Guarantee radio service coverage | MQoS1 | 54.29% | 90.78% | 99.74% | 100.00% | 100.00% |
| | MQoS2 | 46.88% | 75.06% | 94.55% | 100.00% | 100.00% |

Fig.7 shows the probability density function of the received signal strength at STPs and DPs. It summarizes the signal propagation characteristics across the service area. We can observe that in case of low installation budget (0.5 million US$), the signal qualities at DPs are much higher than those of STPs. This means that in case of low budget, the design tries to provide better signal qualities in the area where target users exist. As the installation budget increases (1.5 million US$), the signal qualities at STPs rise and become about the same level as those of DPs. This means the signal qualities could spread more evenly in the service area.

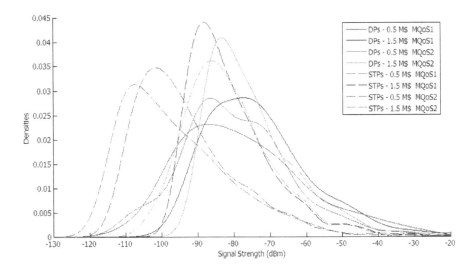

**Fig. 7.** PDF graph of signal propagation characteristic at DPs and STPs

## 5   Conclusions

In this paper, we present a study of the WiMAX network planning problem and de-velop integer linear programming mathematical models that can optimize the network quality of services by determining optimal locations to install base stations (BSs) and relay station (RSs) and determining optimal interconnections between BSs and RSs in the multi-hop manner.

Numerical results show that the proposed network planning model can greatly improve the network quality of services in term of the user access data rate and the network service coverage compared with those of other techniques. Specially, the proposed model could determine network configurations that result in high network performances when taking into account the budget limitation in the network planning processes. Our ongoing research aims to further investigate and analyze the effects of using multiple objective functions on the network quality of service optimization.

## Acknowledgment

This work was supported by the research fund from Suranaree University of Technology, Thailand.

## References

1. Maraj, A., Imeri, I.: WiMAX Integration in NGN Network, Architecture, Protocols and Services. WSEAS Transactions on Communications 7(8), 708–717 (2009)
2. Li, B., Qin, Y., Low, C.P., Gwee, C.L.: A survey on mobile WiMAX. IEEE Communication Magazine, 70–75 (2007)
3. Chen, J., Li, M., Wang, N., Huang, Y.: An Adaptive Cross-layer Bandwidth Scheduling Strategy for the Speed-Sensitive Strategy in Hierarchical Cellular Networks. WSEAS Transactions on Communications 7(8), 545–555 (2009)
4. Kadhim, M.A., Ismail, W.: Implementation of WIMAX IEEE802.16d Baseband Transceiver on Multi-Core Software-Defined Radio Platform. WSEAS Transactions on Communications 9(5), 301–311 (2010)
5. Hurley, S.: Automatic base station selection and configuration in mobile networks. In: IEEE 52$^{nd}$ Vehicular Technology Conference, vol. 6, pp. 2585–2592. IEEE Press, New York (2000)
6. Rawnsley, R.K., Hurley, S.: Towards automatic cell planning. In: IEEE 11$^{th}$ Personal, Indoor and Mobile Radio Communications Symposium, vol. 2, pp. 1583–1588. IEEE Press, New York (2000)
7. Hamad-Ameen, J.: Cell Planning in GSM Mobile. WSEAS Transactions on Communications 7(5), 393 398 (2008)
8. Fragoso, J.G., Galvan-Tejada, G.M.: Cell planning based on the WiMAX standard for home access: a practical case. In: The 2$^{nd}$ Electrical and Electronics Engineering Conference, pp. 89–92 (2005)
9. Neves, P.: WiMAX for emergency services: an empirical evaluation. In: Next Generation Mobile Applications, Services and Technologies Conference, pp. 340–345 (2007)
10. Lannoo, B.: Business scenarios for a WiMAX deployment in Belgium. In: IEEE Mobile WiMAX Symposium, pp. 132–137. IEEE Press, New York (2007)
11. Theodoros, T., Kostantinos, V.: WiMAX network planning and system's performance evaluation. In: IEEE Wireless Communications and Networking Conference, pp. 1948–1953. IEEE Press, New York (2007)
12. Marques, M.: Design and planning of IEEE 802.16 networks. In: IEEE 18$^{th}$ Personal, Indoor and Mobile Radio Communications Symposium, pp. 1–5. IEEE Press, New York (2007)
13. Teterin, V., Hurley, S., Allen, S.M.: Optimizing performance of WiMAX networks through automated site selection. In: Convergence of Telecommunications, Networking and Broadcasting Conference (2007)
14. Mousavi, M., Chamberlanda, S., Quintero, A.: A new approach for designing WiMAX networks. In: Electrical and Computer Engineering Conference, pp. 487–490 (2007)
15. Teterin, V., Hurley, S., Allen, S.M.: A staged optimization framework for cost optimized WiMAX network design. In: IEEE 4$^{th}$ Wireless and Mobile Communications Conference, pp. 185–190. IEEE Press, New York (2008)

16. Yu, Y., Murphy, S., Murphy, L.: Planning base station and relay station locations in IEEE 802.16j multi-hop relay networks. In: Consumer Communications and Networking Conference, pp. 922–926 (2008)
17. Ahson, S., Ilyas, M.: WiMAX handbook. CRC Press, London (2008)
18. Erceg, V., Hari, K.V.S.: Channel models for fixed wireless applications. In: Technical report, IEEE 802.16 Broadband Wireless Access Working Group (2001)
19. Erceg, V., Greenstein, L.J.: An empirically based path loss model for wireless channels in suburban environments. IEEE Journal on Selected Areas of Communications 17, 1205–1211 (1999)
20. Nuaymi, L.: WiMAX technology for broadband wireless access. John Wiley, Chichester (2007)
21. Abate, Z.: WiMax RF systems engineering. Artech House, Boston (2009)
22. Katz, M.D., Fitzek, F.H.P.: WiMAX evolution: emerging technologies and applications. John Wiley & Sons, Chichester (2009)

# An Application of Game Theory for the Selection of Traffic Routing Method in Interconnected NGN

A. Kostić-Ljubisavljević, V. Radonjić,
S. Mladenović, and V. Aćimović-Raspopović

University of Belgrade,
Faculty of Transport and Traffic Engineering,
Belgrade, Serbia
a.kostic@sf.bg.ac.rs

**Abstract.** In this paper, the impact of various dynamic traffic routing methods on different performances of interconnected telecommunications network with the application of bill-and-keep interconnection charging is presented. For the purpose of our research, we developed the software for Routing and Interconnection Simulation (RIS). We conducted two-stage analysis. First stage is concerning the shortest path routing, the three-hop routing, the random path routing and the last successful path routing, and their influence on certain network performance parameters. In second stage the coordination game theory model is proposed in order to determine the one routing method that provides the best results for all operators in terms of costs per link.

**Keywords:** interconnection, NGN, bill-and-keep, routing, costs per link, coordination game.

## 1 Introduction

Next Generation Networks (NGN) are expected to provide capabilities to support enhanced mobility, security, Quality of Service (QoS) and scalable routing. They should ensure potential to use both static and dynamic traffic routing schemes in order to select the proper routing paths between the originating and the terminating node according to the desired QoS. Interconnection is one of the most important issues to be considered in NGN performance analysis. Interconnection enables telecommunication operators to provide services from competing operators to their own end-users, and to deliver their services to other users using all available network resources. In interconnection scenarios with several network operators, it should be ensured seamless services operations across the NGN infrastructure and related accounting and charging support. In order to obtain as many as possible users, and by that increase their own revenue, telecommunication operators have to offer and provide services with adequate quality and at a reasonable price. One of the biggest issues that arise from such operators aim is a problem of charging the service of interconnection [1], [2]. There are a large number of approaches used and suggested for solving this problem in current telecommunication networks [3], [4], [5]. The most common are bill-and-keep, cost-based, revenue sharing, retail minus, etc. As in traditional networks, in

V. Snasel, J. Platos, and E. El-Qawasmeh (Eds.): ICDIPC 2011, Part II, CCIS 189, pp. 107–122, 2011.
© Springer-Verlag Berlin Heidelberg 2011

NGN many different concepts are suggested for interconnection charging [6], [7], [8]. In this paper, we shall present some results of our research that addresses the impact of various dynamic traffic routing methods application on different performances of interconnected telecommunications network when bill-and-keep interconnection charging is applied.

Bill-and-keep approach means that operators do not charge each other for interconnection service. Each operator *bills* its end-users in accordance to the output traffic it generates, and *keeps* all income arising from it. This method assumes that if there were interconnection payments, they would cancel each other out, resulting in no gain or loss for either operator. Further, by forgoing payments, operators avoid the administrative burden of billing for exchanged traffic [3]. The bill-and-keep method is the most appropriate in situations where the traffic between operators is in balance. Otherwise, one of the operators will have revenue losses because of greater traffic termination in its network.

One of many definitions for traffic routing states that routing is an indispensable telecommunications network function that connects a call from origin to destination, and is at the heart of the architecture, design, and operation of any network [9]. The other presents routing as the act of forwarding network packets from a source network to a destination network [10]. No matter how routing is explicitly defined, one thing is sure: routing is one of the most important functions of every telecommunication network. Our research addressed the following dynamic routing methods: the shortest path routing – *spr*; the three-hop routing (paths can contain only four nodes) – *thr*; the random path routing (paths are selected in a random way from the set of possible routing paths) – *rpr* and the last successful path routing – *lspr*.

In this paper, optimisation problems including link utilization and the effects of various dynamic traffic routing methods on different network performances are presented. The optimization problem of selection the one routing method with aim of maximising network performances and efficiency is solved using the proposed coordination game theory model. The model is proposed in order to determine the one routing method that provides minimization of costs per link for all operators.

In order to determine how properly selected methods of dynamic routing with bill-and keep charging affects network performances, we have developed the Software for Routing and Interconnection Simulation (RIS). After the analysis of simulation results, we applied ranked coordination game in order to determine one routing method that provides the best results for all operators in terms of costs. For that purpose, we propose a coordination game theory model.

This paper is organized as follows. After the literature review in Section 2, the problem statement is given in Section 3. In Section 4 RIS is briefly described. Two-stage analysis of simulation results is discussed in Section 5. In Section 6 concluding remarks are given.

## 2   Litereture Review

During our research we focus on references concerning dynamic routing, interconnection charging methods, NGN interconnection, game theory etc.

There are many routing methods employed in telecommunications networks worldwide, which are classified in different ways [9], [11], [12]. The most common classifications distinguish fixed and dynamic routing methods. Dynamic telecommunication traffic routing is the convenient way of adjusting to frequent changes in intensity and traffic distribution among significant network resources and it allows better usage of available resources. Unlike the methods with fixed routing rules, dynamic routing is based on a different approach: traffic is assigned to those paths where the free links are available. Substantial savings in network investment costs can be achieved by choosing the appropriate dynamic traffic routing method. In addition to savings, other advantages of the dynamic routing compared to fixed routing are discussed in [9], [11], [12]. There are numerous different dynamic routing methods whose primary goal is to optimize the network performance by better utilization of its resources [9], [11], [12], [13], [14]. Shortest path routing is one of the most commonly used methods with application in various telecommunication networks [15], [16], [17]. The three-hop routing is explained in more details and some of its possible applications are presented in [18]. One of many methods from the self-learning group is the last successful path routing and one of the applications is given in [19].

NGN must allow the continuity and interoperability with existing networks and, at the same time, enable the implementation of new capabilities [20], [21]. The introduction of NGN could change locations and functions of points of interconnection. It requires working with legacy networks. Introducing NGN also opens up the possibility of changing the pricing of interconnection according to applied arrangements such as bill-and-keep (sender-keeps-all) or Calling Party Network Pays (CPNP) [8].

Problem of interconnection, especially interconnection charging is the object of interest for many scientists and practitioners worldwide. Some experts suggest that interconnection regimes developed for the internet or for traditional telecommunication networks are unlikely to be appropriate in most NGN contexts [6]. In [8] the major accent is placed on regulations concerning NGN interconnection. Main question is what to charge. Marcus analysed all major interconnection charging issues on retail and wholesale level. International regulatory organisations have developed studies about NGN interconnections [22], [23], [24]. European Regulatory Group ERG has very thoroughly analysed NGN interconnection billing. By the term billing, they consider charging (e.g. CPNP, bill-and-keep) and pricing (e.g. element based, capacity based or QoS based), and they considered it on both retail and wholesale level. In [25] Cadmann had another look at current interconnect charging principles. He stated that bill-and-keep would be more likely to promote efficiency gains when applied on NGN. Many scientific and practical experts agree about assumption that bill-and-keep will be the most appropriate for NGN interconnection [6], [7], [8], [22], [23], [24], [25].

Game theory as a mathematical theory of conflict situation can be applied in telecommunications for congestion control, resource allocation, quality of service provisioning, network security, spectrum sharing, routing, etc [26], [27], [28], [29], [30], [31], [32], [33], [34], [35], [36], [37]. It consists of a set of analytical tools that predict the outcome of complex interactions among rational players. In [38] continuation game setting has been applied for examining the two competing networks' equilibrium choices of routing methods and prices. For solving both routing and pricing problems in mobile ad hoc networks, authors in [39] suggest a model that consists of several connected games. The aim of maximizing network operators' revenues can be achieved if Nash equilibrium is obtained in each game of the proposed model.

## 3 Problem Statement

A network is represented by an undirected graph $N(O_n, L)$. Here, $O_n$ is the set of nodes of operator $n$, where $n = 0$ indexes the incumbent operators network and $n = 1, 2, 3...$ indexes the other operators. Let $L$ denote the set of undirected links. Each link can be represented by a pair $(r_i, r_j)$, where $r_i$ and $r_j$ denote the originated and terminated nodes of that link, respectively. A path between each node pair can be represented as a sequence $P = (r_O, r_2, \ldots, r_T)$, where $r_O$ and $r_T$ are the originating and terminating nodes of the path, and $r_1, \ldots, r_{k-1}$ are transit nodes.

Let us consider the situation in which three telecommunication operators A, B, and C are interconnected as shown in Figure 1. The operator's A network consists of nodes 1, 2 and 4; the operator's B network of nodes 3, 5, 6, 7 and 8; the operator's C network of nodes 9 and 10, and corresponding links respectively.

The observed network is characterized by the link capacity, the link cost, the node capacity, and the node cost.

We assumed that all links in the network have equal capacity. The link cost is defined as the cost of the operator for carrying connection that is originated, transited through, or terminated in the network. In this paper, we introduce the "cost factor of interconnection". This factor multiplies the link cost in case when a link is used for carrying traffic originated and/or terminated in other interconnected networks.

The node capacity is considered here as an average number of connection requests that can be generated at any node. The node capacity is normalized to one. If links entering and leaving the node are free, each node can forward all transit traffic. Each node is generating connection requests that are represented by Poisson traffic [40], [41], [42], [43], [44] with a mean value as the multiple of pre-defined capacity of the node. We made software experiments with 10 possible values of the multiple of offered traffic in interval from 0,5 to 5.

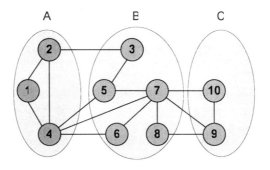

**Fig. 1.** Network used in the analysis

The node cost is a parameter that represents the cost of forwarding connections through the observed node. Depending on a function of a given node, the cost can be related to generation, transition and termination of a connection. For all nodes, we defined that the costs of generating and terminating connections are equal. The cost of transition is the half of generation/termination cost.

The term connection will be concerned as an end-user request for bundle of services offered by an operator. End-users are grouped around the observed nodes in the network. Bundle of services presents a group of selected broadband services. In [45] the term broadband access, which should be provided to each end-user, means the permanent access to the resources of telecommunications networks with bit rates not less than 4 Mb/s.

The period, which is seven times longer than the mean duration of connection, is simulated, while omitting from data analysis intervals that are equal to average duration of the connection at the beginning and the end of simulation. Duration of the connection is viewed as a random variable that has an exponential distribution.

Further, we propose ranked coordination game between operators. Generally, co-ordination refers to the situation where each player must choose strategy[1] that is valuable only if the other players make the complementary selections. In coordination game players are encouraged to coordinate with each other while unilateral deviations do not have an immediate benefit [46], [47]. The game we propose refers to a situation where all operators can agree on a ranking of the considered routing methods or, at least, can agree on a solution that is the best for all. The preferences of each operator can be expressed with preference relations, which define the ranking of the consequences, i.e. routing methods according to the cost minimization criteria.

The proposed game setting is as follows. Suppose a strategy $n^p \in N$ has the property that $c_i(n^p) < c_i(n')$, $\forall\, n' \in N\ \forall\, i$, where $N$ is a set of strategies for all players and $c_i$ is the player $i$'s cost associated to strategy $n^p$. If this property holds, then all players agree that the cost derived from the strategy $n^p$ is preferable to every other strategy. If such a strategy exists, then it is referred to as a dominant one. The dominant equilibrium has three important properties [46], [47], [48]. First, the best strategy is selected collectively. Second, the dominant equilibrium is therefore Pareto efficient. There would be no Pareto improvements upon this outcome if players select several different strategies. Third, if one was to consider cooperative solutions, then if the players were able to work in groups rather than individually and unilaterally making their choices cooperatively, no group could improve upon the dominant equilibrium.

# 4   Software for Routing and Interconnection Simulation

Software for Routing and Interconnection Simulation provides the ability to perform a numerous of experiments and thus to obtain a large number of output data. It simulates the handling of traffic demands in the telecommunications network and performs statistical processing of the relevant parameters. In the structure of the RIS, which is schematically shown in Figure 2, several logical units can be pointed out.

---

[1] Basic components of a game are players (decision makers), their strategies and consequences of the strategies (outcome).

*Network initialisation* - In mathematical terms, the telecommunication network is represented as a graph. Node attributes are the node capacity and node cost, and link attributes are the start (originated) and end (terminating) node as well as the link cost. The main task of initialization unit is the representation of actual network by data structures suitable for the simulation process.

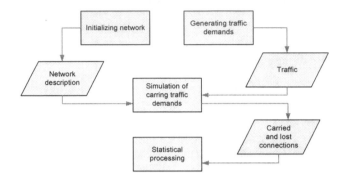

**Fig. 2.** Structure of the developed software

*Traffic demands generation* – For each node, connection requests are represented by Poisson traffic, with a mean value as the multiple of pre-defined capacity of the node. The parameter related to the multiple of traffic intensity (from 0,5 to 5) is entered from input mask, and capacities of nodes are entered from the input file. Attributes of connection request are source node, destination node, moment of generation and duration.

*Simulation of carrying traffic demands* - For a given network and offered telecommunications traffic, the RIS user selects one of the offered methods of routing and one of the offered interconnection charging methods[2]. In addition to these data, the charging rate for the bundle of services should also be chosen, and entered from input mask. The process of simulation after that can be activated. The connection can be carried out or lost. "The track" about each carried or lost connection is saved in an output file.

*Statistical processing* - Outputs from the previous stage give the possibility of forming a large number of statistics related to connections, nodes, links, paths, costs, and so on. For each offered traffic intensity, routing and interconnection charging method and statistic data for each operator are related to:

-   The number of connections that are generated, transited and terminated for each node, and for each operator;
-   Number of realized connections between node pairs;
-   Average costs of all realized connections between node pairs;
-   Costs of connections;
-   Percentage of link usage;
-   Revenues obtained by carrying the connections;
-   Data about used paths (links, connections, usage time).

---

[2] In this paper, we present only the analysis with one of the possible interconnection charging methods (bill-and-keep). RIS software has the ability to perform simulation with cost-based interconnection charging principle, also.

All logical units described above have been implemented as program units in Microsoft Visual Basic 2005 environment [49]. Because the RIS is modularly structured, it can be enhanced with additional functions. The spiral model of RIS, according to authors' opinion, is the model of the first choice for software development for this kind of applications. The RIS has been developed incrementally, by developing a series of prototypes, considering increasing requirements of our research. They have been verified according to [50]. In this stage of our research, the second prototype of the RIS is developed.

The RIS was developed with the ability to change a numerous inputs: network topology, node and link capacity, node and link cost, average number of traffic demands, etc. In order to obtain correct conclusions, after performing adequate statistical analysis with obtained output data, it is necessary that they are derived after "enough" large number of experiments.

## 5   Two-Stage Analysis of Simulation Results

In this section, two-stage analysis will be presented. In the first stage, the analysis performed by processing the numerous data we obtained by running multiple experiments with RIS will be explained. In the second stage, we propose and apply the game theory model in order to find the dominant routing method for the whole network. For purpose of this research, we observed and analyzed several network performances parameters: average link utilization, average lost of connections and average costs per link. The traffic load of each link is observed in details, and in order to obtain the results more statistically valid, we calculated the mean value and standard deviation.

Figure 3 presents mean value of percentage of link utilisation of all the links in observed network. It can be noticed that for the lowest traffic intensities *rpr* method provides slightly higher link utilisation than others. For higher traffic loads, *lspr* can be isolated as a routing method with the worst average link utilisation in whole network, while other three methods give better and very similar results.

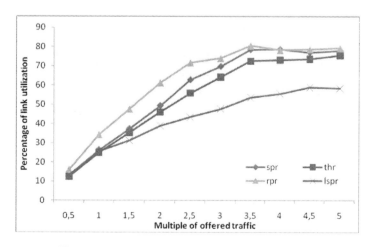

**Fig. 3.** Average link utilisation for the whole network

As the addition to link utilisation analysis in the whole network, we analyzed link utilisation for every telecommunication operators concerned. In Figure 4 link utilization of all operators for applied routing methods is presented. Since link utilisation improves with the traffic growth, we decide to present here only results obtained for heavy traffic load.

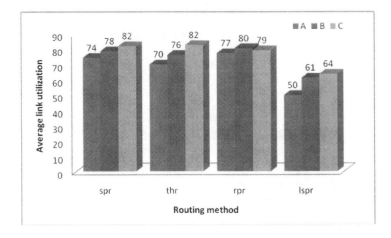

**Fig. 4.** Average link utilisation under heavy traffic load

We noticed that *lspr* method shows the worst performances for all three operators, so in the next phase of our research, we shall focus on that method to be positive about our further decisions.

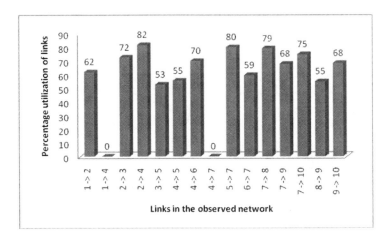

**Fig. 5.** Percentage of link utilisation for *lspr* method

Figure 5 presents detailed analysis of link utilisation for all links in the network when *lspr* method is applied. In this figure, the extreme case of heavy traffic is shown. It can be noticed that *lspr* method provides unused links even at higher intensities of traffic, while some links are loaded with more than 80%.

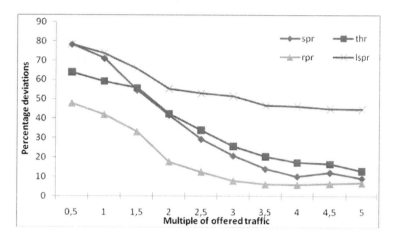

**Fig. 6.** Percentage deviations from the average utilisation of links for bill-and-keep approach

After that, we analyzed traffic load balance. For that purpose, we used percentage deviations from the average utilization of links. There is significant difference among applied routing methods, which is shown in Figure 6. For all routing methods, the traffic load balancing improves with increasing intensity of traffic in the network. As we have already pointed out, the traffic load balance is very significant for bill-and-keep interconnection charging.

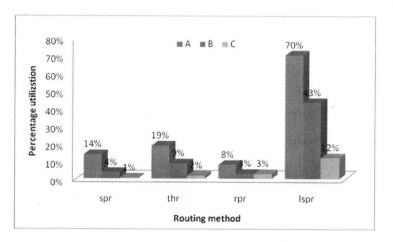

**Fig. 7.** Percentage deviations from the average usage of links for each operator in case of very high traffic

Since operators A, B and C have different configurations of links and nodes, and different traffic demand generating in each node, it was logical to expect some differences among results concerning percentage deviations. Figure 7 shows the case of the heaviest traffic load in the network. A significant load balancing for all three network operators can be noticed. The worst performance was also obtained in this case when the *lspr* method was applied.

The operator C shows the best performance having the least deviation for all four routing methods.

In addition to this analysis, we performed analysis of one of the most important parameter in process of analyzing network performances: the percentage of lost connections. In Figure 8 the dependence of average percentage of lost connections for applied routing methods with bill-and-keep charging method is presented. It can be observed that there ware no connection losses with low traffic intensities for routing methods *spr*, *thr* and *rpr*. However, method *lspr* provides very significant connection loses even for the small network loads.

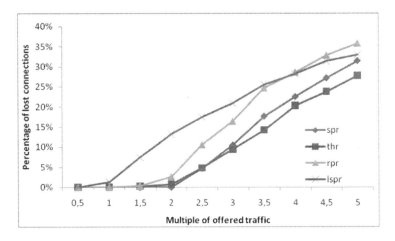

**Fig. 8.** Average percentage of lost connections with bill-and-keep

Figure 8 indicates that traffic could be classified into three major types of traffic load:

- low traffic load – range of [0.5; 2],
- normal traffic load – range of (2; 4] and
- high traffic load – range of (4; 5].

We will conclude the first stage of the analysis with the examination of very important parameter of network performances – average costs per link. By the term average costs per link we consider cumulative costs in whole network divided by number of links. From previous analyses, it can be realized that *lspr* method shows worst results for all considered parameters. Since our goal is to find the most appropriate routing method when bill-and-keep is applied in the network, we decided to omit that method from our further analysis. The major reason for such a decision is the worst performances regarding traffic load balancing.

In Figure 9 the average link costs for applied routing methods are presented. It can be noticed that there is very little difference in results among routing methods concerning all observed values of offered traffic.

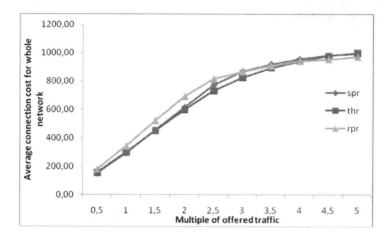

**Fig. 9.** Average connection cost for all routing methods

In the second stage of the analyses, we proposed and applied the ranked coordination game between three operators for finding the dominant network strategy, i.e. the best routing method. In this game, we derived fitted cost functions depending of traffic intensity. These functions define the reaction curves for each operator using selected routing methods, that is, its average costs per link as a function of traffic intensity. We considered three types of traffic load: low, normal and high traffic load.

Figure 10 represents operators $\Lambda$, B and C reaction curves i.e. average costs per link dependence of traffic intensity in a range of [0.5; 5] for routing methods *spr*, *thr* and *rpr*. Based on those graphs, for each operator and traffic load, we defined a strategy set $N = (n^1, n^2, n^3)$ which actually defines rank of routing methods for each operator, such that:

- $n^1$ is rank of the *spr* routing method for observed operator and traffic load,
- $n^2$ is rank of the *thr* routing method for observed operator and traffic load and
- $n^3$ is rank of the *rpr* routing method for observed operator and traffic load.

Each strategy from strategy set $N$ can take values 1, 2 and 3, meaning the best strategy, second best strategy choice and worst strategy choice, respectively. In Table 1 routing strategies of all three operators for all observed types of traffic load are presented.

From Figure 10 and Table 1 it is obvious that routing method *rpr* is not appropriate for either operator because it would drive up to higher costs in comparison to *spr* and *thr*. If $c_i$ represents average costs per link for operator $i$, mathematical formulation of this statement is $c_i(n^3) > c_i(n')$, $\forall\, n' \in N\ \forall\, i$. It can be seen that for all operators *spr* is preferred strategy for low traffic load, i.e. $c_i(n^1) < c_i(n')$, $\forall\, n' \in N\ \forall\, i$ . Method *thr* is their best response strategy for normal and high traffic load, i.e. $c_i(n^2) < c_i(n')$, $\forall\, n' \in N$

∀ *i*. Considering that telecommunication network is usually designed for normal or high traffic load, dominant equilibrium strategy in this game is to choose routing method *thr*. As it is explained in the problem statement, dominant equilibrium defined in this way is Pareto efficient. In case of normal and high traffic load this result coincides with result obtained from analysis of connections lost.

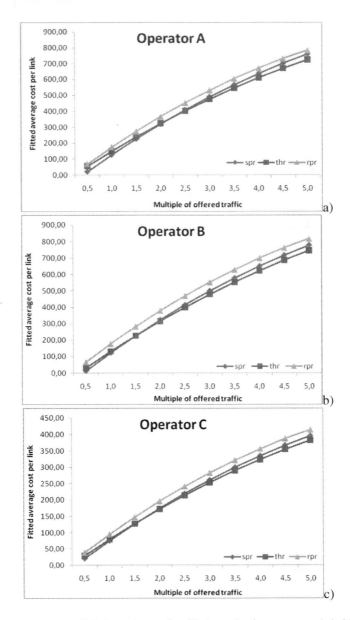

**Fig. 10.** Average costs per link dependence of traffic intensity for operators a) A, b) B and c) C

**Table 1.** Routing strategies of operators A, B and C in ranked coordination game for low, normal and high traffic load

|   | low | normal | high |
|---|-----|--------|------|
| A | (1,2,3) | (2,1,3) | (2,1,3) |
| B | (1,2,3) | (2,1,3) | (2,1,3) |
| C | (1,2,3) | (2,1,3) | (2,1,3) |

# 6 Conclusions

The main goal of our research, presented in this paper, was to analyze how various methods of dynamic traffic routing can affect the performances of telecommunications network in which several telecommunications operators coexist. For the purpose of this research, we developed the original software, RIS. Its main task is the traffic simulation in interconnected telecommunication network. In this paper, two-stage analysis of network performances under different routing methods in interconnected telecommunication network is shown. First stage of the analysis is conducted on those network performance parameters that are of crucial importance when bill-and-keep interconnection charging is applied. Those parameters are link utilisation, load balancing and link costs for whole network and for all considered operators separately. In this stage, we decide to omit one of the routing methods from further analysis since it shows the significantly worse performances concerning all parameters of importance.

In second stage of our research, we proposed and applied the ranked coordination game between three operators for finding the routing method that is the best suitable for all. We based this analysis on average costs per link and three types of traffic load: low, normal and high traffic load. The proposed game showed that the dominant equilibrium strategy for each operator is to choose the three-hop routing method.

## Acknowledgement

This work is partially supported by the Ministry of the Science and Technological Development of the Republic of Serbia, grant number TR32025.

## References

1. Armstrong, M.: Network Interconnections in Telecommunications. Economic Journal 108, 545–564 (1998)
2. Armstrong, M.: Network Interconnection with Asymmetric Networks and Heterogeneous Calling Patterns. Information Economics and Policy 16, 375–390 (2004)
3. ITU-D Question 6-1/, Report on Interconnection (2006),
   http://www.itu.int/publ/D-STG-SG01.06.1-2006
4. http://www.erg.eu.int/documents/erg/index_en.htm
5. http://www.itu.int/ITU-D/finance/costmodels/

6. Dodd, M., Jung, A., Mitchell, B., Paterson, P., Reynolds, P.: Bill-and-keep and the Economics of Interconnection in Next Generation Networks. Telecommunications Policy 33, 324–337 (2009)
7. Radojičić, V., Kostić-Ljubisavljević, A.: Inteconnection of Next Generation Networks. In: Proceedings of XXVII PosTel, pp. 341–350 (2009); (original in Serbian)
8. Marcus, J.S.: Interconnection on an IP-based NGN Environment. In: Global Symposium for Regulators, Dubai, United Arab Emirates (2007),
   http://www.itu.int/ITU-D/treg/Events/Seminars/GSR/
   GSR07/Documents_presentations/
   Session_III%20Scott%20Marcus_interconnect.pdf
9. Ash, G.R.: Dynamic Routing in Telecommunication Networks. McGraw'Hill, New York (1998)
10. Horak, R.: Webster's New World Telecom Dictionary. Wiley Publishing, Inc., Chichester (2008)
11. Medhi, D., Ramasamy, K.: Network Routing: Algorithms, Protocols, and Architectures. Morgan Kaufmann is an imprint of Elsevier, San Francisco (2007)
12. Pioro, M., Medhi, D.: Routing, Flow, and Capacity Design in Communication and Computer Networks. Elsevier, Amsterdam (2004)
13. Aćimović-Raspopović, V., Kostić-Ljubisavljević, A., Radojičić, V.: Dynamic Routing Design under Forecast Uncertainty, Proceedings of TELSIKS, pp. 30-34 (2003)
14. Gunnar, A., Johansson, M.: Robust Load Balancing Under Traffic Uncertainty—Tractable Models and Efficient Algorithms, Telecomunnication Systems (2010) (published online)
15. Kwon, S., Shroff, N.B.: Analysis of Shortest Path Routing for Large Multi-Hop Wireless Networks. Journal IEEE/ACM Transactions on Networking 17(3), 857–869 (2009)
16. Saad, M., Luo, Z.Q.: Design of WDM Networks Under Economy of Scale Pricing and Shortest Path Routing. IEEE Journal on Selected Areas in Communications 24(4), 26–36 (2006)
17. Puzmanová, R.: Routing and Switching, Time of Convergence? Addison Wesley, Reading (2002)
18. Shen, Z.L.H.: A Distributed Three-hop Routing Protocol to Increase the Capacity of Hybrid Networks. In: Proceedings of ICPP 2009, pp. 277–284 (2009)
19. Chao, D., Yong, Z., Yinglei, T., Zhang, Z., Jiansong, G.: A Self-learning Multicast Routing Algorithm for Multi-rate WiFi Mesh Network. In: Proceedings of IC-BNMT 2009, pp. 513–518 (2009)
20. ITU-T NGN FG Proceedings Part II, ITU (2005), http://www.itu.int/ITU-T/ngn/files/NGN_FG-book_II.pdf
21. ITU-T Recommendation Y.2012 Functional Requirements and Architecture of Next Generation Networks Geneva (2004)
22. Project Team on IP-Interconnection and NGN, ERG (07)09, (2007),
   http://www.cmt.es/es/publicaciones/anexos/ERG%2807%2909_rept
   _on_ip_interconn.pdf
23. Report on Next Generation Access - Economic Analysis and Regulatory Principles, ERG (09)17, (2009), http://www.erg.eu.int/doc/
   publications/erg0917ngaeconomicanalysis_regulatoryprinciples_
   report_090603_v1.pdf
24. Study on the Future of Interconnection Charging Methods, European Commission, Ref. 2009-70-MR-EC-Future of Interconnection Charging Methods (2010),
   http://www.teraconsultants.fr/assets/publications/PDF/
   2009-70-MR-draft-final-study%28consult%29.pdf

25. Cadman, R.: NGN Interconnection: Charging Principles and Economic Efficiency, NGNuk, London (2007)
26. Douligeris, C., Mazumdar, R.: A Game Theoretic Perspective to Flow Control in Telecommunication Networks. Journal of the Franklin Institute 329(2), 383–402 (1992)
27. Menasche, D.S., Figueiredo, D.R., Souza, E.S.: An Evolutionary Game-theoretic Approach to Congestion Control. Performance Evaluation 62(1-4), 295–312 (2005)
28. Orda, A., Rom, N., Shimkin, N.: Competitive Routing in Multi-user communication networks. IEEE/ACM Transactions on Networking 1, 614–627 (1993)
29. Altman, E., Basar, T., Jimenez, T., Shimkin, N.: Competitive Routing in Networks with Polynomial Cost. IEEE Transactions on Automatic Control 47, 92–96 (2002)
30. Lazar, A., Orda, A., Pendarakis, D.: Virtual Path Bandwidth Allocation in Multi-user Networks. IEEE/ACM Transactions on Networking 5(6), 861–871 (1997)
31. Jing, Q., Zheng, Z.: Distributed Resource Allocation Based on Game Theory in Multi-cell OFDMA Systems. International Journal of Wireless Information Networks 16(1-2), 44–50 (2009)
32. Chen, S., Park, K.: An Architecture for Noncooperative QoS Provision in Many-switch Systems. In: Proceedings of IEEE INFOCOM, New York, USA, pp. 864–872 (1999)
33. Bouras, C., Sevasti, A.: Pricing QoS over Transport Networks. Internet Research 14(2), 167–174 (2004)
34. Michiardi, P., Molva, R.: Game Theoretic Analysis of Security in Mobile Ad Hoc Networks, Technical Report rr-02-070, Institut Eurecom, France (2002)
35. Jin, S., Yin, L., Li, X.: A Game Theoretical Attack-Defense Model Oriented to Network Security Risk Assessment. In: International Conference on Computer Science and Software Engineering, vol. 3, pp. 1097–1103 (2008)
36. Suris, J.E., DaSilva, L., Han, Z., MacKenzie, A.: Cooperative Game Theory Approach for Distributed Spectrum Sharing. In: Proceedings of IEEE International Conference on Communications, Glasgow, Scotland, pp. 5282–5287 (2007)
37. Bennis, M.: Spectrum Sharing for Future Mobile Cellular Systems, PhD dissertation, Faculty of Technology - Department of Electrical and Information Engineering, University of Oulu, Finland (2009)
38. Hermalin, B., Katz, M.: Your Network or Mine? The Economics of Routing Rules. RAND Journal of Economics 3, 692–719 (2006)
39. Ji, Z., Yu, W., Liu, K.J.R.: A Game Theoretical Framework for Dynamic Pricing-Based Routing in Self-Organized MANETs. IEEE Journal on Selected Areas in Communications 26(7), 1204–1217 (2008)
40. Iversen, V. B.: Teletraffic Engineering and Network Planning, http://oldwww.com.dtu.dk/teletraffic/handbook/telenook.pdf
41. Hu, H.: Poisson Distribution and Application (2008), http://sces.phys.utk.edu/~moreo/mm08/Haohu.pdf
42. Ghazel, C., Saïdane, L.: Dimensioning of Next Generation Networks Signaling Gateway for Improving a Quality of Service Target. In: Proceedings of 2008 Second International Conference on Future Generation Communication and Networking, pp. 275–278 (2008)
43. Zhao, Z., Liu, Q., Guan, H.: A Method and Simulation Study: Network Dimensioning of the Broadband Residential Ethernet-based Access Network, Nokia white paper (2004), http://oldwww.com.dtu.dk/teletraffic/papers/3_5_Zhao.pdf
44. Krithikaivasan, B., Deka, K., Medhi, D.: Adaptive Bandwidth Provisioning Envelope Based on Discrete Temporal Network Measurements. In: Proceedings of IEEE INFOCOM, Hong Kong, vol. 3, pp. 1786–1796 (March 2004)

45. Strategy of Development of Broadband Access in the Republic of Serbia up to 2012 Goverment of Republic of Serbia- strategije/Strategija%20i%20akcioni%20plan%20razvoj%20sirokopojasnog%20pristupa.pdf (2009), http://www.mtid.gov.rs/upload/documents/propisi/ (original in Serbian)
46. Blume, L.E.: The Statistical Mechanics of Strategic Interaction. Games and Economic Behavior 5, 387–424 (1993)
47. Albers, S.: On the Value of Coordination in Network Design. In: Proceedings of the 19th Annual ACM-SIAM Symposium on Discrete Algorithms (SODA), pp. 294–303 (2008)
48. Menache, I., Ozdaglar, A.: Network Games – Theory, models and Dynamics. Morgan&Claypool (2011)
49. http://msdn.microsoft.com/library
50. IEEE Standard 1012-2004 for Software Verification and Validation standard/1012-2004.html (2004), http://standards.ieee.org/findstds/

# Unpredictable Random Number Generator Based on Hardware Performance Counters

Alin Suciu, Sebastian Banescu, and Kinga Marton

Technical University of Cluj-Napoca, Computer Science Department,
28, G. Baritiu St., 400027, Cluj-Napoca, Romania
{alin.suciu,sebastian.banescu,kinga.marton}@cs.utcluj.ro
http://www.cs.utcluj.ro

**Abstract.** Originally intended for design evaluation and performance analysis, hardware performance counters (HPCs) enable the monitoring of hardware events, yet are noisy by their very nature. The causes of variations in the counter values are so complex that are nearly impossible to determine. Hence, while being a major issue in the process of accurately evaluating software products, the unpredictability exhibited by HPCs offer a high potential for random number generation. In the present paper we propose a new unpredictable random number generator (URNG) based on HPCs and analyze the feasibility of producing cryptographic quality randomness. The experiments performed on the proposed generator show that the quality and throughput of the new design is comparable to those exhibited by the well known HAVEG URNG [1]. The results of thorough statistical testing prove the high randomness quality of the produced sequences enabling the generator to be considered a suitable candidate for integration in cryptographic applications.

**Keywords:** unpredictable random number generator, hardware performance counters, statistical testing.

## 1 Introduction

Almost every cryptographic technique requires randomness for providing the desired security functionality, and the level of security exhibited by a cryptographic primitive is highly reliant on the quality of the employed random number generator (RNG) [2]. Consequently, cryptographic systems are constantly increasing their demand for high quality RNGs, and the focus is not only on the quality of produced randomness but also on the availability, accessability and throughput of these RNGs.

In designing a random number generator for cryptographic purposes one has to consider two major aspects: the uniform distribution and independence of generated values, thus providing the two major ingredients of randomness: unpredictability and irreproducibility. According to the degree of unpredictability and irreproducibility present in the employed random sequences, a cryptosystem may be able to satisfy the desired security requirements, for example may ensure

V. Snasel, J. Platos, and E. El-Qawasmeh (Eds.): ICDIPC 2011, Part II, CCIS 189, pp. 123–137, 2011.
© Springer-Verlag Berlin Heidelberg 2011

the indistiguishability of every cryptographically protected message and hence provide the secrecy of the encrypted information.

Based on the nature of the entropy source the generators rely on, RNGs can be classified in three categories: true random number generators (TRNGs), pseudo random number generators (PRNGs) and unpredictable random number generators (URNGs), a brief description of these categories is provided in the following (based on [2]):

1. **True Random Number Generators (TRNGs)**. TRNGs extract randomness by sampling and digitizing natural physical phenomena (like thermal noise, jitter, radiation, etc.), the unpredictability of the generated values being guaranteed by physical laws. While TRNGs offer the highest level of nondeterminism and irreproducibility they do not necessarily present perfectly uniform distribution and independence hence their output needs to be filtered (post processed) in order to reduce possible bias (tendency towards a particular value) and correlation, and make the output more similar to a statistically perfect random sequence. Nonetheless true random sources need specialized hardware, the generators are expensive and some of them are slow and impractical.

2. **Pseudo Random Number Generators (PRNGs)**. PRNGs extract randomness from an initial value, called seed, which is expanded by means of a deterministic recursive formula, providing a modality for generating random sequences using only software methods. As a result, the effective entropy and irreproducibility level resumes to the unpredictability of the seed value (that is therefore recommended to be obtained from a true random number sequence) and the output is completely determined by the starting state of the generator - the seed. Still, the practical features of PRNGs such as high generation speed, good statistical properties and no need for additional hardware devices, made these generators very attractive and are the most widely used RNGs. In cryptographic systems they are represented by the Cryptographically Secure PRNGs - CSPRNGs based on cryptographic primitives or mathematical problems considered to be extremely difficult to solve, and hence are exposed to possible compromise if advances in technology should reveal solutions to the problems the generators rely on.

3. **Unpredictable Random Number Generators (URNGs)**. URNGs are a practical approximation of TRNGs, based on the unpredictability induced by the complexity of the underlying phenomenon that the generator is based upon (e.g. volatile internal processor states [1], human-computer interaction [3,4], race conditions [5]). These generators usually extract randomness from easily available devices, like computer components, and may provide a high level of randomness, but special attention must be given to the way components built for being deterministic can be employed for generating randomness, as thorough knowledge of the underlying phenomenon may ease the prediction of internal states and hence next values. URNGs exhibit certain characteristics of both TRNGs and PRNGs being based on the behaviour of hardware devices like TRNGs are, yet URNGs perform a deterministic

sequence of operations like PRNGs do, nevertheless the impact of the multitude of events and parameters is so complex and any intervention in the generation process disturbs the internal state in such a way that it is impossible for an adversary to model and predict the produced output.

In this paper we introduce a new URNG that exploits hardware performance counters (HPC) which where originally designed for performing low level performance analysis and design validations, but exposed to the complexity and the multitude of effects that operating system functions exert on these special purpose registers they exhibit a certain variation that is unpredictable and hence can be employed as the source of randomness for the proposed generator. The proposed generator shows excellent statistical quality of the produced output as well as a high generation speed - the provided throughput makes the generator suitable for integration in today's cryptographic systems. The generator is highly available, since HPCs are implemented on the majority of currently used processor architectures (x86, PowerPC, UltraSPARC, Cray, MIPS).

The rest of the paper is organized as follows. In Section 2 we first briefly present HPCs in general and highlight the characteristic that enables their use for random number generation. In section 3 the formal model of the generator is provided followed by the description of several experiments conducted on the proposed generator. Then, in section 4 we present the experimental results that show the generators suitability for integration in cryptographic systems. Finally in section 5 we conclude and present further developments.

## 2   Hardware Performance Counters

Many current architectures provide Hardware Performance Counters(HPCs) enabling the performance evaluation of software applications or operating systems and the validation of hardware designs and simulators during runtime. The detailed results of hardware related activities are logged by HPCs, allowing developers and software vendors to enhance the software code until the desired level of performance is achieved.

The set of events that can be monitored is dependent on the specific microprocessor, and furthermore, the types and numbers of hardware counters vary from one processor architecture to another and even within the same family of processors, but usually several HPCs are integrated in a single CPU enabling the low-level and low-overhead performance analysis or tuning to be conducted for several hardware events at the same time.

HPCs consist of two registers – a control register and a count register – through which the specific HPC value can be accessed, read, changed and set, reflecting the number of occurrences of a specific hardware event such as data cache accesses and misses, instruction counts, stalls in the pipeline, TLB misses, retired instructions, hardware interrupts and various other events.

The major difficulty in carrying out performance analyses using HPCs is represented by the noisy nature of the counters, a problem addressed in several research publications. Leif Uhsadel et al. in [6] investigate various sources of noise HCPs are exposed to and emphasize that the impact of noise sources is dependent on the considered event, the system architecture and the used driver and API. In [7] the authors investigate whether HPCs can be trusted and emphasize that subtle changes in the way experiments are conducted can have a significant impact on the observed results. Their focus is on the determinism of the retired instructions performance counters on a variety of single-core x86 processors, yet could not completely determine and neutralize the causes of the variations that produce nondeterminism. In [8] the authors show that although certain variations can be minimized, others are very difficult or nearly impossible to compensate, and the only counters that can come close to deterministic behaviour, on the tested x86 systems, are limited to the class of retired instruction counters, which may still exhibit variations as shown in [7,8] due to operating system interaction, program layout, multiprocessor variations, hardware implementation details or measurement overheads.

In this context, where the behaviour of performance counters during the execution of a program is characterized by a significant level of unpredictability that it is extremely difficult to link back to the source code and furthermore, considering the significant nondeterminism introduced by the concurrent execution of multiple instructions facing race conditions in super-scalar processors and multi-core systems, we find it natural to investigate the feasibility of using HPCs in generating random number sequences.

The hardware performance counters are very low level hardware resources and accessing them programmatically requires the existence of a suitable driver and a high level interface, such as the Performance Application Programming Interface (PAPI) [9] we employed in working with HPCs. PAPI runs on several hardware platforms and operating systems allowing user level programs (C and Fortran) to efficiently access the performance counters. In order to provide a cross platform implementation, the focus of this work is restricted to the fixed number of *preset events*, common to all CPU vendors and models, and does not consider the arbitrary number of *native events* which are specific to each model and vendor.

# 3   Generating Random Bits Using Hardware Events

Consider a simple test program that records the number of *Level1 Cache Hits* before and after performing a hundred iterations of an empty *for* loop (the only operation is the iterator incrementation), and prints the difference between the two values of the counter. Running this program multiple times subsequently on the same machine results in different counter values each time. These variations are caused by the myriad of other processes and services launched by the operating system running in parallel with the test program and having their own specific impact on the total number of L1 cache hits. In an idyllic, sequential environment where time is of no importance and processes do not compete for resources the program would most certainly print the same exact value.

Theoretically, subsequent runs might obtain identical outputs if the exact same conditions in which the program previously ran is recreated. This would imply bringing the CPU and all other processes and hardware components in the same state as in the previous execution of the program. This would pose a nearly impossible task even using the most advanced technologies since the processor would have to be frozen in a stable state, and all its internal parameters need to be recorded. Furthermore, there is the even more difficult task of bringing all other hardware components and processes in the same state which would be practically unattainable even for highly experienced users trying to reproduce the exact same counter values.

Thus we consider as entropy source the unpredictable variation of the value of hardware performance counters during the execution of the test program. The number of each preset event is sampled and recorded using PAPI in a similar manner to the one described above, where the value of the counters are sampled and written to an output file at each iteration of the *for* loop.

### 3.1 Formal Model of the Generator

We model the proposed generator as $\mathbf{G}_B(\epsilon_k, \beta, \delta, n)$, where the meaning of parameters is as follows:

- $\epsilon_k$ is an arbitrary event from the set of *preset events* E, $\epsilon_k \in \mathbf{E}$;
- $\beta$ is the number of bits written to the output file each time the event is sampled. The group of $\beta$-bits are taken from the least significant part of the 64-bit value associated to the sampled counter;
- $\delta$ is the intended delay between two successive samples of the hardware counters expressed as number of instructions to be performed between two successive counter samples.
- $n$ is the total number of samples taken for an HPC – equal to the number of iterations of the *for* loop in the test program presented at the beginning of this section.

The result of an execution is an output file of size $\left\lceil \frac{n \times \beta}{8} \right\rceil$ bytes. Several experiments were conducted in order to determine the appropriate values of the above parameters for producing high statistical quality randomness together with maximizing the throughput of $\mathbf{G}_B$. The system used in these experiments has two Intel Xeon processors, model E5405 with clock speed 2Ghz, a Linux Ubuntu 9.10 operating system and PAPI 3.7.1 with the included perfCtr HPC driver.

### 3.2 Sample Length

The optimum value for the number of bits ($\beta$) produced at each sampling step is dependent on the specific event the counter is set to capture, since some events have higher frequency rates and present a higher level of unpredictability than others.

The value of the hardware counter is captured by PAPI in form of a 64-bit integer, hence the value of ($\beta$) is limited to a maximum of 64.

The first experiment investigates the outputs produced by the generator $\mathbf{G}_B$ for each event $\epsilon_k$ belonging to $\mathbf{E}$ with an intended 0 delay until 8 MB output data is recorded considering the maximum value for $\beta$. Hence, this first experiment can be formalized as $\mathbf{G}_B(\epsilon_k, 64, 0, 2^{20})$ for each $\epsilon_k \in \mathbf{E}$.

Inspecting the $\|\mathbf{E}\|$ output files, of size 8 MB each, a very important conclusion can be drawn: the most significant half of each quad-word remains constant throughout all runs. The following 3 bytes increase monotonically and cannot be used to collect entropy. The least significant byte of the quad-word presents a non-uniform behavior showing potential for a good unpredictability source. These observations are graphically represented in Figure 1. Hence the optimal value for $\beta$ is chosen to be 8 bits - the least significant 8 bits of each sample.

**Fig. 1.** Quad-word sampled from HPCs

A second experiment further analyses the quality of outputs constructed of $\beta = 8$ bit samples aiming to discover whether the quality of these sequences is significantly different compared to the sequences constructed of nibbles, couples of bits or single bits sampled from the least significant byte of the quad-word. The following instances of the generator were performed for each event $\epsilon_k \in \mathbf{E}$:

- $\mathbf{G}_B(\epsilon_k, 8, 0, 2^{20})$, i.e. sample the least significant byte for 1 Mega iterations;
- $\mathbf{G}_B(\epsilon_k, 4, 0, 2^{21})$, i.e. sample the least significant nibble for 2 Mega iterations;
- $\mathbf{G}_B(\epsilon_k, 2, 0, 2^{22})$, i.e. sample the least significant couple of bits for 4 Mega iterations;
- $\mathbf{G}_B(\epsilon_k, 1, 0, 2^{23})$, i.e. sample the least significant bit for 8 Mega iterations.

Each 1 MB output file produced by the above instances was subject to statistical randomness testing using the Rabbit battery of statistical tests from TestU01 test suite [10]. The test results show that the statistical quality of the generated files presents no significant improvement as the value of $\beta$ decreases below 8 bits, but instead the throughput shows a significant decline.

### 3.3   Throughput Inspection

The goal of this experiment is to measure the throughput of the generator instances applied in the previous experiment having the same conditions where $\beta \in \{1, 2, 4, 8\}$ and the throughput ($db$) is measured in Bytes/second. The results highlight the natural tendency for the throughput to double as the number of sampled bits doubles, and show its high dependency on the type of event the hardware counter samples. The results are presented in the following – note that values are expressed as intervals:

- $db(\mathbf{G}_B(\epsilon_k, 8, 0, 2^{20})) = [175, 285]\, KB/second;$
- $db(\mathbf{G}_B(\epsilon_k, 4, 0, 2^{21})) = [88, 142]\, KB/second;$
- $db(\mathbf{G}_B(\epsilon_k, 2, 0, 2^{22})) = [44, 71]\, KB/second;$
- $db(\mathbf{G}_B(\epsilon_k, 1, 0, 2^{23})) = [22, 35]\, KB/second.$

## 3.4   Combining Multiple Counters

PAPI allows the access to multiple counters at the same time, the number of which are limited by the number of hardware counters integrated in the employed microprocessor – a number generally between 2 and 5 for most processors. The goal of this experiment is to inspect the statistical quality of the generator when several different events are counted in the same run and the mixing of counter values is performed using a bitwise XOR.

The experiment can be formally expressed as $\forall e_i, e_j \in \mathbf{E}$ run $\mathbf{G}_B(\epsilon_i, 8, 0, 2^{20}) \oplus$ $\mathbf{G}_B(\epsilon_j, 8, 0, 2^{20})$ resulting in the generation of $\binom{\|E\|}{2}$ output files each subject to statistical testing using the Rabbit battery of tests. The results prove that the statistical quality of mixed outputs generated in this experiment is not superior to the case where single events are counted in each run. The result of the extended experiment which mixes three different performance counters and generates $\binom{\|E\|}{3}$ output files, reconfirmed the above statement.

## 3.5   Mixing at Bit Level

The goal of this experiment is to statistically analyze the quality of files generated by XOR-ing groups of bits from the recorded least significant byte of each sample. The following three XOR-ing strategies illustrated in Figure 2 are considered for each event $\epsilon_k \in \mathbf{E}$:

- $(b_7 \oplus b_6), (b_5 \oplus b_4), (b_3 \oplus b_2), (b_1 \oplus b_0)$ which produces 4 bits per sample;
- $(b_7 \oplus b_6 \oplus b_5 \oplus b_4), (b_3 \oplus b_2 \oplus b_1 \oplus b_0)$ which produces 2 bits per sample;
- $(b_7 \oplus b_6 \oplus b_5 \oplus b_4 \oplus b_3 \oplus b_2 \oplus b_1 \oplus b_0)$ which produces 1 bit per sample.

The 1 MB output files generated by each of the above XOR-ing strategies were statistically tested using the Rabbit battery. The results show a slight increase in the randomness quality of the output as more bits were XOR-ed together. However this approach also leads to a severe decrease in throughput, similar to the one presented in Subsection 3.3. The increasing tendency of the quality versus the decreasing rate of the throughput is graphically represented in Figure 3. The statistical quality is expressed as the number of passed tests from the Rabbit battery of TestU01. The throughput is expressed in tens of kilo-bytes per second. The horizontal axis of the graph represents the number of bits XOR-ed together to produce a single bit in the output.

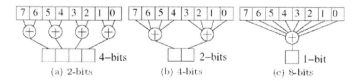

**Fig. 2.** XOR-ing strategies within the sampled byte

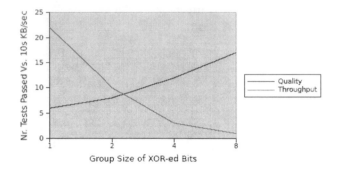

**Fig. 3.** Statistical quality and throughput for the total instructions issued event

As a results of this whitening process the randomness quality of generated sequences has improved and the files generated by XOR-ing groups of 8 bits exhibit the highest randomness quality achieved by the above strategies, but the quality still remains under 60% of the passed Rabbit tests.

### 3.6   Multi-threaded Counting

Within the present experiment $k$ instances of the basic generator are run concurrently inside a multi-threaded application, where $k \in \{1, 2, 4, 8, 16, 32\}$. This extension of the random number generator is denoted by $\mathbf{G}_P(\epsilon_i, \beta, \delta, n, k)$ where $k$ indicates the number of concurrent threads. Every such instance generates $k$ output files. The goal of this experiment is to analyze how the statistical quality of the output files is influenced by increasing the value of $k$.

This experiment was performed on three different test-beds and results show that the statistical quality of the output files increases slightly as the value of $k$ becomes larger. This trend is presented in Figure 4, which shows the number of tests passed from the Rabbit battery of TestU01 for the Total Number of Cycles event on the 8-core test system.

The output files for different instances of $\mathbf{G}_B$ exhibit similar quality levels, with no particular thread standing significantly out with regard to the statistical

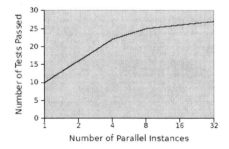

**Fig. 4.** Statistical quality increases as more concurrent threads are employed

quality. Each concurrent thread running an instance of the generator - focused on a specific event counter - exerts a certain influence on (interferes with) all other event counters showing a stronger impact on the variation of the values leading to a higher level of unpredictability due to the operating system's preemptive scheduler. Furthermore, since threads were not bound to kernel threads, the results returned by PAPI calls of unbound user level threads is most likely inaccurate.

On the other hand, when each concurrent thread samples the same event counter, the statistical tests performed on the output file constructed by concatenating each thread's individual output data show a significant decrease of the randomness quality due to the correlation between subsequences in the appended output files. Consequently, this method of combining the generated randomness is rejected.

### 3.7   Thread Level Combination

The experiment from Subsection 3.6 showed that by launching several instances of the basic generator in parallel, the statistical quality of the generated sequences can be significantly improved without sacrificing the throughput, if each concurrent thread focuses on a separate event counter, but when concatenating outputs of concurrent threads sampling the same event, the generated output shows poor statistical quality. Therefore, the method used for combining the results has to be chosen as to maintain the entropy present in each output file. Hence in order to mix the outputs of $k$ concurrent instances of the basic generator using the XOR operation, at first all the sampled bytes have to be recorded in memory – XOR-ing the bytes on the fly is not possible since no synchronization mechanism is used.

This variant of the generator is formally modeled as $\mathbf{G}_{P_{XOR}}(\epsilon_i, \beta, \delta, n, k)$ for all events in $\mathbf{E}$ and produces one single output file of $\frac{n \times \beta}{8}$ bytes, each byte being the result of XOR-ing the $k$ bytes from all concurrent threads corresponding to the same sample index. An illustration of this experiment is shown in Figure 5.

Two concrete implementations are considered and developed, one based on POSIX threads (Pthreads) and the other using OpenMP parallel programming API [11]. The two solutions though conceptually and semantically identical and

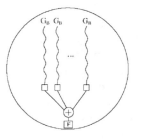

**Fig. 5.** XOR-ing several instances of $\mathbf{G}_B$ ran in parallel

provide similar throughput, exhibit different output quality, the former Pthreads based approach produces good outputs with a good statistical quality, but is exceeded by the latter. The two major OpenMP directive used is *parallel* and *for* without any kind of explicit synchronization mechanisms.

Due to the synchronization involved at the end of the experiment, generating large random files requires an excessive amount of memory, since each thread stores its individual data in memory until finally consumed by the XOR operation. For example if a 1 GB file of high statistical quality numbers needs to be generated it is recommended to use at least 8 instances of the basic generator, resulting in a memory consumption of 8 GB. In order to overcome this drawback, smaller chunks of the larger output file were generated and appended to one another. These large files were then thoroughly tested for identifying possible deviations from randomness.

The results of this experiment show the best randomness quality obtained so far, and although not all the output files exhibit a high statistical quality, the vast majority shows a significant improvement compared to the results obtained in the experiment from Subsection 3.6. Each of the 1 MB output files passed all tests of the Rabbit battery from TestU01. The results for larger output files: 8, 16, 32, 64, 128, 256, 512 and 1024 MB are presented in a later section.

The variant of this experiment where each thread samples a different event is denoted by $\mathbf{G}_{DP_{XOR}}(\xi, \beta, \delta, n, k)$, where $\xi \subset \mathbf{E}$ represents a subset of events, and $\|\xi\| = k$. The other parameters have the same meanings as before. As expected, the randomness tests performed on the generated $\binom{\|E\|}{k}$ output files for each different value of $k$ show an even higher statistical quality of the produced randomness compared to the ones obtained for $\mathbf{G}_{P_{XOR}}$.

## 4    Testing and Results

Concluding the previously presented experiments, the best results are achieved when XOR-ing the outputs obtained by several threads each running an instance of the basic random number generator $\mathbf{G}_B(\epsilon_k, \beta, \delta, n)$. In comparison to the original generator version where the best result obtained in subsequent experiments passed 28.9% of the tests in an isolated case, the best configuration denoted by $\mathbf{G}_{P_{XOR}}(\epsilon, \beta, \delta, n, k)$ shows a significant improvement, the majority of the outputs pass over 60% of the tests from the *Rabbit* battery, furthermore, a set of 18 event counters were identified for which the the output randomness passes over 90% of the tests.

Besides the *Rabbit* battery of statistical tests, which is one of the most complete test suites, two other well known test suites – *Alphabit* and *NIST STS* [12] – were also employed for a more thorough inspection of the generated randomness.

The memory constraints mentioned in Subsection 3.7 limit the generation of very large files, thus our next experiment considers only output files of up to 128 MB generated by uninterrupted runs of the $\mathbf{G}_{P_{XOR}}$ generator. From the large set of *preset events* we further focus only on those event counters that offer a remarkable statistical quality. These events are:

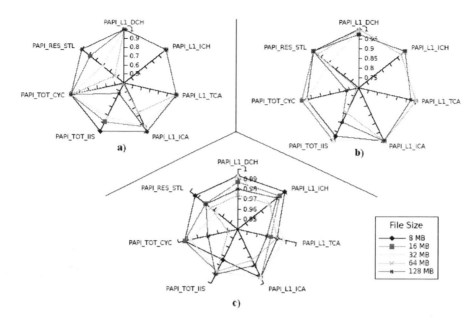

**Fig. 6.** Ratio of a) Alphabit battery tests b) Rabbit battery tests and c) NIST tests passed by $\mathbf{G}_{P_{XOR}}$ output files

- level 1 data cache hits (PAPI_L1_DCH);
- level 1 instruction cache hits (PAPI_L1_ICH);
- level 1 total cache accesses (PAPI_L1_TCA);
- level 1 instruction cache accesses (PAPI_L1_ICA);
- total number of instructions issued (PAPI_TOT_IIS);
- total number of cycles (PAPI_TOT_CYC);
- number of cycles processor is stalled on resouce (PAPI_RES_STL).

The graphical representation of the results obtained after testing output files of: 8 MB, 16 MB, 32 MB, 64 MB and 128 MB (considered as a single bit sequence) with the *Alphabit* and the *Rabbit* batteries of *TestU01* and the *NIST test suite* respectively are shown in Figure 6.

The problem of generating even larger files, larger than 128 MB, can be mitigated by successively running instances of $\mathbf{G}_{P_{XOR}}$ and concatenating the smaller output files. Aiming to thoroughly test the proposed RNG, five files of size 1 GB are generated for each of the seven previously mentioned events. These five files specific for each event are created by concatenating:

- 128 chunks of 8 MB,
- 64 chunks of 16 MB,
- 32 chunks of 32 MB,
- 16 chunks of 64 MB and
- 8 chunks of 128 MB.

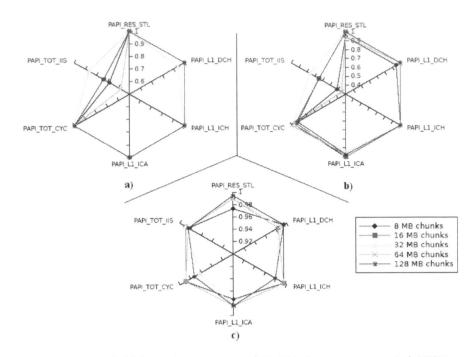

**Fig. 7.** Ratio of a) Alphabit battery tests b) Rabbit battery tests and c) NIST tests passed by 1 GB output files of $\mathbf{G}_{P_{XOR}}$

All files (each considered as a single bit sequence) were subject to the *Alphabit* and textitRabbit batteries of *TestU01* and the *NIST test suite* respectively . The result of these tests are presented in Figure 7.

The result of the above mentioned statistical tests for each of the events except the *Total Number of Instructions Issued* are very satisfactory and enable the generator to be employed for providing high quality randomness for secure cryptographic applications. The event representing the *Total Number of Instructions Issued* failed a large proportion of the two batteries of tests from *TestU01* but passed over 98% of the *NIST test suite*, proving once again the critical importance of using multiple different statistical test batteries in evaluating the quality of RNGs in order to provide a higher confidence in the employed generator.

The next experiment, named *Zoom Testing*, applies the *NIST test suite* which enables the testing of files at various levels, for an even more extensive testing of each 1 GB file considered as 1, 2, 4, 8, 16, 32, 64 and 128 distinct sequences. The results show an average pass rate of over 94%, for all events except the *Total Number of Instructions Issued*. Graphical results are given in Figure 8 for the event representing the *Data Cache Hits*.

As mentioned in the introduction of the paper the throughput is one of the main concerns when designing random number generators, hence the next and final experiment evaluates the generation rate at which the output is produced by our proposed URNG on a system having two cores of 1.75 GHz each. The

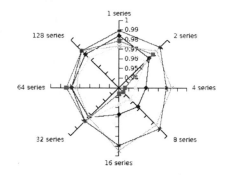

**Fig. 8.** Ratio of NIST tests passed by 1 GB output files (considered as distinct sequences) generated by $\mathbf{G}_{P_{XOR}}$ sampling the Data Cache Hits event

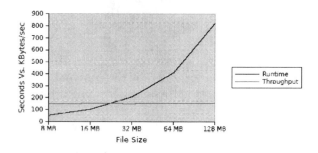

**Fig. 9.** Runtime Versus the Throughput of $\mathbf{G}_{P_{XOR}}$

approximate throughput obtained after measuring the time needed to generate different file sizes is approximately 150 KB per second. The results given in Figure 9. show that the runtime of the generator increases linearly with the size of the output file, hence the throughput remains constant at a level which makes the proposed generator comparable to the state of the art HAVEG algorithm [1] which produces between 8 and 64 KB per operating system interrupt.

## 5    Conclusions and Further Work

We have proposed a new unpredictable random number generator based on the sampling of hardware performance counters and presented several implementation versions that show how HPCs, usually applied for performance analysis or design evaluation, can be successfully employed in generating high quality random number sequences.

For cross-platform compatibility reasons we have only considered HPCs associated to *preset events* and through several experiments we have identified a subset of these HPCs that can be employed as sources of high unpredictability within the proposed generator.

The advantage of the URNG we propose over a TRNG is mainly the reduced cost and availability, while it is clear that the TRNG offers true random bits not just unpredictable random bits. On the other hand, when compared to a PRNG our generator offers several advantages: about the same uniformity of the output, unpredictability, non periodicity, the lack of seeding (hence there is no way to reproduce a generated sequence based on a seed). The main disadvantage of our generator when compared to a PRNG is the lower throughput; this is the price we must pay for obtaining the unpredictability of the output.

The statistical quality of the generated randomness was thoroughly tested using the well known statistical test suites: *Alphabit* and *Rabbit* batteries of *TestU01* and the *NIST test suite*, the results showing the high randomness quality of generated sequences, nonetheless carrying forth the major importance of applying multiple statistical test suites in order to increase the confidence in the generator.

Furthermore, these experiments also emphasize issues that have to be considered such as: the choice of the sampled events, the decrease in randomness quality when concatenating the outputs of concurrent threads sampling the same event counter and the memory requirements for mixing the output files of concurrent threads.

The throughput of the proposed generator is approximately 150 KB/s, a value comparable with the throughput exhibited by the state of the art HAVEG generator. Therefore all aspects regarding the unpredictability, throughput and availability of the randomness source and the quality of the generated sequences prove the proposed unpredictable random number generator's suitability for integration in security systems for providing cryptographic randomness.

In the future we intend to increase the unpredictability of certain hardware events by careful manipulation of the $\delta$ parameter of the generator, which was kept constant (zero) in all the experiments performed so far.

Furthermore, the method we propose for generating random numbers can be applied to other processor architectures (PowerPC, UltraSPARC, Cray, MIPS) and/or operating systems.

# References

1. Seznec, A., Sendrier, N.: HAVEGE: A user-level software heuristic for generating empirically strong random numbers. ACM Trans. Model. Comput. Simul. 13 (2003)
2. Marton, K., Suciu, A., Ignat, I.: Randomness in digital cryptography: A survey. Romanian Journal of Information Science and Technology 13, 219–240 (2010)
3. Suciu, A., Marton, K., Antal, Z.: Data flow entropy collector. In: SYNASC 2008. 10th International Symposium on Symbolic and Numeric Algorithms for Scientific Computing, pp. 445–448. IEEE Computer Society, Los Alamitos (2008)
4. Gutterman, Z., Benny, Pinkas, R.T.: Analysis of the Linux random number generator. In: IEEE Symposium on Security and Privacy, pp. 371–385 (2006)
5. Colesa, A., Tudoran, R., Banescu, S.: Software random number generation based on race conditions. In: SYNASC 2008: 10th International Symposium on Symbolic and Numeric Algorithms for Scientific Computing, pp. 439–444 (2008)
6. Uhsadel, L., Georges, A., Verbauwhede, I.: Exploiting hardware performance counters. In: 5th Workshop on Fault Diagnosis and Tolerance in Cryptography, pp. 59–67 (2008)

7. Weaver, V., McKee, S.: Can hardware performance counters be trusted? In: IEEE International Symposium on Workload Characterization, pp. 141–150 (2008)
8. Weaver, V., Dongarra, J.: Can hardware performance counters produce expected, deterministic results? In: The 3rd Workshop on Functionality of Hardware Performance Monitoring (2010)
9. Browne, S., et al.: A portable programming interface for performance evaluation on modern processors. The International Journal of High Performance Computing Applications 14, 189–204 (2000)
10. L'Ecuyer, P., Simard, R.: TestU01: A C library for empirical testing of random number generators. ACM Transactions on Mathematical Software 33 (2007)
11. Sato, M.: OpenMP: Parallel programming API for shared memory multiprocessors and on-chip multiprocessors. In: ISSS 2002: Proceedings of the 15th International Symposium on System Synthesis pp. 109–111. ACM, New York (2002)
12. Rukhin, A., et al.: NIST Special Publication 800-22: A statistical test suite for random and pseudorandom number generators for cryptographic applications. Technical report, National Institute of Standards and Technology (2010)

# Software Controlled High Efficient and Accurate Microstepping Unit for Embedded Systems

Petr Olivka and Michal Krumnikl

Department of Computer Science
Faculty of Electrical Engineering and Computer Science
VSB-Technical University of Ostrava
tr. 17. listopadu, 708 33, Ostrava, Czech Republic
petr.olivka@vsb.cz, michal.krumnikl@vsb.cz
http://www.cs.vsb.cz

**Abstract.** In this paper, we present a novel design of a microstepping control unit. The goal is to improve the efficiency and compactness of current control units. An effective hardware implementation based on a single microcontroller and L6202 is proposed. By performing the computation of the duty cycle inside the microcontroller PIC18F2455, we have achieved superior positioning accuracy. The unit is designed as a small module, suitable for embedded applications.

**Keywords:** microstepping, control unit, duty cycle computation, microcontroller, step motor, drivers, embedded applications.

## 1 Introduction

Many industrial devices, such as robots, mechanical positioning systems, etc., are composed of small mechanical components in which a step motor is often used as an actuator. Precise positioning is very important, especially when several actuators run at the same time or are in different patterns of the movement. The manufacturers design the step motors to maintain a fixed step for one turn, thus making it possible to achieve such accurate movements. However, there are a lot of applications, which require even more sensitive control. Slow movements, fluent acceleration and deceleration or better accuracy in positioning are often demanded. These requirements can be achieved using a special control technology, known as microstepping. The principle, in short, can be described as a division of a current level in a motor winding. In this way, the step motor can be controlled to operate in more steps than it was originally designed to. While it is theoretically possible to control the step motor continuously, in reality an internal friction will divide this motion into small steps. In practice, we usually use at most 8 or 16 microsteps between two mechanical positions.

Nowadays, there are many units available on the market, designed especially for microstepping control. Nevertheless, a problem arises when we want to use these units in small devices. We are facing the problems related to dimensions,

V. Snasel, J. Platos, and E. El-Qawasmeh (Eds.): ICDIPC 2011, Part II, CCIS 189, pp. 138–146, 2011.

excessive design, efficiency and necessity of cooling, communication interface and protocol, good technical documentation, price and availability on a local market.

In this paper, we will present the current state of the art of microstepping units and propose a novel design, which will outperform the current units in efficiency and compactness.

The remainder of this paper is organized as follows: The opening section discusses the current research and development in the field of microstepping units. Next, in the Section 2 we will specify the requirements and our design goals. We will continue by introducing the design and deriving its main characteristics. In the Section 4 we will focus on the accuracy of proposed microstepping unit. Finally we will summarize the results and provide an outlook on further research.

## 2   State-of-the-Art of Microstepping Units

The invention of microstepping is usually attributed to Larry Durkos, a mechanical engineer of American Monitor Corporation. Microstepping is actually sine cosine microstepping in which the winding current approximates a sinusoidal AC waveform. This allows stopping and holding a position between two standard step positions. Additionally, it provides smoother operations at low speeds.

The basic principles of microstepping can be found in [1]. The paper is primarily focused on simulation and demonstration of the microstepping technique, providing the fundamental mathematical background for calculating the current flow in both phases. It does not cover hardware implementation of microstepping.

An effective hardware implementation of a three phase driver for a two phase step motor is proposed in [3]. The current generated by the PWM is measured and used as a feedback for real-time correction. This allows achieving high precision. Because the control is computationally demanding, digital signal processors are needed for floating point calculations. The authors cover the subject in theory but omit the practical realization. [2] also describes the principles and general characteristics of a software controlled microstepping unit.

Most current designs are based on a general purpose microcontroller. The author of [4] have used C8051F005 as a kernel, combined with L297/298 step motor driving chips. IC L298 is a dual H-bridge in a single package; however, it does not have catch diodes and has less effective integrated bipolar transistors. [5] adopted a similar approach, using PIC18F2331 microcontroller to drive external power circuits using the PWM control signal. The paper covers mainly the software part; hardware is not described in detail. Moreover, the proposed processor is not suitable for USB communication.

Additional inspiration can be found in commercially available units. Manufacturers tend to design universal solutions with a wide range of operational parameters. Let us take a look at some typical examples of commercial devices.

CD30 and CD40 control units [6] are high-end devices with an optional microstepping feature. They are universally designed for a wide range of step motors with a current limitation of up to 4A. Unfortunately, these units are very spacious and heavy, primarily designed for stationary applications and not suitable for embedded systems.

Another example is the control unit EM-136 [7], designed for currents up to 4A, with dimensions of 9x8x4 cm and a weight of 100g without a cooler. This unit is unnecessary large, especially in applications where only small step motors are required.

The last example is the microstepping unit R208 [8]. It is a small unit, which supports the current up to 2A, but lacks the standardised interface, despite the fact that it uses the standard DB-9 connector. In order to achieve standard communication interface, it is necessary to add an additional microprocessor with USART, $I^2C$ or USB interface. This is the only way it is possible to integrate this unit in applications with other devices.

Motivated by this, we have developed a new microstepping unit in the same general class, but with higher efficiency and smaller dimensions.

## 3   Microstepping Unit Design

At first, we should specify the technical requirements. Since we are focusing on embedded applications, we need to design a control unit for two phase step motors with a power supply of 24V and maximum current 1A. Our focus is to create a solution which is as simple as possible. Moreover, the solution must be tiny and light without the necessity of cooling. It should be constructed with minimum parts and integrated circuits.

In order to accomplish our goal, we have broken the task into several stages. In the first stage we will start with the design of the circuit itself. We have taken an integrated approach that takes advantage of the current technology. We have looked over the options and checked the majority of integrated circuits available on the market. We require an IC with an integrated H-bridge. During our search for the best solution, we have eliminated ICs with a half bridge, ICs without integrated catch diodes and ICs for high current applications. After comparing the parameters, we have selected the most suitable IC - ST Microelectronics L6202.

L6202 [9] is an integrated circuit realized with Multipower-BCD technology, which combines isolated DMOS power transistors with CMOS and bipolar circuits on the same chip. The technical parameters are as follows:

- supply voltage up to 48V,
- current up to 1.5A,
- operating frequency up to 100kHz,
- TTL and CMOS compatible input of control logic,
- high efficiency,
- internal logic supply.

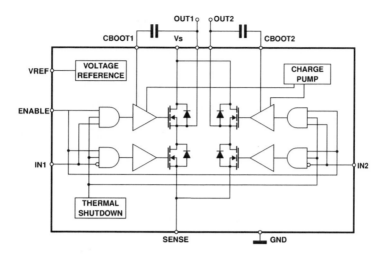

**Fig. 1.** IC L6202 Block Diagram

Only three small capacitors are needed to create a fully functional electric circuit; no additional parts are required. Fig. 1 is a block diagram of L6202 integrated circuit.

### 3.1    IC L6202 Thermal Analysis

Our observations indicate that the IC L6202 has optimal parameters for the design of the microstepping unit. The only parameter we have to carefully observe is the power dissipation. The manufacturer presents this unit as a high efficient device, thus we expect operations without need of a cooler.

We can divide the electrical pulse from the integrated circuit into 4 parts: rising edge, ON, falling edge and OFF period. See Fig. 2. The dissipation energy can be calculated according to the formulas available in the technical documentation.

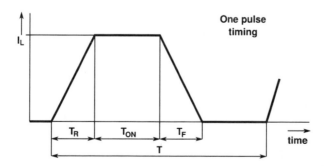

**Fig. 2.** Timing Diagram of Current in El. Circuit Over One Period

The dissipation energy on rising edge is defined as follows:

$$E_{ON/OFF} = R_{DS} * I_L^2 * T_r * 2/3. \tag{1}$$

The dissipation energy on falling edge can be rewritten similarly as:

$$E_{OFF/ON} = R_{DS} * I_L^2 * T_f * 2/3. \tag{2}$$

The dissipation energy during the period when two transistors are opened is:

$$E_{ON} = R_{DS} * I_L^2 * T_{ON} * 2. \tag{3}$$

Finally, the quiescent energy is formulated as:

$$E_Q = V_S * I_Q * T. \tag{4}$$

At this point we shall explain the symbols in the formulas above:

$R_{DS}$ is the internal resistance of an opened transistor, $0.3\Omega$ at $25°C$,
  $V_S$ is the supply voltage, expected maximum is 24V,
  $I_Q$ is the quiescent supply current, typically 10mA,
  $I_L$ is the load current, expected maximum is 1A.

At this stage, it is necessary to determine the worst case operating conditions. The worst situation that may occur is when the microstepping unit stops the step motor in a position, when one phase is fully opened. Which means one integrated circuit is continuously opened with the maximum current flow. In such situations we can compute the maximum dissipation power according to formulas 3 and 4:

$$P_{DIS} = V_S * I_Q + R_{DS} * I_L^2 * 2. \tag{5}$$

The resistance of transistors $R_{DS}$ depends on the chip temperature. Value $0.3\Omega$ is a normalized value for the temperature of $25°C$. The temperature dependency of $R_{DS}$ is shown in Fig. 3. For our applications we do not expect operating temperatures higher than $100°C$. The coefficient $\alpha$ from Fig. 3 is $\alpha = 1.4$ for $100°C$. The maximum proposed supply voltage $V_S$ is 24V and the quiescent current is 10 mA [9]. Using the following modified formula, we can compute the maximum dissipation power of the integrated circuit:

$$P_{MAX} = V_S * I_Q + \alpha * R_{DS} * I_L^2 * 2 = 1.08W. \tag{6}$$

The maximum dissipation power, calculated as described by formula 6, indicates the high efficiency of the construction. Knowing the dissipation power, we can look at Fig. 4.

Sufficient cooling for our application is achieved with a $2cm^2$ copper area on the board. Additional increasing of the copper area is not efficient. The copper area with $l = 1.5cm$ will increase the occupied cooling area to $4.5cm^2$ and decrease the thermal resistance only by $5°C$.

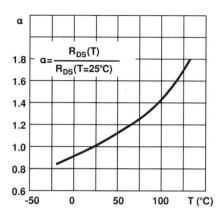

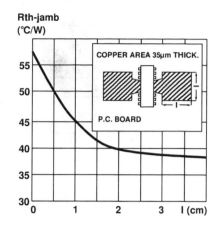

**Fig. 3.** Normalised $R_{DS}$ at $25°C$ vs. Temperature Typical Value

**Fig. 4.** Thermal Resistance Junction-Ambient vs. Copper Area

## 3.2 Accuracy of Microstepping

Our goal is to use the microstepping unit for more than a driver of a step motor. We want to use our unit for positioning as well. For this purpose, we need to check the precision of the microstepping unit. During our experiments we have used the two phase step motor SPA 42/100 with 100 steps per revolution. We have mounted a laser pointer on a motor axis and measured the microsteps using the projections on the wall at a distance of 4 meters. Our control unit was set to 8 microsteps.

The theoretical shift between two microsteps is expected to be 31.4mm $(\tan{(360/100/8)} * 4000)$. The measured values are in Tab. 1 line 1. The table contains medium values taken over ten experiments.

The difference between the expected theoretical shift and measured values was unexpectedly great. Therefore, we have checked the behaviour of other microstepping units. All small microstepping units controlled by pulse wide modulation showed similar inaccuracy. In continuous motion this inaccuracy is eliminated by motor inertia. However, if we intend to use it for positioning, we must avoid this undesirable inaccuracy.

**Table 1.** Measured Microstepping Accuracy

| $\mu$step | 1 | 2 | 3 | 4 | 5 | 6 | 7 | 8 |
|---|---|---|---|---|---|---|---|---|
| 1. measured steps | 18.4 | 30.2 | 40.5 | 34.7 | 35.9 | 42.1 | 31.5 | 18.8 |
| 2. optimised accuracy | 29.0 | 30.2 | 33.5 | 33.1 | 34.0 | 32.7 | 30.5 | 29.7 |

**Table 2.** Nonlinear Dependency of Current vs. Duty Cycle

| $\mu$step | 0 | 1 | 2 | 3 | 4 | 5 | 6 | 7 | 8 |
|---|---|---|---|---|---|---|---|---|---|
| Duty cycle % | 0.0 | 6.25 | 12.5 | 18.75 | 25.0 | 31.25 | 37.5 | 43.75 | 50.0 |
| Current mA | 0 | 3 | 6 | 11 | 18 | 25 | 34 | 43 | 53 |

| $\mu$step | 9 | 10 | 11 | 12 | 13 | 14 | 15 | 16 |
|---|---|---|---|---|---|---|---|---|
| Duty cycle % | 56.25 | 62.5 | 68.75 | 75.0 | 81.25 | 87.5 | 93.75 | 100.0 |
| Current mA | 63 | 72 | 84 | 96 | 115 | 138 | 157 | 171 |

In order to achieve precise positioning we need to improve the precision of current feeding. The $I_1$ and $I_2$ in formula 7 are current in the first and second stator windings. Phase shift is $\pi/2$. The sum of currents in both stator windings must be a constant [1]:

$$\varphi_2 = \pi/2 - \varphi_1$$

$$\sin\varphi_2 = \sin(\pi/2 - \varphi_1) = \cos\varphi_1$$

$$I_{const} = \sqrt{(I_{max}sin\varphi_1)^2 + (I_{max}cos\varphi_1)^2} = \sqrt{I_1^2 + I_2^2} \tag{7}$$

First experiments showed that direct use of PWM leads to irregular current feeding. In the further step, we have to focus on discovering the sources of this inaccuracy.

During the measurements, we discovered nonlinear dependency of current vs. pulse wide modulation. The main cause of this phenomenon is nonlinear behaviour of the electrical circuit in step motor coils, mentioned also in [3]. The results of our measurements (for 16 microsteps) are shown in Tab. 2.

The nonlinearity is clearly visible on the left side of Fig. 5. This nonlinearity complicates the computation of a corresponding duty cycle for a phase shift. It is clear that straightforward usage of the following formula is impossible:

$$DC = 100 * sin\varphi \tag{8}$$

Figure 5 is the illustration of this observation; the real duty cycle has to be approximated from the measured curve. The following formula for duty cycle computation is therefore more general:

$$DC' = f(sin\varphi) \tag{9}$$

Appropriate approximation is computed in the control software according to the corresponding table. The conversion table can be easily modified for any step motor, providing better accuracy. The results of the motor used in our experimental configuration is in Tab. 1 line 2. Measured accuracy is within 10% deviation range from the expected value. By taking into account the internal friction of the step motor, the results cannot be better. The full diagram is shown in Fig. 6.

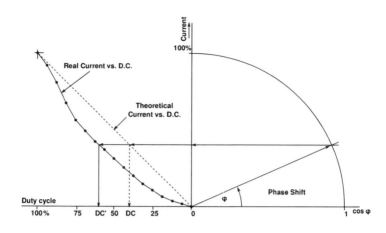

**Fig. 5.** Duty Cycle for Phase Shift

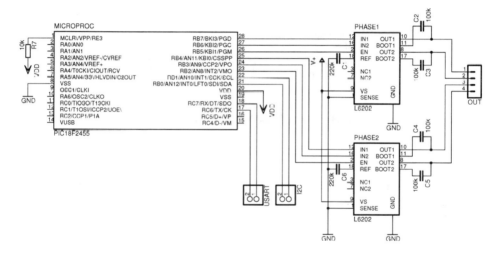

**Fig. 6.** Microsteping Unit Circuit Diagram

## 4    Conclusion

In this paper, we have proposed a novel design of the microstepping control unit. A non-linearity correction feature built into the driving software provides accuracy up to the level of motor internal friction. The final design is small and light-weight, suitable for easy installation into the embedded applications. No cooling is required. The control unit supports $I^2C$, USART and USB connections.

The main contribution of this paper is the implementation of the non-linear correction algorithm inside the microcontroller software. The firmware is not computationally demanding and does not require expensive digital signal processor or additional current sensors.

# References

1. Akdogan, E., Topuz, V., Akbas, A.: An education tool study on mechatronics: emulation of stepper motor driving systems by using a microcontroller based system interface. In: ICM 2004: Proceedings of the IEEE International Conference on Mechatronics, pp. 509–511 (2004); ISBN: 0-7803-8599-3
2. Houška, P., Ondroušek, V., Věchet, S., Březina, T.: Control units for small electric drives with universal software interface. In: Recent Advances in Mechatronics 2007, Part 1, pp. 185–189 (2007), doi:7/978-3-540-73956-2_37
3. Yodsanti, C., Konghirun, M.: Implementation of two-axis highly accurate position control of space-vector PWM based microstepping bipolar drive. In: ICEMS 2008: International Conference on Electrical Machines and Systems, pp. 1027–1031 (2008); ISBN: 978-1-4244-3826-6
4. Li, Z.-q., Jie, Z., Ren, S.-j.: Control system of fine drive for step motor based on SCM. Mechanical and Electrical Engineering Magazine (2007); ISSN 1001-4551
5. Ge, C., Xv, F.-y., Jia, M.-p., Hu, J.-z.: Stepper motor microstepping controller based on PIC. Mechanical and Electrical Engineering Magazine (January 2009); ISSN 1001-4551
6. MICROCON, s.r.o. datasheet, http://www.microcon.cz/pdf2011/02-04.pdf
7. Electromen Oy Ltd datasheet, http://www.electromen.com/pdf/EN_em-136.pdf
8. Lin Engineering datasheet,
   http://www.linengineering.com/LinE/contents/step-motors/pdf/
   Product_Guides/Lin_RG_R208.pdf
9. STMicroelectronics datasheet,
   http://www.st.com/internet/com/TECHNICAL_RESOURCES/
   TECHNICL_LITERATURE/DATASHEET/CD00000089.pdf

# 3-D versus 2-D Animation in Multimedia Application: Is the Extra Effort Worth It?

Riaza Mohd Rias[1] and Halimah Badioze Zaman[2]

[1] Universiti Technologi Mara, Shah Alam
riaza@tmsk.uitm.edu.my
[2] Universiti Kebangsaan Malaysia, Bangi
hbz@ftsm.ukm.my

**Abstract.** Does animation play a role in multimedia learning? Animation in multimedia is said to be beneficial to learning especially when the learning material demands visual movements. The emergence of 3-Dimensional animated visuals has extended the presentation mode in multimedia learning. It is said that animated visuals in a 3-D representation not only possess motivational value that promotes positive attitudes toward instruction but also facilitate learning when the subject matter requires dynamic motion and 3-D visual cue. The field of computer science, especially in operating systems concepts uses an array of abstract concepts such as virtual memory, paging, fragmentations etc to describe and explain the underlying processes. Various studies together with our own observations strongly indicate that students often find these concepts difficult to learn, as they cannot easily be demonstrated. This study investigates the effects of animation on student understanding when studying a complex domain in computer science, that is, the subject of memory management concepts in operating systems. A multimedia learning system was developed in two different versions: 2-D animation and 3-D animation. A hundred and one students took part in this study and they were assigned into one of these groups. All the students who took part in this experiment had low prior knowledge in this subject and after viewing the treatment, they were asked to take a test which tested them for recall and transfer knowledge. This test was used to determine if, in fact, improved learning actually occurred and which version of the animation produced the better outcome. Initial analysis of results indicates no statistical difference between the scores for the two versions and suggests that animations, by themselves, do not necessarily improve student understanding.

**Keywords:** multimedia learning, animation, 3-D animation, memory management.

## 1 Introduction

According to Mayer (2001), multimedia learning is learning from words and pictures and multimedia instructional message or multimedia instructional presentation (or multimedia instruction) is presentation involving words and pictures that is intended to foster learning.

V. Snasel, J. Platos, and E. El-Qawasmeh (Eds.): ICDIPC 2011, Part II, CCIS 189, pp. 147–154, 2011.
© Springer-Verlag Berlin Heidelberg 2011

Based on various studies by researchers (Khalili & Shashaani 1994; Wan Fatimah & Halimah 2005, Faridah & Halimah 2008) the effects of multimedia on learning suggest that multimedia can improve learning performance, irrespective of subject matter, but specifically Mathematics, Sciences and Language. In other studies (Seel & Schenk 2003; Adamczyk et al. 2009) which have compared learning during non multimedia-based and multimedia-based learning, have reported improved learning with the use of multimedia technology.

The present study is aimed at deepening some findings on the benefits of animated instructions whether in a 2 dimensional or a 3 dimensional form. We used a theoretical framework on multimedia learning (Mayer 2001) as a basis for this study.

One of the factors cited as to whether multimedia is effective at improving learning performance, is the difficulty of the learning material being learned (Macaulay & Pantazi 2006). Operating Systems (OS) is a field studied in Computer Science, Information Science and Computer Engineering. Some of its topics require a careful and detailed explanation from the lecturer, as they often involve many theoretical concepts and somewhat complex calculations, demanding a certain degree of abstraction from the students if they are to gain full understanding (Maia et al. 2005). The traditional course model, in which the lecturer follows the knowledge presented in a text book, prepares and exhibits slides and presents some theoretical exercises has been found to be insufficient, to assure a précised comprehension of what is being taught (Maia et al. 2005). Without a practical vision, the students tend to lose touch of the introduced concepts and therefore face difficulties when it comes to solving problems in tests and examinations.

## Animation for Computer Science Education

There have been many literatures on the use of animations in computer science related subjects in the past years. The intuition of computer scientists has led many to believe that animations must provide a learning benefit, but prior experimental studies dating back to the early 90s have provided mixed results.

A study on computer algorithms and data structure examined students learning about the algorithm by reading only a textual explanation and students learning about the algorithm using the text and interacting with an animation of the algorithm (Stasko et al. 1993). Each group had an identical amount of time to study the algorithm, which was followed by a post-test including a variety of questions about the algorithm. The post-test was mostly questions about the procedural, methodological operations of the pairing heap, but it included a few concept-oriented questions as well. There was no significant difference in the two groups' performances on the post-test, but the trend favored the animation group.

Grissom, McNally, and Naps (2003) conducted research to measure the effect of varying levels of student engagement with algorithm visualisation to learn simple sorting algorithms. The three levels of engagement studied were: not seeing any visualisation; viewing visualisation for a short period in the classroom; and interacting directly with the visualisations for an extended period outside of the classroom. Results of their study revealed that algorithm visualisation has a bigger impact on learning when students go beyond merely viewing visualisation and are required to engage in additional activities structured around the visualisation. The researchers also state that it is important that visualisations used by students be consistent with algorithms in their textbooks, or else the visualisations may serve more to confuse them than to aid them.

English and Rainwater (2006) studied the instructional effectiveness of using animations to teach 32 learning objectives in an undergraduate operating systems course. The animations were created using Macromedia Flash$^{TM}$ and were employed as primary pedagogical tools during classroom instruction. In general, descriptions and diagrams served as the basis for reproduction in animated form. The animations were viewed in class by students, as presented as part of the lecture by the instructor at the appropriate point in class when the learning unit was discussed. Pretest scores were obtained by administering the pretest at the beginning of the semester. Posttest scores were acquired by selective inclusion of questions in regular examinations as pertinent to material covered in class. Findings of this study parallels previous research studies which indicate that animations are not effective in conveying information for all learning objectives; i.e. some learning objectives, especially those that are less procedural and more conceptual, are more difficult for students to learn from animation. A closer look at the learning objectives which profited from animation in this study reveals that animations were more beneficial in the sub-topics of *processes*, *memory management* and *virtual memory*. Animations which were designed for these units were generally procedural in structure (English & Rainwater 2006).

In the use of 3-Dimensional animation, Suffern (2000) was inspired to design an effective instructional animation for computer graphics education, with the notion that 3-D animation are effective in their assigned tasks because they focus on concepts and processes that are difficult or impossible to see without animation. They also use a minimalist approach making the animations as simple as possible, focused on what is relevant and interactive, where it allows students to explore viewing systems and tracing transparent objects and visualising the formation of marble. This system is used by computer science students who have prior knowledge experience with 3-D computer graphics. Unfortunately, the author had not carried out any testing on their effectiveness with respect to static graphics. Nevertheless, general feedback from student surveys found that they could really 'see' the processes discussed because the processes were animated and that they learned from the animations.

In the context of our research, we wondered if a 3-D animation is any better than 2-D animation. In a recent study conducted by Schanze (2003) which focused on students in the first two years of chemistry instruction (15 to 16- year old students in German grammar schools) investigated weather the use of 3-D simulations lead to a better understanding of chemical structures than conventional 2-D figures. Schanze's results indicate that chemistry beginners can profit from computer-based 3-D simulations which led to better understanding of chemical structures than 2-D figures.

## 2  Method

Participants were 101 first year students from the Faculty of Computer Sciences at UiTM, Shah Alam. These students had no prior knowledge in this subject (all computer sciences students are supposed to take this subject in their third semester) and were assumed to be homogenous in terms of age, education and cultural background. To be certain, a prior knowledge survey and demographic survey questions were filled out by these participants and they had either none or very little knowledge in the area of operating systems and memory management concepts. These students were than divided r into 2 groups. Group 1(G1) viewed the version with 2-D animation and the group (G2) viewed the 3-D animated version. All the text contents in these versions were the same and in accordance with the syllabus (Silberschatz at al. 2006) for the subject taught.

The self-paced multimedia-based instruction explains on the memory management concepts which consist of background on memory management, swapping technique, contiguous allocation technique and paging technique. Then the students were asked to view the multimedia instructions which were installed in each computer in the computer lab during the two hour lab session. The students could take their time to view the slides and re-visit the slides as often as they wanted within that time frame. The animation was self-paced and interactive. Students could view the animation with the play button and they could rewind, pause or stop according to their individual needs. After the treatment, each participant had to take a test. This test was divided into two parts, which are, the recall test and transfer test. Recall test asked questions which required them to recall or remember some basic facts mentioned in the slides and the transfer test required them to solve some problems based on the knowledge learned in the multimedia learning system they had viewed. All questions were in a multiple choice form, except for one, where the students had to label a diagram. All students answered the questions with paper and pencil. This test procedure followed the conventional paradigm used to evaluate the mental model constructed during multimedia learning (Mayer & Anderson 1992).

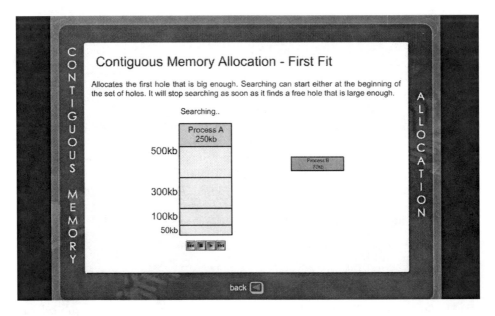

**Fig. 1.** Snapshot of Contiguous Memory Allocation with 2-D animation

## 3   Results

Based on the Independent Sample *t*-test in Table 1, there is no significant effect for visual dimension for neither 2-D nor 3-D animated group on the recall score for low prior knowledge students since the *p*-value is greater than α=0.05, Also, there is no significant effect for visual dimension for either 3-D or 2-D on the transfer score for these students since the *p*-value is greater than α=0.05. However, when the mean score test is observed, the percentage of score for the recall and transfer tests are higher for students who viewed the 3-D version (76.8% and 35.3%) as compared to students who viewed the 2-D version (63.5% and 34.5%). The figure difference between the recall and transfer test is vast even though the number of questions are total scores are divided equally. This is because, the recall test questions are straightforward and require students to remember some facts they had learnt. Whereas, the transfer questions require students to solve problems based on facts and formulas shown in the treatment.

**Table 1.** Independent Sample *t*-test on Recall Score

| Dimension | Mean | Std. Deviation | N | t-value | p-value |
|---|---|---|---|---|---|
| 2 D Animation | 61.3208 | 18.19105 | 53 | -1.313 | 0.192 |
| 3 D Animation | 66.2500 | 19.52903 | 48 | | |

**Table 2.** Independent Sample *t* test on Transfer Score

| Dimension | Mean | Std. Deviation | N | t-value | p-value |
|---|---|---|---|---|---|
| 2-D Animation | 37.1968 | 17.79431 | 53 | 1.057 | 0.293 |
| 3-D Animation | 33.3333 | 18.94603 | 48 | | |

**Table 3.** Mean score test

| Experimental Group | Mean Score Test (%) | |
|---|---|---|
| | Recall | Transfer |
| 2-D Animation & Text | 63.5 | 34.5 |
| 3-D Animation & Text | 76.8 | 35.3 |

**Fig. 2.** Snapshot of contiguous memory allocation with 3-D animation

## 4 Discussion and Conclusion

Findings of the experiment conducted showed that there was no significant effect on 2-D or 3-D animated group on the recall scores and transfer scores for students. This means that there were no advantages of 3-D animation over 2-D animation in generating better recall knowledge amongst the students. Nevertheless, from the mean score test, it is evident that students who viewed the 3-D animated version scored better than the 2-D group. However, in statistical terms, the figures are not significant enough to conclude that the 3-D animated treatment was more effective for student learning.

When the mean scores were analyzed, it was obvious that students performed better in recall questions than transfer questions. This was because transfer questions were problem based and students, who were especially those with low prior knowledge, could not understand all the concepts enough to solve some of the more complex problems.

The non-significance of the findings can be analysed from two standpoints. First, the differences of visual display at the encoding and retrieval time negatively influenced learning gains. The post-test questions in the experiment were presented in two-dimensional format for all experimental groups. The students under the condition of 3-Dimensional animation studied the learning material in 3-D format while they were provided with post-test questions in 2-D format. The 3-D representation was used as an encoding and retrieval cue, confused the students in the 3-D animated group, and they did not take advantage of the 3-D animated representation of learning material to answer the post-test.

Consistency between encoding and retrieval cues was suggested by Paivio (1991). The effects of instructional visuals were maximized when the same kind of pictorial cues were used at retrieving and encoding time. Similar findings were found in a study by Hye (1999) who compared the use of 3-D graphics in student learning and attitude, with that of 2-D graphics in learning the "Motion of the Earth and Moon" in space. The study found no significant gain in students learning in both the groups where the argument was partly blamed on the differences of visual cues at encoding and retrieval time, which is similar to the arguments of the existing study. Kulhavy et al. (1994) conducted a study of map structures and retrieval task. The samples studied a city map and were given different conditions at retrieval. The more the original encoding structure of the map was disrupted at retrieval time, the more the students were bewildered. Students recalled better when the intact map structure was provided at retrieval time, which had been also provided at the encoding time.

Other reasons on why the use of 2-D and 3-D animation did not have a significant impact on the test scores (particularly the transfer test), could be due to the quality of animation implemented. Much time and effort was invested in the design of the animation and the graphics used in the 2-D version can be considered to be typical for those found in the textbook (Silberschatz et al. 2006). However, the animation used for 3-D representation was entirely the idea of the author which had incorporated a constructivist approach and used items such as trucks, excavators, racks and boxes (as metaphors to depict the idea of arranging boxes in a warehouse to that of an operating system arranging data to the respective addresses in memory).

A possibility of the results outcome could also be because the participants had no prior knowledge in this subject and therefore found it difficult to absorb some important concepts and ideas from the multimedia learning software. Further research would be carried out on students who have high prior knowledge in this subject as a comparison to this study.

Time taken for completion of the tests was not one of the research objectives. However, it was interesting to observe that samples from the 3-D groups completed their learning process faster than the other group. Thus, time would be a factor that should be investigated in future research conducted.

Practically, the results of the study has raised some questions to the practice of instructional designer, is it really worth it to design and develop instructions utilizing 3-D animated strategies versus simply using static graphics and 2-D animation if the later have been shown to be at least as effective ? In future design, maybe it is better to utilize static graphics and 2-D animation as much as possible and use 3-D animation only when the use of animation is justified.

# References

1. Khalili, A., Shashaani, L.: The effectiveness of computer applications: A meta-analysis. Journal of Research on Computing in Education 27, 48–61 (1994)
2. Wan Fatimah, W.A., Halimah, B.Z.: Design and Preliminary evaluation of a multimedia courseware for visualizing geometric transformations. Studies in Science, Mathematics and Technical Education 2(1), 10–23 (2005)

3. Faridah, H., Halimah, B.Z.: Development of interactive multimedia courseware using Problem based learning for Mathematics Form 4 (PBL Math-Set). In: Proceedings of the International Symposium on Information Technology 2008 (ITSim 2008), August 26-29. KLCC, Kuala Lumpur (2008); IEEE Cat No. CFP0833E-PRT. ISBN 978-1-4244-2327-9.Pp 1346-1351

4. Seel, N.M., Schenk, K.: Multimedia Environments as Cognitive Tools for Enhancing Model-Based Learning and Problem Solving. An Evaluation Report. Evaluation and Program Planning 26(2), 215–224 (2003)

5. Adamczyk, C., Holzer, M., Putz, R., Fisher, M.: Student learning preferences and the impact of a multimedia learning tool in the dissection course at the University of Munich. Annals of Annatomy 191(4), 339–348 (2009)

6. Macaulay, M., Pantazi, I.: Material Difficulty and the effectiveness of Multimedia in Learning. International Journal of Instructional Media 33(2), 187–195 (2006)

7. Maia, L.P., Machado, F.B., Pacheco Jr., A.C.: A constructivist framework for operating systems education: A pedagogical using the Sosim. Paper read at ITiCSE 2005, at Monte de Caparica, Portugal, June 27 - 29 (2005)

8. Stasko, J.T., Badre, A., Lewis, C.: Do algorithm animations assist learning? An empirical study and analysis. In: INTERCHI 1993 Conference on Human Factors in Computing Systems, pp. 61–66 (1993)

9. Grissom, S., McNally, M., Naps, T.: Algorithm visualization in CS Education. In: ACM Symposium on Software Visualization, pp. 87–94 (2003)

10. English, Brian, M., Rainwater, S.B.: The effectiveness of animations in an undergraduate operating systems course. JCSC 21(5), 53–59 (2006)

11. Suffern, K.G.: Effective Instructional Animation in 3D Computer Graphics Education. Paper read at ACE, at Melbourne, Australia (2000)

12. Schanze, S.: Do computer-based three-dimensional simulations help chemistry beginners to understand chemical structures? A preliminary study (on-line) (2003), http://www1.phys.uu.nl/esera2003/programme/pdf%5c149s.pdf (November 15, 2007)

13. Silberschatz, A., Galvin, P.B., Gagne, G.: Operating System Principles, 7th edn. John Wiley & Sons, NJ (2006)

14. Mayer, R.E.: Multimedia Learning. Cambridge University Press, New York (2001)

15. Mayer, R.E., Anderson, R.B.: The instructive animation: Helping students build connections between words and pictures in multimedia learning. Journal of Educational Psychology 84(4), 444–452 (1992)

16. Paivio, A.: Dual-coding theory: Retrospect and current status. Canadian Journal of Psychology 45, 255–287 (1991)

17. Moon, H.S.: The effects of 3D interactive animated graphics on student learning and attitudes in computer-based instructions. PhD Thesis. Faculty of Graduate School, University of Southern California, Los Angeles (1999)

# Multi-path Construction for Bypassing Holes in Wireless Sensor Networks

Sheng-Tzong Cheng and Jia-Shing Shih

Department of Computer Science and Information Engineering,
National Cheng Kung University, Tainan, R.O.C.
stcheng@mail.ncku.edu.tw,
jason@csie.ncku.edu.tw

**Abstract.** Holes in wireless sensor networks are the geographical region without enough available sensor nodes. When a hole exists in the wireless sensor network, it often causes traditional routing algorithms to fail. In most of the previous works, the routing hole problem was addressed by using the static detour path to route data packets along the boundaries of holes. As a result, the energy of sensor nodes on the static path depletes quickly, and the hole size enlarges. In this paper, we propose a scheme for bypassing holes in wireless sensor networks by exploiting energy-aware multiple paths. Our approach not only takes into account the shorter path to bypass the hole, but also eases the loading of the sensor nodes on the boundaries of holes. Simulation results show that the proposed scheme can achieve short detour paths, low energy consumption and network load balancing.

**Keywords:** Wireless sensor networks, hole problem, bypassing holes, routing algorithms, load balancing.

## 1 Introduction

A typical wireless sensor network (WSN) is formed by a large number of distributed sensor nodes with an information collector [1]. Because sensor nodes have stringent limitations on resources, energy efficiency is a crucial issue of protocols design in WSNs. Traditional routing protocols in wireless networks such as mobile ad-hoc networks cannot work well in the WSNs where sensor nodes are static in most cases. Geographic routing with greedy forwarding has been considered as an attractive approach [2][3] for WSNs because it is a simple, efficient and scalable strategy. It only requires the location of information of sensor nodes. The holes problem consists of a region in the WSN where no sensor nodes inside or the available nodes can participate in the actual routing of the data [9][10]. Holes are hardly avoided in practice. It often causes traditional geographic routing algorithms to fail. There have been many approaches proposed to solve the routing hole problem [11-13]. The routing hole problem is always addressed by using the static detour path or by the perimeter mode to route data packets along the boundaries of the holes. But it's makes uneven energy consumption result of the whole network.

In this paper, we proposed a scheme for bypassing holes in the wireless sensor network by exploiting the energy-aware multi-path. The goals of our work are the

V. Snasel, J. Platos, and E. El-Qawasmeh (Eds.): ICDIPC 2011, Part II, CCIS 189, pp. 155–166, 2011.
© Springer-Verlag Berlin Heidelberg 2011

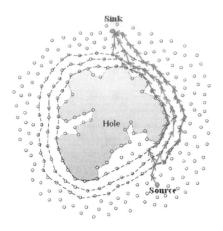

**Fig. 1.** Multiple paths from a source node to the sink in our work

following: First, we model the shape of holes by convex hulls to prevent the packets fall into the holes and to help them to bypass the holes more efficiently. Secondly, we determine which direction is better for bypassing the hole when a data packet encounters it. Finally, we construct energy aware multiple bypass paths for balancing the load of the nodes on the boundary of the hole. Fig. 1 is a schematic diagram which shows multiple paths on the dashed lines, thus the source node can select one from them dynamically to forward packets to the sink in our work.

## 2 System Model

The environment of wireless sensor networks in our work based on the following assumptions: First, sensor nodes are placed in a two-dimensional space R2. Second, the sink and sensor nodes are stationary. Finally, each node can get the location information of itself and all its one-hop neighbors, which can be made available using the GPS or other location services [4-8].

The system architecture is shown in Fig. 2. The proposed scheme consists of three phases: The hole shape modeling phase, the multi-path construction phase, and the bypassing path selection phase. In phase 1, we form a convex hull to model the shape of a hole. In phase 2, we construct multiple detour paths around the hole. After the second phase is finished, whenever packets are transported to the sensor nodes which are located on these multiple paths, they can select the next node to forward packets according to the algorithm we proposed in phase 3.

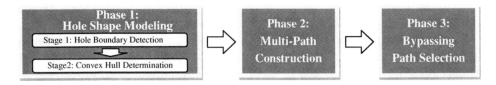

**Fig. 2.** The system architecture

## 2.1 Hole Shape Modeling

There are two stages in the hole shape modeling phase: Stage 1 can find out the locations of all sensor nodes on the boundary of the hole. Stage 2 finds out a convex hull which is the best approximate shape of the hole.

### 2.1.1 Hole Boundary Detection

When a source node has data, it sends the data to the destination $D$ by using geographic greedy forwarding. When a node receives the data packet, if it cannot find any one-hop neighbor closer to the destination $D$ than itself, we name this node as stuck node and denote it as node $v_{ini}(1)$, which represent the initiator node of the first hole boundary detection process.

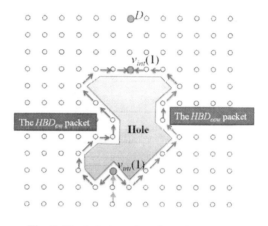

**Fig. 3.** The hole boundary detection process

In order to facilitate the description, we take the grid topology as an example shown in Fig. 3. Each sensor node can communicate with its eight adjacent neighbor nodes. After node $v_{ini}(1)$ detected itself is a stuck node, it sends out a clockwise Hole Boundary Detection ($HBD_{cw}$) packet to the first edge counterclockwise about node $v_{ini}(1)$ from the line segment $\overline{D v_{ini}(1)}$, and then inserts its own location and the unique sensor ID of node $v_{ini}(1)$ into the $HBD_{cw}$ packet. If a $HBD_{cw}$ packet arrive at node $x$ from node $y$, the next edge traversed is the next one sequentially counterclockwise about node $x$ from edge($x$, $y$). The $HBD_{cw}$ packet will be forwarded along the boundary of the hole in clockwise by the long-known right hand rule.

Node $v_{ini}(1)$ also sends out a counterclockwise Hole Boundary Detection ($HBD_{ccw}$) packet to the first edge clockwise about node $v_{ini}(1)$ from the line segment $\overline{D v_{ini}(1)}$. Similarly, node $v_{ini}(1)$ inserts its own sensor ID and location into the $HBD_{ccw}$ packet. If a $HBD_{ccw}$ packet arrives at node $w$ from node $z$, the next edge traversed is the next one sequentially clockwise about node $w$ from edge($w$, $z$). The $HBD_{ccw}$ packet will be forwarded along the boundary of the hole counterclockwise by the left hand rule. After a node receives both $HBD_{cw}$ and $HBD_{ccw}$ packets, it no longer forwards both of them. We denote this node as node $v_{int}(1)$, which represents the first intersection node between the $HBD_{cw}$ and $HBD_{ccw}$ packets. The mission of $HBD_{cw}$ and $HBD_{ccw}$ packets is to track the location of all nodes on the boundary of the hole. Each node which has received the $HBD$ packets will insert its own location into the $HBD$ packets, and then forward it.

### 2.1.2 Hole Boundary Detection

A convex polygon is a simple polygon whose interior is a convex set. The following properties of a simple polygon are all equivalent to convexity: First, every internal angle is less than 180 degrees. Secondly, every line segment between two vertices remains inside or on the boundary of the polygon. The convex hull is typically represented by a sequence of the vertices of the line segments forming the boundary of the convex polygon, ordered along that boundary. A convex hull has the best approximation shape of the hole and we strongly recommend that data packets should be forwarded along the convex hull of the hole.

```
1. function left_turn(node₁, node₂, node₃)
2.    return (x₁ − x₀) * (y₂ − y₀) - (y₁ − y₀) * (x₂ − x₀);
3.
4. sort nodes in H by the angle that they and node Min make with the x-axis.
5. let n = number of nodes in H;
6. let Stack[0] = H[n-1];
7. let Stack[1] = H[0] = node Min;
8. let Stack[2] = H[1];
9.
10. // We denote t as the index on the top of the Stack.
11. let t = 2;
12. for (i = 2; i < n; i++)
13.    while (left_turn(Stack[t-1], Stack[t], H[i]) < 0) do
14.        t--;
15.    end while;
16.    t++;
17.    Stack[t] = H[i];
18. end for;
```

**Fig. 4.** The pseudo code for the convex hull determination

Fig. 4 depicts the pseudo code for the convex hull determination. After the end of hole detection process, node $v_{int}(1)$ can get the location of all sensor nodes on the boundary of the hole from the $HBD_{cw}$ and $HBD_{ccw}$ packets. We denote the set $H$ as the set of these sensor nodes. Node $v_{int}(1)$ can find out which sensor nodes are on the convex hull of the hole from $H$ by using the Graham scan [14].

The algorithm proceeds by considering all the nodes in the sorted array $H$ in sequence. For each node, it is determined whether the move from the two previously considered nodes to this node is a left turn or a right turn. For three nodes with coordinates $(x_0, y_0)$, $(x_1, y_1)$ and $(x_2, y_2)$, we compute the direction of the cross product of the two vectors defined by the nodes $(x_0, y_0)$, $(x_1, y_1)$ and $(x_0, y_0)$, $(x_2, y_2)$, characterized by the sign of the expression $(x_1 − x_0)(y_2 − y_0) - (y_1 − y_0)(x_2 − x_0)$ to determine whether three nodes constitute a left turn or a right turn. If the result is zero, the nodes are collinear; if it is positive, the three nodes constitute a left turn, otherwise a right turn. The $Stack$ will eventually contain all nodes on the convex hull in a counterclockwise order after this process finishes.

## 2.2 Multi-path Construction

Before we describe how to construct multiple paths, we define the path length of each path and thus determine how many paths we need to build. The method of multi-path construction will be described in this section.

### 2.2.1 Path Length Definition and the Number of Paths

During the first phase, node $v_{int}(k)$ can get the locations of all sensor nodes located on the boundary of the hole, thus it can find out the nodes on the convex hull of the hole among these sensor nodes, where $k$ represents the node $v_{int}(k)$ belongs to the $k$-th path. The set $C(k)$ is denoted as the set of the nodes on the convex hull, and the *sink* represents the sink node. Then node $v_{int}(k)$ selects two nodes $v_a(k)$ and $v_b(k)$ so that the angle (which is equal to or smaller than 180 degrees) between $\overline{v_a(k)sink}$ and $\overline{v_b(k)sink}$ is the biggest angle among the angles between any two nodes in $C(k)$. For three nodes $v_a(k)$, *sink* and $v_b(k)$ with coordinates $(x_a, y_a)$, $(x_s, y_s)$ and $(x_b, y_b)$. The direction of the cross product of the two vectors is defined by nodes $(x_s, y_s)$, $(x_a, y_a)$ and $(x_s, y_s)$, $(x_b, y_b)$. We compute the sign of the expression $(x_a - x_s)(y_b - y_s) - (y_a - y_s)(x_b - x_s)$ to determine whether three nodes constitute a left turn or a right turn. If nodes $v_a(k)$, *sink* and $v_b(k)$ constitute a left turn, node $v_a(k)$ is denoted as $v_{ccw}(k)$ and node $v_b(k)$ as $v_{cw}(k)$, otherwise node $v_a(k)$ is denoted as $v_{cw}(k)$ and node $v_b(k)$ as $v_{ccw}(k)$.

We suppose that nodes $\{c_0(k), c_1(k), c_2(k) \dots c_n(k)\}$ are convex hull vertices on the $k$-th path in counterclockwise order. Nodes $\{g_0(k), g_1(k), g_2(k) \dots g_m(k)\}$ are convex hull vertices on the $k$-th path from $v_{ccw}(k)$ to $v_{cw}(k)$ in counterclockwise order. We define the path length of the $k$-th path as following equation (1):

$$PathLength(k) = \frac{1}{2}\left\{ \begin{array}{l} Distance(v_{cw}(k), sink) + Distance(v_{ccw}(k), sink) \\ + \sum_{i=0}^{n-1} Distance(c_i(k), c_{i+1}(k)) - \sum_{j=0}^{m-1} Distance(g_j(k), g_{j+1}(k)) \end{array} \right\} \quad (1)$$

These boundary nodes are located on the first path by the scheme we proposed in this paper. The more detour paths we construct, the more load of boundary nodes on the first path can be reduced. However, if data packets are transported by the paths which have longer path length than the first path, it means they travel a longer distance to the sink, thus the additional overhead of the sensor nodes on these paths is increasing.

We define the number of sensor nodes on the $k$-th path is expressed as *NodesQuantity(k)*. If we built $k$ paths, the load reduction of the first path can be expressed as $[(k-1)/k]$ * *NodesQuantity*(1) and the additional overhead from the second path to the $k$-th path can be expressed as equation (2):

$$\sum_{i=2}^{k}[NodesQuantity(i) - NodesQuantity(1)] \quad (2)$$

In practice, it is difficult to know the number of sensor nodes of each path. But we know that the number of sensor nodes of each path is usually proportional to the length of each path, so we can replace *NodesQuantity(i)* by *PathLength(i)* in equation (2). Considering the above circumstances, if we built $k$ paths, the load reduction can be expressed as following equation (3):

$$LoadReduction(k) = \left\{ \begin{array}{ll} \dfrac{k-1}{k} PathLength(1) - \displaystyle\sum_{i=2}^{k}[PathLength(i) - PathLength(1)] : k > 1 \\ 0 \qquad\qquad\qquad\qquad\qquad\qquad\qquad\qquad\qquad\quad : k = 1 \end{array} \right\} \quad (3)$$

### 2.2.2 Path Construction

After node $v_{int}(k)$ is calculated $LoadReduction(k)$ by the equation (1) and (3), it sends out the *Convex Hull Information (CHI)* packets to node $v_{cw}(k)$ and $v_{ccw}(k)$. The *CHI* packets consist of the following information: the sensor ID of $v_{int}(k)$, $LoadReduction(k)$, the location of node $v_{cw}(k)$ and $v_{ccw}(k)$, and the location of all nodes on the convex hull.

We suppose that nodes $\{q_0(k), q_1(k), q_2(k), \ldots q_n(k)\}$ are convex-hull vertices on the $k$-th path from $v_{cw}(k)$ to $v_{ccw}(k)$ in a counterclockwise order, and let $v_{cw}(k)$ as $q_0(k)$, and $v_{ccw}(k)$ as $q_n(k)$. After node $q_0(k)$ receives the *CHI* packet, it chooses the location of node $q_1(k)$ as the destination of the counterclockwise *Path Construction ($PC_{ccw}$)* packet and forwards this packet to node $q_1(k)$ by the greedy perimeter stateless routing algorithm. Node $q_i(k)$ receiving this packet will select the location of node $q_{i+1}(k)$ as the destination of the $PC_{ccw}$ packet and then forward this packet to node $q_{i+1}(k)$ by greedy perimeter stateless routing algorithm too.

After node $q_n(k)$ receives the *CHI* packet, it chooses the location of node $q_{n-1}(k)$ as the destination of the clockwise *Path Construction ($PC_{cw}$)* packet and forwards this packet to node $q_{n-1}(k)$ by the greedy perimeter stateless routing algorithm. Node $q_j(k)$ receiving the $PC_{cw}$ packet will select the location of node $q_{j-1}(k)$ as the destination of the $PC_{cw}$ packet and then forward this packet to node $q_{j-1}(k)$ by greedy perimeter stateless routing algorithm too. If a node detects its absolute difference of the hop counts from node $v_{cw}(k)$ to itself and the hop counts from node $v_{ccw}(k)$ to itself is smaller than two hops after it receives both $PC_{cw}$ and $PC_{ccw}$ packets, it no longer forwards $PC_{cw}$ and $PC_{ccw}$ packets. The *PC* packets consist of the sensor ID of $v_{int}(k)$, $LoadReduction(k)$, the hop counts from the received node to $v_{cw}(k)$ or $v_{ccw}(k)$, and the locations of nodes $\{q_0(k), q_1(k), q_2(k), \ldots q_n(k)\}$. The Demonstration of the first path construction process is shown in Fig. 5, nodes $\{q_0(1), q_1(1), q_2(1), \ldots q_8(1)\}$ are represented by the black solid points. The number beside each node represents the hop counts from node $v_{cw}(1)$ or $v_{ccw}(1)$ to each node.

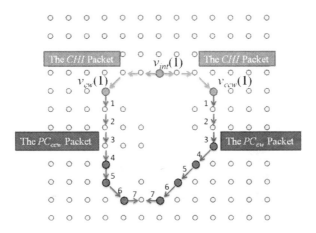

**Fig. 5.** Demonstration of the first path construction process

If a node $u$ receives the $PC_{ccw}$ packet from a node $w$, it performs the following actions: First, if *LoadRuduction(k)* with the $PC_{cw}$ packet or the $PC_{ccw}$ packet is a negative number, it regards itself as an "*outer path node*", otherwise an "*path node*". Secondly, if node $u$ receives the $PC_{ccw}$ packet, it marked itself is located on the "*clockwise region*" of the hole, and records the hop counts from node $v_{cw}(k)$ to itself. If node $u$ receives the $PC_{cw}$ packet, it marks itself is located on the "*counterclockwise region*" of the hole, and records the hop counts from node $v_{ccw}(k)$ to itself. Finally, node $u$ announces its all one-hop neighbors the following things: whether node $u$ is an "*outer path node*", or an "*path node*", whether node $u$ is located on the "*clockwise region*" or "*counterclockwise region*" and the hop counts from node $u$ to $v_{cw}(k)$ or $v_{ccw}(k)$. If a sensor node does not belong to the "*path nodes*" and "*outer path nodes*", it belongs to a "*normal node*". If there is a sensor node $w$ which belongs to the "*normal nodes*" outside of the hole forwards the data packet to a "*path node*" on the $k$-th path, we regard node $w$ as the node $v_{ini}(k+1)$, and then construct the $(k+1)$-th path. All "*path nodes*" on the $k$-th path will be considered in the area of a hole during the $(k+1)$-path construction. Fig. 6 shows a flowchart of a multi-path construction.

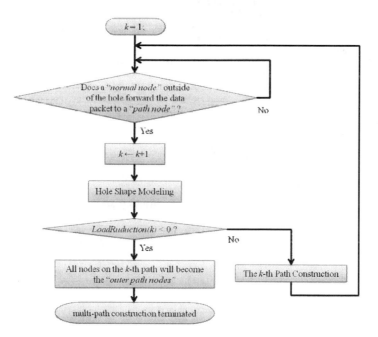

**Fig. 6.** A flowchart of multi-path construction

## 2.3 Bypassing Path Selection

We propose a bypassing path selection strategy with energy awareness; its concept is like the topographic map. The consumed energy of each sensor node is transformed to the elevation, the more energy a sensor node has consumed, the higher its elevation is. When transmitting packets, each sensor node will insert its elevation value in the packet. Thus, each node can update its neighbors' current elevation without additional energy consumption.

The movement of data packets on the paths we construct is determined by the composition of two principles: First, data packets are like water naturally flowing from higher elevation to lower elevation; they will move in the direction that the elevation decreases most. Secondly, data packets should move toward the position of the sink. When a node $u(i)$ ($i$ represents on the $i$-th path) which belongs to "*path nodes*" receives a data packet, it forwards this packet to a neighbor which has the lowest elevation in an established candidate list. If more than one node has the lowest elevation, node $u(i)$ forwards the packet to the node which is located on the lowest order path among them.

```
 1.  function candidate_election(node u(i)) {
 2.    let n = number of neighbors of node u(i)
 3.    for (a = 0; a < n; a++)
 4.      let w(j) = Neighbor[a] of node u(i);
 5.      if node u(i) ∈ "clockwise region" then
 6.        if hop counts from w(j) to v_cw(j) < hop counts from u(i) to v_cw(i) or
 7.          hop counts from w(j) to v_ccw(j) < hop counts from u(i) to v_cw(i) then
 8.            Adding w(j) to the CandidateList
 9.        end if
10.      else if node u(i) ∈ "counterclockwise region" then
11.        if hop counts from w(j) to v_cw(j) < hop counts from u(i) to v_ccw(i) or
12.          hop counts from w(j) to v_ccw(j) < hop counts from u(i) to v_ccw(i) then
13.            Adding w(j) to the CandidateList
14.        end if
15.      end if
16.    end for;
17.  }
18.
19.  if node u(i) ∈ "path node" then
20.    candidate_election(u(i));
21.    Find the node y(g) which has the lowest elevation from the CandidateList;
22.    if more than one node has the lowest elevation then
23.      Find the node z(h) which has the lowest order path from them;
24.      Forward the data packet to z(h);
25.    else
26.      Forward the data packet to y(g);
27.    end if
28.  end if
```

**Fig. 7.** The pseudo code of the data packet forwarding strategy

Node $u(i)$ establishes the candidate list under the following conditions: First, if node $u(i)$ is located on the "*clockwise region*" of the hole; For all neighbors of node $u(i)$, if the hop counts from neighbor $w(j)$ to node $v_{cw}(j)$ or node $v_{ccw}(j)$ is smaller than the hop counts from $u(i)$ to node $v_{cw}(i)$, then add $w(j)$ to the candidate list. Secondly, if node $u(i)$ is located on the "*counterclockwise region*" of the hole; For all neighbors of node $u(i)$, if the hop counts from neighbor $w(j)$ to node $v_{cw}(j)$ or node $v_{ccw}(j)$ is smaller than the hop counts from $u(i)$ to node $v_{ccw}(i)$, add $w(j)$ to the candidate list. Fig. 7 depicts the pseudo code of the data packet forwarding strategy.

## 3   Performance Simulation

We compare our scheme with the virtual circle scheme [13], using a simulator built in C++. The size of the wireless sensor network is set to a rectangular region with 400m x 400m. Sensor nodes are deployed uniformly at random in the network. The sink is deployed at the centre of the most northern point of the network. The radius of the transmission range of each sensor node is set to 50m. We randomly generate 10,000 data packets from the source nodes. We adapt the transmission power consumption model in the work [15].We test the networks when the number of nodes varies from 200 to 800. We set a rectangular hole and a T shape hole in the center of the network. The area of the rectangular hole is about 160m x 80m. The T shape hole consists of two cross rectangular holes which cover about 120m x 60m respectively. Each point in the following figures is the average of 100 runs. We compare average routing path length, energy consumption and energy variance between two schemes.

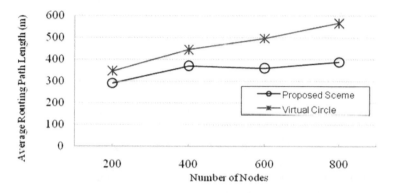

**Fig. 8.** The average routing path length with a T shape hole

Fig. 8 show the average routing path length versus the number of nodes. We form the convex hull which is the best approximation shape of the hole for the packet to bypass the hole efficiently. The data packet also can determine which direction has

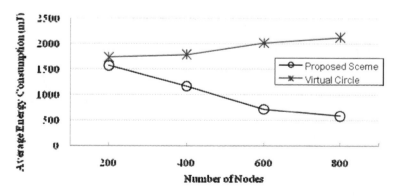

**Fig. 9.** The average energy consumption with a T shape hole

the shorter path to the sink. In the virtual circle scheme, data packets always use the tangent line of the virtual circle as the detour path to bypass the hole. It can be seen that the routing path by the virtual circle is longer than our proposed scheme.

The average energy consumption versus the number of nodes are shown in Fig. 9, we observe that the average energy consumption of bypassing path in our proposed scheme is less than the virtual circle scheme. It means that our scheme saves more energy of sensor nodes than the virtual circle scheme, thus the lifetime of the network can be further prolonged.

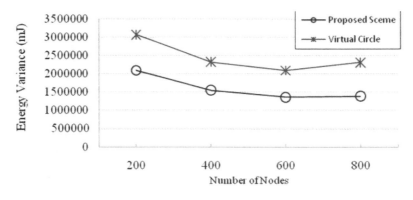

**Fig. 10.** The energy variance with a T shape hole

Fig. 10 show the energy variance at different densities. In the virtual circle scheme, the data packets always route the static path when it encounters the hole. The static detour path may lead to the traffic loading concentrated on the nodes which are on the detour path, and result in uneven energy consumption of the whole network. We construct energy-aware multiple paths for bypassing the hole so that more sensor nodes are involved in routing efforts to share the load on the boundary nodes. Therefore the energy variance of our scheme is less than the virtual circle, which means we have the better performance for balancing the load of the entire network.

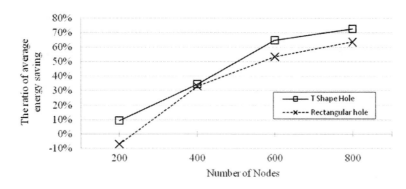

**Fig. 11.** The ratio of average energy-saving with a rectangular hole and a T shape hole

In Fig.11, we compared the proposed scheme and the virtual circle scheme to understand how much ratio of energy-saving to improve. In rectangular hole and low densities, the shape of rectangular hole is not clear. It's almost like a circle shape. Therefore, the virtual circle scheme is better than our proposed scheme by low densities in Fig. 11. When density of deployment become higher, the shape of rectangular hole is clearer. Our proposed scheme is better than virtual circle scheme.

In 800 nodes, our proposed scheme is more than the virtual circle scheme increases the efficiency of 63.56%. Fig. 11 also shows the ratio of average energy-saving with a T shape hole. In this scenario, our proposed scheme is better than virtual scheme at different densities. Specially in 800 nodes, Higher density of deployment increases the efficiency of 72.65% .In generally, when density of deployment is getting higher, then efficiency of energy-saving will getting better.

# 4 Conclusions

In this paper, we propose a scheme for bypassing holes in wireless sensor networks. Our proposed scheme has three features: First, we solve the local minimum phenomenon in the geographic greedy forwarding and prevent data packets from entering the stuck area of the hole. Second, we direct data packets to the direction with the shorter path to bypass the hole when they encounter the hole. Finally, we construct an energy-aware multi-path for balancing the load of the nodes located on the boundary of the hole. Our approach can ease the deterioration of the hole diffusion problem. Simulation results show that our proposed scheme can reduce and balance the energy consumption of the sensor nodes so that the lifetime of the whole wireless sensor network can be prolonged. In the future, we will extend our approach to adapt multiple holes which are close to each other.

The major contributions of paper are as follows:

- Provide a scheme to solve the Holes problem of WSN environment, and sensor can delivered packets bypassing holes to the sink.
- To solve the problem of edge nodes energy exhausted rapidly, we provide a scheme to balance the transmit power load of the edge nodes of hole. Our proposed scheme can delivered packets by different path of boundaries of holes, and extend life time of the edge nodes.
- Because we can balance power consumption and extend life time of edge nodes. So we can collect more sensor data of Holes boundaries.
- Compare with Virtual Circle scheme and our proposed scheme, we improve 40% average efficient of power consumption, and prolong life-time of edge nodes. In higher density of deployment, makes efficient improve obviously.

# References

1. Akyildiz, I.F., Su, W., Sankarasubramaniam, Y., Cayirci, E.: A survey on sensor networks. IEEE Communications Magazine 40, 102–114 (2002)
2. Zhao, F., Guibas, L.: Wireless Sensor Networks, an Information Processing Approach. Elsevier, Amsterdam (2004)

3. Karl, H., Willig, A.: Protocols and Architectures for Wireless Sensor Networks. Wiley, Chichester (2005)
4. Bulusu, N., Heidemann, J., Estrin, D.: GPS-less low cost outdoor localization for very small devices. IEEE Personal Communications Magazine 7(5), 28–34 (2000)
5. Carus, A., Urpi, A., Chessa, S., De, S.: GPS-free coordinate assignment and routing in wireless sensor networks. In: Proc. 24th Annu. Joint Conf. IEEE Comput. Commun. Soc (INFOCOM 2005), pp. 150–160 (2005)
6. Li, J., Jannotti, J., De Couto, D., Karger, D., Morris, R.: A scalable location service for geographic ad-hoc routing. In: Proceedings of Mobicom, pp. 243–254 (2000)
7. Rao, A., Papadimitriou, C., Shenker, S., Stoica, I.: Geographic routing without location information. In: Proc. of Mobicom, pp. 96–108 (2003)
8. Fonseca, R., Ratnasamy, S., Culler, D., Shenker, S., Stoica, I.: Beacon vector routing: Scalable point-to-point in wireless sensornets. In: Intel Research, IRB-TR 2004, vol. 12 (2004)
9. Ahmed, N., Kanhere, S.S., Jha, S.: The holes problem in wireless sensor networks: a survey. ACM SIGMOBILE Mobile Computing and Communications 9(2), 4–18 (2005)
10. Khan, I.F., Javed, M.Y.: A Survey on Routing Protocols and Challenge of Holes in Wireless Sensor Networks. Advanced Computer Theory and Engineering, 161–165 (2008)
11. Karp, B., Kung, H.T.: GPSR: Greedy Perimeter Stateless Routing for Wireless Networks. In: Proc. of the 6th Annual ACM/IEEE Int'l Conf. on Mobile Computing and Networking, pp. 243–254 (2000)
12. Fang, Q., Gao, J., Guibas, L.J.: Locating and Bypassing Routing Holes in Sensor Networks. In: Proc. of IEEE INFOCOM 2004, vol. 4, pp. 2458–2468 (March 2004)
13. Yu, F., Choi, Y., Park, S., Lee, E., Tian, Y., Kim, S.: An Edge Nodes Energy Efficient Hole Modeling in Wireless Sensor Networks. In: Proc. IEEE Global Telecommunications Conference (GLOBECOM), pp. 4724–4728 (2007)
14. Graham, R.L.: An Efficient Algorithm for Determining the Convex Hull of a Finite Planar Set. Information Processing Letters 1, 132–133 (1972)
15. The CMU Monarch Project, The CMU Monarch Project's Wireless and Mobility extensions to NS, http://www.isi.edu/nsnam/ns/ (accessed September 2007)

# On the Usability of Vehicle-to-Roadside Communications Using IEEE 802.11b/g Unplanned Wireless Networks

Martin Milata, Michal Krumnikl, and Pavel Moravec

VŠB - Technical University of Ostrava, FEECS
Department of Computer Science, 17. listopadu 15/2172,
70833 Ostrava-Poruba, Czech Republic
{Martin.Milata,Michal.Krumnikl,Pavel.Moravec}@vsb.cz

**Abstract.** Wireless networks are achieving a widespread penetration thanks to a variety of low cost solutions; cities are overcrowded with IEEE 802.11 access points. While connecting a notebook to a wireless network is simple, a vehicle connection to a roadside unit is still one of the most challenging topic.

In this paper, we introduce a novel solution for vehicle-to-roadside communications using the standard IEEE 802.11b/g network devices. Despite the existence of IEEE 802.11p standard, we exploit IEEE 802.11b/g, which is available and can be already used for the real world applications.

The proposed solution is composed of two layers. A wireless connection layer is responsible for network switching. The upper roaming layer is a proxy and tunneling module providing reliable connection for rapidly changing network environment. The system is designed to provide secure roaming capability on GSM, UMTS, HSDPA and WiFi networks.

Proposed solution was experimentally verified and used as a part of projects involving a vehicle-to-Internet applications.

**Keywords:** vehicle-to-roadside communications, IEEE 802.11 wireless networks, unplanned wireless networks, network roaming, proxy servers, tunneling services.

## 1 Introduction

Recent years have brought forth an impressive expansion of wireless networks all over the world. Cities are overcrowded with IEEE 802.11 access points, most of them are deployed by private users, sharing the internet connection among the home devices. In bigger agglomerations, some part of the access points are operated by cities and non-profit organizations. They are part of city networks, transferring data from camera systems, traffic infrastructure etc.

While connecting a notebook to a wireless network can be easily achieved, vehicle connection to a roadside unit is still one of the challenging topic. Vehicle moving on a road can create only a short term connection with particular access

V. Snasel, J. Platos, and E. El-Qawasmeh (Eds.): ICDIPC 2011, Part II, CCIS 189, pp. 167–177, 2011.

point. For most applications we need to create a fault-tolerant encapsulation preserving the communications endpoints, since the connection parameters will vary from access point to access point.

In this paper, we introduce a solution for vehicle-to-roadside communications using the standard IEEE 802.11b/g network devices. The reason for using these networks is that they are already available on current hardware platforms and can be used for tests in real world environments. IEEE 802.11p standard, which extends the IEEE 802.11 standard to add wireless access in vehicular environments (WAVE), was not available at the time of writing the paper.

The proposed solution is composed of a wireless connection layer, performing the access point discovery, measuring and validating the signal strength, maintaining a database of access points within the vehicle's range and associating with the proper access points. Above this layer is a proxy/tunneling module providing reliable connection for rapidly changing network environment. The system is designed to provide secure roaming capability on GSM, UMTS, HSDPA and WiFi networks. This system was implemented and thoroughly tested.

To further investigate the applicability of proposed solution, we conducted several experiments in which we measured the main characteristics: bandwidth, discovery scan duration and re-association delays. The experiments took place inside the university campus and two cities in Czech Republic and Germany. We created an on-board unit (OBU) based on Intel Atom architecture, equipped with wireless interface and HC25 Siemens HSDPA modem.

Our paper is organized as follows. In the following section, we present the related works. The Section 3 describes the network switching and roaming features. In the Section 4, we will describe the test environment, followed by the experimental results in the Section 5. Our paper ends with a discussion of achieved results.

## 2  Related Works

Many studies have investigated the possibility of using 802.11 based networks for vehicle-to-internet communications. Experiments have been made to measure the bandwidth, mean duration between successful associations and other connectivity parameters during typical driving through the city [1,2,3]. The patterns and causes of packet loss were analyzed in order to improve the design of routing and error-correction protocols [4]. Latest research and reports provides new strategies for handoffs [5,6] and data transfers [7], improving the overall network performance.

Several algorithms have been developed to address the problems related to 802.11 based networks. Protocols exploiting the basestation diversity to minimize disruptions and support interactive applications have been proposed [8].

Despite the fact that the 802.11 based networks are growing in popularity, we have to address the communication problem in areas where they are unavailable. The solution lies in the integration of diverse wireless networks such as WLANs and WWANs. Vertical handoff solution where users can move among various types of networks efficiently and seamlessly were proposed [9]. Efficient interface management during vertical handoff is necessary to reduce the power consumption [10].

Algorithms for vertical handoff must evaluate additional factors, such as monetary cost, offered services, network conditions, and user preferences. Several optimizations of handoff decision algorithms can be found in [11]. A comparison of the performance of vertical handoff decision algorithms was presented by [12].

## 3   Network Switching and Roaming

Data transmissions are crucial part for vehicle applications. In this chapter, we firstly present our approach for roaming between WiFi and GSM network. Then we present the solution of roaming between the access points within the WiFi network. At this point, we simplify the description of our implementation by considering only the integral parts. A more detailed description of the algorithm is out of the range of this paper.

### 3.1   Roaming between the WiFi and GSM Networks

During the communication with the servers and other roadside infrastructure, the OBU needs to be able to send and receive data utilizing the available network connections as much as possible, while reacting quickly to the fact that each of the connections may become unavailable. The TCP (transmission control protocol) is not very suitable for such task since it has to keep the same address through the whole connection. On the other hand, using the UDP (user datagram protocol) to send datagrams is possible, but we would have to solve the problems with flow control and missing/duplicate/out-of-order packets. We are looking for a solution that would utilize strong points of both, whilst negating their weak points. Our solution should have the following properties:

- React quickly to the connection changes, i.e., to solve the problem when a new connection becomes available and when the connection we were using gets lost.
- Allow transparent change of network connection when transferring user data without the need to resend the data we have already send or restart the connection.
- Operate in NATed (i.e., private) networks.

In addition, it would be advantageous if our solution was able to provide the transport for already existing applications (without the support of vehicle-to-infrastructure environment). In this way we can immediately use several existing applications for telemetry transport, navigation and image broadcasting. To satisfy this, we need to implement some additional functionality:

- Encrypt the transmitted data at least in public unencrypted WiFi networks, or WEP encrypted WiFi networks (which use weak cryptosystem).

- Be able to retransmit data when packets get lost and keep the connection active for short periods of time without the network connectivity (e.g., driving through a tunnel).
- Offer a way of preventing man-in-the middle attacks on the OBU server.
- Offer a way of connecting from the server to the OBU for remote monitoring/controlling purposes.

When we summarize the requests, our solution will have to use the UDP protocol (or IP datagrams, but there would be bigger problems with NATed networks) so that the packets might have a different IP address. The communication channel should be encrypted and a ready-made solution for it would be preferable. Ideally a virtual private network (VPN) with server could be built to achieve the desired goals. From the free VPN software, we have chosen OpenVPN 2.0.9 (currently 2.1.4) due to several reasons: the UDP protocol support; supports the tunnels to multiple clients encrypted with different encryption keys; the clients and the server are authorized to each other with the use of asymmetric cryptography; each client can have a different key, on the other hand, all clients may share the same key which is different from server; the client IP addresses and routing information can be set up from the server; user scripts can be run on server upon client connection/disconnection.

The VPN client is available for different operating systems. We can choose whether the clients should be able to communicate with each other, or only with the server. This way we can provide also the transport among the vehicles, in terms of vehicle-to-vehicle communication.

In our experiments, we have used the OpenVPN in the UDP client-server mode with same certificates for all OBUs (in the future, it would be advisable to generate a certificate for each OBU). The clients have used the automatic default gateway selection (GSM/WiFi) through a module described later in this section, which is primarily used for the WiFi network selection. As such, the outgoing IP address was changing in UDP datagrams. We have found out that changing the source address (and even port) is not supported in OpenVPN in the client-server mode, due to the security considerations, which does not fully correspond with the information mentioned in the OpenVPN manual. Due to this limitation, the OpenVPN connection had to be reset, which caused the connection to be unavailable for approximately 10-15 s.

As a result, we have developed an UDP proxy, which runs both, on the server and on the client. The client part of proxy listens for new connections on a specified UDP port and forwards all traffic to the server side. Figure 1 illustrates such example for two clients (OBUs). Each OpenVPN connection has a separate 32 bit client ID (CID) that is assigned at the beginning of communication by the server. The server forwards all traffic to the OpenVPN port, each OpenVPN connection has a separate source UDP port. As a result, all transfers are identified either by the client ID (between the client and server parts of the proxy), or by forwarding the UDP port on the server side of the UDP proxy. The responses are sent to the most recent valid combination of the client IP address and UDP port. We have also supplied a set of scripts for both OBU and server that

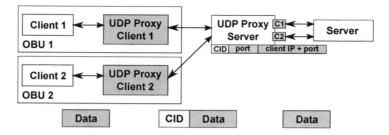

**Fig. 1.** OpenVPN Communication via UDP Proxy

automatically start the UDP proxy server and the client and register the OBUs dynamically after connection. In such way they are accessible from the server.

We have tested this setup in both the laboratory and live environment. The connection was stable. When transferring data, the time needed to change the connection was between approximately 140 ms (N=4751, $\sigma$=201 ms). When the connection was lost (no WiFi or GSM signal) and the connection timed out on the server, the time to restart the VPN was 18 seconds (N=131, $\sigma$=6.6 s).

This setup is considered to be secure, with low probability of possible connection hijacking due to the 32 bit ID. Since the data is encrypted, it is not possible to change it through basic man-in-the-middle attacks. On the other hand, the proxy currently forwards all traffic to the OpenVPN server, which handles all incoming data. As an additional feature, we could supply a pre-shared secret for both the client and server parts of the proxy, thus filtering possible attacks and invalid initial connections. Such approach is possible, but should the need arise, it could be solved by setting the firewall rules as well.

### 3.2 Wireless Communication with the Usage of the 802.11b/g Network

The Wireless LANs based on the standard 802.11 have their place in the vehicle-to-roadside communication at this time. Their usage brings many advantages like wide broadband throughput and simple and inexpensive implementation of the network. Some 802.11 standards allow the data transfers through the shared channel at speeds up to 54Mbps. The new devices that implement 802.11n standard are theoretically able to transfer data at speed up to 108Mbps. To achieve that, the parts of the wireless network must be compatible with each other. The speed of the WiFi networks is still higher in comparison with other mobile technologies like UMTS or other 3G mobile telecommunication technologies.

One of the main disadvantage of the WiFi networks is a poor capability of roaming between the access points. The direct support for roaming in the existing wireless adapters is usually bad and the problem must be solved in the software. New handoff procedure which reduces the MAC layer handoff latency was introduced [13]. Modified client-side with a transport protocol (CTP) has been suggested [14]. Stream Control Transmission Protocol [15] or Mobile IP [16] was proposed as well.

To meet all vehicle-to-infrastructure requirements, the following issues must be taken into an account:

- Scanning the available wireless networks within the range of the wireless client.
- Selecting one of them on the basis of signal to noise ratio or on the basis of counting the missing beacons, which represents the link quality.
- Re-association to the new access point in a specified network.
- Obtaining the IP address (through the dynamic or static configuration).
- Switching between the WiFi and modem connection (setting, maintenance, and manipulation with the default route for routing the IP traffic).

Searching for the available access points that provide the wireless network is the most time consuming operation. Moreover, it is not possible to transfer data through WiFi during the scan. Not only for this reason, it is not a good idea to perform the scans periodically. Scanning should be performed only when nothing else is in progress. As a result of scanning, a list of networks, within the range of the wireless client, is usually obtained.

The list of the wireless networks is not usually sorted in a required manner. We need to find the criteria for their comparison, such as the quality of the signal, the signal-to-noise ratio etc. Effective selection of the network can be based on the calculated line quality. Its value reflects best the actual state of the channel. Other parameters may also be used in the calculation of composite metrics.

Based on the previous selection of the network, the client attempts to associate with it (in fact with the access point that propagates it). It may happen that the association procedure is not successful. Also, its duration may vary. The possible delay depends on the security aspects, especially on the verification mechanism that is used for the client authentication. In case of an unsecured wireless network, the time that is needed to associate with the access point may be close to 40 ms. In the enterprise secured network, the association time can even exceed 10 seconds. In a high dynamic mobile network, the association time should be as short as possible. Therefore, an open network without any security seems to be the best solution in this case.

After a successful association with the access point, it is necessary to set/verify the IP stack setup. If the IP parameters have not been configured yet, it is necessary to do so. At this time, there are two possibilities: The first is the static configuration. It is quick, but not too scalable. The second approach is a dynamic IP parameters assignment via DHCP. This method is prone to errors, but also much more complex and slower.

In addition to the layer 2 (L2) roaming itself, it is needed to implement the switch between the WiFi connection and the connection via HSDPA modem or other secondary network. The permanent dial-up connection makes it possible to do so by simply changing the records in the routing table (e.g., the default gateway priority). If the WiFi network is available, data can be routed through the simple handling of the default route for the network traffic. In this way, switching between the network connections is implemented effectively and quickly.

### 3.3   Implementation

We have created a single thread application implementing the fast roaming and the dynamic selection of the network connection. The whole application was programmed in C language using the standard C library that is used to manage the wireless network interfaces. No special hardware was required. The choice of the wireless adapter, however, significantly influences the speed of WiFi communication.

After the application starts, it searches for the available wireless networks and selects a candidate for the association based on the quality of lines. In case that there is no wireless network within the range of the network adapter, the application continues in periodical scans until the client does reach the specified radio network. After the successful selection of the wireless network the OBU tries to associate with it. The list of other networks is retained for possible future re-association. Should the association fail, the next available network will be selected from the list and the association process will be retried.

After associating with the access point, the application inspects whether the IP address of the wireless interface and the default gateway are set. If so, it automatically starts periodically checking the availability of the default gateway. If not, both addresses are requested via DHCP. The connection must be verified by testing the availability of the default gateway. This is because the wireless network itself does not provide an active detection of faulty connections. If the communication with the default gateway fails, the application tries to associate to another access point if it is available. If such a point does not exist, it is necessary to carry out new searching for the available networks. The behavior of the program is shown in Figure 2.

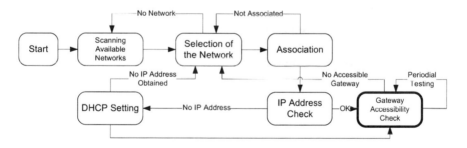

**Fig. 2.** State Diagram of the Algorithm Behavior

The time interval between the periodic tests of the availability of the default gateway was set to 200 ms. If the test fails three times, the connection is declared to be unavailable. Therefore, the detection of failure takes approximately 600 ms ($N=4121$, $\sigma=12$ ms). The default time in which the client must associate with a new access point is set to 100 ms. The new connection must be established during this time; another access point will be selected otherwise.

## 4   Tests

For a verification of our algorithm, we have created a testing environment. We used a homogeneous network with the infrastructure based on the Cisco devices. The testing environment contained 10 access points that were interconnected through a wired infrastructure to the Cisco Wireless LAN Controller (WLC). The whole testing area was continuously covered by the WiFi signal of the quality that was acceptable for roaming between the APs. The data traffic from the wireless network was directly forwarded to the main server.

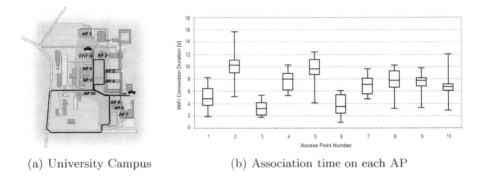

(a) University Campus            (b) Association time on each AP

**Fig. 3.** Testing Environment in the University Campus

Figure 3(a) shows the test environment in the university campus. The algorithm that has been developed was tested in a laboratory environment firstly. The main and final tests, however, were carried out in the real environment under the real-life outdoor conditions. The behavior in the real-life environment has been tested in the cars equipped with the prototype OBUs. Figure 3(b) shows the box plot of the connection time on each access point during the tests in the real-life environment inside the university campus. The overall results of testing are described below.

Two wireless adapters were tested. The first one was the high gain 802.11b adapter with the WLA-54L chipset manufactured by ZyDAS; the second was an adapter from Ralink with the RT2571WF chipset. The roaming software was created to run with both of them. The adapters were connected to the OBU via the Universal Serial Bus (USB); the default driver for Linux was used. Both devices provide the connectors for the external antennas. A 5dBi external antenna located on the roof of the vehicle was used during the tests. In this way, a better level of WiFi signal was obtained.

## 5   Results

We have tested several aspects of vertical and horizontal handovers. We have verified the ability of establishing the initial WiFi connection, which required obtaining the IP address via DHCP. In addition, the active re-association was tested too (if the original access point became unavailable) and the ability to roam between the modem and WiFi connection has been tested as well.

Figures 4(a) and 4(b) shows two typical situations of a vehicle leaving the area covered by WiFi connection and roaming to GSM network (a) and vehicle moving inside the area covered by WiFi networks, roaming between the access points (b). The plots depict the total bandwidth during the handovers. During the tests we have been continuously monitoring TCP sequence numbers to verify the proper operation of tunneled connections. Field tests have shown that no packets were lost during the handovers.

The initial establishing of the WiFi connection has been proven to be the most time consuming. Obtaining the IP address through the DHCP protocol was the critical part of the connection process. The time that was required to obtain the IP address was approximately 3.8 s (N=240, $\sigma$=1.2 s). The time needed for the re-association was 805 ms (N=2338, $\sigma$=405 ms). The longer time has been caused by the fact that we had to add an additional time for network scanning. When comparing the results to [14], we should take into an account that our solution is based solely on non-modified hardware and standard software. In this context, the results are very satisfactory.

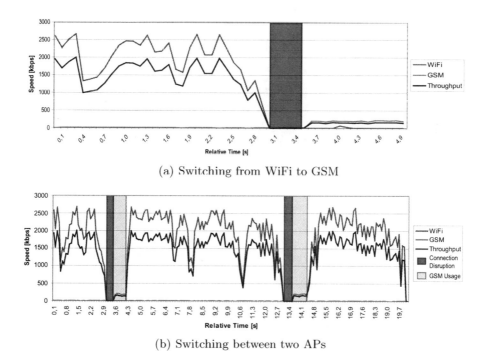

(a) Switching from WiFi to GSM

(b) Switching between two APs

**Fig. 4.** Dead Connection Detection and Recovery (a), (b)

The testing procedure of the availability of the default gateway (that was set for the WiFi network) takes approximately 39 ms ($N=5.10^5$, $\sigma=23$ ms) in the case of its availability. After that, the network traffic could be routed through its gateway. If the gateway had not been available, the next access point had to be selected if available. The best candidate for association is selected according to the algorithm described in Section 3.3.

The total amount of 3.5 GB were transferred, composed of 1.3 GB of images and 2.2 GB of video sequences from on-board cameras. This approach was also successfully used in our other projects.

## 6    Conclusions

This paper describes the wireless connection layers which provide the fault-tolerant encapsulation preserving the communications endpoints. This solution is designed to operate on GSM, UMTS, HSDPA and WiFi networks. In contrast to similar solutions [7,5,6], our system is designed to operate on the standard 802.11 based networks. It does not require any modification to hardware, drivers or access points. With one standard wireless adapter we are able to provide fault tolerant, fully transparent communication channel.

To summarize, there are two main contribution of this paper: the tunneling module, which encapsulates the OpenVPN packets, and the roaming algorithm capable of switching between the wireless and GSM/UMTS/HSDPA networks. This work was successfully used as a part of projects involving transfer of image and telemetry data from vehicle fleet to servers, where it was further processed.

## References

1. Bychkovsky, V., Hull, B., Miu, A., Balakrishnan, H., Madden, S.: A measurement study of vehicular internet access using in situ wi-fi networks. In: Proceedings of the 12th Annual International Conference on Mobile Computing and Networking, MobiCom 2006, pp. 50–61. ACM, New York (2006), http://doi.acm.org/10.1145/1161089.1161097
2. Mahajan, R., Zahorjan, J., Zill, B.: Understanding wifi-based connectivity from moving vehicles. In: Proceedings of the 7th ACM SIGCOMM Conference on Internet Measurement, IMC 2007, pp. 321–326. ACM, New York (2007), http://doi.acm.org/10.1145/1298306.1298351
3. Amdouni, I., Filali, F.: On the feasibility of vehicle-to-internet communications using unplanned wireless networks. In: IEEE 17th International Conference on Telecommunications (ICT), pp. 393–400 (2010)
4. Aguayo, D., Bicket, J., Biswas, S., Judd, G., Morris, R.: Link-level measurements from an 802.11b mesh network. SIGCOMM Comput. Commun. Rev. 34, 121–132 (2004), http://doi.acm.org/10.1145/1030194.1015482
5. Brik, V., Mishra, A., Banerjee, S.: Eliminating handoff latencies in 802.11 wlans using multiple radios: applications, experience, and evaluation. In: Proceedings of the 5th ACM SIGCOMM Conference on Internet Measurement, IMC 2005, pp. 27–27. USENIX Association, Berkeley (2005), http://portal.acm.org/citation.cfm?id=1251086.1251113

6. Ramani, I., Savage, S.: Syncscan: practical fast handoff for 802.11 infrastructure networks. In: Proceedings IEEE 24th Annual Joint Conference of the IEEE Computer and Communications Societies, INFOCOM 2005, vol. 1, pp. 675–684 (2005)
7. Deshpande, P., Kashyap, A., Sung, C., Das, S.R.: Predictive methods for improved vehicular wifi access. In: Proceedings of the 7th International Conference on Mobile Systems, Applications, and Services, MobiSys 2009, pp. 263–276. ACM, New York (2009), http://doi.acm.org/10.1145/1555816.1555843
8. Balasubramanian, A., Mahajan, R., Venkataramani, A., Levine, B.N., Zahorjan, J.: Interactive wifi connectivity for moving vehicles. SIGCOMM Comput. Commun. Rev. 38, 427–438 (2008), http://doi.acm.org/10.1145/1402946.1403006
9. Hasswa, A., Nasser, N., Hossanein, H.: Generic vertical handoff decision function for heterogeneous wireless. In: Second IFIP International Conference Wireless and Optical Communications Networks, WOCN 2005, pp. 239–243 (2005)
10. Chen, W.T., Shu, Y.Y.: Active application oriented vertical handoff in next-generation wireless networks. In: Wireless Communications and Networking Conference, vol. 3, pp. 1383–1388. IEEE, Los Alamitos (2005)
11. Zhu, F., McNair, J.: Multiservice vertical handoff decision algorithms. EURASIP J. Wirel. Commun. Netw. 52–52 (April 2006), http://dx.doi.org/10.1155/WCN/2006/25861
12. Stevens-Navarro, E., Wong, V.: Comparison between vertical handoff decision algorithms for heterogeneous wireless networks. In: IEEE 63rd Vehicular Technology Conference, VTC 2006-Spring, vol. 2, pp. 947–951 (2006)
13. Shin, S., Forte, A.G., Rawat, A.S., Schulzrinne, H.: Reducing mac layer handoff latency in ieee 802.11 wireless lans. In: Proceedings of the second international workshop on Mobility management & wireless access protocols, MobiWac 2004, pp. 19–26. ACM, New York (2004), http://doi.acm.org/10.1145/1023783.023788
14. Eriksson, J., Balakrishnan, H., Madden, S.: Cabernet: vehicular content delivery using wifi. In: Proceedings of the 14th ACM International Conference on Mobile Computing and Networking, MobiCom 2008, pp. 199–210. ACM, New York (2008), http://doi.acm.org/10.1145/1409944.1409968
15. Ma, L., Yu, F., Leung, V., Randhawa, T.: A new method to support umts/wlan vertical handover using sctp. IEEE Wireless Communications 11(4), 44–51 (2004)
16. Andersson, K., Ahlund, C., Gukhool, B., Cherkaoui, S.: Mobility management for highly mobile users and vehicular networks in heterogeneous environments. In: 33rd IEEE Conference on Local Computer Networks, LCN 2008, pp. 593–599 (2008)

# A Comparative Study of Aspect-Oriented and Object-Oriented Implementations: Pervasive System Use Case

Benamar Abdelkrim[1], Belkhatir Noureddine[2], and Bendimerad Fethi Tarik[1]

[1] University of Tlemcen, BP 119, 13000, Algeria
[2] LIG Laboratory, University of Grenoble, Rue de la chimie, 38041, France
{a_benamar, ft_bendimerad}@mail.-univ-tlemcen.dz,
Noureddine.Belkhatir@imag.fr

**Abstract.** Pervasive computing is becoming a reality. On the one hand, they will be deployed into a diversity of small devices and appliances, and on the other hand, they must be aware of highly changing execution contexts. Adaptation is the key crosscutting concern of pervasive computing applications. In this paper, we discuss our experience of implementing an adaptive display environment using Aspect-oriented programming. We compare the aspect-oriented implementation with independently developed object-oriented implementation of the environment. The comparison demonstrates that an aspect-oriented approach is indeed more effective in modularizing adaptation in a reusable, maintainable and evolvable fashion. It also reduces the complexity of the implementation with respect to the above three desirable attributes. At the same time, our experience challenges some of the existing conceptions about aspect granularity within an application and also highlights the need for development guidelines and idioms.

**Keywords:** pervasive computing, adaptation, crosscutting properties, aspect-oriented and object-oriented implementation.

## 1 Introduction

Pervasive systems will be naturally integrated as part of our environment. In pervasive systems we can found a great diversity of computing facilities (computers, PDAs, smartphones, sensors and so on) and high diversity of networks technologies (mobiles ad-hoc networks, sensors/ actuators, etc). This means that a pervasive application have to deal with static and dynamic changes, so its architecture should be well modularized to facilitate its adaptation to the evolution of devices and environment. Then is a big problem how to tackle these high diversity environments.

Regarding this issue we can resume the main problems of pervasive systems in:

- Hardware heterogeneity: the embedded systems and mobiles devices have different capacities and constraints, such as the amount of available memory, communications kinds or computations capacity.
- Dynamism of the application environments: the pervasive system has to be able to react in an automatic way to the environment changes, i.e. they must support a dynamic auto-adaptation and reconfiguration.

V. Snasel, J. Platos, and E. El-Qawasmeh (Eds.): ICDIPC 2011, Part II, CCIS 189, pp. 178–192, 2011.
© Springer-Verlag Berlin Heidelberg 2011

– Management of the application evolution: hardware and software technologies in pervasive system are evolving and changing continuously, then these systems have to be easily to maintain and evolve.

Implementing adaptation in a pervasive environment is a challenging task as the adaptation concern affects multiple elements (devices, services, etc.) in the environment. The problem is further compounded by the fact that the elements are often geographically distributed and in many instances there is no central node controlling the operation of the pervasive environment. Therefore, the distribution concern has to be catered for across the various elements forming the environment.

Aspect-Oriented Programming (AOP) [11] has been proposed as a means to effectively modularize such crosscutting properties, i.e., properties that have a broadly scoped effect on a system. Not only does AOP support improved separation of crosscutting concerns, it promises to provide such separation in a manner that promotes reusability, maintainability and evolvability. However, few application studies exist so far to demonstrate the effectiveness of AOP-based implementations with respect to these quality attributes. It is important to investigate the effectiveness of AOP to improve reusability, maintainability and evolvability in a pervasive environment as such environments are aimed at underpinning the next generation of applications. From an AOP perspective, such an investigation would inform the design of AOP languages, frameworks and methodologies to better serve such emerging adaptive, distributed environments. From a pervasive computing viewpoint, such a study would provide insight into a new modularization technique that promises to provide an effective means to develop, maintain, reuse and evolve crosscutting concerns, such as adaptation and distribution, which are at the heart of pervasive applications.

In this paper we present our experience with using AOP to modularize adaptation in a pervasive environment supporting users to navigate their way to destinations and events across the Tlemcen university campus. We have chosen to use AspectJ [2], an aspect language for Java to implement our application. Our choice is driven by the maturity of the language, its compiler and availability of effective tool support.

The remainder of this paper is organized as follows. Section 2 introduces an overview of pervasive computing and dynamic reconfiguration. Section 3 describes the pervasive navigation environment in more detail. Section 4 discusses the Aspect-Oriented (AO) and Object-Oriented (OO) implementations of the environment in question. We must emphasize that these implementations have been carried out completely independently of each other. This has ensured that no biases for or against a particular development technique have crept into the comparison study. Section 5 discusses some related work while section 6 concludes the paper and identifies directions for future work.

## 2  Backgrounds

### 2.1  Pervasive Computing

To stress the challenge that comes with pervasive systems, we consider a typical ubiquitous scenario where one student plays also the role of administrator of an online student forum regarding main events in the campus. She is interested in news concerning her campus and accesses the web via a smartphone which is both General Packet Radio Service (GPRS) and IEEE 802.11/Wireless Fidelity (WiFi) enabled. While exploiting GPRS, she prefers having an imageless version of the news, but when she switches to the campus WiFi connection, which is fast and costless, she wants to get full web pages, while keeping on working in a seamless way. In both cases, content layout must be adapted to fit the smartphone display she uses and news must be formatted according to her forum style sheets. Besides, as she often drives to the campus, she wants to learn about news also via phone calls: when this happens, she authenticates by spelling a secret password and a synthesized voice reads to her the only news that matches her customized preferences. The above and similar ubiquity scenarios stress many currently debated research fields, such as mobility support and context awareness, multimodality and multi-channel access to content, content aggregation and service composition, variously interconnected.

Mobility needs are usually grouped into three categories: user, terminal and service mobility [4]. User mobility allows users to have a uniform and consistent view of their specific working environment (user preferences and/or service requirements) independent of their current location. Terminal mobility allows devices to move and (re)connect to different networks while remaining reachable and keeping communication sessions consistent. Resource mobility allows resources to move across different locations and still remain available independent of their physical location and the position of their clients.

Context-awareness refers to the capability of leveraging conditions of the user herself and of her surrounding physical and computational environment to provide more relevant or brand new services. To provide a brief example, a printing service could leverage user position and identity to choose the nearest printer to which she is authorized to send a document to. Though location is certainly a common and preeminent piece of context, there is much more to context than position and identity. Services can also exploit time notion, knowledge of device capabilities and user preferences to process requests in the most suitable way, as well as discover and interact with other computing-capable objects or query the environment features for available pieces of information. For instance, web browser requests usually convey device software capabilities by declaring the client software version, the available support for graphical formats and so on. An exhaustive definition of context could be actually illusive, since it can in general refer to every known piece of information about user and environment. Thus, the most reasonable solution for obtaining ubiquitous context is probably to assemble context information from a combination of context related services [1], possibly deployed both at client side and at network infrastructure or server side.

Device heterogeneity calls for multimodal interfaces and content adaptation: users often need to access some unique content or application via different user interfaces and they also need to obtain information presented according to their preferences or device features. As an example, a user may request a service by using one of different input modes, such as keyboard, hand-writing or speech recognition, gestures and so on. In response, she could get different corresponding output formats, such as a text-only document, an image or a vocal reading. We refer to multi-channel access as the ability of providing a same service or information content through different media channels and platforms.

## 2.2 Adaptation of Distributed Software Systems

Adaptation proved, along the years, to be a major issue towards the development of dependable distributed software systems. In principle, we may distinguish three basic types of adaptation situations based on the targeted needs [15]. First, we have corrective adaptation that aims at dealing with faults causing failures in the constituents of a system. Second, we have perfective adaptation that targets changes performed towards meeting the evolving functional and non-functional requirements of the system. Finally, we have adaptive reconfiguration aiming at the proper functioning of devices and their hosted applications that are dynamically integrated in a computing system without prior knowledge of the functional constraints (e.g., available functionalities and resources) imposed by this system. The first two types of adaptation were typically targeted by stationary distributed systems. On the other hand, the need for the last type of adaptation arose with the latest emergence of pervasive computing systems. An in between evolution with respect to these two system domains were nomadic computing systems, which added wide area mobility to stationary distributed systems and were a precursor to pervasive computing systems. There, mobility makes the computing environment less predictable than in stationary systems, thus as well implying the need for adaptive reconfiguration, to a lesser extent, however, than in pervasive systems.

Adaptation in stationary distributed systems – architecturally modeled in terms of components and connectors [9] – concerns adding, removing or substituting components or connectors. Changes should take place at runtime to avoid compromising the availability of the overall system.

Being one step further, pervasive computing systems aim at making computational power available everywhere. Mobile and stationary devices will dynamically connect and coordinate to seamlessly help people in accomplishing their tasks. For this vision to become reality, systems must adapt themselves with respect to the constantly changing conditions of the pervasive environment: (i) the highly dynamic character of the computing and networking environment due to the intense use of the wireless medium and the mobility of the users; (ii) the resource constraints of mobile devices, e.g., in terms of CPU, memory and battery power; and (iii) the high heterogeneity of integrated technologies in terms of networks, devices and software infrastructures.

# 3 The Pervasive Display Environment

The pervasive environment that we are developing involves a set of display devices, such as PDA and smartphone to be deployed at strategic public locations across the Tlemcen university campus. Furthermore, the prototype is aimed at supporting a range of applications including, but not limited to, displaying news, disseminating information on upcoming events and assisting visitors (and also staff and students) in navigating their way around campus.

We have chosen to focus on the navigation application for the purpose of two prototype implementations, including OO and AO. Visitors often need to find their way to various destinations around campus. The destination can be a physical location such as a building, department or auditorium or it can be an event such as a conference being hosted in a particular building. Furthermore, each new display added to the environment must adapt its specific properties to those of the environment.

The UML diagram of the environment is shown in Fig. 1.

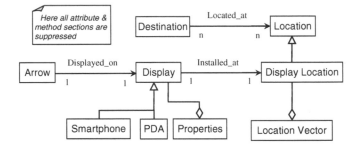

**Fig. 1.** UML diagram of pervasive environment

The objects represented by the classes in Fig. 1 are as follows:

- Destination: includes building, department, event, etc.
- Location: is based on coordinates on the campus map.
- Display Location: design whereas a display has been installed.
- Location Vector: determine which way a display is facing and whether it has been moved.
- Display: is an abstract class representing a display.
- PDA and smartphone: are specific types of display.
- Properties: design the specific characteristics of display.
- Arrow: denotes the data to be displayed to assist with navigation.

## 3.1 Aspect-Oriented Implementation

In bellow, we explore whether we can modularize adaptation in a reusable, maintainable and evolvable manner using AOP when developing our pervasive environment. For this purpose we need to address three specific facets of adaptation within our pervasive environment. The first two are application independent and relate to any application deployed in the environment while the third is specific to the navigation application:

- Display management: As the environment expands more displays will be incorporated into it. All new displays must have their specific properties adapted for use within the pervasive environment. Furthermore, although the UML diagram in Fig. 1 only shows two specific types of displays, smartphone and PDA, it is conceivable that other types of display devices may be added to the environment as they become available.

- Content management: The navigation content (an arrow in this case) is only one type of content to be displayed on the devices. There are other types of content that also need to be delivered to the devices. Furthermore, as new displays are added, the content already being displayed within the environment has to be made available on them as well.
- Display adaptation: As a new destination is added or an existing destination changed (e.g., change of venue for an event), the displays need to be adapted to guide the users to the correct destination. Furthermore, if a display is moved to a different location it should be adapted to display the content in a correct fashion based on its new location.

We have modularized each of these facets of the adaptation concern using AspectJ aspects.

### 3.1.1  Display Manager Aspect

The `DisplayManager` aspect encapsulates all functionality relating to incorporation of new displays or adaptation of their properties to the pervasive environment. The aspect maintains a collection of all displays incorporated into the environment and has a public method to traverse the collection. This is useful for other elements of the system, especially the `ContentManager` aspect, which needs to access all the displays in the system from time to time as new content becomes available.

The `DisplayIncorporation` pointcut captures all calls to the static method introduced into the `Display` class. An `after` advice then adds the incorporated display to the display collections in the aspect as well as adapts the properties of the newly incorporated display to the pervasive environment.

Note that although the `DisplayManager` aspect affects only a single class, nevertheless it encapsulates a coherent concern. This use of an aspect is, therefore, very much in line with good separation of concerns practice.

### 3.1.2  Content Manager Aspect

The `ContentManager` aspect declares all types of content and must implement the `Content` interface. Note that in this case there is only one type of content `Arrow`, shown but in practice the pervasive environment displays a variety of content. The `Content` interface provides an application independent point of reference for the pointcuts within the aspect, hence decoupling content management from the type of content being managed. Any classes that manipulate content in the pervasive applications deployed in the environment are required to implement the `ContentManipulator` interface, which specifies a number of methods for content addition, removal and update. Like the `Content` interface, the `ContentManipulator` interface also provides an application-independent point of reference to capture all content manipulation behavior within the applications in the environment, including the navigation application.

The contentAddition pointcut traps calls to addContent methods in all application classes manipulating content. An after advice for the pointcut then traverses all the displays registered with the DisplayManager and updates them with the new content. The contentDeletion and contentUpdate pointcuts and their associated advice perform similar functions upon content deletion and update.

The pushContentOnNewDisplay pointcut captures the instantiation of all sub-classes of the Display class. An after advice then pushes the available content onto the newly instantiated display.

### 3.1.3 Display Adaptation Aspect

While the DisplayManager and ContentManager aspects are application independent and handle adaptation facets that span across applications in the pervasive environment, the DisplayAdaptation aspect, is specific to the navigation application. The destinationChanged pointcut in this aspect captures the change in location of an existing destination or the creation of a new destination. An after advice for the pointcut invokes the adaptation rules for the displays to adapt the content accordingly.

The displayMoved pointcut identifies that a display has been moved by capturing the change in its location vector. An associated after advice then proceeds to adapt the content of the moved display and any neighboring displays accordingly.

### 3.1.4 Discussion

The three aspects used (e.g., DisplayManager, ContentManager and DisplayAdaptation) clearly demonstrate that AOP constructs provide an effective means to modularize both aplication independent and application specific facets of adaptation in a pervasive environment. The use of aspects makes it easier to not only adapt the environment to changes in content but also makes it possible to react to the reorganization of the displays in an effective fashion. Furthermore, any changes to the adaptation characteristics of the environment or the navigation application are localized within the aspects hence avoiding changes to multiple elements of the system that would have otherwise been required.

There are also interesting observations to be made about the design of the adaptation concern. Firstly, the use of Content and ContentManipulator as application independent points of reference makes it possible to decouple the ContentManager from application-specific content and content manipulation operations. Moreover, this technique allows to decouple the persistence concern from application-specific data. On the other hand, we can observe that the notion of one large aspect (or one in any other AOP technique) modularizing a crosscutting concern does not make sense in the case of the adaptation aspect either. The three aspects and the Content and ContentManipulator interfaces together modularize adaptation (as shown in Fig. 2). While different classes and aspects modularize specific facets of the adaptation concern, it is the framework binding them together that, in fact, aspectises this particular crosscutting concern.

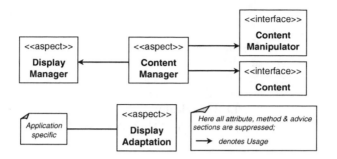

**Fig. 2.** Framework modularizing Adaptation

## 3.2   Object-Oriented Implementation

The OO implementation for pervasive display environment uses a regular client-server distribution model and XML based content transformation and adaptation. It consists of a central content server and an arbitrary number of autonomous displays units. The content server is responsible for storing content and pushing updates out to the displays. Content is generated by a number of applications running on the same physical host as the server. Since the displays are equipped with a GPS receiver and an electronic compass, the content server is ignorant of the position and capabilities of each display; each display receives the same generic (i.e., position-unspecific) content and decides on its own how best to adapt the content.

As shown in Fig. 3, the `DisplayManager` class in the content server keeps track of all connected displays by managing a collection of IP addresses and providing methods for traversing it. Displays contact the content server to explicitly connect and disconnect from it. The content server manages content for several applications, each of which is an independent process running on the same physical host as the server. The content is represented as an XML file or, more specifically, as an instance of the `GenericContent` class. Generic content consists of a collection of multimedia objects and adaptation rules. In the navigation application, the `ContentCreator` computes its content from two pieces of information: a campus map and the destination to which users should be guided.

The output is an image object depicting an arrow and rules of how to rotate this object depending on a display's position. Note, however, that the adaptation is performed by the display and not by the content server (or application).

The main class in the display unit is the `ContentTransformer`. It takes as input positional information delivered from the sensor subsystem and uses it to adapt a generic content file in a position-aware manner. This is done by evaluating the adaptation rules contained in the `GenericContent` file. The result is an instance of the `AdaptedContent` class. The implementation does not focus on modularizing the distribution behavior. However, it handles the three specific facets of adaptation introduced in Section 3.1 as follows:

– Display management: Flexible display management is achieved by strictly limiting the knowledge and server (application) needs to have about individual displays.

Thus new displays can be incorporated by simply registering with the server, regardless of their specific characteristics.

- Content management: Flexible content management is achieved by introducing a common content representation format for all applications.
- Content adaptation: By strictly separating the roles and responsibilities between the application (content creation), server (content management) and display (content adaptation) it is possible to dynamically adapt the content in a position-aware manner. New content can be accommodated by pushing it out to all connected displays.

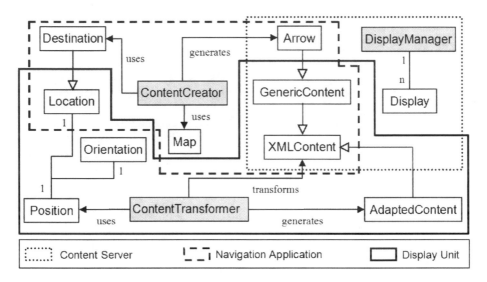

**Fig. 3.** The OO system architecture

### 3.3 Comparing the AO and OO Implementations

We now compare the two implementations of our pervasive display environment with regards to modularity, reusability, maintainability and evolvability as well as the complexity of each implementation in realizing the above properties.

### 3.3.1 Modularity

We can observe that the aspect-based framework for pervasive environment helps us to modularize the adaptation concern effectively. This framework use application-independent points of reference to decouple themselves from the details of individual applications within the environment. At the same time, the aspectisation of adaptation caters for application-specific facets of this particular concern. The use of aspects makes it easier for us to keep the application-specific element of adaptation separate from the application-independent elements. This is a direct consequence for choosing the right level of granularity for the aspects in our design and avoiding the temptation to modularize a concern using one large aspect module. The AO implementation initially has some development overhead due to the changes introduced to the past increment (in this case adaptation) when a new increment is introduced. However, the guidelines we have inferred from this experience can help minimize such revisions during incremental development.

The XML-based content management and transformation approach used in the OO implementation make it possible to modularize the various facets of adaptation.

### 3.3.2 Reusability

The AO implementation of adaptation lends itself to a high degree of domain-specific reuse, e.g., pervasive environments of a similar sort manipulating and sharing information. Furthermore, new applications and content can be seamlessly deployed within the environment as long as they implement the *ContentManipulator* and *Content* interfaces respectively.

In a similar fashion, adaptation behavior in OO implementation is also highly reusable in a domain-specific manner. The content generation and transformation approach is generic. However, the transformer might need to be extended to deal with other types of content from new applications. This is in contrast with the AO implementation where the adaptation aspect framework does not need to be modified as new applications are deployed.

### 3.3.3 Maintainability

The revisiting of the previous increment in our AO approach provides us with some insights into its maintainability. The changes to adaptation behavior are limited to the two application-independent aspects, ContentManager and DisplayManager. The application-specific adaptation behavior is isolated from these and hence remains unchanged.

In OO implementation, though the adaptation code is modularized through the XML-based content management and transformation approach, any changes to it are likely to carry a significant overhead as there is a significant code bloat arising from the inclusion of the XML processing code.

### 3.3.4 Evolvability

Similar to maintainability, evolvability is facilitated by the AO implementation by keeping the adaptation behavior modularized in the aspect-based framework. Any updates or changes to application-independent or application-specific adaptation behavior are localized to that particular aspect framework. However, application evolution is a more intensive and difficult task as crosscutting properties are not modularized effectively.

The adaptation behavior in OO implementation is also quite evolvable albeit it is complex to do so due to the significant amount of XML processing code.

### 3.3.5 Complexity

AO and OO implementations provide modularity mechanisms which are easy to understand and use. In case of the AO implementation, the aspect framework is fairly straightforward to use. Same is the case for adaptation mechanism in OO implementation.

In terms of reuse, maintainability and evolvability, the aspect framework in the AO implementation provide a simple yet effective set of abstractions that one can employ, change or evolve.

In case of OO implementation, the XML processing code poses significant complexity when one is trying to adapt it for reuse or maintenance or evolving it in line with changes to requirements for the pervasive environment.

Table 1 summarizes our comparative analysis of AO and OO implementations.

**Table 1.** Comparative overview of AO and OO implementations

| Implementation Property | AO implementation | OO implementation |
|---|---|---|
| Modularity | Yes | Yes |
| Reusability | Domain & Application Specific | Domain & Application Specific |
| Maintainability | Good | Average |
| Evolvability | Good | Poor |
| Complexity | Low | Medium |

## 4   Related Works

Efforts in supporting ubiquity greatly concentrate now on developing services and middleware platform logic. Current ubiquitous and mobile environments obey some standards and specifications, presenting solutions for specific ubiquity aspects. Research follows some main directions, mostly concerned with design guidelines and feature standardization, middleware proposals and the idea of providing toolkits to create 'ubiquity-enabled' applications. However, these research directions tend to evolve separately from each other, focusing on particular problems or goals, and they altogether lack a unified approach to ubiquity support.

Román and Campbell [18] propose a middleware-based application framework for the purpose. The framework is specifically geared towards device rich, mobile environments. Popovici *et al.* [16] discuss the use of the aspect-oriented middleware platform, PROSE, to support dynamic adaptation of mobile robots to different production needs. The Distributed Aspect and Object Platform (DAOP) [17] reifies the architecture specification, provided using its own architecture description language, which can then be adapted at runtime in line with the adaptation requirements of the application. The platform has been used to construct adaptive environments for collaborative work. All these platforms focus on supporting adaptation with distribution support provided by the middleware platform itself. Our application study of AOP is, therefore, complementary to these approaches as it focuses on evaluating a general purpose AOP technique, in this case AspectJ, to develop adaptive, distributed pervasive environments. In this sense, our AO implementation of the pervasive environment can be seen as a kind of middleware providing distribution and adaptation support for applications being deployed within the environment.

Brooks *et al.* [5] discuss aspect-oriented design of an adaptive sensor network supporting military applications. Their adaptive environment is developed using a custom-built, petri-net based solution while our comparative study is based on using general purpose AO and OO techniques. Furthermore, the nature of their sensor network, and applications supported by it, results in complex aspect interactions which requires a resolution model more elaborate than that of AspectJ. In case of our pervasive environment, the aspect interactions are fairly simple and can be easily handled and resolved by AspectJ.

Soares *et al.* [21] have focused on development of persistence and distribution aspects as separate increments to a system. Our experience provides further insight into the mechanics of such an incremental approach. The AO implementation of our pervasive environment shows that though such an incremental approach is viable, there has to be significant communication across the increments to avoid overhead of revisiting aspects developed in earlier increments.

Some researchers, such as Murphy *et al.* [14] and Baniassad *et al.* [3] have undertaken empirical studies of developers using AOP techniques. Our application experience is orthogonal to such studies as we analytically compare different implementations of the same environment. Ethnographic studies of such comparative implementations would provide interesting insights into the way developers approach the modularization of crosscutting concerns both with and without AOP techniques.

Adaptation is a recurring theme in pervasive computing. A major thrust of systems-level research in pervasive computing is aimed at building context-aware systems [20] that exhibit adaptive behavior, i.e., systems that can adapt at runtime to the user's tasks and needs, and to the availability of system resources such as network bandwidth. The main strategy to achieve this goal is to provide generic system and application platforms with built-in adaptation capabilities. Examples of such platforms are the context-aware and component-based middleware [13], context-awareness simulation toolkit [12], collaborative context-aware [7] and context information [8]. More recently, another approach is based on the use of explicit software architecture models to monitor a system and guide dynamic change to it. Di Ferdinando *et al.* [6] propose to exploit pervasive technologies to autonomously adapt the contents to the evolution of the interests among an audience, and validated the ideas behind it through experimental execution of a prototype platform on a test-bed of distributed machines. Gopalan and Znati [10] propose a resource and location aware framework based on geographical mapping, to support the large-scale deployment of heterogeneous applications in ubiquitous environments. Roy *et al.* [19] provide a context mediation framework based on efficient context-aware data fusion and semantic-based context delivery. In this framework, contexts are first fused by an active fusion technique based on dynamic bayesian networks and ontology, and further mediated using a composable ontological rule-based model with the involvement of users or application developers. Both of these architecture-based approaches aim at enabling a system to self-repair or self-heal in order to recover from an unwanted system state. However, all of the abovementioned approaches focus on short-term adaptation concerns; so far not much attention has been paid to post-deployment issues of pervasive systems such as maintainability, evolvability and long-term adaptation.

# 5  Conclusion

This paper has described our experience of using AOP, specifically AspectJ, to implement an adaptive pervasive display environment. We have also undertaken OO and AO implementations of the same environment developed completely independently of each other. The two implementations give us a strong basis to compare the modularization of the key crosscutting concern, which is adaptation in pervasive computing environments. We have derived our comparison criteria from some of the key motivations behind AOP, i.e., the development of more modular, reusable, evolvable and maintainable representations of crosscutting concerns. At the same time, we have compared the two implementations for complexity of realizing the above quality attributes with regards to adaptation. Our comparison clearly demonstrates that an AO approach facilitates modularization of adaptation and distribution code in our pervasive environment in a manner which is more reusable, evolvable and maintainable compared to the OO implementation. While the OO approach modularize some facets of adaptation concern – an XML based content generation and transformation approach to modularize adaptation – the AO approach does so in a manner that is less complex, avoids unwanted code bloat and is more intuitive to reuse, maintain and evolve.

Our experience also provides interesting insights into development of AO applications. We can observe from the realization of adaptation concerns that the notion of one single, large aspect module (in this case a single AspectJ aspect) encapsulating a crosscutting concern does not make sense. One needs to modularize different facets of a crosscutting concerns using abstractions most suited for the purpose, i.e., aspects, classes or interfaces, and the resulting framework that binds these facets together is, in fact, the aspect modularizing the crosscutting concern. There is another argument for such an approach clearly visible from our implementation. Had we not separated application-independent and application specific facets of adaptation using different AspectJ aspects, the changes to adaptation code required when the distribution aspect was introduced would have been much more difficult to achieve. Our fine-grained modularization facilitated analysis of our design decisions and easy and effective implementation of any refactorings to the existing, aspectised adaptation code. Our application experience also helps us better understand whether closely related aspects, such as adaptation, can indeed be developed in complete isolation in different system increments. We can see that, though this is an attractive proposition, in reality the semantics of such increments are too intertwined to allow strict isolation. In case of our pervasive environment, the design of our adaptation aspect framework would have been better informed had we taken into account the semantics of the distribution concern and the specific distribution architecture to be employed in the following increment.

We can also observe some interesting development styles for AO applications. We have used interfaces as application-independent points of reference to decouple the aspect frameworks (modularizing the crosscutting concerns) from the other concerns in the system. Similar, application-independent points of reference were employed to modularize persistence using AOP. We can see that such an approach works well for aspect-base decoupling especially to improve reusability, maintainability and evolvability of aspects implemented with approaches like AspectJ which, otherwise, require pointcuts to be specified with direct references to the signature of elements in the base. The use of application-independent points of reference offers a level of indirection to avoid such direct references hence significantly reducing, and in our case eliminating, the impact of changes to the signature of the base on the aspects and vice versa.

From a pervasive computing perspective, our application provides an opportunity to evaluate the suitability of an emerging development technique. One of the key points to note in our AO implementation is the focus on the more longer term qualities such as reusability, evolvability and maintainability. Most existing research in pervasive computing focuses on meeting the short-term adaptation needs of the applications and such long-term qualities are often ignored in system design. Our application brings forth AOP as a viable option to develop pervasive environments that are responsive to needs imposed by such long-term quality attributes without compromising the focus on short-term adaptability needs of applications.

Our future work will focus on studies of developers working on similar, independently developed, multiple implementations of systems, involving a variety of systems from a wide range of domains. This will not only provide further opportunities for comparative studies of the implementations but also make it possible for us to study how developers approach the modularization of a crosscutting concern and how challenging the task becomes if AOP tools and techniques are not being employed. Such studies are a key to understanding the full potential of AO techniques.

# References

1. Abowd, G.D., Mynatt, E.D.: Charting Past, Present, and Future Research in Ubiquitous Computing. ACM Transactions on Computer Human Interaction 7(1) (2000)
2. AspectJ Project, http://www.eclipse.org/aspectj/
3. Baniassad, E.L.A., Murphy, G.C., Schwanninger, M., Kircher, C.: Managing Crosscutting Concerns during Software Evolution Tasks: an Inquisitive Study. In: 1st ACM Aspect-Oriented Software Development, pp. 120–126. ACM Press, New York (2002)
4. Bellavista, P., Corradi, A., Montanari, R., Stefanelli, C.: Dynamic Binding in Mobile Applications. IEEE Internet Computing 7(2), 34–42 (2003)
5. Brooks, R.R., Zhu, M., Lamb, J., Iyengar, S.S.: Aspect-oriented Design of Sensor Networks. Parallel and Distributed Computing 64(7), 853–865 (2004)
6. Di Ferdinando, A., Rosi, A., Lent, R., Manzalini, A., Zambonelli, F.: MyAds: A System for Adaptive Pervasive Advertisements. Pervasive and Mobile Computing 5, 385–401 (2009)
7. Ejigu, D., Scuturici, M., Brunie, L.: CoCA: A Collaborative Context-aware Service Platform for Pervasive Computing. In: 4th IEEE International Conference on Information Technology, pp. 297–302. IEEE Press, Las Vegas (2007)
8. Euzenat, J., Pierson, J., Ramparany, F.: A Dynamic Context Management for Pervasive Applications. Knowledge Engineering 23(1), 21–49 (2008)
9. Garlan, D., Shaw, M.: An Introduction to Software Architecture. Technical report, CMU-CS-94-166. Carnegie Mellon University (1994)
10. Gopalan, A., Znati, T.: SARA: a Service Architecture for Resource aware Ubiquitous Environments. Pervasive and Mobile Computing 6, 1–20 (2010)

11. Kiczales, G., Lamping, J., Mendhekar, A., Maeda, C., Videira, C., Loingtier, J.M.: Aspect-oriented Programming. In: Aksit, M., Auletta, V. (eds.) ECOOP 1997. LNCS, vol. 1241, pp. 220–242. Springer, Heidelberg (1997)
12. Kim, I.S., Lee, Y.L., Lee, H.H.: CAST Middleware: Security Middleware of Context-awareness Simulation Toolkit for Ubiquitous Computing Research Environment. In: Huang, D.S. (eds.), ICIC 2006. LNCS, vol. 344, pp. 506–513. Springer, Heidelberg (2006)
13. Kuo, Z., Yanni, W., Zhenkun, Z., Xiaoge, W., Yu, C.: A component-based reflective middleware approach to context-aware adaptive systems. In: Lowe, D.G., Gaedke, M. (eds.) ICWE 2005. LNCS, vol. 3579, pp. 429–434. Springer, Heidelberg (2005)
14. Murphy, G.C., Walker, R.J., Baniassad, E.L.A.: Evaluating Emerging Software Development Technologies. Lessons Learned from Evaluating Aspect-oriented Programming. IEEE Transactions on Software Engineering 25(4), 438–455 (1999)
15. Oreizy, P., Medvidovic, N., Taylor, R.N.: Architecture-based Runtime Software Evolution. In: ACM International Conference on Software Engineering, pp. 177–186. ACM Press, Kyoto (1998)
16. Popovici, A., Frei, A., Alonso, G.: A Proactive Middleware Platform for Mobile Computing. In: Endler, M., Schmidt, D.C. (eds.) Middleware 2003. LNCS, vol. 2672, pp. 455–473. Springer, Heidelberg (2003)
17. Pinto, M., Fuentes, L., Troya, J.M.: DAOP-ADL: An Architecture Description Language for Dynamic Component and Aspect-Based Development. In: Pfenning, F., Macko, M. (eds.) GPCE 2003. LNCS, vol. 2830, pp. 118–137. Springer, Heidelberg (2003)
18. Roman, M., Hess, C.K., Cerqueira, R., Ranganathan, A., Campbell, R.H., Nahrstedt, K.: GAIA: A Middleware Infrastructure to Enable Active Spaces. IEEE Pervasive Computing 1(4), 74–83 (2002)
19. Roy, N., Gu, T., Das, S.K.: Supporting Pervasive Computing Applications with Active Context Fusion and Semantic Context Delivery. Pervasive and Mobile Computing 6, 21–42 (2010)
20. Smailagic, A., Siewiorek, D.P., Anhalt, J.: Towards Context aware Computing: Experiences and Lessons Learned. IEEE Journal on Intelligent Systems 16(3), 38–46 (2001)
21. Soares, S., Laureano, E., Borba, P.: Implementing Distribution and Persistence Aspects with AspectJ. In: ACM Conference on Object-Oriented Programming Systems, Languages, and Applications, pp. 174–190. ACM Press, New York (2002)

# Review of Power Quality Disturbances Classification Using Variable Size Detector (V-Detector)

Kamarulazhar Daud, Noraliza Hamzah, Saiful Zaimy Yahaya,
Mohd Affandi Shafie, and Harapajan Singh Nagindar Singh

Faculty of Electrical Engineering,
Universiti Teknologi MARA, Malaysia
40450,Shah Alam, Malaysia
kamarul@ppinang.uitm.edu.my, noralizah@salam.uitm.edu.my,
saiful053@ppinang.uitm.edu.my,
mohdaffandi370@ppinang.uitm.edu.my, harapajan@gmail.com

**Abstract.** The variable size detector (V-detector) is a real-valued negative selection algorithm with variable-sized detector. The V-detector algorithm is a kind of negative selection algorithm (NSA) inspired by biological immune system (BIS).This paper overviewed the theory of basis V-detector algorithm and typical improved V-detector algorithm summarized their applications in the area of power quality disturbances classification. The comparison between the traditional and V-detector method shows the method has good applicability and effectiveness for power quality disturbances classification. The analysis directions of a new dimension of studying about the power quality (PQ) disturbance classification are also forwarded. All of these showed that the V-detector based methods have great potential for the future development in the power quality or others field of studies.

**Keywords:** Power quality (PQ) disturbance; V-detector algorithm; artificial immune systems (AIS), negative selection algorithm (NSA).

## 1 Introduction

The electrical power quality (PQ) has become an increasing concern in recent years, due to the increasing use of sensitive power electronic devices and nonlinear loads in the industry. The study report in [1] showed that, just in US economy is losing between \$104 billion and \$164 billion a year to outages and another \$15 billion to \$24 billion to PQ phenomena. Poor PQ may cause many problems for affected loads, such as malfunction, instabilities, short lifetime, and so on. Poor quality is attributed due to the various power line disturbances like voltage sag, swell, impulse, and oscillatory transients, multiple notches, momentary interruptions, harmonics, and voltage flicker, etc. In order to improve power quality, we have to detect and classify the type of disturbances, locate the sources of disturbances, compute the parameters and also find the effective methods to mitigate them.

A variety of methodologies of classification of PQ disturbances have been proposed in the past decade [2]. Normally, feature extraction techniques are used to

V. Snasel, J. Platos, and E. El-Qawasmeh (Eds.): ICDIPC 2011, Part II, CCIS 189, pp. 193–198, 2011.
© Springer-Verlag Berlin Heidelberg 2011

extract the features and characterization of PQ disturbances. Feature extraction can be done from transformed domain, such as Fourier transform, wavelet transform and s-transform. After these features are extracted, artificial intelligence (AI) tools can be applied to these features to obtain the classification [3,4,5,6].

AI techniques have been applied successfully in power engineering fields. Artificial immune systems (AIS), inspired by immunology, are new approaches that imitate the immune system's function of learning and memory [7,8,9]. The negative selection algorithm (NSA) is one of the most successful methods in AIS, and its typical applications include change detection, fault detection, virus detection and network intrusion detection [10].The NSA proposed firstly by Forrest et al [11] used binary representation for self and non-self space. This algorithm is inspired by the mechanism of T-cell maturation and self tolerance in the immune system, and believed to have distinct process from alternative methods and be able to provide unique results with better quality [12]. V-detector algorithm takes advantage of negative selection to create a set of detectors covering the whole non self region of the feature space [13].

## 2   V-Detector and Its Application in Power Quality Disturbance Classification

### 2.1   V-Detector Algorithms

V-detector algorithm was formally proposed by Z. Ji and D. Dasgupta in [13]. It operates on (normalized) vectors of real-values attributes being points in the d-dimensional unit hypercube, $U = [0,1]^d$. Each self samples, $s_i \in S$, is represented as a hypersphere with center at $c_s \in U$ and constant radius $r_s$ , i.e. $s_i = (c_i, r_s)$, i = 1,.....,$l$, where $l$ is the number of self samples. Every point $u \in U$ belonging to any hypersphere is considered as a self element. Also detectors $d_j$ are represented as hyperspheres: $d_j = (c_j, r_j)$, j = 1,...,$m$, where $m$ is a number of detectors. In contrast to self elements, the radius $r_j$ is not fixed but is computed as the Euclidean distance from a randomly chosen center $c_j$ to the nearest self element (this distance must be greater than $r_s$, otherwise detector is nor created). Formally we define $r_j$ as

$$r_j = \min_{1 \le i \le l} dist(cj, ci) - rs \tag{1}$$

There are several versions of the V-detector. The algorithm of V-detector from [14] is the latest and most mature version. It took the most of advantages from the other versions. The basic and core idea from [11] based on principles of self/nonself discrimination in the immune system. Since the V-detector is a kind of NSA and used the idea of variable size, the generated detectors can cover more effective non-self space compared with other NSAs for real value representation [13]. But, as one of the new NSA variations, the V-detector has some unique features to be more reliable and efficient in some application field than previous NSAs [15]. The V-detector uses real-valued representation which is different from binary representation of traditional negative selection. In some cases, real-valued representation is more reasonable and efficient [16]. It can cover non-self space more effectively than the method that uses constant-sized detectors can. Then, the boundary aware method proposed by the V-detector can identify boundary between self and no-self regions more effectively than traditional point-wise method can [17]. Furthermore, the V-detector does not compute the number of the needed detectors, but detectors are generated by using statistical estimate and hypothesis testing to meet the coverage requirement [17]. Experimental results in [13] demonstrated that V-detector scheme is more effective in using smaller number of detectors because of their variable sizes. It provides a more concise representation of the anomaly detectors derived from the normal data. The detector set generated by the V-detector is more reliable because the estimated coverage instead of the arbitrary number of detectors is obtained by the algorithm at the end of the run.

## 2.2  Power Quality Disturbance Classification with V-Detector

Power quality analysis comprises various kinds of electrical disturbances such as voltage sags, voltage swells, harmonic distortions, flickers, imbalances, oscillatory transients, and momentary interruptions, etc. In order to classify the electrical disturbances, D. Li et al in [18] used the V-detector operated on a unitary hypercube space after the features extracted by the S-transform. The non-self detectors are first generated to cover the non-self region, and then new class-detectors to identify each class are proliferated based on the previous existing detectors. Every new PQ disturbances datum is classified by checking if it is covered by one or more detectors.

The current fault diagnosis methods can be divided into three categories. The first category is based on process model, which is mature in theory, but it needs reliable process mathematical model. However, the actual process is usually complicated and accurate model is hardly to be found. When the model is not accurate, the method usually cannot have good robustness. The second category is the method based on signal processing, which is mathematical model without process. It filters the input/output data of the system directly and carries out fault diagnosis and forecasting through the analysis of the characteristics of the data after filtering. The method does not need process model, but needs to make certain hypothesis of the fault signals, besides the computing work is heavy. There are some difficulties to realize real-time on-line fault detection and forecasting. The last category is based on artificial intelligence technology. The method does not need accurate mathematical model and it can have the function of self-learning, at the same time, it can integrate the expert knowledge into fault diagnosis effectively, which is not only the research focus of fault diagnosis and accident prediction methods in the current industrial process, but also the development trend of future fault diagnosis technology. The fault sample is hard to be obtained. For most equipment, data reflecting the operating status of the equipment is normal are easy to get, but the failure data are hard to obtain. The problem to be solved is how to carry out equipment fault detection and diagnosis research under the circumstance of knowing mass data of normal running status of the equipment. X.Yue et al in [19] presented the artificial immune system that promising potential in fault detection and diagnosis because of the nature similarity of both biological immune system and fault detection system.

Real-valued negative selection compared with the binary representation, real-valued representation of the most important feature is that self/non-self space corresponds to a subset of $R^n$, normalized to the super-rectangular space $[0,1]^n$, where $n$ is defined as the space dimension. The distance between two points uses Euclidean distance calculation, where every element is represented as n-dimensional point or simply as a vector represented by a list of $n$ real numbers.

The Euclidean distance $d$ is the (standard) distance between any two vectors x={x1,x2,...,xn}, y={y1,y2,....,yn}, defined as:

$$\text{Euclidean } (x,y) = \left(\sum_{i=1}^{n} |x - y|^2\right)^{1/2} \tag{2}$$

The volume of a $n$-dimensional hypersphere with radius $r$ can be calculated as follows:

$$V(n,r) = r^n \bullet \frac{\pi^{n/2}}{\Gamma(\frac{n}{2}+1)} \tag{3}$$

Real-valued representation's search space is usually continuous, and it is suitable for network feature which cannot use binary representation effectively. In the real-valued representation, it generally represents detector in the form of hypersphere or hypercube. The matching rule is expressed by the membership function of the detector, which is a function of the detector-antigen Euclidean distance and the radius of the detector.

Input: S=set of points $\in[0,1]^n$ gathered from normal behavior of a system.

Output: D=set of hyperspheres, which recognizing a proportion $c_0$ of the total space $[0,1]^n$, expert the normal points.

Detector generation: While covered proportion $c_0$ is not reached, generate hyperspheres.

Classification: If unseen point lies within a hypersphere, it does not belong to the normal behavior of the system and is classified as an anomaly.

A. Chmielewski and S. T Wierzchon in [20] proposed the selected structures to speed up the performance of real valued negative selection V-detector algorithm that was comparable to Support Vector Machine, SVM (the achieved learning time was much better and detection rate, false alarm rate, classification time was comparable with SVM). Performed experiments proposed in [20] confirm that tree-based structures can increase the efficiency of V-detector algorithm, especially for huge-sized multidimensional dataset.

The proposed AIS in [21] based fault diagnosis technique provides a relatively simple and fast method for detecting plant faults in normal processes of machines. This system is designed to detect intermittent fault as well as normal permanent faults and thus contributes towards reducing plant-production time. But, [21] also have limitations for certain faults require a larger number of detectors to guarantee an acceptable level of detection.

The disadvantage of method proposed in [14-15] is that the generated excessive invalid detectors cannot cover some holes at the boundary between self and non-self regions.

## 3  Improved V-Detector Methods and Theirs Application in Power Quality Disturbance Classification

An improved V-detector algorithm in [22] divides the collection of self samples into boundary selves and non-boundary selves, where the identifying and recording mechanism of boundary self are introduced during the generation of detectors. The results showed that the new algorithm covers the holes existed in boundary between self region and non-self region more effectively than traditional negative selection. The advantages of the improved algorithm is when the undetectable holes existing in original algorithm are reduced by recording and judging boundary self. So that, the detectors generated by the improved algorithm obtain more diversity and also the number of detectors will be increased slowly with the increasing of target coverage.

## 4  Conclusion

From the overview of Power Quality (PQ) disturbances classification with the basis of V-detector algorithm (from the Negative Selection Algorithm) and its improved modified methods, we believe that V-detector provides good performance and satisfied with power quality disturbance classification. All these showed that V-detector algorithm based methods has great potential for the future development in term of power quality disturbances classification and also in others area of study. But, certain algorithm that proposed in [14-15], generated excessive invalid detectors and cannot cover some holes at the boundary between self and non-self regions. As the novel and improved algorithms based on V-detector had been designed, we can also apply and modify the method in the area of Power Quality disturbances classification and get new frameworks with great values for the future.

## References

1. CEIDS (Consortium for Electric Infrastructure to Support a Digital Society), The Cost of Power Disturbances to Industrial and Digital Economy Companies Executive Summary (2001)
2. Ibrahim, W.R.A., Morcos, M.M.: Artificial intelligence and advanced mathematical tools for power quality applications: a survey. IEEE Trans. Power Del. 17(2), 668–673 (2002)
3. Salem, M.E., Mohamed, A., Abdul Samad, S.: Rule based system for power quality disturbance classification incorporating S-tranfrom features. Journal of Expert Systems with Applications 37, 3229–3235 (2009)
4. Uyar, M., Yildirim, S., Gencoglu, M.T.: An expert system based on S-transform and neural network for automatic classification of power quality disturbances. Journal of Expert System with Application 36, 5962–5975 (2009)
5. Talaat, N., Ilic, M.: ANNs Based on Subtractive Cluster Feature for Classifying Power Quality. In: 40th North American Power Symposium, pp. 1–7 (2008)
6. Gargoom, A.M., Ertugrul, N., Soong, W.L.: Investigation of Effective Automatic Recognition Systems of Power Quality Events. IEEE Trans. on Power Delivery 22(4) (2007)

7. Hofmeyr, S., F. S.: Architecture for an artificial immune system. Evolutionary Computation 8, 443–473 (2000)
8. De Castro, L.N., Timmis, J.: Artificial immune systems as a novel soft computing paradigm. Soft Computing 7, 526–544 (2003)
9. Hart, E., Timmis, J.: Application areas of AIS:The past, the present and the future. Applied Soft Computing Journal 8, 191–201 (2008)
10. Li, T.: Computer Immunology. Publishing House of Electronics Industry, Beijing (2008)
11. Forrest, S., Perelson, A.S., Allen, L., Cherukuri, R.: Self-Nonself Discrimination in a Computer. In: Proceedings of IEEE Computer Society Symposium on Research in Security and Privacy, pp. 202–212. IEEE, Computer Soc Press, Los Alamitos (1994)
12. Garrett, S.M.: How do we evaluate artificial immune system? Evolutionary Computation 13(2), 145–177 (2005)
13. Ji, Z., Dasgupta, D.: Real-valued negative selection algorithm with variable-sized detectors. In: Deb, K., et al. (eds.) GECCO 2004. LNCS, vol. 3102, pp. 287–298. Springer, Heidelberg (2004)
14. Ji, Z., Dasgupta, D.: Estimating the detector coverage in a negative selection algorithm. Presented at Genetic and Evolutionary Computation Conference (GECCO 2005), Washington (2005)
15. Ji, Z., Dasgupta, D.: Applicability issues of the real-valued negative selection algorithms. Presented at Genetic and Evolutionary Computation Conference (GECCO 2006), Washington (2006)
16. González, F., Dasgupta, D., Niño, L.F.: A randomized real-valued negative selection algorithm. In: Timmis, J., Bentley, P.J., Hart, E. (eds.) ICARIS 2003. LNCS, vol. 2787, pp. 261–272. Springer, Heidelberg (2003)
17. Li, G., Li, T., Zeng, J., Li, H.: Significant Level in V-detector Generation Algorithm. In: 2009 Asia Pacific Conference on Information Processing, pp. 513–516. IEEE Computer Society Press, Los Alamitos (2009)
18. Li, D., Das, S., Panigrahi, B.K., Pahwa, A.: A new method for power quality disturbance classification based on the proliferating V-detectors algorithm. In: 40th North American Power Symposium (NAPSOP), pp. 1–6 (2008)
19. Yue, X., Wen, D., Ma, H., Zhang, J.: Fault Detection Based on Real-value Negative Selection Algorithm of Artificial immune System. In: International Conference on Intelligent Computing and Cognitive Informatics, pp. 243–246. IEEE Computer Society Press, Los Alamitos (2010)
20. Chmielewski, A.,, S.: V-detector algorithm with tree-based structures. In: Proc. of the International Multiconference on Computer Science and Information Technology, pp. 11–16 (2006)
21. Govender, P., Mensah, D.A.K.: Fault Diagnosis Based on the Artificial Immune Algorithm and Negative Selection. In: Proc. of IEEE 17th International Conference on Industrial Engineering and Engineering Management, pp. 418–423 (2010)
22. Li, G., Li, T., Zeng, J., Li, H.: An improved V-detector algorithm of identifying boundary self. In: Proc. of 8th International Conference on Machine Learning and Cybernatics, pp. 3209–3214 (2009)

# Classifying Sleep Disturbance Using Sleep Stage 2 and Wavelet-Based Features

Sang-Hong Lee and Joon S. Lim[*]

IT College, Kyungwon University, Korea
{shleedosa,jslim}@kyungwon.ac.kr

**Abstract.** This paper classified sleep disturbance using non rapid eye movement-sleep (REM) stage 2 and a neural network with weighted fuzzy membership functions (NEWFM). In this paper, wavelet-based features using EEG signals in non-REM stage 2 were used to classify subjects who have mild difficulty falling asleep and healthy subjects. At the first phase, detail coefficients and approximation coefficients were extracted using the wavelet transform (WT) with Fpz-Cz/Pz-Oz EEG at non-REM stage 2. At the second phase, using statistical methods, including frequency distributions and the amounts of variability in frequency distributions extracted in the first stage, 40 features were extracted each from Fpz-Cz/Pz-Oz EEG. In the final phase, 80 features extracted at the second phase were used as inputs of NEWFM. In performance results, the accuracy, specificity, and sensitivity were 91.70%, 91.73%, and 91.67%, respectively.

**Keywords:** NEWFM, Wavelet Transforms, REM, non-REM, Sleep Disturbance.

## 1 Introduction

Though sleep can be defined from different perspectives, it is usually defined as the state where a sleeper is inactive with the suspension of the ability to respond and recognize the outer environment. Sleep arises in the brain activity; however it is closely related to physiological changes in the other parts of a body. Among disorders that can occur during sleep, sleep apnea syndrome and sleep disturbance are the major sleep disorders. The sleep apnea syndrome refers to the case where a sleeper is without breath for more than five times within the span of one hour or more than 30 times within the span of seven hours. In this case, sleep is disturbed, both qualitatively and quantitatively. Human sleep is categorized into periods of rapid eye movement-sleep (REM) and non-REM (NREM). The stages of sleep that are widely used in sleep medicine are divided into sleep stage 1, sleep stage 2, sleep stage 3 and sleep stage 4 according to the 1968 standards centered on electroencephalogram (EEG),

---

[*] Corresponding author.

V. Snasel, J. Platos, and E. El-Qawasmeh (Eds.): ICDIPC 2011, Part II, CCIS 189, pp. 199–206, 2011.

electrooculogram (EOG), and electromyogram (EMG). A research that is concerned with sleep is often connected with the sleep apnea syndrome [8][9][10]. Moreover, a research that is about the stages of sleep is usually conducted on the same research subjects' hours of sleep [11][12].

In this paper, wavelet-based features using EEG signals in sleep stage 2 were used to classify subjects who have mild difficulty falling asleep and healthy subjects along with the use of Fpz-Cz/Pz-Oz EEG [3]. At the first phase, detail coefficients and approximation coefficients were extracted using the wavelet transform (WT) with Fpz-Cz/Pz-Oz EEG at sleep stage 2. At the second phase, using statistical methods, including frequency distributions and the amounts of variability in frequency distributions extracted in the first stage, 40 features were extracted each from Fpz-Cz/Pz-Oz EEG. In the final phase, 80 features extracted at the second phase were used as inputs of NEWFM. In performance results, the accuracy, specificity, and sensitivity were 91.70%, 91.73%, and 91.67%, respectively. Furthermore, this paper has made the interpretation of the features possible by suggesting 80 fuzzy membership functions of the 80 features [5][6].

## 2   Overview of Sleep Disturbance Classification Model

Fig. 1 shows the sleep disturbance classification model which is proposed in this paper. The sleep disturbance classification model consists of three steps. In the first step, EEG signals are filtered by remove some noise using wavelet transforms. In the second step, statistical methods, including frequency distributions and the amounts of variability in frequency distributions are used for extracting initial input with the preprocessed sleep EEG signals. In the final step, we measured the performance of the features using NEWFM.

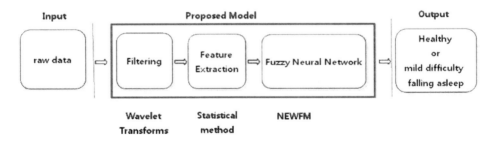

**Fig. 1.** Diagram of Sleep Disturbance Classification Model

### 2.1   Data Description

The recordings were obtained from Caucasian males and females (21 - 35 years old) without any medication; they contain horizontal EOG, Fpz-Cz/Pz-Oz EEG, each sampled at 100 Hz. The sc* recordings also contain the submental-EMG envelope, oro-nasal airflow, rectal body temperature and an event marker, all sampled at 1 Hz. The st* recordings contain submental EMG sampled at 100 Hz and an event marker sampled at 1 Hz. Hypnograms are manually scored according to Rechtschaffen & Kales based on Fpz-Cz/Pz-Oz EEG instead of C4-A1/C3-A2 EEG in Fig. 2.

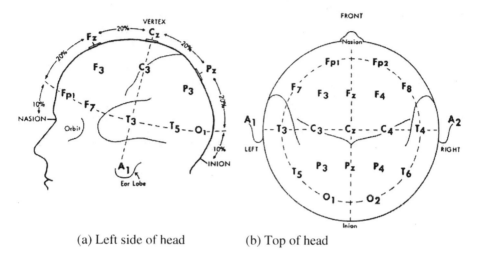

(a) Left side of head          (b) Top of head

**Fig. 2.** International (10-20) electrode placement

The sleep stages W, 1, 2, 3, 4, R, M and 'unscored' are coded in the file as binaries 0, 1, 2, 3, 4, 5, 6 and 9. The 4 sc* recordings were obtained in 1989 from ambulatory healthy volunteers during 24 hours in their normal daily life, using a modified cassette tape recorder. The 4 st* recordings were obtained in 1994 from subjects who had mild difficulty falling asleep but were otherwise healthy, during a night in the hospital, using a miniature telemetry system with very good signal quality. The EEG signals of the sleep stage 2 based on Fpz-Cz/Pz-Oz EEG are used in this paper.

## 2.1 Feature Extraction (Wavelet Transforms)

In this study, Haar WT which is at scale level 5 was conducted with Fpz-Cz/Pz-Oz EEG signals. From the detail coefficients and approximation coefficients which are wavelet coefficients at level 2 through level 5 implemented as such, we extracted 40 features to be used as inputs in this study as follows using the statistical methods described in Table 1. Features 1, 2, and 3, explained in Table 1, represent the frequency distributions of Fpz-Cz/Pz-Oz EEG and features 4 and 5 represent the amounts of variability in the frequency distributions.

In this study, we composed experimental groups consisting of 80 inputs extracted from Fpz-Cz/Pz-Oz EEG signals by the statistical methods described in Table 1. We composed the experimental groups as shown in Table 2 using 2982 experimental groups of healthy subjects and 2321 experimental groups of subjects who have mild difficulty falling asleep. We divided the experimental groups into the first half and the latter half as training sets and test sets, respectively.

**Table 1.** Feature Extraction Description

| No | Feature Extraction Description |
|----|-------------------------------|
| 1 | Mean of the absolute values of the coefficients in each sub-band. |
| 2 | Median of the coefficients in each sub-band. |
| 3 | Average power of the wavelet coefficients in each sub-band. |
| 4 | Standard deviation of the coefficients in each sub-band. |
| 5 | Ratio of the absolute mean values of adjacent sub-bands. |

**Table 2.** Number of Training and Test Sets

| Class | Training sets | Testing sets | Total sets |
|-------|---------------|--------------|------------|
| Subjects who have mild difficulty falling asleep | 1161 | 1160 | 2321 |
| Healthy subjects | 1491 | 1491 | 2982 |
| Total sets | 2652 | 2651 | 5303 |

## 2.2 Network with Weighted Fuzzy Membership Function (NEWFM)

A neural network with weighted fuzzy membership function (NEWFM) is a supervised classification neuro-fuzzy system using the bounded sum of weighted fuzzy membership functions (BSWFMs) [4][5][6]. The structure of the NEWFM, illustrated in Fig. 3, comprises three layers namely the input, hyperbox, and class layer. The input layer contains $n$ input nodes for an $n$ featured input pattern. The hyperbox layer consists of $m$ hyperbox nodes. Each hyperbox node $B_l$ to be connected to a class node contains $n$ BSWFMs for $n$ input nodes. The output layer is composed of $p$ class nodes. Each class node is connected to one or more hyperbox nodes. An $h$th input pattern can be recorded as $I_h=\{A_h=(a_1, a_2, \ldots , a_n), class\}$, where $class$ is the result of classification and $A_h$ is $n$ features of an input pattern. In this paper, using the feature extraction method explained in Table 1, 80 features were extracted from the approximation coefficients and detail coefficients, and these 80 features were used as inputs of the NEWFM as shown in Fig. 3.

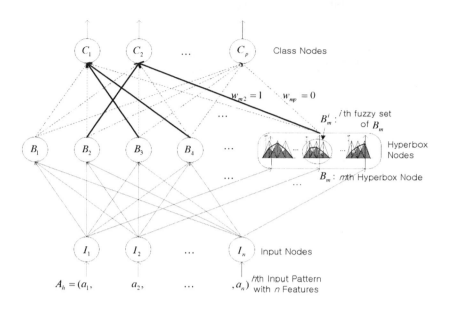

**Fig. 3.** Structure of NEWFM

## 4   Experimental Results

In this study, NEWFM shows in Table 3 as classification performances: TP (True Positive) refers to cases where subjects who have mild difficulty falling asleep are classified as subjects who have mild difficulty falling asleep and TN (True Negative) refers to cases where healthy subjects are classified as healthy subjects. FP (False Positive) refers to cases where subjects who have mild difficulty falling asleep are classified as healthy subjects and FN (False Negative) refers to cases where healthy subjects are classified as subjects who have mild difficulty falling asleep. The sensitivity, specificity, and accuracy obtained as shown in Table 4 are defined per equation (1).

$$Sensitivity = \frac{TP}{TP + FN} \times 100$$

$$Specificity = \frac{TN}{TN + FP} \times 100 \tag{1}$$

$$Accuracy = \frac{TP + TN}{TP + FN + TN + FP} \times 100$$

**Table 3.** Confusion matrix of classification results

| Subjects who have mild difficulty falling asleep | TP | FN |
|---|---|---|
| | 1034 | 94 |
| Healthy subjects | FP | TN |
| | 126 | 1397 |

**Table 4.** Performance Results for NEWFM

| | Accuracy | Specificity | Sensitivity |
|---|---|---|---|
| Performance Results (%) | 91.70 | 91.73 | 91.67 |

Fig. 4 and Fig. 5 show the examples of fuzzy membership functions with respect to the 4 features from Fpz-Cz/Pz-Oz EEG signals, respectively, among 40 initial features. These represent the BSWFM (bounded sum of weighted fuzzy membership functions) described in [4][5][6]. Through these, the difference in healthy subjects and subjects who have mild difficulty falling asleep with respect to the 40 features could be visualized and analyzed accordingly.

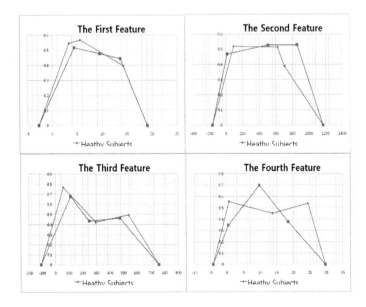

**Fig. 4.** Examples of the BSWFM of the 4 features among 40 features in Fpz-Cz EEG signals

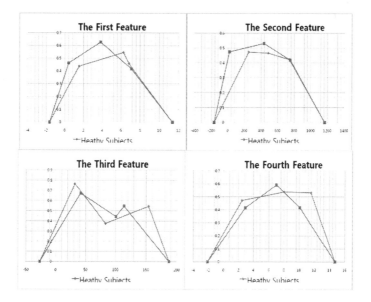

**Fig. 5.** Examples of the BSWFM of the 4 features among 40 features in Pz-Oz EEG signals

## 5 Concluding Remarks

In this study, wavelet-based features using EEG signals in sleep stage 2 were used to classify subjects who have mild difficulty falling asleep and healthy subjects along with the use of Fpz-Cz/Pz-Oz EEG. At the first phase, detail coefficients and approximation coefficients were extracted using the wavelet transform (WT) with Fpz-Cz/Pz-Oz EEG at sleep stage 2. At the second phase, using statistical methods, including frequency distributions and the amounts of variability in frequency distributions extracted in the first stage, 40 features were extracted each from Fpz-Cz/Pz-Oz EEG. In the final phase, 80 features extracted at the second phase were used as inputs of NEWFM. In performance results, the accuracy, specificity, and sensitivity were 91.70%, 91.73%, and 91.67%, respectively. Furthermore, this paper has made the interpretation of the features possible by suggesting 80 fuzzy membership functions of the 80 features.

## Acknowledgement

"This research was supported by the MKE(The Ministry of Knowledge Economy), Korea, under the 'National hrd support program for convergence information technology' support program supervised by the NIPA(National IT Industry Promotion Agency)" (NIPA-2011-C6150-1101-0001).

# References

1. Rechtschaffen, A., Kales, A.: A Manual of Standardized Terminology, Techniques and Scoring System for Sleep Stages of Human Subjects. Brain Information Service/Brain Research Institute, UCLA (1968)
2. Aserinsky, E., Kleitman, N.: Regularly occurring periods of eye motility, and concomitant phenomena, during sleep. Science 118, 273–274 (1953)
3. http://www.physionet.org/physiobank/database/sleep-edf/
4. Lee, S.-H., Lim, J.S.: Forecasting KOSPI based on a neural network with weighted fuzzy membership functions. Expert Systems with Applications 38, 4259–4263 (2011)
5. Lim, J.S.: Finding Features for Real-Time Premature Ventricular Contraction Detection Using a Fuzzy Neural Network System. IEEE Transactions on Neural Networks 20, 522–527 (2009)
6. Lim, J.S., Wang, D., Kim, Y.-S., Gupta, S.: A neuro-fuzzy approach for diagnosis of antibody deficiency syndrome. Neurocomputing 69, 969–974 (2006)
7. Sher, A.E.: Treating Obstructive sleep apnea syndrome - a complex task. West J. Med. 162, 170–172 (1995)
8. Lee, J.-M., Kim, D.-J., Kim, I.-Y., Park, K.-S., Kim, S.I.: Detrended fuctuation analysis of EEG in sleep apnea using MIT=BIH polysomnography data. Computers in Biology and Medicine 32, 37–47 (2002)
9. Chung, Y.-S.: Pathophysiology and Diagnosis of Sleep Apnea. The KJAsEM 20(1) (August 2010)
10. Übeyli, E.D., Cvetkovic, D., Holland, G., Cosic, I.: Adaptive neuro-fuzzy inference system employing wavelet coefficients for detection of alterations in sleep EEG activity during hypopnoea episodes. Digital Signal Processing 20, 678–691 (2010)
11. Acharya, R., Faust, O., Kannathal, N., Chua, T., Laxminarayanb, S.: Non-linear analysis of EEG signals at various sleep stages. Computer Methods and Programs in Biomedicine 80, 37–45 (2005)
12. Güneş, S., Polat, K., Yosunkaya, Ş.: Efficient sleep stage recognition system based on EEG signal using k-means clustering based feature weighting. Expert Systems with Applications 37, 7922–7928 (2010)

# Automated Text Summarization: Sentence Refinement Approach

Shaidah Jusoh[1], Abdulsalam M. Masoud[2], and Hejab M. Alfawareh[1]

[1] Faculty of Science & Information Technology,
Zarqa University, Zarqa, Jordan
[2] College of Arts & Science, Unoversiti Utara Malaysia,
Sintok, 06010 Kedah, Malaysia
Zarqa University, Zarqa Jodan
{shaidah,hejab}@zpu.edu.jo

**Abstract.** Automated text summarization is a process of deriving a shorter version of a text document from an original text. The most well known and widely used technique for automated text summarization is sentence extraction technique. Using this technique, sentences are extracted based on certain features that have been decided. In this paper, a new technique called sentence refinement is introduced as an improvement of the technique. In this approach, a sentence is refined; unimportant words or phrases exist in the extracted sentences are omitted. A summarization tool has been developed based on the proposed approach. The tool was tested using English and Malay texts. Extrinsic and intrinsic measurement methods have been used in evaluating generated summaries. Results show the proposed approach is promising.

**Keywords:** summarization, sentence extraction, sentence refinement.

## 1 Introduction

In this era, an automated summarization tool has become a desirable tool for many people. The tool may allow a human reader to retrieve important information from texts in an easy and faster way. It could be utilized by busy managers to scan relevance information, researches to have a quick glance on relevance research articles, students to have a quick understanding on subject matters, and so on. Technically, summarization is a process of deriving a shorter version of text from an original text, by selecting important contents. Reference in [1] defined, "text summarization is the process of distilling the most important information from a source to produce a shorter version for a particular user or task". Thus, summarization can be considered as a distilling process to obtain the most important information from a source text. Summarization process aims at interpreting the source text, understanding and analyzing the meaning being imparted to it, and finally creating a summary [1].

The basic idea of automated summarization is to make a user understands an eventual meaning of a text which has been presented in a short time, and in the form

V. Snasel, J. Platos, and E. El-Qawasmeh (Eds.): ICDIPC 2011, Part II, CCIS 189, pp. 207–218, 2011.

of a relatively shorter text. This shorter text, which is a subset of the original text, may not really convey all the details of the original text, but it certainly aim at conveying the basic and actual idea of the text [2]. Research community in this area have been putting effort to apply automated text summarization in various applications such as document classifications, information retrieval, document extraction, knowledge sharing, and so on. However, to the best of our knowledge, none text summarizer tool that can produce an accurate summary text has been developed so far. Most of the developed tools try to produce somehow an acceptable summary for a given text. Therefore research work in automated text summarization is still not mature, and many researchers in the area are exploring various techniques to produce a better summary. This paper suggests that a better summary can be obtained by reducing the length of an original text to be shorter and refining sentences to be more precise. An approach to achieve the mentioned goal is introduced. The paper is organized as follows; related work is presented in section 2, the proposed approach is presented in section 3, experiment and results are discussed in section 4, and the conclusion and the future work of the research are presented in section 5.

## 2   Related Work

### 2.1   Automated Text Summarization Techniques

A wide variety of techniques have been applied to condense content information in a text, from pure statistical approaches to those using closer analysis of text structure involving linguistic and heuristic methods (anafora resolution, named entity recognition, lexical chains, etc,). Many algorithms for feature reduction, feature transformation and feature weighting are directly related to text summarization. However, most of the working summarization systems are based on the extraction of a certain number of sentences found in the text. These sentences are seen to express most of the concepts present in the document [3],[4],[5], [6],[7]. Sentence extraction technique is usually statistical, linguistics, and heuristic methods, or a combination of all those techniques in order to generate a summary. The summary is not syntactically or content wise altered. In sentence extraction technique, a score is normally computed for each sentence based on features such as the sentence position and the frequency of words. Using these features, the most important sentences in a document are extracted. A summary is a collection of extracted sentences from the original text.

Some researchers have been trying to rearrange information in a text to produce a readable text; moving from extraction to abstraction. A sentence abstraction technique was introduced for the purpose. However, the major issue of using sentence abstraction [8] technique is the text processor has to understand the whole text and generate a summary as a human does. Although this technique may produce a better summary, however, this technique is very difficult to be implemented, and there is no evidence of its successful rate. Sentence extraction is less difficult to be implemented, and there is an evidence of it successful rate although it is conducted without understanding the context. Furthermore, in a manual abstraction process, an editor would have to acknowledge six editing operations: reducing the sentences; combine them; transform them syntactically; paraphrasing its lexical; generalize and specify; and re-ordering the sentences [9]. Thus, automated abstraction requires a computer system to have the knowledge of a human editor, and this requires lots of computing time. Another possible technique is text categorization. Basically, text categorization is a task of assigning pre-defined categories to free-text documents. Using this technique, a result of the summarization algorithm is a list of key-paragraphs, key-phrases or key-words that have been considered to be the most relevant ones.

## 2.2 Existing Summarization Tools

**Brevity Document Summarizer**
Brevity was developed by Lextek International Company [10] that specialist in full-text search technologies and generating document summaries. The summaries can be customized as a user wish. It can highlight either the key sentences or words in a document. Lextek claimed that Brevity is able to generate an accurate document summary, highlight the important sentences and words, and finding the most key parts in a document.

**Copernic Summarizer**
Copernic Summarizer has been developed by Copernic Inc, the search software specialist [11]. To generate document summaries, the Copernic summarizer uses the statistical model (S-Model) and knowledge intensive processes which is (K-Process). It is able to generate summary reports with key concepts and key sentences in four languages (English, Spanish, German, and French) in many forms such as text documents, hyperlinks, website, and emails.

**Inxight Summarizer**
Inxight Summarizer has been developed by Inxight Federal Systems Company. It is one of the development kits that Inxight introduced to help developers incorporate summarization into their intelligent solution search systems [12]. It basically finds key sentences in a text document.

**FociSum**
Columbia University showed how the extraction technology of the information could be used to classify relevant term types, such as people, places, and technical terms, which can be the focus of documents, despite the domain of the document. By using several features, for instance frequency and term type, the system can identify "the foci" in the text and find relationships between them. So, the summary in this system is based on the sentences and clauses that cover the foci and their plausible relationships [13].

## 3   Sentence Refinement Approach

As presented in the literature, the most common technique for automated text summarization is sentence extraction. In this paper a sentence refinement is introduced as an improvement of the traditional approach. A framework of an automated text summarization with sentence extraction and sentence refinement is illustrated in Fig. 1. The framework consists of 6 steps: paragraph segmentation, sentence tokenization, keyword identification, sentence extraction, sentence refinement, and summary generation.

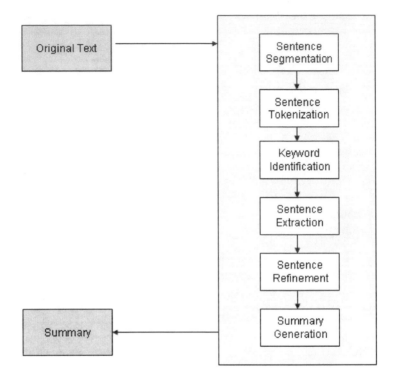

**Fig. 1.** An automated text summarization framework

## Paragraph Segmentation

Paragraph segmentation is a process of segmenting a paragraph into several sentences. The challenging issue is how to recognize the start and the end of each sentence in a paragraph. The simplest way of parsing a paragraph is by using a full stop (.), an exclamation mark (!) and a question mark (?) as an end marker. Although the exclamation and question marks may handle the parsing process correctly, but the full stop mark does not the same. For example, in a sentence "The poster cost Mr. Ali $24.65" , the dot symbol here does not mean the full stop symbol. To resolve this problem, a split method is applied in this approach. Using a split method, each character '.', '!', '?' is treated as a potential end of sentence marker, rather than a definite end of sentence marker. The paragraph parser scans an input paragraph and each time the potential end of sentence marker appears, it will decide either it would be the definite end of sentence marker or not, by using a set of rules.

## Sentence Tokenization

Sentence tokenization is a process of breaking a sentence into a list of tokens. The parser that parses a sentence into a list of tokens (words) is called tokenizer. It is often more useful to represent a text as a list of tokens. Each token is assigned with its part of speech (POS).

## Keyword Identification

Thematic words and title words are taken as keywords. The thematic words are classified based on the subject matter  or  the domain of the text. For example, if the subject matter is business news, then words such as *bank, money, finance, exchange rate, inflation rate, economy, US dollars* are classified as thematic words.

In this work, all words which are classified as noun POS in the title of the texts are also taken as keywords. Keyword identification is a process of searching similar words to the keywords in each sentence of the text. A sentence that may have one or more keywords is marked as a key sentence in the text.

## Sentence Extraction

Sentence extraction is a process of extracting important sentences from the text. A sentence is extracted from the text based on the following features:

1. The first and the second sentence of each paragraph.
2. The key sentences
3. The last sentence of the last paragraph

## Sentence Refinement

Each of the extracted sentences will be examined if it is possible to be refined or not. Refinement is a process of omitting unnecessary words or phrases which do not give a significant meaning to a sentence. In other word, refinement process will ensure that an extracted sentence becomes shorter and precise. This technique stimulates how a human reader manually summarizes a text. Each extracted sentence is scanned whether it contains unnecessary words and phrases or not. Examples of unnecessary words and phrases include "too", "also", at the end of a sentence, "that's why", "normally", "technically", "academically speaking", "furthermore", in the beginning of a sentence. A phrase which appears in a quotation is refined also.

## Summary Generation

Summary generation is a process of combining the refined sentences together to form a summary.

# 4   Experiments and Results

The proposed summarization framework has been implemented using Visual C++. The developed tool is named as **SRAETS.**  It has been customized to support two languages; English and Malay. In the Malay version, insignificant Malay words and phrases which may occur in a sentence have been identified. Examples of the words are "lagi", "juga", "adapun", "walaubagaimanapun", and "manakala". Examples of phrases are "dan sebagainya," "ketika ini", "sambil menambah", "sementara itu", "disamping itu". For example the meaning of a sentence "*Sementara itu, Ahmad Zahid berkata, projek perintis itu tidak menjejaskan sistem pentadbiran sedia ada antara kedua-dua kementerian yang terbabit dan ia akan diteruskan dalam beberapa projek lain*" remains unchanged even though the phrase "sementara itu" is removed.

Two types of experiments have been conducted; first by using English texts and second by using Malay texts. 100 English texts (Business news articles) in the domain of business have been used to evaluate the English version while 40 Malay texts have been used to evaluate the Malay version. The results of the first 50 English texts are presented in Table 1. Fig. 2 and Fig. 4 show examples of original texts, and Fig. 3 and Fig. 5 show the generated summaries of the texts.

Evaluation is an important task in automatic text summarization. Evaluating summaries can be either using intrinsic or extrinsic measures. One of the extrinsic methods is based on the Compression Ratio (CR) rate. The CR rate is calculated as (*the length of summary text*) / (*the length of full text*) * *100*. The length is measured based on the number of words in texts. The compression ratio is used as an evaluation measurement tool for both versions; English and Malay. Table 1 presents the CR rate of the first 50 English datasets, while Table 2 presents the CR for the Malay datasets. Each table presents 4 types of information: text identifier (ID), the original number of words in the text (OT), the number of words in a generated summary (ST) and the compression ratio rate. As we can see from both tables, some datasets have high CR rate and some have low CR rate. The CR rate somehow has been influenced by the length of extracted sentences. Although sentence refinement technique has been applied, it is possible that the extracted sentences do not contain a list of omitted words or phrases.

---

**Redtone tambah pelaburan RM10j**

REDTONE International Bhd (Redtone) akan melabur kira-kira RM10 juta lagi untuk membina infrastruktur stesen bumi (BS) dan peralatan berkaitan lain bagi memperkukuhkan capaian akses Internet tanpa wayar berkelajuan tinggi di Sabah dan Sarawak. Ketua Eksekutifnya, Zainal Amanshah, berkata pelaburan tambahan itu yang akan dibuat tahun ini, bakal menyaksikan pembinaan 19 lagi BS secara berperingkat di Sabah dan Sarawak yang masih belum mendapat kemudahan perkhidmatan internet berkelajuan tinggi berkenaan. Katanya, pembinaan 19 lagi BS itu adalah tambahan kepada 11 yang sudah beroperasi ketika ini, iaitu lima di kawasan Kota Kinabalu seperti Bukit Tiga, POS Malaysia, Radiant Court, TM Putatan, dan Lintas Square,manakala enam lagi di sekitar Kuching iaitu di Bukit Djin, Jalan Pending, Muara Tabuan, BDC Crystals, Jalan Dogan, dan Jalan Astana. Beliau berkata, dalam usaha memenuhi matlamat syarikat untuk membolehkan kemudahan internet berkelajuan tinggi dapat diakses oleh semua lapisan pengguna di kedua-dua negeri terbabit, pihaknya komited untuk meluaskan lagi capaian akses kemudahan itu ke kawasan lain. Ini termasuk kawasan sekitar TM Penampang, Delta Heights Apartment, Megalong Shopping Complex, Celcom Tower Inanam, dan Courtyard Hotel One Borneo di Kota Kinabalu, manakala empat lagi di sekitar Kuching seperti di Bintawa, CIDB Petrajaya, Lee Ling Matang, dan MJC Batu Kawa, katanya kepada Berita Harian ketika ditemui di Petaling Jaya, baru-baru ini. Beliau berkata demikian ketika ditanya mengenai kemajuan kerja syarikat itu dalam meluaskan lagi capaian liputan WiMAX di Sabah dan Sarawak.

---

**Fig. 2.** An example of datasets for Malay texts. The first line at the top is the title of the text

REDTONE International Bhd akan melabur kira-kira RM10 juta lagi untuk membina infrastruktur stesen bumi (BS) dan peralatan berkaitan lain bagi mem-perkukuhkan capaian akses Internet tanpa wayar berkelajuan tinggi di Sabah dan Sarawak. Ketua Eksekutifnya, Zainal Amanshah, berkata pelaburan tambahan itu yang akan dibuat tahun ini, bakal menyaksikan pembinaan 19 lagi BS secara berperingkat di Sabah dan Sarawak yang masih belum mendapat kemudahan perkhidmatan internet berkelajuan tinggi berkenaan. Katanya, pembinaan 19 lagi BS itu adalah tambahan kepada 11 yang sudah beroperasi ketika ini, iaitu lima di kawasan Kota Kinabalu seperti Bukit Tiga, POS Malaysia, Radiant Court, TM Putatan, dan Lintas Square, manakala enam lagi di sekitar Kuching iaitu di Bukit Djin, Jalan Pending, Muara Tabuan, BDC Crystals, Jalan Dogan, dan Jalan Astana. Beliau berkata, dalam usaha memenuhi matlamat syarikat untuk membolehkan kemudahan internet berkelajuan tinggi dapat diakses oleh semua lapisan pengguna di kedua-dua negeri terbabit, pihaknya komited untuk meluaskan lagi capaian akses kemudahan itu ke kawasan lain. Beliau berkata demikian ketika ditanya mengenai kemajuan kerja syarikat itu dalam meluaskan lagi capaian liputan WiMAX di Sabah dan Sarawak.

**Fig. 3.** A generated summary of the text in Fig. 2

**Business Courses for Go-Getters - Improve to Improve Communication**

Gaining confidence is a part of the curriculum at University of California-Berkeley's Haas School of Business (Haas Undergraduate Business Profile), too. There, undergraduate business students can take an elective on improvisational theater to improve their communication and teamwork skills. In one of the first exercises of the course, students stand face-to-face with a partner and go back and forth with either rhyming words or words that start with a particular letter. The exercise forces students to give up the preconceptions they have about the other person and react to what their partner actually says. The course, which began in fall 2008, offers more valuable tools than mere communication, says lecturer Cort Worthington. "Improve trains people to be very present in the reality around them," says Worthington. "I don't know if that's sexy or mundane, but it's incredibly empowering." Indeed, a person's mental health and how good they feel about their personal life will influence their job performance. That's why Susan Feinberg, associate professor of management and global business at Rutgers (Rutgers Undergraduate Business Profile), created the course "Love and Money," which helps business students learn to handle their personal finances, discuss money with their families and future spouses, and determine what kind of life they'd like to create for themselves both personally and professionally. "My aim is to give students the tools for a successful life and bring that success into their career," says Feinberg. Among the tasks students must complete is tracking how much they spend and save in a year, creating a feasible budget, and writing a life plan that demonstrates how they envision their life - including family, work, what their legacy will be - in the next five, 20, and 50 years. Although these courses teach skills that will probably always please employers, they seem to have particular relevancy at this moment in time. Undergraduate business programs are well aware that softer skills might be more important than ever and could be the difference between getting the job and being unemployed. "The current environment shows us we failed in some sense," says Kathleen Getz, senior associate dean for Academic Affairs at American University's Kogod School of Business (Kogod Undergraduate Business Profile). "We recognize that, and we're trying very hard to accommodate the workplace."

**Fig. 4.** An example of datasets for English texts. The sentence at the top is the title of the text

Gaining confidence is a part of the curriculum at University of California-Berkeley's Haas School of Business. There, undergraduate business students can take an elective on improvisational theater to improve their communication and teamwork skills. In one of the first exercises of the course, students stand face-to-face with a partner and go back and forth with either rhyming words or words that start with a particular letter. The exercise forces students to give up the preconceptions they have about the other person and react to what their partner actually says. The course, which began in fall 2008 , offers more valuable tools than mere communication. That's why Susan Feinberg, associate professor of management and global business at Rutgers , created the course "Love and Money," which helps business students learn to handle their personal finances, discuss money with their families and future spouses, and determine what kind of life they'd like to create for themselves both personally and professionally. Although these courses teach skills that will probably always please employers, they seem to have particular relevancy at this moment in time. Undergraduate business programs are well aware that softer skills might be more important than ever and could be the difference between getting the job and being unemployed.

**Fig. 5.** A generated summary of the text in Fig.4

**Table 1.** Results of English texts using SRAETS

| ID | OT | ST | CR(%) | ID | OT | ST | CR(%) |
|----|------|------|-------|----|------|------|-------|
| 01 | 633 | 370 | 58.45 | 26 | 1168 | 628 | 53.77 |
| 02 | 393 | 261 | 66.41 | 27 | 218 | 187 | 85.78 |
| 03 | 352 | 150 | 42.61 | 28 | 175 | 127 | 72.57 |
| 04 | 499 | 150 | 30.06 | 29 | 230 | 92 | 40.00 |
| 05 | 401 | 209 | 52.12 | 30 | 254 | 110 | 43.31 |
| 06 | 683 | 190 | 27.82 | 31 | 328 | 84 | 25.61 |
| 07 | 189 | 97 | 51.32 | 32 | 277 | 169 | 61.01 |
| 08 | 478 | 353 | 73.85 | 33 | 297 | 83 | 27.95 |
| 09 | 488 | 265 | 54.30 | 34 | 788 | 237 | 30.08 |
| 10 | 372 | 230 | 61.83 | 35 | 782 | 340 | 43.48 |
| 11 | 287 | 140 | 48.78 | 36 | 335 | 198 | 59.10 |
| 12 | 462 | 323 | 69.91 | 37 | 610 | 346 | 56.72 |
| 13 | 1073 | 394 | 36.72 | 38 | 171 | 143 | 83.63 |
| 14 | 307 | 268 | 87.30 | 39 | 219 | 1340 | 63.96 |
| 15 | 419 | 279 | 66.59 | 40 | 524 | 311 | 59.35 |
| 16 | 505 | 77 | 15.25 | 41 | 354 | 255 | 72.03 |
| 17 | 275 | 188 | 68.36 | 42 | 241 | 112 | 46.47 |
| 18 | 1054 | 699 | 66.32 | 43 | 294 | 214 | 72.79 |
| 19 | 791 | 291 | 36.79 | 44 | 587 | 230 | 39.18 |
| 20 | 184 | 109 | 59.24 | 45 | 324 | 178 | 59.94 |
| 21 | 270 | 143 | 52.96 | 46 | 741 | 198 | 26.72 |
| 22 | 371 | 107 | 28.84 | 47 | 176 | 144 | 81.82 |
| 23 | 511 | 238 | 46.58 | 48 | 430 | 145 | 33.72 |
| 24 | 482 | 300 | 62.24 | 49 | 408 | 174 | 42.65 |
| 25 | 300 | 135 | 45.00 | 50 | 279 | 209 | 74.91 |

**Table 2.** Results of Malay texts using SRAETS

| ID | OT | ST | CR(%) |
|----|-----|-----|-------|
| 01 | 323 | 204 | 63.16 |
| 02 | 349 | 119 | 34.10 |
| 03 | 179 | 85 | 47.49 |
| 04 | 275 | 124 | 45.09 |
| 05 | 200 | 91 | 45.50 |
| 06 | 490 | 227 | 46.33 |
| 07 | 140 | 62 | 44.29 |
| 08 | 192 | 115 | 59.90 |
| 09 | 358 | 103 | 28.77 |
| 10 | 455 | 94 | 20.66 |
| 11 | 610 | 440 | 72.13 |
| 12 | 342 | 256 | 74.85 |
| 13 | 238 | 166 | 69.75 |
| 14 | 159 | 112 | 70.44 |
| 15 | 532 | 124 | 23.31 |
| 16 | 266 | 213 | 80.08 |
| 17 | 611 | 239 | 39.12 |
| 18 | 283 | 84 | 29.68 |
| 19 | 305 | 254 | 83.28 |
| 20 | 324 | 199 | 61.42 |

| ID | OT | ST | CR(%) |
|----|-----|-----|-------|
| 21 | 487 | 139 | 28.54 |
| 22 | 212 | 122 | 57.55 |
| 23 | 317 | 138 | 43.53 |
| 24 | 324 | 73 | 22.53 |
| 25 | 386 | 229 | 59.33 |
| 26 | 194 | 101 | 52.06 |
| 27 | 495 | 275 | 55.56 |
| 28 | 282 | 126 | 44.68 |
| 29 | 323 | 244 | 75.54 |
| 30 | 382 | 202 | 52.88 |
| 31 | 240 | 210 | 87.50 |
| 32 | 213 | 147 | 69.01 |
| 33 | 515 | 88 | 17.09 |
| 34 | 344 | 114 | 33.14 |
| 35 | 345 | 249 | 72.17 |
| 36 | 315 | 67 | 21.27 |
| 37 | 371 | 185 | 49.87 |
| 38 | 119 | 54 | 45.38 |
| 39 | 208 | 80 | 38.46 |
| 40 | 317 | 158 | 49.84 |

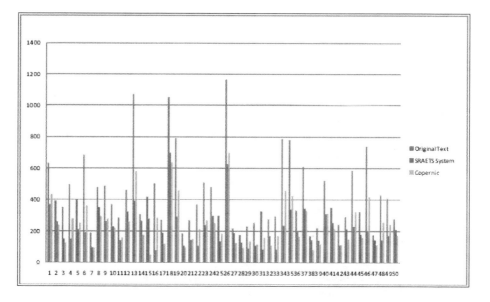

**Fig. 6.** The comparison between word count in  English texts (original texts) and in summaries generated by SRAETS and Copernic. The y-axis represents the number of words and the x-axis represents the dataset ID.

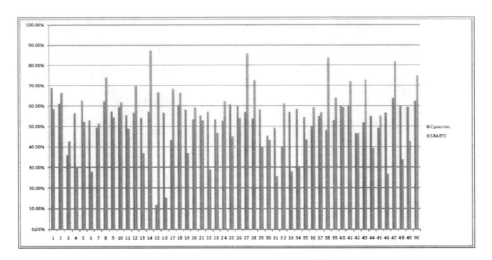

**Fig. 7.** The comparison between CR rate of SRAETS and Copernic. The y-axis represents the CR rate and the x-axis represents dataset ID.

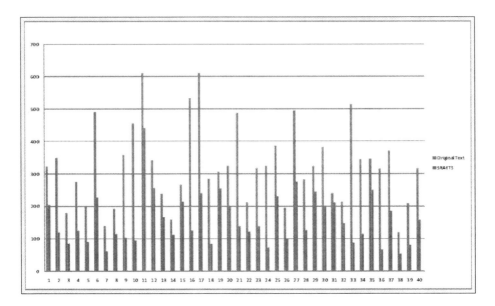

**Fig. 8.** The comparison between word count for original Malay texts (original text) and summaries generated by SRAETS. The y-axis represents the number of words and the x-axis represents the dataset ID.

To evaluate the performance of the proposed approach further, datasets in Table 1 were experimented using a commercial automated text summarization tool, Copernic Summarizer. The obtain results are compared and shown in Fig. 6 and Fig. 7. In overall, CR rate of summaries generated by SRAETS are lower than CR rate of summaries generated by Copernic. This indicates the proposed approach has a better performance. On the other hand, Copernic summarizer tool is not designed for the Malay language texts. Thus, similar comparison cannot be carried out. However, SRAETS shows a great achievement in CR rate for the Malay texts. A graph which is presented in Fig. 8, shows that SRAETS is able to reduce almost half of the original texts.

Besides CR rate, a human expert has been used to evaluate the summaries generated by SRAETS. The expert was asked to rate the summary in two scales; *satisfactory* and *unsatisfactory*. The overall rating that we received was satisfactory.

# 5  Conclusion

This paper has presented a sentence refinement technique as an improvement of the sentence extraction technique for automated text summarization. An automated text summarization tool has been developed in which the technique has been deployed. Two kinds of texts (English and Malay) have been used as test cases. Intrinsic and extrinsic measurement methods have been used to evaluate the generated summaries. A comparison with an existing commercial tool also has been conducted. Obtained results indicate that the propose approach is successful. The results also proved that the sentence refinement technique is applicable to any languages. The future work of this research is to improve the tool (SRAETS) by recognizing more insignificant words or phrases which might be possibly omit from texts and to concentrate on how much information is retained in generated summary texts.

# References

1. Mani, I., Benjamins, J.: Review of Automatic Summarization. Comput. Linguistic 28(2), 221–223 (2002)
2. Mani, I.: Advances in Automatic Text Summarization. MIT Press, Cambridge (1999)
3. Loo, P.K., Tan, C.-L.: Word and sentence extraction using irregular pyramid. In: Lopresti, D.P., Hu, J., Kashi, R.S. (eds.) DAS 2002. LNCS, vol. 2423, p. 307. Springer, Heidelberg (2002)
4. Singla, A., Hakkani, D.: Cross-lingual Sentence Extraction for Information Distillation. In: Cross-Lingual and Multilingual Automatic Speech Recognition Speech Translation (2008)
5. Radev, D.R., Hovy, E., McKeown, K.: Introduction to the Special Sssue on Summarization. Comput. Linguist. 28(4), 399–408 (2002)
6. Matsuo, Y., Ishizuka, M.: Keyword Extraction from a Single Document Using Word co-occurrence Statistical Information. In: Proceedings of the Sixteenth International Florida Artificial Intelligence Research Society Conference, pp. 392–396. AAAI Press, Menlo Park (2003)
7. Mihalcea, R.: Graph-based Ranking Algorithms for Sentence Extraction, Applied to Text Summarization. In: Proceedings of the ACL 2004 on Interactive Poster and Demonstration Sessions (2004)
8. Chan, S.W.K.: Beyond Keyword and Cue-phrase Matching: a Sentence-based Abstraction Technique for Information Extraction. Decis. Support Syst. 42(2), 759–777 (2006)

9. Jeek, K., Steinberger, J.: Automatic Text Summarization: The State of the Art and New Challenges. In: Znalosti 2008, pp. 1–12 (2008)
10. Lextek International, http://www.lextek.com/brevity/
11. Copernic Summarizer, http://www.copernic.com/en/products/summarizer/
12. Inxight-Federal-Systems, http://www.inxightfedsys.com/products/sdks/sum/default.asp
13. FociSum, http://www1.cs.columbia.edu/hjing/sumDemo/FociSum/

# Software-Defined Radio for Versatile Low-Power Wireless Sensor Systems

Sándor Szilvási, Benjámin Babják, Ákos Lédeczi, and Péter Völgyesi*

Institute for Software Integrated Systems, Vanderbilt University,
Nashville, TN, USA
{peter.volgyesi}@vanderbilt.edu

**Abstract.** Traditional wireless sensor network architectures are based on low-power microcontrollers and highly integrated short range radio transceiver chips operating in one of the few ISM bands. This combination provides a convenient and proven approach to design and build inexpensive sensor nodes rapidly. However, the black box nature of these radio chips severely limit experimentation and research with novel and innovative technologies in the wireless infrastructure. Our team previously proposed a revolutionary architecture for wireless nodes based on Flash FPGA devices. This paper shows the first results of our work through the implementation and evaluation of a simple baseband FSK modem in the SmartFusion FPGA fabric. We also demonstrate how we could leverage existing software radio projects to use the baseband modem in a wide range of radio frequency bands.

**Keywords:** Wireless Communication, Low-power Design, Software-defined Radio, FPGA.

## 1 Introduction

Over the past decade the prevailing trend in wireless sensor network (WSN) node design has been to combine common off-the-shelf (COTS) microcontrollers with CMOS short range radio transceivers. This convenient and low-risk approach is supported by several semiconductor companies (e.g., Texas Instruments, Atmel, Microchip, Cypress Semiconductor), many of whom provide these components as chipsets with readily available reference designs. The abundance of these low-cost hardware options enabled the WSN research community to design, prototype and build a vast array of successful "mote" class sensor nodes, such as the Mica [12], XSM [7] and Telos [23] devices, fostering academic research in low-power sensing and wireless communication.

While this almost "ready to eat" design pattern lowered the bar for sensor node design, it also made a huge impact on the variety of research topics within the community. Two notable areas where the implicit constraints inherent in

---

* This work was supported by the National Science Foundation awards 0964592 ("CNS-NeTS") and 1035627 ("CNS-CPS").

V. Snasel, J. Platos, and E. El-Qawasmeh (Eds.): ICDIPC 2011, Part II, CCIS 189, pp. 219–232, 2011.

these hardware platforms prevent progress are: *low-power signal processing* and *innovative RF/wireless technologies* for communication and other middleware services. Albeit our research team was deeply involved in the development of TinyOS [11][18]—a characteristic WSN operating system targeting COTS hardware platforms, we repeatedly encountered these shortcomings of the MCU + RFIC recipe. Using the TinyOS ecosystem we developed and successfully demonstrated several novel applications and key technology components, such as a shooter localization system [26], structural health monitoring application [17], highly accurate time synchronization and time stamping services [20][14] and a localization method with radio interferometric ranging [19]. In these efforts we either had to extend the traditional hardware architecture with custom designed and built components (e.g., FPGA-based cards for parallel signal processing of acoustic emissions, bullet shock waves and muzzle blasts) or we realized that our ideas yielded much higher accuracy and overall performance only if we would have more access to and control over some parts of the RF signal chain (e.g.: radio interferometry, time stamping). We firmly believe that by breaking up the traditional packet-oriented boundary between the radio and the processor a deluge of new research topics will emerge within the WSN scientific community. Innovative media access protocols and ranging technologies, like [15] could be pursued and explored in much more detail.

## 2  Related Work

Our approach and motivation is not entirely new. The mainstream wireless research and development community has long embraced software-defined radio (SRD) architectures, such as the Universal Software Radio Peripheral [9] and GNURadio [10]. This and similar platforms provide the necessary datapaths and computational power for acquiring, processing and emitting sophisticated analog signals tens of megahertz wide selected in an even much wider radio frequency band. Signal processing tasks are implemented on a PC class hardware running desktop operating systems and using standard programming languages and open software frameworks. The performance of the state of the art SRD platforms is sufficient enough to implement WiFi access points, GSM base stations [2] and GPS receivers [13].

Traditional SRD architectures enabled us to experiment with and evaluate new ideas in our WSN research. In these scenarios the SRD platforms provided instrumentation and served as quick prototyping and proof-of-concept vehicles. However, these platforms are not suited well for implementing and deploying WSN applications due to the dependency on PC hardware, large FPGA devices and magnitudes of higher power requirements than it is available on a typical sensor node. Field Programmable Gate Array (FPGA) devices are key elements of SRD platforms: these provide the low-level *plumbing* infrastructure and implement preliminary signal processing tasks (digital up and down conversion, filtering, etc.). The Agile Radio project at Kansas (KUAR) [22] uses an embedded

PC based platform augmented with a Xilinx Virtex-II Pro FPGA. Rice University's Wireless Open-Access Research Platform (WARP) [4] also uses the same FPGA as its baseband processor. Berkeley's Waldo localization platform uses a Xilinx Spartan 3 XC3S1000 FPGA [16]. The WINC2R SDR hardware [21] from the WINLAB group at Rutgers has an embedded CPU and two high-end Xilinx FPGAs, one for baseband processing and another for the network layer. Unfortunately, mainstream CMOS/SRAM-based FPGA architectures (Xilinx Virtex and Spartan and the Altera Stratix and Cyclone families) are not suited well for battery-based operation, mostly due to their significant static power requirements, which cannot be mitigated easily with duty cycling techniques [27].

Recent developments in Flash-based FPGA architectures [3] and a revolutionary new mixed signal device family (Actel SmartFusion [1]) removed most of such barriers. Integrated and configurable analog components provide ideal support for interfacing with various sensor types, the FPGA fabric can be configured for sensor and baseband radio signal processing tasks and the integrated ARM Cortex-M3 processor executes higher-level algorithms and system integration routines. Based on our prior knowledge of the potential benefits and drawbacks of traditional FPGAs in WSN research we quickly embraced the new architecture for building the first compact and low-power software defined radio platform targeting wireless sensor networks [8].

Designing and building such a new platform is a complex endeavor with many unknown challenges and risks. Therefore, we embarked on a more incremental approach, where we could leverage existing and proven hardware and software components. On the analog RF side we already had several URSP radio front-ends in the 433 MHz and 2.4 GHz ISM bands. The new SmartFusion device family is also supported by a readily available low-cost evaluation kit and a more sophisticated development kit. Thus, with the help of a custom designed ADC/DAC and signal conditioning interface circuit board we were able to build the first prototype of the new architecture and to start experiments with the capabilities of the SmartFusion device in RF baseband signal processing. This paper describes the initial results of this work.

## 3   Implementation

We selected a low-power Frequency Shift Keying (FSK) modulator/demodulator (modem) as the initial evaluation tool on the Flash FPGA platform. In the simplest variation of this modulation scheme (binary FSK) the digital information is transmitted using a pair of discrete frequencies around the carrier (center) frequency. Our design was heavily influenced by a similar project for mixed signal microcontrollers [24].

The primary design requirement for the FSK modem was to minimize power consumption and resource utilization of the overall system. A well known technique, often utilized in low-power microcontroller based systems, is precise clock management via clock scaling and duty cycling. Another effective, yet completely different, approach for power reduction in FPGAs is minimizing the amount of

FPGA fabric resources used. This can be achieved by creating designs that are aware of the internal structure of the FPGA. System on Programmable Chips (SoPC) offer further possibilities by taking advantage of their non-general purpose circuitry. These integrated hard-core modules, such as processors and digital communication interfaces, consume less power compared than the FPGA fabric. Furthermore, the programmable analog and interfaces eliminate the need for external DACs and ADCs, which also saves power.

Combining the above mentioned techniques, the high level block diagram of the baseband FSK design is shown in Figure 1. The transmitter and receiver data paths use only the FPGA fabric and the programmable analog parts of the SmartFusion SoPC, whereas the testbed is entirely implemented in software in the Microcontroller Subsystem, that is built around the embedded Cortex-M3 microprocessor. The baseband FSK data paths are connected to the testbed through the AMBA bus matrix.

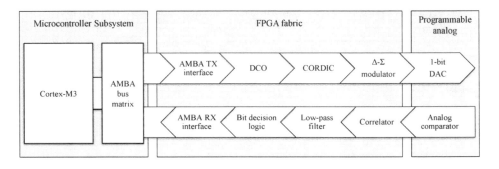

**Fig. 1.** Block diagram of the baseband FSK SmartFusion design

## 3.1    Testbed

The testbed has three main tasks to perform, such as test-vector generation, result-vector comparison and error logging. In the case of the baseband FSK testbed test-vector generation translates to preparing packets with a well defined payload and feeding them into the transmitter data path, see the upper data path in Figure 1. Result-vector comparison works the other way, the payload of the received packet is retrieved from the receiver data path, as shown on the lower data path in Figure 1, and matched against the original payload. The number of mismatching bits in the payload are then stored after each transaction.

Since none of these tasks are time critical and test-vector generation and matching call for complex sequential logic, the entire testbed is realized in software in the Cortex-M3 microprocessor. The processor sets the transmit and receive parameters, sets the transmit payload and gets the received payload via an APB interface defined on the AMBA bus matrix. As the corresponding peripheral registers are mapped into the Cortex-M3 memory space, these transactions are simple register read and write operations. Upon reception of a packet, a bit error rate (BER) counter is incremented according to the mismatches in the transmitted and received payload bits. This BER counter becomes of primary importance when executed in a loop for a large set of different test-vectors as it characterizes the overall BER for the actual transmit and receive parameters. The algorithm for single test transaction is shown in Algorithm 1.

---

**Algorithm 1.** Single transmit-receive transaction

Initialize transmitter and receiver
Start transaction
**while** transaction is not complete **do**
    Wait
**end while**
Compare transmitted and receive payload
Log bit error rate

---

## 3.2   Transmitter Data Path

The transmitter data path resides in FPGA fabric and the Programmable analog blocks of the SmartFusion SoPC as shown in Figure 1. The purpose of the AMBA TX interface is twofold. First, it handles address decoding for registers accessible from the processor AMBA bus, such as the *control, status, baud rate, delta phase low, delta phase high* and *data* registers. Second, it implements a simple state machine that sets the delta phase input and the enable signal of the digitally controlled oscillator (DCO) according the bit values in the data register, using the timing information in the baud register. The DCO acts blindly, as it increments its phase accumulator by the delta phase amount set on its input when enabled and zeros the phase accumulator otherwise. The phase accumulator width is extended to 32 bits in order to reduce phase jitter, however, only the upper 16 bits are used to address the CORDIC module acting as a sinc look-up-table. The CORDIC module is a word-serial implementation of the original algorithm presented by J. Volder [25]. The sine output of the CORDIC module is then fed into a $\Sigma$-$\Delta$ modulator that generates the high-speed, low-resolution input for the 1-bit DAC. This 1-bit DAC also contains a $3^{rd}$ order low-pass filter with a cut-off frequency at 300 kHz. Note that this analog filter in conjunction with the 1-bit DAC and the $\Sigma$-$\Delta$ modulator form a low-hardware cost, high-speed, high-resolution $\Sigma$-$\Delta$ type ADC.

## 3.3   Receiver Data Path

The output of the baseband FSK transmitter is looped back to the Analog comparator found in the Programmable analog block and serves as input for the receiver data path. The receiver data path is depicted in the bottom part of Figure 1. The digital 1-bit output of the Analog comparator is connected to the

*Correlator* block. The Correlator block calculates the XOR combination of the input signal and its delayed samples. The precise selection of this delay is crucial to achieve robust discrimination of logical values, a programmable length *delay line* is utilized. The maximum length of this delay line ultimately limits the achievable maximum delay time of the samples. To extend the maximum delay length, a decimator with programmable down-sampling rate is also incorporated in the Correlator block. One should note, that decimating the signal, that is lowering the sampling frequency, creates a trade-off between the achievable maximum delay time and the time resolution. Figure ref:levels shows correlation values with different delays. The actual values (y-axis) are unitless—measured in squared ADC ticks. However, we are interested in the maximum location only. The comparator output is fed to a 2-stage *CIC filter*. The differential delay length of the filter is also programmable, thus allows for flexible adjustment of the cut-off frequency. The *Bit decision* logic utilizes a timer-based state machine and a thresholding logic to recover the bit values of the payload. These received data bits along with the ready signal are connected to the AMBA *RX interface* module, which in return, makes them accessible for the testbed through the AMBA bus via the data and status registers, respectively. The AMBA RX interface module implements the decoding logic for the rest of the registers holding parameters, such as the baud rate, decimation ratio, correlation delay and differential delay.

## 4    Simulations

Accurate high level simulation of the data paths was a critical step of the design process as it does not just provide a proof of concept, but also serves as a golden reference model when validating the FPGA fabric design. Figure 3 shows the

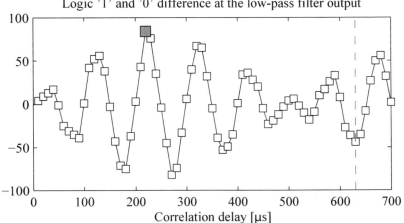

**Fig. 2.** Low-pass filter output level versus correlation delay

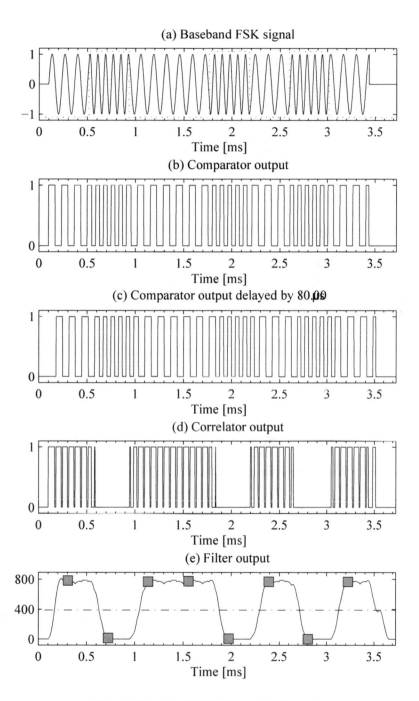

**Fig. 3.** Simulated FSK TX and RX signals

Matlab simulated signals along the receiver data path. The signal in Figure 3 (a) shows the baseband FSK signal ($f_{center} = 10$ kHz, $f_{separation} = 5$ kHz) for a 2400 baud byte transmission of value '01001010'. This waveform is quantized by the Analog comparator resulting in a signal shown in Figure 3 (b). The comparator ouput is correlated by its delayed samples, see Figure 3 (c), to separate the two logic levels. Figure 3 (d) clearly shows that the Correlator output stays low for when the high frequency signal is received and stays high (for most of the time) when the low frequency FSK signal is detected. Thus, averaging it with a low-pass filter resulst in a smooth waveform depicted in Figure 3 (e). Clearly, a simple threshold logic can effectively separate the two logic levels at the decision points as shown by the rectangles in Figure 3 (d). Note, that the decision points yield the byte '10110101', which is exactly the bit-inverse of the transmitted byte, thus can be compensated.

## 5   Radio Frequency Frontends

Just like practically all modern software-radio architectures our implementation follows the partitioning shown on figure 4. On the software side the radio signals are represented in digital form enabling sophisticated and flexible digital signal processing approaches, on the far end the signals are in the analog domain, where conventional analog signal processing and signal conditioning takes place. And just as the mighty beaver connects opposing river banks with its dam, so does our domain conversion card (BeaverBoard) connect the two signal domains.

Digital signal processing tasks are implemented on the SmartFusion evaluation board, while the analog domain is covered by various radio frontend daughter board cards available for the first generation Universal Software Radio Peripheral (USRP). These cards include the LFRX (DC-30 MHz receiver), LFTX (DC-30 MHz transmitter), and the RFX400 (400-500 MHz transceiver). While the first two boards are fairly simple providing only minimal filtering and gain, the RFX400 is much more sophisticated with built-in mixing and quadrature modulation/demodulation capabilities.

The challenge in designing a board that the would connect these off the shelf devices lied in the fact that the radio frontends were developed with a more sophisticated CODEC chip (AD9862) in mind. The AD9862 is a fairly complex mixed-signal front-end processor IC on the USRP, which is capable of 64 MSPS A/D conversion and 128 MSPS D/A conversion. Furthermore, the FPGA on the USRP is an Altera Cyclone EP1C12 device with plenty of free pins dedicated to frontend I/O control. The built-in ADCs and DACs in the Actel SmartFusion A2F200 device were not sufficient for interfacing with the baseband analog signals, and the evaluation board provided only a more limited number (25) of general purpose pins on its mixed signal connector interface.

By carefully checking each I/O pins for the radio frontends and their current use we managed to restrict these to fit in the 25 pins of the mixed signal connector interface. The issue of A/D and D/A conversion proved to be more demanding.

First, we had to decide on sampling rate. Since our intention is to build a low-power platform and we need to to execute all signal processing tasks on the SmartFusion FPGA, we had to restrict ourselves to few MSPS and 12 bits sampling. These constraints meant that the sampling frequency could not be nearly as high as with the USRP. We ended up choosing the Analog Devices AD7357 4.2 MSPS ADC [6] with two channels, and 14 bits of resolution. For the other direction we used the Analog Devices AD5449 2.47 MSPS DAC [5], which had two channels, and 12 bits of resolution.

Due to limited board space proper analog filtering was not implemented, only simple, operational amplifier based first order low pass filters made it into the design. The operational amplifiers also provided a convenient way to set bias voltages.

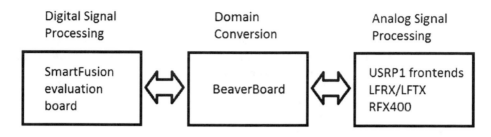

**Fig. 4.** State of the art SRD architecture: Analog (radio frontends for the USRP) and digital (Smartfusion FPGA) signal domain with domain conversion (BeaverBoard built on AD5449 DAC and AD7357 ADC) in between.

In designing the mixed signal interface circuit the primary challenge was to match the output current capabilities of the new DAC with the input current requirements of the RF frontend boards. The original high speed DACs on the USRP provide current outputs form 0 to 20 mA. For the AD5449 DAC that is a R-2R ladder configuration with a typical R of 10 kΩ that would mean a supply voltage of 200 V. Clearly we could only produce a fraction of the required current at the DAC output. A single stage, common-source, PMOS amplifier at the DAC output proved to be unusable in our case because the current range had to go from 0 mA to 20 mA. That range would have resulted in significant nonlinearity at the output of the single stage amplifier.

The circuit shown on figure 5(a) aims at solving this mismatch. The DAC output was converted from current to voltage with a simple operational amplifier stage, then the circuit as seen on the figure was used to generate the current output. The operational amplifier will always regulate its output so that the two op amp inputs have minimal voltage difference. Or in other words, the voltage measured at the inverting input of the amplifier will appear at the non-inverting input as well. That on the other hand is the voltage that can be measured at the bottom of the resistor. The upper part is at supply voltage level, thus the voltage difference is known, thus the current flowing through the transistor is known. Note that current is not flowing into the non-inverting input only through the PMOS transistor. On might think that the transistor is not needed,

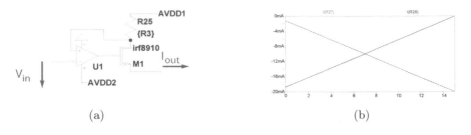

(a)                                                          (b)

**Fig. 5.** LTspice simulation of the circuit providing current output from 0 mA to 20 mA (a) and the simulated differential current outputs (b). The DAC is simulated with 4 bits of resolution giving a range form 0 to 15.

because the output of the amplifier could be connected to the bottom of the resistor. However, in that case—although the voltage would be the same as in the previous case—current would flow into the amplifier through its output, meaning that the current flowing out of the resistor would not necessarily be the output current for the whole circuit.

## 6   Results

The performance of the baseband FSK transmitter and receiver was evaluated using the BER metric with a fixed set of transmitted vectors. The testbed, described in 3.1, was set up to transmit and receive 1000 bits in byte size packets with randomly selected payload. Such a set of transmissions was repeated for baud rates in the range of 2400 to 19200 and for $f_{separation}$ values of 200 Hz to 6000 Hz. The $f_{center}$ was set to constant 50 kHz.

The BER results plotted in Figure 6, which clearly shows that a minimum bandwidth of approximately 1600 Hz is required for reliable transmission at any baud rate. Above that lower $f_{separation}$ limit, communication at baud rates 2400, 4800 and 7200 perform with a BER below 1%. Setting the baud rate to 9600, the BER increases roughly to 6%. This BER may be acceptable in certain applications, however, faster symbol switching rates quickly move the BER to unacceptable levels.

The baseband FSK design comes at a price. That price can be expressed in terms of resource utilization and power consumption. Figure 7 introduces the FPGA fabric usage breakdown among the different design blocks. The overall design takes 85% of the SmartFusion A2F200 device. 2% of that is used for common AMBA bus interface, while 40% and 43% is occupied by the transmitter and receiver interfaces, respectively. The CORDIC module gives almost one third of the transmitter resource usage, which could be reduced by sacrificing bit precision. The TX-APB interface is responsible for almost half of the transmitter resources. The main contributors to this surprisingly large value are the six

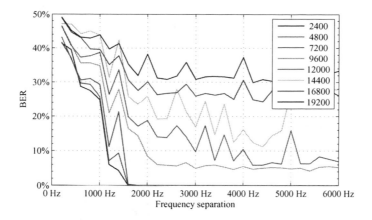

**Fig. 6.** Bit error rate as a function of frequency separation for different baud rates

32-bit registers and the accompanying address decoding logic. Compared these, the resource need of the $\Sigma$-$\Delta$ modulator and the DCO is negligible. In the receiver data path, the main contributors are the RX-APB interface module and the Bit decision logic, claiming one third of the receiver resources each. The former requires large amount of FPGA fabric mainly due to the 32-bit registers and their address decoding logic in it, while the latter needs significant storage area, comparator and counter logic. The Low-pass filter utilizes only one quarter of the receiver logic despite it being a FIR filter with long delay lines. This is due to the hardware-friendly nature of CIC topology and the use of embedded block RAMs. The Correlator block is responsible for approximately one tenth of the receiver data path resource usage, thus it is almost negligible. Note, that as the Microcontroller Subsystem and the Programmable analog blocks are not included as they are not realized in FPGA fabric.

The power consumption of the SmartFusion device is estimated assuming no duty cycling and 80 MHz and 40 MHz clock rates in the Microcontroller Subsystem and the FPGA fabric, respectively. The distribution of the 212 mW total power consumption is shown in Figure 8. According to the chart, the vast majority, 86% of the power is used by the Microcontroller Subsystem, that is by the testbed. The remaining 14% is divided among the transmitter and receiver data paths and the clock network driving them, which corresponds to 12mW, 7mW and 10mW, respectively. Comparing the power and resource usage of the individual blocks it becomes evident that the power consumption is not simply a linear function of the resource utilization. Rather it is heavily dependent on the frequency at the registers and nets change. Thus, the power consumption of the APB interfaces is relatively low, while that of the DCO and CORDIC blocks – operating with wide registers at high speed – is reasonably high.

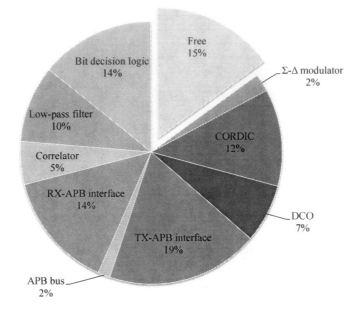

**Fig. 7.** VersaTile (FPGA fabric) resource usage of the baseband FSK SmartFusion design

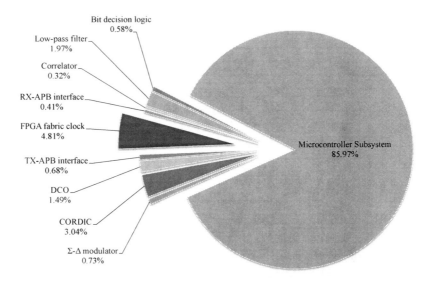

**Fig. 8.** Power usage breakdown of the baseband FSK SmartFusion design (212 mW total)

# References

1. Actel SmartFusion FPGA Device Family,
   http://www.actel.com/products/SmartFusion/default.aspx
2. The OpenBTS Project, http://openbts.sourceforge.net/
3. Actel Corporation. Competitive programmable logic power comparison. White paper (April 2008)
4. Amiri, K., Sun, Y., Murphy, P., Hunter, C., Cavallaro, J.R., Sabharwal, A.: Warp, a unified wireless network testbed for education and research. In: MSE 2007: Proceedings of the 2007 IEEE International Conference on Microelectronic Systems Education, pp. 53–54. IEEE Computer Society, Washington, DC, USA (2007)
5. Analog Devices. AD5449: Dual 12-Bit, High Bandwidth Multiplying DAC with Serial Interface,
   http://www.analog.com/en/digital-to-analog-converters/da-converters/
   ad5449/products/product.html
6. Analog Devices. AD7357: Differential Input, Dual, Simultaneous Sampling, 4.25 MSPS, 14-Bit, SAR ADC,
   http://www.analog.com/en/analog-to-digital-converters/ad-converters/
   ad7357/products/product.html
7. Dutta, P., Grimmer, M., Arora, A., Bibyk, S., Culler, D.: Design of a wireless sensor network platform for detecting rare, random, and ephemeral events. In: Proc. of IPSN/SPOTS (2005)
8. Dutta, P., Kuo, Y.-S., Lédeczi, Á., Schmid, T., Völgyesi, P.: Putting the software radio on a low-caloric diet. In: Ninth ACM Workshop on Hot Topic on Networks, HotNets-IX, p. 20 (2010)
9. Ettus Research LLC (2008), http://www.ettus.com
10. GNU Radio website (2008), http://gnuradio.org
11. Hill, J., Szewczyk, R., Woo, A., Hollar, S., Culler, D., Pister, K.: System architecture directions for networked sensors. In: Proc. of ASPLOS-IX (November 2000)
12. Hill, J., Culler, D.: Mica: a wireless platform for deeply embedded networks. IEEE Micro 22(6), 12–24 (2002)
13. Bertelsen, N., Rinder, P., Jensen, S.H., Borre, K., Akos, D.M.: A Software-Defined GPS and Galileo Receiver. Springer, Heidelberg (2007)
14. Kusý, B., Dutta, P., Levis, P., Maróti, M.: Elapsed time on arrival: a simple and versatile primitive for canonical time synchronization services. International Journal of Ad Hoc and Ubiquitous Computing 2(1) (2006)
15. Lanzisera, S., Lin, D.T., Pister, K.: RF time of flight ranging for wireless sensor network localization. In: Workshop on Intelligent Solutions in Embedded Systems (WISES) (June 2006)
16. Lanzisera, S.: RF Ranging for Location Awareness, Dissertation. University of California, Berkeley (2009)
17. Ledeczi, A., Hay, T., Volgyesi, P., Hay, R., Nadas, A., Jayaraman, S.: Wireless Acoustic Emission Sensor Network for Structural Monitoring. IEEE Sensors Journal (2009)
18. Levis, P., Madden, S., Polastre, J., Szewczyk, R., Whitehouse, K., Woo, A., Gay, D., Hill, J., Welsh, M., Brewer, E., Culle, D.: Tinyos: An operating system for wireless sensor networks. In: Ambient Intelligence. Springer, Heidelberg (2005)
19. Maróti, M., Kusý, B., Balogh, G., Völgyesi, P., Nádas, A., Molnár, K., Dóra, S., Lédeczi, Á.: Radio interferometric geolocation. In: Proc. of ACM SenSys (November 2005)

20. Maróti, M., Kusý, B., Simon, G., Lédeczi, Á.: The flooding time synchronization protocol. In: Proc. of ACM SenSys, pp. 39–49 (November 2004)
21. Miljanic, Z., Seskar, I., Le, K., Raychaudhuri, D.: The winlab network centric cognitive radio hardware platform. Mobile Networks and Applications 13(5), 533–541 (2008)
22. Minden, G.J., Evans, J.B., Searl, L., DePardo, D., Petty, V.R., Rajbanshi, R., Newman, T., Chen, Q., Weidling, F., Guffey, J., Datla, D., Barker, B., Peck, M., Cordill, B., Wyglinski, A.M., Agah, A.: Kuar: A flexible software-defined radio development platform. In: 2nd IEEE International Symposium on New Frontiers in Dynamic Spectrum Access Networks, DySPAN 2007, pp. 428–439 (April 2007)
23. Polastre, J., Szewczyk, R., Culler, D.: Telos: Enabling ultra-low power wireless research. In: Proc. of IPSN/SPOTS (April 2005)
24. Todd Dust, Cypress Semiconductor. AN60594 - PSoC 3 and PSoC 5 - 1200 Baud FSK Modem. Application Note (February 2011)
25. Volder, J.: The cordic computing technique. Papers Presented at the the Western Joint Computer Conference, IRE-AIEE-ACM 1959, March 3-5, pp. 257–261. ACM, New York (1959)
26. Volgyesi, P., Balogh, G., Nadas, A., Nash, C., Ledeczi, A.: Shooter localization and weapon classification with soldier-wearable networked sensors. In: 5th International Conference on Mobile Systems, Applications, and Services, MobiSys (2007)
27. Völgyesi, P., Sallai, J., Szilvási, S., Dutta, P., Lédeczi, Á.: Marmot: A novel low-power platform for wSNs. In: Zavoral, F., Yaghob, J., Pichappan, P., El-Qawasmeh, E. (eds.) NDT 2010. Communications in Computer and Information Science, vol. 88, pp. 274–280. Springer, Heidelberg (2010)

# Implementing Independent Component Analysis in General-Purpose GPU Architectures

Jacquelyne Forgette[1], Renata Wachowiak-Smolíková[2], and Mark Wachowiak[2]

[1] University of Western Ontario
London, ON Canada
jforgett@uwo.ca
[2] Nipissing University
North Bay, ON Canada
{renatas,markw}@nipissingu.ca

**Abstract.** New computational architectures, such as multi-core processors and graphics processing units (GPUs), pose challenges to application developers. Although in the case of general-purpose GPU programming, environments and toolkits such as CUDA and OpenCL have simplified application development, different ways of thinking about memory access, storage, and program execution are required. This paper presents a strategy for implementing a specific signal processing technique for blind-source separation: infomax independent component analysis (ICA). Common linear algebra operations are mapped to a low cost programmable graphics card using the OpenCL programming toolkit. Because many components of ICA are inherently parallel, ICA computations can be accelerated by low cost parallel hardware. Experimental results on simulated and speech signals indicate that efficiency gains and scalability are achievable through general-purpose GPU implementation, and suggest that important applications in telecommunications, speech processing, and biomedical signal analysis can benefit from these new architectures. The utilization of low cost GPUs for programming may potentially facilitate real-time applications of previously offline algorithms.

**Keywords:** General-purpose graphics processing units, GPU, parallel computing, heterogeneous computing, independent component analysis, blind source separation.

## 1   Introduction

Blind source separation (BSS) is the recovery of lost source signals from observed data for which no previous knowledge is available. Independent component analysis (ICA) is one such signal processing method for BSS. ICA analyzes large amounts of observed data (signal mixtures) to recover the individual source signals [1].

A common application of ICA is the separation of speech signals. Other applications include problems in medicine, engineering, business, and other fields. It is also a potentially important technique in mobile telecommunications, where a user's signal must be separated from other users' interfering signals in CDMA (Code-Division

V. Snasel, J. Platos, and E. El-Qawasmeh (Eds.): ICDIPC 2011, Part II, CCIS 189, pp. 233–243, 2011.

Multiple Access) [2]. Certain speech verification and identification procedures also employ ICA for feature extraction [3].

Although its power to solve complex problems is recognized, ICA is considered to be a relatively time consuming algorithm [4]. As the number of signal mixtures and signal length increase, the number of floating point calculations also increases. For larger mixtures, ICA must be computed off-line. Consequently, ICA is not yet considered feasible for real-time applications. However, the problem of throughput can potentially be alleviated through parallel computing.

Processor performance cannot continue to improve indefinitely because the operating voltage of chips cannot be reduced as sharply as in the past with increasing numbers of transistors. Consequently, performance gains are increasingly spearheaded by multi-core and graphics processing unit (GPU) technologies. In fact, *IEEE Spectrum* has named multi-core and the integration of GPU and CPUs as the Number 5 technology of the decade [5].

GPUs are highly parallel processors dedicated to rendering graphics through a fixed function graphics pipeline. It was not until 2001 that part of the graphics pipeline was opened to the application developer. Over the next five years, different parts of the GPU would be exposed to the developer, allowing general purpose use [6]. While general computations were possible, the task needed to be cast in terms of a graphics problem. Programs had to conform to textures, vertices and triangles, making programming awkward. GPU manufacturers have recently added support for random byte addressing and many other requirements of compiled C programs. The generic programming model for the newer GPU architectures introduced the concepts of thread hierarchy, barrier synchronization, and atomic operations to manage and to dispatch parallel tasks [6].

There exist many different technologies for parallel programming, each with unique advantages and disadvantages. Popular GPU programming environments include CUDA by NVIDIA, BROOK+ by AMD, and OpenCL by the Kronos group. OpenCL is an open standard for parallel programming of heterogeneous systems. It can be used to program the CPU, GPU, Cell architecture, clusters, and even mobile devices. OpenCL supports both data and task-based parallel programming models [7].

Different parallel architectures require different parallel programming models. GPUs excel in processing large amounts of data very quickly, and are appropriate for data processing-dominated applications [8]. In a dual-core CPU, the processor can run only two threads in parallel. All NVIDIA GPUs can support at least 768 active threads per multiprocessor, and some can even support up to 1024. The NVIDIA GeForce GTX 280 with 1024 active threads per multiprocessor and 30 multiprocessors can support 30,720 active threads [9].

GPUs have the capability of queuing billions of threads for execution with thousands of threads being active at any time. Even with this level of parallelism, some calculations simply cannot be run in parallel due to dependencies. Linear algebra operations, however, often present excellent opportunities for data parallel computation. The matrix operations generally consist of the same set of operations being performed on all data entries in the matrix. The data level parallelization required fits very well with the execution model of general purpose computation on the graphics processing unit. Through OpenCL, the GPU was chosen as the target platform for the parallel implementation of ICA [9].

In this paper, a specific ICA algorithm based on the Infomax principle is adapted to data-level parallel GPU architectures. This method takes advantage of underutilized hardware found in most personal computers. For long signals with more than $10^6$ samples, a significant performance increase was realized: more than a 50× speedup over the serial calculation. By demonstrating a successful application of GPU computing, the authors hope to motivate its importance to signal processing. High performance computing may therefore be achieved through the use of relatively inexpensive consumer hardware.

## 2  Independent Component Analysis

Independent component analysis is a signal processing technique where large amounts of observed data are analyzed into their contributing factors, known as source signals. This analysis can be written as:

$$\mathbf{x} = \mathbf{As} \tag{1}$$

where $\mathbf{s}$ denotes the independent components of the signal mixtures (sources), $\mathbf{A}$ is the mixing matrix resulting from the observation of the data, and $\mathbf{x}$ is the set of mixtures that were observed. In practical applications, only the observations $\mathbf{x}$ are known.

To recover the sources, an un-mixing matrix must be applied to the mixtures:

$$\mathbf{y} = \mathbf{Wx} \tag{2}$$

where $\mathbf{y}$ denotes the recovered source signals, and $\mathbf{W}$ is the un-mixing matrix computed during blind source separation. The number of recovered source signals must be at least the number of observed mixtures.

ICA uses the statistical principles of independence and normality to compute $\mathbf{W}$. It is assumed that sources are independent of each other, but signal mixtures, as they are linear combinations of the sources, are by definition not independent. Consequently, a strategy for recovering the source signals is to determine signals $\mathbf{y}$ such that all signals are statistically independent. A signal is considered to be a source if its probability density function (PDF) is non-Gaussian. The original source signals can be restored by maximizing the non-Gaussianity of the extracted source signals.

Blind source separation of signals using ICA can be implemented in a number of ways. FastICA [10] maximizes non-Gaussianity, usually negative entropy (negentropy), as a measure of statistical independence. Optimization is performed by a fixed-point iterative Newton-type method. The Infomax principle is used in optimization of artificial neural networks (ANNs), and determines mapping functions to maximize the average mutual information (using Shannon entropy) between the input and output values. This mapping is determined by gradient descent. ICA is one of the most important applications of Infomax [11]. Other ICA algorithms, such as JADE [12] and SOBI [13], also exist. Because ICA methods rely on different paradigms (e.g. FastICA and Infomax are iterative optimization problems while SOBI and JADE compute ICA from cumulants of the data), analytic expressions for computational complexities are difficult to formulate. However, expressions for the numerical complexities of the various approaches can be given in terms of floating point operations (FLOPs). In general, for comparable performance, SOBI requires the fewest number of FLOPs, followed by JADE, while the iterative techniques FastICA and Infomax require the most FLOPs [14]. In comparative studies, usually on EEG signal separation, all algorithms perform robustly. Although Infomax approaches are generally slower than JADE or Fast ICA, and are susceptible to entrapment in local minima (because it a gradient-based technique), they are often favoured because of their simplicity and their straightforward mapping to ANN architectures. Infomax algorithms have been extended to separate mixed subgaussian and supergaussian sources [15]. A field programmable gate array (FPGA) implementation of Infomax ICA, simulating ANNs, was also introduced [16]. The current paper proposes an Infomax ICA implementation based on GPUs, thereby extending the algorithm's utility on low-power computational architectures, such as ANNs and FPGAs. Because ANN computations can be dispatched as matrix operations, the goal of GPU mapping is to increase the efficiency of these operations by carrying them out on simple, but extremely parallel architectures.

In Infomax, the output entropy of an ANN with non-linear outputs is maximized [2]. It has been shown that the Infomax principle is equivalent to maximum likelihood estimation [17]. The non-linear functions used in the neural network are chosen as the cumulative distribution functions corresponding to the density functions in the log-likelihood estimate [2]. Further mathematical details can be found in [1, 2, 10].

The Infomax algorithm utilizes gradient ascent. Gradient ascent is an iterative approach. An iteration consists of several matrix operations, each dependent upon the previous one. Because of these dependencies, opportunities for task-level parallelism are limited. Efficiency gains can be achieved at a finer level by processing matrix operations in parallel. Because GPU programming is also highly scalable, performance can continue to increase by adding more streaming multiprocessors.

## 3   Parallel Execution on GPUs

OpenCL is a standardized, cross-platform parallel computing API based on the C language. It is used on a variety of different devices such as GPU, CPU, Cell processors, and FPGA. It enables portable parallel applications for heterogeneous computing devices. Programming the GPU using OpenCL consists of executing the same program (kernel) on multiple data (single-program-multiple-data, or SPMD). An OpenCL *context*, holding all OpenCL devices (CPUs and GPUs) must be created for the application. There can be more than one device in the context as OpenCL is built to handle many different types of platforms. Each device in the context needs a *command queue*, which stores the list of work that needs to execute on the device. The queue may start with a buffer write to copy the necessary information from the CPU to the device, followed by the kernel execution and finally a buffer read to return the results of the kernel execution.

OpenCL kernels are executed on all individual *workitems*. While workitems and threads share similarities, GPU context switching between workitems is much faster than with CPU threads, as workitem management takes place in hardware. A grid of workitems is organized into *workgroups*. Workgroups are then organized into a grid called the *NDRange* (*n*-dimensional range). The NDRange dimensions must be specified during the kernel launch. The OpenCL execution model is shown in Fig. 1.

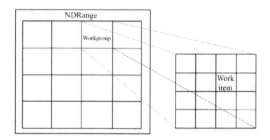

**Fig. 1.** OpenCL execution model

Workitems can be synchronized within a workgroup. The size or indices of the workgroups, workitems and the NDRange can be found using API functions with the dimension as a parameter. For example, `global_size(0)` returns the total width of the NDRange in workitems. Each individual workitem has access to its own registers, its private memory unique to each workitem, local memory shared between all other workitems in the workgroup, and global memory shared between all workitems. Global memory access is costly compared to local memory access. For example, global memory access produces a latency of 400-600 clock cycles compared to 8 clock cycles for local access. Workitems are bundled for execution into *warps*, which are groups of 32 workitems. Warps perform the same instruction in parallel on a processing element. OpenCL hides the latency produced by global memory accesses by scheduling other warps while a warp is waiting for data from global memory.

Depending upon the parallel algorithm, different approaches need to be considered for optimization. For example, matrix-matrix multiplication is a memory-bound operation. Most of the clock cycles are taken by global memory I/O. Shared memory can be used to reduce the number of clock cycles wasted because of latency.

## 4  Methods

There are significant differences between programming processors of different architectures. CPUs, GPUs and other accelerators have their own unique strengths and weaknesses. OpenCL is a common API that supports all such heterogeneous computing, and guarantees correctness and portability [18]. However, performance is not constant, due to differences in architecture and size of memory, and, as a result, kernels need to be optimized for specific target hardware [18]. Furthermore, a direct, naïve porting of linear algebra code may not result in significant performance benefits, due to the specialized nature of GPU architectures.

Infomax is essentially an optimization algorithm. Optimization can be parallelized at the level of (1) the algorithm itself; (2) computation of the similarity metric; or (3) fine-grained linear algebra operations within the algorithm [19]. As Infomax itself is not inherently parallizable due to iteration dependencies, the current ICA implementation concentrates on linear algebra operations, which include matrix multiplication, matrix transpose, matrix addition, vector multiplication, and matrix inverse [1]. The calculation involving the largest data set is matrix multiplication as well as the matrix transpose. Efficient implementations of these functions are imperative to increasing the performance of the algorithm.

The scalar multiplication of a matrix, the matrix inverse, as well as matrix addition and subtraction are the operations being applied to an $M \times M$ matrix, where $M$ is the number of recovered source signals, with $M < 16$ in most cases. With such a small matrix, the overhead incurred in GPU computations make CPU computation quicker.

Running the most expensive operations in parallel and leaving the simpler operations to the CPU is not the most effective alternative. Running the algorithm split between the CPU and the GPU requires that data be transferred between host and device many times during iteration, incurring a large amount of overhead, as data transferred between host and device is 8GB/s. When compared to the access speeds of the device's global memory at 141 GB/s, this is a significant problem to consider [9]. Therefore, leaving the computation results on the GPU for later computations is often the best option, even if certain computations offer no speed increases. Memory can be allocated and operated, and de-allocated on the GPU when needed [9].

When programming for the GPU, memory usage and instruction throughput must be considered [9]. Most importantly, the amount of transfers between the host and the device (CPU to GPU) must be minimized. Data transfers from the host (CPU) to the device (GPU) are done at 8 GB/s. Global memory access from any workitem is achieved at a rate of 141 GB/s – a significant increase over the transfer rate between host and device. For the Nvidia GTX 200 graphics card, the global memory access latency is between 400 and 600 cycles. While global memory access is much quicker than between host and device, it is much too expensive vis-à-vis local memory. Access to local memory from any workitem results in memory latency of only 4 to 6 cycles. Significantly, as most basic arithmetic operations require 4 – 6 cycles, 100 operations are performed for the same amount of time needed for one global memory access. Workitems accessing global memory are switched for those that are ready to carry out operations. Usually a large number of global workitems are desired to be able to properly mask global memory accesses. Context switching masks the latency resulting from access to global memory. For algorithms that access global memory frequently, context switching is not sufficient to hide the large amount of latency.

Utilizing shared memory to decrease the global memory access improves execution time significantly [9]. Frequently-used data are loaded into local memory that is shared among workitems in a workgroup. Workitems in a workgroup cooperate to load the necessary data, and barrier synchronizations are used to ensure that all data are loaded before operations are carried out.

There is another possible optimization on the GPU when data is being accessed from global memory. Each read or write from global memory is done in a 16 byte word. By aligning the reads and writes so that each workitem accesses the memory locations in order, 16 bytes of data can be written or read at the same cost as 1 byte. This optimization is called *memory access coalescing* [6].

The host and the device share an asynchronous relationship running independently of each other. A number of OpenCL function calls return control to the CPU before they complete all their work. This allows the CPU to push functions onto the OpenCL command queue for the GPU to complete. If a function on the CPU depends upon a certain function completing on the GPU, the CPU must be blocked from further execution until all OpenCL calls that were issued are completed.

The asynchronous operation also becomes an obstacle when checking for errors. If an error occurs on the GPU execution, the CPU will be notified when the next command is pushed onto the command queue or if the CPU and GPU are synchronized. The resulting error checking techniques are coarse-grained.

# 5  Results

The ICA algorithm requires operations on both large and small matrices. The large matrix is $M \times N$, where $M$ is the number of recovered sources signals and $N$ is the number of samples in each signal. The small matrix is $M \times M$, where $M$'s order does not usually exceed 10. Operations performed on small matrices yield speed increases on the GPU if pure execution time is measured without reads and writes from the CPU. The additional computing time incured by the overhead from GPU to CPU interaction causes the overall performance of the computation to be below that of the CPU native matrix multiplication. As the size of the matrices increase, performance benefits from running the kernel on the GPU become clear.

Let **C** be the array storing the resulting matrix and let **A** and **B** denote the matrices to be multiplied. The native CPU implementation for performance comparison follows:

```
for i = 0 to height of matrix A
  for k = 0 to width of matrix A
    for j = 0 to width of matrix B
      c[i * (width of B) + j] +=
      a[i *    (width of A) + k] *
      b[k * (width of B) + j]
    end
  end
end
```

In terms of processing time, matrix-matrix multiplication is one of the most expensive operations in the ICA algorithm. Figure 2 shows the log-scaled execution time for matrix multiplication to complete on the GPU (NVIDIA GTX 260) with no need to transfer the data between CPU and GPU. Pure execution without overhead is the time needed for the calculation of the matrix multiplication to complete on the GPU (NVIDIA GTX 260) without any of the overhead needed to transfer the data between CPU and GPU. To measure these times, an event was registered with the enqueN-DRange of the kernel. Once execution was terminated, the event was used to get the exact execution time. The second timing function was on the CPU side, including: allocation of memory on the GPU, transfer of data from host to device, setting kernel arguments, enqueuing the kernel, and transfer of results back to the CPU. The results demonstrate that as the sample size increases, the performance gain over the traditional CPU implementation also increases. However, for small matrices ($N <$ 128), overhead latencies outstrip performance gains.

Three original source signals were chosen: "train", "gong" and "laughter", sample audio signals from Matlab (The Mathworks, Natick MA). The signals were combined in to produce the signal mixtures. Figure 3 illustrates source signals of length $N =$ 100000 and Figure 4 shows their signal mixtures. Given the signal mixtures in Figure 4a, the ICA algorithm running on the GPU with OpenCL was able to separate the mixtures into the recovered signals (see Figure 4b).

The experimental speedup was calculated for various signals lengths and was found to approach 56:1 for a signal length of $5 \times 10^5$ samples. Figure 5 illustrates the effect of the signal length on the performance of the GPU ICA. As the number of samples per signal increase, the ratio of execution time also increases. In fact, if more signals were to be added to the separation, an even larger increase would be expected as performance gains for matrix-matrix multiplication are dependent upon the total number of values in the resulting matrix.

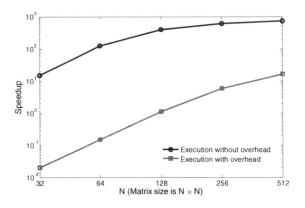

**Fig. 2.** Timing results for matrix-matrix operations required for Infomax ICA

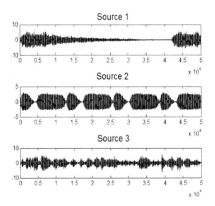

**Fig. 3.** Source signals

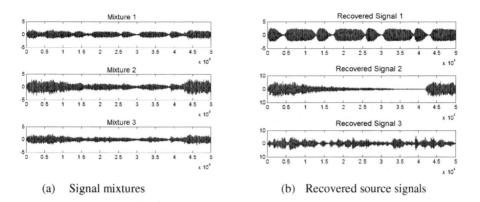

(a)    Signal mixtures                               (b)    Recovered source signals

**Fig. 4.** Signal mixtures and recovered source signals using GPU

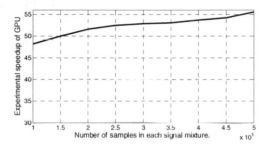

**Fig. 5.** The experimental speedup of ICA. Tests completed on a Dual AMD Athlon FX-70 Dual-core processor system (total of 4 cores), 2.81 GHz with 8GB of RAM. The GPU calculations were completed on an NVIDIA GTX 260.

## 6   Discussion

Results of Infomax ICA on the GPU indicate a significant decrease in running time when compared to the traditional serial implementation on the CPU. With a peak speed-up of close to 56, the ICA algorithm is a good example of how GPUs can accelerate existing algorithms. However, the results also underscore the importance of problem size for GPU parallelism. Speedups are seen for $N > 128$. For smaller matrices, latencies incurred in memory transfer and other overhead result in a decrease in performance – which is not surprising, as most linear algebra operations, including matrix-matrix multiplication, are "fine-grained" operations where the benefits of data parallelism are seen only for large problem sizes.

Parallelism on the GPU, while promising, is limited by the amount of memory available, either global, local, or in registers. However, expansion is possible. OpenCL supports the use of multiple GPUs running the same kernel function, potentially greatly increasing both the size of signals that can be processed using the GPU and the degree of parallelism and speed of calculations.

While double precision support is being added to newer graphics cards, it greatly slows computations. Perfect scalability of matrix-matrix multiplication has been proven to be accelerated using the GPU, even more so than the optimized vendor library CUBLAS 1.1. In fact, for dense matrix-matrix multiplication, a 60% performance increase over CUBLAS 1.1 was achieved [20].

## 7  Conclusions and Future Work

The approach used in this paper to map the Infomax ICA algorithm to the GPU recovers three source signals of length $5 \times 10^5$ samples, equivalent to roughly 10.4 seconds of audio sampled at 48 KHz. Using the GPU, source signals are recovered in only 6.7 seconds. Given 10 seconds of audio every 10 seconds, the algorithm can complete the signal separation before the next segment of audio needs to be analyzed.

In the current implementation, algebraic operations are not as optimized as the operations in CUBLAS 2.0. Use of optimized vendor libraries has the potential to further increase the performance of ICA on the GPU. With the addition of more GPUs, the problem could be partitioned across multiple GPUs splitting the workload as well as improving its running-time. Further improvements would bring real-time ICA processing of large signals much closer to realization.

Even with these improved APIs, significant challenges remain. GPU programming also involves CPU programming; error checking is done in a coarse grained manner as computations on the GPU are asynchronous to those on the CPU. Therefore, debugging is very difficult. NVIDIA has developed the first parallel development environment operating within Microsoft Visual Studio, and provides tools for debugging and profiling both CUDA and OpenCL applications.

The GPU brings powerful high performance computing to relatively inexpensive PCs. The potential for increasing the accessibility of high performance algorithms is promising. With the advent of new tools (development environments, APIs, debuggers, profilers) and the increased availability of GPUs in most consumer computers, high performance computing has become much more accessible.

**Acknowledgments.** This work was supported by research grants from Nipissing University and from the Shared Hierarchical Academic Research Computing Network (SHARCNET).

## References

1. Stone, J.V.: Independent Component Analysis: A Tutorial Introduction. MIT Press, Cambridge (2004)
2. Hyvärinen, A., Oja, E.: Independent Component Analysis: Algorithms and Applications. Neural Networks 13, 411–430 (2000)
3. Ding, P., Kang, X., Zhang, L.: Personal Recognition Using ICA. In: Proceedings ICONIP (2001)
4. Esposito, F., et al.: Real-time Independent Component Analysis of fMRI Time-series. Neuroimage 20(4), 2209–2224 (2003)

5. Moore, S.K.: Multicore CPUs: Processor Proliferation- From Multicore to Many-core to Hard-to-describe-in-a-single-word Core. IEEE Spectrum, 40–42 (January 2011)
6. Kirk, D.B., Hwu, W.W.: Programming Massively Parallel Processors: A Hands on Approach. Morgan Kaufman, Burlington (2010)
7. Mushi, A.: OpenCL Specification Version 1.0. The Kronos Group (2009), http://www.khronos.org/registry/cl
8. Blake, G., Dreslinksi, R.G., Mudge, T.: A Survey of Multicore Processors. IEEE Sig. Proc. Mag. 26(6), 26–37 (2009)
9. NVIDIA OpenCL Best Practices Guide Version 1.0, NVIDIA (August 10, 2009)
10. Hyvärinen, A.: Fast and Robust Fixed-Point Algorithms for Independent Component Analysis. IEEE Transactions on Neural Networks 10(3), 626–634 (1999)
11. Bell, A.J., Sejnowski, T.J.: An Information-Maximization Approach to Blind Separation and Blind Deconvolution. Neural Computation 7, 1129–1159 (1995)
12. Cardoso, J.F.: High-Order Contrasts for Independent Component Analysis. Neural Computation 11, 157–192 (1999)
13. Belouchrani, A., Abed-Meraim, K., Cardoso, J.F., Moulines, E.: A Blind Source Separation Technique Based on Second-Order Statistics. IEEE Transactions on Signal Processing 45, 434–444 (1997)
14. Kachenoura, A., Albera, L., Senhadji, L., Comon, P.: ICA: A Potential Tool for BCI Systems. IEEE Signal Processing Magazine, 57–68 (January 2008)
15. Lee, T.-W., Girolami, M., Sejnowski, T.J.: Independent Component Analysis Using an Extended Infomax Algorithm for Mixed Subgaussian and Supergaussian Sources. Neural Computation 11, 417–441 (1999)
16. Oliva-Moreno, L.N., Arce-Aleman, M.A., Lamont, J.G.: Implementation of Infomax ICA Algorithm for Blind Source Separation. In: Electronics, Robotics and Automotive Mechanics Conference, pp. 447–451. IEEE Press, Los Alamitos (2008)
17. Cardoso, J.F.: Infomax and Maximum Likelihood for Source Separation. IEEE Letters on Signal Processing 4, 112–114 (1997)
18. Stone, J.E., Gohara, D., Shi, G.: OpenCL: A Parallel Programming Standard for Heterogeneous Computing Systems. Computing in Science and Engineering 12(3), 66–73 (2010)
19. Schnabel, R.B.: A View of the Limitations, Opportunities, and Challenges in Parallel Nonlinear Optimization. Parallel Computing 21(3), 875–905 (1995)
20. Volkov, V., Demmel, J.W.: Benchmarking GPUs to Tune Dense Linear Algebra. In: Proc. 2008 ACM/IEEE Conference on Supercomputing, pp. 1–11 (2008)

# Two-Dimensional Signal Adaptive Processing for Airborne Radar

Samira Dib[1], Mourad Barkat[2], Jean-Marie Nicolas[3], and Morad Grimes[1]

[1] University of Jijel, Algeria
[2] King Saud University, Saudia Arabia
[3] Telecom Paris, France
samiradib@yahoo.fr

**Abstract.** In static radars, all the ground returns are received with a Doppler frequency almost null. However, in airborne radars, they present a wide spectrum for the Doppler frequencies because of the platform in motion. Space-time adaptive processing (STAP) was introduced to improve the capacity of radars to detect slow moving targets which can be masked by clutter or jammer. In this paper, we present the principles of STAP and we discuss the properties of optimum detector, as well as problems associated with estimating the adaptive weights such as ambiguities and the high computational cost. The performances are evaluated highlighting the influence of radar parameters on the detection of slow targets. To resolve problem of high computational cost of optimal space-time processing, reduced-rank methods are used. And to resolve Doppler ambiguities staggering of PRF is used. The simulation results are presented and the performances of STAP are discussed.

**Keywords:** Signal processing, Radar, Space-Time Processing, STAP.

## 1 Introduction

In airborne radar systems, the primary goal is to detect, identify, and estimate the parameters of a target in severe interference background. Typically, STAP means the simultaneous processing of the spatial signals received by multiple elements of an array antenna, and the temporal signals provided by the echoes from coherent pulse interval (CPI). For airborne radars, a target in a noisy scenario is shown in Fig. 1. In azimuth projections, the lobe principal of the clutter covers the target; while in Doppler projections, it is covered by the whole spectrum of the white noise and the secondary lobes of the clutter. However, it is clear that the target is separable from the clutter and noise in the two-dimensional field angle-Doppler [1,2]. Space-time processing exploits the fact that the clutter spectrum is basically a narrow ridge. A space-time clutter filter therefore has a narrow clutter notch, so that even slow targets fall into the pass band.

Space-time processing can provide a rejection of such clutter and thus, be able to detect the slow targets. Brennan and Reed [3] first introduced STAP to the radar community in 1973. With the recent advancement of high speed, high performance

V. Snasel, J. Platos, and E. El-Qawasmeh (Eds.): ICDIPC 2011, Part II, CCIS 189, pp. 244–257, 2011.
© Springer-Verlag Berlin Heidelberg 2011

digital signal processors, STAP is becoming an integral part of airborne or space-borne radars for MTI functions. It was proven in [1-14] that STAP algorithms have the ability to detect slowly moving targets that are close to the interference subspace. However, drawbacks that have held back the application of STAP in practice include the great computational cost necessary for implementation and the amount of stationary sample support needed to train the filter. These issues have led to the development of suboptimal reduced-dimension STAP algorithms [6-14].

In this paper, we discuss the effect of radar parameters on the optimal STAP, and the reduced rank STAP (RR STAP) on the airborne radar as well as the staggered PRF on the RR STAP performance in the two cases of known and unknown covariance matrix.

In what follows, we will analyze the influence of the parameters of radar on the target detection using the improvement factor as a study tool. Then, we illustrate the importance of the separation of subspace interference-noise which will reduce the rank of the covariance matrix. In Section 2, we present the mathematical data describing the environment in which the radar operates. Reduced rank STAP processing and staggering PRF are presented in Section 3. Section 4 is devoted to the discussion of the simulation results, while the conclusion illustrating the main results is presented in Section 6.

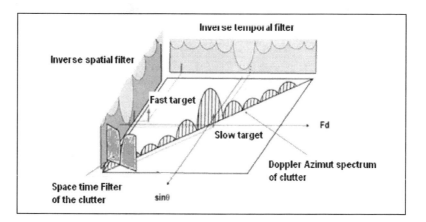

**Fig. 1.** Diagram of two-dimensional filtering

## 2  Space-Time Adaptive Processing (STAP)

The basic principles of space-time adaptive processing (STAP) is defined as a linear combination which adds the spatial samples of the elements of an antenna array and temporal samples of a multiple pulse coherent waveform. To calculate the weight vector adaptive STAP, the statistics of interference environment are determined by forming a covariance matrix. Typically, this matrix is not known a priori and must be estimated from the sample space-time secondary radar as shown in Figure 2.

**Mathematical model of data**

We consider a linear space-time array with $N$ sensors uniformly spaced and $M$ delay elements for each sensor. The radar transmits a coherent range of $M$ pulses at a constant pulse repetition frequency, $PRF$. For each $PRI$ ($PRI = 1/PRF$), the range cells are collected to cover the range constituting a two-dimensional model, called "data cube" of STAP. The data are processed at one range of interest, which corresponds to a slice of the CPI data cube as shown in Figure 3. This 2-D snapshot is a space-time data structure which consists of element space information and PRI space-Doppler information. The snapshot is stocked to form a $MN \times 1$ vector $X$.

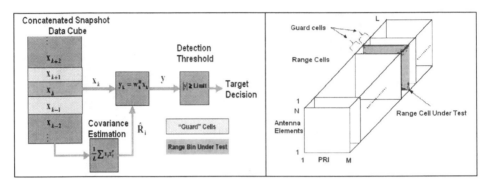

**Fig. 2.** Conventional chain of STAP          **Fig. 3.** Data Cube of STAP

A space time snapshot at range $k$ in the presence of a target is given by [1]

$$X = \alpha S + X_i \tag{1}$$

where, $X_i$ is the vector of interferences (noise, jamming and clutter), $\alpha$ is the target amplitude and S is the space-time steering vector given by $S = S_t \otimes S_s$, $S_t = [1; e^{-j2\pi F_t}; e^{-j2\pi 2F_t}; ...; e^{-j2\pi(M-1)F_t}]$ and $S_s = [1; e^{-j2\pi F_s}; e^{-j2\pi 2F_s}; ...; e^{-j2\pi(N-1)F_s}]$ ;

where $F_t = F_d / PRF$ and $F_s = d.\sin\theta / \lambda$ are, respectively, the normalized Doppler and spatial frequency. $d$ is the distance between the antennas and $\theta$ is the azimuth angle. The optimum weight of the STAP, which maximizes the signal to interference noise ratio SINR, is obtained to be [1]

$$W_{opt} = \alpha R^{-1} S \tag{2}$$

$R$ is the covariance matrix of the interferences, which is supposed to be known and its structure is given by [3]

$$R = E\left[ nn^H \right] = R_c + R_j + R_n \tag{3a}$$

where $R_c$, $R_J$ $R_n$ are the covariance matrices of clutter, jammers and thermal noise, respectively, as follows

$$R_c = \sum_{k=1}^{N_c} \zeta_k \left( S_{tk} \ S_{tk}^H \right) \otimes \left( S_{sk} \ S_{sk}^H \right) \tag{3b}$$

$$R_j = \sum_{i=1}^{N_j} \sum_{j=1}^{N_j} \alpha_i \alpha_j^H \otimes S_{s_i} S_{s_j}^H = AEA^H \tag{3c}$$

and

$$R_n = E[X_n X_n^H] = \sigma^2 I_J \otimes I_K = \sigma^2 I_{KJ} \tag{3d}$$

where $A = [S_{s_1}, S_{s_2}, ...., S_{s_{Nj}}]$ and $E = diag(\sigma^2 \xi_1, \sigma^2 \xi_2, ...., \sigma^2 \xi_{Nj})$.

$\xi_i, i = 1 ........ N_j$, is the jammer to noise ratio (JNR), and is the $\zeta_k$ clutter to noise ratio (CNR). In practice, $R$ is not known and must be estimated from the snapshots. The well-known SMI gives an estimate of the matrix by averaging over the secondary range cells, such that

$$\hat{R} = \frac{1}{L} \sum_{l=1, l \neq k}^{N} X_l X_l^H \tag{4}$$

where $k$ is the test range cell, and $L$ is the number of secondary range cells. The training data should not contain the signal, because it would be considered as interference and suppressed. For this reason, both the range cell under test and any adjacent range cells which might contain significant signal power due to range sidelobes (the so called "guard cells") are usually excluded from the training data. This is illustrated in Fig. 2.The SMI weight vector is then

$$W_{SMI} = \alpha \hat{R}^{-1} S \tag{5}$$

The performance of the processor can be discussed in terms of the Improvement Factor (IF). IF is defined as the ratio of the SINR of the output to that of the input of the Direct Form Processor (DFP) and given by [1]

$$IF_{opt} = \frac{W^H S.S^H W.tr(R)}{W^H R.W.S^H S} \tag{6}$$

$W$ is the optimum weights of the interference plus noise rejection filter.

Note that a notch, which is a reversed peak of the clutter, appears at the frequency in the direction of sight of the radar, while the width of this notch gives a measurement of the detection of slow moving targets.

# 3   STAP with Reduced Rank and Staggered PRF

The objective of the partially adaptive STAP is to reduce the complexity of the problem of adaptation, while maintaining almost the same optimal performance. The partially adaptive algorithms of the STAP consists in transforming the data with a matrix $V \in C^{MN \times r}$ where $r \ll MN$. There are several methods for the covariance matrix rank reduction [3-14], which may differ in the shape of the processor as well as in the selection of the columns of the matrix.

## 3.1   Principal Components Method (PC)

The principal component, PC (also known as the eigencanceler method [5]) is based on the eigenvectors conservation of the matrix of covariance of interferences corresponding to the dominant eigenvalues [7]. The resulting PC-based DFP (Direct Form Processor) weight vector $W = W_{PC\text{-}DFP}$ has the form

$$W_{PC-DFP} = S - \sum_{i=1}^{r} \frac{\lambda_i - \lambda_{\min}}{\lambda} (v_i^H S) v_i \tag{7}$$

Where $\{\lambda_i\}_{i=1}^{MN}$ are the eigenvalues of $R$ and $\{v_i\}_{i=1}^{MN}$ are the associated eigenvectors and $\lambda_1 \geq \lambda_2 \geq ... \geq \lambda_{MN}$ .

## 3.2   SINR Metric Method

The objective is to choose the $r$ columns of $V$ such that the loss in the performances of the SINR will be minimized. Berger and Welsh [8] chose the columns of $V$ as being the eigenvectors of $R$, which minimized the reduction in the performance of the SINR method. Clearly, the partial sum in (7) is maximized by selecting the $r$ columns of $V$ to be the eigenvectors which maximize the quantity [Berger Welsh]

$$\left| v_i^H S \right|^2 / \lambda_i \tag{8}$$

This is referred to as the SINR metric.
    The improvement factor of the reduced rank can then be written as

$$IF_{RR} = S^H V (V^H R V)^{-1} V^H S \frac{tr(V^H R V)}{S^H V . V^H S} \tag{9}$$

## 3.3   STAP with Staggered PRF

It is known that if the PRF has a low value, Doppler ambiguities occur and are caused by the overlapping of the edge lines with the true spectrum. Therefore, the idea of using the change of PRF appeared to solve the problem of Doppler ambiguities. The quadratic change of PRF consists of increasing (or decreasing) the PRI in certain stages. Therefore, the PRI in the temporal frequency of the direction vectors of the target and clutter is multiplied by the term $(1 + \varepsilon.m / M)$ for each impulse $m$ [12].

# 4   Results and Discussion

In this Section, we discuss the influence of some radar parameters and some algorithms, based on the reduction of the rank of the covariance matrix and staggered PRF, on the detection of a target with a low power (SNR=0dB) and with a slow speed. The simulated environment is a linear side looking network of $N$ antennas spaced out by $d$ and $M$ impulses in the CPI. The elevation angle is fixed to 20°. The speed of the airborne radar is $V_R$=100m/s, and the frequency of transmission is 0.3GHz. The environment of interferences consists of five jammers and ground clutter. The jammers are at azimuth angles of 0°, 180°, 60°, 90°, and 72°, respectively, and with respective ratios of jammer to noise (JNRs) of 13dB, 12dB, 11dB, 10dB and 9dB. The clutter to noise ratio (CNR) is set equal to 8dB. This clutter covers the band [30°, 30°]. All the simulations were carried out over 20 Monte Carlo runs.

## 4.1   Sample Size of the Network

In Fig. 4, we plot the improvement factor (IF) versus the normalized Doppler frequency (Ft). It is noted that the clutter notch becomes thinner when the number of antennas increases. This confirms the results obtained in [2]. Similar results are obtained when increasing the number of pulses. It can be concluded that improving the detection can be accomplished by increasing a single parameter (number of antennas or pulses). To achieve good performances, SMI method needs a large number of snaphots which increases the computational cost and time for implementation in real time.

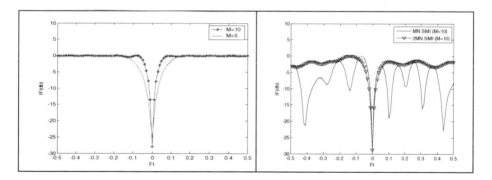

**Fig. 4.** Improvment Factor of the optimal processor, *DFP* with *PRF* =4V$_R$/λ, d/λ=0.5 and *N*=8 : *M*=10, *M*=5 for : (a) known R (b) unknown R

## 4.2   Space Subsampling

Fig. 5(a) shows the IF versus Ft of a scenario where the antennas are spaced at a distance ($d$ =λ) that is to mean, double of the spatial frequency sampling or Nyquist frequency ($F_{Nyquist}$). It is clear that ambiguous notches appear in the sidebands, which is not the case in Fig. 5(b) where the distance between the antennas is ($d = \lambda/2$). In this Figure, we can see that there is disappearance of some ambiguous notches and thus the detection is improved. Similar results are noticed for SMI method but for large number of data. Therefore, we can say that the subsampling in space ($d >= \lambda/2$) leads to a spatial ambiguity or range ambiguity.

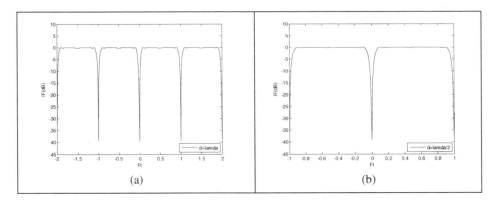

**Fig. 5.** Improvement Factor for known R: (a) $d=\lambda$, (b) $d=\lambda/2$

### 4.3  Temporal Subsampling

From Fig. 6, we note that the notch is thin and leads to the detection of slow targets. In the case where PRF is equal to ($2V_R/\lambda$), we see the appearance of ambiguous notches with speeds associated are called blind velocities and the detection becomes relatively difficult. However, for the case of PRF equal to ($4V_R/\lambda$), we notice that the ambiguous notches are eliminated and thus the detection is improved. We can conclude that the temporal subsampling leads to Doppler ambiguity. This is due to the overlap of the sidebands that becomes more important with the decline in PRF.

The explanation will be more convincing if we consider the problem of sampling and the well known Shannon theorem. Indeed, if one compares the two results in (a) and (b) where it was considered a PRF equal to $F_{Nyquist}$, and a PRF equal to ($F_{Nyquist}$)/2, respectively, although we note the aliasing phenomenon, expressed here by the appearance of sidelobe echoes of clutter.

This analysis can be addressed by using the spectral analysis and varying the PRF. Fig. 7 shows the minimum variance spectra of the received signal in the presence of two jammers for different values of PRF. There is the presence of aliasing of the clutter for high values of PRF. This translates into an increase of range of the covariance matrix as is illustrated in Fig. 8. We can therefore say that the choice of the PRF is essential to ensure good detection.

We can conclude that constant PRF leads to Doppler ambiguities and the clutter spectrum becomes ambiguous so that blind velocities occur.

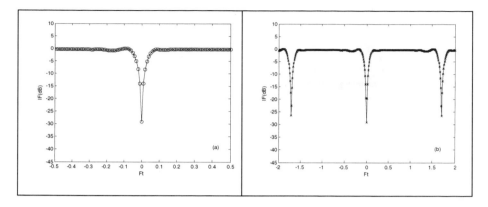

**Fig. 6.** Improvement Factor for the DFP with constant PRF for known and unknown R, $N = 8$, $M = 10$, $d / \lambda = 0.5$: (a) $PRF = 4.V_R / \lambda$, (b) $PRF = 2.V_R / \lambda$

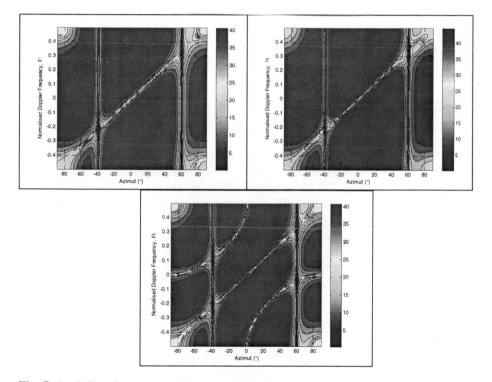

**Fig. 7.** Angle/Doppler spectrum for known R in the presence of two jammers at -40° et 60° with $JNR$=45 dB, $N$=8, $M$=10, CNR = 20 dB, $PRF = 8V_R / \lambda$, $PRF = 4.V_R / \lambda$, $PRF = 2V_R / \lambda$

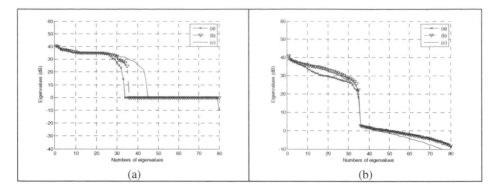

**Fig. 8.** Effect of the PRF on the eigenspectra of the covariance matrix $R$, with $JNR=35$ dB, $N=8$, $M=10$, $CNR = 30$ dB, $J=2$: (a) known $R$ ; (b) 2MN SMI

### 4.4 Influence of Dimension of Processor

Fig. 9 shows the eigenspectra for a known covariance matrix and for an SMI STAP covariance matrix. We note a clear distinction between the interferences subspace and noise subspace. An extension to Brenann's rule, for a number of an effective rank for the covariance matrix of a side-looking radar, has been derived recently in [10] and is given by r $=N+(\beta+J)(M-1)$, where J denotes the number of jammers. The high-input eigenvalue is about $\lambda max=CNR+ 10 \log(NM)(dB))$. This causes a slow convergence which is inherent to adaptive algorithms [15]. These values can actually be read directly from Fig. 9.

On the other hand, we consider three cases: a small number of data ($MN = 20$), average number of data ($MN = 40$), large amounts of data ($MN = 80$). It can be seen clearly from Fig. 10, that an increase in the number of data causes an increase in those of the eigenvalues and the power of the latter itself has increased.

To see the effect of the number of data on the detection of slow target, we consider an unambiguous scenario, $PRF = 4V_R / \lambda$ for $MN = 20$ and $MN = 80$. From Fig. 11, we note that the two notches are relatively thin, which means that the slow moving targets are detected. In addition, the increase in $MN$ leads to an increase in the detection capability, and thus a narrowing of the notch, while the cost of computations becomes increasingly high because it is linked to the number $MN$ x $MN$. However, undulations appear due to the increasing effects of clutter and noise.

### 4.5 Reduction of the Rank Using PC and SINR Metric Methods

It is important to consider the performances of the SINR for each method partially adaptive according to the rank. We notice from Fig. 12 that there is a strong degradation in the performances for a small rank. It is obvious that the method of the PC cannot attain the optimal SINR of exit until the rank is equal to the dimension of the eigenstructure of the noise subspace. The SINR metric is best when the rank is reduced below full dimension.

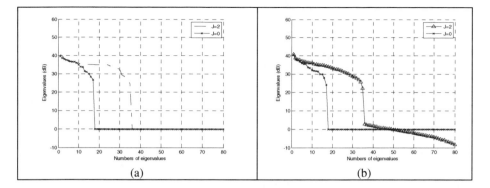

**Fig. 9.** Eigenspectra of the covariance matrix $R$: $JNR$=35 dB, $N$=8, $M$=10, $CNR$ = 30 dB (a) known $R$ ; (b) 2MN SMI

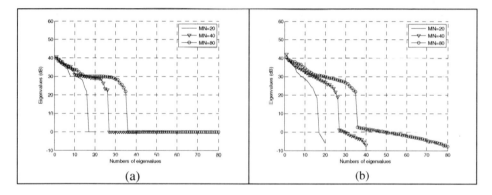

**Fig. 10.** Eigenspectra of the covariance matrix $R$: $JNR$=35 dB, $CNR$ = 30 dB (a) known $R$ ; (b) 2MN SMI

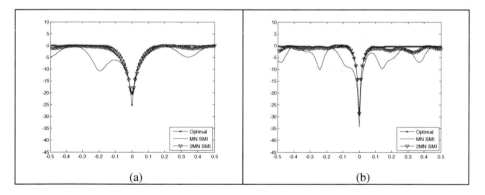

**Fig. 11.** Improvement Factor versus the normalized Doppler frequency for known $R$, $PRF = 4V_R / \lambda$ : (a) MN = 20, (b) MN = 80

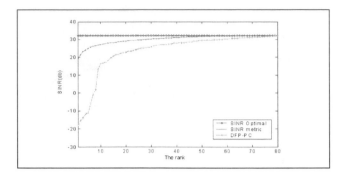

**Fig. 12.** SINR performance versus the rank

In Fig. 13, we show IF versus Ft for the DFP-PC, parameterized by rank $r$. We consider the unambiguous case, $PRF = 4V_R / \lambda$. The same detection results are obtained when $r = 20$ and $r = 40$, and thus to save calculation time, we choose $r=20$ as a good reduction of the rank. We observe that if the rank is very small, the slow moving targets will be removed with the clutter, and thus will not be detected. Similar findings were made for an ambiguous scenario. We can then say that we should not reduce up to the rank to very low values.

The same observations are made in the case of the SINR metric processor.

Fig. 14(a) shows that PC and 2MN SMI methods present acceptable detection performances.

We notice from Fig. 14(b) that there is a strong degradation in the performances for PC and SINR metric methods. Thus, to alleviate this problem of ambiguous notches, we consider the use of staggered PRF technique.

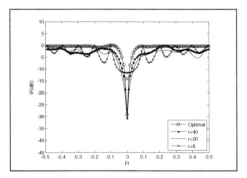

**Fig.13.** Improvement factor for the PC-DFP with different values of $r$ and with $PRF = 4.V_R / \lambda$

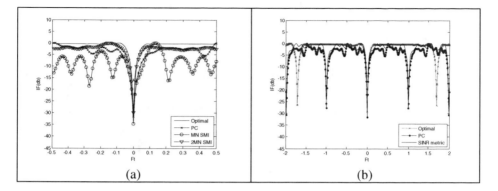

(a)    (b)

**Fig. 14.** Improvement Factor for the DFP with constant PRF for known and unknown R, $N = 8$, $M = 10$, $d / \lambda = 0.5$, $r$=20: (a) $PRF = 4.V_R / \lambda$, (b) $PRF = 2.V_R / \lambda$

### 4.6 Reduction of the Rank with Staggered PRF

Figures 15 and 16 show IF versus Ft with the quadratic change of PRF applied to the PC and SINR metric methods for the two cases of known and SMI method in an ambiguous scenario ( $PRF = 2.V_R / \lambda$ ). We note that the application of the change of the PRF removes the ambiguous notches clutter by leaving undulations in the bandwidth of the STAP filter for any values of the of PRF and number of ambiguous notches. The use of the change of PRF does not have any effect on the detection the slow targets. In addition that SMI method needs only MN snapshots to estimate the covariance matrix, a low number comparatively to the case of constant PRF.

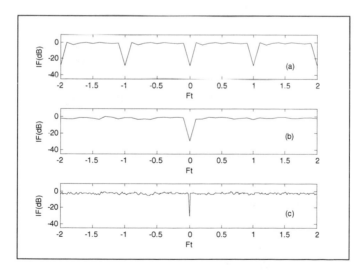

**Fig. 15.** Improvement Factor with PRF=2.$V_R$ /λ, for:(a)  DFP- SINR metric (b) DFP- SINR metric with quadratic change of *PRF* (c) MN SMI- SINR metric with quadratic change of *PRF*

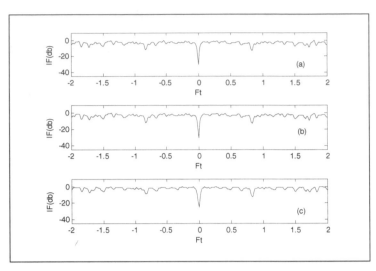

**Fig. 16.** Improvement Factor with PRF=$2.V_R/\lambda$, for: (a) DFP- PC (b) DFP- PC with quadratic change of *PRF* (c) MN SMI- PC with quadratic change of *PRF*

## 5 Conclusion

In this paper, we presented the fundamental concepts of space-time adaptive processing, STAP, while considering a direct form processor. The simulation results are discussed highlighting the influence of various parameters on the performance of radar detection of slow targets. It was shown that to have a good detection, it is recommended to select a PRF greater than or equal to the Nyquist frequency to avoid Doppler ambiguities and take ($d = \lambda/2$) to avoid the range ambiguities. Unfortunately, if radar uses a constant PRF, the clutter suppression will also lead to the suppression of moving target echoes with certain radial velocities, so-called blind velocities. Thus, increasing the PRF is useful for mitigating Doppler ambiguities, and reducing the PRF is useful for achieving unambiguous range. Choosing the PRF of a radar mode therefore involves a compromise between the unambiguous target velocity and the unambiguous range.

In addition, the results concerning the separation of subspace interference-noise can be exploited in algorithms for reducing the rank of the covariance matrix. The results of simulations showed that the reduction of rank has no effect on the detection of slow targets (the width of the notch does not vary) unless the rank is very small. We did the analysis using two methods: PC and SINR metric. The results showed that these methods allow a reduction in the computation time and a reduction of the rank at low values without affecting the detection of slow moving targets. However, some ambiguous notches persist in the bandwidth. To alleviate this problem, we applied the quadratic change of PRF. We showed that this method solves well the problem of ambiguities. We can summarize that Doppler ambiguities can be removed by PRF staggering. While, range ambiguities can be avoided by employing an array antenna with a vertical adaptivity. Also, it is shown that all the algorithms outperform SMI method when the covariance matrix is estimated from a data set with limited support.

# References

1. Ward, J.: Space-Time Adaptive Processing for airborne radar. Technical report 1015, Lincoln Laboratory MIT, USA (1994)
2. Klemm, R.: Space Time Adaptive Processing Principles and applications. The Institution of Electrical Engineers, London (1998)
3. Brennan, L.E., Reed, I.S.: Theory of radar. IEEE transactions on Aerospace and Electronics AES AES9(2), 237–252 (1973)
4. Brennan, L.E., et al.: Comparison of space-time adaptive processing approaches using experimental airborne radar data. In: Proceedings of the 1993 IEEE National Radar Conference, pp. 176–181 (1993)
5. Haimovich.: Eigencanceler. IEEE transactions on Aerospace and Electronics 32(2), 532–542 (1996)
6. Nguyen, H.: Robust Steering Vector Mismatch Techniques for reduced Rank Adaptive Array Signal Processing. PhD dissertation in Electrical and Computer Engineering, Virginia (2002)
7. Goldstein, J.S., Reed, I.S.: Theory of partially adaptive radar. In: Proceedings of the IEEE National Radar Conference IEEE Transactions on Aerospace and Electronics Systems, vol. 33(4), pp. 1309–1325 (1997)
8. Berger, S.D., Welsh, B.M.: Selecting a reduced-rank transformation for STAP, a direct form perspective. IEEE Transactions on Aerospace and Electronics Systems 35(2), 722–729 (1999)
9. Guerci, J.R., et al.: Optimal and adaptive reduced-rank STAP. IEEE Transactions on Aerospace and Electronics Systems 36(2), 647–663 (2000)
10. Richardson, J.G.: STAP covariance matrix structure and its impact on clutter plus jamming suppression solutions. Electronics Letters 37(2), 118–119 (2001)
11. Melvin, W.L.: A STAP Overview. IEEE A&E Systems Magazine 19(1), 19–35 (2004)
12. Klemm, R.: STAP with staggered PRF. In: 5th International Conference on Radar Systems (1991)
13. Dib, S., Barkat, M., Grimes, M.: Analyse du STAP avec valeurs propres et changement de PRF en présence d'une cible interférente. Research And Development Air defence Review (11), 10–16 (2004)
14. Dib, S., Barkat, Nicolas, J.M., Grimes, M.: A Reduced Rank STAP with Change of PRF. In: Proceedings of Eusipco, pp. 95–122 (2007)
15. Kamenetsky, M., Widrow, B.: A variable leaky LMS adaptive algorithm. In: Proceedings of the IEEE conference of the 38thAsilomar on Signals, Systems and Computers, vol. 1, pp. 125–128 (2004)

# Towards Improving the Functioning
# of CloudSim Simulator

Ghalem Belalem and Said Limam

Department of Computer Science, Faculty of Sciences,
University of Oran (ES Senia), PB 1524
El M'Naouer, Oran, Algeria (31000)
Ghalem1dz@gmail.com,
said7dias@hotmail.com

**Abstract.** Cloud computing has become a major force for change in how web design, configure, provision, and manage IT infrastructure. Instead of custom-provisioning individual systems or clusters, an architect or administrator is expected to have hundreds, or even thousands of resources under their control! A variety of approaches have emerged to do this. CloudSim enables seamless modeling, simulation, and experimentation of emerging Cloud computing infrastructures and application services. In the CloudSim simulator there are two fundamental problems: i) Lack of links between Datacenters, this lack of links will lead necessarily to a lack of communication between them and therefore no exchange or shared of any service or information with other datacenters. ii) No possibility to create a virtual machine in more Datacenters. In a first time, we propose to use a ring topology to allow the exchange and the and sharing of information and services between different Datacenter, and in the second time improving the method of creating virtual machines, and by consequence to allow the creation of a virtual machine in several Datacenter, which improves fault tolerance in this type of environment.

**Keywords:** Grid computing, Cloud computing, CloudSim Simulator, Resources management.

## 1 Introduction

The term "cloud computing" comes from a metaphor for the Internet ("the cloud") combined with "computing" which reflects purpose of this paradigm. Cloud computing is also an analogy to well known and mature technologies such as grid computing or high performance computing. In this way, it suggests that cloud computing introduces a new way of making computations. Clouds are sometimes perceived as marketing hype and a way of integrating and selling technologies developed so far such as grid computing, virtualization, service provision, etc. At most they are an evolution of these technologies with added focus on simplicity and usability. Additionally, they usually propose a certain business model. The main reason of this is the fact that the emergence of clouds was led by vendors and

V. Snasel, J. Platos, and E. El-Qawasmeh (Eds.): ICDIPC 2011, Part II, CCIS 189, pp. 258–267, 2011.
© Springer-Verlag Berlin Heidelberg 2011

providers who advertised their offers as a cloud computing service rather than by academia and research communities (as it was in case of Grids) [1].

Cloud computing may be viewed as a resource available as a service for virtual data centers, but cloud computing and virtual data centers are not the same. For example, consider Amazon's S3 Storage Service. This is a data storage service designed for use across the Internet (i.e., the cloud). It is designed to make web-scale computing easier for developers. According to Amazon: Amazon S3 provides a simple web services interface that can be used to store and retrieve any amount of data, at any time, from anywhere on the web. It gives any developer access to the same highly scalable, reliable, fast, inexpensive data storage infrastructure that Amazon uses to run its own global network of web sites. The service aims to maximize benefits of scale and to pass those benefits on to developers [2].

The paper begins by presenting cloud computing an area of rapid evolution. Second, it presents generalized and extensible simulation framework: CloudSim. This simulator enables seamless modeling, simulation, and experimentation of emerging Cloud computing infrastructures and application services [10]. Third, we present our broker policy to deal some problems encountered in CloudSim version b1.0. In section 5, we evaluate the performance of policy presented and report the results obtained finally we conclude the paper.

## 2 Cloud Computing

The cloud is not simply the latest fashionable term for the Internet. Though the Internet is a necessary foundation for the cloud, the cloud is something more than the Internet. The cloud is where you go to use technology when you need it, for as long as you need it, and not a minute more. You do not install anything on your desktop, and you do not pay for the technology when you are not using it [3]. According to the IEEE Computer Society Cloud Computing is:

*"A paradigm in which information is permanently stored in servers on the Internet and cached temporarily on clients that include desktops, entertainment centers, table computers, notebooks, wall computers, handhelds, etc."*

*"Cloud Computing is a type of parallel and distributed system that consists of a collection of computers interconnected, virtualized and presented as a single processing unit based on a SLA with a negotiation mechanism between the service provider and the consumer of this service"* [4].

Cloud computing is typically divided into three levels of service offerings: Software as a Service (SaaS), Platform as a Service (PaaS), and Infrastructure as a service (IaaS). These levels support virtualization and management of differing levels of the solution stack [5].

**Software as a Service (SaaS)**

**SaaS** is a type of cloud computing that delivers applications through a browser to thousands of customers using a multiuser architecture. The focus for SaaS is on the end user as opposed to managed services (described below). For the customer, there are no up-front investment costs in servers or software licensing. For the service provider, with just one product to maintain, costs are relatively low compared to the costs incurred with a conventional hosting model. An example of this model is Google Apps, which provides online access via a web browser to the most common office and business applications used today, all the while keeping the software and user data stored on Google servers.

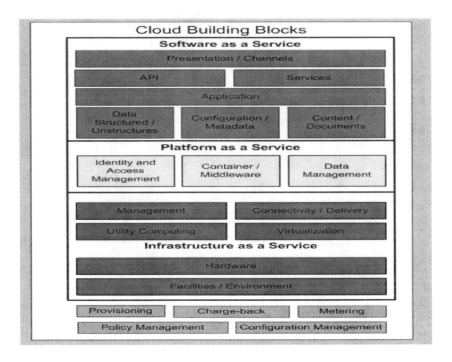

**Fig. 1.** Oracle private cloud [5]

## Platform-as-a-Service (PaaS)

**PaaS** is yet another variation of SaaS. Sometimes referred to simply as web services in the cloud, PaaS is closely related to SaaS but delivers a platform from which to work rather than an application to work with. These service providers offer application programming interfaces (APIs) that enable developers to exploit functionality over the Internet, rather than delivering full-blown applications. This variation of cloud computing delivers development environments to programmers, analysts, and software engineers as a service. An example of this model is the Google App Engine. According to Google [6]., "Google App Engine makes it easy to build an application that runs reliably, even under heavy load and with large amounts of data".

**Infrastructure-as-a-Service (IaaS)**

**IaaS** is the delivery of computer infrastructure (typically a platform virtualization environment) as a service. Rather than purchasing servers, software, data center space or network equipment, clients instead buy those resources as a fully outsourced service. The service is typically billed on a utility computing basis and amount of resources consumed (and therefore the cost) will typically reflect the level of activity. It is an evolution of virtual private server offerings [7].

# 3  CloudSim Toolkit

The recent efforts to design and develop Cloud technologies focus on defining novel methods, policies and mechanisms for efficiently managing Cloud infrastructures. To test these newly developed methods and policies, researchers need tools that allow them to evaluate the hypothesis prior to real deployment in an environment where one can reproduce tests. Especially in the case of Cloud computing, where access to the infrastructure incurs payments in real currency, simulation-based approaches offer significant benefits, as it allows Cloud developers to test performance of their provisioning and service delivery policies in repeatable and controllable environment free of cost, and to tune the performance bottlenecks before deploying on real Clouds.

CloudSim is a new, generalized, and extensible simulation framework that enables seamless modeling, simulation, and experimentation of emerging Cloud computing infrastructures and application services.

CloudSim offers the following novel features: (i) support for modeling and simulation of large scale Cloud computing infrastructure, including data centers on a single physical computing node; and (ii) a self-contained platform for modeling data centers, service brokers, scheduling, and allocations policies.

Figure 2 shows the conception of the CloudSim toolkit [8]. At the lowest layer, we find the SimJava [9] that implements the core functionalities required for higher-level simulation such as queuing and processing of events, creation of system components (services, host, Datacenter, broker, virtual machines), communication between components, and management of the simulation clock.

In the next layer follows the GridSim toolkit that support high level components for modeling multiple Grid components Such as networks, resources, and information services. The CloudSim is implemented as layer by extending the core functionality of the GridSim layer. CloudSim provides support for modeling and simulation of virtualized Datacenters environments such as management interfaces for VMs, memory, storage, and bandwidth. CloudSim layer manages the creation and execution of core entities (VMs, hosts, Datacenters, application) during the simulation period. This layer handle the provisioning of hosts to VMs based on user requests, managing application execution, and dynamic monitoring. The final layer in the simulation stack is the User Code that exposes configuration functionality for hosts (number of machines, their specification and so on), applications (number of tasks and their requirements), VMs, number of users and their application types, and broker scheduling policies. A Cloud application developer can write an application configurations and Cloud scenarios at this layer to perform a cloud computing scenario simulations [1, 10].

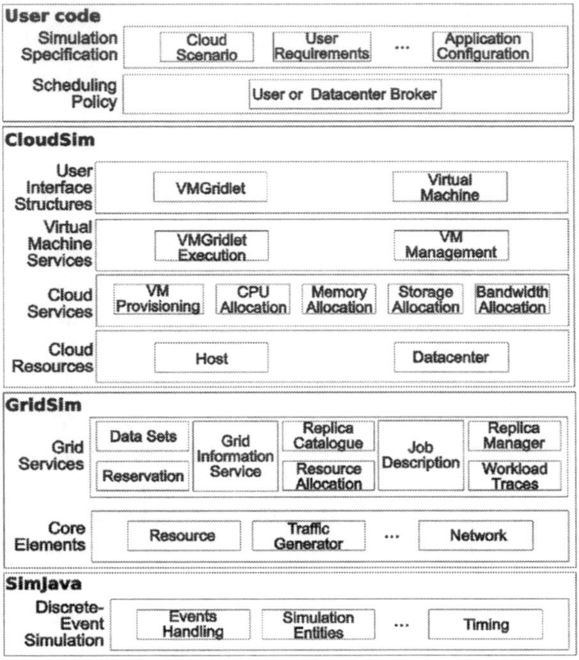

**Fig. 2.** CloudSim Architecture [4]

## 4   Proposed Approach

During the operation of the Simulator CloudSim in our research work for resources management, several problems and inconstancies were identified.

Problems identified in CloudSim Version 1 are:

- When we try to create multiple VMs in several data center, some VMs cannot be created due to a saturation of resource in data centers and cloudlets assigned to this virtual machines not created are lost.

  The creation of VMs in the data center is done sequentially. We send as much vms as possible for this datacenter before trying the next one. when the datacenter is saturated, we try to create in the next and so on, until no longer have DataCenter available, the message "Creation of VM #  __ failed in DataCenter__" appear and cloudlets submitted to these VMs are not run (even after the creation of VM).

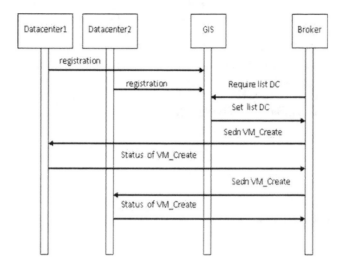

**Fig. 3.** Sequence Diagram of CloudSim before optimization

- There is no link between Datacenters. This lack of links will lead necessarily to a lack of communication between them and therefore no exchange of any service or information on the load of each for a possible load balancing policy. Our solution was to create a "ring topology" of the data center (each datacenter knows his predecessor and his successor).

  Given that each data center has a number of resources available and ready to be dynamically allocated to each request, this number is still limited, which we refer to the first problem. Skip to next Datacenter for allocation of other resources for other VMs, not necessarily the most optimal or most economical for the owner of the data center,

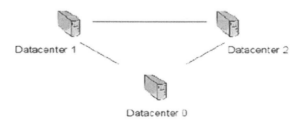

**Fig. 4.** Ring Topology

The main goal for him is to use the Max resources to maximize its gain (or benefit). Indeed, there may have resources already available in the data center, but not enough to create a VM with the number requested.

Our solution is to exploit these resources that are more or less wasted, to gather them from different data center and use it to create VMs that this time are on two or

more data center. This solution is not possible if there are no links between the
different datacenters that can exchange services and information on these VMs. We
have defined for this a search method; this method calculates the number of free
resources in each datacenters. In a possible creation of VM fails, an event is triggered
to call *search method* with a calculation of "threshold" minimum to make a decision
of whether or not a particular data center.

It was considered necessary to take into account a minimum threshold to exceed
for eventual decision to take this or that DataCenter for allocated a virtual machine for
three reasons:

- To minimize the cost of transfer due to exchanges of different services for a
  single VM allocated in several Datacenters
- To reduce the number of Datacenters allocated to a VM: we will take only
  datacenters with a large number of resources available.
- To minimize run time.

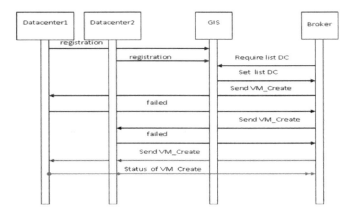

**Fig. 5.** Sequence Diagram of CloudSim Optimized

The following figures (see Fig 6.a, Fig 6.b, and Fig 6.d) show an example of
simulation for an environment containing four datacenters with 4 hosts each, we try to
create five VMs with the following characteristics:

| VMID | Number Of CPUs |
|:----:|:--------------:|
| 1 | 5 |
| 2 | 2 |
| 3 | 4 |
| 4 | 3 |
| 5 | 1 |

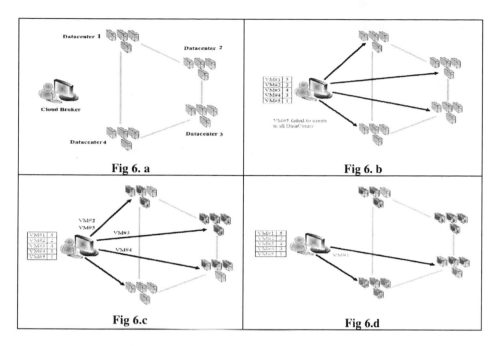

**Fig. 6.** Example of simulation with four datacenters

# 5 Simulation Study

In the first simulation we fixed the Number of datacenters at 6 with 5 host each; the host contain one PE, the number of processor required to virtual machine is 3, we have vary the number of virtual machine that want to create. As the number of virtual machines increase as the number of creation of VMs failed increase and rejection of cloudlet submitted to these VMs increase. The number of virtual machine that can be simultaneously created is 10 and we can create only 6 VMs so we have 12 PEs not used (40 % of resources not used).

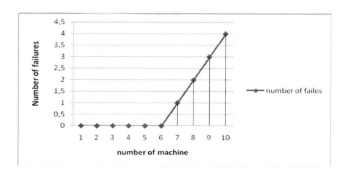

**Fig. 7.** Number of failures in CloudSim

In the second simulation, we fixed the number of datacenter at 15, each datacenter contain 5 hosts with on PE and the description of virtual machines that want to create is given in the following tables:

| VMID | 1 | 2 | 3 | 4 | 5 | 6 | 7 | 8 | 9 | 10 | 11 |
|---|---|---|---|---|---|---|---|---|---|---|---|
| Number of cpus | 3 | 4 | 3 | 4 | 4 | 2 | 3 | 3 | 4 | 4 | 4 |

| VMID | 12 | 13 | 14 | 15 | 16 | 17 | 18 | 19 | 20 | 21 | 22 |
|---|---|---|---|---|---|---|---|---|---|---|---|
| Number of cpus | 2 | 4 | 3 | 3 | 3 | 4 | 3 | 3 | 4 | 3 | 3 |

Figure 8 we show the number of failures for the simple version and our extension, And in Figure 9 we present the resource waste (free resources not used) for both versions.

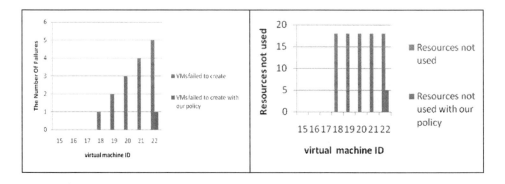

**Fig. 8.** Number of VMs failed to create          **Fig. 9.** Number of waste-resources

The results show that our policy attains much better performance and better resources utilization than the policy used in the version 1. The cases to have VMs failed is not excluded, but significantly reduced.

## 6 Conclusions

The recent efforts to design and develop Cloud technologies focus on defining novel methods, policies and mechanisms for efficiently managing Cloud infrastructures. The principal objective that we aimed at solving; it is the satisfaction of the users, while avoiding rejecting some requests subjected by the customers of Cloud Computing. We have developed own broker policy to create virtual machine in one or more datacenters. We also introduced the links between datacenters to exchange services and information on virtual machines; we use simulation to compare the performance of our proposed policy with the policy version B.0.5 of CloudSim. The simulation results demonstrated that: our policy leads to better performance and better resources utilization.

Several future tracks can be the subject of extension of this work in our laboratory. We can quote: i) To equip the first approach by an agent which makes it possible to select most suitable Datacenter for the assumption of responsibility of the requests; ii) To extend the second approach by a module of balancing enters the various files associated with Cloudlets of Datacenters; iii) Integrating semantic aspect in the cloud can improve performance and quality of service [15], something that already proved in several works in the semantic grid [12,14]; iv) To use a system of multi-agents for negotiation enters the agents with an aim of migrating Cloudlets of Datacenter towards another; v) Improving and optimizing the economic models used for resource management in CloudSim as the business model of English auction [11] and the double auction economic model [13].

# References

1. Rittinghouse, J.-W., Ransome, J.-F.: Cloud Computing: Implementation, Management, and Security. CRC Press Taylor & Francis Group (2009)
2. Amazon Simple Storage Service (Amazon S3), http://aws.amazon.com/s3/
3. Reese, G.: Cloud Application Architectures (April 2009)
4. Buyya, R., Ranjan, R., Calheiros, R.N.: Modeling and Simulation of Scalable Cloud Computing Environments and the CloudSim Toolk
5. Oracle White Paper.: Architectural Strategies for Cloud Computing (August. 2009)
6. Google App Engine, http://code.google.com/intl/fr/appengine/docs/whatisgoogleappengine.html
7. Cloud computing. From Wikipedia, http://en.wikipedia.org/wiki/Cloud_computing
8. Buyya, R., Murshed, M.: GridSim: A Toolkit for the Modeling and Simulation of Distributed Resource Management and Scheduling for Grid Computing. The Journal of Concurrency and Computation: Practice and Experience (CCPE) 14(13-15), 1175–1220 (2002)
9. Howell, F., Mcnab, R.: SimJava:A discrete event simulation library for java. In: Proceedings of the first International Conference on Web-Based Modeling and Simulation (1998)
10. Belalem, G., Tayeb, F.Z., Zaoui, W.: Approaches to Improve the Resources Management in the Simulator CloudSim. In: Zhu, R., Zhang, Y., Liu, B., Liu, C. (eds.) ICICA 2010. LNCS, vol. 6377, pp. 189–196. Springer, Heidelberg (2010)
11. Badica, A., Badica, C.: Formalizing Agent-Based English Auctions Using Finite State Process Algebra. Journal of Universal Computer Science 14(7), 1118–1135 (2008)
12. Flahive, A., Apduhan, B.O., Rahayu, J.W., Taniar, D.: Large scale ontology tailoring and simulation in the Semantic Grid Environment. International Journal of Metadata, Semantics and Ontologies (IJMSO) 1(4), 265–281 (2006)
13. Joita, L., Rana, O.F., Gray, W.A., Miles, J.C.: A Double Auction Economic Model for Grid Services. In: Danelutto, M., Vanneschi, M., Laforenza, D. (eds.) Euro-Par 2004. LNCS, vol. 3149, pp. 409–416. Springer, Heidelberg (2004)
14. Kotsis, G., Taniar, D., Khalil Ibrahim, I., Pardede, E.: Information Integration on Web based Applications and Services. Journal of Universal Computer Science (J. UCS) 15(10), 2026–2027 (2009)
15. Mika, P., Tummarello, G.: Web Semantic in the Clouds. IEEE Intelligent Systems Journal 23(5), 82–87 (2008)

# Towards New Data Access Control Technique Based on Multi Agent System Architecture for Cloud Computing

Amir Mohamed Talib, Rodziah Atan,
Rusli Abdullah, and Masrah Azrifah Azmi Murad

Faculty of Computer Science & IT, Information System Department,
University Putra Malaysia, 43400 UPM,
Serdang, Selangor, Malaysia
ganawa53@yahoo.com,
(rodziah,rusli,masrah)@fsktm.upm.edu.my

**Abstract.** With the rise of the era of "cloud computing", concerns about "Security" continue to increase. Cloud computing environments impose new challenges on access control techniques due to the growing scale and dynamicity of hosts within the cloud infrastructure; we proposed Multi-Agent System (MAS) architecture. This architecture consists of two agents: Cloud Service Provider Agent (CSPA) and Cloud Data Confidentiality Agent (CDConA). CSPA provides a graphical interface to the cloud user that facilitates the access to the services offered by the system. CDConA provides each cloud user by definition and enforcement expressive and flexible access structure as a logic formula over cloud data file attributes. This new access control is named as Formula-Based Cloud Data Access Control (FCDAC). A prototype of our proposed FCDAC will be designed using Prometheus Methodology and implemented using the Java Agent Development Framework Security (JADE-S).

**Keywords:** Cloud Computing, Cloud Data Storage, Cloud Service Provider, Cloud Data Access Control, Multi-Agent System and Confidentiality.

## 1  Introduction

Cloud computing describes applications that are extended to be accessible through the Internet. These cloud applications use large data centers or cloud data storage (CDS) and powerful servers that host Web applications and Web services. Anyone with a suitable Internet connection and a standard browser can access a cloud application. Cloud computing consists of multiple cloud computing service providers (CSPs). In terms of software and hardware, a cloud system is composed of many types of computers, storage devices, communications equipment, and software systems running on such devices.

Cloud storage is composed of thousands of storage devices clustered by network, distributed file systems and other storage middleware to provide cloud storage service for cloud users. The typical structure of cloud storage includes storage resource pool, distributed file system, service level agreements (SLAs), and service interfaces, etc. Globally, they can be divided by physical and logical functions boundaries and

V. Snasel, J. Platos, and E. El-Qawasmeh (Eds.): ICDIPC 2011, Part II, CCIS 189, pp. 268–279, 2011.
© Springer-Verlag Berlin Heidelberg 2011

relationships to provide more compatibilities and interactions. Cloud storage is tending to combined with cloud security, which will provide more robust security [1].

Cloud Data access control issue is mainly related to security policies provided to the users while accessing the data. In a typical scenario, a small business organization can use a cloud provided by some other provider for carrying out its business processes. This organization will have its own security policies based on which each employee can have access to a particular set of data. The security policies may entitle some considerations wherein some of the employees are not given access to certain amount of data. These security policies must be adhered by the cloud to avoid intrusion of data by unauthorized users [2, 3, 4].

Access control regulates accesses to resources by principals. It is one of the most important aspects of the security of a system. A protection state or policy contains all information needed by a reference monitor to enforce access control. The syntax used to represent a policy is called an access control model. In FCDAC, principals are called cloud users. Cloud users get permissions to access resources via membership in roles. We present a new way to realize FCDAC in JADE-S. Our approach focuses not only of providing a cloud user by a user name and password but by define and enforce expressive and flexible access structure for each cloud user as a logic formula over cloud data file attributes.

A multi-agent system (MAS) consists of a number of agents interacting with each other, usually through exchanging messages across a network. The agents in such a system must be able to interact in order to achieve their design objectives, through cooperating, negotiating and coordinating with other agents. The agents may exhibit selfish or benevolent behavior. Selfish agents ask for help from other agents if they are overloaded and never offer help. For example, agents serving VIP (Very Important Person) cloud users for CSP service never help other agents for the same service. Benevolent agents always provide help to other agents because they consider system benefit is the priority. For example, agents serving normal cloud users for CSP service are always ready to help other agents to complete their tasks.

The main contribution of this paper is to introduce the first provably-secure and practical FCDAC that provide access structure of each cloud user by defining it as a logic formula over cloud data file attribute.

In this paper, in section 2 we present a discussion of the related works. Section 3 provides an overview of our research methodology. Section 4 describes our proposed MAS architecture. In, section 5 presents some concluding remarks.

## 2   Related Works

Many existing works close to our work can be found in the areas of "access control of outsourced data" Kallahalla et al [5] proposed Plutus as a cryptographic file system to secure file storage on untrusted servers, Goh et al [6] proposed SiRiUS which is layered over existing file systems such as NFS but provides end-to-end security, Ateniese et al [7] proposed a secure distributed storage scheme based on proxy re-encryption. Specifically, the data owner encrypts blocks of content with symmetric content keys. In [8], Vimercati et al proposed a solution for securing data storage on untrusted servers based on key derivation methods [9]. In this proposed scheme, each file is encrypted with a symmetric key and each user is assigned a secret key.

KAoS uses DAML as the basis for representing and reasoning about policies within Web Services, Grid Computing, and multi-agent system platforms [10]. KAoS also exploits ontology for representing and reasoning about domains describing organizations of human, agent, and other computational actors [11]. Rei is a deontic logic based policy language that is grounded in a semantic representation of policies in RDF-S [12]. However, developers of KAoS augured that the pure OWL based method has difficulty in definition of some types of policy [11].

An access control system is typically described in three ways: access control policies, access control models and access control mechanisms [13]. Policy defines the high level rules according to which access control must be regulated. Model provides a formal representation of the ACPs. Mechanism defines the low level functions that implement the controls imposed by the policy and formally stated in the model.

Access Control Policies can be generally divided into three main policy categories: Discretionary Access Control (DAC), Mandatory Access Control (MAC), and Role-Based Access Control (RBAC). Early DAC models, such as the access control matrix model [14] and the HRU (Harrison–Ruzzo–Ullman) model [15], provide a basic framework for describing DAC policy. In these models, it is the users' discretion to pass their privileges on to other users, leaving DAC policies vulnerable to Trojan Horse attacks [13]. The lattice-based multilevel security policy [16], policies represented by the Bell–LaPadula model [17].

## 3  Research Methodology

This research shall be carried out in five steps that defined as A Secure System Development Life Cycle (SecSDLC) as illustrated in Fig. 1. [18]:

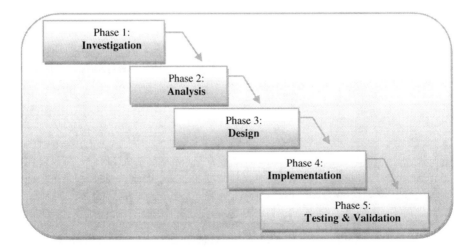

**Fig. 1.** Secure System Development Life Cycle (SecSDLC)

## 3.1 Secure System Development Life Cycle (SecSDLC) Phases

### 3.1.1 Phase 1 - Investigation

This phase defined the processes and goals, and documents them in the program security policies and its attributes. Table 1 shows the investigation phase that proposed data security policies, attributes and its definition.

**Table 1.** Investigation Phase

| DATA SECURITY POLICY | DATA SECURITY POLICY ATTRIBUTES | DESCRIPTION |
|---|---|---|
| Confidentiality | Formula-Based Cloud Data Access Control (FCDAC). | Ensuring that data is not disclosed to unauthorized persons. |

The definitional borders of cloud computing are much debated today. Cloud computing involves the sharing or storage by cloud users of their own information on remote servers owned or operated by others and accesses through the Internet or other connections. Cloud computing services exist in many variations, including data storage sites, video sites, tax preparation sites, personal health record websites and many more. The entire contents of a cloud user's storage device may be stored with a single CSP or with many CSPs. Some of the findings related to the confidentiality issues are:

- Cloud computing has significant implications for the privacy of personal information as well as for the confidentiality of business and governmental information.
- A cloud user's confidentiality risks vary significantly with the terms of service and privacy policy established by the CSP.
- For some types of information and some categories of cloud computing users, confidentiality rights, obligations, and status may change when a cloud user discloses information to a CSP.
- Disclosure and remote storage may have adverse consequences for the legal status of protections for personal or business information.
- The location of information in the cloud may have significant effects on the privacy and confidentiality protections of information and on the privacy obligations of those who process or store the information.
- Information in the cloud may have more than one legal location at the same time with differing legal consequences.
- Laws could oblige a cloud CSP to examine cloud user records for evidence of criminal activity and other matters.
- Legal uncertainties make it difficult to assess the status of information in the cloud as well as the privacy and confidentiality protections available to cloud users.

### 3.1.2  Phase 2 - Analysis

In this phase, our system requirements, components and performance will be analysis using adversary model [19, 3]. We will also evaluate the performance of our secure MAS architecture via implementation of the proposed agents type (Agent Agency). The results of this analysis will be described based on Cloud Data Security Adversary Analysis Approach that considers two types of adversary with different levels of capability as illustrated in Fig. 2.

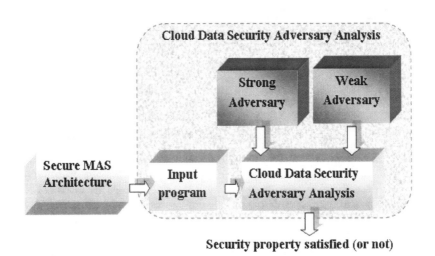

**Fig. 2.** Cloud Data Security Adversary Analysis Approach

> *Weak Adversary:* The adversary is interested in corrupting the user's CDS stored on individual servers. Once a server is comprised, an adversary can pollute the original CDS by modifying or introducing its own fraudulent cloud data to prevent the original cloud data from being retrieved by the cloud user.
> *Strong Adversary:* This is the worst case scenario, in which we assume that the adversary can compromise all the cloud servers so that it can intentionally modify the CDS as long as they are internally consistent. In fact, this is equivalent to the case where all servers are colluding together to hide a cloud data loss or corruption incident.

### 3.1.3  Phase 3 - Design

To ensure the security for CDS under the aforementioned secure MAS architecture, we aim to design efficient mechanisms for confidentially of cloud user's data and achieve the following goal:

> ✓ *Confidentially:* to define and enforce expressive and flexible access structure for each cloud user by defines a logic formula over cloud data file attributes.

MAS design shall be specified to determine the types of agents, events, protocols and agent capabilities, using the Prometheus methodology [20]. The sections below go through each of Prometheus' three phases in more detail and will discuss the notations used by the methodology as well as some specific techniques.

The Prometheus methodology consists of three phases:

❖ *System Specification*: where the system is specified using goals (see Fig. 3.) and scenarios; the system's interface to its environment is described in terms of actions, percepts and external data; and functionalities are defined.

❖ *Architectural design:* where agent types are identified; the system's overall structure is captured in a system overview diagram; and scenarios are developed into interaction protocols.

❖ *Detailed design:* where the details of each agent's internals are developed and defined in terms of capabilities, data, events and plans; process diagrams are used as a stepping stone between interaction protocols and plans.

Each of these phases includes models that focus on the dynamics of the system, (graphical) models that focus on the structure of the system or its components, and textual descriptor forms that provide the details for individual entities.

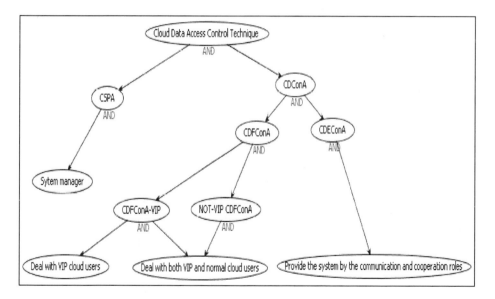

**Fig. 3.** Design Goals

### 3.1.4  Phase 4 - Implementation

Our system architecture will be developed using FIPA compliant JADE-S agent framework version 2.

JADE (Java Agent DEvelopment framework) is a FIPA compliant software framework fully implemented in the Java programming language, which simplifies the implementation of MASs. The platform can be seen as a middleware (Fig. 4) providing a set of useful tools that support the debugging and deployment phase [21, 22, 24].

JADE-S is formed by the combination of the standard version of JADE with the JADE security plug-in [23]. JADE-S includes security features such as user/agent authentication, authorization and secure communication between agents into the same platform. With more details:

- Authentication: a user must be authenticated by providing a username and password, to be able to own or perform actions on a component of the platform. Only authenticated users can own AMS, DF, containers and other agents;
- Authorization: JADE-S uses the concept of Principal as an abstraction for a user account, an agent or a container. A Principal must be authorized by the Java Security Manager. The Security Manager allows or denies the action according to the JADE platform's policy;
- Permissions and Policies: Permission is an object that describes the possibility of performing an action on a certain resource such as a piece of code, but also executes that code. A policy specifies which permissions are available for various principals;
- Certificates and Certification Authority: the Certification Authority (CA) is the entity that signs all the certificates for the whole platform, using a public/private key pair (PKI infrastructure).
- Delegation: this mechanism allows the "lending" of permissions to an agent. Besides the identity certificate, an agent can also own other certificates given to it by other agents;
- Secure Communication: communication between agents on different containers/hosts, are performed using the Secure Socket Layer (SSL) protocol. This enables a solid protection against malicious attempts of packet sniffing.

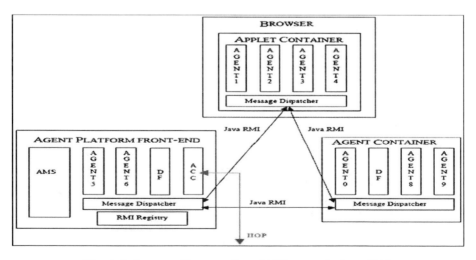

**Fig. 4.** Software architecture of one JADE agent platform ([21])

### 3.1.5  Phase 5 - Testing and Validation

To test and validate our system, we have asked a permission of the Cloud Service Provider (CSP) of Malaysian Institute of Microelectronic Systems (MIMOS) to allow us to test and validate our secure MAS architecture in their cloud computing platform.

In order to test and validate our MAS architecture against the scale of the CDS system, we will measure the times required for the agents to travel around different number of cloud users before and after implementing our MAS technique based on the linearly over the Round Trip Time (RTT) for each agent.

## 4   Proposed MAS Architecture

The MAS architecture consists of two agents: Cloud Service Provider Agent (CSPA) and Cloud Data Confidentiality Agent (CDConA). CSPA interact with the cloud users to fulfill their interests. CDConA provides a Cloud Service Provider (CSP) by definition and enforcement expressive and flexible access structure for each cloud user.

### 4.1  Cloud Service Provider Agent (CSPA)

Is the users' intelligent interface to the system and allow the cloud users to interact with the security service environment. The CSPA provides graphical interfaces to the cloud user for interactions between the system and the cloud user. CSPA act in the system under the behaviour of CSP. It is the only agent that can execute outside the main container of the platform and make remote requests through cloud server. CSPA has the following responsibilities as stated in Table 2.

**Table 2.** Responsibilities of CSPA.

| Agent Name | Responsibilities |
|---|---|
| Cloud Service Provider Agent (CSPA) | ➢ Provide the security service task according to the authorized service level agreements (SLAs) and the original message content sent by the CDConA. |
| | ➢ Receive the security reports and/or alarms from the rest of other agents to respect. |
| | ➢ Monitor specific activities concerning a part of the CDS or a particular cloud user. |
| | ➢ Translate the attack in terms of goals. |
| | ➢ Display the security policies specified by the CSP and the rest of the agents. |
| | ➢ Designing user interfaces that prevent the input of invalid cloud data. |
| | ➢ Creating security reports/ alarm systems. |

## 4.2   Cloud Data Confidentiality Agent (CDConA)

This agent facilitates the security policy of Confidentiality for CDS. Main responsibility of this agent is to provide a CDS by new access control rather than the existing access control lists of identification, authorization and authentication. This agent provides a CSP to define and enforce expressive and flexible access structure for each cloud user. Specifically, the access structure of each cloud user is defined as a logic formula over cloud data file attributes, and is able to represent any desired cloud data file set. This new access control is named as Formula-Based Cloud Data Access Control (FCDAC). This agent is also notifies CSPA in case of any fail caused of the techniques above by sending security reports and/or alarms.

There are two different types of CDConA agents, namely: Cloud Data Flexible Confidentiality Agent (CDFConA) and Cloud Data Expressive Confidentiality Agent (CDEConA). The CDFConA acts as a dispatching center, with the following advantages. Firstly, the CDFConA is the unique access point where authorization agents can contact the CDConA. Secondly, CDFConA acts as the exclusive resource access entry. This makes the SPAs are only able to access the cloud data file via CDFConA.

CDFConA provides cloud users with different security services, such as symmetric encryption/decryption and PKI encryption/decryption. CDFConA is divided into two types of agent based on the exhibited behavior. The first is CDFConA-VIP, which has selfish behavior and only serves for VIP (Very Important Person) cloud users. The second is NOT-VIP CDFConA, which has cooperative behavior and serves for both VIP cloud users and normal cloud users. For example, if CDFConA-VIP agent is overloaded, it sends help request to the first available NOT-VIP CDFConA agent. If this NOT-VIP CDFConA agent is unable to provide the help to CDFConA-VIP agent, the CDFConA-VIP sends the same help request to the next available NOT-VIP CDFConA agent. CDFConA-VIP agents keep sending the same request for help until one of the NOT-VIP CDFConA accepts or it is not overloaded. NOT-VIP CDFConA agents also take the same action as CDFConA-VIP when they are overloaded. However, NOT-VIP CDFConA agent only has knowledge about other NOT-VIP CDFConA agents, but not CDFConA-VIP agents.

### 4.2.1   Cloud Data Flexible Confidentiality Agent (CDFConA)
The architecture of CDFConA consists of five modules, as shown in Fig. 5. Cloud Communication Module provides the agent with the capability to exchange information with other agents, including the CDEConA and CSPA. Cloud Register Module facilitates the registration function for CDConA. Cloud Request Management Module allows the agent to act as the request-dispatching center. Cloud Resource Management Module manages the usage of the cloud resources. Cloud Reasoning Module is the brain of the CDConA. When the request management module and resource management module receive requests, they pass those requests to reasoning module by utilizing the information obtained from the knowledge base and the Confidentiality policy rule.

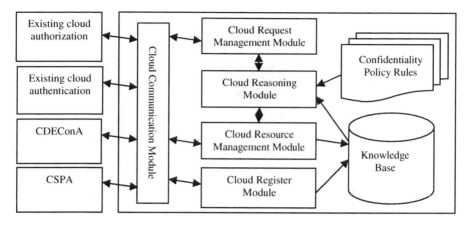

**Fig. 5.** CDFConA Architecture

### 4.2.2 Cloud Data Expressive Confidentiality Agent (CDEConA)

The architecture of the CDEConA consists of two modules, as shown in Fig. 6. *Cloud Communication Module* provides the agent with the capability to exchange information with CSPA and CDFConA. *Cloud Cooperation Module* provides the agent with the following mechanisms. If the CDEConA is registered as CDFConA-VIP it asks for help when it is overloaded. If the CDEConA is registered as NOT-VIP CDFConA, it always offers help to other CDEConAs when it is not overloaded.

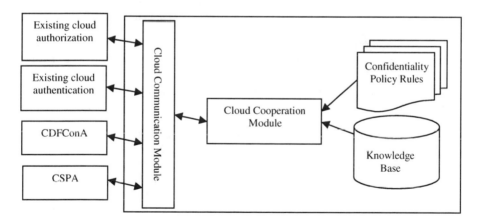

**Fig. 6.** CDEConA Architecture

## 5 Conclusions

This paper proposed a multi agent system for secure cloud data storage. The architecture consists of two types of agents: Cloud Service Provider Agent (CSPA) and Cloud Data Confidentiality Agent (CDConA). CSPA provides a graphical interface to the cloud user that facilitates the access to the services offered by the system. CDConA provides each cloud user by definition and enforcement expressive and flexible access structure as a logic formula over cloud data file attributes. Formula-Based Cloud Data Access Control (FCDAC) is proposed to meet the need of access control in the era of cloud computing by providing enforcement expressive and flexible access structure as a logic formula over cloud data file attributes.

# References

1. Zeng, W., Zhao, Y., Ou, K., Song, W.: Research on Cloud Storage Architecture and Key Technologies, pp. 1044–1048. ACM, New York (2009)
2. Blaze, M., Feigenbaum, J.: The Role of Trust Management in Distributed Systems Security. In: Ryan, M. (ed.) Secure Internet Programming. LNCS, vol. 1603, pp. 185–210. Springer, Heidelberg (1999)
3. Bowers, K.D., Juels, A., Oprea, A.: HAIL: A High-Availability and Integrity Layer for Cloud Storage. In: Cryptology ePrint Archive, pp. 1–8 (2008), http://eprint.iacr.org/
4. Kormann, D., Rubin, A.: Risks of the Passport Single Sign on Protocol. Computer Networks 33(1-6), 51–58 (2000)
5. Kallahalla, M., Riedel, E., Swaminathan, R., Wang, Q., Fu, K.: Plutus: Scalable Secure File Sharing on Untrusted Storage, pp. 29–42. USENIX Association (2003)
6. Goh, E.J., Shacham, H., Modadugu, N., Boneh, D.: SiRiUS: Securing Remote Untrusted Storage, pp. 131–145. Citeseer (2003)
7. Ateniese, G., Fu, K., Green, M., Hohenberger, S.: Improved Proxy Re-encryption Schemes With Applications to Secure Distributed Storage. ACM Transactions on Information and System Security (TISSEC) 9(1), 1–30 (2006)
8. Di Vimercati, S.D.C., Foresti, S., Jajodia, S., Paraboschi, S., Samarati, P.: Over-encryption: Management of Access Control Evolution on Outsourced Data. In: VLDB Endowment, pp. 123–134 (2007)
9. Atallah, M.J., Blanton, M., Fazio, N., Frikken, K.B.: Dynamic and Efficient Key Management for Access Hierarchies. ACM Transactions on Information and System Security (TISSEC) 12(3), 1–43 (2009)
10. Johnson, M., Chang, P., Jeffers, R., Bradshaw, J.M., Soo, V.W., Breedy, M.R., Bunch, L., Kulkarni, S., Lott, J., Suri, N.: KAoS Semantic Policy and Domain Services: An Application of DAML to Web Services-Based Grid Architectures, pp. 32–41. Citeseer (2003)
11. Tonti, G., Bradshaw, J.M., Jeffers, R., Montanari, R., Suri, N., Uszok, A.: Semantic web languages for policy representation and reasoning: A comparison of kAoS, rei, and ponder. In: Fensel, D., Sycara, K., Mylopoulos, J. (eds.) ISWC 2003. LNCS, vol. 2870, pp. 419–437. Springer, Heidelberg (2003)
12. Kagal, L.: Rei: A Policy Language for the Me-centric Project. HP Labs, accessible online, pp. 1-23 (2002), http://www.hpl.hp.com/techreports.html
13. Samarati, P., de Vimercati, S.: Access Control: Policies, Models, and Mechanisms. In: Foundations of Security Analysis and Design, pp. 137–196 (2001)
14. Lampson, B.W.: Protection. ACM SIGOPS Operating Systems Review 8(1), 18–24 (1974)
15. Harrison, M.A., Ruzzo, W.L., Ullman, J.D.: Protection in Operating Systems. Communications of the ACM 19, 461–471 (1976)
16. Denning, D.E.: A Lattice Model of Secure Information Flow. Communications of the ACM 19(5), 236–243 (1976)

17. Bell, D.E., Lapadula, L.J., Mitre, M.A.: orp Bedford. Secure Computer Systems: Mathematical Foundations 1(M74-244), 1–42 (1973)
18. Whitman, M.E., Mattord, H.J.: Management of Information Security, pp. 1–18. Course Technology Press, Boston (2004)
19. Wang, C., Wang, Q., Ren, K., Lou, W.: Ensuring Data Storage Security in Cloud Computing, pp. 1–9. IEEE, Los Alamitos (2009)
20. Padgham, L., Winikoff, M.: Developing Intelligent Agent Systems: A Practical Guide, pp. 1–240. Wiley, Chichester (2004); ISBN: 978-0-470-86120-2
21. Fabio, B., Agostino, P., Giovanni, R.: JADE—A FIPA-Compliant Agent Framework CSELT Internal Technical Report. Part of this report has been also published in Proceedings of PAAM 1999, pp. 97–108 (1999)
22. Bellifemine, F.L., Poggi, A., Rimassa, G.: Developing multi-agent systems with JADE. In: Castelfranchi, C., Lespérance, Y. (eds.) ATAL 2000. LNCS (LNAI), vol. 1986, p. 89. Springer, Heidelberg (2001)
23. Agostino, P., Rimassa, G., Tomaiuolo, M.: Multi-User and Security Support for Multi-Agent Systems. In: Proceedings of WOA Workshop, Modena, Italy, pp. 1–7 (2001)
24. Bellifemine, F., Poggi, A., Rimassa, G.: Developing Multi-Agent Systems with a FIPA-Compliant Agent Framework. Software—Practice and Experience (31), 103–128 (2001)

# Agent-Based MOM for Cross-Platform Communication WorkFlow Management in SOA Systems

Najhan M. Ibrahim, Mohd Fadzil Hassan, and Zain Balfagih

Department of Computer and Information Sciences
Universiti Teknologi PETRONAS,
Bandar Seri Iskandar, 31750 Tronoh, Perak, Malaysia.
hanfast@gmail.com, mfadzil_hassan@petronas.com.my,
z_balfagih@hotmail.com

**Abstract.** A lot of research works in different areas of workflow management can be found in various literatures. Each area of research has its own specification and requirements to manage a complex processing request. Workflow management is significantly important for utilizing heterogeneous communications and resources sharing in SOA systems. Many studies combine the workflow management with agent technology. This requires support from different approaches of implementing agent technology. In this paper, we describe our Agent-based MOM cross-platform communication workflow for SOA systems. We argue that our suggested framework is composing autonomous and flexible interaction for SOA communication. We also illustrate the technologies for cross-platform interoperability communication across wide area computing systems.

**Keywords:** Service Oriented Architecture (SOA), Message Oriented Middleware (MOM), Agent Technology, Web Services, Interoperability.

## 1 Introduction

Service-oriented architecture (SOA) aims to interconnect distributed, loosely coupled, and interoperable components of software owned or provided by different domains. For example, many applications and heterogeneous platforms require a process flow of communication to solve interoperability problem in cross-platform systems [1]. Thus, insuring an interoperable communication between cross-platform systems over Internet is the main problem for Service Oriented Architecture. Workflow management techniques would fulfill these requirements. In addition, Workflow management is a mechanism where a composite of processes is implemented as an interconnected queue of smaller, less complicated tasks [2]. The concept of workflow has been successfully investigated in many areas of research.

Due to the great capabilities of workflow to glue the system components, it has emerged from the SOA systems along with the agent-based technology. Currently, workflow systems for cross-platform are evoking a high degree of interest in research. In this paper we describe our approach in agent-based MOM cross-platform workflow

V. Snasel, J. Platos, and E. El-Qawasmeh (Eds.): ICDIPC 2011, Part II, CCIS 189, pp. 280–288, 2011.

[3]. The remaining of this paper is organized as the following. In section 2 we briefly discuss the background of the research with the implemented methodology. In section III we present a comparative study related to our work and in section 4 we proposed our communication workflow. In the last section, we conclude the paper and discuss the possible future work [2].

## 2  Background and Methodology

Agent-based infrastructures usually facilitate the autonomous communication between distributed and loosely coupled systems. Agent-based technology is a communication architecture that provides interoperability advantage for the cross-platform systems [4]. Currently, different enhancements have been implemented on agent-based communication for different purposes. These enhancements can overcome some interoperability problems but having different kind of technologies and development styles also cause some others interoperability issues. As the software architecture of any organization system is the significant part of the organizations' systems, some requirements needed to be included in the current communication workflow such as 24 by 7 environment, autonomous level, failure recovery and guaranteed transmission. Therefore, existing agent-based technologies still have some barrier of communication on each others [5], [6].

Constructing of flexible, autonomous and generic communication workflow would be a good initial step to achieve interoperability in the SOA system. Currently, researchers within this area are focusing more on the interoperability specification, standardization and requirements. Furthermore, agent-based technology can be useful tool to facilitate cross-platform communication which provides some significant attributes such as auto mouse, adaptive, interactive, support multi-protocol and lightweight implementation of atomic reaction [7].

To evaluate the efficiency of cross-platform communication between different distributed systems and to prove the capability of such communication, generic specifications of the requirements need to be identified. It is also necessary to explore some metrics to measure and evaluate the interoperability [8]. In the context of SOA interoperability, agent-based technology and message oriented middleware (MOM) would be a great combination to develop communication platform for cross-platform infrastructure [9].

Based on our literature reviewed, different extensions of agent-based technology have focused in different kinds of requirements for cross communication. In the following section, we present a table that summarizes the literature studies regarding several attributes of different agent-based deployment for distributed communication where every approach will be discussed in detail in the next section.

## 3  Related Work

Most of Message Oriented Middleware (MOM) is implemented with queued message and store-and-forward capability which is known as Message Queuing Middleware

(MQM). In general, MOM provides a high performance foundation for application interoperability in diverse and complex environments. At the same time, Agent-based technology is one of the well-known software technologies for cross-platform communication. It includes significant attributes such as autonomous, adaptive, interactive, support multi-protocol and lightweight implementation of atomic reaction. Therefore, in our proposed communication workflow, we will combine these two technologies for cross-platform communication [3].

Many research studies found in the literature review is regarding the enhancement of agent-based technology in cross-platform communication. Most of research works are problem specific and some are too general and not specific for one particular issue[10]. Several research works have been conducted to solve different issues of communication such as reliable asynchronous of communication and form-based agent communication language. As shown in Table 1, 12 research works relevant to agent-based extensions derived from literature studies regarding distributed communication of SOA are presented.

Table 1 summarizes and compares different enhancements of agent-based technology with regards to 8 proposed attributes concerning interoperability as highlighted in the first row of the table. We can split these extensions into 2 categories; synchronize and asynchronize communication. The enhancements were selected from several kinds of technologies, in which some of them are very basic using of agent-based technology but they consist of important highlighted points for interoperability of heterogeneous system. The attributes used in the evaluation were essentially selected from generic specification requirement for cross-platform communication and also from seamless interoperability guidelines [1].

The definition of each attributes included in Table 1 can be summarized as follows.

1) Communication type is the type of communication style.

2) 24 by 7 environments can be defined as the availability of application to process others request.

3) Autonomous level refers to the intelligent level of system to manage and implement the request of other systems.

4) Message type means the type of message that used in communication such as SOAP and XML.

5) Software failure recovery is the ability of application itself to recover the failure of transmission.

6) Guaranteed transmission can refer as high levels of application transmit the message to the partner.

7) Scalability is the ability to handle number of requests and number of servants.

8) Follow specifications mean the level of standazition applied to develop the architecture.

**Table 1.** Agent-based framework for cross-platform communication comparison table

| No | Agent-based framework for cross-platform communication | Communication type | Availability and 24x7 support | Autonomous level | Message type | Software failure recovery | Guaranteed transmission | Scalability | Follow Specifications |
|---|---|---|---|---|---|---|---|---|---|
| 1 | An Agent Platform for Reliable Asynchronous Distributed [7] | Asynchronous | Medium | High | ACL | Medium | Low | Low | Medium |
| 2 | Agent-Based Middleware for Web Service Dynamic [11] | Synchronize | Low | High | WSDI | Low | Low | Medium | Medium |
| 3 | XML-based Mobile Agents [6] | Synchronize | Low | High | XML | Low | Low | Low | High |
| 4 | An Agent-Based Distributed Smart Machine [5] | Synchronize | Low | High | KQML / ACL | Medium | Low | Medium | High |
| 5 | An Agent XML based Information Integration Platform [12] | Synchronize | Low | High | SOAP | Low | Low | Low | Medium |
| 6 | A Cross-Platform Agent-based Implementation [13] | Synchronize | Low | High | ACL | High | Low | High | Medium |
| 7 | Communication System among Heterogeneous Multi-Agent System [14] | Synchronize | Low | High | ACL | Low | Medium | Medium | High |
| 8 | FACL (Form-based ACL) [15] | Synchronize | Medium | High | Form-based (ACL) | Low | Medium | Low | Low |
| 9 | ACL Based Agent Communications in Plant Automation [16] | Asynchronous | Medium | High | ACL | Low | Medium | Medium | High ` |
| 10 | Multi-agent Systems for Distributed environment [17] | Synchronize | Low | High | ACL / KQML | Low | High | Medium | High |
| 11 | SOA Compliant FIPA Agent Communication Language [10] | Synchronize | Low | High | ACL | Low | Low | Medium | High |
| 12 | An Agent-Based Distributed Information Systems Architecture [5] | Synchronize | Low | High | ACL | Low | Medium | High | Medium |

L. Bellissard , N. De Palma, A. Freyssinet, M. Herrmann and S. Lacourte [7] introduce a distributed communication model based on autonomous by agents software. Agents act as the glue software components and they provide atomic execution or migration from node to node. A. Lin and P. Maheshwari [11] aims to construct an agent-based middleware for Web service dynamic integration on Peer-to-Peer networks to facilitate the integration of optimal quality of Web services for application integration. R. Steele T. Dillon P. Pandya and Y. Ventsov [6] presents a mobile agent system design based on the use of XML-based agent, the UDDI registry for agent registration and lookup/discovery and XML Web Service calls for mobile agent intercommunication and migration. In these works, the highlighted techniques or requirements are too basic for interoperability communication of heterogeneous distributed information systems. Many attributes were not considered as suggested in interoperability Table 1, such as 24 by 7 environment, software failure recovery, guaranteed transmission and scalability.

Y.C. Kao and M.S. Chen [4] utilized software agent based technology in enhancing remote tool service system by developing related remote service ontology to manage its smart and distributive characteristics. X. Li [11] mentions that to integrate process operation systems effectively, an Agent/XML based information integration platform is proposed. The subsystems are encapsulated as Agents-based on XML and Agent technology. Then based on integration goal of, the Agents distributed in different domains are integrated. The encapsulation of different subsystems was implemented through Agent technology. E. Cervera [12] presents a cross-platform, networked implementation of control tasks based on software agents and streaming technologies.This implementation consists of free, off-the-shelf, software components, resulting in a transparent system whose configuration can be adapted to existing hardware in very different ways, without any modification in the source code. However, according to Table 1 these papers still lack of some generic communication requirement such as scalability, guaranteed transmission, Software failure recovery and it also does not support 24 by 7 environments which is very important for current software architecture.

Y. Yoon, K. Choi and D. Shin [13] suggest and execute the system for translation among heterogeneous service description languages. Any of multi-agent system use the proposed system can expand the service area. T. CHUSHO and K. FUJIWARA [14] describe a multi-agent framework and an agent communication language (ACL) for the MOON (multiagent-oriented office network) systems which are distributed systems of E- commerce. The multi-agent framework is a Java application framework and includes a form-based ACL (FACL) as a common protocol for passing application forms. Q. Feng and G. Lu [15] have tried to use agent communication language (ACL) to implement communications between PABADIS agents. In order to fulfill with the final part of project in which Grasshopper is used as agent developing platform, FIPA ACL is adopted. In contrast, these in papers did not discuss several attributes which are available in other distributed communication architectures such as 24 by 7 environments, software failure recovery, guaranteed of transmissions and Scalability. Therefore, it would be very difficult for this framework to interact with other systems especially if those systems were built based on other interoperability requirements [8].

H. Farooq Ahmad [16] temporarily explores the basic agent systems architecture with highlight on agent communication languages (ACL). Two most accepted agent communication languages, namely FIPA ACL and KQML have been briefly reviewed. This work summarizes generic requirements of the agent system from the viewpoint of FIPA and OMG models. M. AtifNazir, H. Ahmad and H. Suguri [10] address the issue of interoperability between FIPA agents and grid services by suggesting a communication framework for interconnected. SOA compliant FIPA ACL ontology has developed that provides the necessary expressions that not only facilitate to the FIPA specifications but also used by grid services. M. Purvis, S. Cranefield, G. Bush and D. Carter [4] describes framework for building distributed information systems from available resources, based on software agent and distributed technologies. An agent-based architecture is adopted, by messages exchanging via the FIPA agent communication language (ACL). Similar to other research work these efforts did not include some significant interoperability communication attributes such as 24 by 7 environment, software failure recovery, guaranteed transmission, and scalability. Therefore, this study strongly proposes cross-platform interoperability attributes as a based guideline for future cross-platform communication framework.

## 4  The Agent-Based MOM Workflow Management System

Users can describe the interactions between agents by agent communication languages (ACL) which is the basic standard agent communication proposed by FIPA (Foundation for intelligent Physical Agent). Workflow system can coordinate or control the interactions between agents which used to perform tasks, such as message passing and computing tasks. Our approach for workflow management in SOA environments is agent-based MOM Flow Management Systems (AMFMS). AMFMS provides high-level middleware to enable transparent communication between agents over distributed system and resource sharing over a wide-area network.

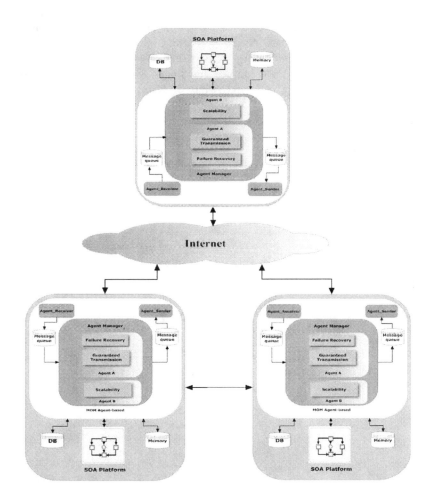

**Fig. 1.** The Architecture of AMFMS

The basic ideas for the AMFMS are very simple: it consists of a collection of federated servers with hosting AMFMS engine in each of SOA system. The partnership of processing resources, which host the AMFMS environment, make their own placement and communication decisions independent of each other. The AMFMS environment provides the necessary framework for the seamless communication and execution of the component parts of the users' requests across the distributed cross-platform system to ensure that the request is fulfilled.

AMFMS architecture has been adopted from a service-oriented perspective, with a high degree of automation that supports flexible collaborations and computations on a large complex application, as shown in Fig.1. In the architecture, workflow applications are central to the architecture of the AMFMS. Workflow engines are distributed across SOA environment.

We adopted the cMOM (Composite-event Based Message-Oriented Middleware) [8] as AMFMS engine. Communication or message passing can manage themselves in one or more workflow engines. AMFMS engine can be interconnected with those SOA services and resources in the engine. AMFMS engines can be dynamically detected and connected into different SOA architectures, such as XML-based architecture, SOAP-based architecture or CORBA-based architecture. Due to the dynamic nature and flexibility of agent-based technology, the AMFMS is suitable for future communication workflow.

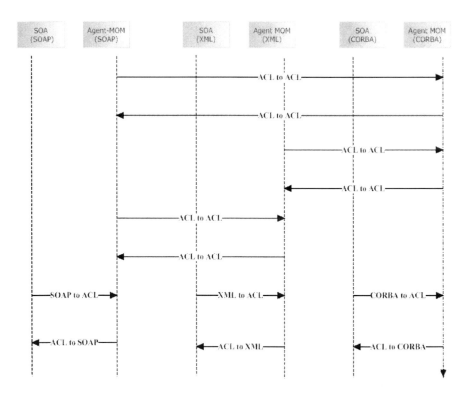

**Fig. 2.** Agent-based MOM Communication Activities

In addition, this communication workflow decreases the level of complexity in cross-platform communication. Classically, SOA architecture needs to deal with middle server such as CA and message brokers. According to [17] SOA system is not required to have any third party in the system between trusted domains. By decreasing such complexity of workflow, it will increase the autonomous level that doesn't need any responds from participant. In agent-based MOM workflow, all components will be two way interaction and the agent-based MOM platform will use the standard messaging proposed by FIPA which is ACL(Agent Communication Language), Each agent will analyze each message priorities and in which action should be taken. For example, SOAP platform need to run some service in CORBA platform where analyzer agent will analyze the message that received by agent-receiver. Then, it will translate it to ACL (Agent communication Language). The sender agent also will identify which platform offer which type of service and which message type they are using [10].

## 5   Conclusion and Future Work

Cross-platform communication has become a significant process in connecting and sharing resources between SOA-based environments. The lack of interoperability awareness in SOA inspires researchers to focus on heterogeneous type of communication flow between SOA systems. We found that some researchers focus on some particular perspective while others have worked to combine several specifications such as scalability, flexibility and resource management. We believe that more research in this area is still needed.

In this paper, agent-based MOM Flow Management System (AMFMS) is proposed. AMFMS enables the communication between different platforms and also for resource sharing across organizations. In AMFMS, we propose a communication based on agent communication language (ACL) which is able to communicate over cross platform. This is to guarantee the exchange of data without any restrictions. The proposed agent-based MOM is for cross-platform environment within SOA system. In the future, the main concern of this research will concentrate on the attributes in the comparative study shown in Table 1 such as software failure recovery, 24 by 7 environments, scalability and guaranteed transmission to construct valuable interoperability cross-platform communication architecture.

## References

1. Ibrahim, M., N.b., Hassan, M.F.B.: A Survey on Different Interoperability frameworks of SOA Systems Towards Seamless Interoperability. In: Escon 2010, IEEE, Kuala Lumpur (2010)
2. Yuan, P., Jin, H., Qi, L., Li, S.: Research on an MOM-based service flow management system. In: Jin, H., Pan, Y., Xiao, N., Sun, J. (eds.) GCC 2004. LNCS, vol. 3251, pp. 783–786. GCC, Heidelberg (2004)
3. Goel, S., Shada, H., Taniar, D.: Asynchronous Messaging Using Message-Oriented-Middleware. In: Liu, J., Cheung, Y.-m., Yin, H. (eds.) IDEAL 2003. LNCS, vol. 2690, pp. 1118–1122. Springer, Heidelberg (2003)

4. Kao, Y.-C., Chen, M.-S.: An Agent-Based Distributed Smart Machine Tool Service System. 3CA IEEE, Los Alamitos (2010)
5. Goel, S., Sharda, H., Taniar, D.: Message-oriented-middleware in a distributed environment. In: Böhme, T., Heyer, G., Unger, H. (eds.) IICS 2003. LNCS, vol. 2877, pp. 93–103. Springer, Heidelberg (2003)
6. Steele, R.: XML-based Mobile Agents. In: Proceedings of the International Conference on Information Technology: Coding and Computing (ITCC 2005), IEEE, Los Alamitos (2005)
7. Bellissard, L., De Palma, A.F.N., Herrmann, M., Lacourte, S.: An Agent Platform for Reliable Asynchronous Distributed Programming. IEEE, France (1999)
8. Yuan, P., Jin, H.: A Composite-Event-Based Message-Oriented Middleware. In: Li, M., Sun, X.-H., Deng, Q.-n., Ni, J. (eds.) GCC 2003. LNCS, vol. 3032, pp. 700–707. Springer, Heidelberg (2004)
9. Lin, A., Maheshwari, P.: Agent-Based Middleware for Web Service Dynamic Integration on Peer-to-Peer Networks. In: Zhang, S., Jarvis, R.A. (eds.) AI 2005. LNCS (LNAI), vol. 3809, pp. 405–414. Springer, Heidelberg (2005)
10. Raja, M.A.N., Ahmad, H.F., Suguri, H.: SOA Compliant FIPA Agent Communication Language. IEEE, Los Alamitos (2008)
11. Li, X.: An Agent/XML based Information Integration Platform for Process Industry. In: 2nd International Conference on Computer Engineering and Technology, IEEE, Los Alamitos (2010)
12. Cervera, E.: A Cross-Platform Agent-based Implementation. IEEE, Los Alamitos (2005)
13. Yoon, Y.-J., Choi, K.-H., Shin, D.-R.: Design and Implementation of Communication System among Heterogeneous Multi-Agent System. In: Fourth International Conference on Networked Computing and Advanced Information Management. IEEE, Los Alamitos (2008)
14. Chusho, T., Fujiwara, K.: A Form-based Agent Communication Language for Enduser-Initiative Agent-Based Application Development. IEEE, Los Alamitos (2000)
15. Feng, Q., Lu, G.: FIPA-ACL Based Agent Communications in Plant Automation. IEEE, Los Alamitos (2003)
16. Ahmad, H.F.: Multi-agent Systems: Overview of a New Paradigm for Distributed Systems. In: HASE 2002. IEEE, Los Alamitos (2002)
17. Louridas, P.: SOAP and Web Services in the IEEE Computer Societ. IEEE, Los Alamitos (2006)

# HSFS: A Compress Filesystem for Metadata Files

Nicola Corriero[1], Emanuele Covino[2],
Giuseppe D'amore[2], and Giovanni Pani[2]

[1] University of Vlora
Department of Computer Science
Shehi Pavaresia, Skela,
Vlora, Albania
corriero@univlora.edu.al
[2] University of Bari
Department of Computer Science
Via Orabona 4, Bari, Italy
{covino,pani}@di.uniba.it,
damore.giuseppe@gmail.com

**Abstract.** In this paper we propose a solution to improve the search among compress data. A Linux filesystem have been implemented by combining the advantages of squashfs (compression) and hixosfs (for research). We test our idea with DICOM file used to store medical images.

**Keywords:** Filesystem, Compression Data, Linux, DICOM, Metadata.

## 1 Introduction

Hospitals and major health organizations are turning today to computers to make secure, fast, reliable and easily accessible in real time and distance learning enormous amounts of information as regards data processing.

The standards provide for the association for medical imaging and the incorporation of accurate and unambiguous information about the patient to whom the data relate to the image data, personal details, medical reports related to some clinical analysis, etc. To do so, systems are able to associate and combine data of different types in a single document, DICOM is the standard format adopted for the treatment of these images (Digital Imaging and Communications in Medicine). For these reasons, forensic images must be retained for a period of not less than 10 years, but we are in the presence of a large number of mages of considerable size, you need to find a method to reduce the commitment of resources, in terms of occupying space in storage devices. GNU / Linux offers an interesting solution, the SquashFS file system. Squashfs is a compressed read-only file system that compress files, inodes and directory, usually used in systems for use minimal storage read-only file. The interest lies on this file system to the mode of operation, mounted the image of the directory containing the compressed files, allows you to manage them as a normal file through the shell or the GUI. So the compression completely transparent to the user.

V. Snasel, J. Platos, and E. El-Qawasmeh (Eds.): ICDIPC 2011, Part II, CCIS 189, pp. 289–300, 2011.
© Springer-Verlag Berlin Heidelberg 2011

In the file in DICOM format, associated with the image, we have the identification data used by applications to manage them. Having to extract these data directly from the compressed files may require an excessive commitment of resources in terms of time.

Similar problem was already addressed in the *Hixos* laboratory, realizing *HixosFS*. *HixosFS* is an Ext2 filesystem extending, modifying and ridefinedo the inode associated with the file, adding a tag whose attributes will be backed up by data that are normally encapsulated in the same file. Based on the experience of HixosFS, we will proceed with the change of SquashFS by making *HSFS* (Hixos Squash File System).

## 2   Problem

The DICOM Standard is structured as a multi-part document in accordance with the guidelines set forth in the document: ISO/IEC Directives, 1989. This was done in order to update the single part without having to republish the entire standard. The current version (2007) consists of 18 parts and is found at the link and http://medical.nema.org, http://www.dclunie.com/.

The general structure of a DICOM file includes a header containing data describing the image, the patient, time and date of acquisition, and more, and the image itself, all in one file. The standard since its first appearance has not definitively established the indivisibility between the image pixel data and data describing the process that led to the formation of the image.

We are in the presence of a large number of images of considerable size.

Examples of these size are:

| Exam | MB/Exam |
|---|---|
| Nuclear Medicine | 1 - 2 |
| Magnetic Resonance | 6 - 12 |
| Ultrasound | 15 - 150 |
| Echocardiography | 150 - 800 |
| Angiography | 600 - 700 |
| Coronary | 700 - 800 |
| TCMS 64 | 700 - 800 |
| CR | 13 |
| DR | 28 |
| Digital Mammograms | 120 |

Dicom images must be retained for a period of not less than 10 years. So we need a lot of space to store these informations and a lot of time to looking for a single exam of a single patient.

## 3   Other Solutions

Normally these situations are handled using PCs with large primary and secondary memories that make possible the use of every operating system and every mean for saving and managing information.

Other approaches of the system require the use of complex databases over servers and/or embedded databases over embedded machines.

## 3.1  Oracle/Mysql

The tools used to handle large quantities of data are very efficient although they require large resources in hardware and software. Installing and executing of applications like Oracle or Mysql, in fact, require large quantities of memory and hard disk space.

## 3.2  Sqlite

In the embedded systems we have evident problems of memory that during the time have solicited light-weight and high-performance ad-hoc solutions. Sqlite is an application that implements all the functionalities of a database using simple text files. This enlighten the execution load of the system and facilitates the integration of the system inside, for example, an embedded system. However, the system installation produces a certain load to the mass memory.

## 3.3  Extended Attributes

Currently Linux is as ext2 [4], ext3, reiserfs allows to manage with metainformation related to a file with *xattr* feature. Patching the kernel with xattr you have a way to extend inode attributes that doesn't physically modify the inode struct. This is possible since in *xattr* the attributes are stored as a couple attribute-value out of the inode as a variable length string. Generally the basic command used to deal with extended attributes in *Xattr* is *attr* that allows to specifies different options to set and get attribute values, to remove attributes to list all of them and then to read or writes these values to standard output. The programs we implemented in our testing scenario are based on this user space tool.

# 4  Our Solution: HSFS

Our proposal is to use a compressed filesystem changed ad-hoc to improve the indexing of files and facilitate the discovery of information. HSFS borns from the benefits in terms of performance for the detection of Hixosfs and compression squashed. The idea is to compress the files via DICOM Squashfs and index the contents of the files in the inode of each file compressed. In this way the image will occupy less space and you can find information without browsing the GB of data, but only in the inode file.

## 4.1  System Architecture

In the preparation of minimal Linux operating systems and integrated each byte of storage device (floppy, flash disk, etc..) is very important, so compression is used wherever possible.

In addition, compressed file systems are usually necessary for archival purposes. That is essential for large public records or even personal archives and it is the latter application that has led us to study this file system. The SquashFS file system brings everything to a new level. This is a read-only file system that allows compression of individual directories or entire file systems, their writing on other devices / partitions or regular files and mount directly (if it is a partition) or through the use the loopback device (if it is a file). The modular and compact SquashFS is brilliant. For archival purposes, squashfs is much more flexible and faster than a tarball. The squashfs distributed software includes a patch for Linux kernel sources (which enables the kernel versions prior to 2.6.34 - support for reading the squashed file system), the instrument *mksquashfs*, you need to create file systems and *unsquashfs* tool that allows you to extract multiple files from an existing squashed file system. The latest released version of the squashed is 4.x, this version was made for the kernel 2.6.34 and later. Support for reading the squashed file system in Linux kernel versions from 2.6.34 is integrated. The previous version, 3.x, made for versions of the Linux kernel prior to 2.6.34, includes a patch to apply. To manage the new information that we intend to include in the structure of an inode is necessary:

– to create a new definition of the VFS inode with new fields;
– to create new syscall to perform operations on the new inode3;
– to create a new definition of inodes in the filesystem SquashFS;
– to change squashfs instruments to allow corroboration of the new fields of the inode;
– to create user space programs to interact with the file system changes.

## 4.2    Hixosfs

*Hixosfs* is as an ext2 Linux filesystem (fs) extension able to classify and to manage metadata files collections in a fast and high performant way. This is allowed since high priority is given to the storing and retrieving of metadata respect tags because they are managed at fs level in kernel mode.

The *hixosfs* core idea is that information regarding the content of a metadata of a file belong to the fs structure itself. Linux fs in general stores common information for a type of file, such as permissions or records of creation and modification times, then the struct to represent a file inside the VFS called inode keeps information about such data. To represent tags physically inside the inode, *hixosfs* reserves a greater amount of memory for the inode to store extra information needed to label a file respect its content such as *album, author, title, year* for music file.

In this paper we explain how the fundamental concepts implemented in *hixosfs* can help to solve problems in embedded systems.

We had to implement two system calls to write and read the new information stored inside the inode: *chtag* and *retag*, the final user recall the syscall by the tools *chtag* and *stattag* with analogous functionality of the well known chown and stats but obviously considering generics tags.

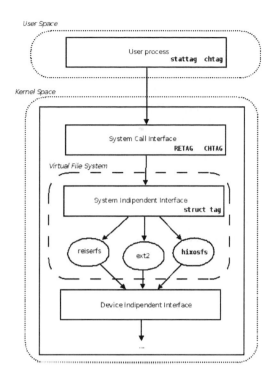

**Fig. 1.** Hixosfs

Hixosfs has been used to tag gps files and mobile devices. In this way all the load has been transfered to the kernel that handles and organizes the hixosfs files as occurrs. The servers and the clients contain partitions that can read and set the hixosfs tags so to manage the database.

The kernel struct for all the file type management is the inode.

The struct tag has four fields for a total of about 100 byte of stored information, theoretically an inode can be extended until 4 kb then it's possible to customize it with many tags for your purpose. It's convenient to choose tags that are most of the time used in the file search to discriminate the files depending their content.

For such reasons we decided to use a generic version of hixosfs with a generic structure in which is possible to insert file representative tags case by case.

```
struct tag {
#ifdef CONFIG_HIXOSFS_TAG
 char tag1[30];
 char tag2[30];
 char tag3[30];
 char tag4[30];
 unsigned int tag_valid;
#endif
}
```

## 4.3  HSFS

DICOM header information are arranged in groups according to the following: Patient, Study, Series and Image. Each attribute has a unique identifier, consisting of two words of bytes, the first on the parent group and second on the same single attribute.

To manage the new information that we intend to include in the structure of an inode is needed:

- create a new definition of the VFS inode with new fields;
- create new syscall to perform operations on the new inode[1],
- to create a new definition of inode in filesystem squashfs;
- modify the squashfs tools to allow the corroboration of the new fields of inode;
- create user space programs to interact with the file system changes.

```
... ... ...
struct squashfs_dicom_inode {
  char tag1[30];
  char tag2[30];
  char tag3[30];
  char tag4[30];
  unsigned int hixos_tag_valid;
};
... ... ...
struct squashfs_reg_inode {
  __le16 inode_type;
  __le16 mode;
  __le16 uid;
  __le16 guid;
  __le32 mtime;
  __le32 inode_number;
  __le32 start_block;
  __le32 fragment;
  __le32 offset;
  __le32 file_size;
/* HSFS Field */
  struct squashfs_dicom_inode dicom;
  __le16 block_list[0];
};
... ... ...
```

The location field *dicom* within the structure *squashfs_reg_inode* is not negligible, must precede the *block_list [0]*.

---

[1] In our case, simply read the values because we work on a read-only filesystem.

```
... ... ...
int squashfs_read_inode(struct inode *inode, long long ino)
{
... ... ...
  switch (type) {
    case SQUASHFS_REG_TYPE: {
... ... ...
/* hsfs changhes /*
       strcpy((inode->i_tag).tag1,(sqsh_ino->dicom.tag1));
       strcpy((inode->i_tag).tag2,(sqsh_ino->dicom.tag2));
       strcpy((inode->i_tag).tag3,(sqsh_ino->dicom.tag3));
       strcpy((inode->i_tag).tag4,(sqsh_ino->dicom.tag4));
/*hsfs changhes /*
... ... ...
```

## User space tools

To use hixosfs features we choose to store inside squashfs_inode informations
about:

- tag1 − > id;
- tag2 − > name;
- tag3 − > patient's birthday;
- tag4 − > study date.

For that reason we need to create some tools to automatic populate tag inside
inode by reading informations from header.

The operation of reading the header of DICOM files in order to validate the
new struct inode filesystem squashfs inserted, was achieved through a feature
included in the program *mksquasfs.c.* The program *mksquashfs.c* is the tool used
to create compressed file and append new files to existing ones.

The definition of the new tag that will contain the extracted values of the
header file that will be used to validate the dicom tag added in the inode
of the filesystem has been included in the file *squashfs_fs.h*, while in the file
*squashfs_swap.h* macro definition is complete SWAP.

Changes made in kernel space allow us to handle the added tag, with the
squashfs tools we can add tags to indicate the data taken with the header of
DICOM files, now we need tools that allow us to extract these data.

In this regard we have developed programs:

*statdicom* and *finddicom*

These programs was applied to files in DICOM format present in a compressed
filesystem, using the syscall RETAG, will allow us to view data stored in the
inode of all files and select certain files that match specific search criteria.

```
$ statdicom --help
Usage: statdicom [OPTION...] FILE
Shows the values of the new tags added to squashfs inode contains
the header data drawn wire type dicom.
  -?, --help                 Give this help list
      --usage                Give a short usage message
  -V, --version              Print program version
$
```

The command *finddicom* allows us to search and display the name of the file in DICOM format, with the relative values of the added inode, which meet certain search criteria passed as arguments to the command itself.

```
$ finddicom --help
Usage: finddicom [OPTION...]
Search for files in DICOM format that meet the attribute values
passed as parameters in the command line.

  -b, --birthdate=BIRTHDATE  Patient's birth date (yyyymmdd)
  -i, --id=ID                Patient ID
  -n, --name=NAME            Patient's name
  -s, --studydate=STUDYDATE  Study date (yyyymmdd)
  -?, --help                 Give this help list
      --usage                Give a short usage message
  -V, --version              Print program version
$
```

## 5    Testing Scenario

The test scenario we were offered by a local medical center analysis that helped us with a set of images in DICOM format.

We have created a folder with images in all the images on DICOM format (with extension. dcm).

We have created an *hsfs* filesystem with the command *mksquashfs*.

```
$ mksquashfs immagini/ immagini.sq -always-use-fragments
Parallel mksquashfs: Using 2 processors
Creating 4.0 filesystem on immagini.sq, block size 131072.
....
```

Then to test the goodness of what we have mounted the squashfs filesystem in */mnt/tmp*. In this way we have the information available for research.

```
$ mount immagini.sq /mnt/tmp -t squashfs -o loop
$ cd /mnt/tmp
/mnt/tmp $ statdicom immagine19.dcm immagine7.dcm
File:  immagine19.dcm
Data study:  20100428
Name Surname:  XXXXXTTI^XXXXXLA
Id:  2804101650
Birthday:  19651128

File:  immagine7.dcm
Data study:  20100604
Name Surname:  XXXXXCCIA^XXXXXA
Id:  0405101520
Birthday:  19660530
/mnt/tmp $
/mnt/tmp $ finddicom -s 20100504
File:  immagine37.dcm
Data study:  20100504
Id:  0405101605
Name Surname:   XXXXXA^XXXXX
Birthday:  19601112

File:  immagine38.dcm
Data study:  20100504
Id:  0405101605
Name Surname:   XXXXXA^XXXXX
Birthday:  19601112
/mnt/tmp $
```

The scenery is running even if there are problems because not very usable. In fact, all operations are currently done using the Linux command line. Our project is to create a more usable interface of the system through a simple web application.

## 6    Test Comparaisons

To test our filesystem we choose to create an ad-hoc minimal Linux distribution with Bash command line and without graphic environment.

The metric chosen for evaluation in testing is the execution time, to have a significant significativity statistical measurements were repeated for each instance created, 10 times, not to distort the data for the presence of demons running.

We choose to compare a database of 20000 empty files managed by: hixosfs, ext2 with xattr, hsfs, a simple *sqlite* database and a *mysql* database.

In cases of databases we populate tables by random data.

Each databases (*sqlite* and *mysql*) is composed by a single table with 5 fields (1 for id e 1 for each of 4 *hixos tag*).

We test time to create file, to change a tag value, to read all tags values, to find a tag value.

We try to create the same conditions between the filesystem usage and database usage.

Here are a set of data (the more interesting) collected during the test.

**Time to read all values: 20000 empty files**

| Hixosfs | Ext2_xattr | HSFS | SQLite | MySQL |
|---------|-----------|------|--------|-------|
| 23,844 | 96,463 | 32,152 | 69,973 | 187,952 |
| 23,922 | 96,867 | 32,106 | 69,748 | 188,606 |
| 23,868 | 96,851 | 32,237 | 69,451 | 188,754 |
| 23,987 | 97,214 | 32,266 | 69,790 | 188,938 |
| 23,780 | 97,350 | 32,252 | 69,489 | 188,995 |
| 23,900 | 96,755 | 32,203 | 70,573 | 189,010 |
| 24,070 | 97,035 | 32,188 | 69,122 | 189,383 |
| 23,966 | 96,968 | 32,164 | 69,234 | 189,270 |
| 24,003 | 97,103 | 32,318 | 69,235 | 189,354 |
| 23,927 | 97,501 | 32,272 | 69,567 | 189,172 |

**Average time to read all values: 20000 empty files**

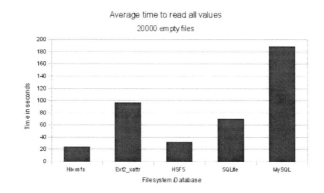

**Fig. 2.** Read all values

**To find a value among tag: 20000 empty files**

| Hixosfs | Ext2_xattr | HSFS | SQLite | MySQL |
|---------|-----------|--------|--------|---------|
| 60,301 | 234,516 | 60,286 | 68,467 | 188,543 |
| 60,527 | 234,867 | 70,285 | 68,708 | 188,931 |
| 60,590 | 235,581 | 70,704 | 68,999 | 188,300 |
| 60,781 | 236,751 | 60,339 | 69,245 | 188,812 |
| 60,681 | 236,469 | 60,296 | 69,309 | 188,874 |
| 60,507 | 235,106 | 60,293 | 69,327 | 189,345 |
| 60,505 | 236,507 | 60,333 | 68,377 | 188,647 |
| 60,574 | 234,757 | 61,271 | 69,690 | 188,651 |
| 60,869 | 235,916 | 60,299 | 70,297 | 189,075 |
| 60,594 | 236,326 | 60,404 | 69,133 | 188,396 |

**Average time to find a value: 20000 empty files**

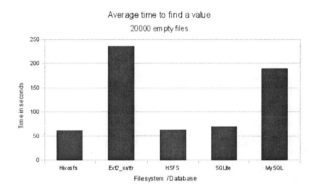

**Fig. 3.** Find a value

The applied test is the test of Student working on the average values of the metric under consideration.

As you can see from the averages of observed values and how the Student test have confirmed HSFS represents a viable alternative for use with the ext2 xattr and common database. The only filesystem appears to be more powerful hixosfs which does not, however, does not present the characteristics of data compression as hsfs.

## 7   Conclusions and Future Works

The assessment of the experimentation carried out, the solution is obviously advantageous to include in the inode file dicom attribute values of interest, this is to allow for a more immediate than reading the same values of the header files directly. While the decision to include the construct of selecting files based on the values passed as parameters to the command finddicom RETAG in the system call, or alternatively to specific command, does not find substantial differences. Even if, where the application on a system not minimal, as the one chosen in the trial (Mvux) could come into play noise conditions that would favor a solution that is acting entirely in kernel space, so with the construct for selection of RETAG file in the system call.

Today, most medical centers have completed or are completing the transition to digital technologies. At its heart is the PACS (Picture Archiving and communcations System), a system capable of receiving digital images from the workstation via the DICOM archive, DICOM send them to other entities, to respond to questions on the studies by other nodes network, to produce transportable media containing digital images. An interesting future development of this work could lead to a test HSFS experiencing any PACS system efficiency, and possibly assess the possible advantages in services telerefertazione.

Furthermore, since Squashfs a filesystem read-only, a possible future evolution might affect the identification of techniques that allow, with operations transparent to the user, change the values of this additional tag in the inode file.

# References

1. DICOM Resources (2005),
   http://star.pst.qub.ac.uk/idl/DICOM_Resources.html
2. The SquashFS archives (2011),
   http://sourceforge.net/projects/squashfs/files/squashfs/
3. Official SquashFS LZMA (2006), http://www.squashfs-lzma.org/
4. Card, Ts'o, Tweedie.: Design and Implementation of the Second Extended Filesystem, http://e2fsprogs.sourceforge.net/ext2intro.html
5. Sqlite (March 2011), http://www.sqlite.org/ Home Page
6. Kernel. Torvalds (March 2011), ww.kernel.org Home Page
7. Hixosfs. Hixos (March 2009), www.di.uniba.it/$\sim$hixos/hixosfs Home Page
8. Corriero, Zhupa: An embedded filesystem for mobile and ubiquitous multimedia. In: MMEDIA 2010 (2010) 978-1-4244-7277-2
9. Corriero, Zhupa: Hixosfs for ubiquitous commerce through bluetooth. In: FUTURETECH 2010 (2010) 978-1-4244-6948-2
10. Corriero, Cozza: The hixosfs music approach vs common musical file management solutions. In: SIGMAP 2009, pp. 189–193 (2009) 978-989-674-007-8
11. Corriero, Cozza: Hixosfs_Music: A Filesystem in Linux Kernel Space for Musical Files. In: MMEDIA 2009 (2009) 978-0-7695-3693-4
12. Rubini.: The "virtual filesystem" in Linux. Kernel Korner,
    http://www.linux.it/$\sim$rubini/docs/vfs/vfs.html
13. Bovet & Cesati. Understandig the linux kernel

# Environment Sound Recognition for Digital Audio Forensics Using Linear Predictive Coding Features

Mubarak Obaid AlQahtani[1] and Abdulaziz S. Al mazyad[2]

[1] Center of Excellence in Information Assurance,
King Saud University,
Riyadh, Saudi Arabia
mukobaid@gmail.com
[2] College of Computer and Information Sciences,
King Saud University,
Riyadh, Saudi Arabia
mazyad@ccis.ksu.edu.sa

**Abstract.** Linear Predictive Coding coefficients are of the main extraction feature in digital forensic. In this paper, we perform several experiments focusing on the problems of environments recognition from audio particularly for forensic application. We investigated the effect of temporal Linear Predictive Coding coefficient as feature extraction on environment sound recognition to compute the Linear Predictive Coding coefficient for each frame for all files. The performance is evaluated against varying number of training sounds and samples per training file and compare with Zero Crossing feature and Moving Picture Experts Group-7 low level description feature. We use K-Nearest Neighbors as classifier feature to detect which the environment for any audio testing file. Experimental results show that higher recognition accuracy is achieved by increasing the number of training files and by decreasing the number of samples per training file.

**Keywords:** Linear Predictive Coding (LPC), Zero Crossing (ZC), Mel frequency cepstral coefficients (MFCC), Moving Picture Experts Group (MPEG), Audio Waveform (AWF), Audio Power (AP), Audio Spectrum Envelop (ASE), Audio Spectrum Centroid (ASC), Audio Spectrum Spread (ASS), Hidden Markov model (HMM), K-Nearest Neighbors (K-NN).

## 1 Introduction

Digital forensics can be defined as the collection of scientific techniques for the preservation, collection, validation, identification, analysis, interpretation, documentation, and presentation of digital evidence derived from digital sources for the purpose of facilitating or furthering the reconstruction of events, usually of a criminal nature [1]. There are several areas of digital forensics: image forensics, audio forensics, video forensics, etc.

In this paper, we concentrate on digital audio forensic. Digital audio forensic is to provide evidence from left over audio files contained in audio / video media in the

V. Snasel, J. Platos, and E. El-Qawasmeh (Eds.): ICDIPC 2011, Part II, CCIS 189, pp. 301–309, 2011.
© Springer-Verlag Berlin Heidelberg 2011

crime spot. This type of forensic can be categorized into four different classes according to its nature: (a) speaker identification / verification / recognition, to find the answer of 'who', (b) speech recognition / enhancement, to find the answer of 'what', (c) environment detection, to find the answer of 'where' or 'situation' and (d) source authentication, to find the answer of 'how'.

A significant amount of research can be found in the area of speech recognition or enhancement [2], speaker recognition [3], and authentication of audio [4]. However, a very few researches can be found in the area of environment recognition for digital audio forensic, where foreground human speech is present in environment recordings. There are many difficulties while dealing with recognition of environment from audio. Unlike speech or speaker recognition cases, different environment sounds may have similar characteristics.

We present in this paper several experiments on environment recognition for digital audio forensics: restaurant, office room, fountain, cafeteria, mall, meeting room, and corridor. We record many files for each environment in different places and different time. Recording files were separated into two types for each environment: training files and testing files. Each file is divided into many fixed-length frames (512 samples) with 256 sample overlapping and calculated linear predictive coding (LPC) coefficient for each frame and keep them in the database. For environment recognition we compute LPC coefficient for each frame from testing file. Then we use K-Nearest Neighbors (K-NN) to compute the distance between LPC coefficients for each frame from testing files and all training files. Finally, comparing the results and reveal a smaller space. Smaller distance means that the environment file of the test is the training environment files. Two types of experiments on environment recognition are performed by varying (a) the number of training files and (b) the number of samples per each training file.

This paper is organized as follows. Section 2 gives a review of related past works. Section 3 describes the data used in the experiments. Section 4 Linear Predictive Coding feature extraction, Section 5 describes classifier feature; Section 6 presents the proposed approach to recognize environment sound. In this section, the experimental results and discussion are also given. Finally, conclusions and future direction are in Section 7.

# 2  Related Past Works

A block diagram of environment recognition from audio file is given in Fig. 1. The procedure is divided into two main blocks: feature extraction and classification. In the feature extraction block, input audio stream is represented into some suitable feature form. Feature dimension reduction is an optional block that minimizes the dimension of feature vector without losing too much information. In a training phase, different types of environment are modeled using the features. In a testing phase, input features are compared against each model to classify the matched environment.

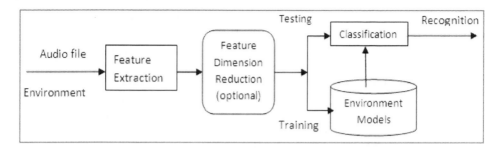

**Fig. 1.** Block diagram of environment recognition from audio files

Most of the previous works in environment detection used Mel frequency cepstral coefficients (MFCC) as features, which are applied not only in environment detection but also in speech and speaker recognition applications [5], and Hidden Markov model (HMM) based classification. While HMMs are widely used in the applications, K-NN classifier is also applied due to its simplicity [6]. As mentioned before, there are not so much works done in this particular area targeted to forensic applications, however, we mention some related works that are of interest in this area. A comprehensive evaluation of a computer and human performance in audio-based context (environment) recognition is presented in [7]. In their work, Eronen et al used several time-domain and spectral-domain features in addition to MFCC. PCA (principal component analysis), ICA (independent component analysis), and LDA (linear discriminated analysis) were used to reduce dimensionality of feature vector. Two types of classifiers were applied separately: K-NN (K = 1), and HMM with number of states and number of mixtures within each state varying from 1 to 4 (and 5), respectively. Nature and outdoors were recognized with highest accuracy (96-97%) and library with the lowest accuracy (35%). Selina et al [8] introduced matching pursuit (MP) technique [9] in environmental sounds recognition. MP provides a way to extract features that can describe sounds where other audio features (e.g. MFCC) fail. In their MP technique, they used Gabor function based time-frequency dictionaries. It was claimed that features with Gabor properties could provide a flexible representation of time and frequency localization of unstructured sounds like environment. They applied K-NN (K = 1), and GMM with 5 mixtures [8, 10]. In [10], they also used SVM (support vector machine) with 2-degree of polynomial as classifier, and reduced the dimension by applying forward feature selection and backward feature selection procedures. Sixty-four dimensional MFCC, plus the spectral centroid were used as features in [11]. They used forensic application like audio files, where both ambient (environmental) sound and human speech were presented. However, they selected only those segments that were quieter than the average power in an audio file for the experiments. They introduced linear autoencoding neural networks for classifying environment. A hybrid autoencoder and GMM was used in their experiments, and 80.05% average accuracy was obtained. Wang et al [12] used three Moving Picture Experts Group (MPEG) audio low level descriptors as features in their work on

environmental sound classification. They proposed a hybrid SVM and K-NN classifier in their work. For SVM, they used three different types of kernel functions: linear
kernel, polynomial, and radial basis kernel. The system with 3 MPEG-7 features
achieved 85.1% accuracy averaged over 12 classes. Ntalampiras et al [13] used
MFCC along with MPEG-7 features to classify urban environments. They exploited a
full use of MPEG-7 low level descriptors, namely, audio waveform, audio power,
audio spectrum centroid, audio spectrum spread, audio spectrum flatness, harmonic
ration, upper limit of harmonicity, and audio fundamental frequency. To detect the
used microphone and the environments of recorded audio signals, Kraetzer et al [14]
extracted 63 statistical features from audio signals. Seven of the features were time
domain: empirical variance, covariance, entropy, LSB ratio, LSB flipping rate, mean
of samples, and median of samples. Besides these temporal features, they used 28
mel-cepstral features and 18 filtered mel-cepstral features. They applied K-NN and
Naïve Bayes classifiers to evaluate microphone and environmental classification.
Their work reported highest 41.54% accuracy obtained by Naïve Bayes classifier with
10 folds cross validation, while 26.49% as its best by simple k-means clustering. They
did not use HMM or GMM for classification.

The same files recorded for these environments have been verified by zero crossing
(ZC) features and MPEG-7 feature. For ZC features the average accuracy rate is 20%
and 40% when the number of samples 500000 and 1000000 respectively when the
training files are six. Figure 2 explains the accuracy is enhancement for ZC feature
when the numbers of samples are decreasing and increase the number of training files
[15].

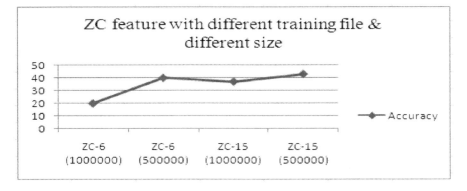

**Fig. 2.** Recognition accuracy for ZC feature

For MPEG-7 feature, we use low-level characteristics, Audio Waveform maximum
(AWF_max), Audio Waveform minimum (AWF_min), Audio Power (AP), Audio
Spectrum Envelop (ASE), Audio Spectrum Centroid (ASC) and Audio Spectrum
Spread (ASS). Table 1 is explain all low-level characteristics for MPEG-7 feature
with different training file and different sample and the accuracy enhancement when
the number of samples are decreasing and increase the number of training file.

**Table 1.** Recognition accuracies for MPEG-7 feature

| Type of experiment | 6 file training | | 15 file training | |
|---|---|---|---|---|
| feature Extraction | 1000000 Sample | 500000 Sample | 1000000 Sample | 500000 Sample |
| AWF_max | 26 | 32 | 24 | 46 |
| AWF_min | 34 | 31 | 44 | 51 |
| AP | 29 | 25 | 26 | 37 |
| ASE | 40 | 55 | 53 | 62 |
| ASC | 41 | 36 | 33 | 49 |
| ASS | 26 | 38 | 65 | 71 |

## 3  Data

We recorded audio signals from seven different scenarios: restaurant, office room fountain cafeteria, mall, meeting room and corridor. The duration for each environment is half hour (30 minutes). Each environment file is separated into many files with fixed number of samples. Sounds were recorded with an IC recorder (ICD-UX71F/UX81F/UX91F). Sampling rate was set to 22.05 KHz and quantization was 16 bit.

## 4  Linear Predictive Coding Extraction Feature

The Linear Predictive Coding method is one of the most popular approaches for processing speech. The most common representation is

$\widehat{x}(n) = \sum_{i=1}^{p} a_i x(n - i)$, Where $\widehat{x}(n)$ is the predicted signal value, $x(n - i)$ the

previous observed values, and $a_i$ the predictor coefficients. The error generated by this estimate is

$e(n) = x(n) - \widehat{x}(n)$, where $x(n)$ is the true signal value. [16]

## 5  K-NN Classifier Feature

We used K-Nearest Neighbor algorithm (KNN) as classifier. K is the most important parameter in a text categorization system based on KNN. In the classification process, K nearest documents to the test one in the training set are determined firstly. Then, the predication can be made according to the category distribution among this K nearest neighbors. KNN is one of the most popular algorithms for text categorization [17]. Many researchers have found that the KNN algorithm achieves very good performance in their experiments on different data sets [18-20]. The nearest neighbors are defined in terms of Euclidean distance. The Euclidean distance or Euclidean metric is the "ordinary" distance between two points that one would measure with a ruler, and is given by the Pythagorean formula.

$$d(p,q) = \sqrt{(p_1 - q_1)^2 + (p_2 - q_2)^2 + \dots + (p_n - q_n)^2} = \sqrt{\sum_{i=1}^{n} (p_i - q_i)^2}$$

# 6   Experimental Results and Discussion

In this section we evaluate the performance of LPC feature extraction. The steps of this experiment are:

1. Recorded many files for each environment in different places and different time.
2. Recording files were separated into two types for each environment: training files and testing files.
3. Each file is divided into many fixed-length frames (512 samples) with 256 sample overlapping
4. Compute LPC coefficient for each frame from training file and keep it in data base.
5. Compute LPC coefficient for each frame from testing file.
6. Use K-NN feature to compute the distance between LPC coefficient for each frame in testing file and all training file.
7. Comparing the results and reveal a smaller space. Smaller distance means that the environment file of the test is the training environment files

Two types of experiments are performed, one with decreasing number of samples per file and the other one with increasing number of training file. First, we decrease number of samples with fixed number of file training to six. Second, the same consideration with the number of training file is fifteen.

**Six training file with different number of samples**

The first six files from each environment' files are used for training, and the last five files for testing. The experiment was made with different number of samples 1000000, 500000 and 100000 samples for each file. The reason of this experiment is to see the affect of decreasing the number of samples. Results are shown in Table 2.

The average accuracy for all environments is 25% when the numbers of sample is 1000000, when we decrease numbers of sample to 500000 the average accuracy for

**Table 2.** Recognition accuracies for six training file.

| file # | 6 - file |
|---|---|
| LPC-(1000000) | 25 |
| LPC- (500000) | 44 |
| LPC- (100000) | 51 |

all environments is enhanced to 44%. Also when we decrease numbers of sample to 100000 samples the average accuracy is increased to 51%. In general the accuracy is increasing when the size of file is decreasing.

### Fifteen training file with different number of samples

In second experiment, we increased the number of training file from six to fifteen file with different number of samples. The accuracy is enhanced when the number of file training is increased. The highest accuracy achieved when the number of sample is 100000. The results are given in table 3.

**Table 3.** Recognition accuracies for fifteen training file

| file # | 15 file |
|--------|---------|
| LPC-(1000000) | 41 |
| LPC- (500000) | 49 |
| LPC- (100000) | 59 |

From table 2 and table 3 the average accuracy increased when we decreased number of sample and increased number of training file.

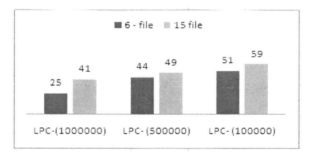

**Fig. 3.** Recognition accuracy for six and fifteen training files used LPC feature

Figure 3 give recognition accuracies (%) for each samples by varying the number of training files. From these figures we can find that by increasing the number of training files, recognition accuracies are increased with all the feature types. However, for the number of samples, the reverse is true. If we decrease the number of samples, the accuracies increase.

Figure 4 explains the comparison for LPC feature, ZC feature and MPEG-7 feature. For ZC feature give us more accuracy when the number of sample is decreasing to 500000 samples and when we increase the number of training file to fifteen file, give us the good accuracy for all different samples. For MPEG-7 feature low-level characteristics, all features give us good enhancement when the number of training file is fifteen. ASS and ASE feature are more accuracy. For LPC feature give us more accuracy when the number of sample is decreasing to 500000 samples and when we increase the number of training file to fifteen file, give us the good accuracy for all different samples.

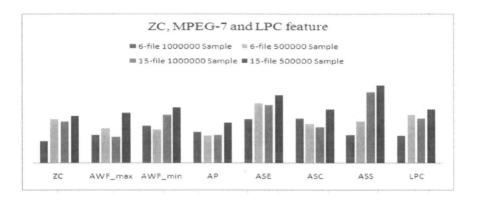

**Fig. 4.** Recognition accuracy for six and fifteen files training used ZC, MPEG-7 and LPC feature.

## 7  Conclusion

In this paper we investigated LPC features for environment sound recognition application and compare with ZC feature and MPEG-7 low level description feature. The experimental results showed significant improvement in accuracy using LPC when we increase number of file training and decrease number of samples. The future work is to study the effect of different types of other features and classifiers in environment recognition for audio forensics to achieve higher performance.

## References

[1] Delp, E., Memon, N., Wu, M.: Digital Forensics. IEEE Signal Process. Magazine, 14–15 (2009)
[2] Broeders, A.P.A.: Forensic Speech and Audio Analysis: the State of the Art in 2000 AD. Actas del I Congreso de la Sociedad Espanola de Acustica Forense, March, 13-24 (2000)
[3] Campbell, W., et al.: Understanding Scores in Forensic Speaker Recognition. In: ISCA Speaker Recognition Workshop, June, 1-8 (2006)
[4] AES AES43-2000: AES Standard for Forensic Purposes - Criteria for the Authentication of Analog Audio Tape Recordings. Journal of the Audio Engineering Society 48(3), 204–214 (2000)
[5] Rabiner, L.R., Juang, B.H.: Fundamentals of Speech Recognition. Prentice Hall, Englewood Cliffs (1993)
[6] Duda, R.O., Hart, P.E., Stork, D.G.: Pattern Classification, 2nd edn. Willey, New York (2001)
[7] Eronen, A.J., et al.: Audio-Based Context Recognition. IEEE Trans. Audio, Speech and Language Process 14(1), 321–329 (2006)

[8] Selina, C., Narayanan, S., Kuo, J.: Environmental sound recognition using MP-based features. In: Proc. IEEE International Conference on Acoustics, Speech and Signal Processing (ICASSP 2008), pp. 1–4 (2008)

[9] Mallat, S., Zhang, Z.: Matching pursuits with time-frequency dictionaries. IEEE Trans. on Signal Processing 41(12), 3397–3415 (1993)

[10] Selina, C., et al.: Where am I? Scene recognition for mobile robots using audio features. In: Proc. IEEE ICME 2006, pp. 885–888 (2006)

[11] Malkin, R.G., Waibel, A.: Classifying user environment for mobile applications using linear autoencoding of ambient audio. In: Proc. ICASSP 2005, pp. 509–512 (2005)

[12] Wang, J.C., et al.: Environmental sound classification using hybrid SVM/KNN classifier and MPEG-7 audio low-level descriptor. In: Proc. IEEE International Joint Conference on Neural Networks, Canada, pp. 1731–1735 (July 2006)

[13] Ntalampiras, S., Potamitis, I., FakotaKis, N.: Automatic recognition of urban environmental sounds events. In: Proc. CIP 2008, pp. 110–113 (2008)

[14] Kraetzer, C., et al.: Digital audio forensics: a first practical evaluation on microphone and environmental classification. In: Proc. ACM MultiMedia Security (MM&Sec), pp. 63–73 (2007)

[15] Alqahtani, M.O., Muhammad, G., Alotibi, Y.: Environment Sound Recognition using Zero Crossing Features and MPEG-7. In: ICADIWT 2010 (2010)

[16] http://en.wikipedia.org/wiki/Linear_prediction

[17] Manning, C.D., Schutze, H.: Foundations of Statistical Natural Language Processing. MIT Press, Cambridge (1999)

[18] Yang, Y., Liu, X.: A Re-examination of Text Categorization Methods. In: Proc. 22nd Annual International ACM SIGIR Conf. Research and Development in Inform. Retrieval, pp. 42–49 (1999)

[19] Joachims, T.: Text Categorization with Support Vector Machines: Learning with Many Relevant Features. In: Proc. Euro. Conf. Machine Learn (1998)

[20] Baoli, L., et al.: A Comparative Study on Automatic Categorization Methods for Chinese Search Engine. In: Proc. Eighth Joint International Computer Conference Hangzhou, pp. 117–120 (2002)

# Improving Code-Based Steganography with Linear Error-Block Codes

Rabiî Dariti and El Mamoun Souidi

Laboratoire de Mathématiques, Informatique et Applications
Faculté des Sciences, Université Mohammed V-Agdal
BP 1014 - Rabat - Morocco
rabiedariti@yahoo.fr, souidi@fsr.ac.ma

**Abstract.** We introduce a steganographic protocol based on linear error block codes. Our method is an extension of Westfeld's F5 algorithm. It allows to grow embedding capacity by exploiting more bits from the cover, in such a way that the probability for each bit to be flipped is related to its influence on the image quality. For example least significant bits (LSB) are the most exposed to alteration. Moreover, linear error-block codes, as a generalization of linear error correcting codes, provide larger and better choices for the codes to use. The results show that with a good choice of parameters, the change rate can also be reduced for an acceptable image quality.

**Keywords:** Linear Error-Block Codes, Steganography, LSB Embedding, F5 algorithm, Syndrome Decoding.

## 1 Introduction

Steganography aims to transfer a secret message through an open channel by using an other message, called the cover. The objective is that the existence of the secret message must be undetectable. This is done at coast of modifying some bits in the cover. A good steganographic scheme should ensure small changes in the cover for large secret message size, as well as keeping the changes made in the cover undetectable for analysts. The best known covers we can use in steganography come from multimedia data. Firstly because it is a digitation of physical quantities (voice, light ...), which produces pseudo-random sequences. Therefore, replacing a segment of bits with other pseudo-random data (an encrypted message) is to be statistically undetectable. Secondly, as multimedia data is presented by large sequences of bits, in general, there are some specific bits that can be flipped without causing any change that can be detected by human senses.

Primitive methods in steganography use a bitmap gray-scale image as a cover. The image is presented as a sequence of pixels and each pixel is presented by an 8-bit vector. This can be generalized to larger encoding and to multi-color images, since a multi-color image is the composition of individual gray-scale images representing basic colors, for example the red, green and blue. To embed

V. Snasel, J. Platos, and E. El-Qawasmeh (Eds.): ICDIPC 2011, Part II, CCIS 189, pp. 310–321, 2011.
© Springer-Verlag Berlin Heidelberg 2011

a secret message we first write it as a sequence of bits, then we select a list of pixels from the cover, and finally we replace the least significant bits (LSBs) of these pixels by the bit sequence representing the message. This method is called LSB embedding.

In 1970, an idea from Crandall [1] was to use an error correcting code to randomize the bits used to hide the secret message. The first implementation of a steganographic algorithm based in codes was in 2001 by Westfeld [2]. He chose to use Hamming codes which allow to embed $t$ message bits within $2^t - 1$ cover bits. A generalization of error correcting codes, called Linear Error-Block codes (LEBC), was introduced in 2006 by Feng et al. [3]. They added a new parameter to a code, called the type, that determines the metric to use to deal with it (calculating distances, weights of codewords, minimum distance etc.). Several works have been published to find optimal LEBCs [3,4,5,6,7]. It is shown in [5] that, in addition to classical perfect linear codes, there exist further perfect LEBCs, some of them have even minimum distance. Although LEBCs are not likely to be useful in correcting errors occurring in binary noisy channels, they have other applications in different fields. Namely, as cited in [3], numerical integration, orthogonal arrays and experimental design.

In this paper, we present a new method of steganography. We use linear error-block codes to handle the bits selected to carry the secret message. Our method is derived from the F5 algorithm [2], and it uses further than the first least significant bit. Actually, the metric used with linear error block codes allows to deal in the same vector with different levels of bits. This means, for example, we can allow to flip one bit from the second LSB level instead of flipping $n$ bits from the first LSB level. Or, we can select different sequences of bits, and order them by their ability to support distortion. The results show that our method offers good security parameters.

This paper is organized as follows. In Section 2 we recall basic definitions and set the notations to use. Section 3 describes how classical linear error correcting codes are applied in steganography. In Section 4 we introduce Linear error-block codes and recall the main tools to be used. Section 5 is our main contribution, it presents our steganographic scheme and motivates the use of Linear Error-Block Codes. The experimental results are given in Section 6. Section 7 involves conclusion and perspective of this work.

## 2    Preliminaries and Notation

A steganographic scheme features two essential components. First one is the cover: the support used to hide the secret message. The most used covers are multimedia files (image, audio or video). Thanks to their pseudo-random properties, they make statistical analysis to detect alteration more difficult, especially if the message is firstly encrypted. The second component is the steganographic protocol, that is the algorithms used to insert data in the cover, and then to extract it. These two algorithms are called respectively embedding (or dissimulation) and retrieval (or extraction). The well known LSB embedding method uses, for example, an image file as a cover, and allows to modify only the least significant bit (LSB) of each pixel in the image. Extensions of this method use further bit levels (the 2nd or/and the third LSBs) if their modification still be imperceptible.

In this paper we consider the cover as a sequence of bits (not necessarily LSBs) taken from an 8-bit gray-scale image. The reliability of a steganographic scheme is assessed with three main ratios [8]. First one is the *embedding rate*, witch presents the percentage of the message bits to the total cover bits.
Second one is the *embedding average distortion*, also called *embedding change rate*. It is the ratio of the changed bits in the cover to the total cover bits. It is well-known that the lower the embedding rate, the more difficult it is to reliably detect the message.

Third parameter is the *embedding efficiency*. It is defined as the average number of random message bits embedded using one embedding change. Clearly schemes with low embedding efficiency are more vulnerable than schemes with higher embedding efficiency. It reflects transparency (undetectability for human senses) of steganographic methods.

It is obvious that embedding capacity is expected to be as large as possible. However, since large size of secret information will lead to more distortions in general, this is contradictory with the expecting of image's transparency. Hence, a vital goal of steganography is to feature algorithms which simultaneously owns high embedding efficiency and large embedding capacity.

We focus in this paper in binary codes although any $q$-ary code can be used with the same technics. We use the following notations:

$m$: the (secret) message,
$x$: the cover,
$y$: the modified cover,
$E()$: the embedding map,
$R()$: the retrieval map.

# 3    Linear Error Correcting Codes in Steganography

The idea of using error correcting codes in steganography was firstly brought up by Crandall [1]. We generalize this method by using linear error-block codes which are a natural generalization of linear error correcting codes [3]. In this section we give an overview of Crandall's method.

Let $\mathcal{C}$ be a linear error correcting code of parity check matrix $H$. The retrieval map requires simply computing the syndrome of the modified cover $R(y) := S(y) = Hy^T$.

The embedding algorithm consists of three steps. First compute $u := S(x) - m$, then find $e_u$ a word of smallest weight among all words of syndrome $u$. This is the syndrome decoding problem. It is equivalent to decode $u$ in $\mathcal{C}$ and get the error vector $e_u$. Finally compute $E(m, x) := x - e_u$.

It is easy to verify that we have

$$R(E(m, x)) = S(x - e_u) = S(x) - S(e_u) = S(x) - u = m. \tag{1}$$

*Remark 1.* The word $e_u$ is chosen of minimum weight in order to have a minimal change rate. Otherwise, we could choose any other word of syndrome $u$ (i.e. in the same coset as $e_u$). Therefore, the uniqueness of $e_u$ is not necessary.

Munuera has proven in [9] that there exists a close relationship between steganographic protocols and error correcting codes. Construction, parameters and properties of both are similar, and the ones can be deduced from the others. In a steganography channel, the messages are the errors, so $t$, the correcting capacity of the code, actually describes how many message bits may be embedded. In other words, the maximum distortion of a carrier word with $t$ embedded characters is $t$. Thus, it should be expected that a perfect code would cause the minimum possible distortion, since the upper limit on $d(x, x')$, the distance between any word and the closest codeword to it, is the covering radius. The corresponding protocols to perfect codes are referred to as maximum length embeddable (MLE) protocols [10]. They result on a maximum embedding efficiency, that is also a minimum change rate for a given embedding capacity.

Hamming codes are a particularly interesting class used in steganography. Firstly, since they are perfect codes with covering radius 1, they embed within one bit alteration the largest possible relative payload $\dfrac{r}{2^r - 1}$, where $r$ is the message length [8]. Secondly, thanks to their fast and simple decoding algorithm, they allow easy and efficient embedding and extracting procedures.

## 4    Linear Error-Block Codes

Linear error-block codes (LEBC) are a generalization of linear error correcting codes. They were introduced in [3], and studied in several works [4,5,6,7]. The authors of [3] defined a special Hamming bound for LEBC with minimum distance even. The codes attaining this bound are thus considered perfect. There exist larger families of perfect linear error-block codes than the classical linear error correcting codes, but all of the known families are of minimum distance either 3 or 4 (in addition to the well known classical perfect codes which are also perfect error-block codes). The existence of more perfect LEBC is still an open problem.

In this section, we first recall preliminary notions to be used. Then we describe linear error-block codes. We discuss the metric used to deal with these codes.

A composition $\pi$ of a positive integer $n$ is given by $n = l_1 m_1 + l_2 m_2 + \cdots + l_r m_r$, where $r, l_1, l_2, \ldots, l_r, m_1, m_2, \ldots, m_r$ are integers $\geq 1$, and is denoted

$$\pi = [m_1]^{l_1} [m_2]^{l_2} \ldots [m_r]^{l_r} \tag{2}$$

If moreover $m_1 > m_2 > \cdots > m_r \geq 1$ then $\pi$ is called a partition.

Let $q$ be a prime power and $\mathbb{F}_q$ be the finite field with $q$ elements. Let $s$, $r$, $l_1, l_2, \ldots, l_r, n_1, n_2, \ldots, n_s$ be the non negative integers given by a partition $\pi$ as

$$s = l_1 + \cdots + l_r,$$
$$n_1 = n_2 = \cdots = n_{l_1} = m_1$$
$$n_{l_1+1} = n_{l_1+2} = \cdots = n_{l_1+l_2} = m_2$$
$$\vdots$$
$$n_{l_1+\cdots+l_{r-1}+1} = n_{l_1+\cdots+l_{r-1}+2} = \cdots = n_s = m_r$$

We can write

$$\pi = [n_1][n_2]\ldots[n_s]. \tag{3}$$

Let $V_i = \mathbb{F}_q^{n_i}$ ($1 \le i \le s$) and $V = V_1 \oplus V_2 \oplus \ldots \oplus V_s = \mathbb{F}_q^n$. Each vector in $V$ can be written uniquely as $v = (v_1, \ldots, v_s)$, $v_i \in V_i$ ($1 \le i \le s$). For any $u = (u_1, \ldots, u_s)$ and $v = (v_1, \ldots, v_s)$ in $V$, the $\pi$-weight $w_\pi(u)$ of $u$ and the $\pi$-distance $d_\pi(u, v)$ of $u$ and $v$ are defined by

$$w_\pi(u) = \sharp\{i/1 \le i \le s, u_i \ne 0 \in V_i\} \text{ and} \tag{4}$$

$$d_\pi(u, v) = w_\pi(u - v) = \sharp\{i/1 \le i \le s, u_i \ne v_i\}. \tag{5}$$

This means that a fixed vector can be of different $\pi$-weights if we change $\pi$. For example, consider the word $v = 1010001101$ of length 10 and the two partitions of the number 10: $\pi = [3][2]^3[1]$ and $\pi' = [3]^2[2][1]^2$. We have $w_\pi(v) = 4$ while $w_{\pi'}(v) = 3$.

An $\mathbb{F}_q$-linear subspace $\mathcal{C}$ of $V$ is called an $[n, k, d]_q$ linear error-block code over $\mathbb{F}_q$ of type $\pi$, where $k = dim_{\mathbb{F}_q}(\mathcal{C})$ and $d = d_\pi(\mathcal{C})$ is the minimum $\pi$-distance of $\mathcal{C}$, which is defined as

$$d = \min\{d_\pi(c, c')/c, c' \in \mathcal{C}, c \ne c'\}$$
$$= \min\{w_\pi(c)/0 \ne c \in \mathcal{C}\}. \tag{6}$$

*Remark 2.* A classical linear error correcting code is a linear error-block code of type $\pi = [1]^n$.

*Remark 3.* A linear error-block code with a composition type is equivalent to some linear error-block code with a partition type.

The difference between decoding linear error block codes and decoding classical linear error correcting codes is the use of the $\pi$-distance instead of the Hamming distance. Therefore, coset leaders are words having minimum $\pi$-weight, although sometimes they are not of minimum Hamming weight.

It is well known that perfect codes have odd minimum distance. Nonetheless, the Hamming bound presented in [3] allows to construct perfect codes with even minimum distance. This is done by considering the sets

$$B'_\pi(c, \frac{d}{2}) = B_\pi(c, \frac{d}{2} - 1) \cup \left\{ x \in V; d_\pi(c, x) = \frac{d}{2} \text{ and } x_1 \neq c_1 \right\} \quad (7)$$

where $B_\pi(c, r) = \{x \in V; d_\pi(x, c) \leq r\}$ is the ball of center a codeword $c$ and radius $r$. The sets $B'_\pi(c, \frac{d}{2})$ are pairwise disjoint. (And if the code is perfect, their union for all codewords $c$ covers the space $V$). A word $x \in V$ is thus decoded as $c$ if $x \in B'_\pi(c, \frac{d}{2})$. Therefore, the decoding algorithm of a code with even minimum distance $d$ corrects, further, error patterns with both $\pi$-weight $d/2$ and non null first block.

To construct a syndrome table, we add the following condition. If a coset of weight $d/2$ has more than one leader, we select among them a word which has a non null first block. Note that the coset leader has not to be unique unless the code is perfect. The maximum likelihood decoding (MLD) [11] is slightly modified.

*Remark 4.* This decoding technique can also be used with classical codes. Therefore, quasi-perfect codes [11] are considered perfect and can perform complete decoding. This makes them more efficient in steganography.

*Example 1.* Let $\pi = [3][2]^2[1]$, if we have to choose a coset leader between the words $e_1 = 000|01|00|1$ and $e_2 = 010|01|00|0$, we select the second one, since they are both of $\pi$-weight 2 and the first block of $e_2$ is not null.

Note that this does not guaranty that every error pattern of $\pi$-weight $d/2$ can be corrected. We present below an example of syndrome decoding of a given linear error-block code.

*Example 2.* Consider $\mathcal{C}$ the binary $[7, 3]$ code of type $\pi = [3][2][1]^2$, defined with its parity check matrix

$$H = \begin{pmatrix} 1 & 1 & 1 & 0 & 0 & 0 & 1 \\ 0 & 1 & 1 & 1 & 1 & 0 & 0 \\ 1 & 0 & 0 & 1 & 0 & 1 & 0 \\ 1 & 0 & 1 & 0 & 0 & 1 & 0 \end{pmatrix}$$

Syndromes are computed by the classical formula $s = Hx^T$, $x \in \mathbb{F}_2^7$. The words which have the same syndrome belong to the same coset. Coset leaders are words which have the minimum $\pi$-weight in their cosets. The syndrome table of the code $\mathcal{C}$ is presented in Table 1. We added two columns to mark, in the first one, the difference between the use of the $\pi$-distance and the Hamming distance, and in the second one, cases where $\pi$-metric decoding is not unique (since $d_\pi = 2$, correction capacity is $t_\pi = 1$). Note that in line 5, since the first block of the right side column word is null, it can not be chosen as a coset leader. In lines 6 and 8, the third column words have $\pi$-weight 2, they also can not be coset leaders. While in the last four lines, all of the right side column words can be a coset leader.

**Table 1.** Syndrome table of the error-block code $\mathcal{C}$

| Coset leader | Syndrome | C.L. using Hamming distance (if different) | Other coset words with minimum $\pi$-weight |
|---|---|---|---|
| 000 00 0 0 | 0000 | - | |
| 100 00 0 0 | 1011 | - | |
| 010 00 0 0 | 1100 | - | |
| 001 00 0 0 | 1101 | - | |
| 101 00 0 0 | 0110 | 0001000 | 000 10 0 0 |
| 110 00 0 0 | 0111 | - or 0000110 | |
| 011 00 0 0 | 0001 | - | |
| 111 00 0 0 | 1010 | 0101000 | |
| 000 01 0 0 | 0100 | - | |
| 000 11 0 0 | 0010 | - | |
| 000 00 1 0 | 0011 | - | |
| 000 00 0 1 | 1000 | - | |
| 100 01 0 0 | 1111 | - or 0100010 | 010 00 1 0 - 001 11 0 0 - 110 00 0 1 |
| 001 01 0 0 | 1001 | - | 011 00 0 1 - 111 00 1 0 - 100 11 0 0 |
| 011 01 0 0 | 0101 | 0001010 or 0010001 | 001 00 0 1 - 101 00 1 0 - 110 11 0 0 |
| 111 01 0 0 | 1110 | 0001001 or 0010010 | 001 00 1 0 - 010 11 0 0 - 101 00 0 1 |

## 5   Linear Error-Block Codes in Steganography

By using the $\pi$-distance, when we correct a single error-block, all the bits in the block are being corrected at once [6], which means that we recover within one error correction not less than one message bit. The maximum recovered bits is the size of the corrected block. In other words, assume that to embed a $k$-bit message we have to modify $r$ bits in the $n$-bit cover. These $r$ bits are located in $r'$ blocks where $r' \leq r$. Thus we have to provoke $r'$ errors, whilst with a classical code we provoke $r$ errors.

However, it may happen, for some partitions, that alteration of a whole block is needed, while if we use a classical code we just need to flip a single bit to embed the same message. In Example 3 (page 319), the coset leader for Hamming distance is $e_u = 0001000$ (Line 5 of Table 1), which looks more interesting to use. Nevertheless, the blocks are distributed over the cover in order to give preferential treatment to each block of bits. The size and the order of the blocks are considered as well. It is clear that the smaller is the block, the less is its probability of distortion. We show in the next subsection that it might be more suitable to flip a whole block rather than a single bit.

Although syndrome decoding using the $\pi$-distance returns coset leaders with more non null bits than Hamming distance, application of linear error-block codes in steganography is motivated by the following vision. In general, pictures feature areas that can better hide distortion than other areas. The human vision system is unable to detect changes in inhomogeneous areas of a digital media, due to the complexity of such areas. For example, if we modify the gray values of pixels in smooth areas of a gray-scale image, they will be more easily noticed by human eyes. In the other hand, the pixels in edged areas may tolerate larger

Inhomogeneous area

Homogeneous area

**Fig. 1.** Embedding 16-valued pixel in two areas of Lena gray-scale image

changes of pixel values without causing noticeable changes (Fig. 1). So, we can keep the changes in the modified image unnoticeable by embedding more data in edged areas than in smooth areas.

Another vision consists of using one or two bits next to the least significant ones. Actually, the least significant bits (LSB) are the most suitable, but we can use further bit levels if this does not cause noticeable change to the image (Fig. 2). There are many embedding methods that uses bit signification levels in different ways [12,13,14]. For our method, there are two possibilities. First one, we select a list $(p_i)_{i \in I}$ of pixels to be modified, and embed the message within (some) bit levels of this list. The pixels must then be located in a sufficiently inhomogeneous area. The second way is by selecting independently, for each bit level $j$, a list $(p_i)_{i \in I_j}$ of pixels to be manipulated. Hence more bits are used, resulting in a larger cover size. If the pixels are strong enough against distortion, higher bit levels can be used but with smaller and smaller block sizes.

We sketch our method in Figure 3. The cover bits are assorted by their ability to hide distortion. Thus, in the previous examples, first level bits refer to the most inhomogeneous areas or to the least significant bits. We can also combine these methods by assorting bits starting from the LSB of the most inhomogeneous area to the last significant bit considered of the most homogeneous area.

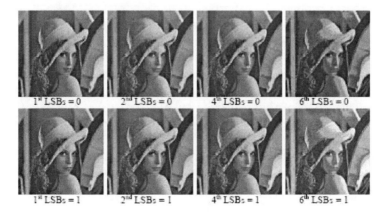

**Fig. 2.** Lena image with different bit levels switched to 0 or 1

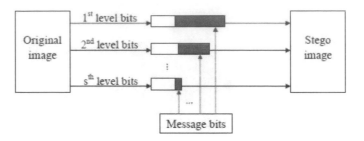

**Fig. 3.** Overview of our embedding method

Now assume we have made $s$ sequences of cover bits assorted by their ability to support distortion in the decreasing sens (i.e. the first sequence bits are the less sensitive to distortion). We note the $i^{th}$ sequence $(a^i_j)_{j=1,2,..,m_i}$. In the next step, we reorder the bits such that the cover will be written as blocks $x = (x_1, x_2, \ldots, x_s)$ where $x_i \in V_i$ is a subsequence of $n_i$ bits of $a^i$ (we use the notation of Section 4). Considering these blocks, a partition $\pi = [n_1][n_2] \ldots [n_s]$ of the size of the cover is defined. And the cover is viewed as a list of vectors $x \in V$. Therefore, the distortion of the first level bits is more probable than the distortion of the second level bits, and so on. The sizes of the blocks are chosen such that the complete distortion of any block (the distortion of all of its bits) has an equal effect on the image change. In the next section we show how is a linear error-block code of type $\pi$ used.

*Remark 5.* If the cover bits have equal influence on image quality, for example only LSBs are used or all the bits are located in an area of a constant homogeneity, then $\pi$ turns to the classical partition $\pi = [1]^n$.

The steganographic protocol we propose follows the same steps as in Section 3. But with the $\pi$-distance, the syndrome decoding seeks coset leaders among vectors with non null first block. Therefore, we can have better image quality since first blocks contain the less sensitive bits. In the following we describe the steps of the embedding/retrieval algorithm and give a practical example.

Let $\mathcal{C}$ be an $[n, k]$ linear error-block code of type $\pi$ and of parity check matrix $H$. The syndrome of a vector $v \in V$ is computed by the product $S(v) = Hv^T$. Hence the retrieval algorithm is defined by $R(y) := S(y) = Hy^T$.

The first step of the embedding algorithm is also simple, it consists of computing $u := S(x) - m$.

Now to accomplish the embedding operation we compute $E(m, x) := x - e_u$ where $e_u$ is the coset leader of $u$. The vector $e_u$ is also the error vector found by decoding $u$ in $\mathcal{C}$. We can compute it by the decoding algorithm presented in Section 4.

*Remark 6.* In our steganographic protocol, we do not need to perform a unique decoding (see Remark 1), so we can choose any coset leader with the only condition that it has minimum $\pi$-weight.

The final step is computing $y = x - e_u$.

*Example 3.* Assume we have a (part of a) cover $x = 0001101$, and that the first block of three bits is located in an area that can hide more distortion than the second block of two bits, and that the remaining two blocks of one bit are more sensitive to distortion. The cover is of size 7 and we just defined the partition $\pi = [3][2][1]^2$. We use the code $\mathcal{C}$ of Example 2. Let $m = 1100$ be the message to hide. We follow the steps:

**Embedding**
1. $u = S(x) - m = 0110$
2. $e_u = 1010000$ (found from the syndrome table)
3. $y = E(x, m) = x - e_u = 1011101$

**Retrieval**
$R(y) = S(y) = 1100$

## 6 Results

The proposed method was tested with 3 different messages to be hidden within the famous Lena gray-scale image of size $256 \times 256$. For each message, we applied several linear error-block codes with deferent partitions. The messages are divided to blocks which have the same size as the code length.

**Table 2.** Steganography performance of a $[7, 3]$ error-block code

| $\pi$ | $s$ | $\rho_\pi$ | $\frac{n-k}{s}$ | $\frac{\rho_\pi}{s}$ |
|---|---|---|---|---|
| $[1]^7$ | 7 | 2 | 0.5714 | 0.2857 |
| $[2][1]^5$ | 6 | 2 | 0.6666 | 0.3333 |
| $[2]^2[1]^3$ | 5 | 2 | 0.8000 | 0.4000 |
| $[3][2][1]^2$ | 4 | 2 | 1.0000 | 0.5000 |
| $[4][2][1]$ | 3 | 2 | 1.3333 | 0.6666 |

**Table 3.** Steganography performance of a $[6, 3]$ error-block code

| $\pi$ | $s$ | $\rho_\pi$ | $\frac{n-k}{s}$ | $\frac{\rho_\pi}{s}$ |
|---|---|---|---|---|
| $[1]^6$ | 6 | 2 | 0.5000 | 0.3333 |
| $[2][1]^4$ | 5 | 1 | 0.6000 | 0.2000 |
| $[3][1]^3$ | 4 | 1 | 0.7500 | 0.2500 |
| $[3][2][1]$ | 3 | 1 | 1.0000 | 0.3333 |
| $[5][1]$ | 2 | 1 | 1.5000 | 0.5000 |

**Table 4.** Steganography performance of a $[9, 3]$ error-block code

| $\pi$ | $s$ | $\rho_\pi$ | $\frac{n-k}{s}$ | $\frac{\rho_\pi}{s}$ |
|---|---|---|---|---|
| $[1]^9$ | 9 | 2 | 0.6666 | 0.2222 |
| $[2]^2[1]^5$ | 7 | 2 | 0.8571 | 0.2857 |
| $[3][2][1]^4$ | 6 | 2 | 1.0000 | 0.3333 |
| $[3][2]^2[1]^2$ | 5 | 2 | 1.2000 | 0.4000 |
| $[4]^2[1]$ | 3 | 2 | 2.0000 | 0.6666 |

Tables 2, 3 and 4 summarizes the results for one block embedding. In order to compare the performance of different partitions, we used the following parameters; $\frac{n-k}{s}$ measures the block-embedding rate, $\rho_\pi$ measures the maximum embeddable blocks, it is also the $\pi$-covering radius of the code defined by

$$\rho_\pi = max\{d_\pi(x, \mathcal{C}), x \in \mathbb{F}_q^n\}. \tag{8}$$

And finally $\frac{\rho_\pi}{s}$ measures the block embedding average distortion.

The results show that a careful selection of the code and the partition is critical. For a fixed code, a partition of a few number of blocks causes a big block-average distortion $\frac{\rho_\pi}{s}$ (if the covering radius $\rho_\pi$ remains unchanged), whilst a big number of blocks causes a small block-embedding rate $\frac{n-k}{s}$. For the $[6, 3]$ code of Table 3, it is clear that the partition $[2][1]^4$ is the best, since it provides the largest block-embedding capacity and the smallest block-embedding distortion.

## 7   Conclusion and Perspective

We introduced in this paper a useful application of linear error-block codes in steganography. Our scheme increases the number of exploitable bits in a given image (cover), and decreases the average distortion with some codes. Specifically, further bits in the image can be exploited such as second least significant bits and/or the pixels located in homogeneous areas. The average distortion is decreased if we succeed to find, for given parameters $n$ and $k$, a linear error-block code with smaller covering radius than the classical one. A major factor to get the maximum benefit from this scheme, besides the choice of codes, is the choice of the cover. Two methods were given to make up a suitable cover. The first method suggests to assort the areas of the cover image regarding their ability to hide distortion, and the second one exploits the second LSBs. We should carefully select the pixels that allow flipping the second (or further) LSBs, since in general not the whole cover pixels are suitable. Forthcoming work involves defining a direct relationship between cover-pixels homogeneity and the optimal partition to use with the code.

Further improvement can be carried to this method by using perfect codes. Actually, there exist large families of perfect linear error-block codes [5]. They have different types, but they are all of covering radius either 1 or 2. It is also of concern to look for LEBCs with good covering properties and with fast decoding algorithms.

# References

1. Crandall, R.: Some Notes on Steganography. Posted on Steganography Mailing List (1998), http://os.inf.tu-dresden.de/~westfeld/crandall.pdf
2. Westfeld, A.: F5-A Steganographic Algorithm. In: IHW 2001: Proceedings of the 4th International Workshop on Information Hiding, pp. 289–302 (2001)
3. Feng, K., Xu, L., Hickernell, F.J.: Linear Error-Block Codes. Finite Fields Appl. 12, 638–652 (2006)
4. Ling, S., Özbüdak, F.: Constructions and Bounds on Linear Error-Block Codes. Designs, Codes and Cryptography 45, 297–316 (2007)
5. Dariti, R., Souidi, E.M.: New Families of Perfect Linear Error-Block Codes (submitted)
6. Dariti, R., Souidi, E.M.: Cyclicity and Decoding of Linear Error-Block Codes. Journal of Theoretical and Applied Information Technology 25(1), 39–42 (2011)
7. Udomkavanicha, P., Jitman, S.: Bounds and Modifications on Linear Error-block Codes. International Mathematical Forum 5(1), 35–50 (2010)
8. Bierbrauer, J., Fridrich, J.: Constructing Good Covering Codes for Applications in Steganography. Transactions on data hiding and multimedia security III 3, 1–22 (2008)
9. Munuera, C.: Steganography and Error Correcting Codes. Signal Process. 87, 1528–1533 (2007)
10. Zhang, W., Li, S.: A Coding Problem in Steganography. Designs, Codes and Cryptography 46(1), 67–81 (2008)
11. van Lint, J.H.: Introduction to Coding Theory, Graduate Texts in Mathematics, 3rd edn., vol. 86. Springer, Berlin (1999)
12. Liao, X., Wen, Q.: Embedding in Two Least Significant Bits with Wet Paper Coding. In: CSSE 2008: Proceedings of the 2008 International Conference on Computer Science and Software Engineering, pp. 555–558 (2008)
13. Zhang, X., Zhang, W., Wang, S.: Efficient Double-Layered Steganographic Embedding. Electronics letters 43, 482 (2007)
14. Zhang, W., Zhang, X., Wang, S.: A Double Layered "Plus-Minus One" Data Embedding Scheme. IEEE Signal Process. Lett. 14(11), 848–851 (2007)

# Vibration of Composite Plate - Mathematical Modelling and Experimental Verification by ESPI

David Seidl[1], Pavol Koštial[1], Zora Jančíková[1], and Soňa Rusnáková[2]

[1] VŠB - Technical University of Ostrava,
Faculty of Metallurgy and Materials Engineering,
17. listopadu 15/2172, 70833 Ostrava - Poruba,
Czech Republic
[2] Tomas Bata University in Zlín, Faculty of Technology,
T. G. Masaryka 275, 762 72 Zlín,
Czech Republic
{David Seidl,Pavol Koštial,Zora Jančíková,
Soňa Rusnáková}@Springer.com

**Abstract.** For observatory of vibrations of composite rectangular plate were used two different methods: mathematical and experimental. Experimental part was done by electronic speckle pattern interferometry (ESPI). This method - ESPI - is very suitable for non-destructive observatory several types of materials - in our experiment it is composite rectangular plate. Results of this method - vibration modes - are applicable especially in designing of various structures. Results of the mathematical modelling are suitable for verifying and comparison with results from ESPI method - they are very comparisonable. In our mathematical modelling program MARC was used with help of the FEM.

**Keywords:** ESPI - electronic speckle pattern interferometry, vibration mode, FEM - finite element method, composite, resonant frequency.

## 1 Introduction

Most of the works on vibration analysis of plates published in the literature are analytical and numerical and very few experimental results are available. Existing modal analysis techniques such as accelerometers and laser Doppler vibrometers are pointwise measurement techniques and are used in conjunction with spectrum analyzers and modal analysis software to characterize the vibration behaviour. In this study, a technique called electronic speckle pattern interferometry (ESPI) optical system is employed to investigate the vibration behaviour of square laminate plate. This method is very convenient to investigated vibration objects because no contact is required compared to classical modal analysis using accelerometers. High-quality interferometric fringes for mode shapes are produced instantly by a video recording system. Based on the fact that clear fringe patterns will appear only at resonant frequencies,

V. Snasel, J. Platos, and E. El-Qawasmeh (Eds.): ICDIPC 2011, Part II, CCIS 189, pp. 322–328, 2011.
© Springer-Verlag Berlin Heidelberg 2011

both resonant frequencies and corresponding mode shapes can be obtained experimentally using the present method. The square plate is most using structural element in industry. The square laminate plate we select for its shape simplicity and undemanding character for clamping. The square laminate plate is fixed by special metal frame on elastic rubber. So we reach all its degree of freedom. The tested object is vibrated by loudspeaker, which is situated behind the tested plate. The boundary conditions are investigated in this study, namely free–free–free–free (FFFF).

The numerical calculations by finite element method are also performed and the results are compared with the experimental measurements. Excellent agreements are obtained for both results of resonant frequencies and mode shapes. ESPI has been recently developed and widely used because it has the advantage of being able to measure surface deformations of engineering components and materials in industrial areas without contact. ESPI was used for tuning and visualization of natural frequencies of Kevlar/epoxy square plate. Numerical calculations by finite element method are also performed and the results are compared with the experimental measurements. Good agreements are obtained for both results. Our experimental setup consists of tested object, laser, CCD-camera, PC, generator, loudspeaker, special optical head, lens, mirrors. Vibration of elastic plates has been widely studied; both from experimental and theoretical points of view [1–4], since plates are important components in many engineering applications. A vast literature exists for the flexural vibration of rectangular plates.

Measurement/monitoring of vibration of machines, equipments and complex structures is necessary to diagnose various problems associated with them so that their breakdown is prevented and also the noise levels can be controlled. Mathematical models for analytical solutions are only symbolic and useful for the idealized systems, where all the assumptions are imposed on the physical problem. Analytical solutions for vibration of membranes and thin plates were considered for simplified cases [5]. In complex cases and in actual operating conditions, it is however, difficult to manage the vibration problem analytically. Measurement of vibration is needed to fulfil two main objectives: the first is to determine the vibration level of the structure or machine under actual operating conditions and the second is to validate theoretical predictions. Due to the pressing need to design lighter, more flexible and less damped structures and on-line monitoring of vibration in factory or shop floor environment, there is a need to develop an accurate and precise vibration measurement/monitoring system. Optical techniques developed for measurement/monitoring of vibrations have wide dynamic range of frequencies. ESPI technique is a full field, non-contact, non-evasive and almost real time method to measure the vibrations of structures subjected to various kinds of loading [6-7]. ESPI is faster in operation and less sensitive to environmental perturbations than holography. In ESPI, the speckle pattern is formed by illuminating the surface of the object by laser light. The object wave is imaged on the photosensitive part of the CCD camera where it is allowed to interfere with an in-line reference beam. The interferograms of two different states of the object are grabbed and subtracted. The speckle correlation fringes are thus displayed on computer monitor using digital techniques.

## 2 Experimental Part: Technique and Methods

The schematic layout of ESPI optical system, as shown in Fig.1, is employ to perform the out-of-plane vibration measurement of the resonant frequencies and mode shape for composite plate. The real experimental setup is on Fig. 2. The mode shape is a specific pattern of vibration executed by a mechanical system at a specific frequency. Different mode shapes will be associated with different frequencies. The experimental technique of ESPI analysis discovers these mode shapes and the frequencies.

Composite plates with all edges free are used to have the ideal boundary conditions for experimental simulation. The resonant frequency and correspondent mode shape for the vibrating plate are determined experimentally using the no - contacting optical method ESPI. A He - Ne laser with wavelength $\lambda = 632,8\ nm$ is used as the coherent light source.

The laser beam is divided into two parts, the reference and object beam, by a beamsplitter. The object beam travels to the specimen and then reflects to the CCD camera via the mirror and reference plate. The CCD camera converts the intensity distribution of the interference pattern of the object into a corresponding video signal. The signal is electronically processed and finally converted into an image on the video monitor.

The experimental procedure of ESPI technique is performed as follows. First, a reference image is taken, after the specimen vibrates, then the second image is taken, and the reference image is subtracted by the image processing system. If the vibrating frequency is not the resonant frequency, only randomly distributed speckles are displayed and no fringe patterns will be shown. However, if the vibrating frequency is in the neighborhood of the resonant frequency, stationary distinct fringe patterns will be observed. Then the function generator is carefully and slowly turned, the number of fringes will increase and the fringe pattern will become clearer as the resonant frequency is approached. The resonant frequencies and corresponding mode shapes can be determined at the same time using the ESPI optical system.

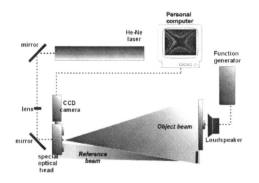

**Fig. 1.** Schematic diagram of ESPI setup          **Fig. 2.** ESPI optical system

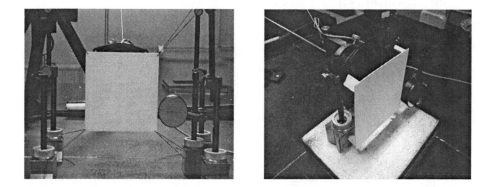

**Fig. 3.** The attachment of the plate on flexible strings and rubbers

The resonant frequency and correspondent mode shape for the vibrating laminate plate are determined experimentally using the non contacting optical method ESPI. Publications [9, 10] detailed describes a principle of this method. Plates are structural elements of great importance and are used extensively in all fields of engineering applications such as aerospace and electronic industry.

The object of observation is Kevlar/epoxy composite plate. The material properties of the plate are: $E = 25, 9\ GPa$, $G = 10, 4\ GPa$, $v = 0, 47$, the dimension of laminate plate *175 x 175 mm*, the density $\rho = 1450\ kg/m^3$, thickness $h = 0,3\ mm$.

Composites are materials consisting of a combination of high-strength stiff fibers embedded in a common matrix (binder) material; for example, graphite fibers and epoxy resin. Composite structures are made of a number of fibers and epoxy resin laminates. These laminates can number from *2* to greater than *50*, and are generally bonded to a substructure such as aluminum or nonmetallic honeycomb. The much stiffer fibres of graphite, boron, and Kevlar epoxies have given composite materials structural properties superior to the metal alloys they have replaced. The use of composites is not new. Fiber glass, for example, has been used for some time in various aircraft components. However, the term advanced composites applies to graphite, boron, and Kevlar, which have fibers of superior strength and stiffness. The use of these advanced composite materials does represent a new application for naval aircraft. [11, 12].

We compared experimental obtained the resonant frequencies by ESPI with the numerical frequencies (FEM). Isotropic materials have physical properties, which are the same in all directions. Orthotropic materials have properties, which are different when measured at right angles to one another. The view on corresponding mode shapes is described on the Figure 4. Numerical results of resonant frequencies and mode shapes are calculated by using the commercially available software, Cosmos finite element package. Comparison of theoretical predicted resonant frequencies with experimental results for the FFFF plate are summarized in the Table 1.

## 3 The Vibration Theory of the Plate

Equation of motion for free vibration of a flat plate of uniform thickness made of homogeneous isotropic material is given by [8]

$$D\nabla^4 w + \rho \frac{\partial^2 w}{\partial t^2} = 0 \qquad (1)$$

where $w$ is the transverse defection, $D = Eh^3/12(1-v^2)$ is the plate stiffness, $E$ the modulus of elasticity, $h$ the thickness of the plate, $v$ the Poisson's ratio of the material of the plate, $\rho$ the mass density per unit area of plate surface, $t$ the time, $\nabla^4$ the biharmonic differential operator (i.e: $\Delta^4 = \Delta^2\Delta^2$ ) and $\Delta^2 = (\partial^2/\partial x^2) + (\partial^2/\partial y^2)$ in rectangular coordinate.

## 4 Results and Conclusion

This study investigates the resonant frequencies and mode shapes of laminate composite plate for out of - plane vibrations by experimental technique ESPI and FEM. It has shown that the ESPI method has the advantages of non-contact, full-field, real-time and high-resolution measurement. Excellent quality of interferometric fringes for mode shapes is presented by a video recording system. [13] For the laminate plate, the resonant frequencies and full-field mode shapes up to nine modes are measured by ESPI and are excellently correlated with FEM results. Excellent agreements between the theoretical predictions and experimental measurements of resonant frequencies and mode shapes are obtained. However, the difference between the experimental measurement and FEM results may result from the determination of the material properties and defects of the composite plate. Composite industry is very popular today, with big volume of different and unexplored materials. As well, we can say that each composite product is original. We determine the type of materials only in productions process. It is shown that this optical method has the advantages of non-contact, real-time and high-resolution measurement for the vibration behaviour of laminate materials.

**Table 1.** Comparison of theoretical predicted resonant frequencies with experimental results for the FFFF plate

| Mode | 1 | 2 | 3 | 4 | 5 | 6 | 7 | 8 | 9 |
|---|---|---|---|---|---|---|---|---|---|
| ESPI (Hz) | 69 | 79 | 156 | 264 | 560 | 640 | 742 | 837 | 1816 |
| FEM (Hz) | 91 | 69 | 132 | 303 | 580 | 736 | 740 | 899 | 1831 |
| Error (%) | 24 | 14 | 18 | 13 | 3 | 13 | 0 | 7 | 1 |

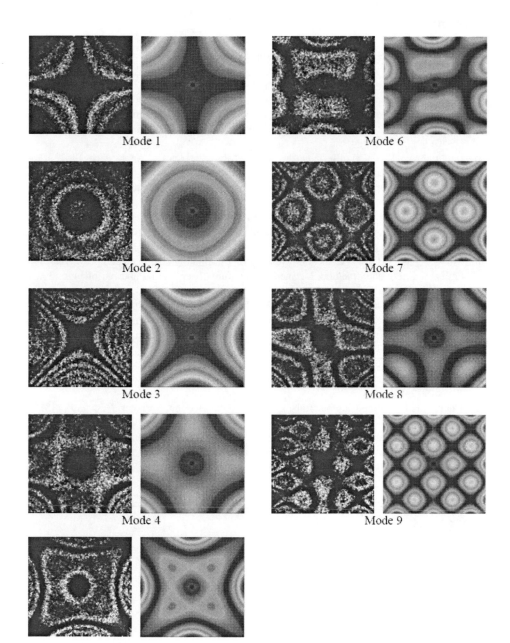

**Fig. 4.** Mode shapes – experimental (ESPI) and analytical (FEM)

# References

1. Caldersmith, G.W.: Vibrations of orthotropic rectangular plates. J. Acoustica 56, 144–152 (1984)
2. Leissa, A.W.: The free vibration of rectangular plates. J. Sound Vib. 31, 257–293 (1973)
3. Stokey, W.F., Harris, C.M.: Vibrations of systems having distributed mass and elasticity in shock and vibration handbook, pp. 7.1–7.37 McGraw-Hill Book Comp, New York (1961)
4. Young, D.: Vibration of rectangular plates by the Ritz method. J. Appl. Mech. 17, 448–453 (1950)
5. Barton, M.V.: Vibration of rectangular and skewcantilever plates. J. Appl. Mech. 18, 129–134 (1951)
6. Fein, H.: Holographic inteferometry: non-destructive tool. J. The Industrial Physicist, 37–38 (1997)
7. Huang, C., Hung, M., Chien, C.: Experimental and numerical investigations of resonant vibration characteristics for piezoceramic plates. J. Acoustical society of America 109(6), 2780–2788 (2001)
8. Ma, C.C., Lin, C.C.: Experimental investigation of vibrating laminated composite plates by optical interferometry method. J. American Institute of aeronautics and Astronautics 39(3), 491–497 (2001)
9. Rusnáková, S., Slabeycius, J., Rusnák, V.: The possibilities of holographic speckle interferometry by investigation of composite materials. In: Photonics Prague 2005, the 5th International Conference on Photonics, Devices and Systems, Praha, pp. 109–115 (2005); ISBN 80-86742-08-3
10. Rusnáková, S., Kopal, I., Koštial, P.: The applications of waveprocess for the study of glass fibre reinforced laminates. J. Current topics in acoustical research 4, 1–10 (2006); ISSN 0972-4818
11. Chawla, K.K.: Composite materials, science and engineering. Springer, New York (1987); ISBN 0-387-96478-9
12. Geier, M.H.: Quality handbook for composite material. I. ASM International (1999)
13. Wang, W.C., Hwang, C.H., Lin, S.Y.: Vibration measurement by the time-average electronic speckle pattern interferometry methods. Applied Optics 35(22), 4502–4509 (1996)

# SIP Registration Burst Load Test

Jan Rozhon and Miroslav Voznak

VSB – Technical University of Ostrava, 17. listopadu 15,
708 33 Ostrava, Czech Republic
{jan.rozhon,miroslav.voznak}@vsb.cz

**Abstract.** The paper deals with performance testing a SIP infrastructure. While
the working methodology for measuring performance and effectiveness of the
SIP B2BUA and SIP Proxy has recently been introduced, the more complex application of this methodology is still missing. This paper tries to fill this gap and
improve the methodology further to better fit into the planned modular design of
the testing platform, which is being designed in the VoIP laboratory of VSB –
Technical University of Ostrava. By separating registrations from calls, we were
able to measure both cases without the need of extensive postprocessing of data
to ensure the data in one case is not affected by the ones from the other case. Furthermore the security vulnerability of the SIP protocol has been harnessed to allow measuring software for performing both registrations and calls together but
in individual processes, which builds the basis for planned and already mentioned modular design of the platform. In this paper the results from separate
registration stress test analysis will be presented as one of the examples of usage
of the mentioned methodology.

**Keywords:** Asterisk, Burst test, Registrations, RFC 6076, SIPp, Stress test.

## 1 Introduction

With our methodology for testing and benchmarking SIP infrastructure finished, we
had the opportunity to perform several series of tests on multiple different platforms.
From these tests we realized, that it would be very beneficial to modify the existing
testing platform to allow us for performing separate test scenarios on each of the important SIP dialogs. This way the movement towards the modular design started.
During this work at the beginning of this year the new RFC 6076 was adopted finally
standardizing most essential measured parameters.

With the parameters standardized we have developed the most important testing
scenarios – the registration test scenario and the call test scenario, both having its
roots in the previously used scenario for complex performance measuring. Each of
those scenarios offers a different perspective when defining the SIP server limits and
can be run either separately to test some special environments or occasions or simultaneously to simulate the real VoIP client behavior. The latter presented a big challenge, because the testing software does not allow running multiple scenarios at once
inherently. However this problem was walked around by exploiting SIP security vulnerability, which allows a client from one address register another. This way the basis
of module based testing platform has been created.

V. Snasel, J. Platos, and E. El-Qawasmeh (Eds.): ICDIPC 2011, Part II, CCIS 189, pp. 329–336, 2011.
© Springer-Verlag Berlin Heidelberg 2011

In this paper we present the example of results gained by testing two different versions of most commonly used VoIP PBX Asterisk focusing on its ability to handle multiple simultaneous registrations coming in several consequent bursts. This example is particularly useful to determine how the SIP server reacts in the case of network failure and consequent restoration of full connectivity, when all the clients try to register at once.

In the given examples the way how the SIP server responds to bursts with high loads can be determined and all the conclusions are made according to information obtained by the measurements on the client side exclusively, because the measurements on the server side are often impossible due to the provider restrictions.

## 2 State of the Art

As stated in the introduction the authors have vast knowledge in the field of performance measurement of SIP servers using open source software testing tool SIPp and cooperatively created the basic methodology and testing platform. This methodology had its foundations in the RFC-draft, which was adopted by the IETF as RFC 6076 this year; therefore the existing methodology is almost entirely compliant with it.

The formerly used testing platform utilized one complex SIP scenario to test both registrations and calls at once, which allowed for complex analysis of the SIP server, but inherently resulted in the call measurement to be affected by the registrations. This issue could have been solved by data postprocessing, when the number of actually created calls was taken as the basis instead of desired call load, but except of this the user of the testing platform could not have simply chosen what type of test he wants and moreover the more complex scenarios which would include automatic answers and more sophisticated SIP dialogs could not have been created. For this reason the modular approach has been adopted.

Apart of the mentioned the proprietary solutions also exist, but they offer limited or nonexistent compliance with IETF standards and could not be considered cost effective.

## 3 Testing Platform and Test Scenario

For the registration test the testing platform must slightly differ from the one presented in complex methodology. The main reason for this comes from the lack of need for UAS part of the testing platform, since only end to end dialogs between client and SIP server will occur. Basically all the computers will act as the initiators of the SIP registration dialogs, which is why they are going to be called UACs (User Agent Servers). For the generation of SIP messages, the well-known testing tool SIPp will be used and to ensure that client computers will not run out of hardware resources, the generated load will be spread among 8 computers. From these assumptions the basic test topology will look as depicted on the Fig. 1.

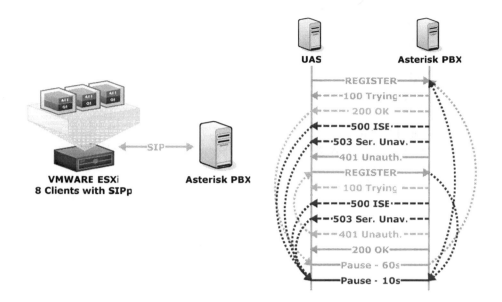

**Fig. 1.** Test topology and flow of SIP messages during the registration dialog. Correct messages are colored in green, while unexpected messages are orange and error messages red. Dotted lines with arrows represent the hop after error or unexpected message is received, or error occurs while transmitting the message.

The virtualization is a useful option because due to the internal limitations of SIPp testing tool it is better to distribute individual SIPp instances each on the separate computer, therefore the usage of physical computers would result in large space and networking requirements.

The main configuration elements of the virtualized computers can be summarized in these points:

- Guest OS Ubuntu 10.10 x64 Server Edition
- 1x Virtual x64 Processor Core @ 2.8 GHz
- 2048 MB Virtual RAM
- 8 GB HDD
- UDP Buffer Size 131 071 B (default size)
- File Descriptor Limit 65535 (ulimit -n)
- Stack Size Limit unlimited (ulimit -s)

The keystone element of the platform – the SIP server is realized on the separate hardware machine with this configuration:

- OS Ubuntu 10.04 x64 Server Edition
- AMD Athlon X2
- 4 GB DDR2 RAM
- 500GB HDD

- UDP Buffer Size 131 071 B (default size)
- File Descriptor Limit 100000 (ulimit -n)
- Stack Size Limit unlimited (ulimit -s)
- Asterisk 1.6.2.16.2
- Asterisk 1.8.2.4
- 100 000 SIP Peers

Both network elements – the host virtualization server and SIP server are interconnected via a gigabit switch to ensure minimal additional delays caused by the network infrastructure.

The measurement is performed only on client devices to reflect the practical situation, when SIP server is not accessible to perform measurement of any kind. On the client devices these values are measured:

- Number of individual SIP messages
- Number of retransmissions
- Number of Timeouts
- Approximated RRD

All the mentioned parameters will be used to determine the SIP servers performance and the last one will be properly described and explained in the next section.

On the Fig. 1 the message flow of the registration dialog is also depicted. The standard messages of the successful registration dialog are colored in green and are followed by 60s long pause after which the reregistration takes place. Additionally out of sequence messages can be received from the SIP server, when the load exceeds the level SIP server can handle without significant delays. These messages are valid part of the SIP dialog and are colored in orange. Each time such a message is received the jump to correct part of the dialog is performed. When the load is even higher, the error messages or timeouts might occur. In this case two 5XX messages are being anticipated and when one of these messages is received or one of the correct dialog messages times out the error jump is performed to a 10s long pause after which another attempt to register is sent.

## 4   Methodology and Limit Definition

The aim of the measurements is to determine how the SIP server Asterisk will respond to high burst loads of SIP registrations. These registrations will be sent in 5 consecutive 1 second long bursts with a given load and the client devices will try to hold these registrations for 15 minutes by sending reregistration requests every 60 second. After the 15 minutes all the measured parameters are logged and the process repeats again with the higher load. If the registration attempt is not successful no matter if this is caused by an error message or timeout, the client will wait for 10 seconds before it tries to register again. This way the SIP server is given the possibility to spread the load to longer period and the real world VoIP client behavior is preserved. Although the way the error messages and timeouts are treated is the same, the severity of these two kinds of errors is different. While receiving the error message causes client not to be able to register for about 10 seconds (the error pause interval), after the message timeout this period is about 42 seconds, which is caused by the timeout mechanism of the SIP protocol. For this reason the timeouts have greater impact on the SIP server's performance evaluation.

Due to the length of the test the client will attempt to send Register message 15 times. In this number the retransmissions are not counted. From this number the limit for determining whether SIP server passed the test successfully or not can be derived. If the number of timeouts exceeds the 1/15 of the total number of unique Register requests sent, it can be interpreted as the clients were not able to register successfully after 45 seconds. To ensure that SIP server has the possibility to recover from the burst, this limit was doubled. Same calculation can be made for the error messages, but with the lower weight caused by the significantly shorter period when the client cannot register. Because no 5XX error message was received during the whole test, this paper's result analysis will work only with the number of 2/15 (~13%) timeouts as limit for successful passing the test.

As defined in the previous section, the approximated RRD is also measured. In the previous work and in the RFC 6076, the RRD (Registration Request Delay) is defined as the time between sending the Register request and receiving the 200 OK response. Approximated RRD in this paper is measured exactly the same way, but due to the limitations of the SIPp in loop scenarios, the time measurement is not possible by the available timers and must be performed by the logging mechanism of the SIPp. To the log no precise time can be written. The most useful possibility is to use the internal clock ticks of the SIPp. One clock tick is loosely comparable with the 1 millisecond, but the precision may vary in higher loads, therefore the measured parameter can be viewed only as the fair approximation of the RRD. Approximated RRD is therefore important not for its absolute values but for its trend change while the load is being increased.

## 5  Result Analysis

In this section the results will be reviewed. In two subsections four charts will be presented and on each of these charts the Asterisk 1.6 will be displayed by the dark brown rounded symbols, while Asterisk 1.8 will be depicted by orange triangles. All the measured parameters are related to the number of simultaneous registrations and each dot in the chart represent a single 15 minutes long step in the test process.

Successful Registration Attempts display the ratio between attempted registrations and success indicating 200 OK responses. The best and optimal value is 100 %, but no architecture is designed to handle huge number off registrations at once, therefore mechanisms which will spread the load to longer interval if the unsuccessful registration occurs are implemented. As mentioned in the previous section the threshold coming from number of timeouts was designated to 13% and because the timeouts were the only error measured during the whole test, this threshold can be used directly on the number of Successful Registration Attempts.

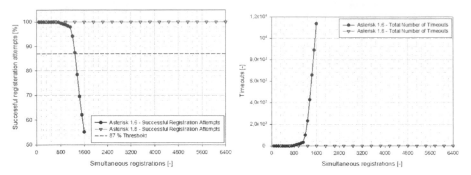

**Fig. 2.** Successful Registration Attempts and Total Number of SIP Message Timeouts

The charts on the Fig. 2 show clearly the difference between two tested architectures. While Asterisk 1.6 starts having problems when the load of 1000 registrations is generated and falls under the designated threshold immediately after 1280 simultaneous registrations, Asterisk 1.8 holds the 100% ratio for the whole time of the test reaching stable behavior even with the load of 6400 simultaneous registrations.

The similar behavior can be seen on the chart depicting the number of SIP timeouts. For Asterisk 1.6 timeouts are the essential problem, on the other hand no timeout occurred while testing Asterisk 1.8.

From this information can be stated that new version of Asterisk handles the burst load of SIP registrations much better than the older one. On this place it would be good to state, that all the parameters were set to defaults on both Asterisks, and same number of SIP peers was used, therefore no external event could have influenced the results.

From already presented information the clear assumption about what Asterisk is better in case of network connectivity failure and subsequent recovery can be made. Now we are going to explore whether the retransmissions and approximated RRD will confirm this assumption.

Approximated RRD was clearly explained in the previous section, therefore no further explanation will be presented. The retransmissions occur when there is long period between sending the message and receiving the appropriate answer. In SIP the standard timer define, that the first retransmission takes place when the response is not received in 500 milliseconds after sending the request. Each subsequent retransmission is sent after doubled interval, until the 4 seconds are reached. When this happens all other retransmission will be sent after 4 seconds giving the following sequence of time periods between the neighboring messages – 500ms, 1s, 2s, 4s, 4s... After the sequence of 9 retransmissions the timeout occurs. The number of retransmissions increases when SIP server cannot successfully process all the messages. In the following charts, the total number of retransmissions means the sum of all retransmissions of all messages in the SIP registration dialog.

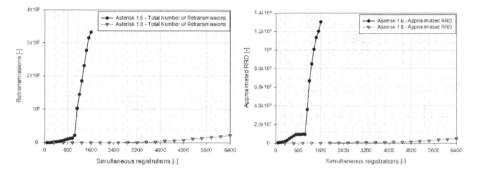

**Fig. 3.** Total Number of Retransmissions and Approximated Registration Request Delay

Both parameters depicted on the Fig. 3 – Total Number of Retransmissions and approximated RRD – share the same trend and underline the knowledge obtained in the previous subsection. Asterisk 1.8 excels again reaching minimal number of retransmissions even for very high loads, while for Asterisk 1.6 the number of 1280 simultaneous registrations is the highest load it can process satisfactorily. If we use the fair approximation of SIPp clock ticks to milliseconds, we can see on the second chart of the Fig. 3, that for higher loads than 1280 registrations, the registration interval takes up to 14 seconds to complete, which is of course unacceptable. Asterisk 1.8 has no significant issues even for 5 times greater load.

## 6 Conclusion

In this paper we presented one of many approaches to stress testing of SIP servers, which was made possible by adopting of modular approach to test scenario design. The presented results showed that the new major version of Asterisk PBX was also a major leap in the effectiveness of handling burst loads of Register requests. The decision was made based on the data collected on the client devices exclusively, but thanks to the possibility of collecting data even on the SIP server we can determine that the limiting factor was the Asterisk's ability to successfully and quickly enough process the UDP segments from the UDP buffers.

The comparison with other work is quite problematic, because no unified approach to stress test SIP server has been widely adopted. Our previous work described in the articles already referenced here [1,2], was focused on measuring overall performance of the SIP server, and that is why the comparison with this newer modular approach would lead to the results without any practical value.

The sowed example of measurements can also be combined with the call tests or there is a possibility to test not the bursts but the slow sequential increase of the number of simultaneous registrations. In other word the possibilities of the newly redesigned platform are vast.

# References

1. Voznak, M., Rozhon, J.: SIP Back to Back User Benchmarking. In: ICWMC 2010, pp. 92–96. IEEE CS, Valencia (2010)
2. Voznak, M., Rozhon, J.: Performance testing and benchmarking of B2BUA and SIP Proxy. In: Conference Proceedings TSP 2010, Baden near Vienna, pp. 497–503 (2010)
3. Malas, D., Morton, A.: Basic Telephony SIP End-to-End Performance Metrics. IETF RFC 6076 (2011), http://www.ietf.org/rfc/rfc6076.txt
4. SIPp development team: SIPp – SIP performance testing tool, http://sipp.sourceforge.net/
5. Rosenberg, J., Schulzrinne, H., Camarillo, G., Johnston, A., Peterson, J., Sparks, R., Handley, M., Schooler, E.: SIP: Session Initiation Protocol. IETF RFC 3261 (2002), http://www.ietf.org/rfc/rfc3261.txt
6. Meggelen, J., Smith, J., Madsen, L.: Asterisk: The Future of Telephony, 2nd edn. O'Reilly, Sebastopol (2007)
7. Wintermeyer, S., Bosch, S.: Practical Asterisk 1.4 and 1.6: From Beginner to Expert. Addison-Wesley Professional, New York (2009)
8. Johnston, A.: SIP: Understanding the Session Initiation Protocol, 3rd edn. Artech House Publishers, Norwood (2009)

# Analysis of M-QAM Data Communication System Using 3D Eye Diagram

Mohamed Al-Wohaishi, Radek Martinek, and Jan Zidek

Department of Measurement and Controll,
VSB - Technical University of Ostrava,
17. listopadu 15/2172,
708 33 Ostrava,
Czech Republic
{Wohaishi,radek.martinek.st1,jan.zidek}@vsb.cz

**Abstract.** When designing digital systems and incorporating a high-speed digital device with the need of quick transfer of large data amounts between chips and peripherals, jitter will be a key parameter to measure. In this paper, we are able to determine the initial phase of a carrier sine wave by performing carrier recovery loop in Digital communication systems of M-ary quadrature amplitude modulation (M-QAM) schemes. It is important for the M-ary QAM carrier re covery circuits to have low phase jitter as well as only four stable phase points as we see below. We examined the effect of channel noise on carrier recovery. More specifically, we examined what behaviour can occur when channel noise is significant enough to prevent carrier locking. We saw the symbols on the 3D Eye Diagram and constellation plot begin to jitter at first, and then settle closer to the ideal symbol locations after a short period of time.

**Keywords:** M-QAM, Jitter, carrier recovery system, 3D Eye Diagram, PLL (phase-locked loop).

## 1 Introduction

Software Defined Radio is a radio communications transceiver system in which all the typical components of a communication system such as mixers, modulators/demodulators, detectors, amplifiers are implemented through software rather than hardware. This approach is helpful because there is a scope of developing a system which is compatible with more than one mobile communication standard [8]. This can be achieved by using reconfigurable hardware and swapping the software for different technologies. In a digital communication system, digital information can be sent and received by subtly changing characteristics of a carrier sine wave. In this case, determining changes in amplitude (ASK) is quite simple. However, detecting changes in phase (PSK and QAM) is much more difficult and requires a process known as carrier recovery [1]. By performing carrier recovery, we are able to determine the initial

V. Snasel, J. Platos, and E. El-Qawasmeh (Eds.): ICDIPC 2011, Part II, CCIS 189, pp. 337–348, 2011.

phase of a carrier sine wave. Thus, it is possible to detect shifts in the phase of this signal.

## 2   System Model

We investigate one of the more widespread in digital TV broadcasting family of modulation schemes, QAM works by using M different combinations of voltage magnitude and phase to represent N bits, as described by the relationship $M = 2^N$. When N is an even integer, the constellation is regular with I and Q each representing $2^{N-1}$ bits. When N is an odd integer, the constellation is not necessarily symmetrical, and finding an optimal distribution of sample points is not straightforward, for which the signal can be generally given by [3]:

$$s(t) = \sqrt{2E_s / T} \left[ I(t) \cos \omega_0 t - Q(t) \sin \omega_0 t \right] \tag{1}$$

Where I (t) and Q(t) are the baseband I and Q waveforms, respectively [3].

$$I(t) = C_0 \sum_n a_n^I \sqrt{T} \sigma(t - nT), \tag{2}$$

$$Q(t) = C_0 \sum_n a_n^Q \sqrt{T} \sigma(t - nT), \tag{3}$$

Here $\sigma(t)$ has unit energy and $C_0$ is chosen so that the normalizing condition is satisfied. This requires averaging over all the pairs $(a_n^I, a_n^Q)$, weighting each by 1/M, the integral in is simply T, so [3]:

$$1/C_0 = \left[ (1/M) \sum_{a^I, a^Q} \left[ (a^I)^2 + (a^Q)^2 \right] \right]^{1/2} . \tag{4}$$

The basic structure of designed communication system comes from the general chain of digital communication system and was implemented using functions from LabVIEW Modulation Toolkit additional library. Our Experiment Model represents the use of LabVIEW Modulation Toolkit. This Experiment demonstrates continuous acquisition and demodulation of a QAM signal see figure 1 below [2].

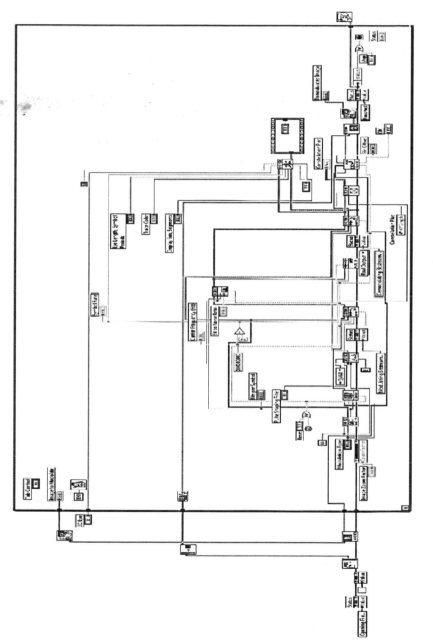

**Fig. 1.** Block diagram of implemented Experiment

## 3  Quadrature Modulation - QAM

Quadrature Amplitude Modulation, QAM, has fast become the dominant modulation mechanism for high speed digital signals. From the wireless 802.11 protocols to ADSL modems to personal communicators for the military, QAM has become a necessary part of our daily lives. With increases in processing power, QAM as a part of software defined radio (SDR) schema is now easily achievable.

QAM is a modulation scheme which is carried out by changing (modulating) the amplitude of two carrier waves. The carrier waves are out of phase by 90 degrees, and are called quadrature carriers - hence the name of the scheme. QAM can be viewed as a combination of ASK and PSK. That means the digital information is carried in both the phase and the amplitude of the carrier signal [4].

Quadrature amplitude modulation, or QAM, extends the idea of PSK to modulating the pulse amplitudes as well as the phases. If forms the basis of TCM coded modulation, and so we will set down some analytical tools. As a generic communication term, QAM implies linear I and Q modulation and carrier, in contrast to PAM, which implies single-channel linear baseband modulation. A general from for a QAM signal is once again Eq, with the data mapped to M two-tuples $(a_n^I, a_n^Q)$, but this time the resulting constellation is more than just the PSK circle. Some QAM signal space constellations are shown in figure 2, see [1].

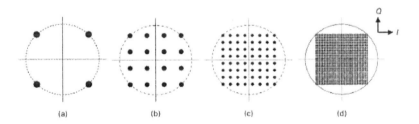

**Fig. 2.** Square QAM constellations: a) 4-QAM (QPSK), b) 16-QAM, c) 64 –QAM, d) 1024-QAM

A common convention is to take the $a_n^I$ and $a_n^Q$, as whole integers, as in the figure, but this requires an extra step to normalize I and Q.

## 4  Jitter and Eye Diagram

Jitter is time-base error. It is caused by varying time delays in the circuit paths from component to component in the signal path. The two most common causes of jitter are poorly-designed Phase Locked Loops (PLL's) and waveform distortion due to mismatched impedances and/or reflections in the signal path. An eye diagram provides the most fundamental intuitive view of jitter [7], as shown in Figure 3. It is a composite view of all the bit periods of a captured waveform superimposed upon each other.

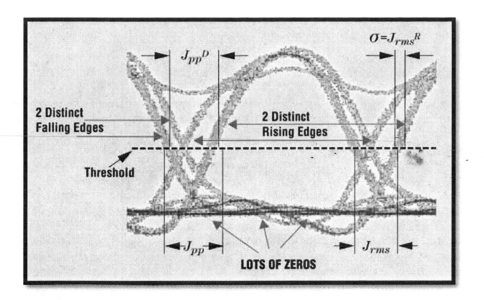

**Fig. 3.** An eye diagram with an irregular shape provides a wealth of information [7]

## 5  Fundamentals of Jitter Analysis

Jitter is fundamentally an expression of phase noise. Mathematically, jitter is the undesired    variation in the phase of a signal given by the term, $\phi$ (t), in the expression:

$$S(t) = P(2\pi f_d\, t + \varphi(t)) \tag{5}$$

Where S is the received signal, P represents the sequence of signal pulses as a function of time, and $f_d$ is the data rate. Jitter isn't measured simply to create statistics; it
is measured because jitter can cause transmission errors. For example if jitter results
in a signal being on the "wrong side" of the transition threshold at the sampling point,

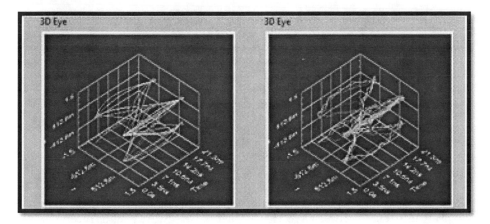

**Fig. 4.** 3D Eye diagram for 4-QAM respectively with Bit to Noise Ratio (100) & (30)

the receiving circuit will interpret that bit differently than the transmitter intended, causing a bit error. See figure 4 from experiment.

## 6  Constellation Diagrams

A constellation diagram is the representation of a digital modulation scheme on the complex plane. The diagram is formed by choosing a set of complex numbers to represent modulation symbols. These points are usually ordered by the gray code sequence. Gray codes are binary sequences where two successive values differ in only one digit. The use of gray codes helps reduce the bit errors. The real and imaginary axes are often called the in-phase and the quadrature. These points are usually arranged in a rectangular grid in QAM, though other arrangements are possible. The number of points in the grid is usually a power of two because in digital communications the data is binary, when start the process to convert the file to a single binary bistream, modulate it using the QAM modulation scheme, and then do the reverse process to reconstruct the original image. The channel to noise ratio is set to a maximum value, so the constellation plot shows the symbols mapped almost perfectly to their ideal positions, and then for both of the phase and the frequency of the carrier are able to be determined correctly. We will also see that the "Image to Modulate" and the "Demodulated Image" match very closely to one another. By decrease the "Bit to Noise Ratio" do 30 then observe the affect in the constellation plot, this means as the Bit to Noise Ratio decreases, the noise floor increases, see Figure 5.

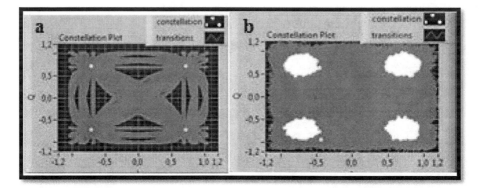

**Fig. 5.** Constellation diagram with Bit to Noise Ratio for 4-QAM a) with 100 b) with 30

Upon reception of the signal, the demodulator examines the received symbol and chooses the closest constellation point based on Euclidean distance. It is possible to transmit more bits per symbols by using a higher-order [5].

## 7  Carrier Recovery Fundamentals

A carrier recovery system is a circuit used to estimate and compensate for frequency and phase differences between a received signal's carrier wave and the receiver's local oscillator for the purpose of coherent demodulation.

When coherent detection is used, the receiver must exploit knowledge of both carrier frequency and phase to detect the signals. Carrier recovery typically entails two subsequent steps: in the first step carrier synchronization parameters are estimated, and in the second the receiving carrier signal is corrected according to the estimates made. These steps must be performed quickly and accurately in burst-mode [6].

A QAM transmitter fundamentally modulates a bit pattern onto a carrier signal with a specific phase and amplitude. On the receiver side, it is absolutely imperative that the receiver is able to detect both the phase and amplitude of that signal. Otherwise, the receiver will not be able to correctly demodulate the incoming signal into the appropriate symbols.

## 8 Results and Discussion

There are two main ways to solving this problem of carrier recovery. The first approach to carrier recovery is to implement a pilot signal. The receiver is able to extract this signal and lock its local oscillator to both the phase and frequency of this signal. The receiver thus uses a phase-locked loop (PLL) to track the pilot signal. The second approach, which is more commonly implemented, is to derive the carrier phase directly from the modulated signal. We used this approach by using the QAM demodulation VI's in LabVIEW, this shown in Figure 6.

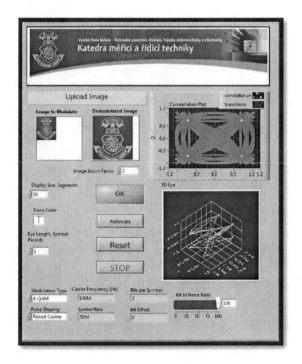

**Fig. 6.** Front-panel: 4-QAM Screenshot with maximum Bit to Noise Ratio

We will examine what behaviour can occur when noise channel noise is significant enough to prevent carrier locking. We work with QAM modulation scheme of (8, 16, 32, 64, 128, and 256) QAM, we use here a prompted file as image (recommended .jpg.).

When start the process to convert the file to a single binary bistream, modulate it using the QAM modulation scheme, and then do the reverse process to reconstruct the original image. Run the QAM modulation scheme of M-QAM, the channel to noise ratio is set to a maximum value, so the constellation plot and 3D eye diagram in Figure 7 shown respectively (8, 16, 32, 64, 128 and 256) M-QAM, the symbols mapped almost perfectly to their ideal positions and an 3D eye diagram of a waveform that is even less ideal. But the characteristic of its irregular shape enables the viewer to learn much about it, and then for both of the phases and the frequency of the carrier are able to be determined correctly.

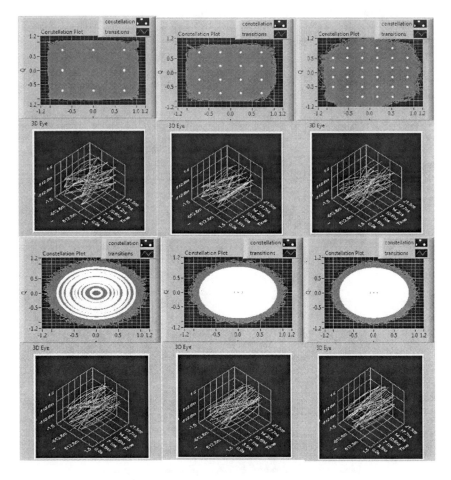

**Fig. 7.** Constellation and 3D Eye diagram for M-QAM with Bit to Noise Ratio (100) respectively for (8, 16, 32, 64, 128 and 256)

To observe the PLL performing carrier recovery by adding enough noise such that the phase and frequency information of the carrier signal can no longer be determined, by slowly decrease the value of Bit to Noise Ratio (current value 30) even more until the constellation plot begins to spin. This gives us two key characteristics. First, while the Demodulated Image is not exactly recovered, it does unclear like the image to modulate. This illustrates that at least some of the symbols are mapped to bits that are close to their expected location. Second and more importantly, notice that the constellation plot is now appears to have a ringed or unclear , that is mean  the constellation plot is now spinning and that the carrier's frequency cannot be properly determined. In Figure 8 below have the constellation plot and 3D eye diagram for the results respectively of all the M-ary QAM (8, 16, 32, 64, 128 and 256) with Bit to Noise Ratio (30).

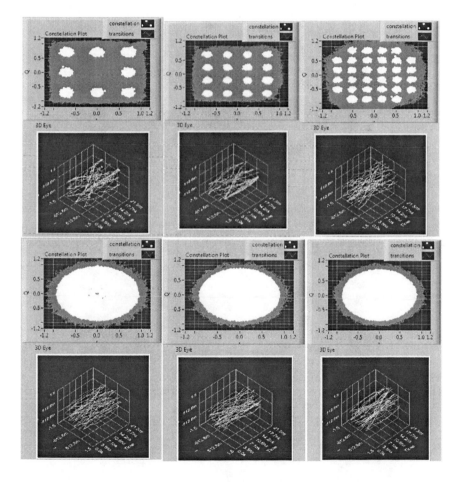

**Fig. 8.** Constellation and 3D Eye diagram for M-QAM with Bit to Noise Ratio (30) respectively for (8, 16, 32, 64, 128 and 256)

We will also see that the "Image to Modulate" in Figure 9 and the "Demodulated Image" in Figure 10 match very closely to one another. By decrease the "Bit to Noise Ratio" do 30 then observe the affect in the constellation plot, this means as the Bit to Noise Ratio decreases, the noise floor increases. As a result, the recovered symbols begin to show jitter from the ideal symbol locations. However, each of these symbols can still be mapped to the correct bit values, and the image is to be recovered correctly.

**Fig. 9.** Demodulated Image with Bit to Noise Ratio 100 respectively for M-ary QAM (8, 16, 32, 64, 128 and 256)

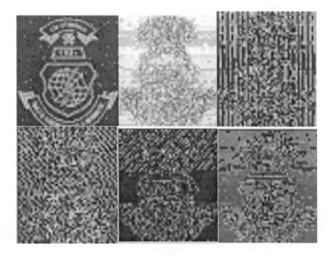

**Fig. 10.** Demodulated Image with Bit to Noise Ratio 30 respectively for M-ary QAM (8, 16, 32, 64, 128 and 256)

# 9  Conclusion

It was clearly observed that the PLL (phase-locked loop) spent at maximum noise, with the number of iterations, before eliminating it from the physical channel; it was also noticed in some instances that the constellation plot seems to show significant PLL jitter at first, but then settles onto the appropriate phase and amplitude. As this demonstration illustrates that carrier recovery is a significant aspect of digital communications systems. We have created 3D eye diagrams to show the relationship among time, in-phase, and quadrature signals. Moreover, the phase-lock loop performs a significant role in allowing the receiver to accurately determine both the phase and frequency of the carrier signal. Here, we observed that channel noise is one of the largest impairments to carrier recovery and that significant noise can even "break" the carrier locking ability of a PLL.

The main contribution of the work is in the creation of a virtual instrument designed for real measurement, applicable in wireless transmission systems. The idea of functionality of such systems comes from the definition of the software radio, which regards the hardware of the transmission system as a universal, generally conceived device.

## Acknowledgement

This project has been carried out under the financial support of the Ministry of Education of the Czech Republic, Project FRVS 498/2011.

## References

1. Martinek, R., Al-Wohaishi, M., Zidek, J.: Software based flexible measuring systems for analysis of digitally modulated systems. In: 9th RoEduNet 2010, Sibiu, Romania, pp. 397–402 (2010); ISSN 2068-1038, ISBN 978-1-4244-7335-9
2. Lu, J., Lcfaicf, K.B., Chunng, J.C.-I., Liou, M.L.: M-PSK and M-QAM BER computation using signal-space concepts. IEEE Transactions on communications 47(2), 181–184 (1999); ISSN: 0090-6778, NSPEC Accession Number: 6212385
3. Martos-Naya, E., Paris, J.F., Fernandez-Plazaola, U., Goldsmith, A.: Exact BER analysis for M-QAM modulation with transmit beam forming under channel prediction errors. Wireless Communications, 36–74 (2008); ISSN: 1536-1276
4. Rao, W., Yuan, K., Guo, Y., Yang, C.: A simple constant modulus algorithm for blind equalization suitable for 16-QAM signal. In: The 9th International Conference on Signal Processing, vol. 2, pp. 1963–1966 (2008); Print ISBN: 978-1-4244-2178-7, INSPEC Accession Number: 10411271
5. Wilson, J.S., Ball, S.: Test and measurement, p. 968. Newnes, USA (2009); ISBN: 978-1-85617-530-2; Illustration: NL language: ENG, Complete Title: Test and Measurement: Know It All

6. Measuring Jitter in Digital Systems, Application Note 1448-1,
   http://www.agilent.com
7. Reinhardt, V.S.: A review of time jitter and digital systems. In: Proceedings of the 2005
   IEEE International Frequency Control Symposium and Exposition, p. 38 (2005); Print
   ISBN: 0-7803-9053-9, INSPEC Accession Number: 8923479
8. Vasudevan, S.K., Sivaraman, R., Alex, Z.C.: Software Defined Radio Implementation
   (With simulation & analysis). International Journal of Computer Applications 4(8),
   0975–8887 (2010)

# Mobile Phone Positioning in GSM Networks Based on Information Retrieval Methods and Data Structures

Tomáš Novosád, Jan Martinovič, Peter Scherer,
Václav Snášel, Roman Šebesta, and Petr Klement

VŠB - Technical University of Ostrava,
Faculty of Electrical Engineering and Computer Science,
17. listopadu 15/2172, 708 33 Ostrava, Czech Republic
{tomas.novosad,jan.martinovic,peter.scherer,vaclav.snasel,
roman.sebesta,petr.klement}@vsb.cz
http://www.cs.vsb.cz

**Abstract.** In this article we present a novel method for mobile phone positioning using a vector space model, suffix trees and an information retrieval approach. The method works with parameters which can be acquired from any common mobile phone without the necessity of installing additional hardware and is handset based. The algorithm is based on a database of previous measurements which are used as an index which looks for the nearest neighbor toward the query measurement. The accuracy of the algorithm is in most cases good enough to accomplish the E9-1-1 requirements on tested data.

**Keywords:** Mobile Phone Positioning, GSM, Information Retrieval, Vector Model, Suffix Tree, Handset Based Localization, Location Based Services.

## 1 Introduction

Determining the position of mobile phone users is one key feature of wireless communication system these days. It is a part of Location Based Service (LBS) which is an information or entertainment service, accessible with mobile devices through the mobile network and utilizing the ability to make use of the geographical position of the mobile device. The crucial moment in this area (year 2001) was the requirement of the The United States Federal Communications Commission (FCC) that, wireless network operators must be able to precisely determine the location of persons calling US emergency assistance service Wireless Enhanced 9-1-1 (E9-1-1) [6]. The information about mobile phone user location must meet FCC accuracy standards, generally to within 50 to 300 meters, depending on the type of technology used. There also exists a wide range of useful applications of mobile phone positioning such as location-based mobile advertising, turn-by-turn navigation to any address etc. [27]. Nowadays there is a wide variety of methods to determine mobile station location. We can broadly divide

V. Snasel, J. Platos, and E. El-Qawasmeh (Eds.): ICDIPC 2011, Part II, CCIS 189, pp. 349–363, 2011.
© Springer-Verlag Berlin Heidelberg 2011

the localization systems into three main categories - network based, handset based and hybrid systems.

The network based systems use the measurement of signals, and these can be applied to any cellular system such as GSM. The most important methods are measurement of signal propagation time (i.e. Time Of Arrival - TOA), Time Difference Of Arrival (TDOA), Angle Of Arrival (AOA) and carrier phase, etc. [4]. The position of the mobile station is then calculated by techniques like trilateration, multilateration and triangulation. Several other methods based on previous ones also exist and some of them have become standard [31,25]. The main disadvantage of all of these approaches is the additional hardware requirements to wireless network infrastructure such as Location Measurement Unit (LMU) devices or Angle Measurement Unit devices (AMU). These electronic devices must be installed on every Base Transceiver Station (BTS) and are also very expensive. On the other hand these techniques are very accurate and successfully meet all of the E9-1-1 standards.

In handset based systems the position of a mobile phone is recognized upon the parameters which the mobile station receives from the wireless network. In GSM networks, these parameters include Cell IDentity code (Cell ID), Base Station Identity Code (BSIC), Received signal Level (RxLev), Timing Advance (TA), Broadcast Control CHannel (BCCH), etc. The mobile station receives the parameters from the serving station and from six neighboring stations as well. One of the main advantage of this system is that it does not require any additional hardware. It has been developed in many research projects in this field and it still remains a great challenge in these days in computer science. For example in [19,20] the authors used artificial neural networks and radio signal strength to locate the mobile device. Another popular approach is space segmentation [21], application of fuzzy logic [12,24,10], hidden Markov models and pattern recognition methods [8,9], data mining techniques [1,13], probabilistic methods [22,23], and many others.

The last of the three is hybrid positioning systems which use a combination of network-based and handset-based technologies for location determination. Currently the most used would be probably Assisted GPS (A-GPS) [2], which uses both GPS and network information to compute the location of the mobile station. Hybrid-based techniques give the best accuracy of the three but inherit the limitations and challenges of network-based and handset-based technologies as well. Different hybrid positioning systems are currently being developed and used in services from Navizon, Xtify, PlaceEngine, SkyHook, Google Maps for Mobile for applications in smart-phones including Apple iPhone, HTC Desire, etc. The main disadvantage of these systems is a necessity of a GPS module installed in the mobile device, which is not a common standard in these days yet.

In this article we introduce a novel method for determining mobile station location in handset based systems. We use values of parameters which the mobile phone receives from the wireless GSM network (from the serving base transceiver station and six neighboring base transceiver stations) as an input to our algorithm - namely base station identity code, cell identity code, broadcast control channel and timing advance. The method is based on a database of such measurements collected in the desired location with GPS positions for each such measurement. All measurements in the database are indexed by suffix tree data structure. After that we extract the attributes from the suffix tree and build a vector model. For evaluation of our method we use measurements which were not previously indexed such as a query to vector model. The result of the query in the vector model (determined location of mobile phone) is simply the first nearest neighbor measurement returned by the system.

## 2   Experimental Data

The data for our experiments were collected in the Czech Republic in the city of Ostrava, location Ostrava - Poruba and adjacent city parts. The scanned area is about 16 $km^2$.

### Measuring Parameters of the GSM Network

First of all we need to record the parameters which are received by the mobile station from the wireless network and exact GPS positions as well. This task is done by the device we call the NAM Logger from NAM Systems company. The NAM Logger is a device for measuring GSM parameters from the wireless network and can determine exact GPS position at a given (measured) place, actual velocity, time of measurement, altitude, identification of country and mobile operator - Mobile Country Code (MCC) and Mobile Network Code (MNC). Next it gives us the following parameters from the serving BTS:

- Cell ID - Cell (antenna) IDentity code
- BCCH - Broadcast Control CHannel (It represents the ARFCN that shows the Absolute Radio Frequency Channel Number, which identifies the BCCH carrier.)
- RxLev - Received signal Level
- BSIC - Base Station Identity Code
- TA - Timing Advance

and the following parameters from 6 neighboring BTS:

- BCCH - Broadcast Control CHannel (It represents the ARFCN that shows the Absolute Radio Frequency Channel Number, which identifies the BCCH carrier.)
- RxLev - Received signal Level
- BSIC - Base Station Identity Code

Thanks to this device we are able to measure the parameters above at a given place with an exact GPS position.

## Collecting the Data

Measuring it-self lies in recording all the above parameters during the passage of the measuring system along a given trace. Recording frequency is set to one measured sample per five seconds, due to the ability of the NAM Logger device. As a test location the Poruba region of the city of Ostrava was selected as well as the adjacent area Martinov and Pustkovec. The average length of every measured trace is about 30 kilometers. During the measuring the GSM and GPS antennas are placed on the roof of a car beside each other. The NAM logger is placed on the rear seats of the car and is powered with a 12V gel battery. During measuring the relief driver has the ability to monitor on-line the recorded parameters on a laptop terminal.

## Data for Experiments

Experimental data was recorded by the process described above. Data was separated into a so-called training set and testing set. The training set does not contain any samples of the testing set and vice versa. The training set consists of 133000 measured samples. Next we have created three different test sets which differ in the location of measurement. We have also experimented with different combinations of measured parameters as an input to our algorithm. After a series of experiments we have found the best attributes for indexing are:

- BSIC - Base Station Identity Code from serving and neighboring BTS
- BCCH - number of broadcast channel from BTS, which provides the signaling information required by the mobile phone to access and identify the network
- TA - Timing Advance from serving BTS
- Cell ID - Cell IDentity code from serving BTS

In table 1 is the example input into our algorithm (except GPS readings). Each line represents one measured sample with an exact GPS position. The first two columns of table 1 represent GPS latitude and GPS longitude position, the next four columns represent parameters from serving base transceiver station and the rest of the columns represent the parameters measured for six neighboring base transceiver stations. **GPS readings are not input into our algorithm, they are used for later evaluation of the algorithm only.**

**Test set - TS1.** First test set consists of 646 measured samples. It is a part of a measurement with three NAM logger devices. The First NAM Logger was placed on the roof of the car, the second was placed inside the box of the car and the third was placed on the rear seats of the car. This test set represents the measurements from the NAM logger placed on the roof of the car. Measuring conducted in locations Ostrava - Poruba, Klimkovice, Vřesina, Dolní Lhota, Čavisov, Zbyslavice and Kyjovice.

**Test set - TS2.** Second test set consists of 1675 measured samples. Measuring conducted with one NAM Logger device in location Ostrava - Poruba.

**Table 1.** Algorithm Input Data

| GPS | GPS | BSIC | BCCH | Cell ID | TA | BSIC1 | BCCH1 | ... | BSIC6 | BCCH6 |
|---|---|---|---|---|---|---|---|---|---|---|
| 49.8227 | 18.1700 | 34 | 29 | 758F | 4 | 34 | 29 | ... | 01 | 60 |
| 49.8230 | 18.1693 | 34 | 29 | 76B4 | 3 | 34 | 29 | ... | FF | 57 |
| 49.8309 | 18.1712 | 2B | 29 | 7541 | 0 | 2B | 29 | ... | 30 | 107 |
| 49.8369 | 18.1561 | 29 | 29 | 7650 | 0 | 29 | 29 | ... | 01 | 60 |
| : | : | : | : | : | : | : | : | ... | : | : |

**Test set - TS3.** Last test set consists of 758 measured samples. Measuring conducted in locations Ostrava - Poruba, Ostrava - Martinov, Ostrava - Pustkovec. It is part of a measurement with three NAM Loggers (same case as test set TS1).

### Data Encoding for Indexing

The objective of this stage is to prepare the data for indexing by suffix trees. The suffix tree can index sequences. The resulting sequence in our case is a sequence of nonnegative integers. For example, let's say we have two samples of a measurement (two sequences of words) from a NAM Logger device:

{34 29 758F 4 34 29 01 60}
{34 29 76B4 3 34 29 FF 57}

After obtaining this sequence of 16 words in this case (measured parameters), we create a dictionary of these words (each unique word receives its own unique non negative integer identifier). The translated sequence appears as follows:

{1 2 3 4 1 2 5 6}
{1 2 7 8 1 2 9 10}

In this way, we encode each sample of measurement from a NAM Logger device. This task is done for training set samples as well as for every sample from test sets. Now we are ready for indexing training samples using suffix trees.

## 3   Background

In this section we describe theoretical background required to understand our algorithm. It consists of high level description of vector space model and suffix trees as well.

### Vector Space Model

The vector model [3] of documents was established in the 1970's. A document in the vector model is represented as a vector. Each dimension of this vector corresponds to a separate term appearing in document collection. If a term occurs in the document, its value in the vector is non-zero.

We use $m$ different terms $t_1, \ldots, t_m$ for indexing $N$ documents. Then each document $d_i$ is represented by a vector:

$$d_i = (w_{i1}, w_{i2}, \ldots, w_{im}),$$

where $w_{ij}$ is the weight of the term $t_j$ in the document $d_i$. The weight of the term in the document vector can be determined in many ways. A common approach uses the so called $tf \times idf$ (Term Frequency $\times$ Inverse Document Frequency) method, in which the weight of the term is determined by these factors: how often the term $t_j$ occurs in the document $d_i$ (the term frequency $tf_{ij}$) and how often it occurs in the whole document collection (the document frequency $df_j$. Precisely, the weight of the term $t_j$ in the document $d_i$ is [11]:

$$w_{ij} = tf_{ij} \times idf_j = tf_{ij} \times \log \frac{n}{df_j}, \tag{1}$$

where $idf$ stands for the inverse document frequency. This method assigns high weights to terms that appear frequently in a small number of documents in the document set.

An index file of the vector model is represented by matrix:

$$D = \begin{pmatrix} w_{11} & w_{12} & \cdots & w_{1m} \\ w_{21} & w_{22} & \cdots & w_{2m} \\ \vdots & \vdots & \ddots & \vdots \\ w_{n1} & w_{n2} & \cdots & w_{Nm} \end{pmatrix},$$

where $i$-th row matches $i$-th document, and $j$-th column matches $j$-th term.

The similarity of two documents in vector model is usually given by the following formula – Cosine Similarity Measure:

$$sim(d_i, d_j) = \frac{\sum_{k=1}^{m} (w_{ik} w_{jk})}{\sqrt{\sum_{k=1}^{m} (w_{ik})^2 \sum_{k=1}^{m} (w_{jk})^2}} \tag{2}$$

For more information, please consult [14,17,3].

## Suffix Trees

A suffix tree is a data structure that allows efficient string matching and querying. Suffix trees have been studied and used extensively, and have been applied to fundamental string problems such as finding the longest repeated substring [28], strings comparisons [5], and text compression [18]. Following this, we describe the suffix tree data structure - its definition, construction algorithms and main characteristics.

The following description of the suffix tree was taken from Gusfield's book *Algorithms on Strings, Trees and Sequences* [7]. Suffix trees commonly dealing with strings as sequence of characters. One major difference is that we treat documents as sequences of words, not characters. A suffix tree of a string is simply a compact trie of all the suffixes of that string. Citation [30]:

**Definition 1.** *A suffix tree T for an m-word string S is a rooted directed tree with exactly m leaves numbered 1 to m. Each internal node, other than the root, has at least two children and each edge is labeled with a nonempty sub-string of words of S. No two edges out of a node can have edge labels beginning with the same word. The key feature of the suffix tree is that for any leaf i, the concate-nation of the edge labels on the path from the root to leaf i exactly spells out the suffix of S that starts at position i, that is it spells out $S[i \dots m]$.*

In cases where one suffix of $S$ matches a prefix of another suffix of $S$ then no suffix tree obeying the above definition is possible since the path for the first suffix would not end at a leaf. To avoid this, we assume the last word of $S$ does not appear anywhere else in the string. This prevents any suffix from being a prefix to another suffix. To achieve this we can add a terminating character, which is not in the language that $S$ is taken from, to the end of $S$

Example of suffix trie of the string *"I know you know I know you#"* is shown in Figure 1. Corresponding suffix tree of the string *"I know you know I know you#"* is presented in Figure 2. There are seven leaves in this example, marked as rectangles and numbered from 1 to 7. The terminating characters are also shown in this figure.

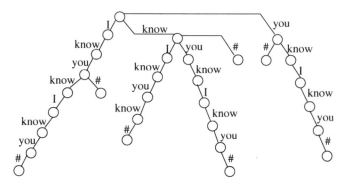

**Fig. 1.** Simple example of suffix trie

In a similar manner, a suffix tree of a set of strings, called a generalized suffix tree [7], is a compact trie of all the suffixes of all the strings in the set [30].

**Definition 2.** *A generalized suffix tree T for a set S of n strings $S_n$, each of length $m_n$, is a rooted directed tree with exactly $\sum m_n$ leaves marked by a two number tuple $(k, l)$ where k ranges from 1 to n and l ranges from 1 to $m_k$. Each internal node, other than the root, has at least two children and each edge is labeled with a nonempty sub-string of words of a string in S. No two edges out*

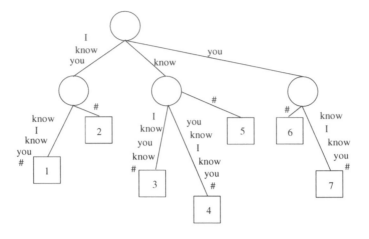

**Fig. 2.** Simple example of suffix tree

*of a node can have edge labels beginning with the same word. For any leaf $(i, j)$, the concatenation of the edge labels on the path from the root to leaf $(i, j)$ exactly spells out the suffix of $S_i$ that starts at position $j$, that is it spells out $S_i[j \dots m_i]$.*

Figure 3 is an example of a generalized suffix tree of the set of three strings - *"Tom knows John #1"*, *"Paul knows John too #2"* and *"Tom knows Paul too #3"* (#1, #2, #3 are unique terminating symbols). The internal nodes of the suffix tree are drawn as circles, and are labeled from $a$ to $f$ for further reference. Leaves are drawn as rectangles. The first number $d_i = (d_1, \dots, d_n)$ in each rectangle indicates the string from which that suffix originates - a unique number that identifies the string. The second number represents the position in that string $d_i$ where the suffix begins. Each string is considered to have a unique terminating symbol.

There are different ways how to construct a suffix tree data structure. The naive, straightforward method to build a suffix tree for a string $S$ of length $L$ takes $O(L^2)$ time. The naive method first enters a single edge for the suffix $S[1 \dots L]$ into the tree. Then it successively enters the suffix $S[i \dots L]$ into the growing tree for $i$ increasing from 2 to $L$. The details of this construction method are not within the bounds of this article. Various suffix tree construction algorithms can be found in [7] (a good book on suffix tree construction algorithms in general).

Several linear time algorithms for constructing suffix trees exist [16,26,28]. To be precise, these algorithms also exhibit a time dependency on the size of the vocabulary (or the alphabet when dealing with character based trees): they actually have a time bound of $O(L \times min(\log |V|, \log L))$, where $L$ is the length of the string and $|V|$ is the size of the language. These methods are more difficult to implement then the naive method, which is sufficiently suitable for our purpose.

We have also made some implementation improvements of the naive method to achieve better than the $O(L^2)$ worst-case time bound. With these improvements,

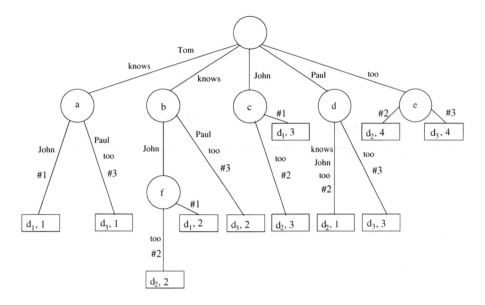

**Fig. 3.** Example of the generalized suffix tree

we have achieved constant access time for finding an appropriate child of the root (this is important because the root node has the same count of child nodes as it is the size of the alphabet - count of terms in document collection) and logarithmic time to find an existing child or to insert a new child node to any other internal nodes of the tree [15]. Next we have also improved the generalized suffix tree data structure to be suitable for large document collections [15].

## 4    Mobile Phone Positioning Algorithm

In this section we describe the algorithm for determining the mobile station location based on database of previously measured samples. Let's suppose we have prepared the data as was was discussed in section 2. A brief description of the algorithm follows:

**Step 1** Insert all encoded measurements of the training set into the generalized suffix tree data structure.

**Step 2** For each query sequence (measurement from training set) construct a vector model.

**Step 3** For each query sequence find nearest neighbor from training set.

### Step 1: Inserting All Measurements into the Suffix Tree

At this stage of the algorithm, we construct a generalized suffix tree of all encoded measurements from the training set. As mentioned in Section 2, we obtain the encoded forms of measurement samples - sequences of positive numbers. All of these sequences are inserted into the generalized suffix tree data structure (section 3).

**Step 2: Build Vector Model for Query Sequence**

Second step of the algorithm covers the procedure for building the matrix representing the vector model index file (section 3) for each query sequence. In a classical vector space model, the document is represented by the terms (which are words) respectively by the weights of the terms. **In our model the document is represented not by the terms but by the common phrases (nodes in the suffix tree)!** - the term in our context is a common phrase i.e. node of the suffix tree.

To be able to build a vector model for query measurement, we have to find all nodes in the suffix tree which match the query sequence - common phrases. Recall the example given in Figure 3: the phrases can be e.g. *"Tom knows John #1"*, *"knows John #1"*, *"John #1"*, etc. (just imagine that *"Tom knows John #1"* is equal to *"34 29 758F #1"*). The **phrase** in our context is an encoded measurement or any of its parts. The document in our context can be seen as an encoded measurement.

For all suffixes of the query sequence we simply traverse the suffix tree from the root and find the longest matching path. All the nodes on the path from the root to the position where a match does not occur represent the common phrases between query sequence and sequences in the training set - attributes of the vector model. In this step we identify the attributes for the vector model (common phrases) as well as documents (measurements) which match the query sequence.

The node in the generalized suffix tree represents the group of the documents sharing the same phrase (group of measurements sharing the same subsequence). Now we can obtain the matrix representing the vector model index file directly from the generalized suffix tree. Each document (measurement) is represented by the nodes of the generalized suffix tree in which it is contained. For computing the weights of the common phrases (nodes matched the query sequence - vector model attributes), we are using a $tf \times idf$ weighting schema as given by Equation 1.

Simple example: Let us say that we have a node containing documents $d_i$. These documents share the same phrase $t_j$. We compute $w_{ij}$ values for all documents appearing in a phrase cluster sharing the phrase $t_j$. This task is done for all nodes identified by the previous stage of the algorithm.

Now we have a complete matrix representing the index file in a vector space model (section 3).

**Step 3: Finding Nearest Neighbor for Query Sequence**

This step of the algorithm is very simple. From the previous stage of the algorithm we have also constructed a query vector - all the nodes found (common phrases). This query vector contains no null element toward the vectors representing the measurements in the index file. Now we need to sort all the documents in the constructed index file against the query document (query measurement). We compute the similarity score residing in formula 2 between all documents in the index file and query sequence and sort them. The highest scoring document from the index file is returned as a result of the query - the first nearest neighbor.

## 5   Evaluation

In this section we present the evaluation of the algorithm for mobile phone positioning. Three test sets were evaluated and compared to a classical vector model. In our previous study we developed a classical vector model approach to document indexing [15]. The key difference is that in a classical vector model the terms are single words whereas in this new approach the terms of the vector model are common phrases - common parts of measurements. As we stated in section 2 we use GPS readings to evaluate our algorithm. For each measurement from test sets the distance (error) in meters is computed with a result of the query, which is the first nearest neighbor found in the training set. Three test sets were analyzed by our algorithm (see Section 2). The total number of training samples is 133000 as was mentioned in Section 2. Following Table 2 presents the results of our experiments. Descriptions of tables 2 are as follows: column *Test Set* stands for a label of test set used, column *Vector Model* means which type of vector model was used for experiment, column *No. of Samples* means number of samples in a given test set, column *>500 m* indicates the number of tested samples for which the distance against the first nearest neighbor was more than 500 meters and the column *Mean Average Error* stands for average measured error between all query samples from test set and their first nearest neighbors found in indexed train set.

**Table 2.** Experimental Results

| Test Set | Vector Model | No. of Samples | >500 m | Mean Average Error |
|----------|--------------|----------------|--------|--------------------|
| TS1 | Classical | 646 | 299 | 229.87 m |
| TS1 | Suffix Tree | 646 | 28 | 131.90 m |
| TS2 | Classical | 1675 | 1150 | 471.89 m |
| TS2 | Suffix Tree | 1675 | 16 | 76.96 m |
| TS3 | Classical | 758 | 201 | 145.04 m |
| TS3 | Suffix Tree | 758 | 17 | 108.94 m |

Following figures 4, 5, 6 depict the results of our experiments. Dark red points on the map represent query samples from test set and the pale yellow ones represent the response to the queries returned by our algorithm - measurements from previously indexed training set (recall the algorithm in section 4). It is obvious that in most cases the response (pale yellow points) of the algorithm matches the query measurements (dark red points). The distance between two green points at the right top corner of the figures represent control distance of 200 meters in a real environment.

**Fig. 4.** Result of localization algorithm for test set TS1

**Fig. 5.** Result of localization algorithm for test set TS2

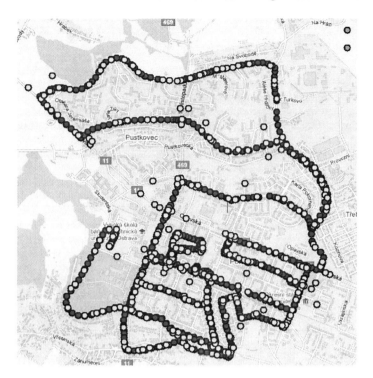

**Fig. 6.** Result of localization algorithm for test set TS3

# 6    Conclusion

In this work we have proposed a novel method for mobile phone localization. The algorithm works with parameters which can be obtained from every common mobile phone and does not require a GPS module to be installed. We have shown that the results are very accurate and in most cases of test measurements accomplish the E9-1-1 requirements in all of the test sets. We have also found the use of suffix trees very useful and realized the suffix tree vector model significantly outperforms the classical vector model in this case. This leads us to the idea that the measured parameters are dependent on ordering as they are received from the wireless network. Also we have found the use of common subsequences very useful towards the use of simple single terms. The disadvantage of the method lies in the fact that the suffix tree is very complicated to store on a persistent device such as a hard drive, so all the computing must be done in memory. This could be complication for large data sets since the suffix tree requires about 10× more space in memory than the input. In future work we want to solve this problem by finding better structures (e.g. suffix arrays, suffix automaton) or algorithm for finding common subsequences and also want to manage an attempt on very large datasets.

# References

1. Ashkenazi, I. B., Moshe, B.: Radio-maps: an experimental study. Report, Ben-Gurion University (2005), http://www.cs.bgu.ac.il/benmoshe/RadioMaps
2. Assisted GPS: A Low-infrastructure approach. GPS World (March 1, 2002), http://www.gpsworld.com/gps/assisted-gps-a-low-infrastructure-approach-734
3. Baeza-Yates, R., Ribeiro-Neto, B.: Modern information retrieval. Addison Wesley, Reading (1999)
4. Drane, C., Macnaughtan, M., Scott, G.: Positioning GSM telephones. IEEE Communication Magazine 36(4), 46–54 (1998)
5. Ehrenfeucht, A., Haussler, D.: A new distance metric on strings computable in linear time. Discrete Applied Math. 20(3), 191–203 (1988)
6. The FCC. Fact Sheet-FCC Wireless 911 Requirements, FCC (January 2001)
7. Gusfield, D.: Algorithms on strings, trees and sequences: Computer Science and Computational Biology. Cambridge University Press, Cambridge (1997)
8. Kennemann, O.: Pattern recognition by hidden Markov models for supporting handover decisions in the GSM system. In: Proc. 6th Nordic Seminar Dig. Mobile Radio Comm., Stockholm, Sweden, pp. 195–202 (1994)
9. Kennemann, O.: Continuous location of moving GSM mobile stations by pattern recognition techniques. In: Proc. 5th Int. Symp. Personal, Indoor, Mobile, Radio Comm., Den Haag, Holland, pp. 630–634 (1994)
10. Kim, S.C., Lee, J.C., Shin, Y.S., Cho, K.-R.: Mobile tracking using fuzzy multi-criteria decision making. In: Jia, X., Wu, J., He, Y. (eds.) MSN 2005. LNCS, vol. 3794, pp. 1051–1058. Springer, Heidelberg (2005)
11. Lee, D.L., Chuang, H., Seamons, K.E.: Document ranking and the vector-space model. IEEE Software, 67–75 (1997)
12. Lee, J.C., Yoo, S.-J., Lee, D.C.: Fuzzy logic adaptive mobile location estimation. In: Jin, H., Gao, G.R., Xu, Z., Chen, H. (eds.) NPC 2004. LNCS, vol. 3222, pp. 626–634. Springer, Heidelberg (2004)
13. Manzuri, M.T., Naderi, A.M.: Mobile positioning using enhanced signature database method and error reduction in location grid. In: WRI International Conference on Communications and Mobile Computing, vol. 2, pp. 175–179 (2009)
14. Manning, C.D., Raghavan, P., Schütze, H.: Introduction to information retrieval. Cambridge University Press, Cambridge (2008)
15. Martinovič, J., Novosád, T., Snášel, V.: Vector model improvement using suffix trees. In: IEEE ICDIM, pp. 180–187 (2007)
16. McCreight, E.: A space-economical suffix tree construction algorithm. Journal of the ACM 23, 262–272 (1976)
17. van Rijsbergen, C.J.: Information retrieval, 2nd edn. Butterworths, London (1979)
18. Rodeh, M., Pratt, V.R., Even, S.: Linear algorithm for data compression via string matching. Journal of the ACM 28(1), 16–24 (1981)
19. Salcic, Z., Chan, E.: Mobile station positioning using GSM cellular phone and artificial neural networks. Wireless Personal Communications 14, 235–254 (2000)
20. Salcic, Z.: GSM mobile station location using reference stations and artificial neural networks. Wireless Personal Communications 19, 205–226 (2001)
21. Simic, M.I., Pejovic, P.V.: An algorithm for determining mobile station location based on space segmentation. IEEE Communications Letters 12(7) (2008)
22. Simic, M.I., Pejovic, P.V.: A probabilistic approach to determine mobile station location with application in cellular networks. Annals of Telecommunications 64(9-10), 639–649 (2009)

23. Simic, M.I., Pejovic, P.V.: A comparison of three methods to determine mobile station location in cellular communication systems. European Transactions on Telecommunications 20(8), 711–721 (2009)
24. Song, H.L.: Automatic vehicle location in cellular communication systems. IEEE Transactions on Vehicular Technology 43, 902–908 (1994)
25. Sun, G., Chen, J., Guo, W., Liu, K.J.R.: Signal processing techniques in network aided positioning a survey of state of the art positioning designs. IEEE Signal Processing Mag. 22(4), 12–23 (2005)
26. Ukkonen, E.: On-line construction of suffix trees. Algorithmica 14, 249–260 (1995)
27. Wang, S., Min, J., Yi, B.K.: Location based services for mobiles: Technologies and standards. In: IEEE International Conference on Communication (ICC), Beijing, China (2008)
28. Weiner, P.: Linear pattern matching algorithms. In: The 14th Annual Symposium on Foundations of Computer Science, pp. 1–11 (1973)
29. Zamir, O., Etzioni, O.: Web document clustering: A feasibility demonstration. In: SIGIR 1998, pp. 46–54 (1998)
30. Zamir, O.: Clustering web documents: A phrase-based method for grouping search engine results. In: Doctoral dissertation, University of Washington (1999)
31. Zhao, Y.: Standardization of mobile phone positioning for 3G systems. IEEE Communications Mag. 40(7), 108–116 (2002)

# The Framework of e-Forensics in the Republic of Croatia

Vladimir Remenar, Dragan Peraković, and Goran Zovak

Faculty of Transport and Traffic Sciences,
Vukelićeva 4, 10000 Zagreb, Croatia
{vladimir.remenar,dragan.perakovic,goran.zovak}@fpz.hr

**Abstract.** With the development of information communication systems and the services they provide, the complexity of the organization of information within information systems is growing. The complexity itself contributes to the increase in the number of electronic incidents and affects the high demands of forensic procedure implementation. It is estimated that in the near future the number of electronic incidents will outgrow the number of classical criminal incidents both financially and quantitatively. Due to the things mentioned above, early identification, discovering and taking legal proceedings against the perpetrator of an electronic incident are necessary. It is necessary to investigate all electronic incidents adequately and promptly and adapt the legal framework and laws related to e-Forensics. e-Forensics is a relatively new discipline within which there is a low level of standardization and consistency. With the purpose of increasing the quality of performing e-Forensics and presenting the evidence in a possible judicial proceeding one has to define the legal framework of e-Forensics. The analysis of current legal standards and methods used to perform e-Forensics is presented in the paper as well as the proposal of performing e-Forensics with defined procedures and methods.

**Keywords:** forensics, e-Forensics, framework, law, Republic of Croatia.

## 1 Introduction

In today's world most of the information is created and saved on electronic media, mostly on hard drives. Computers are becoming extremely important in almost every investigation because of the increase in creating and storing information in digital form which is why e-Forensics represents the basis for discovering the evidence in the $21^{st}$ century.

e-Forensics represents the combination of both technology and science which is trying to establish the way in which computer systems are involved in certain criminal activities. The science in e-Forensics includes knowing the methods and procedures which are used when collecting and analyzing the data i.e. possible evidence. On the other hand the technology represents different tools which enable the employment of e-Forensics methods and procedures. e- Forensics itself is a multidisciplinary skill in which a forensic must have a vast knowledge of network communication protocols, network communications and also about operating systems and file systems. e-Forensics is "who", "what", "when" and "how" on the electronic evidence. The aim of e-Forensics is to try to reconstruct the incidents in computer systems which have

V. Snasel, J. Platos, and E. El-Qawasmeh (Eds.): ICDIPC 2011, Part II, CCIS 189, pp. 364–372, 2011.

been performed by an individual or a group of people and present the gathered evidence in possible judicial proceedings [1].

Although in most of the literature e-Forensics is called computer forensics, computer systems forensics or even digital investigation, those names do not show the real work area of e-Forensics. Computer forensics and Computer systems forensics terms are applied only while performing forensics of computers. And as such they should not be used while performing forensics on entire information and communications systems, its entities and data. Digital forensics term should only be applied while performing forensics on digital evidence because it does not include entities which participate in the process of creating, processing, storage and distribution of data. Due to aforementioned e-Forensics term should be used.

e-Forensics can be defined as a set of actions, procedures and methods in collecting and analyzing the data and entities in information communication system. As shown in Figure 1 information communication system includes all hardware, software, netware, dataware, lifeware and orgware resources as well as entities, products and services.

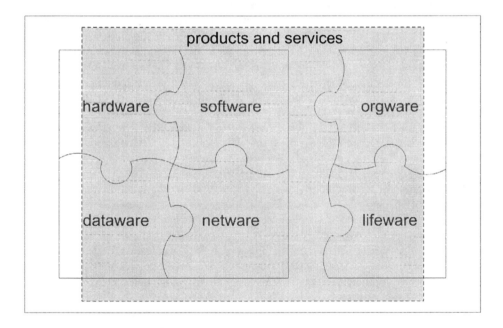

**Fig. 1.** Information communication system

Since the legal framework is often nonexistent, insufficient or out of date the actions and procedures are left to individuals which lessens the possibility of accepting the gathered evidence in judicial proceedings. By defining the framework for carrying out e-Forensics and implementing it in regulations it is possible to achieve a significant progress in the quality of carrying out e-Forensics with the purpose of establishing the facts of a higher quality.

## 2    Regulations in the Republic of Croatia

The Croatian National Parliament passes laws in the Republic of Croatia and they are published in the official gazette of the Republic of Croatia – Narodne novine (NN). Information system security regulations are passed by Office for Information System Security (cro. Zavod za sigurnost informacijskih sustava, ZSIS) which is the central government body for conducting work in the technical field of information security and National Security Council Office (cro. Ured vijeća za nacionalnu sigurnost, UVNS). Additional guidelines and documents are published by the national CERT i.e. CERT at the Croatian Academic Research Network (CARNet). The Croatian National Bank (cro. Hrvatska narodna banka, HNB) issues guidelines for controlling information systems of banks. In the Republic of Croatia there are currently various laws, provisions, decisions, internal rules and guidelines related to information communication technology law regulations.

The fundamental document in the Republic of Croatia relevant to the research of this field is Information Security Law (cro. Zakon o informacijskoj sigurnosti) in which the basic concepts of information security, measures and standards of information security and government bodies for information security such as ZSIS, UVNS and CARNet CERT are defined as well as their authorities and duties. The field of computer crime, i.e. cybercrime, is defined in the Decision on passing the law regarding Confirmation of Convention on Cybercrime. The Convention on Cybercrime represents a form of an international treaty which Croatia ratified in 2003. It was introduced by the European Council on 23rd November 2001 and it became effective on 1st July 2004. Extremely important documents related to the field of security are Regulations on Standards of Information System Security (cro. Pravilnik o standardima sigurnosti informacijskih sustava) and Regulations on Coordination of Prevention and Response to Computer – security Incidents (cro. Pravilnik o koordinaciji prevencije i odgovora na računalno – sigurnosne incidente). The National CARNet CERT has published a vast number of documents, but the only document relevant to the subject of this paper is The Basics of Computer Forensic Analysis.

The procedures of performing e-Forensics are described only in CERT's document, the Basics of Computer Forensic Analysis, which, as the title itself suggests, covers only the basics. The document provides only a suggestion of performing e-Forensics and it has no legal grounds in judicial proceedings. As such it is a good basis for the development of a more detailed document which can serve as a guideline for performing e-Forensics.

The only document which defines performing of forensics is Regulations on Standards of Information System Security. Article 223 of the mentioned regulation provides that in case of computer security incident by a body or a corporation from article 2 (referring to article 1 subsection 2 of Information Security Law) one is obliged to act according to Regulations on Prevention and Response to Computer – security Incidents Coordination (cro. Pravilnik o koordinaciji prevencije i odgovoru na računalno sigurnosne incidente) introduced by ZSIS in 2008. However, according to article 1, subsection 2 of Information Security Law, the mentioned regulations refer only to government bodies, local and regional government and corporations with public authority which use classified and non-classified data. According to afore mentioned, the Croatian laws do not state how private companies and corporations should deal with electronic incidents nor do they state how e-Forensics should be performed so that the evidence can be accepted in judicial proceedings.

Current practices in Croatia in appointing court experts from a certain professional field are not accompanied by technical and technological development of information – communication systems, products and services. In terms of that e-Forensics or expert evaluation of the field of information security is currently performed by court experts who are experts in the "Electrical engineering, electronics, informatics and telecommunication" group specialized in informatics i.e. "telecommunication and informatics".

## 3   e-Forensics Procedures

e-Forensics used to be performed only on permanent data, i.e. the data stored on a certain kind of media even when there is no electrical power available to the media. With the increased usage of information communication systems the need to perform e- Forensics on volatile data, i.e. the data which is not permanently stored on some media but temporarily or in transmission through telecommunication or computer network and their entities, has emerged. The importance of performing e-Forensics on volatile data is constantly growing because of the aforementioned. Whether e- Forensics is being performed on permanent or volatile data the main aim is to identify,

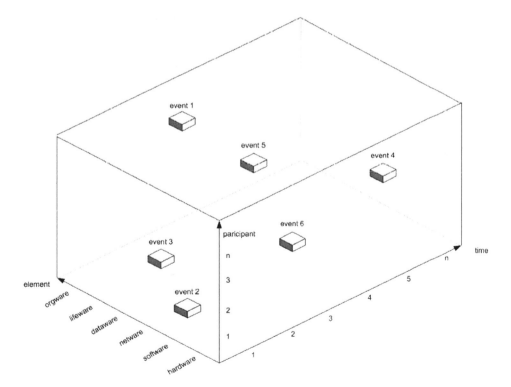

**Fig. 2.** Determining the sequence of the events

gather, store and analyze the data in a way which preserves the integrity of gathered evidence so that those could be used in possible judicial proceedings. At the same time it is necessary to determine how the data was created, modified and / or used and who performed the aforementioned in a time lapse on some information communication system element, as is shown in Figure 2.

During the mentioned steps it is necessary to make detailed records and in the end make a detailed report about what was found and about the performed procedures. In literature it is possible to find different definitions of the steps involved in the performing of e-Forensics. From three – step generalized models which include preservation, searching and reconstruction [2] or preservation, authentication and analysis [3] to five – step models which include consultations with the client, preservation, gathering, discovering, analyzing and testifying [1] and even nine – step models which include identification, preparation, approach strategy, preservation, gathering, testing, analyzing, presenting and returning to the owner[4]. The mentioned models have advantages but there are also some disadvantages like insufficiently defined procedures or the presence of unnecessary procedures with the absence of particularly necessary ones.

## 4   The Suggestion of the Framework for Performing e-Forensics

Based on the conducted research described in chapters 2 and 3, an optimal model for performing e-Forensics in 6 steps, whether on permanent or volatile data, has been designed. The suggested model can be used for performing the procedures of e-Forensics on information communication system as a whole or on its entities. It can be used on computers, computer systems (hardware, software) or telecommunication network and its entities. The suggested model consists of six steps: identification, gathering, preserving, analyzing, documenting and reporting. The sequence of events can be seen in Figure 3.

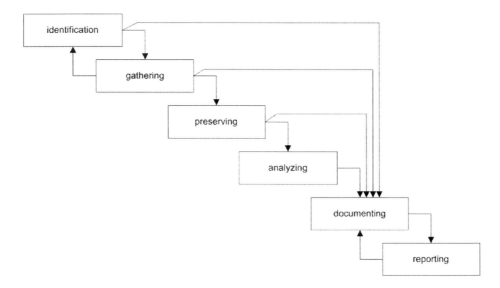

**Fig. 3.** 6 steps of performing e-Forensics

Suggested model is a framework for performing forensics analysis on any entity of information and communication system. As such these steps can be implemented in legislation as steps for performing e-Forensics. Depending on analysed entity of information and communication system (hardware, software, dataware, netware and so on) it is necessary to use specialized tools and procedures necessary for that entity.

## 4.1 Identification

In order to gather relevant and high – quality data it is necessary to identify which data and resources during e-Forensics are needed. By identifying the type of the data (classified and non classified) or resources and possible format of data or resources it is possible to assess the feasibility of e-Forensics, if necessary get all the permits and forms needed and hold consultations with lawyers, owners of the resources and other stakeholders on whose resources e-Forensics is going to be performed. By identifying the data that a person wants to gather and analyze the possibility of making a mistake or destroying the data lessens while the possibility of breaching certain legal regulations during the performing of e-Forensics lessens or even completely disappears by identifying the type of the data. By examining the feasibility one is trying to assess the possibility of gathering and analyzing required data without changing or destroying it and determining whether it is possible to perform e-Forensics on the system which is working or whether it needs to be turned off. Consultations with lawyers are necessary when it is not possible to determine whether or not some constitutional or legal act will be breached during e Forensics. Consultations with the owners of the resources and other stakeholders are necessary when changing the state of the system, for example if it is of the utmost importance that the system is working and it is not possible to turn it off.

## 4.2 Gathering

After identifying the data which need to be analyzed they have to be gathered in their original state, preserving the authenticity. During the gathering of the data it is possible that some new relevant data is found and so one has to go through the step of identifying the new data and then continue with the gathering. During the gathering of the data it is necessary to preserve the data in its original state and mark it unambiguously for later identification with the purpose of proving its authenticity. For that purpose it is possible to use MD5 hash algorithm for calculating a hash value of an evidence file. Gathering itself does not necessarily signify gathering only electronic data but also physical resources like CDs and DVDs, different paper notes etc. Such resources also need to be unambiguously marked, their position must be photographed and other possible physical parameters should be determined.

## 4.3 Preserving

Gathered data or resources must be preserved in their original state before analyzing. In the case of physical resources preserving the resources might mean that the computer has to be transported into a safe laboratory and if not necessary not turned on or connected to the network. If for example dealing with a hard drive or a CD one has to make its identical bit-by-bit copy on which analysis will be performed and the original disc needs to be deposited in a safe place. In the case of electronic evidence one has to provide their copy and the stability of volatile data gathered from telecommunication network or RAM. Before storing the gathered electronic data on a media, the media needs to be disinfected in order to avoid the reappearance of some previously stored data during the analysis. For preserving the authenticity of the original data one has to use various hardware and software solutions which make writing on the media, on which the data is stored, impossible.

### 4.4 Analysis

The analysis of the gathered materials should be performed in a controlled environment and on the previously made copies in order to avoid or at least lessen the possibility of destroying or changing the original data i.e. resources. During the analysis one has to establish the timeline of the events and entities which were involved in the creating, changing or accessing the resource which is being analyzed. For example if the communication in the communication network is being analyzed it is necessary to establish the source, the destination, the entities involved in the communication network and the human factor that initialized or in some way influenced the communication process in a certain time frame. In case an analysis of a computer or a mobile terminal equipment is being performed, the dates of creation, modification and accesses have to be determined for each record individually. Also, possible hidden data of the application and the timeline of the interaction between an individual and the user equipment have to be analyzed. Each analyzed data or resource has to be unambiguously marked, identified and compared with the original using for example MD5 checksum algorithm in order to prove that the data or the resource has not undergone any changes during the analysis.

### 4.5 Documenting

During each of the previous steps one has to make detailed notes and documentation about the undertaken activities. The notes and documentation have to be complete, accurate, comprehensive and without any mistakes or corrections. The notes and documentation should at least contain:

- a warrant for starting the procedures of e-Forensics,
- the documentation about authorisations and responsibilities of the participants in e-Forensics process,
- the exact procedures performed in each of the steps which enable the correct repetition of the undertaken steps,
- for each procedure one has to record the description and the results of that procedure,
- all the unusual occurrences which appeared while e-Forensics was performed,
- all the relevant data about the users of the system on which e-Forensics was performed,
- all the changes which happened while e-Forensics was performed,
- time and date have to be specified for each note.

Notes and documentation have to be stored in a safe place. It is also advisable not to delete the notes but rather mark the incorrect note and write the new correct one.

## 4.6 Reporting

The making of the final report depends on the demands of the organization or bodies for which it is being made. It should at least consist of:

- the data about the organization or individual that asked for e-Forensics,
- the data about the organization or individual that performed e-Forensics,
- an identification mark of the procedure of e-Forensics ,
- the data about the participants involved when e-Forensics was performed,
- the date of starting and finishing all the steps performed in e-Forensics,
- the list and the pictures of all the gathered and analyzed resources as well as their identification marks such as the unique identification mark and possible serial or identification numbers (such as mobile phone IMEI number or SIM card IMSI number),
- the list of all gathered electronic data and their unique identification marks and relevant characteristics (for example time and date of sending and receiving an SMS, time and date and identification mark of the user who accessed a certain file, log, etc),
- the description, time and date of the undertaken steps while e-Forensics was performed,
- the results of e-Forensics,
- the opinion and the conclusion.

## 5  Conclusion

Based on the conducted research numerous inadequacies of a former way of performing forensic procedures in the field of information communication traffic and applying it within Croatian laws have been noticed. An optimal model of performing e-Forensics in 6 steps is presented in the paper. The application of the suggested model with some corrections in Croatian regulations will increase the quality of procedures performed in e-Forensics and the quality of results of a forensic procedure, i.e. unique, unquestionable establishment of facts. In addition, the data about all involved entities will be preserved if applying the suggested model. Based on the suggested model it is possible to define specific rulebooks and guidelines for performing e-Forensics on the specific entity of information and communication system.

## References

1. Wall, C., Paroff, J.: Cracking the Computer Forensics Mystery. Utah Bar Journal 17(4), 10–14 (2004)
2. Carrier, B.: File System Forensic Analysis, 1st edn. Addison-Wesley Professional, Reading (2005)
3. Bidgoli, H.: Handbook of Information Security, 1st edn. Wiley, Chichester (2006)
4. Reith, M., Carr, C., Gunsch, G.: An Examination of Digital Forensic Models. International Journal of Digital Evidence 1(3), 1–12 (2002)
5. Volonino, L.: Electronic Evidence and Coputer Forensics. Communications o f374 V. Remenar, D. Peraković, and G. Zovak AIS 12, 1-23 (October 2003)

6. Taylor, M., Haggerty, J., Gresty, D.: The Legal Aspects of Corporate Computer Forensic Investigations. Computer Law & Security Report 23, 562–566 (2007)
7. Schwerha, J.: Cybercrime: Legal Standar ds Governing the Collection of DigitlEvidence. Information Systems Frontiers 6(2), 133–151 (2004)
8. Meyers, M., Rogers, M.: Computer Forensics: The Need for Standardization and Certification. International Journal of Digital Evidence 3(2), 1–11 (Fall 2004)
9. Legiland, R., Krings, A.: A Formalization of Digital Forensics. International Journal of Digital Evidence 3(2), 1–31 (Fall 2004)
10. Giordano, S.: Electronic Evidence and the Law. Information System Frontiers 6(2), 161–174 (2004)
11. Brenner, S.: U.S. Cybercrime Law: Defining Offenses. Information System Frontiers 6(2), 115–132 (2004)
12. Computer Forensics. US-CERT (2008)
13. Decree for Proclamation of Information Security Law (In Croatian: Odluka oproglašenju Zakona o informacijskoj sigurnosti). Hrvatski Sabor, Zagreb, NN79/ (July 2007)
14. Decree for Proclamation of Law for Affirmation of C onvention on Cybercrime(In Croatian: Odluka o proglašenju Zakona o potvrđivanju Konvencije o kibernetičkom kriminalu). Hrvatski Sabor, Zagreb, NN173/ (July 2002)
15. Basics of Computer Forensics Analysis (In Croatian: Osnove računalne forenzičke analize). CARNet CERT, Zagreb, CCERT-PUBDOC-2006- 11-174 (2006)
16. Rulebook for Coordination of Prevention and Response on Computer Security Incidents (In Croatian: Pravilnik o koordinaciji prevencije i odgovora na računalno-sigurnosne incidente). Zavod za sigurnost informacijskih sustava, Zagreb (2008)
17. Rulebook of Information Systems Security (In Croatian: Pravilnik o standardima sigurnosti informacijskih sustava). Zavod za informacijsku sigurnost, Zagreb (2008)

# Knowledge Based Data Cleaning for Data Warehouse Quality

Louardi Bradji[1,2] and Mahmoud Boufaida[2]

[1] University of Tebessa
12002 Tebessa Algeria
bradjilouardi@yahoo.fr
[2] LIRE laboratory, Mentouri University of Constantine
25017 Constantine Algeria
mboufaida@umc.edu.dz

**Abstract.** This paper describes an approach for improvement the quality of data warehouse and operational databases with using knowledge. The benefit of this approach is three-folds. First, the incorporation of knowledge into data cleaning is successful to meet the user's demands and then the data cleaning can be expanded and modified. The knowledge that can be extracted automatically or manually is stored in repository in order to be used and validated among an appropriate process. Second, the propagation of cleaned data to their original sources in order to validate them by the user so the data cleaning can give valid values but incorrect. In addition, the mutual coherence of data is ensured. Third, the user interaction with data cleaning process is taken account in order to control it. The proposed approach is based in the idea that the quality of data will be assured at the sources and the target of data.

**Keywords:** Data Cleaning, Data Quality, Data Warehouse, Knowledge.

## 1 Introduction

The decision making systems are based on the construction of federated databases and their analysis with intelligent tools such as data mining [1].

Data warehousing is a process that aims at extracting a relevant data from multiple heterogeneous and distributed operational databases and recopying them into a data warehouse (DW), while preserving the changes of data states. The model of the DW describing its data must support the data evolution [2].

Data mining (DM), also known as Knowledge Discovery in Databases (KDD) is defined as "the extraction of implicit, previously unknown, and potentially useful information from data". It encompasses a set of processes performed automatically whose the tasks are to analyze, to identify and to summarize knowledge from large data sets. The DM aims at extracting some tangible knowledge comprehensible and useful [3].

Coherence is the capacity for a system to reflect on the copy of a data the updates which has done on other copies of this data [4]. The update propagation of operational databases to the DW is the subject of several works [5]. However, we did not note works that treat the propagation of cleaned data towards the operational databases.

V. Snasel, J. Platos, and E. El-Qawasmeh (Eds.): ICDIPC 2011, Part II, CCIS 189, pp. 373–384, 2011.
© Springer-Verlag Berlin Heidelberg 2011

Data cleaning is one of the critically important steps in both the DW and DM process. It is used to improve the data quality by using various techniques. Many research works use the methods of DM in the data cleaning. Missing and incomplete values of data represent especially difficult to build good knowledge and draw any conclusions [3], [6].

So, this work proposes an iterative, an interactive and an incremental approach of improvement the quality of data warehouse using knowledge based data cleaning where the knowledge are stored in separate repository in order to facilitate their management . This repository will be used mainly to improve the DW quality and by consequence the knowledge (results obtained by data analysis tools). Moreover the accumulation and availability of knowledge in a repository accelerate and facilitate the decision making process. Our approach is adapted to the DM tools by separating the data set before their loading in three subsets: cleaned, modeled and corrected. Our contribution proposes:

- An incremental building of a knowledge repository, which will be used during the data cleaning process and for improvement of the decisional systems;
- A data cleaning process adapted to the DM tools;
- An Updates propagation process in order to ensure the mutual coherence between the data warehouse and the operational databases from which data warehouse is formed.

The rest of this paper is organized as follows. Section 2 presents the data cleaning process. Then, some related research works will be reviewed in section 3. In section 4, basic concepts of mutual coherence and evidence based medicine are briefly described. Section 5 presents and describes our approach. The experimental results are reported in section 6. Finally, we draw our conclusions and some future research directions.

## 2   Data Cleaning

Data cleaning also called data cleansing or scrubbing, improve the data quality by deals with detecting and removing errors and inconsistencies from data. The data cleaning tools roughly distinguish between single-source and multi-sources problems and between schema and instance related problems [1]. A data cleaning process is executed in the data staging area in order to improve the accuracy of the DW [7].

### 2.1   Data Cleaning Process

In general, data cleaning involves five phases:

- Data Analysis in order to detect the inconsistencies;
- Definition and choice of transformations;
- Verification of the correctness and effectiveness of transformations;
- Execution of the transformation;
- Feedback of cleaned data.

The data cleaning remains expensive and the scripts combining the various operations of cleaning can also introduce new errors [8].

## 2.2  Data Cleaning Implementation

A large variety of tools is available to support data cleaning tasks, in particular for data warehousing. These tools can be divided into data auditing and ETL (Extraction/Transformation/Loading) tools.

**Data auditing tools.** They also called data profiling is define as the application of data mining-algorithms for measuring and (possibly interactive) improving of data quality. Data auditing can be divided into two subtasks, induction of a structural description (structure induction), and data checking that marks deviations as possible data errors and generates probable corrections (deviation detection).

Among the commercial tools of data auditing: ACR/Data d'Unitech Systems and Migration Architect d'Evoke [9].

**ETL tools.** They typically have little built-in data cleaning capabilities but allow the user to specify cleaning functionality. The first part of the process embraces all the actions that are required to extract the data from operational data sources. This also includes pre-cleaning. The second step encompasses all the transformations that the data has to go through in order to fit the DW model. In this phase data is aggregated, cleaned and transformed so that it could be loaded into a DW. The very loading is performed in the last stage. Here also some additional cleaning is possible. Among the commercial tools of the transformation: Potter's Wheel, ARKTOUS, Ajax, .etc [3].

## 2.3  Data Cleaning Approaches

The research tasks on the data cleaning are classified in four great approaches [10]:

- Use of specific transformation rules;
- Use of tools integrating transformations;
- Definition of a conceptual language to express the transformations in the query;
- Generation of mediation query integrating the data cleaning.

# 3  Some Related Works

The most popular data cleaning frameworks include: AJAX, Potter's Wheel, Febrl, FraQL, ARKTOS, IntelliClean, Xclean and ODCF [17, 18, 19, 20]. In all these frameworks, the data cleaning operations will be specified by the end-users through an interface. One of the main drawbacks presented by these frameworks in DW is related to the propagation of cleaned data to their operational databases in order to improve them and avoid to redoing the same data cleaning operation when building other DWs.

Although knowledge provides domain independent information that can be used for successful data cleaning, the issue of knowledge use to support data cleaning has not been dealt with [15]. IntelliClean is the first knowledge based data cleaning tool, which scrubs the data for anomalies [16]. However, this tool presents two majors disadvantages. First, it can only identify and remove duplications and therefore cannot deal with all the data quality problems. Second, it does not permit the knowledge validation, which is an important aspect that alters the quality of data cleaning operations.

In order to deal with the drawbacks mentioned above, we propose a knowledge based data cleaning framework using the mutual coherence mechanism in order to ensure the updates propagation, and the evidence medicine system from which is inspired the process managing knowledge.

## 4   Basic Concepts of Mutual Coherence and Evidence Based Medicine

### 4.1   Mutual Coherence

The coherence in the distributed systems and shared databases is guaranteed by the two phases commit protocol [11]. In the context of data warehouses, it is closely related to the mechanisms of data replication and update propagation techniques.

**Data Replication.** The general problem involved in the data replication is the coherence of the data. The concept of coherence covers various problems. From the viewpoint of the access requests, the management of local concurrent access is concerned with their isolation. From the viewpoint of the data, the management of the copies must ensure their mutual coherence, i.e. all the replica copies must be identical [4].

**Data replication strategies.**   The strategies of replication can be classified in two families: synchronous and asynchronous [12]. In the synchronous replication, whenever a transaction updates a replica copy all the other ones of the same source object are isolated before validating an update. The maintenance of mutual coherence requires to delay the updating operations until all the copies of data are similar, which causes an overcost of response time. The invariant condition of this family of strategy is that replica copies are always mutually coherent. The asynchronous replication offers more flexibility because it distinguishes the data update phase of the update propagation phase. The interest of this strategy is to improve the data availability and transaction response time. The problem is that the copies are not always mutually coherent [13].

**Update propagation methods.** These methods try to maintain constantly the data divergence by propagating the data update as soon as possible. Table 1 presents these methods of propagation and the time of its release [4].

**Table 1.** Propagation methods

| Method | Release |
|---|---|
| Immediate Propagation | As soon as the validation of data updates. |
| Periodic propagation | As soon as the arrival of the primary copy update. |
| Eventual propagation | As soon as the arrival of an event. |

**Replication in Data Warehoue.** After it has been populated, the DW must be refreshed to reflect updates to the operational databases. Refreshing is usually done periodically. It can also be done immediately after every update for On Online Analytical Processing (OLAP) applications that need to see current data. To avoid populating entire tables, only the updates of the source data should be propagated to the data warehouse. This is done using asynchronous replication techniques that perform incremental maintenance of replicas from primary copies [11].

Once the errors are removed, the cleaned data should also replace the dirty data in the original sources in order to give legacy applications the improved data [9]. For data warehousing, the cleaned data is available from the building of data staging area [1].

An important aspect, which is not yet considered by the research works, is the propagation of the cleaned data to the operational databases. Moreover, the scripts combining the various data cleaning operations can also produce new errors. Thus, the validation of the cleaned data is important aspect which will be integrated in Data Cleaning works especially for the biomedical data where the error led to catastrophes.

In this work, we considered these two aspects in order to improve the data and analysis quality in the biomedical data warehouse and operational databases.

## 4.2 Evidence Based Medicine

Evidence based medicine is the conscientious, explicit, and judicious use of current best evidence in making decisions about the care of individual patients. Its task is to complement the existing clinical decision making process with the most accurate and most efficient research evidence. It is used for explicit and validate knowledge collected from books, reviews, health protocols, doctor, etc. Data mining techniques enable us to identify new knowledge which are hidden in data. After it needs to be examined and approved by the higher authority and then transformed into evidence. The incorporation of the evidences in the health decision-making system is the subject of several works. The collection of the evidences is done by a process of four steps: asking answerable questions, accessing the best information, appraising the information for validity and relevance, and applying the information to patient care [14].

The goal of the use of DW and DM to support evidence-based medicine in the domain of clinical pathways is to improve the coordination of care between different clinical departments and so to improve the quality of care and to reduce the length of patient's hospitalization.

## 5   Knowledge Based Data Cleaning for Data Warehouse

On the basis of the idea that the analysis quality is conditioned by the data quality and the fact that the analysis tools generally and DM especially proved their performances in the field of the KDD, we propose in this work a generic, an iterative and an interactive approach for data cleaning based in the uses of knowledge for data warehouse quality (see figure 1).

Our contribution is based on the incremental construction of knowledge repository and the determination of three data sets: a corrected data set, a cleaned data set and a modeled data set to use them in:

- Data cleaning process during the data warehousing in order to improve the DW quality and thereafter reduce the data cleaning operation during the data analysis;
- Improvement of the decision making system: the user can exploit the knowledge directly what allows to accelerate and to facilitate the decision making system where time is an important factor (medical urgency);

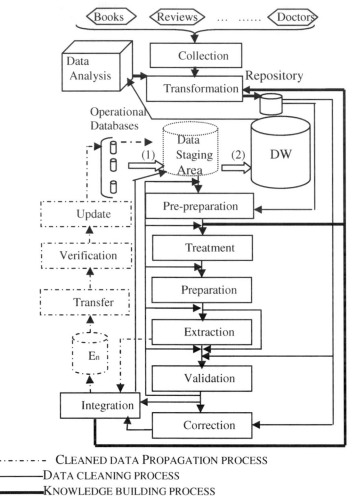

-·-·-·-·-· CLEANED DATA PROPAGATION PROCESS
——————DATA CLEANING PROCESS
████████KNOWLEDGE BUILDING PROCESS
(1): INTEGRATION     (2): CONSTRUCTION

**Fig. 1.** Knowledge based Data Cleaning for Data Warehouse Framework

- Implication of the users in the improvement of the data and knowledge quality: as the cleaning operations can provide errors, the validation of the cleaned data by the operational databases users ensures and improves the data and knowledge quality.

- Improvement of the data quality in the operational databases: there are three replica copies of a data: two ones are materialized in the operational databases and the DW and virtual replica copy in the data staging area built during the data warehousing. The cleaned data should be propagated to the operational databases in order to improve the operational databases quality and thereafter to avoid redoing the cleaning work for future data extractions. This aspect is ensured by the cleaned data propagation process ;

To reach these goals, as shown in figure 1, our approach proposes three processes:

- A data cleaning process adapted to the data analysis by the DM ;
- An update propagation process ;
- A knowledge repository building process.

Before looking at each process in detail, it is important to define the quality measurement proposed to be used in our works.

## 5.1 Quality Measurements

In this work, we have introduced five quality measurements.

**Attribute Cleaned Value Support.** For an attribute A, this support which is denoted $Svn(A)$ is the ratio between the cleaned values of A (denoted $Vn(A)$) and the number of records (denoted m).

$$Svn(A) = Vn(A) / m \tag{1}$$

This support has the following properties:
- $0 \leq Svn(A) \leq 1$;
- $Svn(A) = 1$: each value (instance attribute) of A must be cleaned;
- $Svn(A) = 0$: no value of A will be cleaned.

**Record Cleaned Value Support.** For a record E, this support which is denoted $Tvn(E)$ is the ratio between the cleaned values of E (denoted $Vn(E)$) and the number of attributes (denoted Ne).

$$Tvn(E) = Vn(E) / Ne \tag{2}$$

This support has the following properties:

- $0 \leq Tvn(A) \leq 1$;
- $Tvn(E) = 1$: each value of E must be cleaned
- $Tvn(E) = 0$: no value of E will be cleaned.

**Cleaned Data set.** It contains the cleaned values. It is denoted $E_n$ and has the following proprieties:

- Its records have the $Tvn(Ei) > 0$
- Its attributes have the $Vn(A)$ and $Svn(A) > 0$

**Modeled data set.** It contains the records have the Tvn(E) = 0. It will be used to build the models. This data set is denoted $E_m$ and has the following property:

$$E_m = (\text{Data Staging Area set}) - E_n \qquad (3)$$

**Corrected Data Set.** It contains the cleaned values that are detected invalid and consequently corrected by the user during the verification step of the cleaned data propagation process.

## 5.2   Knowledge Repository Building Process

This process contains two phases (see figure 1). The extraction of knowledge is done during the collection phase by applying a process of four steps described above in subsection 4.2. It can be also extracted during the data cleaning step during data warehousing or during the use of DW by data analysis tools. During the transformation phase these knowledge will be corrected by high authority, then transformed in the form of rules before their storage in the repository.

## 5.3   Data Cleaning Process

It is inspired from the data mining process. As shown in figure 1, it contains seven phases: pre-preparation, treatment, preparation, extraction, validation, correction and integration.

**Pre-preparation.** Several operations will be realized during this phase either automatically or through the intervention of high authority. These operations are:

- Standardization of the names and the formats of data;
- Data transformation: dates in durations, graphic data in coordinates, decomposition of addresses (or reverse) and any common transformation to the all data analysis techniques;
- Data Enrichment: use of taxonomies.

**Treatment.** Moreover the usual operations of elimination of redundant (rows and columns), discretization and regrouping of variables, we have proposed to separate the data in cleaned data and modeled data as follows:

- Invalid Value Marking: this operation aims at identifying and marking the missing, incomplete, and aberrant values. Theses values are generally detected automatically and by various tools especially the graphic and multi-dimensional visualization. Any marked value is known as cleaned value;
- Data Pre-cleaning: it aims at using the knowledge repository to correct certain cleaned values. This operation is capital to reduce the set of cleaned values;
- Construction of cleaning statistic table: this table is a matrix with two dimensions where the lines are the attributes (Ai) and the columns are the Vn(Ai) and Svn(Ai);
- Creation of the attribute cleaned value support: for each table, we added the Tvn(Ei) attribute;

-   Elimination of records and attributes useless: An attribute (resp. record) comprising a high number of cleaned values is useless. So it will be eliminated in order to improve the analysis and data quality. For the implementation of this operations, we introduced two thresholds :

> Sa: threshold of attribute elimination.
> Se: threshold of record elimination.

Elimination is done according to two cases:

-   Case 1: If Tvn(Ei) < Se   then Ei is to be removed.
-   Case 2: If Svn(Ai) < Sa   then Ai is to be removed.

**Preparation.** This phase contains two operations: the data separation and data partition. The data separation aims at dividing the data set in two data sets disjoined: the cleaned data ($E_n$) and modeled data ($E_m$). The data partition aims at sharing $E_m$ into three mutually exclusive data sets data: a training data set, a test data set and a validation data set.

**Extraction.** It is the usual phase of KDD where the extraction of knowledge (models, rules) from the training data set is done by using the data mining techniques [3]. These techniques are multiple and showed their effectiveness in various fields.

**Validation.** After fitting the knowledge on the training data set, it should test its performance on the validation data set. The accuracy of the knowledge on the test data set gives a realistic estimate of the performance of the knowledge on completely unseen data.

**Correction.** In this phase, we proceed to the prediction of the cleaned values. If a cleaned value can be corrected by several knowledge (resp. rules), we propose to choose one of the choices:

-   Choice 1: If the number of knowledge (resp. rules) or the cleaned value set is very large then remove the record which contains the cleaned value;
-   Choice 2: If the number of knowledge  is limited then the correction is done by all rules (one record and three knowledge gives three records);
-   Choice 3: Intervention of the user to decide on the knowledge (resp. rules) to choose.

**Integration.** This phase concern the knowledge (rules) and the cleaned values. The cleaned values will be replaced by the corrected values in the data staging area. The cleaned data set $E_n$ must be also built in order to use it in the next process as shown in figure 1.

### 5.4  Updates Data Propagation Process

This process concerns only the cleaned values. It aims at validating the corrections by users and then at propagating them to the operational databases. This process is of high importance because the error can lead to catastrophes (death, epidemic...) in the medical field for example.

The data cleaning process updates the values on the level of data staging area, which is a replica copy of the operational databases. From this fact, this process ensures the mutual coherence of data and then improves the operational databases quality. The updates propagation process is a crucial for total data quality assurance i.e. the quality of data at the operational databases and data warehouse.

This process does not treat the mutual coherence as being only the propagation of the corrections but it permits to validate them by the users of operational databases.

The knowledge quality assurance is another objective aimed by this process because the corrected data updates by the users implies the update of the knowledge automatically.

If the corrections made during the data cleaning process are updated by the users then the updates propagations to the DW (resp. data staging area) and the knowledge update must be launched.

**Cleaned Data Propagation**. This process contains three phases: a transfer, a verification and an update. It is used to propagate the cleaned values made during the data cleaning process to the operational databases.

As the data cleaning can introduce errors, the choice is done between three values: initial value (Vi), cleaned value (Vn) and the user value (V).

In this process, the selected replication strategy is asynchronous and the update propagation method is the eventual propagation because the cleaned data propagation starts after the integration of cleaned data in the data staging area.

*Transfer.* As the operational databases are distributed and heterogeneous, the transfer consists for each base to:

-   The construction of the cleaned data set according to their operational databases schema;
-   The sending of these data sets to the users of operational databases in order to decide on the corrections.

*Verification.* The user must intervene in order to decide on the corrections done during the data cleaning process. There are three possibilities:

-   If Vn is retained then Vi: = Vn;
-   If Vi is retained then Vn: =Vi (in data staging area and data warehouse);
-   If V is retained then Vi :=V and Vn :=V.

*Update.* This phase contains two tasks:

-   Operational databases updates: the cleaned values Vn and V retained by the users in the precedent phase must immediately replace the initial values in the operational databases;
-   Construction of the Corrected data set $E_v$: this data set contains the cleaned values Vi and V retained by the user in the precedent phase.

**Corrected Data Propagation.** The propagation of the corrections doing by users (when a user refuses the cleaned value) to the DW requires the release of the data warehousing process. This propagation cannot be made constantly because it is costly (time). From this fact, we propose three choices for the propagation: periodical, rebuilding and on request.

*Periodic propagation* . The corrections data set propagation is done during the refreshing of DW and there are two types: rebuild or incremental.

*Rebuilding propagation.* If the volume of corrected data set ($E_v$) is important, the DW is judged of bad quality and thus the analysis quality will be poor. So the rebuilding of DW is necessary. We compute the ratio between the corrected data set and the DW. If this ratio is significant then the DW will be rebuilt.

*On request propagation.* The corrected data set propagation is on request of the DW administrator. Thereafter the data cleaning process contains only the following phases:

- Preparation phase : data transformation;
- Extraction phase : knowledge extraction;
- Integration: knowledge  and cleaned value update .

Let us notice that:

- During the data cleaning, the $E_v$ will be integrated directly in the $E_m$. That ensures knowledge and analysis quality;
- The data cleaning process will be reduced;
- Certain phases and operations of the data cleaning process will be used by the corrected data propagation.

## 6   Case Study and Experimental Results

In order to illustrate the applicability and performances of our work, this section presents the results of a case study of applying the proposed framework to health sector. We have selected in this sector three departments (laboratory, pharmacy and medical services) where each department is operational data sources. The manual inspection of the data sets in these departments reveals a wide number of data quality problems (single-source and multi-sources): missing values, empty fields, misspellings, improper generation of data, domain value violations… duplicate entities).

In order to demonstrate the benefit of our proposal, we have compared its performances to several Data Cleaning tools. We have measured the errors rate before the DW process for each DW and operational databases. Our proposal has given better results for the improvement of data quality but the time consuming is the problem which will be resolved in the next step of our work

## 7   Conclusion

In this paper, we have presented a theoretical approach for the knowledge based data cleaning for data warehouse in order to ensure the data and analysis quality.  This approach allows one to ensure and improve data warehouse and operational databases quality using three processes: knowledge process, updates propagation process and data cleaning process.  The knowledge repository ensures the validity and availability of the knowledge to accelerate the decisional system.  The implication of the users of operational databases is an important aspect because the data cleaning operations can give valid values but incorrect which led to catastrophes conclusions. Our future work is the implementation of this approach with a case study related to a medical organization.

## References

1. Rahm, E., Do, H.H.: Data Cleaning: Problems and Current Approaches. IEEE Data Engineering Bull. 23(4), 3–13 (2000)
2. Raynal, M., Mostéfaoui, A., Roy, M., Agrawal, D., El Abbadi, A.: The lord of the rings: efficient maintenance of views at data warehouse. In: Malkhi, D. (ed.) DISC 2002. LNCS, vol. 2508, pp. 33–47. Springer, Heidelberg (2002)

3. Matyia, D.: Applications of data mining algorithms to analysis of medical data. Master Thesis, Software Engineering, Thesis no: MSE-2007, Blekinge Institute of Technology (2007)
4. Le Pape, C., Gançarski, S., Valduriez, P.: Data Quality Management in a Database Cluster with Lazy Replication. Journal of Digital Information Management (JDIM) 3(2), 82–87 (2005)
5. Favre, C., Bentayeb, F., Boussaid, O.: Evolution of Data Warehouses' Optimization: A Workload Perspective. In: Song, I.-Y., Eder, J., Nguyen, T.M. (eds.) DaWaK 2007. LNCS, vol. 4654, pp. 13–22. Springer, Heidelberg (2007)
6. Lin, J.H., Haug, P.J.: Exploiting missing clinical data in Bayesian network modeling for predicting medical problems. Journal of Biomedical Informatics 41(1), 1–14 (2008)
7. Vassiliadis, P., Quix, C., Vassiliou, Y., Jarke, M.: Data warehouse process management. Journal of Information Systems 26(3), 205–236 (2001)
8. Berti-Équille, L.: La qualité des données comme condition à la qualité des connaissances: un état de l'art. Mesures de qualité pour la fouille de données. Numéro spécial, Revue Nationale des Technologies de l'Information (RNTI),Cépaduès (2004)
9. Luebbers, D., Grimmer, U., Jarke, M.: Systematic Development of Data Mining-Based Data Quality Tools. In: Proceedings of the 29th Intl VLDB Conference, vol. 29, pp. 548–559 (2003)
10. Kedad, Z., Bouzeghoub, M., Soukrane, A.: Génération des requêtes de médiation intégrant le nettoyage des données. Journal of Ingénierie des Systèmes d'Information 7(3), 39–66 (2002)
11. Pacitti, E.: Improving Data Freshness in Replicated Databases. INRIA. Research report 3617 (1999)
12. Sutra, P., Shaprio, M.: Comparing Optimistic Database Replication Techniques. In: 23 Journey of Advanced DataBase (BDA 2007), Marseille, French (2007)
13. Pacitti, E., Simon, E.: Update Propagation Strategies to Improve Freshness of Data in Lazy Master Schemes. INRIA. Research report n° 3233 (1997)
14. Nevena, S., Min Tjoa, A.: The relevance of data warehousing and data mining in the field of evidence-based medicine to support healthcare decision making. In: International Conference on Computer Science (ICCS 2006), Prague, Czech Republic, Informatica, vol. 11 (2006)
15. Oliveira, P., Rodrigues, F., Henriques, P.: An Ontology-based approach for data cleaning. In: Proceedings of the 11the International Conference on Information Quality (ICIQ 2007), pp. 307–320 (2007)
16. Kororoas, A., Lin, S.: Information Quality in Engineering Asset Management. In: Ismael, C., Mario, P. (eds.) Information Quality Management: Theory and Applications, pp. 221–251. Idea Group Publishing, USA (2007)
17. Berti-Equille, L., Dasu, T.: Data Quality Mining: New Research Directions. In: International Conference on Data Mining (ICDM 2009) (2009)
18. Huanzhuo, Y., Di, W., Shuai, C.: An Open Data Cleaning Framework Based on Semantic Rules for Continuous Auditing. In: 2nd International Conference on Computer Engineering and Technology, vol. 2, pp. 158–162. IEEE, Los Alamitos (2010)
19. Lee, M.L., Ling, T.W., Low, W.L.: IntelliClean: A Knowledge Based Intelligent Data Cleaner. In: Proceedings of the 6th ACM SIGKDD conference on Knowledge Discovery and Data Mining, pp. 290–294 (2000)
20. Herbert, K.G., Wang, J.T.L.: Biological data cleaning: a case study. Int. J. of Information Quality 1(1), 60–82 (2007)

# Using Uppaal for Verification of Priority Assignment in Real-Time Databases

Martin Kot*

Center for Applied Cybernetics, Department of Computer Science, FEI,
VSB - Technical University of Ostrava,
17. listopadu 15, 708 33, Ostrava-Poruba, Czech Republic
martin.kot@vsb.cz

**Abstract.** Model checking, as one area of formal verification, is recently subject of an intensive research. Many verification tools intended to check properties of models of systems were developed, mainly at universities. Many researches are also interested in real-time database management systems (RTDBMS). In this paper we show some possibilities of using a verification tool Uppaal on some variants of priority assignment algorithms used in RTDBMS. We present some possible models of such algorithms expressed as nets of timed automata, which are a modeling language of Uppaal and then some simulation and verification possibilities of Uppaal on those models.

**Keywords:** real-time database systems, priority assignment, timed automata, model checking, verification, verification tool, Uppaal.

## 1 Introduction

Many real-time applications need to store some data in a database. It is possible to use traditional database management systems (DBMS). But they are not able to guarantee any bounds on a response time. This is the reason why so-called real-time database management systems (RTDBMS) emerged (e.g. [1,8]). Research in RTDBMS focused on evolution of transaction processing algorithms, priority assignment strategies and concurrency control techniques. There are also some implementations of RTDBMS, e.g., Raima Embedded Database, eXtremeDB etc.

Formal verification is of great interest recently and finds its way quickly from theoretical papers into a real live. It can prove that a system (or more exactly a model of a system) has a desired behavior. The difference between simulation, testing and other classical approaches on the one hand and formal verification on the other hand is that during testing and simulation only some possible computations are chosen. Formal verification can prove correctness of all possible computations. This proves handy mainly in parallel applications where errors

---

* Author acknowledges the support by the Czech Science Foundation - GACR, Grant No. P202/11/0340 and by the Czech Ministry of Education, Grant No. 1M0567.

V. Snasel, J. Platos, and E. El-Qawasmeh (Eds.): ICDIPC 2011, Part II, CCIS 189, pp. 385–399, 2011.

may appear only in one of many possible orders of mutual computations of parallel processes. A drawback of formal verification is that almost all problems are undecidable for models with high descriptive power. It is important to find a model with an appropriate descriptive power to capture a behavior of a system, yet with algorithmically decidable verification problems.

There are two main approaches to fully automated verification – equivalence checking and model checking. Using equivalence checking, two models of systems (usually model of specification and model of implementation) are compared using some behavioral equivalence. In this paper we consider the other approach – so called model checking (see e.g. [4,13]). This form of verification uses a model of a system in some formalism and a property expressed usually in the form of formula in some temporal logic. Model checking algorithm checks whether the property holds for the model of a system. There are quite many automated verification tools which implement model checking algorithms (see e.g. [17] for overview). Those tools use different modeling languages or formalisms and different logics.

The idea of the research described in this paper came from people from real-time area dealing with RTDBMS. They have heard about verification tools and were interested in using such a tool on their experimental database system. They would like to verify and compare different variants of algorithms and protocols used in RTDBMS. A great effort has been devoted to development of some experimental RTDBMS to test different algorithms and to do some simulation studies on them (e.g. [12]). Apart from experimental implementations, there were also some formal models used for simulation (e.g., a model developed by progression from a simple mathematical analysis to complicated simulations, illustrated on concurrency control protocols in [16]). As stated above, formal verification is something quite different (but not always better, it depends on requirements). There are only rare attempts of automated formal verification of real-time database system. We know about one paper ([15]) where authors suggested a new pessimistic concurrency control protocol and verified it using Uppaal. They presented two small models covering only their protocol. And there is a recent book chapter [14] which is devoted to formal verification of real-time databases. But it describes only a case study that considers sensor networks.

There is not any verification tool intended directly for real-time database systems. They are mostly intended for verification of so called reactive systems (system changes its states according to actions/impulses from outside). This means, it is not possible to model data stored in database or particular data changes in transactions. Big problem of almost every verification tools is so called state space explosion. Embedment of database/transaction data into models would lead to too many states and models not manageable by any verification tool. We have chosen the tool Uppaal because it is designed at least for real-time systems. But, it is also supposed to be used on reactive systems, which are quite different from database systems. So we need to find some possibilities how to deal with it. Uppaal is also not able to manage too detailed models. On the other hand, too simple models can not catch important properties of a real system. So our main goal is to find a suitable level of abstraction, a compromise between size (and complexity) of models and catching important properties into models.

One of the most important and crucial parts of all database management systems allowing concurrent access to data records is concurrency control. Some of protocols used for concurrency control author of this paper modeled and verified using Uppaal in [9,10] previously. In this paper, we will concentrate on other important part of real-time database systems – priority assignment and distribution of resources to transactions according to priorities. Ongoing work on this topic was presented as a poster at a local workshop [11].

There are many parameters that can be used for determination of priority of database transaction. Some of them are criticality, deadline, amount of resources already used by transaction etc. There were several algorithms presented for this task. In this paper we will consider some of them presented in [1,6] – First Come First Serve (Section 4), Earliest Deadline (Section 5), Latest Deadline (Section 6), Random Priority (Section 7) and Least Slack (Section 8)). The nature of this paper should be mainly proof of concept. There are not any new informations found about described algorithms or any errors in them discovered. But some general possibilities of modeling using nets of timed automata are shown which can be used for verification and comparison of, e.g., newly designed algorithms in the future. Some simulation and verification possibilities on suggested models are described in Section 9. Models in Sections 4, 5, 6, 7, 8 are designed and described in a way to show as much general possibilities of abstraction and simplification as possible in the small extent of a conference paper.

Before we will discuss concrete models of algorithms, we will shortly describe the tool Uppaal in the Section 2 for readers not experienced of it to understand models describe in this paper. Then we will talk over some general possibilities and assumptions in Section 3.

## 2 Verification Tool Uppaal

Uppaal ([3,5]) is a verification tool for real-time systems. It is jointly developed by Uppsala University and Aalborg University. It is designed to verify systems that can be modeled as networks of timed automata extended with some further features such as integer variables, structured data types, user defined functions, channel synchronization and so on.

A timed automaton is a finite-state automaton extended with clock variables. A dense-time model, where clock variables have real number values and all clocks progress synchronously, is used. In Uppaal, several such automata working in parallel form a network of timed automata.

An automaton has locations and edges. Each location has an optional name and invariant. An invariant is a conjunction of side-effect free expressions of the form $x < e$ or $x \leq e$ where $x$ is a clock variable and $e$ evaluates to an integer. Each automaton has exactly one initial location.

Particular automata in the network synchronize using channels and values can be passed between them using shared (global) variables. A state of the system is defined by the locations of all automata and the values of clocks and discrete variables. The state can be changed in two ways - passing of time (increasing values of all clocks by the same amount) and firing an edge of some automaton (possibly synchronizing with another automaton or other automata).

Some locations may be marked as committed. If at least one automaton is in a committed location, time passing is not possible, and the next change of the state must involve an outgoing edge of at least one of the committed locations.

Each edge may have a select, a guard, a synchronization and an assignment. Select gives a possibility to choose nondeterministically a value from some range. Guard is a side-effect free expression that evaluates to a boolean. The guard must be satisfied when the edge is fired. It can contain not only clocks, constants and logical and comparison operators but also integer and boolean variables and (side-effect free) calls of user defined functions.

Synchronization label is of the form $Expr!$ or $Expr?$ where $Expr$ evaluates to a channel. An edge with $c!$ synchronizes with another edge (of another automaton in the network) with label $c?$. Both edges have to satisfy all firing conditions before synchronization. Sometimes we say that automaton firing an edge labeled by $c!$ sends a message $c$ to the automaton firing an edge labeled by $c?$. There are urgent channels as well – synchronization through such a channel have to be done in the same time instant when it is enabled (it means, time passing is not allowed if a synchronization through urgent channel is enabled) – and broadcast channels (any number of $c?$ labeled edges are synchronized with one $c!$ labeled edge) . An assignment is a comma separated list of expressions with a side-effect. It is used to reset clocks and set values of variables.

Figure 1 shows how some of the described notions are represented graphically in Uppaal. There are 3 locations named A, B and C. Location A is initial and B is committed. Moreover A has an invariant x<=15 with the meaning that the automaton can be in this location only when the value of the clock variable x is less or equal 15. The edge between A and B has the select z:int[0,5] – it nondeterministically chooses an integer value from the range 0 to 5 and stores it in variable z. This edge also has the guard x>=5 && y==0. This means that it can be fired only when the value of the clock variable x is greater or equal 5 and the integer variable y has the value 0. Data types of variables are defined in a declaration section. Further it has synchronization label synchr! and an assignment x=0, y=z resetting the clock variable x and setting the value of z to the integer variable y. This edge can be fired only when some other automaton has an edge labeled synchr? enabled.

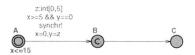

**Fig. 1.** Graphical representation of a timed automaton in Uppaal

Uppaal has some other useful features. Templates are automata with parameters. These parameters are substituted with given arguments in the process declaration. This enables easy construction of several alike automata. Moreover, we can use bounded integer variables (with defined minimal and maximal value), arrays and user defined functions. These are defined in declaration sections. There is one global declaration section where channels, constants, user data types etc. are specified. Each automaton template has own declaration section, where local clocks, variables and functions are specified. And finally, there is a system declaration section, where global variables are declared and automata are created using templates.

Uppaal's query language for requirement specification is based on CTL (Computational Tree Logic, [7]). It consist of path formulae and state formulae. State formulae describe individual states and path formulae quantify over paths or traces of the model. A state formula is an expression that can be evaluated for a state without looking at the behavior of the model. For example it could be a simple comparison of a variable with a constant x <= 5. The syntax of state formulae is similar to the syntax of guards. The only difference is that in a state formula disjunction may be used. There is a special state formula deadlock. It is satisfied in all deadlock states. The state is deadlock if there is not any action transition from the state neither from any of its delay successors. Path formulae can be classified into *reachability*, *safety* and *liveness*. Reachability formulae ask if a given state formula is satisfied by some reachable state. In Uppaal we use $F\Diamond\varphi$ where $\varphi$ is a state formula and we write it as E<> $\varphi$ .

Safety properties are usually of the form: "something bad will never happen". In Uppaal they are defined positively: "something good is always true". We use $A\Box\varphi$ (written as A[] $\varphi$) to express, that a state formula $\varphi$ should be true in all reachable states, and $E\Box\varphi$ (E[] $\varphi$) to say, that there should exist a maximal path such that $\varphi$ is always true. There are two types of liveness properties. Simpler is of the form: "something will eventually happen". We use $A\Diamond\varphi$ (A<> $\varphi$) meaning that a state formula $\varphi$ is eventually satisfied. The other form is: "leads to a response". The formula is $\varphi \leadsto \psi$ (written as $\varphi$ --> $\psi$) with the meaning that whenever $\varphi$ is satisfied, then eventually $\psi$ will be satisfied.

The simulation and formal verification are possible in Uppaal. The simulation can be random or user assisted. It is more suitable for the user of the tool to see if a model is behaving like he want and like it corresponds to the real system. Formal verification should confirm that the system has desired properties expressed using the query language. There are many options and settings for verification algorithm in Uppaal. For example we can change representation of reachable states in memory or the order of search in the state space (breadth first, depth first, random depth first search). Some of the options lead to less memory consumption, some of them speed up the verification. But improvement in one of these two characteristic leads to a degradation of the other usually.

For more exact definitions of modeling and query languages and verification possibilities of Uppaal see [3].

# 3   General Comments and Assumptions

In real-time database systems we consider usually transaction processing. Each transaction incoming to a system is assigned a priority. Resources are than apportioned according to priorities to transactions that are processed concurrently. The number of concurrently processed transactions in system is usually bounded – it is controlled by overload management policy. Incoming transactions have usually a deadline. This can be hard (transaction exceeding deadline becomes nearly useless and can be aborted for the sake of other transactions meeting their deadlines) or soft (the value of transaction exceeding deadline decreases, the priority can be lowered and transaction is processed in the time when there are not any transactions possibly meeting deadlines). In this paper we consider hard deadlines.

Scheduling and computation time assignment is strongly connected with priorities. Hence we will discuss this also in the following sections. Other aspects as, e.g., concurrency control will be omitted to preserve suggested models manageable by Uppaal (for complex models it runs out of memory even for relatively simple queries due to the state space explosion).

There are many possibilities how to model transaction arrival. For example, there can be special automaton serving as a generator of transactions. The models described in this paper are designed for comparison of several different algorithms. Hence we have decided to define incoming transactions statically as an array `inc_trans`. Elements of this array are structures of `release_time` (representing incoming time of transaction since beginning), `deadline_time`(deadline since beginning), `operations` (number of database operations), `received_time` (initially equals zero, it represents computation time already used by this transaction). For simplicity we do not consider exact database records and we even consider that all database operations need the same computational time given by constant `OP_TIME`. All models can be simulated over this array to compare them (see Section 9).

# 4   First Come First Serve

The first and simplest policy assigns the highest priority to the transaction with the earliest release time. Often, release time equals arrival time. This algorithm is not very suitable for real-time database systems because it does not make use of deadline information. It can give more computation time to older transaction instead a newer transaction with more urgent deadline.

We consider that all computation time is assigned to the oldest transaction in a system until it finishes or reaches its deadline. Hence we will need just one copy of automaton depicted on Figure 2. This automaton represents successively all transaction processed by a modeled system.

The state `Inactive` represents situation when there is not any processed transaction. Constant `TRANSACTIONS` contains the overall number of transactions defined in the input array, variable `act_trans` counts processed transactions. Clock variable `time` represents time from the beginning while clock variable `op_time` measures the time of performance of one database operation. If actual transaction ends successfully (number of performed operations `op_done` reaches the number of operations specified for this transaction), the automaton gets through the state `Done` to `Inactive` and it is prepared for representation of next transaction. If the transaction reaches its deadline before successful finish, an abort is modeled by the state `Abort`, it is counted and the automaton goes to the state `Inactive` once again.

The state `Waiting` is intended for the situation when there are more transactions in the input sequence but release time (representing time of arrival in the real system) is not passed yet. If all transactions from the input sequence are processed, automaton goes to the state `End` and the run is deadlocked. It is the only possible deadlock situation of this model (this has been checked using verification possibility of Uppaal).

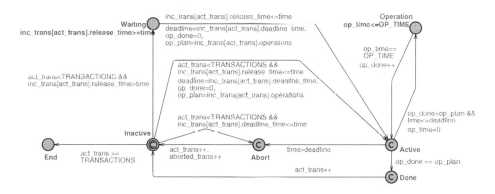

**Fig. 2.** Transaction automaton for FCFS algorithm

## 5   Earliest Deadline

Earliest Deadline is algorithm which gives the highest priority to transaction with the earliest deadline. A disadvantage of this policy is that it can give high priority and hence a big amount of resources to a transaction which is about to miss its deadline anyway.

Assigned priorities can be used in several different ways for distribution of resources. One way is that a transaction with the highest priority gets all resources until it finishes or exceeds its deadline and it is aborted. To show some other general modeling possibilities, we have chosen some other way. We consider several concurrently processed transactions and scheduler distributes computation time between all of them. Transactions with higher priority get more time but no transaction is skipped. All automata representing concurrent transactions are instances of the same template depicted on Figure 3. The number of those instances can be set by a constant `PAR_TRANS`.

Distribution of computation time is controlled by Scheduler Automaton depicted on Figure 5. Priorities to transactions are assigned using Priority Assignment Automaton depicted on Figure 4.

The basic behavior of Transaction automata is the same as in the case of First Come First Serve algorithm. The main modification is the state `Sleep` and its adjacent edges. It represents the situation when this transaction is processed but actually has not assigned resources. An indication of assigned resources is received from Scheduler automaton through the channel `activate[trans_id]`. `trans_id` is unique identifier of each Transaction automaton and `activate` is array of channels. Taking the resources away is announced through the channel `preempt`. There are two more channels – `abort_notif` informs Scheduler automaton that this transaction is aborted and resources are free and `start_notif` is broadcast channel that informs Scheduler about active transaction and simultaneously asks Priority Assignment to compute priority for new transaction (identification of this transaction is shared using global variable `calc_trans`).

There are two auxiliary arrays. `active_trans` contains for each Transaction automaton a flag if it actually represents some transaction and `cor_trans` contains for each Transaction automaton identification of actually represented transaction from input array.

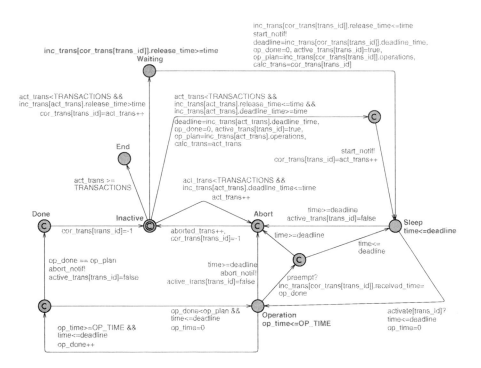

**Fig. 3.** Transaction automaton for Earliest Deadline algorithm

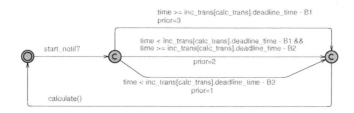

**Fig. 4.** Priority Assignment automaton for Earliest Deadline algorithm

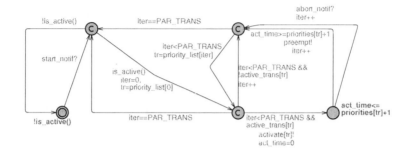

**Fig. 5.** Scheduler automaton for Earliest Deadline algorithm

Scheduler automaton waits in the initial state until it is notified about new transaction. Then it takes iteratively identifications of Transaction automata representing transactions according the priority from the array `priority_list` which is maintained sorted by Priority Assignment automaton. Each Transaction automaton is activated for the time corresponding to its priority (this can be chosen in different ways, in this paper it is directly priority, just for technical reasons increased by one). After all active Transaction automata take a turn, the whole process is repeated again from the automaton representing transaction with the highest priority. Function `is_active` is axillary, it returns true if there is at least one `true` in the array `active_trans`.

Priority Assignment automaton assigns priorities 1, 2 or 3. The highest priority goes to transactions which have at most $B1$ time units until deadline, priority 2 to transactions with $B1$ to $B2$ time units before deadline and priority 1 to all other. Bounds $B1, B2$ can be taken from real modeled algorithm or chosen according to estimated values in incoming transactions. In our case, they were set to such values, that all three priorities were used for transactions from our input sequence. It should be clear how to add more values of priority to the model. Function `calculate()` sorts identifications of Transaction automata in the array `priority_list` according to priorities of transactions they represent.

## 6   Latest Deadline

This policy is the opposite of the Earliest Deadline mapping. It gives higher priority to transactions with later deadlines. This could be a way how to avoid the a disadvantage of Earliest Deadline algorithm which can spend computation time on transactions without a chance to finish before their deadline.

Models for this policy are very similar to models of Earliest Deadline. Just update statements `prior=1` and `prior=3` are switched in Priority Assignment Automaton depicted on Figure 4.

## 7    Random Priority

The Random Priority mapping randomly assigns priorities to transactions without taking any of their characteristics into account. It is mainly used in more complex policy called Adaptive Earliest Deadline (not considered in this paper) for transactions in the group called MISS, but it makes sense to consider it also as a stand-alone policy. To show some other behavior than previously we will consider that scheduler gives repeatedly computation time to the transaction with maximal priority and waits until it finishes (successfully or by abort).

Model of this algorithm can use template depicted on Figure 3 in Section 5 for automata representing concurrent transactions. Scheduler Automaton (Figure 6) is modified in the sense that after synchronization using channel `abort` it looks for an active transaction with the greatest priority and gives unlimited computation time to it. Priorities to transactions are assigned using Priority

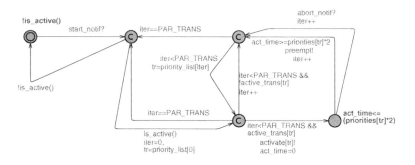

**Fig. 6.** Scheduler automaton for Random Priority algorithm

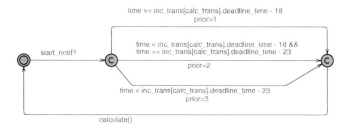

**Fig. 7.** Priority Assignment automaton for Random Priority algorithm

Assignment Automaton depicted on Figure 7. There is not any random number generating function in Uppaal. The only way is to use nondeterminism, e.g., as it is used on Figure 7 (three different transitions enabled in the same time and each assigning other value to a variable).

## 8   Least Slack

Last algorithm we will consider is Least Slack. For a transaction is a slack time $S = d - (t + e - p)$ where $d$ is deadline, $t$ is actual time, $e$ is expected time needed for finishing and $p$ is time already received. The slack is in fact an estimate how long we can delay the execution of a transaction and still meet its deadline. Transactions with smaller slack time get higher priority. If the slack is negative, transaction cannot meet its deadline and should not get any resources.

There are two different versions of this algorithm considered. Static evaluation means that the slack is evaluated only once when a transaction arrives, continuous evaluation means that the slack is recalculated whenever we wish to know priority of a transaction. As we have considered one evaluation of priority after transaction arrival in previous cases, we will now consider continuous evaluation to show something new.

Transaction automata for this algorithm remain the same as in the Section 5. Scheduler automaton is depicted on Figure 8 and Priority Assignment automaton on Figure 9.

Scheduler automaton demands recalculation of priorities through channel `calculate_prior`. After it gets confirmation through channel `calc_done`, it takes active transaction with the highest priority and gives some computational time to corresponding Transaction automaton. This is repeated until there are active transactions and priorities are recalculated before each selection of transaction with highest priority.

Priority Assignment automaton is more complex than in the previous case. This is because it computes always priorities for all transactions, not only one as in the case of Earliest Deadline model. There is one auxiliary priority 0 for Transactions automata that are inactive or representing transactions with negative slack time.

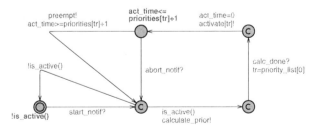

**Fig. 8.** Scheduler automaton for Least Slack algorithm

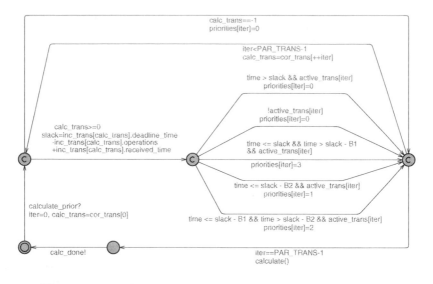

**Fig. 9.** Priority Assignment automaton for Least Slack algorithm

## 9    Simulation and Verification

Uppaal gives essentially two uses for created models - simulation and verification. All models in this paper were designed to use the same specification of input transactions. Hence we are able to use simulation in Uppaal and compare behavior of those models. We used several different sets of input transactions and executed simulation of each model on each set several times. The intention of this paper is not to tell which algorithms or policy is the best, it should just show several possible general abstractions and some ideas how to model such type of algorithms. So, it is not important to discuss whether the input sets were chosen suitably to really compare different algorithms.

Simulation can be used e.g. to compare number of transactions aborted before successful finish. This is counted in all models in variable `aborted_trans`. Table 1 shows this number for three of tried input sets and all modeled protocols.

Two or more numbers in one cell mean that several different runs on the same input have different outcomes because of nondeterminism. All three sets

**Table 1.** Number of aborted transactions

| Protocol | Set 1 | Set 2 | Set 3 |
|----------|-------|-------|-------|
| FCFS     | 7     | 3     | 2     |
| ED       | 9,10  | 7     | 7     |
| LD       | 8     | 5     | 5,6   |
| RP       | 6     | 2     | 1,2,3 |
| Slack    | 6     | 4     | 2     |

have 10 transactions. Set 1 has quite short deadlines and 10 operations per transaction. Set 2 has also 10 operations per transaction but longer deadlines and, on average, bigger intervals between release times. Set 3 has exactly the same release times and deadlines of transactions as set 2 but the number of operations varies between 5 and 15 for different transactions.

Simulation finds only some possible behavior (randomly or chosen by user). We can be interested, e.g., if it is possible, that sometimes is the result worse. Here, formal verification becomes handy. Model of protocol Random Priorities contains more nondeterminism than other presented models hence it was chosen for illustration. Suppose that we want to know if there can be more than 6 aborted transaction for Set 1. We can enter property `E<> aborted_trans > 6` (Is there a path to a state where variable `aborted_trans` contains a number greater than 6?) and run verification. Uppaal says "satisfied" and even shows a run of the model leading to a state where the number of aborted transactions is 8. Next query on reachability of more than 8 aborted transactions is answered negatively. This means that 8 aborted transactions is the worst case for this input and model.

Alternatively, we could be interested in the best case. Still for Random Priority and Set 1, we can ask, if there is a run aborting less than 6 transactions. It is not sufficient to ask `E<> aborted_trans < 6` because this property is satisfied from the beginning. The models are designed in such a way that computation stops (denoted as deadlock in Uppaal) when all transactions are processed (successfully ended or aborted) and there is not any other deadlock situation possible. We can use this and ask for the property `E<> deadlock && aborted_trans<6` (Is there a path to a state where system is deadlocked and where variable `aborted_trans` contains number less than 6?). This property was satisfied and a run with just 5 aborted transactions was found. Next query on less than 5 aborted transactions was answered negatively.

In a similar way we can check other properties of our models. It is useful to combine simulation and verification possibilities of Uppaal as we have done in our example on number of aborted transactions. Using simulation we can find some estimation and using verification we can find out, if there are some worse/better results possible. This is something what can not be usually obtained using testing or simulation only.

# 10   Conclusion

In the previous sections, several timed automata were shown. They form models of different variants of known algorithms for priority assignment and control of resources used in real-time database management systems. Of course, this were not the only possible models. The purpose was to show that some important aspects of the real-time database system, such as a priority assignment, can be modeled using such a relatively simple model as nets of timed automata are. The models can be extended in many different ways to capture more behavior of those policies and thus allow many properties to be described as a formula in the logic of Uppaal and then checked using its verification algorithms. Even on presented models (without any extensions or modifications) some simple properties have been checked and modeled algorithms were compared on several different "bursts" of transactions using simulation and verification possibilities of Uppaal.

Some properties even can not be expressed using Uppaal's modification of CTL. The used CTL e.g. does not support nesting of path quantifiers which excludes the possibility to express directly properties like "there is a reachable state from which all other reachable states satisfy ..." and many other. Automata can be modified to bypass this imperfection, but it can demand a special modification for each query and it also can increase reachable state space. Another possible solution to this problem is to try some other verification tool with other query language which can be our future work.

# References

1. Abbott, R.K., Garcia-Molina, H.: Scheduling real-time transactions: a performance evaluation. ACM Transactions on Database Systems (TODS) 17(3), 513–560 (1992)
2. Alur, R., Dill, D.L.: Automata for modeling real-time systems. Proc. of Int. Colloquium on Algorithms, Languages, and Programming. In: Paterson, M. (ed.) ICALP 1990. LNCS, vol. 443, pp. 322–335. Springer, Heidelberg (1990)
3. Behrmann, G., David, A., Larsen, K. G.: A Tutorial on Uppaal (December 15, 2008), http://www.it.uu.se/research/group/darts/papers/texts/new-tutorial.pdf
4. Berard, B., Bidoit, M., Petit, A., Laroussinie, F., Petrucci, L., Schnoebelen, P.: Systems and Software Verification, Model-Checking Techniques and Tools. Springer, Heidelberg (2001); ISBN: 978-3540415237
5. David, A., Amnell, T.: Uppaal2k: Small Tutorial (December 15, 2008), http://www.it.uu.se/research/group/darts/uppaal/tutorial.ps
6. Haritsa, J.R., Livny, M., Carey, M.J.: Earliest Deadline Scheduling for Real-Time Database Systems. In: Proceedings of Real-Time Systems Symposium 1991, pp. 232–242 (1991); ISBN: 0-8186-2450-7
7. Henzinger, T.A.: Symbolic model checking for real-time systems. Information and computation 111, 193–244 (1994)
8. Kao, B., Garcia-Molina, H.: An Overview of Real-Time Database Systems. In: Advances in Real-Time Systems, pp. 463–486. Prentice-Hall, Inc., Englewood Cliffs (1995)
9. Kot, M.: Modeling selected real-time database concurrency control protocols in Uppaal. Innovations in Systems and Software Engineering 5(2), 129–138 (2009); ISSN: 1614-5046
10. Kot, M.: Modeling Real-Time Database Concurrency Control Protocol Two-Phase-Locking in Uppaal. In: Proceedings of the International Multiconference on Computer Science and Information Technology, vol. 3, pp. 673–678. IEEE Computer Society Press, Los Alamitos (2008); ISBN: 978-83-60810-14-9, ISSN: 1896-7094
11. Kot, M.: Modeling and Verification of Priority Assignment in Real-Time Databases Using Uppaal. In: Proceedings of the Dateso 2010 Annual International Workshop on DAtabases, TExts, Specifications and Objects, CEUR Workshops Proceedings, Sun SITE Central Europe, vol. 567, pp. 147–154 (2010); ISSN: 1613-0073
12. Król, V., Pokorný, J., Černohorský, J.: The V4DB project - support platform for testing the algorithms used in real-time databases. WSEAS Transactions on Information Science & Applications 10(3) (October 2006)

13. McMillan, K.L.: Symbolic Model Checking. Springer, Heidelberg (1993); ISBN: 978-0792393801
14. Neto, P.F.R., Perkusich, M.L.B., De Almeida, H.O., Perkusich, A.: A Formal Verification and Approach for Real-Time Databases. Selected Readings on Database Technologies and Applications, Information Science Reference, 268–295 (2009); ISBN: 978-1-60566-098-1
15. Nyström, D., Nolin, M., Tesanovic, A., Norström, C., Hansson, J.: Pessimistic Concurrency-Control and Versioning to Support Database Pointers in Real-Time Databases. In: Proc. of the $16^{th}$ Euromicro Conference on Real-Time Systems, pp. 261–270. IEEE Computer Society, Los Alamitos (2004)
16. Ulusoy, Ö., Belford, G.G.: A Simulation Model for Distributed Real-Time Database Systems. In: Proceedings of the $25^{th}$ Annual Simulation Symposium, pp. 232–240 (1992); ISBN: 0-8186-2765-4
17. ParaDiSe (Parallel & Distributed Systems Laboratory): Yahoda verification tools database (April 15, 2011), http://anna.fi.muni.cz/yahoda/

# User Modeling to Build Mobile Advertising Algorithm

Mohammed A. Razek[1,3] and Claude Frasson[2]

[1] Azhar university, Faculty of science,
Math.& Computer Science Depart.
Naser City, Cairo, Egypt
[2] Département d'informatique et de recherche opérationnelle
Université de Montréal C.P. 6128,
Succ. Centre-ville, Montréal, Québec Canada H3C 3J7
[3] Development & Research Department,
Deanship of Distance Learning, King Abdulaziz University,
Kingdom of Saudi Arabia, P.O. Box 80254,
Jeddah 21589
{abdelram,frasson}@iro.umontreal.ca

**Abstract.** Digital signage is a form of electronic display that presents information, advertising and other messages. With the merge of mobile technology and exponential growth of broadcasting network, an overwhelmingly amount of digital signage has been made available to dissimilar consumers. This paper presents an algorithm based on Naïve-Bayes technique to build a user modelling to be used for recommending a suitable signage to customers. Our goal is to personalize signage by choosing the proper products to the proper customers. This way is promising to present an automated algorithm to create an adaptable content which can be exchanged more easily and the signs can adapt to the context and audience.

**Keywords:** Mobile marketing, m-advertising, m-business, intelligent Agent, machine learning.

## 1 Introduction

Digital signage is distantly organized distribution and display of digital content across networks. It is used for delivering visual messages at point-of-purchase, or at any other public venue. Nowadays, mobile device technology is growing up rapidly which help in transferring marketing from regular computer to mobile device. Mobile marketing is the use of mobile or wireless personal digital assistants devices to do marketing while costumers are on the move. Mobile-based marketing with very diverse customers may fail because it not succeeds to satisfy various customers' needs. Based on customers' needs, this paper proposes a framework for an intelligent agent aggregating and editing mobile marketing materials.

A major part of this paper present how to formulate the classification problem of mobile advertisings. As we see that digital signage is a term used to describe the display of up to the minute information on electronic devices such as plasma displays, LCD panels, video cubes, projectors, full matrix LED boards, and PC. So if we add a

V. Snasel, J. Platos, and E. El-Qawasmeh (Eds.): ICDIPC 2011, Part II, CCIS 189, pp. 400–410, 2011.

hand held computer, or mobile devices, we can call it a mobile signage.. According to the Interactive Mobile Advertising Platform [7] mobile advertising is defined as "the business of encouraging people to buy products and services using the wireless channel as medium to deliver the advertisement message".

Mobile marketing is a fast developing mobile communication technology which includes Bluetooth, local area wireless networks by Wi-Fi, mobile networks, and related mobile computing devices such as mobile phones, pocket PCs, Tablet PCs, and Personal Data Assistant (PDA). Nowadays, the mobile technology has been rapidly grown up from First Generation 1G (simple functions) to Third Generation 3G (multiple functions) which has different characterizes and functions. We'd like to point out that the development of mobile marketing is not intended to replace the regular marketing, but to improve the value of business. Using m-marketing, companies can directly communicate with their customers without time or location difficulty.

However, there are little identified about how mobile  application  can be effectively included into marketing activities [4],  mobile advertisers are progressively more relying on different modes of interactive technology to advertise and promote their products and services [14]. In the face of this, possible consumers up to now did not have the chance to sign their likes and dislikes with marketing activities via mobile.

Following the above argument, this paper presents an algorithm that aims for designing a mobile agent system called smart mobile marketing agent. The agent architecture is built in order to act well as a mobile application service though surrounded by the mobile environment. This agent based on a machine learning solution, adapts individualized advertising signage to consumers via mobile devices. It takes into consideration consumers' needs, and profiles. In other products, it uses the similarities among user profiles to find which purchases are most similar to that of the requester. The agent tries to know the characteristics of clients and audiences. The method behind the work is to ensure that the mobile signage  is specified to the right person who will not keep away from being ignore it and will not feel  bad when she/he receive it.

In this sense, this paper deals with a new technique, called dominant products approach and how it can be used to make individualized mobile signage. How does it influence signage construction? The dominant products definition is known as "the set of products that best fit an intended category of a target signage". This technique sees a signage as a set of classes, each class contains some products called slave that fall within the range of that product.

In a major part of this paper, we will try to solve answer the following problems challenges: how to construct a method that allows us to find the dominant products from a collection of products; and how to select an intended product. In short, we need to find a way of constructing this context and then using it to construct a signage. We claim that individualizing the context of the products can significantly improve mobile signage. Our idea is to represent the collection as a hierarchy of classes[16]. Each class consists of some dominant products. And each dominant product is linked with a customer who interested to it. The more any signage consists of dominant products, the more closely it is related to its signage goals.

## 2   Related Work

Since 4000BC, advertising was growing progressively. Egyptian was using papyrus to create sales messages and wall posters. In the 17th century, advertisements began to appear in weekly newspapers in England. Modern advertising developed with the rise of mass production in the late 19th and early 20th centuries. There were different types of media could be used to deliver these signage, including traditional media such as newspapers, magazines, television, radio, outdoor or direct mail. In the late of $20^{th}$ and $21^{st}$ century, advertising was taking advantage of the amazing advancements in technology, such as e-advertising and mobile marketing. To overcome the challenges posed by personalized advertising, we need to shed light on related works on twofold: classification, how a mobile agent works, and how filtering, recommendation methodology work.

Bayesian assessment is considered as a comfortable technique for estimating the probability distribution of classes over feature data inputs [19], [3], [10] and [5]. In the Text Classification domain, this is often referred to as Naïve Bayes text classification.

The basic idea of it is to use the joint probabilities of words and categories to assess the probabilities of categories given a signage. The advantage of Naïve Bayes technique over other techniques is based on the assumption of word independence. On other words, the conditional probability of a word given a category is assumed to be independent from the conditional probability of other wards given that category. Consequently, this way makes the computation of the Naïve Bayes classifiers more accurate than the exponential complexity of non-Naïve Bayes techniques because it does not use word combinations as predictors [20].

There are two models of the Naïve Bayes classifiers: multivariate Bernoulli and multinomial mixture model. A signage at multivariate Bernoulli is represented as a vector of binary attributes. However, this vector signifies which words occur and do not occur in the signage, it does not take into account the number of times a word happens in a signage. This approach is more traditional in the field of Bayesian networks, and has been used for text classification by several researchers [8], and [19].

We can see that signage at multinomial technique are represented by the set of word occurrences from the signage. However, the order of the words is lost; the number of occurrences of each word in the signage is taken into account. This approach has also been used for text classification by several researchers [12].

On the other hand, mobile agents can benefit small devices such as PDAs and cellular phones in numerous ways. They can be used to download customized, context-sensitive services to small devices on demand [1]. Mobile agents can also help alleviate bandwidth limitations and support disconnected operation, both significant problems in wireless and mobile environments. However, to achieve these capabilities, small devices must be able to support mobile agents.

A great deal of work has been done on building systems that use filtering to recommend an item. Two approaches are particularly important in this context: collaborative filtering and matchmaking systems. Two approaches to collaborative filtering systems, in turn, are prevalent: Collaborative Filtering (CF) and Content-Based (CB) methods [13]. CF systems build user profiles of user ratings of available classs. They use the similarities among user profiles to figure out which one is most similar to that of the requester. Using positive training examples, Pazzani [15] represented user profile as a vector of weighted products. For predicting, he applied CF to the user ratings matrix.

In Fab [9], the relevance feedback of user is used to classify a personal filter. Moreover, another filter is related to this topic. Each item is classified by the topic filter which is used to classify the item related to the user relevance feedback. In another approach, Cotter et al. [4], CB and CF approaches are allowed to create distinct recommendations and therefore to merge their advertising prediction directly. Horting Hatches and Egg [2] is an alternative, graph-based technique in which nodes are users; edges between nodes indicate the degree of similarity between two users. Advertising predictions are produced by walking the graph to nearby nodes and combining the opinions of the nearby users. Koller [9] is a matchmaking system that allows users to find agents for needed services. It can store various types of advertisement coming from various applications.

Our method differs from these by using the credibilities of users rather than the ratings from users [17]. For effective filtering, we have created a new classification method called a Pyramid Collaborative Filtering Model (PCFM). It depends on three classification techniques: domain filtering, user model filtering, and credibility filtering. The next subsection sheds light on the guide agent framework.

## 3   Methodology of the Classification

To specify the main signage for specific costumers, three questions must be answered: How can we construct dominant products for each class? How can the system decide which intended products to choose? And how can it select products that must be added to the original signage? The following subsections answer these questions in detail.

The signage consists of $m$   classes; each class has an image and a little information about price with a product's specifications. In general, suppose that $C$ is a finite set of categories organized in a hierarchy. Each category contains some products which are pre-classified under the categories of $C$ [6].

The question now is how can we use those products to construct dominant products of the corresponding mobile signage-cart? The challenge is how to determine those products. Actually, the more those products are related to its domain knowledge, the more any mobile signage-cart consists of dominant products.

Now, how we can construct a signage. To illustrate the classification problem, suppose the signage is represented as a collection of $m$   classes, i.e. $C = \{C_k\}_{k=1}^m$ [6]. In this definition, each class is represented by a finite set of products $C_k = \{d_j^k \mid j = 1,...,n\}$. Where $d_j^k$ represent the frequency of product $d_j$ which belongs to class $C_k$. This frequency is computed as follows:

$$d_j^k = \frac{n_j}{F_{max} \times N}$$

Where $n_v$ represents the number of items of the product $d_j^k$ had been sold, N represents the total number of receipts, and $F_{max}$ represents the maximum number of items for a product had been sold, and calculates as follow: $F_{max} = \underset{v=1,...,n}{Max} \{n_v\}$

Our goal is to choose the concepts (class) and the products which can represent the mobile signage. To do that, this paper uses naïve Bayes classification to create signage-cart as presented in next section.

## 4   Naïve Bayes Classification

Basically, the Naïve-Bayes classifier views signage as set of conditionally independent products $X = \{x_1, x_2,..., x_n\}$ which is represented as a collection of $m$ classes. We can see it as a function that maps an input feature set $X$ to the corresponding class $c_k$, where $c_k \in C = \{C_k\}_{k=1}^m$. Now, Naïve-Bayes classifier is looking for which classes should be added to the signage and consequently which products included in each class.

As discussed in the previous section, for each signage $S$, we only test the existence of currently dominant products of class to apply as features. This set is $X$, and can be updated over time. The signage $S$ thus contains a subset of the products in $X$. We would like to calculate the probability that this signage $S$ is in each of the different classes $c_k$. We use Bayes theorem to estimate this probability:

$$P(C = c_k \mid S) = \frac{P(S \mid C = c_k)P(C = c_k)}{P(S)}, \tag{1}$$

Where $P(C = c_k)$ is the prior probability that any random signage belongs to the class $c_k$, and $P(S)$ is the likelihood of signage $S$. Since $P(S)$ is constant for any particular signage $S$, it can be dropped. If we suppose that the features of the signage $S$ consists of $X' = (x_1, x_2,..., x_m)$ which are conditionally independent, given the category variable C, this simplifies the computation of $P(S \mid C = c_k)$ as follows:

$$P(S \mid C = c_k) = P(X' \mid c_k) = \prod_{i=1}^{m} P(x_i \mid c_k). \tag{2}$$

Since the Bayesian approach is only using $P(S \mid C = c_k)$ for classifying a new signage, thus to predict the best class $B(X')$ given the signage vector $X' = (x_1, x_2, ..., x_m)$, we simply need to compute the maximum a posteriori value of $B(X')$:

$$B(X') = \arg\max_{c_k \in C} P(C = c_k \mid S) \tag{3}$$

$$= \arg\max_{c_k \in C} \frac{P(S \mid c_k)P(c_k)}{P(S)} \tag{4}$$

$$= \arg\max_{c_k \in C} P(c_k) \prod_{i=1}^{m} P(x_i \mid c_k) \tag{5}$$

Computing $P(c_k)$ is straightforward. Following [Nigam 00], given the training data, the prior probability of a class is typically determined by the maximum likelihood estimate as the fraction of signage in it, giving

$$P(c_k) = \frac{n_{c_k}}{N^t}, \tag{6}$$

Where $N^t$ represents the total number of training signage in all classes and $n_{c_k}$ is the number of examples belonging to class $c_k$.

As mentioned above, there are two distinct classifiers which build on the Naïve Bayes Classification: Multivariate Bernoulli and multinomial mixture model. The difference lies in calculating $P(S \mid c_k)$. Whilst the multivariate Bernoulli model considers binary features which points to the appearance or non-appearance of a term $x_j$ in a particular signage $S$, the multinomial mixture model uses plain term frequencies in a signage. This research is dealing with the multivariate Bernoulli model. The likelihood of a signage given the class is calculated as follows:

$$P(S \mid c_k) = \prod_{i=1}^{m} P(x_i \mid c_k)^{I(x_i,S)} (1 - P(x_i \mid c_k))^{(1-I(x_i,S))} \,, \tag{7}$$

where

$$I(x_i, D) = \begin{cases} 1 & x_i \in D \\ 0 & x_i \notin D \end{cases},$$

and according to the training data, we can compute $P(x_i \mid c_k)$ by:

$$P(x_i \mid c_k) = \frac{1 + N_{c_k}(x_i, S)}{2 + N_{c_k}(S)} \,, \tag{8}$$

Where $N_{c_k}(x_i, S)$ represents the number of signage belonging to class $c_k$ in which term $x_j$ appears at least once, and $N_{c_k}(S)$ is the total number of signage in class $c_k$.

Simply, to decide which class $c_k$ to be added to a signage $S$, we briefly outline the steps from formula (1) to (8):

$$P(C = c_k \mid S) = \underset{c_k \in C}{\arg\max} \begin{cases} \dfrac{n_{c_k}}{N^t} \prod_{i=1}^{m} \dfrac{1 + N_{c_k}(x_i,S)}{2 + N_{c_k}(S)} & x_i \in S \\ \dfrac{n_{c_k}}{N^t} \prod_{i=1}^{m} \dfrac{1 + N_{c_k}(S) - N_{c_k}(x_i,S)}{2 + N_{c_k}(S)} & x_i \notin S \end{cases} \tag{9}$$

## 5   User Modelling Algorithm

In this section, we will discuss all stages in the process of identifying the suitable products that meet costumer' $(U_i)$ needs.  Suppose that the store keep an information about their customers  about their mobile number, their address and all products they have been bought. The algorithm will looking for a similar costumer who has almost the same characteristics  of the known customer.  The first step shows how to find a customer whose bought similar products that $U_i$ needs. Suppose that we have classified all customer related to equation(9). Accordingly,

$$U^k = \{U_i^k \mid i = 1,...,m\}$$

We can say that $U_i^k$ is a person $U_i$ who buy a product classified in a class $c_k$.
To comput the similarity between two person, we follows the next algoritm
Suppose that

***Step 1: similarity( $U_i^k$ , $U_j^k$ )***

- For           each           customer           $U_i^k, U_j^k \in U^k$,

  $Q(U_i^k) = \{w_i \in C_k \mid i = 1,...m \geq 1\}$,    where    $Q(U_i^k)$ represents

  products        $w_i$      that      included      in      $C_k$,           and

  $Q(U_j^k) = \{v_j \in C_k \mid j = 1,...r \geq 1\}$,    where    $Q(U_j^k)$ represents

  products  $v_i$  that included in $C_k$,

We can evaluate the dominant meaning  similarity $S(U_i^k, U_j^k)$               (1)

$$S(U_i^k, U_j^k) = \frac{1}{m} \sum_{i=1}^{m} \frac{1}{r} \left[ \sum_{j=1}^{r} \Theta(w_i, v_j) \right],$$

where               $\Theta(w_i, v_j) = \begin{cases} 1 & w_i = v_j \\ 0 & w_i \neq v_j \end{cases}$

- For k If  $S(U_i^k, U_j^k) \geq 0.5$ return $U_i^k, U_j^k$ are similar for a concept $C_k$.

## 5.1  Classification Algorithm

In this subsection, we explain how to extract the main concept of the signage given
some products, and how to formulate Signage for a customer. Researchers have used
many techniques to traverse the graph[11]. For a large problem space, the graph's
nodes must be searched in an organized way. Starting from a specific state (node) and
moving toward a specific goal could solve the problem. We can use a Depth-First
Search (DFS), a Breadth First Search (BFS), and a Best-First-Search [18].
    To do so, we use the hill climbing search algorithm with some modifications. It
uses Search List to keep track of the current fringe and maintain states. It chooses
node "C" as a starting point. We mark this node to show that it has been visited. The
Search List applies a heuristic evaluation to the edges. This is represented by the
value of $P_{i,j}$, where $P_{i,j}$  represents the dominant product distance.

Initially, the Search List consists of the generated children that we intend to consider during the search. Suppose that we search for a child from the Search List. After being opened, it can be expanded and removed. The proposed algorithm ends when a request product is extracted from the Search List (success), when we try to extract a child while it is empty (failure), or, in some cases, or when we generate a goal state (success). The input of our traverse algorithm is requested product $d_v^k$, and the output would be requested concept $C_r$. The pseudo-code for this algorithm search is as follows:

---

TRAVERSEDMG (Requested product $d_v^k, U_i^k, P(C = c_k \mid S)$ )

1. Compute $Q(U_i^k) = \{ w_i \in C_k \mid i = 1,...m \geq 1 \}$
2. Put Search List= [Starting point].
3. While Search List $\neq$ [ ] do begin

    1.    If  Starting point, choose $w_i \equiv d_v^k$ and $C_r = P(C = c_k \mid S)$,

    2.    Remove the leftmost state from Search List, call it X.

    3.    If X = $d_v^k$ then $C_r$ = paraent (X),   exit successfully and return $C_r$.

    4.    If not begin
        1.    Generate children and edges of X.
        2.    For each children of X
            1.    Calculate the edge heuristic value $H$.
            2.    Sort children related to $H$ as decreasing order.
            3.    Add sorted children to Front of Search List.
4.    If the goal has been found, announce success and return $C_r$.

---

At each iteration, it removes the first element from the Search List. If it meets the requested product, the algorithm returns to its parents (which led to the concept). If the first element is not a requested product, the algorithm generates its children and then applies heuristic evaluation $H$  to its edges. These states (children) are sorted in decreasing order according to heuristic values before being inserted at the top of the Search List.  This brings the best state to the front of the Search list.

## 6  Conclusion

This paper presented a new algorithm based on based on Naïve-Bayes technique to build a user modelling to be used for recommending a suitable signage to customers. It presents a way to personalize signage by choosing the proper products to the proper customers. The method classified products as classes, each class consists of some dominant products. And each dominant product is linked with a customer who interested to them. The user modeling based on Naïve-Bayes technique can suggest a new mobile signage which might be more close to what the customer needs.

# References

1. Adler, M., Bradshaw, J.M., Mahan, M., Suri, N.: Applying Mobile Agents to Enable Dynamic, Context-Aware Interactions for Mobile Phone Users. In: Pierre, S., Glitho, R.H. (eds.) MATA 2001. LNCS, vol. 2164, p. 184. Springer, Heidelberg (2001)
2. Aggarwal, C.C., Wolf, J.L.: Horting Hatches an Egg: A New Graph-theoretic Approach to Collaborative Filtering. In: Proc. of the ACM KDD 1999 Conference, San Diego, CA, pp. 201–212 (1999)
3. Balasubramanian, S., Peterson, R.A., Jarvenpaa, S.L.: Exploring the Implications of M-Commerce for Markets and Marketing. Journal of the Academy of Marketing Science 30(4), 348–361 (2002)
4. Cotter, P., Smyth, B.: PTV: Intelligent personalized TV guides. In: Twelfth Conference on Innovative applications of Artificial Intelligence, pp. 957–964 (2000)
5. Friedman, N., Geiger, D., Goldszmidt, M.: Bayesian network classifiers. Machine Learning 29, 131–163 (1997)
6. Bardesi, H.J., Razek, M.A.: Towards Smart Algorithm to Build Mobile Advertising. In: CSREA EEE, pp. 310–314 (2010)
7. IMAP Global System Framework – Business Model, Research Report (2003), http://www.imapproject.org/imapproject/downloadroot/ublic1/D 2-2003.pdf (last accessed at December 20, 2003)
8. Kalt, T., Croft, W, B,: A new probabilistic model of text classification and retrieval. Technical Report IR-78, University of Massachusetts Center for Intelligent Information Retrieval (1996), http://ciir.cs.umass.edu/publications/index.shtml
9. Koller, D., Sahami, M.: Hierarchically classifying products using very few products. In: Proc. of the 14th International Conference on Machine Learning (ICML 1997), pp. 170–178 (1997)
10. Leah, S., Bruce Croft, W.: Combining classifiers in text categorization. In: ACM SIGIR 1996 (1996)
11. Luger, G.F.: Artificial Intelligence: Structures and Strategies for Complex Problem Solving. Addison Wesley, Reading (2002)
12. Nigam, K., McCallum, A., Thrun, S., Mitchell, T.: Text classification from labeled and unlabeled documents using EM. Machine Learning 39(2/3), 103–134 (2000)
13. Paolucci, M., Niu, Z, K. S. K.: Matchmaking to Support Intelligent Agents for Portfolio Management. In: Proc. of the AAAI (2000)
14. Pavlou, P.A., Stewart, D.W.: Measuring the Effects and Effectiveness of Interactive Advertising: A Research Agenda. Journal of Interactive Advertising 1(1) (2000)
15. Pazzani, M.J.: A framework for collaborative, content-based and demographic filtering. Artificial Intelligence Review 13(5-6), 393–408 (1999)
16. Razek, M.A., Frasson, C., Kaltenbach, M.: Pyramid collaborative filtering technique for an intelligent autonomous guide agent. International Journal of Intelligent Systems 22(10), 1065–1154 (2007)
17. Razek, M., Frasson, C., Kaltenbach, M.: A Confident Agent: Toward More Effective Intelligent Distance Learning Environments. Accepted in ICMLA 2002, Las Vegas, USA, June 24-27 (2002)

18. Russel, S.J., Norvig, P.: Artificial Intelligence: A Modern Approach, 2nd edn. Prentice Hall, Upper Saddle River (2003)
19. Sahami, M., Dumais, S., Heckerman, D., Horvitz, E.: A bayesian approach to filtering junk e-mail. In: AAAI 1998 Workshop on Learning for Text Categorization (1998)
20. Yang, Y., Liu, X.: A re-examination of text categorization methods. In: Proceedings of ACM SIGIR Conference on Research and Development in Information Retrieval (SIGIR 1999), pp. 42–49 (1999)

# Use of Multi-level State Diagrams for Robot Cooperation in an Indoor Environment

Bogdan Czejdo[1], Sambit Bhattacharya[1], and Mikolaj Baszun[2]

[1] Department of Mathematics and Computer Science
Fayetteville State University
Fayetteville, NC 28301, USA
{bczejdo,sbhattac}@uncfsu.edu
[2] Department of Electronics and Information Technology
Warsaw University of Technology
Nowowiejska 15/19, 00-665 Warsaw, Poland

**Abstract.** This paper describes the syntax and semantics of multi-level state diagrams to support probabilistic behavior of cooperating robots. The techniques were presented to analyze these diagrams by combining individual robots behaviors into a single finite graph describing a complete system. It is shown how to use state abstraction and transition abstraction to create, verify and combine large probabilistic state diagrams. The paper also describes how to use probabilistic state diagrams to design and evaluate robot games.

**Keywords:** autonomous robot navigation, probabilistic robot behavior, cooperating robots, game theoretic approach.

## 1 Introduction

This paper addresses the problems in the area of robot navigation in an indoor environment [1, 2]. We assume that the robot not only responds directly to the environment [3, 4] but also to actions of other robots [5]. State diagrams [7, 8] have been previously used to describe the robot behavior [9]. Typically, the appropriate software is developed manually based on such models. To accelerate the development process we have created a new tool with a simple graphical interface for the interactive design of state diagrams and automatic code generation (GISAC) [10]. Such an interface can be very useful for the rapid modification of robot reactive behavior since it allows the developers to incrementally modify the graphical design and the generated code in response to changing requirements [10].

In this paper we describe the graphical interface for interactive design of multi-level state diagrams, integration of multiple state diagrams and automatic code generation (GISAC 2). The multi-level state diagrams allowed us to model more advanced interactions between autonomous robots and ensuring the correctness of robot interactions. When rapid modifications of robot behavior are required, the rapid checking of robot interactions is crucial. The model checking method for state diagrams can offer the robot behavior designer a set of ready-to-use algorithms and techniques for the analysis of complete system properties.

V. Snasel, J. Platos, and E. El-Qawasmeh (Eds.): ICDIPC 2011, Part II, CCIS 189, pp. 411–425, 2011.

In our studies we addressed the following research questions: (1) how to design multi-level state diagrams to support probabilistic behavior of cooperating robots, (2) how to combine individual robots' diagrams into a single probabilistic graph describing a complete system, (3) how to use techniques such as state abstraction and transition abstraction to create, and combine large probabilistic state diagrams, (4) how to perform automatic model verification and code generation of state diagrams for cooperating robots, and (5) how to design and evaluate robot games using probabilistic state diagrams.

The organization of the paper is as follows. In Section 2 we describe a sample indoor environment referred to as environmental resources. The environmental triggers described in Section 3 can be used for specifying robot behavior. In Section 4 we discuss a state diagram for a single robot with probabilistic transitions for robot navigation. In Section 5 we describe probabilistic state diagrams for cooperating robots. In Section 6 we show how probabilistic state diagrams can be used for robot game design and analysis.

## 2   Environmental Resources

From the point of view of the robot programmer it is important to determine the type of an indoor environment. In general, an indoor environment can be known or unknown. In this paper we will concentrate on describing robot behavior in a known environment. The known environment is typically described by a topological map identifying all landmarks and accessible places for robot occupancy and movement. One of the representations of a topological map can be a graph [1, 2] showing all accessible places in the form of nodes and the ways to get to these places in the form of graph paths.

Any topological map in the form of a graph can be also interpreted as a graph of environmental resources. It means that each node of the graph can be also interpreted as a resource and when the robot position is associated with this node we claim that the robot acquired the resource. The link between two nodes can be interpreted as a constraint in acquiring resources by a robot. Such an interpretation of a topological graph allows us to apply known resource allocation algorithms for the description of multiple robot behavior.

Let us assume, for our case study, the indoor environment of a corridor in the "I" shape that has two doors leading to two rooms. The topological graph interpreted also as an environmental resource graph can be constructed as shown in Figure 1.

The following nodes corresponding to environmental resources can be identified: (a) the beginning of corridor called "Corridor Beginning", (b) in front of the first door called "Door 1 Front", (c) between walls in the middle of the corridor called in short form "Corridor Middle ", (c) in front of the second door called "Door 2 Front", (d) between walls at the end of the corridor called in short form "Corridor End", (e) inside room 1 called in short form "Room 1", and (f) inside room 2 called in short form "Room 2". The link between two nodes e.g. "Corridor Beginning" and "Door 1 Front" can be interpreted as follows: if the robot is assigned a resource "Corridor Beginning" it should first acquire resource "Door 1 Front" before releasing resource "Corridor Beginning".

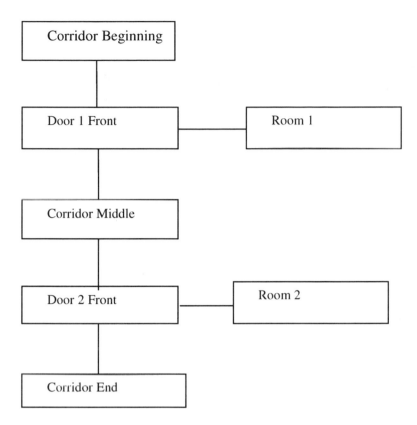

**Fig. 1.** An Environmental Resource Graph

## 3  Environmental Triggers

Different topological places i.e. different resources would usually generate different values for the robot's sensors. The sensor signal processing algorithms i.e. algorithms describing a translation of robot sensor signals into a high level signals that can be used to directly identify the environment. We will refer to these high level signals as the environmental triggers.

In our previous papers [10], we extensively studied the environmental triggers to identify wall of the corridor, end of the corridor, doors, door opening etc. Let us summarize the previous results. Various computer vision techniques can be used to create such environmental triggers. The Hough transform is widely used in computer vision for detecting line segments and regular geometric features such as line segments and circles in images. More specifically, Progressive Probabilistic Hough Transform [11] can be used for detecting naturally occurring lines in indoor images of corridors and hallways [10]. The histogram based difference methods can be used for discriminating between corridor features and for recognition of major landmark objects [2] such as doors and wall surfaces between them.

Using Hough transform we can implement the environmental triggers to allow the robot to direct itself to the middle of the corridor. The OrientationPointToLeft and OrientationPointToRight triggers are used to identify the misalignment.

Histogram based difference measurement can be used during indoor robot navigation to solve the significant problem of recognition of major landmark objects [2] such as doors and wall surfaces between them. When the robot moves beside a door and the edge of the camera detects the door pattern then the environmental trigger DoorPatternDetected becomes True otherwise this condition is False. Similarly, when the robot moves beside a wall and the edge of the camera detects wall pattern then the environmental trigger WallPatternDetected becomes True.

The other triggers e.g. MiddleOfDoorDetected can be derived based on previous triggers. When the trigger WallPatternDetected changes from False to True a robot odometer is initialized and the trigger MiddleOfDoorDetected becomes False. When the value of that odometer is equal or greater than half of the width of the door, then the trigger MiddleOfDoorDetected becomes True.

In addition the triggers MiddleDoorOrientationPointToLeft and MiddleDoorOrientationPointToRight are computed based on the hybrid analysis combining Hough Transform with histogram analysis. More specifically, the algorithm selects vertical lines separating surfaces based on histogram based differences and computes the orientation point as a point in the middle of these lines.

We also used simple environmental triggers such as Obstacle whose value was generated by a simple infrared sensor.

In this paper, we extended previous studies to include situations when the robot might not be able to recognize the landmarks or can recognize them with a certain probability. There are two cases here. The first case is when the existence of the landmark is immaterial for the robot behavior. For example, if the robot does not need to enter the door it might be immaterial if it cannot recognize the door. In such a case the reduction of the resource graph can be performed by removing unnecessary nodes.

The second case is when the existence of the landmark is crucial for robot behavior. The proposed techniques in this paper namely, probabilistic state diagrams can be used to model such behavior.

## 4 State Diagrams with Probabilistic Transitions for Robot Navigation

The deterministic state diagrams are well described in literature [7, 8]. Generally, the deterministic state diagram, in addition to states, has transitions consisting of triggers that cause the transition of the robot from one state to another, and actions, that are invoked during a transition. Triggers are expressed by Boolean conditions evaluated continuously to respond to changes in the environment.

To specify state diagrams we use the notation based on Universal Modeling Language (UML) [11] where a state is indicated by a box and a transition is indicated by an arrow with a label. The first part of the transition label (before the slash) specifies the trigger and the part after the slash specifies the action to be invoked during the transition [11]. The syntax of probabilistic specifications is described in the literature [6] as an additional third component specifying the probability of the entire transition.

State diagrams that are explicitly location dependent can be convenient to specify robot behavior for several reasons. Firstly, the diagram can be constructed by relatively simple transformation of environmental resource diagram. Second, probabilistic components can be added relatively easily. Thirdly, the behavior of cooperating robots can be described by concurrent state diagrams and all well-established techniques for concurrent program analysis with limited resources can be used i.e. deadlock detection or deadlock avoidance algorithms. The analysis of concurrency can be done automatically and the robot program can be directly generated from state diagram model.

Based on environmental graph and corresponding environmental triggers we can rapidly specify the various location dependent state diagram. For example, let us consider Behavior 1 of a robot: start from the corridor beginning, then follow the corridor until encountering the middle of the first door, then randomly either (a) turn itself towards the door, and then enter the room and stop, or (b) continue to follow the corridor until encountering the middle of the second door, then turn itself towards this door, and then enter the room and stop.

In order to model such behavior a two-level model is used. The higher, more abstract level can be obtained by transforming the environmental graph i.e. converting non-directional to directional edges and providing the necessary triggers, actions and probabilities. On the higher level the model describes only how the need for use of environmental resources is changing without specifying how each resource is used. The second level model describes the robot behavior for each environmental resource. The models can be refined into an "implementable" model. By implementable model we mean the model specific enough so that it can be used to generate the program for the robot.

The higher level model, in our case study, is represented by the state diagram shown in Figure 2. It specifies the robot Behavior 1 in some detail dividing it into several phases:

- Phase 1. Initially the robot is in the "Corridor Beginning" state. In this state, the forward command is executed until it recognizes the door. This built-in command engages the motors to move the robot forward.
- Phase 2. When robot stays in the "Door 1 Front" state it continues moving forward until it reaches the door opening. After detecting the door it either enters Room 1 or continues going forward. The decision is randomly selected, each option with the probability 0.5.
- Phase 3. In the state "Room 1" it continuously moves forward until encountering the end of room 1.
- Phase 4. In the "Corridor Middle" state the robot moves forward until encountering another door.
- Phase 5. When robot stays in the "Door 2 Front" state it continues moving forward until it reaches the door opening. After detecting the door it enters room 2.
- Phase 6. In the state "Room 2" it continuously moves forward until encountering the end of room 2.

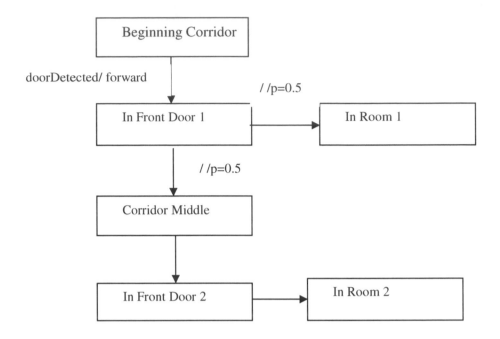

**Fig. 2.** Higher-level State Diagram to describe Behavior 1

Creation of a high-level state diagram can be accomplished by using our graphical interface for interactive design of multi-level state diagrams (GISAC2). The interface supports the following functions:

- Creation of the environmental graph by selecting menu operators createResource, and createResourceLink.
- Converting the environmental graph into high-level state diagram by selecting menu operators deleteResource, duplicateResource, convertResourceLink, and addLabel (to add triggers, actions and probabilities).

There are several issues, however, that need to be discussed related to the syntax and the semantics of probabilistic specifications. Generally, in the transition of probabilistic state diagrams there can be a probability expression in a trigger, probability of action, and third component specifying the probability of that transition e.g. p=0.5 as shown in Figure 2.

The second-level diagrams describe all details of behavior associated with the environmental resource. Let us describe these diagrams in an order. Second level Diagram 1 (Phase 1) is associated with the environmental resource "Corridor Beginning". State diagram shown in Figure 3 includes typical robot actions such as forward, and environmental triggers such as doorDetected. Initially the robot is in the "START" state and with no trigger, the transition to the "Moving" state takes place. During the time of the transition, the forward command is executed. This built-in command engages the motors to move the robot forward. Once the trigger doorDetected becomes true the transition to the exit state (modeled as a black rectangle) takes place that is linked to the state "In Door 1 Front" in the higher level diagram.

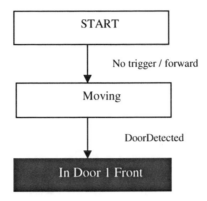

**Fig. 3.** Second-level State Diagram 1 to describe Phase 1

Creation of a second-level state diagram can be accomplished using our graphical interface for interactive design of multi-level state diagrams (GISAC 2). The interface supports the creation of the second-level state diagram by selecting traditional operators as described in [9].

The second-level Diagram 2 (Phase 2) is associated with the environmental resource "In Door 2 front". Initially the robot is in the "START" state and with no trigger, the transition to the "Moving 1" state takes place. The robot stays in the "Moving 1" state (and continues moving forward) until it detects the middle of the door, and the trigger condition MiddleOfDoorDetected becomes True. Detecting the middle of the door triggers the probabilistic transitions to either the "Turning" or "Moving 2" states. Each transition can have a different action therefore the appropriate action needs to be selected i.e. the transition to "Turning" state is associated with action to turn left whereas the transition to "Moving 2" is associated with action to move forward. While in the "Turning" state detecting the room triggers the transitions to "Room 1" state. While in the "Moving 2" state detecting the room triggers the transitions to the "Corridor Middle" state.

The second-level Diagram 3 (Phase 3) is associated with the environmental resource "In Room 1". Initially the robot is in the "START" state and with no trigger, the transition to the "Moving" state takes place the robot moves forward to room 1 until encountering the obstacle (the end of room 1).

The second-level Diagram 4 (Phase 4) is associated with the environmental resource "Corridor Middle". Initially the robot is in the "START" state and with no trigger, the transition to the "Moving" state takes place the robot moves forward until encountering the door.

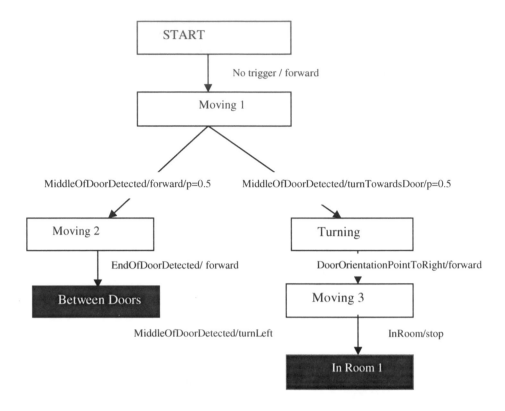

**Fig. 4.** Second-level State Diagram 2 to describe robot behavior

The second-level Diagram 5 (Phase 5) is associated with the environmental resource "In Door 2 front". Initially the robot is in the "START" state and with no triggers, the transition to the "Moving 1" state takes place. The robot stays in the "Moving 1" state (and continues moving forward) until it detects the middle of the door, and the trigger condition MiddleOfDoorDetected becomes True. Detecting the middle of the door triggers the transition to the "Turning" state. While in the "Turning" state detecting the room triggers the transitions to "Room 2" state.

The second-level Diagram 6 (Phase 6) is associated with the environmental resource "Room 2". Initially the robot is in the "START" state and with no trigger; the transition to the "Moving" state takes place the robot moves forward to room 2 until encountering the obstacle (the end of room 2).

There several additional issues that need to be discussed: (a) For a more complex robot behavior, when the robot "visits" the same environmental resource several times, the graph node for the environmental resource needs to be duplicated. The process of creation of a high-level state diagram is very similar. (b) There are many abstractions that allow handling large state diagrams. The abstract (high-level) was described in this section but also the abstract (high level) transition are possible (c) The state diagram fragment reusability is convenient. (d) The probability can be also introduced for actions e.g. random speed of the robot. Since all actions are specified in state diagrams as a second component of the transition we can represent action randomness by random transitions. (e) The probabilistic state diagrams can have cycles involving probability transitions. Let us assume that when robots reach any of the room they are moved to the beginning of the corridor. Let us call it Behavior 2. This repetitive robot behavior can be described by a new state diagram with an additional transition (with No Trigger and No Action) between "Room1" state and "Corridor Beginning".

The models described in this section can be converted to a code and executed. In our experiments we generated the code in the Python language for the Scribbler robot [4].

## 5   Interactions of Robots

The probabilistic state diagrams described in the previous section can be used to generate code for several interacting robots. In this section we discuss the use of state diagrams to describe and ensure the proper interactions between autonomous robots. Since in our approach we create explicit state diagrams based on environmental resource graph, we can take advantage of many theoretical and practical solutions in:

(a) geometrical modeling of robot movement [1, 2, 3],
(b) resource allocation algorithms,
(c) model checking [12, 17],

and apply them for verification of robot behavior. Most solutions can be applied for both static verification of robot behavior and the dynamic verification when the robot is in the middle of execution of a program. The geometrical modeling of the robot movement is typically related with spatial path description and can be done for both static and dynamic analyses. Resource allocation algorithms for deadlock avoidance can be used for dynamic verification to avoid collisions of moving robots assuming that they can stop and wait while doing their tasks.

The model checking provides a most general methodology [13, 14, 15, 16] that can be used not only for deadlock avoidance or detection but also for detection and verification of wide variety robot interaction characteristics. Typically the model checking is based on finite-state methods [14] that can be applied directly to our state diagrams and therefore it can be of important practical use for verifying robot behaviors. The model checking method can offer the robot behavior designer a set of ready-to-use algorithms and techniques for the analysis of complete system properties. In our research activities we extended the previous studies to include probabilistic state diagrams to provide a foundation for the description of robot probabilistic behavior, and the study of checking of state diagrams describing probabilistic robot behaviors.

Conceptually, the approach is as follows. First, out of the specifications of the robots' behavior by state diagrams we build a possibly large but finite graph containing all possible (reachable) system states and all possible transitions among them. This graph defines the behavioral model of the set of robots. Each path in the graph represents an allowable execution or a (part of a) behavior of a system. The graph contains all possible executions or behaviors. The property list will be used for the graph correctness specification. We concentrated on an investigation of the probabilistic features of model checking. The probabilistic properties can be specified as a simple probability variable or as more complex probability distributions. Then, given the system model and the probabilistic property, an exhaustive search of the system's state graph will be performed, aimed at deciding whether the desired probabilistic property holds.

We have to deal with the exponential explosion of the state space size similar as others [15, 16].There are many proposed and implemented solutions but the exponential growth of state space is still a real threat [17]. We included in our research a study of multiple forms of reduction of state space, aimed at removing the states and transitions which are irrelevant for the evaluation of a given formula. We also investigated the usefulness of compositional model checking, where some individual parts of a system (of a more acceptable size) are subject to an exhaustive state space search while the conclusion as to the performance of the whole system is reached by combining the results obtained for the individual parts.

Let us consider again the state diagram for Robot behavior as specified in Figure 2. Let us assume that we have two robots. Robot 1 behavior is exactly as in Figure 2. Robot 2 behavior is almost identical except that it starts from the end of the corridor. In some cases the behavior of robots can be independent but in general they can interact as in our example. The analysis of combined diagram might be necessary. There is a need for analytical transformations to investigate how the probability of reaching a given state by the first robot affects the reachability of the states by the second robot.

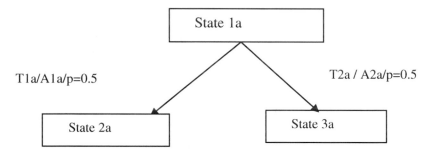

**Fig. 5.** A state diagram to describe Behavior 1 in an abstract form

To be specific let us discuss the necessary analytical transformations in case of two robots acting according to the state diagram 2, 3 and 4. First, some form of reduction of state space is necessary to make the combined diagram manageable. One of the forms of the reduction is based on state abstraction. We will reduce the diagram by make abstract states from the fragments that do not require probabilistic transitions. As a result for Behavior 1 we obtained the abstract state diagram as shown in Figure 5.

As discussed before, out of the specifications of the 2 robots' behavior  by state diagrams we  build a possibly a  single finite graph containing all possible (reachable) system states and all possible transitions among them as shown in Figure 6.

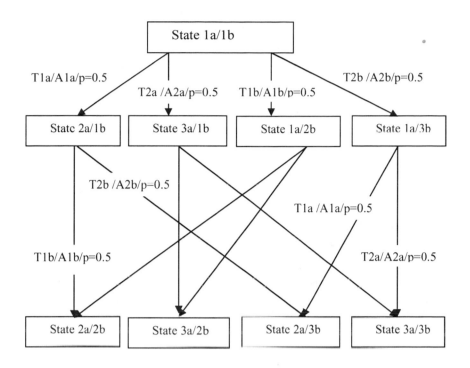

**Fig. 6.** A single graph for the a complete system of cooperating robots

The system properties can be checked against the graph. We can use both analytical and simulation mode to do it. For example, the probability of entering room 1 by two robots can be computed based on analytical mode. The result is 0.5\*0.5=0.25 since this is a final event and therefore it is time independent.

There are also time dependent events that can be checked. For example, state 2a/3b can be disallowed based on the fact that robots will collide when the first robot tries to get to the door 2 while robot 2 has chosen door 1 and is moving towards it. If the both robots start the movement about the same time the probability can be computed the simple way. More complex probabilistic computations are required when probability of robots' movement is a function of time.

The most typical analysis of the combined graph is checking the provided parameters e.g. restrictions on using environmental resources. The robot movement collisions can be a case to consider. Once the needed environment resources are specified for each robot, the potential "bottlenecks" can be identified.

The single combined graph can be also used in the simulation mode. As a result, our system allows us to ask the queries like: what is the probability of a given state together by robot 1 and the robot 2.

The above discussion shows that there are tasks related to multi-level probabilistic state diagram that can be automated. Our GISAC 2 system supporting probabilistic state diagrams implements five main tasks as shown in Figure 7. First, it uses a graphical interface to specify the resource graph. Second, it allows a user to convert the resource graph into a probabilistic state diagram using similar graphical interface. Third, it can simulate execution of the probabilistic state diagrams. Fourth, it can analyze combined diagrams e.g. computes combined probabilities if requested. Fifth, it generates the code which can be executed by robots.

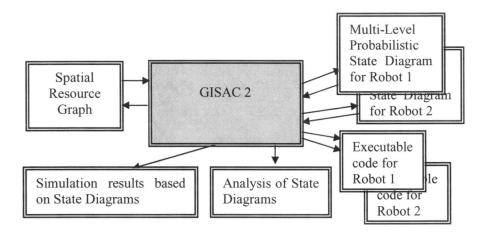

**Fig. 7.** Architecture of a system supporting modeling of behavior of cooperating robots

# 6   Interactions of Robots and Game Theory

Game Theory is a probabilistic model that allows "players" to investigate their options to maximize their returns/advantage [20]. During game different payoffs are assigned to each possible move. A player is constantly attempting to increase his/her payoffs as much as possible in each move.

James Waldegrave is accredited for being the first one to discuss game theory while analyzing a card game in year 1713 [21]. However, it took many more years, until 1928, for game theory was recognized as a unique field of study [21]. There are many practical applications of game theory in Biology, Economics, Political Science, Computer Science, Logic, and Philosophy, [20, 21].

A strategy is a plan that is used during a game session. A strategy consists of many moves. While a move is a single step made during a game. There are two types of strategies, pure strategy and mix strategy.

• Pure Strategy – A player knows the pros and cons of every move and as a result the player makes each move with certainty.

• Mix Strategy– A player has possible moves and a probability distribution (collection of weights). A player would use a mixed strategy if he/she doesn't have a preference between many pure strategies. In addition, he would keep the opponent guessing because the opponent can benefit from knowing the next move.

Using a game theory for analyzing robot behavior is also a promising area as shown in the literature [5, 18]. We experimented with several games involving robots. In this paper we use, as a case study, a game based on the prisoner's dilemma [19]. Our game was designed to involve two robots. The following assumptions were made for the new game.

1. There are two rooms Room 1 and Room 2.

2. Robots need to go to one of the Rooms to collect an award. Choosing the room is referred as choosing strategy in the game theory terminology

3. If Robot 1 enters Room 1, it will collect either 9 points award or nothing depending on the choice of the second robot as described in Table 1.

4. If Robot 1 enters Room 2, it will collect either 10 points award or 5 points award depending on the choice of the second robot as described again in Table 1.

**Table 1.** Strategies and Payoffs Table for our Robot game

| Payoffs (P1,P2) P1 for Row P2 for Column | Room 1 | Room 2 |
|---|---|---|
| Room 1 | (9 ,9) | (0,10) |
| Room 2 | (10, 0) | (5, 5) |

The game theory can recommend what say Robot 1 should do. In game theoretic terminology it is referred as dominant strategy. The dominant strategy is typically computed by summing up all awards for the given raw (strategy). In our case the dominant strategy is to get award in Room 2 since the sum 10+5 is greater than 9+0. It is clear that such computation is made based on the assumption of the random choice of the room by Robot 2.

It can be also seen that if Robot 1 and Robot 2 would always choose Room 1 they will benefit more since each time they would collect award of 9 points. That sort of inconsistency was referred as the "dilemma" in the original prisoner's dilemma game. In literature [20] this type of the result is also often referred as "inefficiency". Game theorists need to tackle the obvious "inefficiency" of the outcome. One way is to "learn" of other partner strategies by playing it more than once. In such a repeated game, patterns of cooperation can be established [20].

The probabilistic state diagrams described in the previous sections are a good foundation for designing and evaluating robot games using game theory and the GI-SAC 2 system supporting interactions of robots can be used for game implementation as shown in Figure 8.

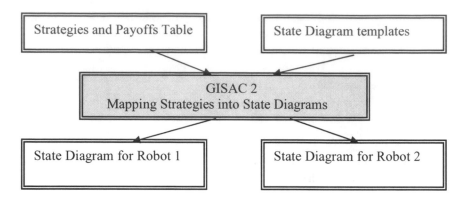

**Fig. 8.** Architecture of a Probabilistic State Diagram Processing System enhanced with Strategies and Payoffs

First, the state diagram template(s) are designed to describe possible robot behaviors as described in the previous section. The state diagram shown in Figure 2, after minor modification, can serve a template for our Award Room game. Next, Strategies and Payoffs Table (such as shown in Table 1) can be used to assign probabilities to the different robot behaviors. Depending on the goal, we can adjust the probabilities for Robot 1 and/or Robot 2 so that the probabilities will reflect the dominant strategy.

We can also use our system to design games between human with a robot, and "learn" of other partner strategies by playing it more than once. Probabilistic state diagrams can be a good foundation for experiments to establish the best cooperation patterns.

## 7  Summary

In this paper, we have presented a novel approach for autonomous robot navigation in a known indoor environment using probabilistic state diagram integrated with computer vision techniques. Triggers were developed for state diagram based to detect to changes in the environment and respond according to a given probabilistic specifications. The probabilistic specifications allowed us to model more advanced interactions between autonomous robots. We addressed the problem of ensuring the correctness of robot interactions. The techniques were presented to verify and analyze individual probabilistic robots' behaviors, and combine individual robots' behaviors into a single finite graph describing a complete system. It was shown how to use techniques such as state abstraction and transition abstraction to create, verify and combine large probabilistic state diagrams. The paper also addressed the potential of using probabilistic state diagrams to design and evaluate robot games.

**Acknowledgments.** We acknowledge the ORISE (Oak Ridge faculty program), NSF (award id: 0959958), grant from the Graduate School of Fayetteville State University and the Belk Foundation for supporting this research.

# References

1. Murphy, R.: Introduction to AI Robotics. MIT Press, Cambridge (2000)
2. Desouza, G.N., Kak, A.C.: Vision for mobile robot navigation: a survey. IEEE Transactions on Pattern Analysis and Machine Intelligence 24(2), 237–267 (2002)
3. Blank, D.: Robots make computer science personal. Communications of the ACM 49(12) (2006)
4. Kumar, D. (ed.): Learning Computing with Robots (Python), 1st edn. Institute for Personal Robots in Education (2007)
5. Meng, Y.: Multi-Robot Searching using Game Theory Based Approach. Journal of Advanced Robotics Systems (2008)
6. Czejdo, B.D., Bhattacharya, S., Czejdo, J.: Use of Probabilistic State Diagrams for Robot Navigation in an Indoor Environment. In: Proceedings of the Annual International Conference on Advanced Topics in Artificial Intelligence, ATAI, pp. A-97 to A-102 (2010)
7. Harel, D.: On visual formalisms. Communications of the ACM 31(5), 514–530 (1988)
8. Rumbaugh, J., Blaha, M., Premerlani, W., Eddy, F., Lorensen, W.: Object-Oriented Modeling and Design. Prentice Hall, New Jersey (1990)
9. Czejdo, B.D., Bhattacharya, S.: Programming robots with state diagrams. Journal of Computing Sciences in Colleges 24(5), 19–26 (2009)
10. Bhattacharya, S., Czejdo, B.D., Mobley, S.: An Integrated Computer Vision and Infrared Sensor Based Approach to Autonomous Robot Navigation in an Indoor Environment. In: Proceedings of the 7th International Conference on Computing, Communications and Control Technologies (2009)
11. Galamhos, C., Matas, J., Kittler, J.: Progressive probabilistic Hough transform for line detection. In: Conference on Computer Vision and Pattern Recognition, vol. 1, pp. 560–566. IEEE Computer Society, Los Alamitos (1999)
12. McMillan, K.L.: Symbolic Model Checking. Kluwer Academic Publishers, Dordrecht (1993)
13. Peled, D.A.: Software Reliability Methods. Springer, Heidelberg (2001)
14. Clarke, E.M., Wing, J.M.: Formal methods; State of the Art and Future Directions. ACM Computing Surveys 28(4), 627–643 (1996)
15. Bryant, R.E.: Binary Decision Diagrams: Enabling Technologies for Formal Verification. In: Proc. IEEE/ACM Int. Conf. on Computer-Aided Design, pp. 236–243 (1995)
16. Holzmann, G.J.: The Model Checker SPIN. IEEE Trans. on SE 23(5), 279–295 (1997)
17. Berard, B. (ed.): Systems and Software Verification: Model-Checking Techniques and Tools. Springer, Heidelberg (2001)
18. Montemerlo, E.: Game-Theoretic Control for Robot Teams, doctoral dissertation, tech. report CMU-RI-TR-05-36, Robotics Institute, Carnegie Mellon University (August. 2005)
19. Kuhn, S.: Prisoner's Dilemma (Stanford Encyclopedia of Philosophy). Stanford Encyclopedia of Philosophy (October 22, 2007),
    http://plato.stanford.edu/entries/prisonerdilemma
20. Turocy, T., von Stengel, B.: GameTheory, CDAMResearch Report LSE-CDAM-2001-09 (2001)
21. Walker, P., Chronology of Game Theory. Economics and Finance - University of Canterbury - New Zealand (2010),
    http://www.econ.canterbury.ac.nz/personal_pages/
    paul_walker/gt/hist.htm

# VANET Security Framework for Safety Applications Using Trusted Hardware

Asif Ali Wagan, Bilal Munir Mughal, and Halabi Hasbullah

Department of Computer and Information Sciences
Universiti Teknologi PETRONAS,
Bandar Sri Iskandar, 31750 Tronoh, Perak, Malaysia
asifwaggan@gmail.com

**Abstract.** Vehicular ad hoc network has caught much attention from research-ers in industry and academia. Security is one of the main issues that must be addressed for successful deployment of VANETs. Many researchers have pro-posed security protocols and frameworks. Since no standards have been fina-lized as yet, much of the early research works regarding security has become obsolete. Efficiency and reliability are two of the core issues that need to be re-solved. In this paper a security framework is proposed for efficient periodic and event-driven messages. Proposed framework uses TPM hardware to reduce processing time for secure messaging. Framework is based upon two major components i.e. smart utilization of symmetric and asymmetric security me-thods and a trusted grouping scheme. Furthermore, simulations were carried out to highlight the potential bottlenecks created by processing delays while using trial security standard for VANET.

**Keywords:** Reliability; Security Framework; Trusted Hardware; VANET.

## 1 Introduction

Vehicular Ad hoc Network (VANET) is well established growing technology that many researches and projects are implementing now days. VANET is a special branch of ad hoc network (MANET) and soon it is expected to become part of real world applications. Motivation to use VANET comes from road safety, increasing accidents on road, increasing death ratio and injuries. The basic idea of VANET is to have communication between vehicle to vehicle (V2V) and vehicle to roadside infrastruc-ture (V2I) as shown in figure 1. Vehicles broadcast messages which contain informa-tion about road conditions (hazard, curve, etc) and vehicle position, speed, direction etc. VANET has many prominent characteristics which makes it better than other ad hoc networks. Those characteristics include vehicles moving at high speeds, fast changing topology, and short interface time among nodes.

In North America, 5.9 GHz (5.850-5.925) frequency band was selected for short to medium range communication and is known as DSRC (Dedicated Short Range Com-munication). WAVE (Wireless Access in Vehicular Environment) is the IEEE default trial layered architecture for VANET testing. WAVE comprises of IEEE 1609.x pro-tocol and 802.11p (an 802.11a variant for VANET) [1], [2]. WAVE works on DSRC multichannel environment.

V. Snasel, J. Platos, and E. El-Qawasmeh (Eds.): ICDIPC 2011, Part II, CCIS 189, pp. 426–439, 2011.
© Springer-Verlag Berlin Heidelberg 2011

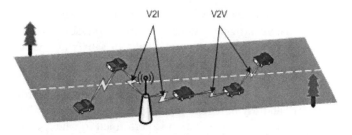

**Fig. 1.** VANET Communication: Vehicle-to-Vehicle (V2V) and Vehicle-to-Infrastructure (V2I)

Like other wireless technologies, security is an essential requirement for successful implementation of VANET. Elliptic Curve Digital Signature Algorithm (ECDSA) has been used as default security protocol. ECDSA key size is very small but ECDSA provides same level of security as RSA algorithm. There are two security methods used in security namely symmetric and asymmetric. The symmetric method generates one Secret Key (SK). SK is used to encrypt data and the same SK is used to decryption. But symmetric method lacks non repudiation due to symmetric cryptography mechanism. However symmetric methods are fast enough in terms of encryption/decryption speed than asymmetric methods. Whereas digital signature is an asymmetric method; it is more secure in comparison to symmetric cryptography. Digital signature method generates two keys; one key is called private key that is used for signing (encryption) while verification (decryption) key is called public key. The basic idea is that private key is used in signing the message for authentication of user. But private key is never disclosed to any other party and it is also impossible to calculate private key part form given public key part. Public key part is used for verification of signature to proof authenticity of recipient and public part is only shared with authorized parties. This process normally involves a trusted third party.

VANET security requirements have been well studied and there are several security requirements identified for VANET environment. Some of the well-known security requirements are defined as below.

1. **Authentication:** As demonstrated in [2], [3], it is a process of identifying source node by verifying source node credential. In the VANET environment, when a vehicle receives a message from source, this receiver vehicle will verify source node signature (private key) through its public key.
2. **Privacy:** As demonstrated in [2], [3], privacy is directly related to vehicle or user personal information; if vehicle identity has been disclosed then unauthorized user can easily use that information for his/her own benefit.
3. **Non-Repudiation:** As defined in [2], [3], it is a process of identifying a user when user is denying that a sent message is originated by him. In this situation non-repudiation provides a guarantee to the receiver that, if bogus information is contained in a received message, that sender can be identified and s/he cannot deny from it because there is evidence inside the message.
4. **Availability:** As demonstrated in [2], [3], it is related to communication part. In any circumstances vehicles are able to communicate to each other or Road Side Unit (RSU). Sometimes the service is jam or channels are busy and due to these problem message cannot be received by recipient.

Recently various protocols have been proposed by researchers to overcome security attacks in VANET. These provide message integrity, privacy and non repudiation. However, it is reviewed that these protocols lacks in satisfying the requirements of safety applications. It is also reviewed that various studies also have been conducted to reduce the high computational cost in VANET. Despite of that there is high computational cost. In order to address this problem, a security framework is proposed by combining the symmetric and asymmetric cryptography techniques and that builds trust among vehicles on the road. The simulation is performed in which various algorithms are compared that reduces computation cost. This framework provides the security and contributes towards reduction of computation cost accordingly.

The rest of this paper is organized as follows. Section 2 is literature review, Section 3 is methodology. In section 4 simulation and results are discussed and finally conclusion and future directions in Section 5 are provided.

## 2   Literature Review

Due to high computational cost incurred by default trail asymmetric Public key Infrastructure (PKI) scheme which is ECDSA, researchers have proposed many alternate schemes [3] - [13]. However most of the schemes are based on other tradeoffs with regard to processing overhead such as large message size, communication delay, and higher bandwidth utilization. Symmetric method provides a faster processing solution but it comes at the cost of reduced security. This problem can be mitigated to some extent by building trust among communicating nodes. A combination of asymmetric and symmetric methods can be used to build trust while reducing the processing overhead and achieving maximum security.

In [3], authors give details of VANET's threats, possible security requirements and its solutions. This study also compares default PKI mechanism with NTRUEncrypt mechanism which is fast in verification but large in key size as compared to default mechanism. NTRU may not be appropriate for VANET's environment due to scarce bandwidth situation and is likely to result in longer transmission delays.

In [4], TPM is a hardware chip introduced to implement in VANET environment. It has been noted that TPM can benefit VANET technology. However TPM have to be designed according to the requirements of VANET architecture. Currently TPM is being used with RSA method which is faster in verification but at the same time RSA has larger key size.

In [5], authors gave the idea of secure message aggregation. There are two methods which are concatenated signature and onion signature. The first method is called concatenated signature as in this technique sender broadcasts a message and the receiver verifies the message and appends its signature. After appending signature, the receiver will rebroadcast that message. As this process continues, receiver has no need to verify additional signatures. In second method which is onion signature scheme, a receiver over signs the message and then rebroadcast new message. This message contains signatures, the old signature and the last receiver's signature. So, next hop verifies only the last signature. If signature is invalid it will be discarded and a new process of signature generation will be started. However this method has a computational overhead.

In [6], group formation is done by dividing geographical area into small size of cells (cell size depend on transmission range). If any vehicle enters in a cell, it will automatically know that this vehicle belongs to which group. The group leader is a vehicle which is nearest to cell center. If there are many vehicles close to cell center then selection of group leader is done by the vehicle having lower identity. This method will select a group leader; however this technique creates frequently changing group leaders.

In [7], a symmetric cryptography mechanism TESLA (Time Efficient Stream Loss-tolerant Authentication) is introduced. TESLA is a faster cryptography mechanism due to its symmetric nature but lacks non-repudiation property. In this scheme, receiver has to store message and Message Authentication Code (MAC) until the sender discloses the key (delay key disclosure). TESLA may lead to vulnerability against possible memory attacks. VANET Authentication using Signatures and TESLA++ (VAST) is a hybrid framework which is the combination of TESLA and ECDSA. VAST carries both signatures ECDSA and TESLA in case of emergency, where non repudiation requires ECDSA signature verification. However, due to carrying both signatures, it will increase size of packet significantly.

In [8], the suggested scheme depends on two techniques which are Convoy Member Authentication (CMA) and Vehicle Sequence Authentication (VSA). CMA and VSA are used to verify the actual position of vehicle. CMA checks weather vehicle is on same direction whereas VSA is concerned with vehicles sequence. The proposed schemes are also utilized to tackle different kind of attacks such as Sybil and position cheating.

Study [9], gives the concept of blind signature scheme. Vehicle sends a message to another vehicle to sign a message without knowing what information the message contains. Study [10] presents architecture for safety and business applications such as internet; service announcement. They proposed two schemes namely EAP-Kerberos and EAP-TLS. These schemes provide AAA. EAP-Kerberos is a scheme that mutually authenticates user to user or access point or service provider at entry point. It can be suitable for business point of view. However due to its on-line real-time security requirements; it may not be suitable for VANET. This is due to on-line system probable disconnections and delays, which could lead to a network wide calamity.

In [10], the highway is divided into small segments and these segments are monitored by RSU. Each segment is divided into equal size and each RSU is placed in such way that they are overlapping. Vehicles form a group by location and time interval. Furthermore, RSU divides segments into splits. Each split has it unique key for communication. Vehicles between two splits acts as relay node, however placing RSU along the entire road is not feasible in VANET environment. As it can raise the deployment cost significantly.

Proposed in [11], is security architecture with the supports TPM. The basic concept is that every vehicle is embedded with TPM and vehicles are preloaded with a set number of cryptography keys to provide anonymity. That pair of cryptography keys are used for short time to create pseudonym. On need basis, memory sticks can be used to create new key pairs.

Proposed in [12], is an identity based scheme for VANETs to cover security and privacy. The Trusted Third Party (TTP) is used to generate private keys for users after an authentication task is completed. TTP does not contain any record for binding keys. After authentication user gets a key. That key can be used for further operations such as encryption, decryption, signing and verification. This scheme is not utilized for Certificate Authority (CA) or Key Distribution Center (KDC). The four levels are proposed in the scheme. First level is setup (initializes all system parameters and computes all public and private keys). The second level is extract (private key is computed). Third level is encryption. In this level data is encrypted by using blowfish algorithm. The last level is decryption. In this level data is decrypted by same blow-fish algorithm.

In study [13], a scheme is proposed that is based on rough set theory. This study also introduces Mobile Trusted Module (MTM). MTM is divided into Mobile Local-owner Trusted Module (MLTM) and Mobile Remote Owner trusted Module (MRTM). MLTM works the same way as TPM. MLTM users can use near local device and perform activities. MRTM cannot access directly any local device as MLTM. MRTM performs all activities to restart in safe boot and certifies that all engines are capable to perform in rightly manner.

## 3   Methodology

### 3.1   Framework

The proposed framework is divided into four parts which are message dispatcher, TPM, group leader, group members and cell as illustrate in figure 2. In this figure we have explained each element step by step and the complete detail of components that how they are interrelated to each other. Security is a key element for successful deployment of VANET applications. Periodic and event-driven messages roles are highly notified in this connection, particularly for life-safety applications, for which their transmissions must be fast and secure. We propose a framework which is based on combination of hybrid cryptography schemes and also supports TPM chip. The goal of this framework is to achieve trust among vehicles to create a trusted group on road by using default PKI mechanism. Framework which is shown in figure 2, have also been discussed by the authors of this study in [14].

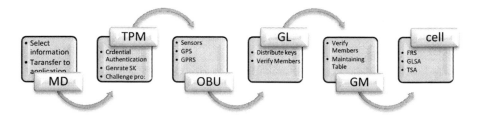

**Fig. 2.** The proposed VANET security framework

### 3.1.1 Message Dispatcher

Message Dispatcher (MD) works between application and other layers. It works in both directions, that is, lower layers to application and from application layer to lower layers. It receives information from application layers and extracts similar information. MD will collect similar information in one packet and broadcast it to receiving end. At recipient, MD sorts out all information and distributes among required applications [20].

### 3.1.2 Trusted Platform Module

TPM is integrated chip which comes with hardware to provide security features. TPM contain all cryptography functions. TPM provides reliability of system by using challenge procedure. TPM perform operation in protected location plus it store all there elements in that protected location. TPM define an integrity procedure where it save measured digest in protected location of system and use that digest for ensure that system running in trusted environment. TPM not only provide a hardware security it also store values from initial booting [2][21], TPM elements PCR, SML, EK, AIK, for our framework we adopt TPM chip which provides cryptographic engines; asymmetric (RSA/ECC), symmetric (SMS4/AES)[15], random number generator, and hash.

The Core Root of Trust for Measurement (CRTM) is programming code. CRTM is used in TPM to provide reliability of running components of a system. CRTM operates from starting of system and before Basic input/output system (BIOS). CRTM measures BIOS routines and save that valuable information in PCR registered. After storing values in PCR, CRTM transfers control to Bios. Bios will check hardware components and boot-loader routines and save that information in PCR. After that control is transferred to the boot loader to assess routines of Operating System (OS) kernel and before transferring control to OS, boot loader saves the assessed information into PCR. In this manner all components are measured step by step so that one can verify from PCR saved values that current system running on trustworthy environment [21].

### 3.1.3 Group Leader (GL)

Role of GL is to generate secret key by using random generator engine and distribute to group members. Whenever new GL is selected it generates a new key as frequently changing the key reduces risk of key theft. Symmetric key will be utilized only once for a safety applications message between vehicles. Once it is used, it will be discarded and automatically a new secret key will be generated. Normal communication is done by ECC. Symmetric key is transferred via secure asymmetric scheme called elliptic curve diffie hellman (ECDH) [20]. ECDH is asymmetric algorithm. This algorithm used to create communication securely between nodes.

### 3.1.4 Group Members

Every vehicle in cell is not considered as a group member until that vehicle authenticates itself from GL or present group members in a cell. After authentication process, vehicle gets secret key for the future usage. This vehicle is considered as a group member after all process are complete. If any vehicle provides invalid credentials, neither that vehicle is considered as a group member nor it gets a secret key. However the vehicle still can communicate with normal ECDSA. This is one of the advantages of our framework that without joining the group; vehicles are still able to communicate with neighboring vehicles.

### 3.1.5  Key Distribution

Group leader distributes key to group members and group member also can share secret key with other members after credential verification. The secret key is only used for low latency safety applications. The periodic safety applications and few event driven applications are requires very short time. To see the list of safety applications, please go through the study referred as [20]. Those applications that require sufficient time in reacting to a driver behavior uses default method (ECDSA).

### 3.1.6  Cell

It is possible to divide a highway and urban area in fixed and variable size. This technique improves the performance of VANET and it is also important for group formation. There are different type of techniques that are used to create hop some of with the help of road side unit, navigation map on vehicles and global position. In our framework we create fixed size of cell in circle shape further we created segments in the cell to reduce load and easy selection of group leader. We design three segments in each cell as illustrate in figure 3, a group selection segment called common Group Leader Select Area (GLSA).every vehicle maintaining table which called vehicle position and speed measured table (VPSM).VPSM table contains all vehicles position and speed according there speed and position we select the group leader, the advantage of this table is to easy selection.

Forward Segment Area (FSA) is next segment form GLSA. FSA contain information about next and present cells. Vehicle work as relay node vehicles between two cells, relay vehicle contain both secret keys from present cell and also from next cell. FSA segment get information from Trailing Segment Area (TSA) . FSA and TSA both contain larger areas then GLSA. Whereas TSA is entrance point of cell, its size is same as FSA.

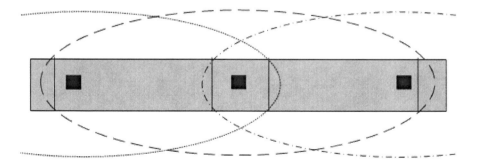

**Fig. 3.** Road Segments

Next two equations are described which are used to calculate communication duration between two vehicles as defined in [16], [17]. These vehicles are moving in towards each other in different lanes.

$$Lifetime_{link} = \frac{R - \left| d_{ij} \right|}{\left| v_i - v_j \right|}. \tag{1}$$

$$Lifetime_{link} = \frac{\sqrt{R^2 - w^2} + s.\sqrt{d_{ij}^2 - w^2}}{v_i + v_j} \tag{2}$$

In equation 1 & 2, 'R' represent range, 'dij' is the absolute distance between two vehicles (I & j), 'Vi' and 'Vj' are velocities of 'i' and 'j' vehicles. In equation (2), 'w' is representing separation distance among two vehicles (vehicle 'i' and vehicle 'j').

### 3.2 Group Communication

Group communication describes several steps how a vehicle joins the group and after approving credential gets a secret key figure 4. Furthermore if any vehicle cannot satisfy that vehicle discarded and cannot get a secret key.

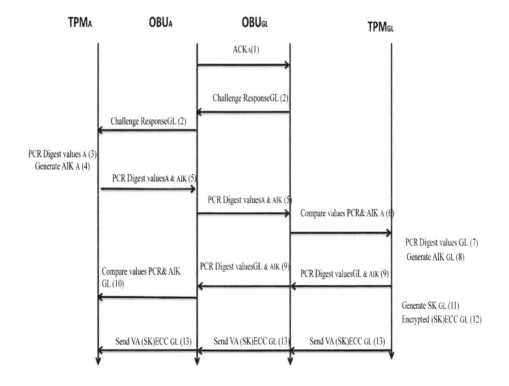

**Fig. 4.** Group Communication

**Step 1**: VA sends an acknowledge (Ack) message to VGL.

**Step 2**: VGL receives request from vehicle VA and sends challenge response to VA.

**Step 3**: VA receives the challenge response from VGL. Vehicle VA Collocate PCR digest values and SML values.

**Step 4** : VA generates attestation identity key and encrypts  PCR and SML values. VA (PCRA) encryptedAIK(Pr) sends to VGL.

**Step 5 & 6**: VGL will receive message from VA and compare values. If hash values are equal then further operation is processed else message communication is discarded. VGL (PCRA )DecryptAIK (Pub) = comparison of hash values.

**Step 7**: VGL Collocates PCR digest values and SML values.

**Step 8**: VGL Generates attention identity key and encryptes  PCR and SML values. VGL (PCRGL) encryptedAIK(Pr) sends to VA.

**Step 9 & 10**: VA will receive message from VGL and compares values.  If hash values are equal then further operation is processed else message communication is discarded. VA (PCRA) DecryptAIK (Pub) = comparison of hash values.

**Step 11 & 12:** VGL Generates Secret Key (SK) encryptedECC(PR) and sends to vehicle VA.

**Step13:** VA will receive the secret key and store it for future communication.

## 4   Simulation Settings and Results

The network was simulated on network simulator 2 (ns2 version 2.34). The simulation takes place in the probabilistic fading environment. For this we configured the Nakagami model. Furthermore the highway simulation scenario was designed to create a realistic environment. Therefore six lanes were created (three lanes in each direction). The three lanes were designed according to different distances. The most

**Table 1.** Simulation Parameters

| Parameters | Value |
|---|---|
| Antenna height | 1.5 |
| Vehicles | 384 |
| Simulation time | 20 sec |
| Distance between  vehicles | 30 meter, 40 meters, 50 meters |
| Message size | 100, 200, 300…1000 |
| Broadcast interval | 100 ms |
| Interval variance | 0.05 ms |
| Communication Range | 300 meters |
| Propagation Model | Nakagami |
| Radio System | 5.9 GHz (DSRC) |
| Bandwidth | 6 (Mbps) |
| Lane | 6 (three in each direction) |

inner lane nodes were placed at the distance of 50 meters from each other. The outer most lane nodes were placed at a distance of 30 meters from each other and middle lane nodes were placed at a distance of 40 meters from each other. The other three were also designed accordingly. In the simulation, total number of vehicles placed was 384, and each vehicle broadcasted a message in 100 milliseconds. The communication range of the vehicle was set around 300 meters and the message size varied from 100 to 1000 bytes. The simulation running time was 20 seconds. Rest of the simulation parameters are defined in table 1.

### 4.1   End to End delay

End to End delay results are shown in figures 5 and 6, which were taken from highway simulation scenario for increasing message and distance respectively. Figure 5 is showing that as a message size increases, delay also increases drastically. The RSA and Group signature schemes are around 800-900 hundreds byte, it is noticed that both these schemes are highest in communication delay. RSA and Group signature schemes take 9-12 milliseconds to broadcast a message. It is also noticed in figure 5 that increasing distance is not affecting much but it clearly shows that RSA and group signature schemes are still highest in delay among other schemes. That is a reason that why large size methods are not appropriate for many VANET safety applications. Furthermore, if ECDSA scheme utilizes message size which is around 350 bytes, it is included in cryptography overhead, payload and protocol type etc. The present issue is processing capability with ECDSA, which makes ECDSA unsuitable.

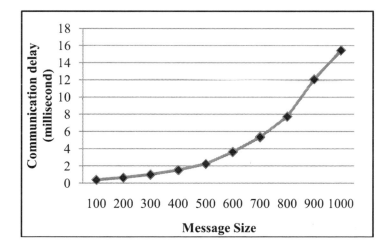

**Fig. 5.** Communication delay with increasing message size

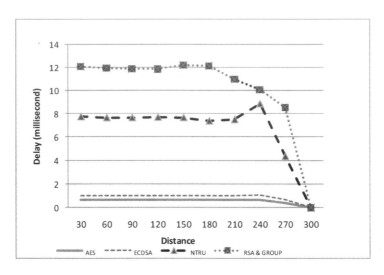

**Fig. 6.** Communication delay at different distance

## 4.2 Message Drop Ratio

As noticed in figure 7, the increase in message size also significantly effects MDR. It validates the statement that a small message size are efficiently utilized then large size of methods such as RSA,NTRU and Group mechanism. The sizes of these methods are between 800 to 900 bytes. It is noticed that when message size is 800 bytes and above, the number of drop messages increased drastically, around 13000-14000 messages dropped in 20 seconds. It means 650 messages dropped in a second, which is

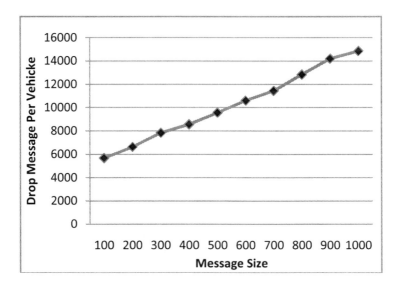

**Fig. 7.** Message Drop by Per vehicle

about 70% percentage of total sent messages. ECDSA MDR 7000 in 20 seconds, it means 350 messages dropped in a second, the total broadcasted messages in communication range are 840 in a second, which means 45% percentage.

## 4.3 Packet Delivery Ratio

Figure 8 shows that increasing message size is dropping receiving message ratio and figure 9 also shows that even increasing distance between vehicles affect packet delivery ratio drastically. RSA and group schemes are highest among comparing

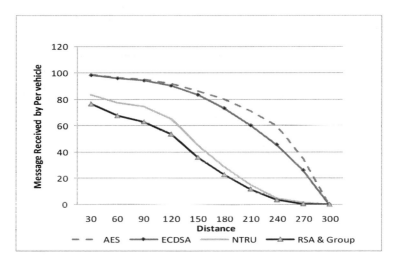

**Fig. 8.** Packet Delivery Ratio at different distances

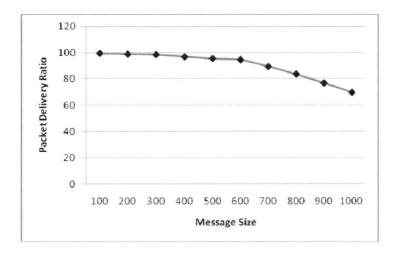

**Fig. 9.** Packet Delivery Ratio with increasing in message size

protocol, there message size are between 800-900 bytes. Even NTRU is also heavily drops its packet receiving ratio. It is noticed that ECDSA and AES methods have highest packet receiving ratios, even AES is superior then all methods, it increased the probability of message receiving in emergency case. It is also noted that vehicle located at 300 meters was not receiving any packet from broadcasting vehicles.

### 4.4 Analysis of Results

From the above results it can be summarized that large message size is not feasible for VANET applications, it is noticed that data message size of 300 bytes or less the performance is much better. However small security protocol like ECDSA has total message size of 300 bytes (including cryptography material) but due to computational cost this method is also not satisfactory. Currently many applications mainly event driven applications have low latency and time is critical for them. To overcome this issue our proposed framework design balances use of security protocols according to the need of applications. Those applications where time is critical we proposed symmetric method which is quite efficient in processing and where security is critical we proposed ECDSA protocol. Trusted platform module was used to create trust among vehicles. Creating group in the proposed framework was to increase the efficiency because it requires only 5 messages by any new vehicle to join a group.

## 5 Conclusion

In this paper a security framework for VANET is proposed that is based on trusted platform hardware for creating trust between vehicles. This proposed framework ensures fast authentication for event driven broadcast messages through symmetric security method which helps in reducing processing delay. Default trial standard is recommended for periodic messages only. Simulations were performed in realistic highway scenarios to measure the effects of message size on packet drop ratio, packet delivery ratio and communication delay.

Proposed framework lacks hardware implementation as only software simulation was performed in this study. Therefore it will be interesting to implement this proposed framework in a real case scenario with hardware implementation.

## References

1. Jiang, D., Taliwal, V., Meier, A., Holfelder, W., Herrtwich, R.: Design of 5.9 GHz DSRC-based vehicular safety communication. IEEE Wireless Communications 13(5), 36–43 (2006)
2. IEEE 802.11p: Towards an International Standard for Wireless Access in Vehicular Environments (May 2008), http://dx.doi.org/10.1109/VETECS.2008.458
3. Raya, M., Hubaux, J.P.: The security of vehicular ad hoc networks. In: Proc. of the 3rd ACM workshop on Security of ad hoc and sensor networks, SASN 2005 (2005)
4. Guette, G., Bryce, C.: Using TPMs to Secure Vehicular Ad-Hoc Networks (VANETs). In: IFIP International Federation for Information Processing (2008)

5. Raya, M., Aziz, A., Hubaux, J.P.: Efficient secure aggregation in VANETs. In: VANET 2006: Proc. of the 3rd. International Workshop on Vehicular ad hoc Networks (2006)
6. Studer, A., Bai, F., Bellur, B., Perrig, A.: Flexible, Extensible and Efficient VANET Authentication. In: Proc. of the 6th Embedded Security in Cars (ESCAR) Workshop (November 2008)
7. Ahren, S., Mark, L., Adrian, P.: Efficient mechanisms to provide convoy member and vehicle sequence authentication in VANETs. In: Proc. of the SecureComm 2007 (2007)
8. Chun, T.L., Min, S.H., Yen, P.C.: A secure and efficient communication scheme with authenticated key establishment and privacy preserving for vehicular ad hoc networks. ACM 31(12), 2803–2814 (2008)
9. Moustafa, H., Bourdon, G., Gourhant, Y.: AAA in vehicular communication on highways with ad hoc networking support: a proposed architecture. In: Proc. of the 2nd ACM International Workshop on Vehicular ad hoc Networks (September 2005)
10. Verma, M., Huang, D.: SeGCom: secure group communication in VANETs. In: Proceedings of the 6th IEEE Conference on Consumer Communications and Networking Conference, Las Vegas, NV, USA, January 11-13, pp. 1160–1164 (2009)
11. Guette, G., Heen, O.: A TPM-based architecture for improved security and anonymity in vehicular ad hoc networks, . In: Vehicular Networking Conference (VNC), October 28-30, pp. 1–7. IEEE, Los Alamitos (2009)
12. Yeun, C.Y., Al-Qutayri, M., Khalifa, F.A.-H.: Efficient secrurity implementation for emerging vanets. Ubiquitous Computing and Communication Journal (2009)
13. Li, B., Wang, J., Dong, T., Liu, Y.: An new approach to access VANETs. In: ISECS International Colloquium on Computing, Communication, Control, and Management, CCCM 2009, August 8-9, vol. 2, pp. 482–485 (2009)
14. Wagan, A.A., Mughal, B.M., Hasbullah, H.: VANET Security Framework for Trusted Grouping using TPM Hardware. In: ICCSN 2010, February 26-28 (2010)
15. Huanguo, Z., Zhongping, Q., Qi, Y.: esign and Implementation of the TPM Chip J3210. In: 3rd. Asia-Pacific Trusted Infrastructure Technologies Conference (APTC 2008), October 14-17, pp. 72–78 (2008)
16. Kumar, D., Kherani, A.A., Altman, E.: Route lifetime based optimal hop selection in vanet on highway: an analytical viewpoint. IEEE Transactions on Vehicular Technology (2007)
17. Namboodiri, V., Gao, L.: Prediction Based Routing for Vehicular Ad Hoc Networks. In: Proc. of Vehicular Ad Hoc Networks VANET 2004 (2004)
18. Chen, Q., Schmidt-Eisenlohr, F., Jiang, D.: Overhaul of IEEE 802.11 Modeling and Simulation in NS-2 (802.11Ext),
http://dsn.tm.uni-karlsruhe.de/download/
Documentation-NS-2-80211Ext-2008-02-22.pdf
19. Khan, A., Sadhu, S., Yeleswarapu, M.: A comparative analysis of DSRC and 802.11 over Vehicular Ad hoc Networks, Project Report, Department of Computer Science, University of Californai, Santa Barbara (2009)
20. Hartenstein, H., Laberteaux, K.: VANET Vehicular Applications and Inter-Networking Technologies (February 5, 2010)
21. Trusted Computing Group: TPM main specification. Main Specification Version 1.2 rev. 85, Trusted Computing Group (February 2005)

# Technology Resources and E-Commerce Impact on Business Performance

Muhammad Jehangir[1], P.D.D. Dominic[1],
Alan Giffin Downe[2], and Naseebullah[1]

[1] Department of Computer and Information Sciences
[2] Department of Management and Humanities
Universiti Teknologi PETRONAS
Bandar Seri Iskandar, Tronoh Perak, Malaysia
janisbg22@yahoo.com

**Abstract.** Many firms around the world have adopted E-commerce to enhance competitive advantage and business performance. E-commerce is now an important model in today's business environment and is often considered a key dimension in generating a firm value, despite the fact that many firms still have difficulty generating the anticipated returns of E-Commerce technology investments. To date, researchers have attempted to develop range of strategies for E-commerce success but uptake in business environments has proven slow and inconsistent. In this paper we proposed a model that offers a strategic framework for generating value from E-commerce, using technology resources factors, IT infrastructure, IT-human resources to facilitate business outcomes. A regression analysis was performed on survey data from 243 Malaysian firms. Results indicated that technology resources are the key drivers of E-commerce and lead to better business performance.

**Keywords:** E-commerce, Technology resources, Marketing, Business performance.

## 1 Introduction

In using Internet-mediated business strategy, today's organizations need to be more tactically focused than ever before [1]. To gain a competitive advantage, within the digital business environment many firms have chosen to invest in the technologies. Derstyne (2001) defined E-commerce as "business and market processes operations on the internet or World Wide Web technology, it contains a group of technologies to communicate, gather information and conduct business with companies or customers. E-commerce offers opportunities to firms in highly competitive or turbulent market environments and can become a core component of business strategies that generates value by allowing organizations, suppliers, customers and consumers to exchange information about business activities, goods and services [2]. In particular, it has a potential to provide and facilitate an efficient operations of supply chain [3]. Some previous studies have reported that the adoption and usage of this technology requires appropriate strategies and sufficient organizational resources [4], [5]. What is

V. Snasel, J. Platos, and E. El-Qawasmeh (Eds.): ICDIPC 2011, Part II, CCIS 189, pp. 440–447, 2011.

important, however, is not necessarily the size of the resource investment – including financial, technical and human resources – but the manner in which they are assigned strategically and used [6]. It is through the strategic allocation and positioning of complementary resources that firms are able to serve customers effectively and increase productivity [7]. The purpose of this paper is to offer a strategic framework for conceptualizing the relationship between various organizational resources and business performance within firms that have adopted an E-commerce business model. The relative contribution of information technology (IT) and of human resource capabilities to E-commerce implementation and business performance are evaluated, and implications for strategy development are highlighted.

## 2   Theoretical Model and Justification of Hypotheses

It has been well established that a firm's technological capabilities positively contribute to its business performance and that organizational resource is a key to enhancing competitive advantage [7]. The Resource Based View (RBV) and the Dynamic Capabilities Theory (DCT) have been used to highlight the importance of organizational resources. RBV explains that the nature of the resources and its attributes are essential in building strategies [8]. DCT explains that the manner in which a firm's resources are integrated, configured and deployed is instrumental in sustaining its performance within the marketplace [9]. A range of capabilities have been identified to account for the success of IT implementation and the achievement of better strategic performance. However, IT is not capable alone of preserving a firm's competitive advantage, but that it must be complemented with other resources to achieve better results [10].

In this paper we have proposed the theoretical model illustrated in figure 1. This framework is intended to provide a foundation for strategizing about technology resources, E-commerce and their relationships to business performance. The impact of technology and human resources on the perceived effectiveness of E-commerce and reported business performance was evaluated.

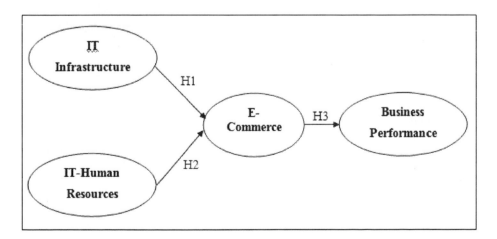

**Fig. 1.** Research Model

## IT Infrastructure

IT infrastructure refers to technologies adopted by the organization. Kohli and Jaworski [11] pointed out that IT infrastructure is a set of tools and capabilities which offer a stage or base for business applications. In other study, IT infrastructure was identified as a successful predictor of technology implementation [12]. Organizations lacking strong IT infrastructure may not take the risk of implementing new technologies [13]. A sound IT infrastructure is the basis for the adoption of new technologies. A firm's IT infrastructure includes the tools which represent the IT resources in which it has invested, including but not necessarily limited to the networking system, computers and their accessories, software, hardware systems, and so on. Several researchers have concluded that a sound IT infrastructure is a positive factor for technology implementation [14], [15], [16], [17]. The successful implementation of E-commerce technology relies on a strong IT infrastructure [18]. Therefore,

H1:  IT infrastructure significantly has a positive relationship with E-commerce capability.

## IT-Related Human Resources

IT-related human resources refer to the skills and know-how of individuals within the firm, with respect to the effective operation of IT effectively for business processes [19]. Organizations with high levels of technically competent users of IT tend to achieve better business performance than firms with lower levels of IT-related human resources [20]. The lack of IT expertise can be a barrier of to technology implementation and usage. Therefore, IT-related human resources should have a positive relationship to the implementation of E-commerce and its use. Therefore,

H2:  IT-related human resources have positive relationship with E-commerce capability

## E-commerce and Business Performance

E-commerce technology can be used in a variety of ways to enhance business performance. It can provide an effective and efficient order processing system, to improve inventory management. It can reduce cost and increase customization the products and services, to enhance consumer satisfaction [21]. It can facilitate timely data exchange and prompt response to customers in online business environments [22]. It can be beneficial to online procurement or sales practices, by creating cost savings, shorter order cycle times and more productive interactions between customers and suppliers [23]. It can also be helpful in enhancing the effectiveness of supply chains by providing real-time information about product or services availability, shipment status, and production obligations [24]. In the present study, E-commerce measured by the firms' website characteristics and richness. Business performance was measured by the financial and non-financial performance of the organizations after the implementation of E-commerce. Therefore,

H4:  E-commerce has a positive relationship with business performance

# 3  Methodology

Survey respondents were drawn from the population of Malaysian manufacturing firms reporting the use of online business. Organizations were randomly selected from an online database of Malaysian firms (www.101panduan.com.my). A total of 500 organizations were chosen for data collection. Online survey distribution was supplemented by the personal administration of surveys in selected cases. After 12 unusable responses were discarded, the response rate was 48.6% (n=243). Surveys were directed to senior management of each organization, with the rationale that these would be the individuals within the firm charged with IT-related decision making responsibilities. Data were then analyzed by using SPSS version 11.5.

# 4  Results and Discussions

## *Sample Characteristics*

Table 1 shows characteristics of firms reported by respondents.

**Table 1.** Company General Information

| General Information | Descriptions | freq |
|---|---|---|
| Full Time Employees | Less than 50 | 45 |
| | 50-100 | 51 |
| | 100-200 | 63 |
| | 200-300 | 49 |
| | 300-500 | 21 |
| | More than 500 | 14 |
| Annual Average Revenue | Less than RM500,000 | 13 |
| | RM500,000-RM1Million | 29 |
| | RM1Million-RM10Million | 64 |
| | RM10Million-RM25Million | 72 |
| | RM25Million-RM50Million | 48 |
| | RM50Million-RM1Billion | 6 |
| | More than RM1Billion | 9 |
| Annual Average EC Transactions | Less than 100,000 | 38 |
| | RM100,000-RM20,000 | 54 |
| | RM200,000-RM50,000 | 81 |
| | RM500,000-RM1Million | 51 |
| | RM1Million-RM10Millions | 16 |
| | More than RM10Millions | 3 |

Results indicated that firms in the sample had a well developed IT infrastructure and good internet facilities.

Table 2 summarizes characteristics of individual respondents. Most respondents were male, well educated and holding key positions.

**Table 2.** Demographics of the respondents

| Respondent's Information | Descriptions | freq |
|---|---|---|
| Gender | Male | 141 |
| | Female | 102 |
| Position | CEO | 55 |
| | Director | 53 |
| | General Manager | 41 |
| | IT Manager | 49 |
| | Business Manager | 45 |
| Education | PhD | 6 |
| | Master | 75 |
| | Bachelor | 125 |
| | Diploma | 47 |

Statistical analyses were performed using SPSS 11.5 to test the reliability of items in the instrument and to test hypotheses.

*Construct reliability*

Cronbach's alpha was calculated to test internal consistency reliability of the survey instrument. It measures the degree to which items are free from random error that may have an effect on the results. Table 3 shows the results of this analysis. All scales achieved an acceptable Cronbach's alpha ($>.70$).

**Table 3.** Construct reliability

| Factors | No of Items | Reliability Analysis Cronbach's alpha |
|---|---|---|
| IT Infrastructure (ITINF) | 8 | 0.701 |
| IT-Human Resources (ITHR) | 11 | 0.712 |
| E-commerce (EC) | 6 | 0.821 |
| Business performance (BPR) | 12 | 0.776 |

*Hypotheses Testing*

All three hypotheses were supported. The results indicate that IT-related human resources and IT infrastructure are the strongest predictors of E-commerce capability. E-commerce also contributes significantly to firms' business performance. These findings are consistent with the RBV [8] and DCT [9] concepts that stresses on the utilization and allocation of the resources for generating competitive advantage. In this study the IT infrastructure and IT-human resources were deployed in E-commerce environment to analyze the firms' business performance. Table 4 shows the regression results of the hypotheses.

**Table 4.** Hypotheses Testing

| Hypothesis and Results | | | | Conclusion | |
|---|---|---|---|---|---|
| $H_1$: ITINF --------> EC | | | | | |
| R | $R^2$ | F | $p$ | | |
| .700 | .490 | 274.10 | .000 | Significant | Supported |
| $H_2$: ITHR -------->EC | | | | | |
| R | $R^2$ | F | $p$ | | |
| .671 | .408 | 232.12 | .000 | Significant | Supported |
| $H_3$: EC ---------> BPR | | | | | |
| R | $R^2$ | F | $p$ | | |
| .584 | .341 | 147.115 | .000 | Significant | Supported |

### $H_1$: T infrastructure and E-commerce capability

To analyze the relationship between IT infrastructure and E-commerce capability the regression analysis was used. The results indicate the F-ratio 274.10 and strong significant level of 0.000, which suggests the positive relationship of IT infrastructure with E-commerce capability. The results also show the R-value is 0.700 and R-square value is 0.462, which shows 46% variance of IT infrastructure is accounted in E-commerce capability.

### $H_2$: IT-human resources and E-commerce capability

Hypothesis $H_2$ was tested to see the relationship of the IT-human resources and E-commerce capability. The results show that there is a positive relationship between the IT-human resources factor and E-commerce capability factor with the F-ratio of 232.12 and p-value 0.00. R-square is .408, which indicates that 40% variance of IT-human resources is accounted in E-commerce capability factor.

### $H_3$: E-commerce capability and Business Performance

Hypothesis $H_3$ was tested to analyze the relationship of the E-commerce capability and business performance. The results indicate the F-ratio 147.115 and significant p-value of 0.00, which suggests the positive relationship between E-commerce capability and business performance. The results also show the R-value is 0.584 and

R-square value is 0.341, which shows 34% variance of E-commerce capability is accounted in business performance.

## 5  Conclusion and Future Work

This study provided a theoretical model that combines the technology resources factors in E-commerce environment to enhance business performance. The significant relationship of all three hypothesis of the study indicates the importance of each factor of the theoretical model. IT infrastructure and IT-human resources shape the E-commerce capability that positively influenced on business performance. The results of this study are also consistent with the concepts of RBV and DCT. Both of the theories explained the importance of the organizational resources. However, this study provides the integration of technology resources and its deployment in E-commerce environment to achieve better outcomes. The results suggest that managers must pay attention to the integration, reconfiguration and allocation of the organizational resources and most importantly to the technology resources in the implementation of E-commerce. This study highlights the importance of the technology resources that would be helpful for the managers in making the decisions and strategies for the use and implantation of E-commerce.

This study is single test of one data sample that collected from the manufacturing industries. It does not include other industry sectors. To test the model in other sector may provide different insights. The theoretical model can be also extended with including other organizational resources for attaining more results and implications.

## References

1. Dowlatshahi, S., Cao, Q.: The relationships among virtual enterprise, information technology, and business performance in agile manufacturing: An industry perspective. European Journal of Operational Research 174, 835–860 (2006)
2. Romero, C.Q.: DiegoRodríguez Rodríguez E-Commerce and efficiency at the firm level. Int. J. Production Economics 126, 299–305 (2010)
3. Leea, S.-G., Koob, C., Nam, K.: Cumulative strategic capability and performance of early movers and followers in the cyber market. International Journal of Information Management 30, 239–255 (2010)
4. Ordanini, A., Rubera, G.: How does the application of an IT service innovation affect firm performance? A theoretical framework and empirical analysis on e-Commerce. Information & Management 47, 60–67 (2010)
5. Barney, J.B.: Firm resources and sustained competitive advantage. Journal of Management 17, 99–120 (1991)
6. Zhuang, Y., Lederer, A.L.: A resource-based view of electronic commerce. Information & Management 43, 251–261 (2006)
7. Broadbenta, M., Weillb, P., Neoc, B.S.: Strategic context and patterns of IT infrastructure capability. Journal of Strategic Information Systems 8, 157–187 (1999)
8. Barney, J.B.: Is the resource-based "view" a useful perspective for strategic management research? Yes. The Academy of Management Review 26(1), 41–56 (2001)

9. Teece, D.J., Pisano, G., Shuen, A.: Dynamic capabilities and strategic management. Strategic Management Journal 18(7), 509–533 (1997)
10. Zott, C.: Dynamic capabilities and the emergence of intraindustry differential firm performance: Insights from a simulation study. Strategic Management Journal 24(2), 97–125 (2003)
11. Broadbent, M., Weill, P., Clair, D.S.: The Implications of Information Technology Infrastructure for Business Process Redesign. MIS Quart. 23(2), 159–182 (1999)
12. Kohli, A.K., Jaworski, B.J.: Market orientation: The construct research propositions, and managerial implications. International Journal of Marketing 54(2), 1–18 (1990)
13. Hui, L.Y.: An Empirical Investigation on the Determinants of E-procurement Adoption in Chinese Manufacturing Enterprises. In: 15th International Conference on Management Science & Engineering, Long Beach USA, pp. 32–37 (2008)
14. Wu, F., Mahajan, V., Balasubramanian, S.: An analysis of e-business adoption and its impacts on business performance. Journal of the Academy of Marketing Science 31, 425–447 (2003)
15. Aik, N.K.: Survey on Electronic Procurement Implementation in Malaysia Construction Companies, Master Thesis, Universiti Teknologi Malaysia (2005)
16. Carayannis, E., Popescu, D.: Profiling a methodology for economic growth and convergence: learning from the EU c-procurement experience for central and eastern European countries. Technovation 25, 1–14 (2005)
17. Harland, C., Caldwell, N., Powell, P., Zheng, J.: Barriers to supply chain information integration: SMEs adrift of eLands. Journal of Operations Management 25, 1234–1254 (2007)
18. Kaliannan, M., Awang, H., Raman, M.: Government purchasing: A review of E-procurement system in Malaysia. The Journal of Knowledge Economy & Knowledge Management IV (2009)
19. Capon, N., Glazer, R.: Marketing and Technology: A Strategic Co alignment. The Journal of Marketing 51(3), 1–14 (1987)
20. Wong, C.H., Sloan, B.: Use of ICT for E-Procurement in the UK Construction Industry: A Survey of SMES Readiness. In: Proceedings of ARCOM Twentieth Annual (2004)
21. Teoa, T.S.H., Ranganathan, C.: Adopters and non-adopters of business-to-business electronic commerce in Singapore. Information & Management 42, 89–102 (2004)
22. Johnston, R.B., Mak, H.C.: An Emerging Vision of Internet-Enabled Supply Chain Electronic Commerce. International Journal of Electronic Commerce 4(4), 43–60 (2000)
23. Zhu, K.: The Complementary of Information Technology Infrastructure and E-Commerce Capability: A Resource-Based Assessment of Their Business Value. Journal of Management Information Systems 21(1), 167–202 (2004)
24. Saffu, K., Walker, J.H.: Strategic value and electronic commerce adoption among small and medium-sized enterprises in a transitional economy. Journal of Business & Industrial Marketing 23(6), 395–404 (2008)

# A Mitigation Approach to the Privacy and Malware Threats of Social Network Services

SeyedHossein Mohtasebi and Ali Dehghantanha

Asia Pacific University College of Technology and Innovation,
Kuala Lumpur, Malaysia
{shmohtasebi,dehqan}@gmail.com

**Abstract.** In the past few years, there has been a substantial growth in the number of users who employ social network services (SNS) for communicating and sharing information with their friends. Notwithstanding many plus points of SNSs, they have some drawbacks which can be potentially misused by perpetrators for their destructive goals. Owing to a massive amount of personal data stored and exchanged on SNSs and the simplicity of gaining access to the vast majority of data using illegitimate methods like social engineering techniques, these services are highly vulnerable to privacy intrusion threats. Moreover, the tremendous number of users of SNSs and a variety of communication features provided by these services, make SNSs as a suitable target for virus authors to employ them for infecting users' machines. This paper investigates threats, vulnerabilities, and risks that endanger privacy of SNS users. It also encompasses techniques used by cybercriminals for propagating malicious software (malware) and launching attacks against victims' machines through these services. The paper eventually presents a set of recommendations to eliminate or mitigate the privacy and malware risks of SNS.

**Keywords:** Social network service; privacy; malware.

## 1 Introduction

Over recent years, the number of SNS users has dramatically increased. At the time of writing only Facebook as one of the prominent SNSs has more than 500 million active users and facebook.com is the second most visited website on the Internet [1,2]. Events happened across the Middle East and North Africa in early 2011 that many of which were organized by SNSs are evident that social networks are not just an entertainment websites, but one the most important and effective communication assets in today's world [3,4,5]. Nonetheless there have been always privacy and secrecy concerns about misusing the uploaded personal information by Internet perpetrators such as cyberstalkers and even adversaries who target an organization that a user works for. Additionally, SNSs are a perfect platform for virus authors to spread their malwares faster than traditional methods since the structure of SNSs is the combination of almost

V. Snasel, J. Platos, and E. El-Qawasmeh (Eds.): ICDIPC 2011, Part II, CCIS 189, pp. 448–459, 2011.

all long-established Internet communications channels like email and instant messaging (IM). Furthermore, some SNSs enable developers to share their applications and as a result, it facilitates distributing malwares that are covered in the form of a useful application.

The main contributions of this paper are to review the privacy and malware threats of SNS to find appropriate methods for mitigating the vulnerabilities and consequently circumventing the identified threats. The remainder of this paper proceeds as follows: Section 2 studies the potential dangers regarding privacy issues within SNS. It also delves into functionality of malwares that employ SNS for propagating themselves or launching attack against third parties' machines. Section 3 offers a holistic approach to reduction the security risks that are caused by the privacy and malware threats of SNS. Finally, the last section concludes this paper and discusses future work.

## 2   Literature Review

In order to eliminate or at least reduce SNS risks, it is important to identify threats that could exploit the vulnerabilities of SNSs. Current SNSs are facing myriad threats; this work is, however, mainly focusing on privacy intrusion and malware infection. This section is intended to review state of the art of the privacy and malware threats of current SNSs.

### 2.1   Privacy Threats

As a general rule, users need to provide SNS with some basic information such as name and email address to create profile. In most SNSs, registered users may invite their friends whether or not they are member of the SNS. Some SNSs also suggest users to provide them with email account name and password to send invitation to all emails saved on their address books. Once a profile is created, the owner of the profile can articulate and share information which is the most particular characteristic of SNS [6]. SNS typically provides users with diverse ways of communications. Users can post public messages in various forms like text, photo etc. on their personal space provided by SNS [7]. Users are also able to privately communicate with their friends who are member of the same SNS by using the features of the SNS like IM [7]. Furthermore, some SNSs host applications which can be employed by participants for simultaneous activities such as online games [7].

In addition to personal profiles and public pages like those made for bands, celebrities, campaigns etc. many organizations take advantage of SNS to advertise their products or services and at the same time to stay in touch with people. With respect to hundreds of millions of users of SNSs and the immense amount of data shared on them, social networks are treasures of personal and corporate data. Over and above SNS which has full access to all data, a lot of data can be garnered by both third parties that transmit data and also cybercriminals who employ social engineering techniques [8,9,10].

G'alvez-Cruz [11] defines privacy as a due that enables users to have (1) control of disclosure, (2) control of personal data, and (3) the right of being left alone. Additionally, Cutillo et al. [10] state that an ideal SNS should fulfill the following privacy requirements:

- End-to-end confidentiality: All interactions are needed to be confidential and only sender and receiver should have access to data;
- Privacy: Personal information of a user should not be disclosed to any party apart from those explicitly mentioned by the user;
- Access control: Users should be able to manage access controls of their profiles as well as attributes of their profiles. Users should be also allowed to grant permission to another user or a group of users;
- Authentication: For satisfying the previous requirements, a receiver of a message should be able to authenticate the sender of the message as well as the attribute message;
- Data integrity: For each exchanged message whether it is a response or a request, origin authentication and also modification detection are needed to be performed;
- Availability: Public data has to be always available and all messages should be delivered at any time.

According to Bonneau et al. [12], SNSs with enhanced privacy policy have better functionality as well as higher growth rate compared to those with inferior privacy strategy. They also observed that long-standing SNSs, in comparison with newer ones, have more extensive privacy policy [12]. This can be concluded that people are more interested in joining SNSs with exhaustive privacy policy and strategy. Overall, the threats of SNS, regarding privacy issues are classified as follows [8,9]:

1. Browsing user activities: Public personal information on users' profiles is vulnerable to be downloaded by third parties such as search engines and social network aggregators and consequently there is a risk of developing a history record of each user over time [8]. Moreover, even after removing a profile, owing to established links to other users, some information such as sent messages may still remain available to users who have been in touch with the removed user [8,9,13]. Furthermore, information about users' online behaviors, like visited profiles, and also the specification of network settings such as the IP address of users' machines may be monitored and logged by Internet service providers (ISP) and other similar third parties [8,9,10]. These vulnerabilities could, by unauthorized access to the recorded data, result in privacy leakage risk.

2. Disclosing user's identity: The majority of SNSs encourage users to share a profile image [6]. Shared uploaded images are vulnerable to be examined by face recognition tools that ascertain the real identity of users who create their profiles under pseudonyms [8]. Additionally, there is a risk that technologies like Content-Based Image Retrieval (CBIR), by inspecting the specifications of an image, could reveal details such as the place which the image was taken

[8,9]. Moreover, many people may not be aware of usage of their personal images or videos by other users within SNSs as in most SNSs users are able to share any images and videos regardless of who in the images or videos are. Users often also give a description of each shared file. Furthermore, some SNSs allow users to tag images of other users and link them to the profiles of the owners of the images which enables visitors to get more details by few clicks [8]. There is, therefore, a high risk of exposing the identity and location of users even sometimes without their knowledge [7].

3. Cyber-stalking, cyber-bullying, harassing, and slandering: The most ideal privacy level is sharing information to only user's friends or a group of users; this rule is, however, vulnerable to cybercriminals who pose themselves as a friend using a fake name and image to gain access to all information shared by nave users [8]. Particularly, many participants desire to be connected to more users and have many friends in their friend list [8] which makes them more vulnerable to cyber-stalking, cyber-bullying, and harassing threats. There is also a risk that stalkers, especially those whose account name has been added to a target user's friend list, could achieve precious information (e.g. date of birth, spouse name, address etc.) from the profile of the victim. Moreover, cybercriminals may keep their targets' activities on SNS under surveillance by constantly browsing profiles [8]. Due to many channels of communication of SNS, culprits have many options for sending offensive messages, images, videos etc. to intrude on victims' private lives. As long as SNSs are vulnerable to creating fraudulent profiles, perpetrators are simply able to create fake profiles and start posting slanders and canards [8].

4. Eavesdropping: Hundreds of millions of users everyday connect to SNSs from mobile devices [1,14]. It is also expected that many users connect to the Internet from public places through vulnerable wireless access points. Additionally, most current SNSs do not provide secure communication layer [15] and as a result of these vulnerabilities, there is a risk of transmitted data being captured by sniffing tools.

5. Penetrating into corporate systems: Hackers reconnoiter any resources that help them to penetrate into their victims' systems and SNS is no exception but a valuable asset that enable them to trace and manipulate employees of target corporation for gaining information [8,9]. A 2010 survey conducted by Sophos found that 59% of employers believe their personnel's behavior on SNS could put their company's security in danger [16].

There are also two architecture styles for managing SNS that impact upon privacy issues. The first style is centralized architecture (aka client-server) which is used by many of the current SNSs [7]. The second style is decentralized architecture (aka peer-to-peer) which implementing that is not as simple as the centralized style [7]. In decentralized architecture users who store their data in different domains can get connected to each other [18]. Users are, thus, able to choose any servers that provide better services including appropriate level of privacy preservation [18]. Above all, in this style users are allowed to keep their information even in their own personal servers [18]. Diaspora [19] is an exemplar of decentralized SNSs.

According to Zhang et al. [7] access control methods of many of the current SNSs are deliberately weak. They also argue that there is a challenge of making a trade-off between privacy and the following factors:

- Social network searching: It is unattainable to hide all the information of a user's profile but allow other users to find the user by social searching [7]. The same is true of traversing friends' profiles [7];
- Social network interaction: There is a privacy breach risk through common friends [7]. Details of users (e.g. school name, interests etc.) might be exposed through the profiles of their friends [7];
- Data mining: SNS data may be studied for analyzing social behaviors which in that social network is considered as graphs and users are their vertexes and relationships are their edges [7,17]. To avoid privacy breach and make data anonymous the usual way is replacing identities of users with meaningless characters [7]. However this approach is quite vulnerable as by exploring information of graph topology there is risk of the exposure of the real identity of the users [7,17]. Removing private data on the other hand, reduces the accuracy of the results [7].

## 2.2   Malware Threats

The large number of users who are widely distributed across the world and joined with one another by trust relationships and also application sharing feature which some SNSs provide altogether make SNSs as an appropriate platform for unlawful activities such as propagating malwares [20]. SNS malwares are generally classified as follows:

1. Spam, hoax, and scam messages: Spammers need to make fraudulent accounts or compromise accounts of existing users to propagate spam messages [21]. Spam messages are sent to users in various ways depending on communication channels of SNS. Additionally, spammers might employ SNS spamming tools and behind fake accounts with attractive names invite users and send hoax and scam messages to victims in an automated fashion [8]. They typically embed a malicious link in each spam message to forward users to a compromised website and infect victims' machines whether by exploiting the vulnerabilities of the installed software on users' machines or running Trojan horses [8,16]. Perpetrator may also comment on users' posts on public pages in order to lure visitors to click on malicious link mentioned in their comments [8]. Moreover, spammers sometimes use URL obfuscation technique for hiding real address of malicious links [21]. Although a spammer usually needs to establish a friendship relation to users before posting any spam message on victims' profile wall, but once the connection is established, there is a high risk that the spammer will have spam message rapidly spread as the victims' friends see the message on their friends' profile rather

than on a strange webpage [22]. Domain blocking [21] is a common method employed by SNSs in order to confront link-spam messages.
2. Malicious application: SNSs that allow developers to share their applications are potentially vulnerable to malicious applications that by using social engineering techniques entice users to run them. These malwares are categorized as follows:

   - Data stealing application: In some SNSs once a user installs an application, the application has access to the considerable amount of their account's information [20]. There is, therefore, a risk that the details of users who install the application could be collected by malware authors [20].
   - Malicious applet: SNSs that are capable of sharing applications with embedded Java applets may make their users vulnerable to malicious Java applets that by using some techniques gain access to the disks of users who have run them [20].
   - Survey scam: For installing these applications users mostly need to grant them the permission of posting messages on their profile's wall [23]. This authorization enables malware to advertise itself using victims' profiles [23]. Once application is installed, by running application and few clicks, victims will be forwarded to a compromised website that tempt visitors into entering their personal information to make money, while filling in the website's form just provides perpetrator with financial benefits [16,23].
   - Distributed denial-of-service (DDoS) attack: In this technique attackers develop applications which include Uniform Resource Identifiers (URI) pointing to resources such as images and videos hosted by victims' servers [20]. When SNS users install and run one of these applications, it starts downloading resources from the victim's server and consequently on a large scale there is a high risk of target server being crashed [20]. At the time of writing, Facebook copies external images that are used by a Facebook application, to its own server, Makridakis et al. [20] have, however, shown that URIs can be embedded in hidden frames for preventing Facebook from copying them.
3. Cross Site Scripting (XSS) attack: In this method, worm authors insert malicious codes to their profiles and once a user visits one of the compromised profiles, without the user interaction, the XSS worm makes the profile of the visitor infected as well and likewise it spreads the worm [24]. These worms may be also distributed by exploiting the vulnerabilities of application programming interfaces (API) whereby users run on their mobile phones to get connected to SNS [25].
4. Command-and-Control (C&C) worm: In this technique, after creating fake profiles manually or automatically by zombies [20], hackers upload their commands which are normally encrypted to the fraudulent profiles [26,27]. When malware developed by the hackers infects a machine it makes a connection to each profile specified in the malware code to get the latest commands [26,27].

A remarkable point to note is that the hackers rely on free legitimate servers and consequently blocking the malware connections and also forensic investigation are more difficult than when they use their own domain name and servers for launching attacks.

5. Phishing attack: Phisher can achieve more accurate details about a user through SNS and apply collected information for personalizing and launching attack against the user [8]. Beyond the numerous communication channels of SNSs, knowing the user's personal information such as their workplace increases the risk of a successful phishing attack as phisher could have more chance to persuade the user into revealing their confidential information.

# 3    Proposed Mitigation Approach

Our proposed recommendations for dealing with current SNS threats are divided into four parts as follows: (1) user education and awareness, (2) privacy preservation strategies, (3) surveillance and ascertainment, and (4) application evaluation and code review which are explained in the rest of this section.

## 3.1    User Education and Awareness

As we have seen in the previous section most of the SNS threats rely on social engineering techniques. Hence educating users and simplifying privacy settings and warning messages are effective ways to avoid users from being deceived. Additionally, providing non-English users with translated privacy policy, terms of use, and privacy protection settings which has been implemented in some SNSs like Facebook is an invaluable effort in making all users aware of privacy intrusion threats and hinder the expose of the user identity. Furthermore, it is advised that legislation on illegal activities that can be potentially committed within SNS such as propagating spam messages, harassment etc., to be delineated in privacy policy and terms of use pages. It is suggested that in addition to international related law, in each country voluntary institutions or organizations collect and organize domestic Acts and legislation and provide them for all SNSs to be published on their websites. It may thwart some, but not all, perpetrators like cyber-stalkers and most importantly, it makes users familiar with their legal rights in cyberspace and in SNS in particular.

Sending out straightforward security newsletters on a regular schedule and warning users about malwares that are in progress as well as common social engineering techniques may impede the distribution of spam messages, malicious applications, and phishing attacks.

Additionally, educating employees to know how to safely use SNS without exposing any data pertaining to the companies they work for, rather than obligating them not to use SNS can reduce the risk of corporate data leakage. SNS can prepare a set of guidelines to be employed by companies for educating their personnel in regard to SNS surfing.

## 3.2     Privacy Preservation Strategies

When it comes to privacy preservation, the decentralized architecture outdoes the centralized style. It must be taken into consideration that any chosen architecture should, as far as possible, meet the privacy requirements cited in Subsection 2.1.

It is also recommended that all data on a user who deletes their account are permanently removed. This includes information that was posted or uploaded by deleted participant earlier and currently is stored on other profiles or pages that the user used to be in touch with them.

Moreover, there are some de-identification techniques [8,28] that SNS may employ against face recognition tools. SNS should warn users about the potential risks of using personal image on their profiles. Furthermore, users who want to have their profile kept secluded should be able to ensconce all their personal data stored on SNS including profile names and images from social searching, aggregators, and friends of friends. It is also advised that tagging another user requires the permission of the user who is tagged. Not to mention the user should be able to remove the tag anytime. Additionally, algorithms that insure preservation of edge anonymity should be used in social network graphs in order to keep users' identities confidential.

With respect to eavesdropping threat, all data transmitted between SNS and users need to be encrypted and secured by protocols like the Transport Layer Security (TLS). Although using these protocols might slow down the transmission process, but applying secure protocols should not be restricted to the login phase as many users may connect to SNS and transfer their personal information from public places using wireless access points. Many activities of users on SNS will be protected from intermediate third parties and sniffers if transmitted data is encrypted by secure protocols.

It should be noted that proper procedures are needed to be followed for securing and protecting SNS networks and data stored on its storage systems.

## 3.3     Surveillance and Ascertainment

It is advised that public pages are grouped into two categories namely, official and unofficial. For creating an official page, user has to provide SNS with more details to prove the page would belong to the same individual or organization. Pages marked as official need to be listed in SNS search result higher than unofficial ones and visitors should be informed that there is no assurance for authenticity of unofficial pages. The same pattern can be applied to normal users. Since 2009 Twitter has implemented a similar method for background check of its prominent users [29]. Categorizing profiles and pages as official and unofficial can reduce the number of the visitors of the fake profiles and as spammers and virus authors employ fraudulent profiles to distribute spam messages and application malwares, this method may hinder the propagation progress. SNS can also organize volunteers in different fields such as art, politics etc. and they explore the authenticity of public pages that their owners have requested for official mark.

The common method for dealing with cyber-bullying and harassment messages is removing sender by offended user. Users should nevertheless be able to report incident and SNS needs to take serious actions against offenders like blocking their profile account. SNS may specify that they might provide information to law enforcement agencies and authorized forensic experts for investigation purposes if an offended user files a formal complaint and search warrant is issued. Conversely, SNS should not violate the freedom of speech and the privacy of any users aside from offender.

Furthermore, beyond the existence of a mechanism for blocking fake accounts, users should be able to report comment-spam messages as well. SNS needs to block full URL address of spam-link instead of all addresses that start with the same domain name. It is also suggested that when the number of times that the same message has been sent to users reaches a predetermined value, SNS provides new users who receive the message with a statistics options that specify the number of users who have reported the message as spam. It is obvious that this value should be far less than the value that SNS considers for blocking spam messages.

Finding profiles compromised with C&C commands is not an easy task as hackers may use common words that any other users might enter in their profile. However hackers often make numerous profiles and right after that thousands connections are made to their profiles. It is not unusual thousands users visit a profile but when lots of connections are made to a profile which its age is only few hours, SNS can employ methods like Completely Automated Public Turing Test To Tell Computers and Humans Apart (CAPTCHA) [30] to verify whether the profile is requested by a human or a computer program. Virus' authors may, however, handle the situation by either increasing connection time interval of zombies or limiting the number of zombies that connect to a profile. Consequently, it is necessary for SNS to frequently examine the functionality of new C&C malwares or have agreements with computer security companies to get rigorous information concerning this kind of malwares and update the connection limitation control.

### 3.4   Application Evaluation and Code Review

With regard to malicious applications, the most sophisticated solution is that SNS experts investigate applications including their source codes before they are shared. Applications should have access to users' details as little as possible. It is advised that SNS fully informs users about data that may be collected by the requested application. Moreover, there should be a feature that allows users to report suspicious behaviors of applications. Not to mention users need to be able to delete any applications anytime. There should be also proper procedures that enable third parties that their servers are under attack of SNS application to report incidents.

XSS worms have been one of the most challenging malwares on the Internet. Unless the codes of all webpages and web applications are examined and tested thoroughly, SNS are very vulnerable to XSS worms and other types of cyber attacks like SQL injection. Thus rather than enabling users to add scripts like JavaScript codes, SNS can provide them with graphical user interfaces (GUI) that allow user to design their profiles without having access to page codes. Furthermore, GUIs' functionalities and all codes of default templates need to be tested for any vulnerability before being accessible to users. Code testing and preventing users having direct access to their profiles' codes are the finest way for dealing with XSS worms. Application testing can also reduce the number of SNS malwares like data stealing applications, malicious applets, survey scams, and those used for DDoS attacks.

Table 1 summarizes the threats that are addressed by the recommendations of this work. Although the proposed mitigation approach relies on having many regulators who constantly support users, audit public pages, and test applications, but it is believed significant parts of these jobs can be done by voluntary users.

**Table 1.** The proposed mitigation approach in relation to the identified threats

| Threat | Education and Awareness | Privacy Strategies | Surveillance | Application Evaluation |
|---|---|---|---|---|
| Browsing user activities | X | X | X | |
| Disclosing user identity | X | X | | |
| Harassing and slandering | X | | X | |
| Eavesdropping | | X | | |
| Penetrating into corporation | X | | | |
| Unsolicited message | X | | X | |
| Malicious application | X | | X | X |
| XSS worm | | | | X |
| C&C worm | | | X | |
| Phishing attack | X | | X | |

## 4   Conclusion and Future Work

It has been discussed that current privacy policies are not comprehensive enough and there are many vulnerabilities that perpetrators can exploit them to get access to shared personal information of users. Additionally, SNSs especially those that provide users with application sharing feature can be misused for malware and spam propagation. The work presents a mitigation approach to preserving users' data as well as deterring virus authors to distribute malwares through SNS. Although the proposed approach complies with the definition of privacy cited in Section 2, but this work has some weaknesses in addressing privacy preservation. Further research should be conducted into preventing shared personal information from being downloaded by users who have view permission to the profile of the owner of the information. Moreover, the criteria of courts to have jurisdiction over SNS-related cases whereby SNSs should be subject to their judgments are open to dispute. We will continue to improve the mitigation approach and we hope that the work will eventually, by further research, lead to a comprehensive framework of secure SNS.

# References

1. Statistics Facebook (2011),
   http://www.facebook.com/press/info.php?statistics
2. Facebook.com Site Info (2011), www.alexa.com/siteinfo/facebook.com
3. Giglio, M.: Tunisia Protests: The Facebook Revolution (2011),
   http://news.yahoo.com/s/dailybeast/20110115/ts_dailybeast/
   1186_tunisaproteststhefacebookrevolution
4. Hauslohner, A.: Is Egypt About to Have a Facebook Revolution? (2011),
   www.time.com/time/world/article/0,8599,2044142,00.html
5. Giglio, M.: Inside Egypt's Facebook Revolt (2011),
   www.newsweek.com/2011/01/27/inside-egypt-s-facebook-revolt.html
6. Boyd, D.M., Ellison, N.B.: Social network sites: definition, history, and scholarship. Journal of Computer-Mediated Communication 13(1) (2007)
7. Zhang, C., Sun, J., Zhu, X., Fang, Y.: Privacy and security for online social networks: challenges and opportunities. IEEE Network 24(4), 13–18 (2010)
8. Hogben, G.: Security Issues and Recommendations for Online Social Networks, Position Paper. ENISA, European Network and Information Security Agency (2007)
9. Huber, M., Mulazzani, M., Weippl, E.: Social networking sites security: Quo Vadis, Social Computing (SocialCom). In: 2010 IEEE Second International Conference, pp. 1117–1122 (2010)
10. Cutillo, L.A., Molva, R., Strufe, T.: Privacy preserving social networking through decentralization, Wireless On-Demand Network Systems and Services. In: WONS 2009: Sixth International Conference, pp. 145–152 (2009)
11. G'alvez-Cruz, D.C.: An environment for protecting the privacy of e-shoppers, Ph.D. dissertation, Department of Computing Science, University of Glasgow (2009)
12. Bonneau, J., Preibusch, S.: The Privacy Jungle: On the Market for Privacy in Social Networks. In: Eighth Workshop on the Economics of Information Security, WEIS (2009)
13. Privacy Policy Facebook (2011), www.facebook.com/policy.php
14. Wu, C.: A Better Mobile Experience (2011),
   http://blog.facebook.com/blog.php?post=496520902130
15. Huber, M., Mulazzani, M., Weippl, E., Kitzler, G., Goluch, S.: Friend-in-the-middle Attacks: Exploiting Social Networking Sites for Spam, Internet Computing. IEEE, Los Alamitos (2011)
16. Sophos security threat report 2011 (2011),
   https://secure.sophos.com/securitywhitepapers/
   sophos-security-threat-report-2011-wpna
17. Zhang, L., Zhang, W.: Edge Anonymity in Social Network Graphs. In: CSE 2009:International Conference on Computational Science and Engineering, vol. 4, pp. 1–8 (2009)
18. Seong, S. W., Seo, J., Nasielski, M., Sengupta, D., Hangal, S., Teh, S.K., Chu, R., Dodson, B., Lam, M. S.: Preserving Privacy with PrPl: a Decentralized Social Networking Infrastructure (2010), http://prpl.stanford.edu/papers/pets10.pdf

19. Diaspora, https://joindiaspora.com
20. Makridakis, A., Athanasopoulos, E., Antonatos, S., Antoniades, D., Ioannidis, S., Markatos, E.P.: Understanding the behavior of malicious applications in social networks. IEEE Network 24(5), 14–19 (2010)
21. Thomas, K., Nicol, D.M.: The Koobface botnet and the rise of social malware. In: 2010 5th International Conference on Malicious and Unwanted Software (MAL-WARE), pp. 63–70 (2010)
22. Robertson, M., Pan, Y., Yuan, B.: A social approach to security: using social networks to help detect malicious web content. In: 2010 International Conference on Intelligent Systems and Knowledge Engineering (ISKE), pp. 436–441 (2010)
23. Cluley, G.: How to clean up your Facebook profile after a survey scam (2010), www.youtube.com/watch?v=0r-qR0Y300w
24. Faghani, M.R., Saidi, H.: Malware propagation in Online Social Networks. In: 2009 4th International Conference on Malicious and Unwanted Software (MALWARE), pp. 8–14 (2009)
25. Wueest, C.: New XSS Facebook Worm Allows Automatic Wall Posts (2011), http://www.symantec.com/connect/blogs/new-xss-facebook-worm-allows-automatic-wall-posts
26. Cybercriminals Now Using Public Social Networks to Give Command and Control Orders to Banking Trojans (2010), http://blogs.rsa.com/rsafarl/cybercriminals-now-using-public-social-networks-to-give-command-and-control-orders-to-banking-trojans
27. Fisher, D.: Attackers Moving to Social Networks for Command and Control (2010), http://threatpost.com/en_us/blogs/attackers-moving-social-networks-command-and-control-071910
28. Agrawal, P., Narayanan, P.J.: Person De-identification in Videos. IEEE Transactions on Circuits and Systems for Video Technology (99) (2011)
29. McCarthy, C.: Twitter power players get shiny 'verified' badges (2009), http://news.cnet.com/8301-13577_3-10263759-36.html
30. The Official CAPTCHA Site, www.captcha.net

# Cooperative Multiagents Detection and Beamforming with Spherical Array Sensors

Belkacem Benadda and Fethi Tarik Bendimerad

Dept. of Electrical and Electronic Engineering,
University of Abou Bekr Belkaid,
BP 230 Pole Chetouane 13000
Tlemcen Algeria
{benadda.belkacem, ftbendimerad}@gmail.com

**Abstract.** In this paper multi-agents systems are presented as a new design paradigm that allows an efficient use of multiprocessor architectures and distributed systems architectures currently widely available and preferred. Moreover, in our case, multiagent systems will bring the concepts of artificial intelligence, collaboration principles, autonomy, proactive behavior and communications possibility. Adopting a multiagent approach on spherical array sensors for both sources detection and spatial filtering will provide several issues: simultaneous several signals acquisition, effective spatial filttering, optimal performance under the imposed environment circumstances and prompt reaction and treatment.

**Keywords:** Array Sensors, Acquisition, Beam-forming, Space filtering, source detection, multiagent systems.

## 1 Introduction

The world is observed through sensors. Their objective consists on the transformation of specified physical entity into electrical signal. The measurement of physical entity is often masked by the perception of other undesirable phenomena, called noise [1-6]. The signals spectral characteristics can be used for discrimination and selection between useful signal and undesired signals [1-6] (see Fig.1). This technique can be used, only if the useful signal and the noises have distinct frequential bands. This situation is not satisfied in all cases. Often useful signal and noises have encroached frequential bands and the frequential filter cannot be effective (see Fig.2) [1-6].

On the other hand, if in an environment, signals share the same frequency band they have certainly, for a given observer, different arrival directions [6-12]. Indeed, it is practically impossible that two information sources operate in the same frequency band and have the same geometrical coordinates. The purpose of this work is to create a complete multiagents system able to detect environmental sources and listen to them simultaneously. In our case, multiagent systems are presented as new paradigm used to design intelligent independent systems. To accomplish this specific task, several agents with different goals, must cooperate on the system. In this paper we are using

V. Snasel, J. Platos, and E. El-Qawasmeh (Eds.): ICDIPC 2011, Part II, CCIS 189, pp. 460–469, 2011.

spherical array sensors combined with multiagents system. By this system we are implementing cooperating agents for detection and beamforming.

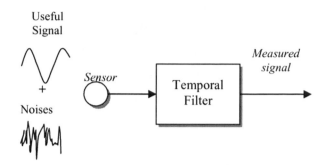

**Fig. 1.** The temporal acquisition diagram [5,6]

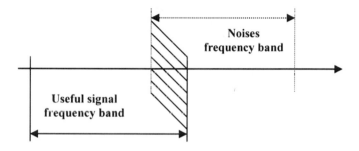

**Fig. 2.** The temporal acquisition limitation [5,6].

## 2  Array Sensors Modeling

Array sensors are formed with multiple elementary sensors, each one with a geometrical position in space and considered as independent observer in respect to a well-defined origin as shown in Fig.3 [5,7-12]. Arbitrary spherical array sensors architecture is shown on Fig.4. Each sensor provides a measure, if the array is composed with "N" sensors then the overall answer of the array will be writes in vectorial form by (1) [5,7]:

$$X(t)=\begin{pmatrix} x_1(t) \\ x_2(t) \\ \vdots \\ x_N(t) \end{pmatrix} \tag{1}$$

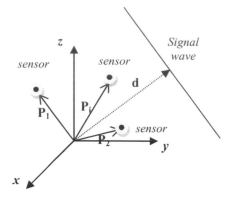

**Fig. 3.** Array sensors general disposition [5,7].

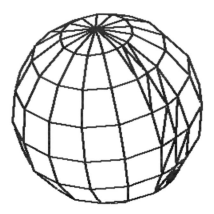

**Fig. 4.** Sensors disposition on spherical array

## 2.1 Propagation Channel Modeling

The propagation channel is defined as the medium used by the different signals between transmitters and receivers [1,13,14]. Ideal connection is achieved if the received signal is exclusively the same as the emitted one without distortion. Alas, in reality the channel will alter the signals by adding: noise, attenuation, fading, absorption, dispersion, refraction, reflection, Faraday rotation, glitter, Dependence of polarization, Doppler Effect, and multipath (see Fig.5) [1,13,14].

We have used the block diagram model shown on Fig.6, to simulate the channel effects. In this diagram, we modeled the multipath, fading and time propagation effects by equation (2) based on narrowband signals [2].

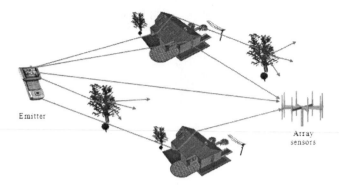

**Fig. 5.** The channel: fading, absorption, dispersion, refraction, reflection and multipath, effects

$$h(t, \tau) = \sum_{i=1}^{N} x(t) e^{j\varphi_i(t)} \delta(\tau - \tau_i(t)) \tag{2}$$

With $x(t)$ signal from the emitter, $\varphi_i(t)$ path rank $i$ propagation phase shift, $\tau_i(t)$ time propagation delay associated with path rank $i$.

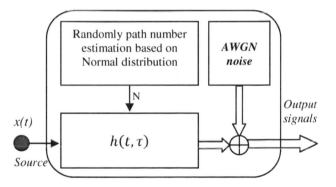

**Fig. 6.** Implementation synoptic for channel: multipath, fading, propagation delays and noise effects

## 2.2 Array Sensors Signals Specifications

The array response, detailed by equation (3), is a linear composition of the noise $B(t)$ and $S_i(t)$ the incident signals on the array sensors. Obviously, based on the channel model, the number of incident signals "$L$" is greater than the source number.

$$X(t) = \sum_{i=1}^{L} S_i(t) \tag{3}$$

For any signal $S_i(t)$, the various sensors outputs are identical except a certain delay which corresponds to the wave propagation time [5,12]:

$$S_i(t) = \begin{bmatrix} s_i(t - \tau_1) \\ s_i(t - \tau_2) \\ \vdots \\ s_i(t - \tau_M) \end{bmatrix} \qquad (4)$$

with "$M$" the array sensors number.

If we know signal $S_i(t)$ arrival direction specified by the unit vector "$d$" (see Fig.3), the various propagation delays can be estimated by (see Fig.7) [5]:

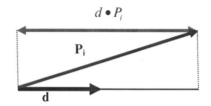

**Fig. 7.** Vector Pi dot product projection principle to estimate sensor rank i time propagation delay [5]

$$\tau_i = \frac{d \bullet P_i}{c} \qquad (5)$$

where "$c$" is the propagation velocity and vector "$Pi$" the sensor rank $i$ position.

## 3   The Detection Strategy

In our case the array sensors detection problem is formulated by two points:

- the estimation of the incident signals number "$L$",
- the different arrival directions determination.

To carry out spatial signals separation. Fig.8 describes the strategy we have adopted. The different phases, proposed and implemented, with our strategy are describe on the following sections.

### 3.1   Treatment and Data Alignment Phases

In this work we have considered only narrow band signals; the treatment phase will implement a passband filter. However, the alignment phase will perform an amplitude normalization to cope with the channel attenuation phenomena. Practically this is done through an emitter power control [10].

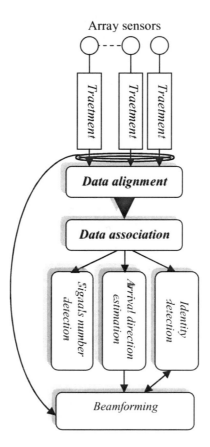

**Fig. 8.** The different phases adopted on the detection spatial filtering strategy

### 3.2 Data Association Phase

In this phase we will regroup the measures from different "M" sensors in a single entity. According to equations (4) and (5) we can write:

$$X(t) = \sum_{i=1}^{L} s_i(t) \times S_i \qquad (6)$$

where $S_i$ denote the array space vector. With narrow band assumption, the array space vector expressed by equation:

$$S_i = \begin{bmatrix} e^{-j\varphi_1} \\ e^{-j\varphi_2} \\ \vdots \\ e^{-j\varphi_M} \end{bmatrix} \tag{7}$$

with $|\varphi_m| \leq \pi$ propagation phase delay. The matrix notation of the array response can be written by:

$$X(t) = A.[s_1(t) \quad s_2(t) \quad \cdots \quad s_L(t)]^T \tag{8}$$

where "$A$" denote the array manifold matrix (9):

$$A = [S_1 \quad S_2 \quad \cdots \quad S_L] \tag{9}$$

It is now possible to calculate the correlation matrix "$R$" associated with the measures from the two last phases by (10), which can be expressed with the manifold matrix by the equation (11).

$$R = E\{X(t).X(t)^H\} \tag{10}$$

$$R = A.S.A^H + R_{GWN} \tag{11}$$

where "$R_{GWN}$" the noise correlation matrix. This matrix is diagonal expressed by (12).

$$R_{GWN} = A.(\sigma^2.I).A^H \tag{12}$$

In this case $\sigma^2$ represent the noise variance, considered the same as the noise power.

The association phase will estimate the correlation matrix "$R$" from the different sensors outputs and in a limited observation time "$k$". The estimated matrix is carried out by [2-4]:

$$\hat{R} = \frac{1}{K}\sum_{k=1}^{K} X(k).X(k)^H \tag{13}$$

For important "$k$" values, the matrix "$\hat{R}$" is considered as a good approximation.

### 3.3 Detection and Beamforming Phases

The detection phase based on the preceding ones, is divided onto three parts:

- Incident signals number detection,
- Detection of signals arrival directions,
- Identity detection, this part is introduced to correct the multipath effect by removing redundant signals,

The various sensors responses within the network must be combined by a suitable processing method in order to spatially extract the signals on the different detected directions [7-12]. Indeed, the detection result, specially the detected incident directions, will be used to implement spatial filtering approach based on a quadratic error optimization algorithm [4,7]. The beamforming phase, after acquisition and demodulation, cooperate with the identity detection to remove redundant signals or improve the acquisition quality.

## 4  Multiagents Implementation

Multiagents systems with the characteristics of artificial intelligence, collaborations, proactivity, autonomy, and data exchange capabilities, provide us, an interesting opportunity to implement the above strategy. The predominant behavior implemented on our multiagent system is shown on Fig.9.

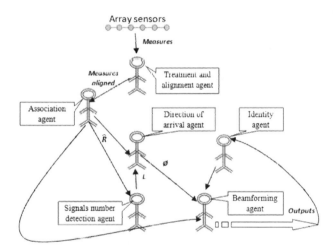

**Fig. 9.** The proposed predominant behavior for our multiagents system

## 5  Simulations and Results

We have done simulations for different array sensors architectures. We present in Fig.10 the beam patterns for 144 sensors spherical array; the signals arrival directions are imposed to [-148° -78° ; -25° 10°; -15° 30°; 45° 70°; 80° 110°]. In this case the system automatically detects the sources. Fig.10 shows that we have five simultaneous acquisition and space filtering on random jam directions.

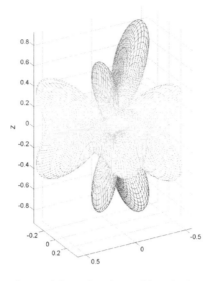

**Fig. 10.** Multagents detection and beamforming, with spherical regular array 144 sensors. [-148° -78° ; -25° 10°; -15° 30°; 45° 70°; 80° 110°] as signals arrival directions

A second application involves 60 microphones as a spherical and regular array. In this second case we want to measure a source with (45° 45°) as the useful direction. The result (see Fig. 11) shows the effective filtering performed by our mutliagents system.

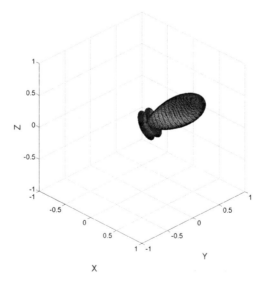

**Fig. 11.** Multagents detection and beamforming, with spherical regular array 60 microphones. [45°, 45°] the direction of the useful signal

# 6 Conclusion

The results presented in this paper, show that the proposed multiagents systems with spherical array sensors architecture has ensure effective cooperation between the different detection and beamforming techniques. This cooperation allowed in the same time the source number detection and the directions of arrival detection,

As well as the ability to perform simultaneous acquisition of several mobile and transient environment sources avoiding duplication caused by the channel multipath effect.

# References

1. Kirianaki, N.V., Yurish, S.Y., Shpak, N.O., Deynega, V.P.: Data acquisition and signal processing for smart sensors. John Wiley & Sons, Chichester (2007)
2. Coulon, F.: Theorie et traitement des signaux, PPUR (1996)
3. Kunt, M.: Techniques modernes de traitement numerique des signaux, Vol.1, PPUR (1991)
4. Manolakis, D.G., Ingle, V.K., Kogon, S.M.: Statistical and adaptive signal processing spectral estimation, signal modeling, adaptivefiltering, and array processing. Artech House, Boston (2005)
5. Benadda, B.: Réseaux de neurones pour l'adaptation de réseaux de capteurs, thèse de magistère d'électronique option signaux et systèmes, Faculté des sciences de l'ingénieur (2001)
6. Benadda, B., Bendimerad, F.T.: Multiagent linear array sensors modelling, Communications in Computer and Information Science part 2, vol. 88, pp. 366–375. Springer, Heidelberg (2010)
7. Benadda, B., Bendimerad, F.T.: Quadratic error optimization algorithm applied to 3D space distributed array sensors. Journal of Applied Sciences Research, 1320–1324 (October 2009)
8. Robert, J.M.: Phased array theory and technology. Proceedings of the IEEE 70(3), 246–302 (1982)
9. Winters, H.: Smart antennas for wireless systems. IEEE Personal Communications 1, 23–27 (1998)
10. Robert, J.M.: Phased array antenna handbook. Artech House, Boston (2005)
11. Krim, H., Viberg, M.: Two decades of array signal processing research. IEEE Signal Processing Magazine, 67–94 (July 1996)
12. Prabhakar, S.N.: Sensor array signal processing. CRC Press, Boca Raton (2000)
13. Vern, A.D.: Wireless data technologies. John Wiley & Sons, Chichester (2003)
14. Jay Guo, Y.: Advances in mobile radio access networks. Artech House, Boston (2004)

# New Method: Mapping of 802.11e into MPLS Domains, Conception and Experimentation

Jawad Oubaha, Adel Echchaachoui,
Ali Ouacha, and Mohammed Elkoutbi

SI2M Laboratory,
RIS Team ENSIAS Rabat, Morocco
Jawadoubaha@yahoo.fr, adel@aznet.ma,
ouacha_ali@yahoo.fr, elkoutbi@ensias.ma

**Abstract.** Mapping between two heterogeneous networks, Multi Protocol Label Switching (MPLS) and IEEE 802.11e is choice of future technology as it has ability to perform traffic engineering and create the corresponds between LSP (Label Switch Path) and AC (Access Category). This paper discusses the mapping between IEEE 802.11 MPLS integration to achieve quality of service on MPLS networks. MPLS and 802.11e is very useful approach for today's internet to ensure the Quality of service the end to end. It talks about different approaches to map 802.11e Access Categories (AC) to Label Switched Path (LSP) and their advantages. It then introduces the concept of encapsulated LSPs to achieve future QoS, which requires further study to examine its practicability.

**Keywords:** MPLS, 802.11e, Mapping, Access Category (AC),Type of Service (ToS), Forward Equivalent Class (FEC) and Label.

## 1 Introduction

The Wireless Applications are increasingly used in the business world and also the transmission of real time and multimedia traffic over the IP network [1][2].

This situation requires the differentiation of services between users by the resource sharing and assigning of priority, consequently the quality of service the end to end assured. Best effort is a IP network service in which the network doesn't provide any guarantees that a data packet is received or that a user is given a guaranteed quality of service level or a priority. IP network is trying to improve its transmission and find solutions to adapt to this growing demand by providing different services like VoIP (Voice over IP) [13] [14], Differentiated Service (DiffServ), and MPLS (Multi Protocol Label Switching), and also provide the new technology that supports quality of service as IEEE 802.11e wireless network. Section 2.A explains 802.11e. In order to manage the packet data and exploit the backup paths, MPLS gives the differentiated services and the speed of layer 2 switching lacked in IP network. MPLS is a promising solution to take over the next generation IP networks Section 2.B explains the MPLS. MPLS can be combined with IEEE 802.11e to provide quality of service

V. Snasel, J. Platos, and E. El-Qawasmeh (Eds.): ICDIPC 2011, Part II, CCIS 189, pp. 470–483, 2011.

along with traffic engineering as both have many notions of treatment in common. Section 3 explains the IEEE 802.11e MPLS networks. Section 4: Discussion, describes the concept of encapsulated LSP for future QoS needs. Then section 5 experimentation of model L-LSP_E-LSP  and Section 6 concludes the paper..

# 2  Mapping Context

## 2.1  QoS Support Mechanism of IEEE 802.11e

To differentiate service depending its priority, there are wireless priority schemes currently under discussion. IEEE 802.11 Task Group E currently defines some enhancements in the MAC level, called 802.11e, which introduces EDCF and EPCF[3]. Stations, which operate under 802.11e, are called enhanced stations, and an enhanced Access Point, which may optionally work as the centralized controller for all other stations within the same BSS, is called the Hybrid Coordinator (HC). BSS includes an 802.11e-compliant HC and stations. The HC will typically reside  within an 802.11e AP. In the next paragraph, we discuss 802.11e-compliant enhanced stations by stations. The EDCF is used in the CP only, while the EPCF is used in both phases, which creates this new coordination function hybrid.

### Enhanced Distributed Coordination Function

EDCF is an enhanced version of DCF also using the CSMA / CA. The contention access method to the channel is called EDCA (Enhanced Distributed Channel Access) The enhancements EDCF are described below[3]:

- EDCF provides service differentiation by introducing four access classes AC (Access Category) representing 4 priorities with different parameters, which will be seen in detail later.
- 8 priorities, TC (Traffic Category) according to IEEE 802.1D are mapped on the 4 AC(Fig. 1).
- No stations (specifically entity AC) can occupy the channel during longer than a certain limit. By introducing the concept of TXOP [AC] (Transmission Opportunity) representing a time interval during which backoff entity (corresponding to an AC) has the right to emit. Called the TXOP EDCA-TXOP [4]is defined by its initial time and duration. Its maximum TXOPlimit is uniformly distributed in the QBSS (QoS BSS) in each Beacon. The TXOP can thus limit the transmission times in order provide a certain QoS.
- No entity has the right to exceed the value of TBTT. This means, that during CP transmission of a frame, can only to take place if the complete transmission can to occur before the arrival of the next beacon (separated from the previous TBTT) [5]. In this way the delays beacon will be monitored and the time constraints flows better verified.
- If the same station in the early transmission of two streams of two entities coincide, we have a virtual collision is the priority flow is issued.
- Possibility of direct exchange of frames between two stations without going through the AP, using the protocol DLP (Direct Link Protocol) [6].

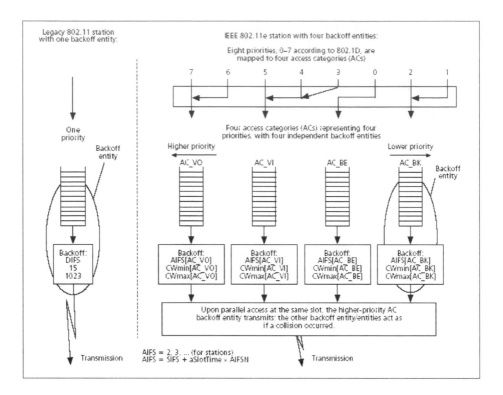

**Fig. 1.** 802.11 and 802.11e stations with four ACs by station

## Access Categories (AC) parameters in EDCA

- Four AC with different parameters exist with EDCA, they are designated by the flows that use them: AC_VO (voice), AC_VI (video) AC_BE (Best Effort), and AC_BK (Background).
- Replaces DIFS (Distributed Inter Frames Spacing) by AIFS [AC] (Arbitration IFS), with:
  AIFS [AC] =SIFS + **AIFSN** [AC] x SlotTime where **AIFSN** [AC] $\geq 2$ ,
  With AIFS [AC] $\geq$ DIFS and AIFSN [AC] has the lowest value for the highest priority (Audio=video
    <data.) (Fig. 2)
- CWmin [AC] and CWmax [AC] vary with the AC (Audio <Video <Data).
- Persistence Factor PF, in the first, differs by AC, then set the value by 2:
  with CWnew = (CWold +1) x PF -1.

As in DCF access, the backoff has to wait for the medium being idle for AIFS, when the medium is determined busy which the counter reaches zero, the counter continue to count down with AIFS again A big difference from the legacy DCF is that when the medium is determined as being idle for the period of AIFS, the backoff counter is reduced by one beginning the last time interval of the AIFS period. however in the legacy DCF, the backoff counter is reduced by one beginning the first slot time after the DIFS period. After any transmission failure attempt a new CW is calculated with using of the persistence factor PF[TC], enlarged CW is drawn, to minimize the probability of a new collision. then in legacy 802.11 CW is always doubled after any failure access as PF equivalent to 2[3].

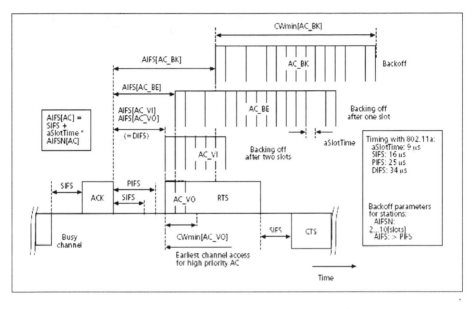

**Fig. 2.** Parameters for different priorities in EDCA

### Hybrid Coordination Function

HCF (Enhanced Point Coordination Function) describes more rules than EDCF offering more control of transmissions. The HCF allocates bandwidth and transmission opportunities (TXOPs) using a hybrid coordinator (HC) that gets the highest access priority. HCF uses a centralized polling with a approach similar to PCF. During Contention Period, each TXOP starts as defined by the EDCF rules, after AIFS backoff time, or when the station receives from the HC a special poll frame, assigned as the QoS Contention-Free (CF)-Poll. The HC sends this QoS CF-Poll after it listen for the wireless media to be idle for PIFS. The QoS CF-Poll specifies TXOP, during this time interval the station has the right to transmit. During the Contention Free Period, only the polled station is authorized to transmit. The CFP ends after the time announced by a CF-End frame from the HC or in the beacon frame or[3][6].

HCF is an enhanced version of the principle of the PCF. It has the following additional properties:

- PCF works only for the CFP, while HCF works in the CFP and the CP, hence the name of Hybrid.
- Provides a management policies and a deterministic channel access by controlling the channel by the hybrid coordinator HC (Hybrid Coordinator).

- Detecting the channel as being free for PIFS, is shorter than AIFS, gives the HC high priority on EDCF, which allows it to issue even during the CP.
- HCF model can to provide guaranteed services with higher probability than pure EDCF.
- A signaling protocol can be used to facilitate admission control and to specify the flow needs.

As for EDCA TXOP (EDCF access) is limited so HCCA (HCF access) can provide the better service in the required time. The TXOP in HCCA-TXOP is called polled, it is allocated by the HC, and is limited by TXOPlimit.

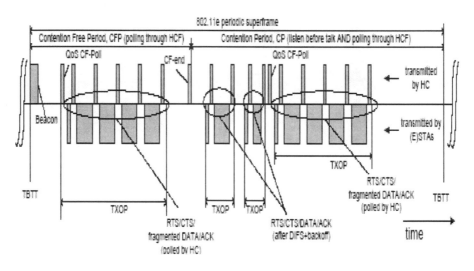

**Fig. 3.** 802.11e superframe. Using TXOP. The polled-TXOP exist in CP andCFP

In order to provide quantitative QoS services, HCF requires a signaling process that informs the HC about the transmission requirements of each traffic stream at each station. Using this information, the HC will determine which stations need to be polled, when, and which TXOP should be granted. TXOP is granted per-station—that is, the HC does not specify which traffic stream should be transmitted on the channel. It is up to the station to select the traffic stream to be transmitted.

## 2.2 Multi Protocol Label Switching

MPLS is a new technology, developed and standardized by the IETF, using mechanisms switching labels intended to reduce the cost of routing network layer while giving it better performance, greater scalability and greater flexibility in restoration services network layer. MPLS is a switching technology using labels. In a MPLS network, incoming packets are assigned a "label" by a "LER (label edge router)" according to their forwarding equivalence class (FEC) [7]. Packets are forwarded along a "label switch path (LSP)" where each "LSR (label switch router)" makes forwarding decisions based solely on the contents of the label, eliminating the need to look for its

IP address. At each hop, the LSR takes off the existing label and applies a new label for the next hop. Next hop also decides how to forward the packet by reading just the label on the packet. These established paths, Label Switch Paths (LSPs) can guarantee a certain level of performance, to route around network congestion, or to create IP tunnels for network-based virtual private networks. This technology can more easily integrate technologies such as QoS, VPNs or VoIP, makes it a flagship technologies of tomorrow already appreciated by the majority of Internet service providers as well as by some major companies. This demand has encouraged the evolution of these different networks which at the same time increased the complexity of managing all these networks. In terms of improvements, MPLS allows better management of routing, switching and transfer packages, through networks of new generation.

But that's not all because the MPLS is more able to solve many problems outlined above by improving four major aspects[9]:

- Possibility to define in advance the path that will take data or types of data sent over the network (Traffic Engineering).

- Ease of creating tunnels and IP VPNs (Virtual Private Network) level including Internet service providers, and solving problems related to the multiplication of them.

- Independence protocols layers 2 and 3 of the OSI model with support for IPv6, IPv4 layer 3, and Ethernet, Token Ring, FDDI, ATM, Frame Relay and PPP layer 2 .

- Interaction between the existing routing protocols such as OSPF (Open Shortest Path First) and BGP (Border Gateway Protocol).

The architecture is based on MPLS mechanisms switching labels linking Layer 2 of the OSI model (switching) with the layer 3 of the OSI model (routing). Moreover, switching conducted layer 2 is independent of the technology used.

The networks now use the analysis of headers layer 3 of the OSI model to make decisions on the transmission of packets. however, MPLS is based on two distinct components to reach its decisions: the control plan and data plane.

- The data plan can be used to transmit data packets based on the labels, which carry based on a database of transmission labels maintained by a switch of labels.

- The control plan maintains information transmission labels to groups of switches labels.

| Label (20 bits) | Exp (3 bits) | S (1 bit) | TTL (8 bits) |
|-----------------|--------------|-----------|--------------|

**Fig. 4.** MPLS header

Label is generated according to routing protocol. This label is used to forward the packet. The traffic is encapsulated in MPLS header. MPLS header is 32 bit long and composed of label (20 bits), Exp (3 bits) for experimental use, S (stacking bit, 1bit), Time To LifeTTL (8 bits). (Figure 4) backbone ingress routers examine the MPLS header to make forwarding decision (Label switch Path) and swap the label with appropriate label for next hop. Egress router performs the withdrawal and removes the MPLS header. Two neighboring routers Label known as label distribution peers decide on a label to bind a particular FEC. FEC is used to define the association of traffic with the same distination, the traffic have the same FEC will be assigned by the same label, different FECs and their associated labels are used. In order to transmit packets and establish an FEC, MPLS is based on the following parameters[7][8]:

- Source and/or destination IP address
- Source and/or destination port numbers
- IP protocol ID (PID)
- IPv4 Differentiated Service (DS) code point
- IPv6 flow label.

The assignment of label is made by the downstream LSR by either "downstream-on demand" operation or "unsolicited downstream label" operation. Label binding is local and does not represent the FEC. It is the agreement between two LSRs for binding to a particular FEC. The path through one or more LSRs, followed by packets is called LSP (Label Switched Path)[10]. MPLS uses two methods for choosing the LSP for a FEC, which is called route selection: Hop-By-Hop routing and Explicit Routing.

## 3   Mapping between MPLS and 802.11e

IEEE 802.11e and MPLS help solve the IP quality problem. IEEE 802.11e uses the IP TOS (type of service) field to classify traffic into different classes at the boundary node to provide QoS. MPLS also classifies traffic into different FECs with which it can provide QoS. MPLS networks support IEEE 802.11e by mapping IEEE 802.11e ACs (Access Categories) onto LSPs. The ToS of a packet determines the priority of the nodes and MPLS label of a packet determines the route of the packet. MPLS IEEE 802.11e network combines these to features best match traffic engineering and QoS[11] [12].

Common factor in terms of quality of service, constituting a real reason to achieve our approach:

- Complexity is pushed to edge routers.
- Classification of traffic at edge routers
- Labeling of packets after classifying them
- Transit routers treat packets according to the labels
- Labels are short and of fixed length
- Aggregation support

When a IEEE 802.11e packet arrives into a MPLS network, ingress LSR examines the TOS field of IP datagram to check the 802.11e priority information. The incoming traffic is mapped to appropriate LSP.

MPLS can map IEEE 802.11e traffic to MPLS traffic in several ways. Multiple ACs can be mapped to single LSP or a single AC is mapped to single LSP. When multiple ACs are mapped to a single LSP, Exp field in MPLS is used to specify PHB. This method is called EXP-Inferred-PSC LSP (E-LSP). When a single AC is mapped to a single LSP, it is Label-Only-Inferred-PSC LSP (LLSP).

**E-LSP:** EXP field of MPLS header (3 bits) is used to specify ACs. Label can be used to make a forwarding decision and EXP field can be used to determine how to treat the packet. all ACs take the same explicit path, with a different priority treatment.

**L-LSP:** A separate LSP can be established for a single FEC AC combination. In this case, the LSR can infer the path as well as treatment of the packet from the label of the packet. The EXP field encodes the drop precedence of the packets.

When a network supporting less than 8 ACs classifications, E-LSP is very useful. It combines the traffic engineering capabilities of MPLS with QoS provided by ToS field. LSR needs to map EXP field to AC. This mapping needs to be configured. L-LSP supports arbitrarily large number of <FEC, AC> combinations. Different LSPs are used for different types of ACs. Ingress router sets the EXP field in accordance with the drop precedence of the packet and sends it on to correct LSP for specified AC. Transit routers read the label along with EXP field and act accordingly. Mapping of Label to AC is signaled and EXP to drop precedence is well known.

# 4  Analysis

Though L-LSP is the answer for MPLS IEEE 802.11e with many types of PHBs defined. in the other side E-LSP is very useful in a network with limited number of traffic classifications (until 8 classes), E-LSP serves our purpose. Using different trade-off and combinations of techniques, operate in the MPLS network, can provide a quality of service from the end to end and enhanced service.

The main technique is not permanent usage of resources and labels. Labels will be assigned whenever a particular AC uses the network or defined the EXP field.

In future, QoS is going to be must demanding enhanced methods for ensuring QoS. Internet applications require high granularity of QoS, will demand more number of ACs in 802.11e.Internet service providers have many customers, who need intermittent connections. the labels associated with a customer can be used for other, when such customers are not using the network. Thus the total number of labels used will not exeed the scope and will still support more numbers of traffic classifications. MPLS is going to be the technology increasingly used as it provides traffic engineering capabilities and QoS. Currently, if MPLS technology is expanded to embrace new QoS, rather than defining new standards for QoS. 802.11e can be extended to provide high granularity of QoS using MPLS. One approach to provide such high granular 802.11e is the use of encapsulated LSPs; EXP field of LSP deciding the QoS and the other field deciding the path[13].

Labels denoted could be static as well as dynamic. The assumption is the classes of service do not change as frequently as the network itself. In that case, static use of labels, which means the fixed association of label and service, will reduce the processing time of LSRs minimize the memory load. By verifying the E-LSP, LSR knows what how to treat the packet. LSR can then check L-LSP to look up the table just to make forwarding decision. Static Label-Service association will not require LSRs to swap signaling messages with their neighbors[14].

Main policy MPLS of the ISP must define the QoS mapping for the label–Service association. This information is assigned to all other LSR using signaling protocols.

In the case, dynamic labels are used, labels specifying different classes of services should also be exchanged through signaling protocols. For this approach each each MPLS router is composed of two separate databases: one for traffic classes(data plan) and the other for path decisions(control plan). Use of L-LSPs and E-LSPS together eliminate the need establishing different LSPs for different classes thus eliminating the need to maintain large number of labels as label as same labels can be used for denoting different service as well as forwarding decision. E-LSP will determine the service and the L-LSP will determine the path. This approach needs further study to verify its feasibility.

# 5 Experimentation

In the first, we will present the experimentation of the interconnection that unites two technologies: IEEE802.11e and MPLS. 802.11e that present here a transmission system of data assuring the link between peripherals by the waves radio and MPLS is the technology that permits to simplify the administration of a network backbone by adding new particularly interesting functionalities for the management of the quality of service. We will pass in a second time to give the result of the comparison between the two methods of creation of LSP: E-LSP and L-LSP.

The model of the MPLS-WiFi experimentation is constituted of:

- Three machines: 2LER and a LSR that present the MPLS backbone.
- Two access points WiFi Linksys WAP54G 802.11g (54Mbps) of cisco.
- Two PC Windows that are connected via access points to the MPLS backbone.

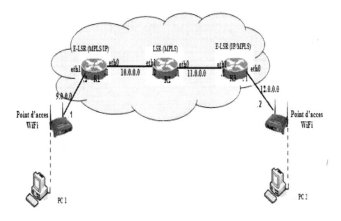

**Fig. 5.** Mapping model

The figure 5 shows names of machines, interfaces and the IP addresses used.

The PC1/PC2 are the machines server/customer that will be used to transfer the FTP/UDP applications, this last will pass by the MPLS backbone constituted by the machines R1, R2 and R3.

## 5.1   Comparison between the E-LSP and L-LSP Mechanisms

- **E-LSP** mechanisms

On the PC1 machine (server) launch two flows video in two ports 1235 and 1236. in the other side PC2 (customer) we configured the opening of these two flows networks by listening to these two ports.

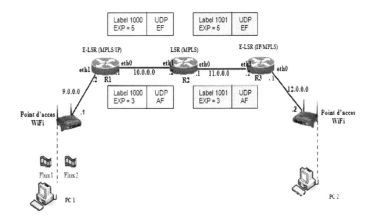

**Fig. 6.** E-LSP mechnism with QoS

## Description

- PC1 sends two UDP flows on the two ports 1235 and 1236 toward PC2.

- The R1 machine is going to make a classification according to the port destination, then the AC-EXP mapping will be established while copying the three bits the most meaningful, finally the label "1000" is added.

The following figure illustrates the parameters used in this scenario.

| ToS | EXP | Label | Specified bandwidth | Port source |
|------|-----|-------|---------------------|-------------|
| 0x1A | 3 | 1000 | 2400kbit/s | 1235 |
| 0x2E | 5 | 1000 | 4400kbit/s | 1236 |

**Fig. 7.** QoS (L-LSP) configuration of UDP flow

- It will give to the packet (EXP=5) a big priority and to the packets (EXP=3) a minor priority while offering to each a specified bandwidth.

- The R2 machine is going to exchange label 1000-->1001 and may suppress packets in case of congestion according to the priority defined.

- The R3 machine suppresses the label 1001 and routes packets toward the PC2.

The following graph shows the domination of the bandwidth of the flow (port 1236) that has the biggest priority and less packets to compared to the second flow (port 1235).

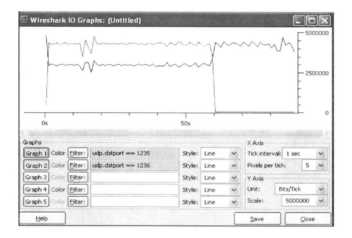

**Fig. 8.** Throughput Variation of two Flows UDP(E-LSP)

While taking the result of this experimentation as a basis, we conclude that the configuration that we adopted to the departure permitted us to give a big priority to the UDP flow (port 1236) in relation to the second flow (port 1235).

- **L-LSP mechanism**

We exercised the same experimentation, but this time the R1, R2 and R3 machines have been configured to support the L-LSP mechanism, this last can offer the differentiation of service while using the MPLS label, The EXP field contains information of loss solely.

**Description**

- PC1 sends two flows UDP in two ports 1235 et 1236 toward PC2.

- The R1 machine is going to make a classification according to the port destination, then she will add the label "1000" for the first flow and the label "2000" for the second, now the label has a duplicate role: used in the commutation of label to define the destination, and to identify the class of service The EXP field used also to identify the priority of loss.

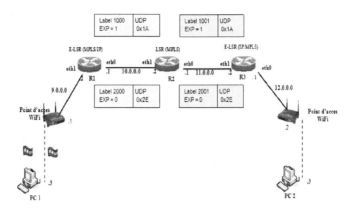

**Fig. 8.** L-LSP mechanism with QoS

The following figure contains the parameters used in this connection.

| ToS | EXP | Label | Specified bandwidth | Port source |
|------|------|-------|---------------------|-------------|
| 0x1A | 1 | 1000 | 1600kbit/s | 1235 |
| 0x2E | 0 | 2000 | 4400kbit/s | 1236 |

**Fig. 9.** QoS (L-LSP) configuration of UDP flow

- It will give to packet "0x1A" (Label=2000, EXP=0) a major priority and to packets "0x2E " (the label=1000, EXP=1) a minor priority while offering to each a specified bandwidth.

- The R2 machines is going to exchange labels 1000--->1001, and 2000--->2001 and to suppress packets in case of congestion according to the priority (EXP field) has already definite.

- The R3 machine suppresses labels 1001 and 2001 and routes packets toward PC2.

The following graph has the same pace that the one gotten by the E-LSP mechanism, what demonstrates that the two mechanisms offer the same quality of service.

Although the two E-LSP and L-LSP mechanisms use two manners to differentiate services, they offer the same quality of service.

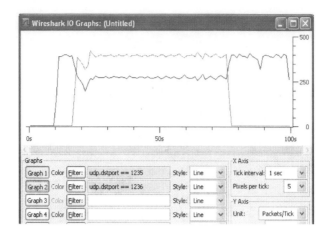

**Fig. 10.** Throughput Variation of two Flows UDP(L-LSP)

## 5.2 Result of the Comparison

- In the E-LSP, the label is a means to indicate the destination of packets, the EXP field is used to specify the class of service.

- In The L-LSP, the label is not used only to determine the destination of the FEC but as the class of service, the EXP field serves to define the priority of loss.

- The L-LSP method is more complex because the LSR must define different LSP toward the same destination.

- The MPLS nodes use  MPLS him to distinguish the different classes of the traffic.

- The MPLS network cannot offer a guaranteed bandwidth, but only the minimal passing bandwidth by class of service that can be saturated.

## 6  Conclusion

The aim of this paper was to  propose a for finding the best mapping between several heterogeneous system by used the flows with different priority, and we described how MPLS and 802.11e work together. It explained different approaches to incorporate the IEEE 802.11e into MPLS networks, and also showed the importance of our approach and its role in providing QoS the end to end. This paper designed to develop mechanisms capable of providing a quality of service between two mechanisms of QoS to accomplish future QoS supporting many types of traffic classification and 802.11e into MPLS networks, and also showed the importance of our approach and its role in providing QoS the end to end. This paper designed to develop mechanisms capable of providing a quality of service between two mechanisms of QoS to accomplish future QoS supporting many types of traffic classification and offered more choices of service according to Access Categories.

# References

1. IEEE 802.11 WG, Wireless Lan Medium Access Control and Physical-Layer (PHY) Specifications, standard (1999)
2. IEEE 802.11e, "Wireless Lan Medium Access Control(MAC)Enhancements for Quality of Service (QoS)" 802.11e Draft8.0 (2004)
3. Heusse, M., Rousseau, F., Berger-Sabbatel, G., Duda, A.: Performance Anomaly of 802.11b. In: IEEE INFOCOM (2003)
4. Mangold, S., Choi, S., May, P., Klein, O., Hiertz, G., Stibor, L.: IEEE 802.11e Wireless LAN for Quality of Service. In: Proc. European Wireless 2002, Florence, Italy (February 2002)
5. Choi, S., del Prado, J., Garg, A., Hoeben, M., Mangold, S., Shankar, S., Wentink, M.: Multiple Frame Exchanges during EDCF TXOP. IEEE 802.11-01/566r3 (January 2002)
6. Blake, S.: An Architecture for DifferentiatedServices, RFC 2475 (December 1998)
7. Rosen, E., Viswanathan, A., Callon, R.: Multiprotocol Label Switching Architecture., RFC 3031 (January 2001)
8. Uyless Black, MPLS and label Switching Networks, Prentice Hall, Upper Saddle River (2002)
9. Davie, B., Rekhter, Y.: MPLSTechnology and Applications. Morgan Kaufmann, San Francisco (2000)
10. Trimintzios, P., et al.: A Management and Control Architecture for Providing IP Differentiated Services in MPLS-based Networks. IEEE Comunication Magazine (May 2001)
11. Trimintzios, P., et al.: A Management and Control Architecture for Providing IP Differentiated Services inMPLS-based Networks. IEEE Comunication Magazine (May 2001)
12. Maâlaoui, K., Belghith, A., Bonnin, J., Tezeghdanti, M.: Performance evaluation of QoS routing algorithms. In: IEEE International Conference on Computer Systems and Applications (AICCSA), January 3-6. IEEE Computer Society, Cairo (2005)
13. Kochkar, H., Ikenaga, T., Kawahara, K., Oie, Y.: Multi-class QoS routing strategies based on the network state. Computer Communications 28(11), 1348–1355 (2005)

# Reusability Assessment of Task Knowledge Patterns through Metrics

Cheah Wai Shiang and Edwin Mit

Faculty of Computer Science & IT,
UNIMAS 94300 Kota Samarahan Sarawak, Malaysia
c.waishiang@gmail.com, edwin@fit.unimas.my

**Abstract.** Reusability assessment of patterns is needed to help pattern designers and pattern developers to check whether a pattern is well-designed. Hence, the outcome from the assessment can be used to improve the current patterns and also to reveal the potential of reusing the patterns in software development. This paper presents the reusability assessment of task knowledge patterns through the proposed metrics. This is a continuous effort to evaluate the potential reuse of the proposed task knowledge patterns for multi agent system development. The reusability assessment proposed in this paper further elaborates reusability assessment by synthesizing how to evaluate the genericity of a task knowledge pattern (aka. agent patterns) and its similarity to other patterns in tackling a particular problem. The hypothesis is that a pattern is reusable when it is descriptive and expressive. A case study will be presented to showcase that the outcome of the assessment can help to improve the effort to design the task knowledge patterns for reuse purposes. Furthermore, the outcome of the assessment allows the pattern developer to communicate their patterns in quantitative manner. The two main contributions of this paper are first, to determine the design quality of agent patterns and secondly, the introduction of a novel designs metrics for agent patterns and the process to assess the potential reuse of task knowledge patterns.

**Keywords:** Reusability assessment, agent patterns.

## 1 Introduction

The notion of task is important when developing an agent system. Adopted from [1], task knowledge is defined as how experts solve specific task; an expert's problem solving capability or problem solving methods; the knowledge about problem solving [2]; the knowledge people have of the tasks they performed [3].

Task knowledge is formed into a template knowledge model to prevent the developer for reinventing the wheel during the application development [5]. The template knowledge model is also known as an expertise model and is viewed as design patterns or "knowledge patterns" for tasks. It contains a predefined knowledge that is represented in the form of reusable model sets for developers.

The knowledge patterns are reused during the analysis phase of MAS-CommonKADS. For example, the assessment template knowledge model is used to

V. Snasel, J. Platos, and E. El-Qawasmeh (Eds.): ICDIPC 2011, Part II, CCIS 189, pp. 484–496, 2011.

guide the task of coordinating a meeting. Instead of working iteratively to detail the task to coordinate a meeting, the assessment template knowledge model is selected to further detail it. The assessment template knowledge model is a "knowledge patterns" that describes how to make a decision from a collection of user requests [5].

Based on the observation of the task knowledge patterns, it has been noted that there is a certain inadequacy and inconsistency when it comes to reusing the task knowledge patterns during the development of adviser finder multi agent system [6]. As a result, the task knowledge patterns are introduced [6]. The task knowledge patterns are used in the early stage of agent development. The template structure supports the sharing of knowledge at a higher level of abstraction (viz. owner's perspective) and provides the complete knowledge elements description for task knowledge within the agent context. The knowledge is designed to be modeled in an agent context as agent developers are familiar with the agent concepts. Reader can refer to [6] for more detailed description of the task knowledge patterns.

This paper presents our work in assessing the task knowledge patterns. It is our continuous effort to evaluate the potential reuse of the proposed task knowledge patterns for multi agent system development. We present how to estimate the potential reuse of the task knowledge patterns through assessing the quality of the patterns with the proposed design metrics. Furthermore, we showcase how to reveal the potential reuse of the patterns with similar kinds through the assessment values.

Assessing the quality of the agent patterns will provide answer to the question: 'What is the potential reuse of the patterns?' Our hypothesis is that a pattern is reusable when it is descriptive and expressive. We showcase that the outcome of the assessment can improve the effort to design task knowledge patterns for reuse in which a case study is presented.

This work contributes in determining the design quality of agent patterns. A novel design metrics for agent patterns and process to assess the potential reuse of task knowledge patterns are introduced.

This paper consists of four sections. Section 2 presents the background study of this research. The effort in assessing the software patterns which form the background knowledge in this work is described. Section 3 will present the reusability assessment of task knowledge patterns. In this section, a case study is presented to assess the task knowledge patterns of information finding through the proposed metrics. Furthermore, the reuse potential of the patterns with similar kinds is revealed and followed by a discussion on the improvement of the designed task knowledge pattern. The paper concludes by Section 4.

## 2   Background

Patterns consist of various pattern elements that explicitly describe the problem, solution and consequences in clear structure. It encourages the developer or designer to communicate the ideas by explicitly presenting the concepts within the pattern [13, 14]. One way to reveal the potential reuse of the patterns is to demonstrate how the patterns support the maintainability of software development within a controlled experiment. Another way is to assess the design quality of the agent patterns as inspired by Araban and Sajeeve [8].

The reusability assessment of software components is introduced by Saeed Araban at the University of Melbourne [8] [16]. The aim of the research is to estimate the potential reuse of software components. The outcome of this research has lead to the improvement on the effort of designing for reuse purposes among the developers.

In the work [8], object oriented metrics are used to measure the criteria to ease reuse and design with reuse among two object oriented software components. The software components that have been used for the reusability assessment are the Java package and the Eiffel libraries. From the analysis of the result, the author concluded that Java has a better design for reuse due to the minimum number of children as compared to Eiffel.

The object oriented metrics that have been used are weighted method per class (WMF), number of children (NOC), coupling between object (CBO), just to name a few. The summary of the metrics used is as follow:

***Weighted Methods per Class, WMF,***

$$\text{WMC} = \sum_{i=1}^{n} C_i$$

WMF is also known as the number of methods by Harisson [10]. It is used to calculate the number of methods occurrences within a class.

***Number of Attribute, NOA.*** The number of attributes is referred to as the total number of attributes that are defined within a class.

***Response For a Class, RFC.*** Response for a class is used to measure the method invocation after receiving a message. It calculates the methods that are potentially executed in response to a message received by a class or object. Also, it is used to measure the connection of the potential communication between the classes and methods. The RFC [12] is defined as,

$$\text{RFC} = |\text{RS}|, \text{ where RS, the response set of the class, is given by}$$
$$\text{RS} = M_i \cup_{all\ j} \{R_{ij}\}$$

In which, the response set involves the counting of M, the set of all methods in a class, and $R_i$, the set of methods called by method $i$ in the class. Such methods in R are positioned remotely. Li & Henry [12] defined RFC as a coupling measurement as RFC does not only include the method directly involved by a method but also the method called by other methods in other classes.

***Coupling between Objects, CBO.*** Generally, coupling involves identifying the frequency of connections between the classes and types of connections between the classes like interaction coupling and content coupling. CBO is one of the couplings metrics which is used to determine the relationship among classes. Measuring the CBO happens when methods of one class use the methods or attributes of the others. CBO is also known as fan-out within the traditional software metric. Fan-out is defined as element like attribute or method that the class depends on. The CBO is defined below.

*CBO = total number of other classes to which it is coupled.*

This section summarizes the object oriented metrics that are used for reusability assessment of the software component. It is worth exploring how those practices are used to introduce the reusability assessment of agent patterns by treating the object oriented metrics as baseline concept to measure the agent oriented models in the task knowledge patterns as shown in the following section. Since this involves agent models, object oriented metrics are inadequate for measuring the agent models. It has been suggested that when proposing the metrics, determining the quality characteristic and who direct it is needed. The definition of the metrics must not be ambiguous or over emphasis. This is needed to facilitate in data collection from the raw data. In addition, effort is required to demonstrate and support the usefulness and significance of the set of proposed metrics through empirical evaluation or case study [9], [11].

## 3   Design Metrics of Agent Oriented Models for Task Knowledge Patterns

The metrics [15, 17] to measure the complexity of patterns are presented in this section. The metrics proposed in this section are related to the agent models in which the patterns are designed upon on. The complexity of the agent models reflects the explicitness of a task knowledge pattern. The common object oriented metrics is refined like weighted methods per class, size metrics, response for a class and coupling between objects to introduce the reusability assessment on task knowledge patterns. The refinement is needed as the notion of object oriented metrics like the number of classes, the dependency of classes and so on is not adequate to measure the agent models.

Altogether, five metrics for complexity analysis such as weighted goals per goal model, number of responsibility, number of domain, number of association for goal and goal coverage will be presented in this paper. The design metrics are described as below.

**Overall goals per goal *(OG)***
*Definition: OG* = number of goals + quality goals.

The overall goal per goal is defined as the total number of goals that are required to be achieved in order to solve a particular problem. In a goal model, goals, sub-goals and quality goal model an overall achievement of the goal. In order to fulfil a goal, it is required to fulfil the sub-goals as well as the quality of the goal given. The minimum number of *OG* is one. The *OG* includes the count of an initiate goal (e.g. root goal or sub-root goal) as the root goal contributes to the overall achievement of the goals. The *OG* can be measured for a particular sub-goal regardless of whether it is a root goal, sub-goal or quality goal and regardless of the hierarchy and sequence of goals arrangement.

By having a higher value of *OG*, this introduces the complexity of the pattern. However, this also increases the explicitness of the pattern by explicitly describing the goals that are required to be achieved for the task accomplishment. In fact, a higher value of *OG* increases the likelihood for reuse. According to Araban & Sajeev [8], software components that are measured with a higher value of weighted method per class, WMC are easier to reuse. The WMC is the number of functionalities in a class. The higher the value of WMC is, the higher the number of functions that are useful for application development also.

Figure 1 shows an example of measuring the overall goals per goal for a task knowledge pattern of information finding. In Figure 1, the value of *OG* for the overall goal model is 11. It includes the sub-goals of organising result, accepting user request

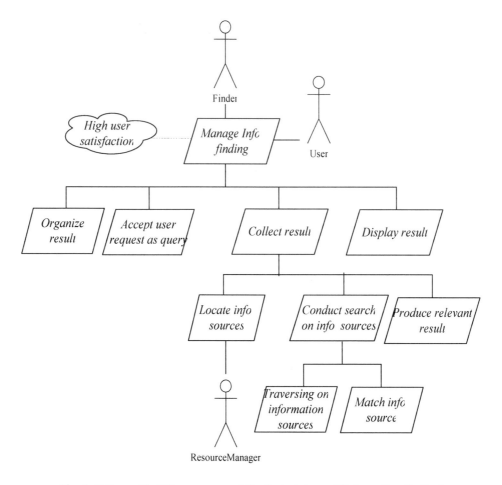

**Fig. 1.** $OG_{root} = 11$, $OG_{organizeQuery} = 7$ for the task type of 'information finding'

as query, and collecting result. The latter has been further divided into the sub-goals of locating information sources, conducting search, producing relevant result, and displaying result, and with the addition of the quality of the goal 'high user satisfaction'. Here, the value of *OG* for the subgoal 'Collect result' can be to be seven. This value of *OG* is calculated based on the goal of collecting result, sub-goals of locating information sources, conducting search, producing relevant result, traversing on information sources, and matching information source, and including the quality of the goal for high user satisfaction. The quality of the goal is applied to the highest-level goal 'Manage information finding' and all its subgoals.

**Number of Responsibilities *(NoR)***
*Definition: NoR* = The number of responsibilities.

This metric involves counting the number of responsibilities listed for a particular role in its role model. The role model models the role being played within an organization. High value of responsibilities may increase the reusability of the pattern as it explicitly lists the subtasks required to be performed by that role in order to achieve the goal(s).

**Number of Domain Entities (*NoD*)**
*Definition: NoD* = The number of domain entities.

This metric involves counting the number of domain entities within a domain model. Domain entities explicitly describe the knowledge items that are required for fulfilling the responsibilities and achieving the goals directly or indirectly related to them. As a result, the higher the value of *NoD* is, the more likely the knowledge embodied in the domain entities is to be reuse.

**Number of Quality Goals per Goal (*NoQ*)**
*Definition: NoQ* = The number of quality goals that are related to a goal.

Harrison et. al [10] have proposed the 'number of associations per class' metric as an inter-class coupling metric. In this research, the number of associations per goal is redefined as the number of quality goal that are associated with a particular goal, either directly or through its parent goals. A quality goal describes a non-functionality requirement in relation to a goal. In Figure 1, the value of *NoQ* for any goal including the goal of the model is one. The goal 'Manage information finding' is characterised with the quality of the goal 'High user satisfaction'. This quality of the goal explicitly represents an extra effort that is required for achieving the goal 'Manage information finding'. A higher number of *NoA* will increase the likelihood of reuse because the corresponding goal of the model explicitly describes the additional and "softer" knowledge elements that are required in solving the problem.

**Response for Goal** *(RFG)*
*Definition: RFG* = the number of goals + the number of quality goals + the number of roles for a goal.

Similar to the response for class, RFC in object oriented metrics, the *RFG* identifies the coverage of a particular goal. The *RFG* metric indicates various aspects of the subgoals that have been modelled for a goal together with the associations that support the achieving of the goal. The metric indicates the achieving of the subgoals together with the achievement of the parent goal. The *RFG* metric also includes the relevant quality of the goals and the roles that are required for achieving the goal. Overall, the value of *RFG* expresses the number of aspects of a problem that have to be considered to achieve the goal. From Figure 1, the *RFG* for the root goal 'Manage information finding' is calculated as 14. This value means that in order to achieve the goal 'Manage information finding' it's the sub-goals and the roles that are relied upon are taken into consideration. Another example, the *RFG* for the sub-goal 'Collect result' is 11. This value expresses that in order to fulfil the goal, it is required to fulfil the sub-goals of locating information sources, conducting search on information sources, and producing relevant result, in addition to the quality of the goal 'High user satisfaction' and also taken into consideration the involvement of the Finder, User, and ResourceManager roles.

Five design metrics have been introduced for assessing the different levels of task knowledge representation. In fact, the metrics can be used to assess the reusability of the task knowledge patterns as described next. In the following section, how to reveal the potential reuse of the task knowledge patterns through the proposed metrics will be demonstrated.

# 4   Validation of Task Knowledge Patterns through Metrics

Several patterns for the same problem may exist due to the differences of patterns proposed by different people. This research has drafted several examples that model the task knowledge through agent models. Each of the examples models the shared experience through the goal model, role model, organization model, and domain model. The challenges are how to measure the quality of various versions of the patterns and how to show the differences among those patterns. The answer is through reusability assessment. In other words, the quality of patterns can be measured through the proposed metrics.

In this section how a pattern developer can estimate the reuse potential of a task knowledge pattern will be demonstrated. This is followed by the demonstration of how to handle the reusability assessment of the task knowledge patterns of information finding. Figure 2 shows the goal model, role model, and domain model that are used for describing the task knowledge pattern of information finding.

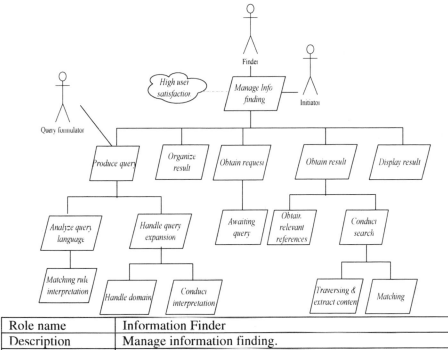

| Role name | Information Finder |
|---|---|
| Description | Manage information finding. |
| Responsibilities | -Query language analyse<br>-Receive incoming query for information finding<br>-obtaining relevant references<br>-Traversing on documents given<br>-Searching through the content by giving the references<br>-Perform matching<br>-Perform ranking and combination of searched result<br>-Display the relevant returned |
| Constraints | - |

| Role name | Query formulator |
|---|---|
| Description | Organize query. |
| Responsibilities | -Concept interpretation to identify the relevant topics of discussion<br>-Analyse query language<br>-Obtain domain<br>-Context interpretation to understand a particular concept based on personal preferences<br>-Relating the requests to others concepts<br>-Concept expansion for original user query<br>-Filtering concept expansion to produce relevant returned to user<br>-generate query |
| Constraints | -query formation is depending on the query that received. |

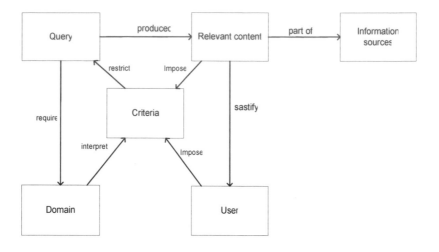

**Fig. 2.** Goal model, role model and domain model from our earlier work on the task knowledge pattern, 'TKP' of information finding

In the following description, the reusability assessment of the task knowledge pattern that is modeled in Figure 2 is presented. This is followed by the reusability assessment of eight task knowledge patterns of information finding as presented in [7]. Further elaboration of the estimation values is given at the end of this section.

**Table 1.** Assessment of task knowledge pattern, 'TKP' of information finding

| | NoR | 16 |
|---|---|---|
| | NoD | 6 |
| Assessment of task knowledge pattern shown in Figure 6.5 | RFG | 20 |
| | OG | 17 |
| | NoQ | 1 |

The result of the reusability assessment of the task knowledge pattern that is modeled in Figure 2 is shown in Table 1. The values in Table 1 show the measurements for the overall goal model, role model, and domain model of the TKP pattern. The values have been calculated as follows:

The $NoR$ = Number of responsibilities$_{informationFinding}$
  = Number of responsibilities for the role of InformationFinder +
    Number of responsibilities for the role of QueryFormulator
  = 8 + 8
  = 16
The $NoD$ = Number of domains(D)$_{informationFinding}$
  = D1:Query + D2:RelevantContent + D3:Information Sources + D4:Criteria
    +D5:Domain + D6:User
  = 6

The $RFG$ = Number of goals(G)$_{informationFinding}$ + Quality goal(QG)$_{informationFinding}$ + Role(R)$_{informationFinding}$

= G1:Manage Info finding + G2:Produce query + G3:Analyze query language +G4:Matching rule interpretation + G5:Handle query expansion + G6:Handle domain + G7:Conduct interpretation + G8:Organize result + G9:Obtain request + G10:Awaiting query + G11:Obtain result + G12:Obtain relevant references +G13:Conduct search + G14:Traversing & extract content + G15:Matching + G16:Display result + QG: High user satisfaction + R1: Finder + R2:Initiator + R3:QueryFormulator

= 16G+ 1QG + 3R

= 20

The $OG$ = Number of goals(G)$_{information\ Finding}$ + Quality goal(QG)$_{informationFinding}$

= G1:Manage Info finding + G2:Produce query + G3:Analyze query language + G4:Matching rule interpretation + G5:Handle query expansion + G6:Handle domain + G7:Conduct interpretation + G8:Organize result + G9:Obtain request + G10:Awaiting query + G11:Obtain result + G12:Obtain relevant references +G13:Conduct search + G14:Traversing & extract content + G15:Matching + G16:Display result + QG:High user satisfaction

= 16G + 1QG

= 17

The $NoQ$ = Number of quality goals $_{informationFinding}$

= QG:High user satisfaction

= 1

The number of responsibilities for the task type (NoR) is 16. The number of domain entities (NoD), which have been explicitly modeled in the pattern is 6. The overall goals per goal (OG) is 17. This value expresses that expanding or reformulating a user query to increase the number of relevant results returned may be required for information finding. In addition, the user should be allowed to provide his/her preferences other than the solution given as well as the returned documents should be arranged accordingly. The response for the root goal (RFG) is 20. Two roles have been shown to be important when conducting the task of information finding. These roles are managing the finding, which involve handling of queries, conducting search, ranking, and combining results, and supporting query interpretation and expansion. The number of quality goals (NoQ) for this type of taskis 1. Achieving the quality of the goal; user satisfaction is important in information finding. Hence, the solution must be able to return a collection of relevant results either according to the user preferences or within a certain degree of relevance. For example, when performing a query, efficiency of the retrieval should be considered. In such a case, the time required for returning the results becomes an aspect to the solution.

Table 2 presents the metrics that characterise the task knowledge patterns of information finding: *if1, if2, if3, if4, if5, if6, if7, if8* and *TKP*. This is the outcome based on the reusability assessment through the proposed design metrics.

Once the result is obtained, the explicitness and comprehensiveness of the patterns can be determined through the following guidelines.

1.  A pattern is claimed to be explicit and comprehensive if it has the best score on each of the metrics listed in the Section 3.
2.  An agent will play a role and serve its responsibilities towards achieving the goal(s). If the pattern has explicitly described the goals and responsibilities in detail, the pattern is claimed to be explicit and comprehensive.
3.  A pattern that scores well in RFG but scores low for NoA, NoR and NoD as compared to others pattern is claimed to be explicit due to the reason that having a higher number of RFG has indicated the explicitness of the goals and the person in charge (i.e. role) in achieving the goals. This is important as goals and role are important elements for agent paradigm as mentioned in the previous guideline.

**Table 2.** The values of metrics for the task knowledge patterns of information finding

| Pattern | OG | RFG | NoQ | NoR | NoD |
|---------|----|----|----|----|----|
| TKP | 17 | 20 | 1 | 16 | 6 |
| if1 | 10 | 12 | 3 | 12 | 7 |
| if2 | 4 | 6 | 1 | 8 | 4 |
| if3 | 12 | 16 | 0 | 19 | 5 |
| if4 | 5 | 7 | 0 | 5 | 4 |
| if5 | 6 | 8 | 0 | 5 | 2 |
| if6 | 4 | 7 | 0 | 10 | 4 |
| if7 | 8 | 10 | 0 | 12 | 3 |
| if8 | 8 | 11 | 1 | 13 | 4 |

Presented in Table 2, the highest values of the metrics OG, RFG, NoD, NoQ, and NoR characterize the pattern modeled in Figure 2. This finding indicates the explicitness of the task knowledge pattern (TKP). This is a comprehensive task knowledge pattern because it has been derived from various articles. This confirms our initial assumption that the TKP pattern is more reusable as compared to the others because it takes into consideration more sub-goals and other elements. This finding complies with the claim that having a higher number of methods in an OO class leads to more reusability of the corresponding software component [8]. A further observation from the results presented in Table 2 is that the next pattern in terms of comprehensiveness and explicitness is the *if3*. This is because *if3* pattern has scored slightly less number of goals and response for goal as compared to TKP. Other than that, the pattern of *if3* has scored well as compared to the others.

The three remaining groups of people, if1, if7 and if8 have produced slightly less comprehensive task knowledge patterns. These patterns are *if1*, *if7* and if8 accordingly. Finally, the level of explicitness for the rest of the patterns can be arranged accordingly: the pattern that described at *if2* to the pattern that described from *if5*, *if6* and *if4*. Adopted from the guideline 3, the RFG for *if5* is higher than *if4* and *if6* although *if6* scored 10 in NoR. As a result, we claim that the pattern of *if5* is more explicit as compared to *if6*.

In this section, estimating potential reuse of the task knowledge patterns is explained. Based on the estimation value, we may improved our task knowledge pattern

(TKP) that is modeled in Figure 2 with an additional quality goal (appropriate manner), additional responsibilities (e.g., monitoring and recording troubleshooting cases) and additional domain entities (e.g. error) that have been derived from the patterns *if1*, *if2*, and *if3* modeled. The improvement is needed to reduce the level of explicitness on a particular element within the pattern. In addition, the improvement is required to make our TKP pattern more comprehensive and explicit which we believe will lead to better reusability of the pattern. In fact, this is entirely true based on our experience in developing a multi agent advice finder system through the adoption of task knowledge patterns [7].

# 5  Conclusion and Future Work

A novel reusability assessment method for task knowledge patterns is introduced in this paper to estimate the quality of the patterns. Estimating the potential reuse of the patterns is needed to help the pattern designer or pattern developer to check if the pattern is well-designed. The reusability assessment proposed in this paper further elaborates reusability assessment by synthesizing how to evaluate the genericity of a task knowledge pattern and its similarity to other patterns in tackling a particular problem. Several design metrics are introduced to measure the complexity of the task knowledge patterns. With the help of the metrics, the values received from measurements can be used to improve the patterns. As a continuation from this work, we are working on extending our assessment method to others agent patterns. As mentioned before, knowing the design quality of agent patterns is important. In fact, we believe that by understanding the potential reuse of the patterns will better improve the adoption of agent technology to wider software practitioners, in which there is much more to explore in future.

**Acknowledgments.** The author would like to thank Universiti Malaysia Sarawak (UNIMAS) and Professor Leon Sterling for providing the support in working on this research.

# References

1. Studer, R., Benjamins, V.R., et al.: Knowledge engineering: principles and methods. Data & Knowledge Engineering 25(1-2), 161–197 (1998)
2. Chandrasekaran, B., Josephson, J.R., et al.: The ontology of tasks and methods. In: Proceedings of the Eleventh Workshop on Knowledge Acquisition, Modelling and Management (KAW 1998), pp. 18–23 (1997)
3. Annamalai, M.: Modelling knowledge for scientific collaboration on the semantic web, The Melbourne University. PhD (2006)
4. Henderson-Sellers, B., Giorgini, P.: Agent-oriented methodologies, Idea Group Pub., USA (2005)
5. Schreiber, G.: Knowledge engineering and management: the CommonKADS methodology. MIT press, Cambridge (2000)
6. WaiShiang, C.: Patterns for Agent oriented software development, The Melbourne University. PhD (2010)

7. WaiShiang, C., Sterling, L., Taverter, K.: Task knowledge patterns reuse in multi-agent system development. In: Proceedings of the 13$^{th}$ International Conference on Principles and Practice of Multi-Agent Systems (PRIMA-2010),, Kolkata, India (November 2010)
8. Araban, S., Sajeev, A.S.M.: Reusability analysis of four standard object-oriented class libraries. In: Dosch, W., Lee, R.Y., Wu, C. (eds.) SERA 2004. LNCS, vol. 3647, pp. 171–186. Springer, Heidelberg (2006)
9. Harrison, R., Counsell, S., et al.: An overview of object-oriented design metrics. In: 8th International Workshop on Software Technology and Engineering Practice, pp. 230–235 (1997)
10. Harrison, R., Counsell, S., et al.: An overview of object-oriented design metrics. In: Proceedings on Eighth IEEE International Workshop on incorporating Computer Aided Software Engineering, pp. 230–234 (1997)
11. Genero, M., Piattini-Velthuis, M., et al.: Metrics for UML models. UML and Model Engineering 5(1) (2004)
12. Li, W., Henry, S.: Object-oriented metrics that predict maintainability. Journal of systems and software 23(2), 111–122 (1993)
13. Beck, K., Crocker, R., et al.: Industrial experience with design patterns. In: Proceedings of the 18th international conference on Software engineering, pp. 103–114. IEEE Computer Society, Los Alamitos (1996)
14. Chung, E.S., Hong, J.I., et al.: Development and evaluation of emerging design patterns for ubiquitous computing. In: Proceedings of the 5th conference on Designing interactive systems: processes, practices, methods, and techniques, pp. 233–242. ACM, New York (2004)
15. Marchesi, M.: OOA metrics for the Unified Modeling Language. In: Proceedings of the Second Euromicro Conference on Software Maintenance and Reengineering, pp. 67–73 (1998)
16. Boxall, M.A.S., Araban, S.: Interface metrics for reusability analysis of components. In: Australian Software Engineering Conference, pp .40-51 (2004)
17. Genero, M., Piattini, M., et al.: A survey of metrics for uml class diagrams. Journal of Object Technology 4(9), 59–92 (2005)
18. Gruhn, V., Laue, R.: Complexity metrics for business process models. In: Witold Abramowicz and Heinrich C. Mayer, editors, 9th international conference on business information systems (BIS 2006). Lecture Notes in Informatics, vol. 85, pp. 1–12 (2006)

# Personal Recognition Using Multi-angles Gait Sequences

Connie Tee[1], Michael Kah Ong Goh[1], and Andrew Beng Jin Teoh[2]

[1] Multimedia University, Jalan Ayer Keroh Lama,
75450, Melaka, Malaysia
{tee.connie,michael.goh}@mmu.edu.my
[2] Electrical and Electronic Engineering Department,
Yonsei University, Seoul, South Korea
bjteoh@yonsei.ac.kr

**Abstract.** This paper presents an automatic gait recognition system which recognizes a person by the way he/she walks. The gait signature is obtained based on the contour width information of the silhouette of a person. Using this statistical shape information, we could capture the compact structural and dynamic features of the walking pattern. As the extracted contour width feature is large in size, Fisher Discriminant Analysis is used to reduce the dimension of the feature set. After that, a modified Probabilistic Neural Networks is deployed to classify the reduced feature set. Satisfactory result could be achieved when we fused gait images from multiple viewing angles. In this research, we aim to identify the complete gait cycle of each subjects. Every person walks at difference paces and thus different numbers of frame sizes are required to record the walking pattern. As such, it is not robust and feasible if we take a fixed number of video frames to process the gait sequences for all subjects. We endeavor to find an efficient method to identify the complete gait cycle of each individual. In this case, we could work on succinct representation of the gait pattern which is invariant to walking speed for each individual.

**Keywords:** gait recognition, statistical shape analysis, Fisher Discriminant Analysis, Probabilistic Neural Networks.

## 1 Introduction

Recently, gait recognition has emerged as an attractive alternative to biometric technology due to its ability to identify a person at a distance. Gait recognition is used to signify the identity of a person based on the way the person walks [1]. This is an interesting property to recognize a person, especially in surveillance or forensic applications where other biometrics may be inoperable. For example in a bank robbery, it is not possible to obtain face or fingerprint impressions when masks or hand gloves are worn. Therefore, gait appears as a unique biometric feature in this case to allow possible tracking of people's identities.

Gait has a number of advantages as compared to the other biometric characteristics. Firstly, gait is unique to each individual. Every person has a distinctive way of walking due to the different biomechanical and biological compositions of the body [2]. Human locomotion is a complex action which involves coordinated movements of the

V. Snasel, J. Platos, and E. El-Qawasmeh (Eds.): ICDIPC 2011, Part II, CCIS 189, pp. 497–508, 2011.
© Springer-Verlag Berlin Heidelberg 2011

limbs, torso, joints, and interaction among them. The variations in body structures like height, girth, and skeletal dimension can also provide cue for personal recognition. Secondly, gait is unobtrusive. Unlike other biometrics like fingerprint or retina scans which require careful and close contact with the sensor, gait recognition does not require much cooperation from the users. This unobtrusive nature makes it suitable for wide range of surveillance and security applications. Thirdly, gait can be used for recognition at a distance. Most of the biometrics such as iris, face, and fingerprint require medium to high quality images to obtain promising recognition performance. However, these good quality images can only be acquired when the users are standing close to the sensors or with specialized sensing hardware. When these controlled environments are not applicable, like in most of the surveillance systems in real-life, these biometrics features are rendered of little use. Therefore, gait appears as an attractive solution because gait is discernable even from a great distance. Lastly, gait is difficult to disguise or conceal. In many personal identification scenarios, especially those involving serious crimes, many prominent biometric features are obscured. For instance, the face may be hidden and the hand is obscured. However, people need to walk so their gait is apparent. Attempt to disguise the way a person walks will make it appears even more awkward. In a crime scene, criminals would want to leave at speed and does not want to provoke attention to minimize the chance of capture. Therefore, it is extremely hard for the criminals to masquerade the way they walk at the crime scene without drawing attention to themselves. These wealth of advantages make gait recognition a graceful technology to complement the existing biometric applications.

There are two main approaches for gait recognition, namely model-based [3][5] and appearance-based [2],[6],[7],[8]. The model-based approach explicitly models the human body based on body parts such as foot, torso, hand, and leg. Model matching is usually performed in each frame to measure the shape or dynamics parameters. Cunado et al. [3] assumed legs as an interlinked pendulum, and gait signature was derived from the thigh joint trajectories as frequency signals. Johnson and Bobick [4] used activity-specific static body parameters for gait recognition without directly analyzing gait dynamic. Yam et al. [5] recognized people based on walking and running sequences and explored the relationship between the movements that were expressed as a mapping based on phase modulation. Usually, the model-based approaches are easy to be understood. However, these methods require high computational cost due to the complex matching and searching processes involved.

On the contrary, the appearance-based approach is more straight-forward. These methods generally apply some statistical theories to characterize the entire motion pattern using a compact representation without considering the underlying motion structure. BenAbdelkader et al. [2] obtained eigengaits by using image self-similarity plots. Lu and Zhang [6] proposed to use Independent Component Analysis (ICA) to extract gait feature from human silhouettes. Tao et al. [7] also applied similar approach to represent the gait sequences using Gabor gait and Tensor gait features. On the other hand, Kale et al. [8] modeled the temporal state-transition nature of gait by using Hidden Markov Model (HMM). The appearance-based approaches are more frequently used due to its simpler implementation process and computational cost.

In this paper, we propose an efficient gait recognition system by using Fisher Discriminant Analysis (FDA) and modified Probabilistic Neural Networks (PNN). We first extract the binary silhouettes from the gait sequences. The reason we work on silhouette images is because silhouette images are invariant to changes in clothing color/texture and also lighting condition. After that, we obtain the contour width information from the silhouettes and applied FDA to reduce the dimension of the feature set. The extracted feature has the advantage of ease of representation and low computational cost. Then we deploy a modified PNN as the classifier. As the gait sequences we used are composed of multi-view angles datasets [9], the scores obtained from each viewing angles are fused to obtain the final result. The overall framework of the proposed system is depicted in Fig. 1.

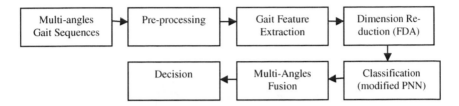

**Fig. 1.** Framework of the proposed system

The contributions of this paper are two-fold. Firstly, we modify the pattern layer of PNN in order to characterize the gait signatures more effectively. Secondly, we analyze the motion model of the human gait in order to determine the walking cycle of each person. By learning the walking cycles, we could find a compact representation of the walking pattern for each individual. Figure 2 illustrates the five stances corresponding to one walking cycle of a subject. Being able to identify the walking cycle is important because every person walks at different paces. Some people transit between the successive stances very quickly as they walk very fast, and vice versa. If we fix a number of video frames for analysis for every person, the video frames for the person who is walking fast may contain repeating walking pattern; while the video frames for the person who is walking slowly will not be able to capture the entire walking pattern for that person. Therefore, we endeavor to identify the gait cycle of each subject (which may encompass varying number of video frames), and use this compact representation to process the gait motion more precisely.

## 2  Proposed System

### 2.1  Pre-processing

Given a video sequence, we use the background subtraction technique [10] to obtain the silhouette of the subject. The background-subtracted silhouette images may contain holes, noise or shadow elements. Therefore, we apply some morphological operations to fill the holes and remove the noises.

After obtaining the silhouette images, the gait cycle for each subject could be identified by measuring the separation point of the feet. The walking cycle of a person comprises a generic periodic pattern, with an associated frequency spectrum [3]. Let say the walk starts by lifting the right foot and moving forward. When the right foot strikes the floor ("heel-strike"), the left leg flexes and lifts from the ground ("heel-off"). The body moves by interchanging the movement between the left and right foot lifting and striking the floor, forming a periodic gait cycle (Fig. 2).

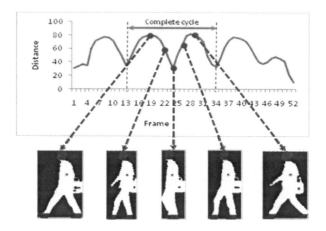

**Fig. 2.** Five stances corresponding to a gait cycle

A complete gait cycle could be determined by analyzing the gait signature graph and locating the local minimal of the graph (Fig. 2). The gait signature is constructed based on separation between the two legs. The start of the gait cycle is signified by the second local minima point detected in the graph. We do not consider the first local minima because it may contain some erroneous "heel-strike" or "heel-off" events. The complete gait cycle could be extracted by taking two consecutive temporal transitions between the "heel-strike" and "heel-off" phases as indicated by the positions of two successive local minima points in the gait signature.

The gait cycle for each person comprises different lengths depending on the speed the person walks. The frame sequences to capture a slow walking pattern may be longer than that of a fast walking pattern. We analyzed the frame sequences of all subjects in our dataset and found that the average number of frames to characterize a complete gait cycle is about 20 frames. Therefore, we take this number to optimally represent the gait cycle for the subjects in our experiment. For some slow-moving subjects with longer frame sequences, we "interpolate" the frame sequence length by taking alternative walking poses to reduce the number of frame sequences. For fast-moving subjects whose frame numbers are less than 20, we "extrapolate" the frame sequence by taking a few more frames beyond the end of the walking cycle to make up the figure. The frame sequences containing the gait cycle is then extracted from the whole video sequence for further processing. Instead of having to work on lengthy frame sequences containing repeating walking patterns, we can focus on a compact representation of the gait movement for analysis.

## 2.2  Gait Feature Extraction

Based on the pre-processed silhouette images, the contour of the subject could be traced. We obtain the width features of the contour along each row of the image and store them as the feature set. Assume that $F$ denotes the number of frames in a gait sequence, and $R$ refers to the number of row encompassing the subject contour. The sequence of width vector of the gait cycle of a subject can be represented by $X = \{x_1^{w_i}, x_2^{w_i}, ..., x_F^{w_i}\}$, where $w_i$ refers to the vector corresponding to each row in an image, and $i = 1, 2, ..., R$. Some sample contour width features extracted from two different subjects are depicted in Fig. 3.

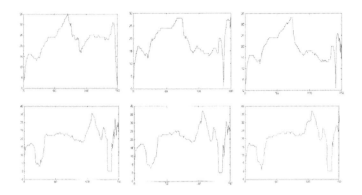

**Fig. 3.** The extracted contour width features from two subjects (depicted in different rows)

One advantage of representing the gait signature using the contour shape information is that we do not need to consider the underlying dynamics of the walking motion. It is sometimes difficult to compute the joint angle, for instance, due to self-occlusion of limbs and joint angle singularities. Therefore, the contour/shape representation enable us to study the gait sequence from a holistic point of view by implicitly characterizing the structural statistics of the spatio-temporal patterns generated by the silhouette of the walking person. Note that $X$ is a high-dimensional vector and modeling this feature set requires a lot computational cost. Therefore, some dimension reduction technique is used to minimize the size of this feature set.

## 2.3  Dimension Reduction Using FDA

FDA is a popular dimension reduction technique in the pattern recognition field [11]. FDA maximizes the ratio of between-class scatter to that of within-class scatter. In other words, it projects images such that images of the same class are close to each other while images of different classes are far apart. More formally, consider a set of $M$ images having $c$ classes of images, with each class containing $n$ set images, $i_1, i_2, ..., i_n$. Let the mean of images in each class and the total mean of all images be represented by $\widetilde{m}_c$ and $m$, respectively, the images in each class are centered as,

$$\phi_n^c = i_n^c - \tilde{m}_c \tag{1}$$

and the class mean is centered as,

$$\omega_c = \tilde{m}_c - m \tag{2}$$

The centered images are then combined side by side into a data matrix. By using this data matrix, an orthonormal basis $U$ is obtained by calculating the full set of eigenvectors of the covariance matrix $\phi_n^{cT}\phi_n^c$. The centered images are then projected into this orthonormal basis as follow,

$$\widehat{\phi_n^c} = U^T \phi_n^c \tag{3}$$

The centered means are also projected into the orthonormal basis as,

$$\widehat{\omega}_c = U^T \omega_c \tag{4}$$

Based on this information, the within class scatter matrix $S_W$ is calculated as,

$$S_W = \sum_{j=1}^{c} \sum_{k=1}^{n_j} \widehat{\phi}_k^j \widehat{\phi}_k^{j^T} \tag{5}$$

and the between class scatter matrix $S_B$ is calculated as,

$$S_B = \sum_{j=1}^{C} n_j \tilde{\omega}_j \tilde{\omega}_j^T \tag{6}$$

The generalized eigenvectors V and eigenvalues $\lambda$ of the within class and between class scatter matrix are solved as follow,

$$S_B V = \lambda S_W V \tag{7}$$

The eigenvectors are sorted according to their associated eigenvalues. The first M-1 eigenvectors are kept as the Fisher basis vectors, $W$. The rotated images, $\alpha_M$ where $\alpha_M = U^T i_M$ are projected into the Fisher basis by

$$\varpi_{nk} = W^T \alpha_M \tag{8}$$

where $n = 1, \dots, M$ and $k = 1, \dots, M-1$.

The weights obtained is used to form a vector $\Upsilon_n = [\varpi_{n1}, \varpi_{n2}, \dots, \varpi_{nK}]$ that describes the contribution of each fisher basis in representing the input image. In this research, the contour width feature, $X$, is input to FDA. The original dimension of $X$ is $R \times F$. This size can be reduced to only $c-1$ after FDA processing.

## 2.4 Classification Using Modified PNN

We modify an ordinary PNN to classify the gait features. In general, a PNN consists of three layers – a pattern, summation and output layers (apart from the input layer) [12]. The pattern layer contains one neuron for each input vector in the training set, while the summation layer contains one neuron for each user class to be recognized. The output layer merely holds the maximum value of the summation neurons to yield the final outcome (probability score). The network can simply be established by setting the weights of the network using the training set. The modifiable weights of the first layer are set by $\omega_{ij} = x_{ij}^t$ where $\omega_{ij}$ denoting the weight between $i$th neuron of the input layer and $j$th neuron in the pattern layer, and $x_{ij}^t$ is the $i$th element of the contour width feature, $X, j$ in training set. The second layer weights are set by $\omega_{jk} = T_{jk}$, where $\omega_{jk}$ is the weight between neuron $j$ in pattern layer and neuron $k$ of the output layer, and 1 is assigned to $T_{jk}$ if pattern $j$ of the training set belongs to user $k$ and 0 otherwise.

After the network is trained, it can be used for classification task. In this paper, the outcome of the pattern layer is changed to $out_j = \exp\left(-\left(\sum_{i=1}^{m}(x_i - \omega_{ij})\right)/\sigma\right)$, instead of inner product which is used in standard PNN. Note that $out_j$ is the output of neuron $j$ in pattern layer, and $x_i$ refers to $i$th element of the input. $\sigma$ is the smoothing parameter of the Gaussian kernel which is the only independent parameter that can be decided by the user. The input of the summation layer is calculated by the equation

$in_k = \sum_{j=1}^{n} out_j \times \omega_{jk}$   where $in_k$ is the input of neuron $k$ in output layer. The outputs of the summation layer are binary values, i.e 1 is assigned to $out_k$ if $in_k$ is larger than the input of others neurons and 0 otherwise.

In the experiment, we are using cross-validation to estimate the accuracy of the method more reliably. The smoothing parameters ($\sigma_1, \sigma_2,...,$ and $\sigma_j$) need to be carefully determined in order to obtain an optimal network. For convenience sake, a straightforward procedure is used to select the best value for $\sigma$. Firstly, an arbitrary value of $\sigma$ is chosen to train the network, and then test it on a test set. This procedure is repeated for other $\sigma$'s values and the $\sigma$ giving the least errors is selected. In this research, 0.1 appears to be best $\sigma$.

The motivation of using the modified PNN is driven by its ability to better characterize the gait features and its generalization property. Besides, PNN only requires one epoch of training which is good for online application.

## 3   Experimental Results

### 3.1   Experiment Setup

In this research, we use the publicly available CASIA gait database: Database B [9]. The gait data in this database consists of views from eleven different angles (Fig. 4).

Besides, the database also contains subjects walking under different conditions like walking with coats or bags (Fig. 5). There are ten walking sequences for each subject, with six samples containing subjects walking under normal condition, two samples with subjects walking with coats, and two samples with subjects carrying bags.

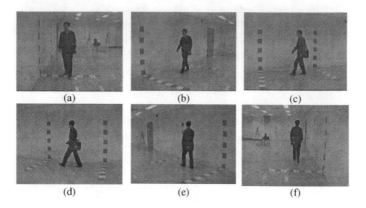

**Fig. 4.** Sample walking sequences from different viewing angles at, (a) 0°, (b) 36°, (c) 72°, (d) 108°, (e) 144°, (f) 180°

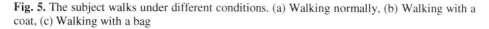

**Fig. 5.** The subject walks under different conditions. (a) Walking normally, (b) Walking with a coat, (c) Walking with a bag

We selected the first fifty subjects in the database to be used in this research. Among the ten gait sequences for each subject, we used three samples under the normal walking condition as gallery set. The remaining seven samples under the normal walking condition (three samples), walking with coats (two samples) and bags (two samples) are used as the probe sets.

To consolidate the gait sequences for the different viewing angles, the sum-rule based fusion rule is adopted in this research. This fusion method is selected because of its good performance as compared to AND- and OR-fusion rules, or even more sophisticated techniques like neural networks [13] and decision trees [14].

### 3.2 Verification Performance under Different Viewing Angles

We have conducted a number of experiments to testify the performance of the proposed method. The four important biometric performance measurements criterion namely False Rejection Rate (FRR), False Acceptance Rate (FAR), Equal Error Rate

(EER), and Genuine Acceptance Rate (GAR) are used to evaluate the performance of the system. FRR refers to the percentage of clients or authorized person that the biometric system fails to accept while FAR represents the percentage of imposters or unauthorized person that the biometric system fails to reject. EER is an error rate where FAR is equals, or almost equals, to FRR. On the other hand, GAR denotes the percentage of clients or authorized person that the biometric system correctly accepts.

The first experiment was carried out to assess the performance of the system under different viewing angles. From Table 1, we observe that the results for the different viewing angles are quite disparate. For example, the EER for the $0°$ view is about 9%, but the EER for the $36°$ view is as high as 25%. We conjecture that this may be due to the different amount of discriminative information that can be solicited from the different viewing angles. The gait pattern perceived from $90°$, for instance, is evidently more distinguishable than that perceived from $54°$. Therefore, although the images taken from different angles may be good for reconstructing some geometrical information of the subjects, they might be of little use in contributing to the overall recognition accuracy of the system.

Table 1. Performance of the System Under Different Viewing Angles.

| Viewing Angles | GAR (%) | FAR (%) | FRR (%) | EER (%) |
| --- | --- | --- | --- | --- |
| $0°$ | 90.50 | 9.52 | 9.50 | 9.51 |
| $18°$ | 88.00 | 37.41 | 12.00 | 24.71 |
| $36°$ | 57.00 | 8.04 | 43.00 | 25.52 |
| $54°$ | 65.25 | 6.03 | 34.75 | 20.39 |
| $72°$ | 88.75 | 16.39 | 11.25 | 13.82 |
| $90°$ | 85.5 | 15.90 | 14.50 | 15.20 |
| $108°$ | 90.00 | 16.64 | 10.00 | 13.32 |
| $126°$ | 89.75 | 17.04 | 10.25 | 13.65 |
| $144°$ | 88.25 | 19.35 | 11.75 | 15.55 |
| $162°$ | 89.00 | 22.81 | 11.00 | 16.41 |
| $180°$ | 74.00 | 5.74 | 26.00 | 15.87 |

## 3.3 Fusion Results

In this experiment, we evaluate the performance of the system when we combine images taken from the different viewing angles. The comparisons among fusing different number of viewing angles are illustrated in Fig. 6. When we fuse the images from all the eleven angles, GAR of 90.50% is achieved. When we reduce the number of viewing angles, with the aim of reducing the computational complexity, the results surprising do not degrade adversely (we discard the worst performing angles in reducing the fusion size). In fact, some fusion sizes could even retain the performance of fusing all the angles. For example, the GARs for fusing the best ten, nine, and eight angles are 90.47%, 90.25%, and 90.50%, respectively. Nevertheless, the drop in performance starts to appear evident when we fuse only seven or less angles. GARs of 89.75% and 87.50% were obtained, for instance, for the fusion of seven and six angles. Therefore, to strike a balance between accuracy and computational complexity, fusing the best eight viewing angles appears to be the optimal solution.

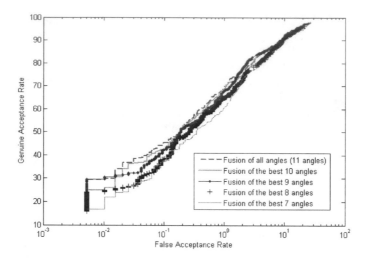

**Fig. 6.** The subject walks under different conditions. (a) Walking normally, (b) Walking with a coat, (c) Walking with a bag.

### 3.4 Influence of Feature Dimensionality

Besides evaluating the accuracy of the proposed method, we also want to investigate influence of the dimensionality of the features used in this research. We vary the feature sizes by taking different number of gait cycles. We analyze the impact of taking different number of gait cycles on accuracy of the system (measured in terms of EER) and the processing time. A standard PC with Intel Core 2 Quad processor (2.4 GHz) and 3072 MB RAM is used in this study.

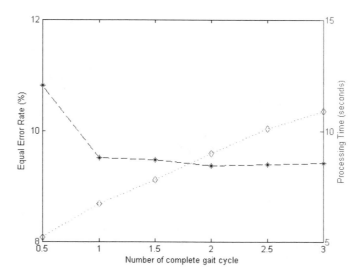

**Fig. 7.** Influence of feature dimensionality.

Fig. 7 depicts the EER and processing time when different number of gait cycles are used. We observe that as we increase the number of gait cycles to be used in the experiment, the processing time increases accordingly. However, when we look at the EER, there is not much improvement gain when we increase the number of gait cycles. Therefore, taking one complete gait cycle is the best threshold between accuracy and processing time in this research.

### 3.5 Performance Gain by Using Modified PNN

In this experiment, we want to assess the effectiveness of using the modified PNN as compared to the standard PNN. The comparative result is shown in Fig. 8. We observe that an improvement gain of about 5% could be achieved with the use of the modified PNN in our research.

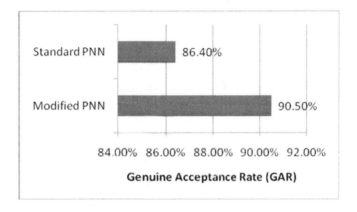

**Fig. 8.** Performance gain by using modified PNN

## 4 Conclusions and Future Works

We propose an automatic gait recognition system based on the contour width feature obtained from the silhouette images of a person. The advantage of representing the gait feature using contour shape information is that we do not need to consider the underlying dynamics of the walking motion. As the resulting feature size is large, FDA is used to reduce the dimension of the feature set. After that, a modified PNN is deployed to classify the reduced gait features. Experiment shows that the modified PNN is able to yield an improvement gain of 5% as compared to the standard PNN. In this research, we find that the images taken from different viewing angles contribute different amount of discriminative information that can be used for recognition. Therefore, we postulate that the images taken from different angles may be good for reconstructing some geometrical information of the subjects, but they might not be very useful in improving the overall recognition accuracy of the system. In this research, satisfactory performance can be achieved when we fuse eight or more viewing angles of the gait images together.

In the future, we want to explore more methods which could represent the gait features more effectively. In particular, we wish to obtain good performance by using only a few viewing angles. Besides, we also want to investigate the performance of gait recognition under different conditions like varying walking paces, wearing different clothing/footwear, or carrying objects. Lastly, we plan to extend our work to classify more gait motions such as walking and running. This will enable us to explore the possibility of activity independent person recognition.

**Acknowledgments.** Portions of the research in this paper use the CASIA Gait Database collected by Institute of Automation, Chinese Academy of Sciences.

# References

1. Little, J.J., Boyd, J.E.: Recognising People by Their Gait: The Shape of Motion. International Journal of Computer Vision 14, 83–105 (1998)
2. Ben Abdelkader, C., Culter, R., Nanda, H., Davis, L.: EigenGait: Motion-based Recognition of People using Image Self-similarity. In: Proc. Int. Conf, Audio- and Video-Based Person Authentication, pp. 284–294 (2001)
3. Cunado, D., Nixon, M., Carter, J.: Automatic Extraction and Description of Human Gait Models for Recognition Purposes. Computer Vision and Image Understanding 90(1), 1–41 (2003)
4. Bobick, A., Johnson, A.: Gait Recognition using Static Activity-specific Parameters. In: Proc. Int. Conf. Computer Vision and Pattern Recognition (2001)
5. Yam, C., Nixon, M., Carter, J.: On the Relationship of Human Walking and Running: Automatic Person Identification by Gait. In: Proc. Int. Conf. Pattern Recognition, vol. 1, pp. 287–290 (2002)
6. Lu, J., Zhang, E.: Gait Recognition for Human Identification based on ICA and Fuzzy SVM Through Multiple Views Fusion. Pattern Recognition Letters 28, 2401–2411 (2007)
7. Tao, D., Li, X., Wu, X., Maybank, S.J.: General Tensor Discriminant Analysis and Gabor Features for Gait Recognition. IEEE Transactions on Pattern Analysis and Machine Intelligence 29(10), 1700–1715 (2007)
8. Kale, A., Sundaresan, A., Rajagopalan, A.N., Cuntoor, N.P., Roy–Chowdhury, A.K., Kruger, V., Chellappa, R.: Identification of Humans using Gait. IEEE Trans. Image Processing 13(9), 163–173 (2004)
9. CASIA Gait Database, http://www.sinobiometrics.com
10. Elgammal, A., Harwood, D., Davis, L.: Non-parametric Model for Background Subtraction. In: FRAME-RATE Workshop. IEEE, Los Alamitos (1999)
11. Martinez, A.M., Kak, A.C.: PCA versus LDA. IEEE Transactions on Pattern Analysis and Machine Intelligence 23(2), 228–233 (2004)
12. Specht, D.F.: Probabilistic Neural Networks. Neural Networks 3(1), 109–118 (1990)
13. Ross, A.A., Nadakumar, K., Jain, A.K.: Handbook of Multibiometrics. Springer, Heidelberg (2006)
14. Wang, Y., Tan, T., Jain, A.: Combining Face and Iris Biometrics for Identity Verification. In: Kittler, J., Nixon, M.S. (eds.) AVBPA 2003. LNCS, vol. 2688, pp. 805–813. Springer, Heidelberg (2003)

# Performance Comparison of Direction-of-Arrival Estimation Algorithms for Towed Array Sonar System

H. Qayyum[*] and Muhammad Ashraf

Department of Electronic Engineering,
Mohammad Ali Jinnah University, Islamabad
hamzaqayyum02@yahoo.com

**Abstract.** Under water acoustic signatures can vary significantly under different environmental conditions. Finding direction-of-arrival (DOA) using towed array in under water environment requires algorithm robustness against variable acoustic signatures. The algorithm should be capable of performing source separation and localization extremely well in complex environments. Concurrently, the algorithm should not be much complex because it will be used in real time and systems needs to identify a target instantly. Array size is another important issue in target positioning because fewer sensors could lead to small size and require less computational cost.

In this paper, we present a comparison of the conventional direction-of-arrival algorithm with 2DFFT, MVDR and MUSIC algorithms for the purpose of finding DOA in underwater acoustics. The comparison would be focused on array size, source separation/resolution, signals type and complexity. We showed the DOA results of different algorithms on a simulated signal with given SNRs (Signal to Noise Ratio) and discuss issues such as resolution, computational complexity, and array size.

**Keywords:** Direction of Arrival, Conventional Beamforming, MVDR and Towed array.

## 1 Introduction

The purpose of any beamforming algorithm is to determine the DOA of one or more signals. Towed arrays are widely used in underwater acoustics for estimating the horizontal directionality of the acoustic field. Several spectral based techniques have been developed for estimating the DOA by using the data acquired by the signal radiated by the target. Among these, adaptive beamforming and eigen space based methods are the most commonly used methods [1]. Conventional beamforming utilizes a delay and sum technique to steer the array in a desired direction independently of the array data, so the conventional beamformer exhibits side lobes that do not completely attenuate the interfering signal. Therefore, this technique suffers from poor resolution and high side lobe problems [2]. 2-Dimensional Fast Fourier Transform (2DFFT) algorithm [3] is also used to determine the DOA of signals transmitted by different sources. Its

---

[*] Corresponding author.

V. Snasel, J. Platos, and E. El-Qawasmeh (Eds.): ICDIPC 2011, Part II, CCIS 189, pp. 509–517, 2011.

resolution is totally dependent upon the number of sensor elements. Unconstrained Minimum Variance Distortionless Response (MVDR) [4] is an optimum beam former in which weights are calculated to minimize output power subject to a unity gain constraint in the steering direction. The steering direction is the bearing that the array is "steered" toward to look for a particular incoming signal. The MUltiple SIgnal Classification (MUSIC) [5] algorithm is a high-resolution DOA estimation algorithm based on exploiting the eigen structure of the spatial covariance matrix [6]. It is a noise subspace based method, and it has been proved that the standard MUSIC method possesses a certain degree of inherent robustness to steering vector errors. However, for small sample data size and low SNR, the performance of MUSIC is degraded.

This paper is arranged as follows: the received signal model is given in Section 2. An overview of the Beamforming algorithms for equally spaced straight-line towed arrays is presented in Section 3. In Section 4, simulation results of different algorithms in term of resolution, signal type and computational complexity are plotted. Finally, Section 5 summarizes main results of this study.

## 2   Received Signal Model

Consider an array of $N$ equally spaced elements and $L$ sources transmitting the signal. At time $t$, let $s_l(t)$ represents the signal transmitted by the $l^{th}$ source, with $0 \leq l \leq (L-1)$, and let $x_i(t)$ be the signal incident at $i^{th}$ array element, with $0 \leq i \leq (N-1)$. Considering that the incoming signal from the $l^{th}$ source reaches the array element with an angle denoted by $\theta_l$, the gain provided by the array element for such an angle is represented by $a_i(\theta_l)$. If $n_{x,i}(t)$ represents the noise components, then the description of the received signal as a function of transmitted signals is given by [6]

$$x_i(t) = \sum_{l=0}^{l=L-11} s_i(t)\, a_i(\theta_l) + n_{x,i} \tag{1}$$

By defining the following auxiliary vectors and matrices in the discrete-time domain $k$

$$x(k) = [x_0(k)\, x_1(k) \cdots x_{N-1}(k)]^T \tag{2}$$

$$n_x(k) = [n_{x,0}(k)\, n_{x,1}(k) \cdots n_{x,N-1}(k)]^T \tag{3}$$

$$s(k) = [s_0(k)\, s_1(k) \cdots s_{L-1}(k)]^T \tag{4}$$

$$A = \begin{bmatrix} a_0(\theta_0) & \cdots & a_0(\theta_{L-1}) \\ \vdots & \ddots & \vdots \\ a_{N-1}(\theta_0) & \cdots & a_{N-1}(\theta_{L-1}) \end{bmatrix} \tag{5}$$

Then the input-to-output relationship given in Eq.(1) can be rewritten as

$$x(k) = As(k) + n_x(k) \tag{6}$$

## 3  Beamforming Algorithms for Equally Spaced Straight Line Towed Arrays

Beamforming is a well-known technique to observe the directionality of the acoustic field sampled by a hydrophone array. To observe signals from a given direction, the beamformer coherently adds the hydrophone outputs by adjusting their relative delays for that direction. Consider the pair of identical omnidirectional sensors shown in Fig.1, which are spaced apart by a distance $d$. Let a signal $x(t)$ is incident on two sensor elements from a direction $\varphi$ with respect to the array normal. It can be seen that element 2 experiences a time delay $\tau$ with respect to element 1 as given below

$$\tau = \frac{d\sin\varphi}{c} \tag{7}$$

Similarly in a line array of $N$ sensor elements, where the elements are equally spaced, a time delay of $n$th element will be $n\tau$ with respect to element 1.

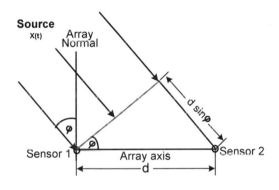

**Fig. 1.** Pair of identical omnidirectional sensor elements

### 3.1  Conventional Beam Forming (CBF)

In the beamforming operation the array output can be given by the sum of $N$ sensor element signals

$$y(t) = \sum_{n=0}^{n=N-1} x(t - n\tau) \tag{8}$$

The illustration of equation (8) is shown in Fig. 2

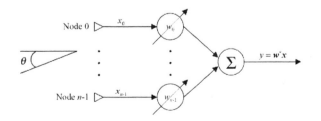

**Fig. 2.** Conventional BeamForming (CBF) structure [6 ]

The beamforming is usually performed in the frequency domain, in that case the relative delays are replaced by the equivalent phases. If $x(t)$ is a narrowband signal having centre frequency $f_0$, then the time delay $\tau$ corresponds to a phase shift of $\frac{2\pi d}{\lambda_0} \sin\varphi$. In frequency domain the beamforming operation $y(t)$ for a given frequency bin can be written as [6]

$$y(n) = \sum_{n=0}^{n=N-1} x(n) \, e^{\frac{-j\omega d \sin(\varphi)}{c}} \tag{9}$$

Among the sensors $\varphi_1, \varphi_2, \ldots \varphi_L$ are the DOAs of $d$ multi path signals from $L$ sources. When dealing $L$ source locations the steering vectors can be combined into steering matrix as,

$$s = [s(\varphi_1), s(\varphi_2), \cdots s(\varphi_L)] \tag{10}$$

It contains the information about the array geometry and the directions of the impinging signals. The response of the array to a source at a location $i$, in the absence of noise, is a column vector $s(\varphi_i)$, in the direction of $\varphi_i$. It is called the steering vector, which can be formulated as

$$s(\varphi_i) = \left[1, \; e^{\left\{j\frac{\omega}{c}d\sin(\varphi i)\right\}}, \cdots \; e^{\left\{j\frac{\omega}{c}(N-1)d\sin(\varphi i)\right\}}\right]^T \tag{11}$$

The cross-spectral density matrix, $R$, is the autocorrelation of the vector of frequency-domain sensor outputs

$$R = E\{XX^*\} \tag{12}$$

The matrix $R$ is also referred to as the covariance or correlation matrix in time-domain algorithms. The output power per steering direction is defined as the expected value of the squared magnitude of the beamformer output and given as

$$\text{Power} = E\{|y|^2\} = W^* E\{XX^*\}W^* = W^*RW \tag{13}$$

In CBF, the weight vector $W$ is equal to the steering vector $(S)$ then power is given as

$$\text{Power}_{CBF} = S^*RS \tag{14}$$

After calculation and plotting $\text{Power}_{CBF}$, the peaks formed correspond to the angle of arrival.

## 3.2  MVDR Beamforming

The goal of beamforming is to estimate the desired signal $s$ as a linear combination of the data collected at the array. In other words, we would like to determine an $N \times 1$ vector weights $w$ such that $w*S$ is a good estimate of $g$ (gain). The beamformer that results from minimizing the variance of the noise component of $w*S$, subject to a constraint of gain 1 in the look direction, is known as the MVDR beamformer. The corresponding weight vector $w$ is the solution to the following optimization problem is

$$Min_w P = w*Rw \; constrained \; to \; w*s = 1 \qquad (15)$$

The optimization problem in Eq. (15) has an elegant closed-form solution [4] given by

$$w = \frac{R^{-1}s}{s*R^{-1}s} \qquad (16)$$

*In* MVDR [4], the beamformer output is given as

$$Power_{MVDR} = \frac{1}{s*R^{-1}s} \qquad (17)$$

When $Power_{MVDR}$ is plotted, peaks appear at the angles of arrival of the incident angle.

### 3.3  MUSIC Algorithm

MUSIC is a powerful algorithm to determine DOA, it is based on the assumption that the desired signal array response is orthogonal to the noise subspace ($E_n$) [5]:

$$E_n^*.s(\theta) = 0 \quad \theta = \{\theta_1, \theta_2, \theta_3, \cdots \theta_D\} \qquad (18)$$

The MUSIC power spectrum is defined as [5]:

$$P_{MUSIC}(\theta) = \frac{1}{|a(\theta)*E_nE_n^*a(\theta)|} \qquad (19)$$

By examining the denominator in Eq. (19) it is evident that peaks in the MUSIC power spectrum occur at angles $\theta$ for which the array manifold matrix A is orthogonal to the noise subspace matrix $E_n$. Those angles $\theta$ define the desired directions-of-arrival of the signals impinging on the sensor array.

### 3.4  2-Dimensional Fast Fourier Transform (2DFFT) Algorithm

In 2DFFT signals from each array element are sampled simultaneously at rate $f_s$, yielding a multichannel time series $x_{n\ m}$. *N-point* FFTs are taken along each channel as given by [2]

$$X_n(i) = \sum_{m=0}^{N-1} x_{n\ m} e^{-j(2\Pi/N)mi} \qquad (20)$$

Now each along-channel FFT bin index will be considered separately. The $N$-point sequence of complex values representing the same bin index for all channels is processed with a cross-channel FFT.

$$X(i,k) = \sum_{m=0}^{M-1} X_n(i)e^{-j(2\Pi/M)nk} \tag{21}$$

## 4   Simulation Results

In this work numerical simulations of the received signal using four different types of beamforming algorithms were performed in Matlab. In simulation, linear equi-spaced array of sensors with 1.5 m inter-element spacing and 1024 number of data points were selected for each estimate.

### 4.1   Performance Evaluation of Correlated and Un-correlated Signals

In this section the results of various algorithms, considering correlated and un-correlated sources are discussed. For both correlated and un-correlated signals the number of sensor elements was 128 and angle of arrival were 20° and 80°. Fig 3 shows the result of algorithms considering the input signal as correlated signals. In case of correlated signals all four algorithms are giving accurate results that can be seen as sharp peaks in Fig. 3. However, the peak width that corresponds to the resolution of an algorithm is different for different algorithms.

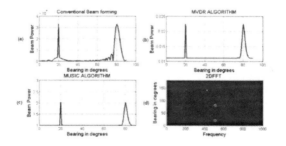

**Fig. 3.** Spectrum generated by various algorithms using correlated signals, (a) CBF (b) MVDR (c) MUSIC (d) 2DFFT

Fig 4 shows results of various algorithms for un-correlated signals. It can be seen that results of all the four algorithms has been changed. In case of un-correlated signal these algorithms give correct result for only one angle or one signal, this shows that in Fig. 4 peak at 80° is correct. These algorithms give correct result for only those signals whose frequency is being used to generate the steering vector. Thus these algorithms are not sensitive to un-correlated signals.

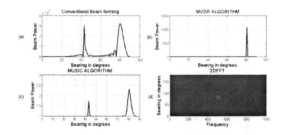

**Fig. 4.** Spectrum generated by various algorithms using un-correlated signals, (a) CBF (b) MVDR (c) MUSIC (d) 2DFFT

## 4.2 Resolution of Algorithms

Fig. 5 shows the result of MUSIC algorithm when the number of sensor elements were varied. In this case the angle of arrival was selected $28^{\circ}$ and $30^{\circ}$, the source separation was $2^{\circ}$. In case of 32 sensors the MUSIC algorithm gave only one peak at output, which shows MUSIC is unable to distinguish between two signals with source separation of $2^{\circ}$. But when the numbers of sensors were increased up to 64 the MUSIC algorithm can distinguish easily between two signals that can be seen as two definite peaks in Fig 5. Moreover, the peak width of 96 sensors is less than that of 64 sensors indicating that the resolution of algorithm increases with the increase in number of sensors.

The technique mentioned above was used to get peaks or results of different algorithms. The results of various algorithms were then plotted in Fig. 6. The MUSIC can distinguish between the signals of two sources separated by 7.5° when 16 sensors were used. Whereas the sources separated by 1.5° can be distinguished by 128 sensors. It can be seen that the resolution of various algorithms increases as the number of sensors increases. Fig. 6 also shows that the resolution of MUSIC and MVDR is better than that of CBF and 2DFFT in case of less number of sensors. Whereas when the numbers of sensors were more than 128 the resolution of all four algorithms is almost same.

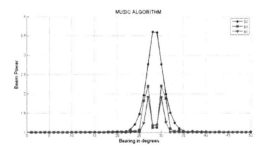

**Fig. 5.** Spectrum generated by MUSIC for different number of sensors, (●) 32 sensors, (■) 64 sensors and (▼) 96 sensors

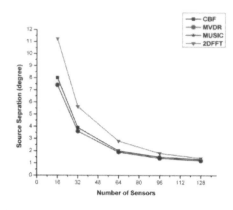

**Fig. 6.** Comparison of the resolution of various algorithms

## 4.3 Computational Complexity

The computational complexity is one of the major parameter while selecting an algorithm. In this work we executed each algorithm one hundred times and then average out the execution time of each algorithm. The Fig. 7 shows the average computational time of each algorithm. If we compare computational complexity of these algorithms, MVDR is the most complex. But the signal resolution of MVDR and MUSIC was almost equal (see Fig. 6), thereby the less computational time of MUSIC makes it more efficient than MVDR.

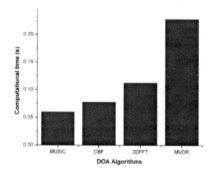

**Fig. 7.** Comparison of the computational time of various algorithms

## 5 Conclusions

In this paper we have presented the comparison between four direction-of-arrival (CBF, 2DFFT, MVDR and MUSIC) algorithms focusing on resolution, type of signal and computational complexity. Simulation results show that all four algorithms are not sensitive to un-correlated signals. The results obtained from simulation shows that the resolution of an algorithm is directly proportional to number of sensors. For a fixed number of sensors the resolution of MUSIC is better as compared to other three algorithms. Moreover, the computational complexity was calculated: MUSIC was least complex whereas MVDR was most complex algorithm.

# References

[1] Roy, R., Kailath, T.: ESPRIT-Estimation of Signal Parameters via Rotational Invariance Techniques. IEEE Trans. Acoust. Speech, Signal Process. 37(7), 984–995 (1989)
[2] Hou, S.Y., Chang, S.H., Hung, H.S., Chen, J.-Y.: Dsp-based Implementation of a Real-Time DOA Estimator for Underwater Acoustic Sources. Journal of Marine Science and Technology 17(4), 320–325 (2009)
[3] Defatta, D.J.: Joseph.G.Lucas and William.S.Hodkiss. Digital Signal Processing A System Approach
[4] Benesty, J., Chen, J., Huang, Y.: A Generalized MVDR Spectrum. IEEE Signal Processing Letters 12(12) (December 2005)
[5] Bakhar, Vani, R.M., Hunagund, P.V.: Eigen Structure Based Direction of Arrival Estimation Algorithms for Smart Antenna Systems. ICJNS 9(11) (November 2009)
[6] Ferreira, T.N., Netto, S.L., Diniz, P.S.R.: Low Complexity Covariannce-Based DoA Estimation Algorithm. In: Proceedings of the 15th European Signal Processing Conference, Poznam, Poland, pp. 100–104 (September 2007)

# Platform for Dynamic Adaptation of Learning Content for Pervasive Learning Environments

Amal Elhamdaoui[1,2], Mounia Abik[1], and Rachida Ajhoun[1]

[1] Ecole National Supérieure d'Informatique et d'Analyse des systèmes,
Université Mohamed-V Soussi, Rabat, Morocco
[2] Insitut Royal de la culture Amazighe, Rabat, Morocco
elhamdaoui@ircam.ma, abik@ensias.ma, ajhoun@ensias.ma

**Abstract.** With the evolution and convergence of wireless technologies, mobile devices and sensors, the mobile and ubiquitous learning have appeared next to the e-learning. Far from being simple extensions of distance learning, they pose several challenges. Most of learning content used in learning platforms are built to be consumed on broadband networks and powerful terminals. However, technological advances have allowed their access over low-flow wireless networks, and terminals with limited resources such as ubiquitous and mobile devices. With this type of access, there is a strong need for learning content adaptation systems. Our work focuses on pervasive learning environments which are the new trends of distant learning and proposes to solve a big range of constraints posed by the use of various technologies in learning. We are interested in studying the various limitations of learning in pervasive environments and the development of a platform for dynamic adaptation of learning content, taking into account the challenges posed by the evolving learning context.

**Keywords:** m-learning, u-learning, p-learning, Context, Adaptation of Content, MPEG-21 DIA UED.

## 1 Introduction

The new evolution of information technology is described by a variety of terms including: mobile computing, ubiquitous computing and ambient intelligence. This development refers to the use of increasingly smaller sizes processors that communicate spontaneously with each other and the use of sensors which, thanks to their very small size, will be integrated in objects of everyday life becoming almost invisible to users. Recently, with the technological evolution of mobile devices and their availability on the market, users want information as quickly as possible, anywhere and anytime. Consequently, the mobile phone is no longer just a simple text or voice communications and is no longer isolated from the Internet; it allows the user to interact with different services located on different servers [2]. This evolution leads us to integrate this type of equipments in our learning systems [1].

Mobile computing applied to distance learning "m-learning" is an area of recent research. The m-learning has emerged as a new trend of e-Learning that takes into

V. Snasel, J. Platos, and E. El-Qawasmeh (Eds.): ICDIPC 2011, Part II, CCIS 189, pp. 518–529, 2011.

account the mobility of learners and has the same educational goals as the e-Learning. However, Access to learning content with different mobile means of communication raises issues of compatibility and relevance: relevance with the preferences of the learner, compatibility of transmitted data with the capacity of the network and access device [9] [10] [11], ergonomics of the display on the device, etc [12] [15].

Considered as a technological evolution of e-learning; m-learning which challenges much more difficulties in terms of technology limitations must provide a satisfactory learning experience [13]. To provide learners with a transparent and permanent access to learning content through any environment, the information sent to the learner must be adapted to specific conditions of their use (device characteristics, constraints of communication networks, learner preferences...) [19] [20]. Designing this adaptation is the core of our study.

The work presented in this article is part of the project MADAR-Learning and aims to demonstrate the feasibility of a new area of functionalities: pervasive learning that beyond the integration of networks and communication technologies develops innovative and original ways of learning [23].

This article is organized as follows: the first section discusses the learning evolution and the need for an environment of adaptable learning content to the learner's current context. The second section presents the architecture of our adaptive system and presents solutions that describe the context: CC / PP, UAProf and MPEG DIA, which help and guide infrastructure of content adaptation.

## 2   E-Learning to P-Learning: Overview of Learning Evolution

### 2.1   E-Learning

The e-learning was raised to address the constraints of classical learning (spatiotemporal constraints, untargeted learning...) and exploiting the new information technologies. The coupling of technology to learning has created new needs in E-learning: Pedagogical and Technical needs [24]. Among these needs, we give the three issues of technical challenges [25] [27]: *Accessibility* for facilitating learning resources discovery, *Reusability* of the same content according to the context and *Durability* of learning resources. Two major e-learning pedagogical challenges are raised according to various existing learning currents (constructivist, differentiated ...): *Collaborative* learning based on constructivist, psycho-cognitive and socio-cognitive theories, and *personalization* of the learning process according to the learner's profile and characteristics [28].

Many standards were established to fulfill technical and pedagogical needs. We cite as example, the learning object indexation and structuring, and learning participants profile design (individual or group) [29]. In the other hand, many learning platforms were developed allowing a convivial learning environment and also providing learners tracking. These platforms have become pedagogically perfect by combining four actors: the learner, administrator, author and teacher. Then, by adopting new standardization works of integrating the learning to the various services provided by learning platforms, e-learning has reached a higher level of maturity and has been able to answer several technical and pedagogical needs. However, following the advanced networking and telecommunications, e-learning has been extended to provide another form of remote learning called m-Learning.

## 2.2 m-Learning

Mobile learning is a learning environment that allows courses access and communication between the main users via mobile technologies [31]. Users fully exploit the technological environment to ensure the various learning services, including mentoring, access to educational content and collaborative work. This new mode of communication has a big success and quickly became very popular, because of the various facilities provider to the users. Even though the mobile learning brought new opportunities, there still the same challenges that we noted in e-learning environment and adds several technical and pedagogical challenges to overcome.

The integration of mobile technologies in the learning process was responsible for several technical requirements: *Device with Small screen, connectivity, throughput, variety of hardware and software features, capacity of devices and mobility,* this mobility is an extremely important advantage of M-learning [32], but it supposes a permanent connectivity which is not usually available. Learning solution requires at the same time a disconnection management [4].

In addition to these technical problems, pedagogical challenges remain a fertile field of research and include different areas: *learning in real context, collaborative learning, more creativity and more autonomy* and *personalization need.*

Until now, due to the existence of a set of challenges only the application of mobile technology in education does not ensure effectively the expectations of learners. To meet the various challenges of m-learning, a new form of learning is established called p-learning (Pervasive Learning).

## 2.3 P-Learning

Pervasive learning is a social process that connects learners to communities of devices, people and situations, including other pervasive leaning situations, and proposes to solve a maximum of challenges posed by the use of various technologies in learning. Among many proposed definitions for pervasive learning we found: « pervasive learning refers to an environment for the student where the computer becomes completely transparent and where the machine adapts to human needs. Access is everywhere, no matter the location of the equipment. This dimension calls for new paradigms to reduce the gap between the mechanical representation and human relations in a communicating space. The learner is at the center of an ecosystem that allows learning through a network of services and access. The learner structure his learning through human interaction / network that takes into account the ubiquity of a spatial, temporal and cognitive multi dimension, as well as multiple channels and multiple access methods tailored to the learner »[35].

By consequence, a fundamental functionality of pervasive learning is to present to the learner relevant information or services in the right place, in the right time and in a seamless way. It allows learning in various contexts but also across different changing contexts. To provide learners with a transparent and permanent access to learning resources through any environment, the information sent to learner must be adapted

[21]. The usefulness of adaptability and context awareness is derived from the ability to better support a variety of learners [18] in varying contexts [16] [17] [22]. The recent research on adaptability and context awareness have turned towards supporting pervasive environments in order to support a situated learning process for an anyway and everyway training through a pervasive environment [23]. The adaptability and context awareness are most of the research topics addressed to develop a platform for dynamic adaptation of learning content for pervasive learning environments in our MADAR-learning project. Consequently, two keys inputs are involved: the acquisition and management of the context of learning situation and provide solution to multiple constraints or "possibilities" provided by the use of technology in learning process [36].

The Context has a variety of definitions in the pervasive computing literature (Chen & Kotz [37], Strang & Linnhoff-Popien [38], daCosta, Yamin & Geyer [39]). The definition of context which is the most widely used was given by Dey [40] saying that: «Context is any information that can be used to characterize the situation of entities (i.e. whether a person, place or object) that are considered relevant to the interaction between a user and an application, including the user and the application themselves ». From this definition and because of the need to adapt learning content to the context, the context in our project covers all information that characterizes the learning situation of the learning entities. This information is related to the device, network, preferences of participant in learning (learner, group of learners) [41] and the technical environment. According to this information, four dimensions or profile of context has been defined; each profile contains much information that constitutes the context parameters (figure 1):

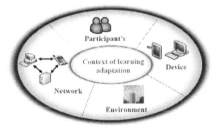

**Fig. 1.** Context of learning adaptation [19]

## 3    Platform for Dynamic Adaptation of Learning Content for Pervasive Learning Environments

The main objective of our work is to propose an adaptation system for learning content to enable transparent adaptation and facilitate the migration to future pervasive learning environment. Generally, Content adaptation solutions can determine the identity and characteristics of a particular device by using the header fields of HTTP requests. They use "User-Agent" which contains information about the browser, the operating system and sometimes material information. And « Accept header » that contains the list of formats supported by the device. However the available information in the HTTP header is not sufficient for a detailed description about device features. For this propose, we have designed an adaptation architecture that consists of collecting the current context parameters (terminal capabilities, network capabilities, preferences and environment parameters of participant in learning), generating the rules for adaptation (adapting what and how?) then adapting the requested content for the learner. Figure 3 represents the architecture of our adaptation platform that is positioned as an intermediate layer between the learner current context (learner's preferences, device, network…) and the learning content database. Our architecture is inspired by the platform VISNET[].

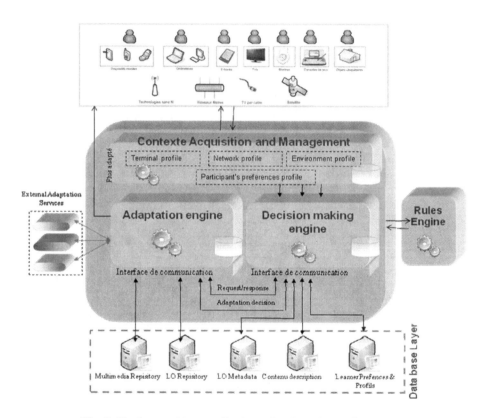

**Fig. 2.** Platform architecture for dynamic adaptation to the context

## 3.1   Learner Context Level

The learning context contains four main elements:

**Device:** Recently, with technological development, a wide variety of devices can play the role of terminals exist such as personal digital assistants (PDA), laptops, mobile phones, TVs, e-books, games consoles etc. However, since these devices have different features, it is necessary to adapt contents according to their characteristics. In fact, because of the over use of mobile devices, the adaptation according to the device has become more and more important. This adaptation is based on the particular characteristics of each type of device. Those characteristics are classified into two types of information: hardware information (Type of terminal (PC, PDA, mobile phone), mark, model, memory, audio characteristics, screen type, screen size, screen resolution, processor...) and software information (Name of the operating system, operating system version, applications, audio format, video format, pictures format, types of protocol, ...).

**Network:** We can classify Network parameters by two types. The first concerns the static ones that include the type of networks supported by device and its theoretical characteristics (theoretical download and upload speed ...). The second concerns the dynamic parameters wherein the parameters change across the time (Current used network, current connection speed and the quality of service offered by the network). In a wireless network where the network condition is more unstable than the wired network, adapting the content to the network condition will help learners to obtain part of important information with acceptable waiting time. For example, when the network bandwidth is low, only text and small images are shown on the mobile device. Mechanisms like this will facilitate information acquisition process across different hardware devices and network conditions.

**Environment:** To be able to include authentic learning scenarios in the real-world, learning solutions should include parameters of learner's environment such us learner location [42], time, proximity to services or other devices or objects and other parameters such us temperature, motion, light and all environmental or activity context. We can classify environment parameters into tree classes: Objects and services proximity (Bluetooth, Wi-Fi RFID) [43], localization parameters (Cell ID, GPS) [44], and Sensors parameters (light sensors, temperature sensors, smoke detectors, motion sensors, and touch sensors).

**Participant's preferences:** A participant in learning is either a learner (an individual learner) or a group of learners (collaborative learning). Consequently, two types of profiles exist: The learner preferences profile that gathers information about the learner, such as his content preferences (text, audio, video...), and to the human machine interfaces preferences (text size, language preference, color choice...) etc. The group preferences profile that gathers information about the collaborative learning includes the group preferences and the type of group interaction. The communication and interactions within a group of learners aims at achieving a collaborative activity. This activity associates roles to the environment of the communication to reach its objectives. This environment can bear different interaction types (synchronous or asynchronous) and different communication tools and services (forum, chat, audio conferencing...).

### 3.2 Database Layer

The main objective of our work is to propose an adaptation system for learning content to enable transparent adaptation and facilitate the migration to future pervasive learning environment. However, in the current context of technological convergence and the explosion of networks and mobile terminals, the consumption of learning object poses a mismatch between the media content that is likely to be represented with different content encoding formats at different quality levels [14], and context of use, which is the main obstacle to fulfilling the promise of pervasive learning. Detailed descriptions of content are needed and this must be arranged as a description of learning objects. This doesn't just imply the need of metadata about learning objects, but another level of description detailing the multimedia learning content.

MPEG-7 includes a rich set of descriptors and description schemes by both the content (audio and visual) and semantic / text [8]. The MPEG-7 descriptions of content may include [49]:

- Information describing the creation and production processes of the content (director, title, short feature movie).
- Information related to the usage of the content (copyright pointers, usage history, and broadcast schedule).
- Information of the storage features of the content (storage format, encoding).
- Structural information on spatial, temporal or spatio-temporal components of the content (scene cuts, segmentation in regions, region motion tracking).
- Information about low level features in the content (colors, textures, sound timbres, melody description).
- Conceptual information of the reality captured by the content (objects and events, interactions among objects).
- Information about how to browse the content in an efficient way (summaries, variations, spatial and frequency subbands,).
- Information about collections of objects.
- Information about the interaction of the user with the content (user preferences, usage history).

The scope of action of MPEG-7 only applies to multimedia content. Consequently, inserting a new description layer of multimedia content (MPEG-7) above proposed standards such as LOM model that is more focused on describing educational information will facilitate adaptation decisions. Our choice of using MPEG-7 for description of content is also encouraged by the possibility that the descriptors in MPEG-7 can be used as such, but can also be extended by means of a registration authority so that the encoding formats that are yet to be defined could be taken into account.

### 3.3   Treatments Layer

Our platform is designed in a model of multilevel distributed applications. The adaptation logic is divided into components according to the function assigned to each component. Three main components are identified: Context Acquisition & management, decision making engine and adaptation engine. Each component of the architecture meets one of these challenges: Collection management, decisions making and implementation of the decision.

#### Context Acquisition & management

Managing all the information that describes the execution context of applications is centralized in a Context Acquisition & Management layer. The context manager provides the collection, annotation, automatic composition and management on the context.

To annotate context parameters, several solutions exist as CC/PP [46], UAProf [20] and WURFL [45] for describing the characteristics of mobile devices [30] [26] [7]. The Composite Capabilities/Preference Profile (CC/PP) is given by the W3C as the first recommendation based on RDF for the description of mobile devices and user preferences [5]. The User Agent Profile (UAProf) specification is a concrete implementation of the CC/PP developed by the Open Mobile Alliance [20]. This specification contains information about six components: HardwarePlatform, SoftwarePlatform, NetworkCharacteristics, BrowserUA, WapCharacteristics et PushCharacteristics [33]. The Wireless Universal Resource File (WURFL) is a project that provides a universal open source file (wurfl.xml), containing the description of the information about more than 1500 devices [45].

Several solutions for m-learning content adaptation architecture are based on UAProf or WURFL for describing the characteristics of mobile devices. However, in the pervasive need the context does not only consists of mobile devices dimension, but of other dimensions, namely the network characteristics (current used speed of the network), information about the physical environment of the learner and his preferences. These dimensions have to be described under the same standard description language that must be widely accepted to be manipulated by all sorts of machines and software. For this reason, we chose to use the "Usage environment description" tools or "UED of the MPEG-21 DIA considered as the standardization initiative to represent a more complete context of content adaptation [3]. The UED allows the description of terminal capabilities, network characteristics, user preferences and characteristics of the natural environment.

UED parameters used in our context adaptation are summarized in Table 1:

**Table 1.** Summary list of context parameters [48]

| Context Profile | Context information | Context Parameters |
|---|---|---|
| **Terminal capabilities** | Codec capabilities | AudioCapabilities, GraphicsCapabilities, ImageCapabilities, SceneGraphCapabilitiesTransportCapbilities,VideoCapabilities |
| | DisplayCapability | Resolution, SizeChar, ScreenSize, olorBitDepth, ColorPrimaries,CharacterSetCode, DisplayDevice RenderingFormat |
| | AudioOutputsCapability | sampligFrequency, bitsPerSample, llowFrequency, hightFrequency, dynamicRange, signalNoiseRatio power, numChannels |
| | UserInteractionInput | Stringinput, keyInput, Microphone, MouseTrackball, Pen, Tablet |
| | Device Properties | Device class, PowerCharacteristics,Storage characteristics, Data I/O characteristics,IPMP Support, CPU Benchmark |
| **Network characteristics** | Network Capability | maxCapacity, minGuaranted, InSequenceDelivery, errorDelivery, errorConnexion |
| | Network Condition | Availabale Bandwidth, Delay, Error |
| **Natural environment characteristics** | Location | DS Location |
| | Time | DS Time |
| | Audio Environment | Noise level, NoiseFrequencySpectrum |
| | Illumination Characteristics | TypeOfillumination, ColorTemperature, ChromaticityIlluminance |

**Table 1.** (*continued*)

| User Preferences | DisplayPresentationPreferences | ColorTemperaturePrference ;BrightnessPreference; SaturationPreference ;ContrastPreference ; StereoscopicVideoConversion |
|---|---|---|
| | Audiovisual Presentation | volumeControlFrequencyEqualizer, Adible, frequencyRange, AdioOutputDevice, BalancePreference, Soudfield, SoniferousSpeed) |
| | GraphicsPresentationPreferences | GeometryEmphasis,TextureEmphasis,AnimationEmphasis,AvatarPreference |
| | ConversionPreference | GeneralResourceConversions,SpecificResourceConversions |
| | PresentationPriorityPreference | GeneralResourcePriorities,SpecificResourcePriorities (Modality.Genre,Object) |
| | FocusOfAttention | Roi, URL, updateinterval, TextFocusOfAttention,SceneObjectFocusOfAttention |
| | MobilityCharacterisctics | UpdateInterval, Directivity,Erraticity |
| | Destination | Time,Location,DestinationClass,DestinationName |

## Decision making engine

The decision making engine Is based on the outputs of the context manager 'The UED description tools', the profile of the learner or the learner's group (IMS-LIP and IMS-Enterprise [12] formalize the learner & the group profile), the MPEG-7 Metadata, the Learning Object Metadata, the Universal Description Constraints and Terminal and network quality of service of the DIA part of MPEG-21. Decision making engine is based on these inputs to generate a set of rules to define what to adapt and to what it will be adapted. Same as the VISINET II project [], we use Terminal and Network Quality of Service and  UCD (Universal Constraint Description) to describe constraints for adaptation. The UCD is the link between "AdaptationQoS" and UED [48]. With this tool, different types of constraints that affect the adaptation process can be described using XML syntax [6]. We use a rules engine to define rules. A rule may be charged, discharged or amended in memory without resetting the rules engine. Then, the rules engine optimizes the performance of rules by arranging the most efficient way possible.

## Adaptation engine

Based on rules provided by decision making engine, the adaptation engine selects the services necessary to adapt the learning content. The objective of this adaptation layer is to attach, detach, dynamically reconfigured, compose and combine the appropriate services that provide elementary adaptation operations to adapt learning resources, activities or situations based on adaptation rules. Adaptation engine contains all generated rules during the user access session to the learning system, and delegate and allows adaptation to adaptation services (video adaptation, translation, audio processing, and change of layout). Types of adaptation can be: Transmoder; Transcoder, Traduction, etc.

# 4  Conclusion

As we note through this paper, during the last decade several learning environments have emerged: e-learning then the m-learning and recently the p-learning. Migration to a pervasive environment requires the use of standards to describe the content and context. These standards will help for dynamic adaptation of content to the learner context, especially that the sphere of context parameters and types of content evolves more and more. The main objective of our work is to propose an adaptation system for learning content. Our platform is based on standards describing the context and content for facilitate the migration to future pervasive learning environment. Our future work focus on several components, firstly, the modules developed for context management is still in a prototype, we plan in the near future to finalize its development.

# References

1. Benlamri, R., Berri, J., Atif, Y.: A Framework for Ontology-aware Instructional Design and Planning. International Journal of E-Learning Knowledge Society 2(1), 83–96 (2006)
2. Tatar, D., Roschelle, J., Vahey, P.: Penuel: Handhelds go to school: Lessons learned. IEEE Computer 36(9), 30–37 (2003)
3. Nam, J., Ro, Y.M., Huh, Y., Kim, M.: Visual Content Adaptation According to User Perception Characteristics. IEEE Transactions of Multimedia 7(3), 435–445 (2005)
4. Vasiliou, A., Economides, A.A.: Mobile collaborative learning using multicast MANETs. International Journal of Mobile Communications (IJMC) 5(4), 423–444 (2007)
5. Resource Description Framework (RDF), http://www.w3.org/RDF/
6. Extensible Markup Language (XML) 1.0, 2 edn., http://www.w3.org/TR/REC-xml
7. Qing, T., Kinshuk: Client Mobile Software Design Principles for Mobile Learning Systems. International Journal of Interactive Mobile Technologies (iJIM) 3(1) (2009)
8. Lonsdale, P., Chris, B., Sharples, M., Arvanitis, T.N.: A context awareness architecture for facilitating mobile learning. In: 2nd European conference on learning with mobile devices (mLearn 2003), London, UK, May 19-20, pp. 79–85 (2003)
9. Tretiakov, Kinshuk, A.: A unified approach to mobile adaptation of educational content. In: Proceedings of the IEEE International Conference on Advanced Learning Technologies (ICALT 2004). IEEE, Los Alamitos (2004)
10. Yau, J., Joy, M.: Architecture of a context-aware and adaptive learning schedule for learning Java. In: Proceedings Seventh IEEE International Conference on Advanced Learning Technologies (ICALT), pp. 1–5 (2007)
11. Yau, J., Joy, M.: A context-aware and adaptive learning schedule framework for supporting learners' daily routines. In: Proceedings Second International Conference on Systems (ICONS 2007), pp. 1–6. IEEE, Los Alamitos (2007)
12. Vassileva, J.: DCG + GTE: Dynamic courseware generation with teaching expertise. Instructional Science 26(3/4), 317–332 (1998)
13. Kurzel, F., Slay, J., Chau, Y.: Towards an adaptive multimedia learning environment. Informing Science InSITE - Where Parallels Intersect (2002)

14. Wang, H.-C., Li, T.-Y., Chang, C.-Y.: Adaptive presentation for effective Web-based learning of 3D content. In: Proceedings of the IEEE International Conference on Advanced Learning Technologies (ICALT 2004). IEEE, Los Alamitos (2004)
15. Klett, F.: The challenge in learning design concepts: Personalization and adaptation in virtual arrangements. In: Proceedings ITHET 6th Annual International Conference. IEEE, Los Alamitos (2005)
16. Kelly, D., Tangney, B.: Adapting to intelligence profile in an adaptive educational system. Interacting with Computers 18, 385–409 (2006)
17. Kay, K.: Learner control. User Modeling and User-Adapted Interaction 11, 111–127 (2001)
18. Elhamdaoui, A., Abik, M., Ajhoun, R.: Toward an adaptation system of learning Content in pervasive environment. In: Proceedings of the 10st International Conference on e-Learning, e-Business, Enterprise Information Systems, and e-Government (EEE 2010), WORLDCOMP 2010 congress, USA, July 12-15 (2010)
19. Wolpers, M., Grohmann, G.: PROLEARN: Technology enhanced learning and knowledge distribution for the corporate world. International Journal of Knowledge and Learning 1(1-2), 44–61 (2005)
20. Goh, T.T., Kinshuk, Lin, T.: Developing an adaptive mobile learning system. In: Proceedings of the International Conference on Computer in Education 2003, December 2-5, pp. 1062–1065. AACE, Hong Kong (2003)
21. Lytras, M.D.: Teaching in the Knowledge society: An art of passion. International Journal of Teaching and Case Studies 1(1/2), 1–9 (2007)
22. Freysen, J.B.: M-learning: an educational perspective. Dans Book of Mobile learning anytime everywhere, pp. 73–76 (2004)
23. Abik, M.: Normalisation et Personnalisation des Situations d'Apprentissage. Thèse de doctorat en informatique, 196p (2009)
24. Procena.: Rapport du Groupe de travail sur l'interopérabilité entre les environnements numériques d'apprentissage. CREPUQ (2007),
    http://www.ccrti.umontreal.ca/documents/ENA_et_Normes.pdf
25. Hassan, M., Al-Sadi, J.: A New Mo-bile Learning Adaptation Model. Inter-national Journal of Interactive Mobile Technologies (iJIM) 3(4) (2009)
26. Arnaud, M.: Problématique de la normalisation pour la formation en ligne. Journée "Normes et standards éducatifs, Lyon, France (2004)
27. Ajhoun, R., Elhamdaoui, A., El Bouzekri, Y., El Idrissi, D.N., Abik, M.: Enhancing learning through the latest technologies. ENSIAS, Mohammed-V Souissi University
28. IMS-Enterprise. IMS Enterprise Information Model Version 1.1 (2002),
    http://www.imsglobal.org/enterprise/index.html
29. Magal-Royo, T., Fajarnes, P., Tor-tajada Montañana, G.I., Defez Garcia, B.: Evaluation Methods on Usability of M-learning Environments. International Journal of Interactive Mobile Technologies (iJIM), 1(1) (2007)
30. Korean, L.I.P.: Model Research Team. A Learner Information Item for m-learning. ISO/IEC JTC1 SC36 WG3 N0139. Working Document (2005),
    http://isotc.iso.org/livelink/livelink/fetch/2000/
    2122/327993/806742/1056984/36N1288_Mobile_Learning_
    Applications.pdf?nodeid=5441346&vernum=0
31. Calvé, A., Dominique, A.: Mobile learning: les avantages du papier virtuel FI 1 – 3 février, Haute Ecole Valaisanne, Sierre (2004)

32. User Agent Profile version 2.0; OMA specification (2006),
    http://www.openmobilealliance.org/release_program/docs/
    UAProf/V2_0-20060206-A/OMA-TS-UAProf-V2_0-20060206-A.pdf
33. Elhamdaoui, A., Abik, M.: Adaptation of E-services for Mobile and Ubiquitous
    environments. In: Proceedings of the 1st International Conference on Next Generation
    Networks and Services (NGNS 2009), Rabat (2009)
34. Preteux, F., Vaucelle, A., Henda, M.B., Hudrisier, H.: Pervasive learning and
    normalization. In: Proceedings of Workshop Emap 2008, TELECOM ParisTech (2008)
35. Elhamdaoui, A., Abik, M.: Adaptation System of learning content to learner's current
    context. In: Proceedings of the 1st International Conference on Next Generation Networks
    and Services (NGNS 2010), Rabat (2010)
36. Chen, G., Kotz, D.: A Survey of Context-Aware Mobile Computing Research. Technical
    Report. UMI Order Number: TR2000-381, Dartmouth College (2000)
37. Strang, T., Linnhoff-Popien, C.: A Context Modeling Survey. In: Indulska, J., De Roure,
    D. (eds.) Proc. of First International Workshop on Context Modeling, Reasoning and
    Management (UbiComp 2004), Nottingham, England (2004)
38. Costa, C., Yamin, A., Geyer, C.: Toward a General Software Infrastucture for Ubiquitous
    Computing. IEEE Pervasive Computing 7(1), 64–73 (2008)
39. Dey, A.K., Abowd, G.D.: CybreMinder: A context-aware system for supporting reminders.
    In: Thomas, P., Gellersen, H.-W. (eds.) HUC 2000. LNCS, vol. 1927, pp. 172–186.
    Springer, Heidelberg (2000)
40. Abik, M., Ajhoun, R.: Normalization and Personalization of Learning Situation: NPLS.
    International Journal of Emerging Technologies in Learning (iJET) 4(2) (2009); ISSN:
    1863-0383
41. Becker, C., Durr, F.: On location models for ubiquitous computing. Personal Ubiquitous
    Computing 9, 20–31 (2005)
42. Schilit, B.N., Theimer, M.M.: Disseminating active map information to mobile hosts.
    IEEE Networks 8(5), 22–32 (1994)
43. Ryan, N., Pascoe, J., Morse, D.: Enhanced reality fieldwork: The context-aware
    archaeological assistant. Computer Applications in Archaeology, British Archaeological
    Reports, Oxford (1998)
44. Wireless Universal Resource File WURFL,
    http://wurfl.sourceforge.net/help_doc.php
45. Composite Capability/Preference Profiles (CC/PP): Structure and Vocabularies 2.0
    (January 15, 2004), http://www.w3.org/TR/CCPP-struct-vocab2/
46. Zebedee, J., Martin, P., Wilson, K., Powley, W.: Context-Aware Mobile and Ubiquitous
    Computing for Enhanced Usability. In: An Adaptable Context Management Framework
    for Pervasive Computing, p. 115 (2009)
47. Kasutani, E.: New Frontiers in Universal Multimedia Access, ITS Report 04.22, Lausanne,
    EPFL, pp. 26-40 September (2004)
48. Martínez, J.M.: MPEG-7 Overview (version 10), ISO/IEC JTC1/SC29/WG11N6828
    (October 2004)
49. Carreras1, A., Andrade, M.T., Masterton, T., Arachchi, H.K., Barbosa, V., Dogan, S.,
    Delgado, J., Kondoz, A.M.: Contextual information in virtual collaboration systems
    beyond current standars. In: Universitat politécnica de catalunya, WIAMIS (2009)

# A Theoretical Scheme to Implement MAC Protocols in VANETs Employing Cognitive Radio[*]

Shankar Yanamandram and Hamid Shahnasser

San Francisco State University
San Francisco, CA, USA
shankary@sfsu.edu

**Abstract.** Vehicular communications have the capacity to open up a plethora of service applications and most importantly, increasing road safety by providing warning messages. To enable these features, it is necessary to establish MAC protocols which not only offer good QoS and fairness but also address other concerns of Vehicular Ad-hoc Networks (VANETs). As VANETs pose greater challenges compared to conventional Ad-hoc networks like MANETs, it is required to implement effective medium access schemes which address efficient use of spectrum, minimization of packet delay, as well as authentication, security and prioritized delivery of safety messages. In this paper, we study novel concepts of three recently proposed MAC protocols for VANETs. We provide a theoretical approach in implementing multiple MAC protocols for VANETs, which use cognitive radio technology, by combining some of the novel features proposed in the reviewed protocols.

**Keywords:** Vehicular Ad-Hoc Networks, VANETs, Cognitive Radio, MAC protocols.

## 1 Introduction

### 1.1 VANETs

The universal networking standard defined by the IEEE has several sections. IEEE 802.11 standard defines Wireless Local Area Networks (WLANs). Wireless networking was revolutionized with the introduction of dual role capabilities of transmission and reception to nodes in a wireless network. Mobile Ad-Hoc Networks (MANETs), as these networks are called, introduced several concepts which were apt for implementation in vehicular communication and creating Intelligent Transportation Systems (ITS). Research in combining MANET concepts in vehicular communications ushered in Vehicular Ad-hoc Networks (VANETs). VANETs form inherent concepts and part of ITS which aim at modernizing transportation systems by improving their safety, entertainment and efficiency. VANETs have the capabilities to perform Vehicle-to-Vehicle communication (V2V) and Vehicle-to-Infrastructure communication

---

[*] This work has been partially supported by UNCFSP's NASA Science and Technology Institute Grant.

V. Snasel, J. Platos, and E. El-Qawasmeh (Eds.): ICDIPC 2011, Part II, CCIS 189, pp. 530–537, 2011.
© Springer-Verlag Berlin Heidelberg 2011

(V2I) which will enable efficient delivery of emergency and other safety messages to vehicles. Besides safety message delivery, VANETs will also enable smooth traffic flow, internet connectivity in vehicles, other custom applications in vehicles.

## 1.2 VANETs – Features and Challenges

VANETs will enable ITS to build robust networks for effective inter vehicular communication. VANETs are a prime example of the implementation of MANETs. However, due to highly dynamic positions of vehicles, VANETs will have a unique structure and will also present several challenges in their implementation.

An On-Board Unit (OBU) present in every vehicle will communicate with other vehicular nodes and Road Side Units (RSUs). RSUs may be connected to the internet via a network backbone for increased applications. Such a network employing both V2V and V2I communication is known as a Hybrid network.

VANETs have a few unique features that make their implementation challenging. Features like high nodal speeds, extreme dynamicity of the network, and transmission reliability pose unique challenges in creating efficient VANETs. The features and challenges of VANETs have been discussed in detail by Yanamandram and Shahnasser [1].

Owing to these exceptional network conditions, efficient MAC and routing protocols have to be proposed exclusively for VANETs. In this paper, we mainly look at the possibility of combining novel features of previously proposed MAC protocols for VANETs. We theoretically propose a scheme to implement MAC protocols in VANETs which use next generation cognitive radio devices.

## 1.3 Organization of the Paper

Prime importance has to be accorded to research work on medium access in VANETs. The unique features presented by VANETs and the arduous challenges posed to tackle these features make the efficient implementation of VANETs challenging. The features and challenges of VANETs are discussed in Section 1. In Section 2, we discuss three previously proposed novel MAC protocols which are based on the DSRC band and highlight their features. We provide a theoretical scheme to implement MAC protocols in VANETs which make use of next generation cognitive radio technology in Section 3. We evaluate and analyze the proposed scheme in section 4 and we conclude this paper in Section 5.

## 2 DSRC Based MAC Protocols

Yanamandram and Shahnasser [1] have analyzed three recently proposed MAC protocols which consider the DSRC band in their implementation. In this paper, we apply some novel concepts presented by Secure VANET MAC [2], Cognitive Mac Protocol (CMV) [3] and Vehicular Self Organizing MAC protocol (VeSOMAC) [4] protocols to create a medium access scheme for VANETs. These protocols introduce various aspects to create an efficient MAC protocol for VANETs namely:

- Message priority and Security while accessing channels for emergency and non emergency messages (Secure VANET protocol)[1][2]. Secure VANET MAC considers message security and message priority while transmitting a message in a VANET and hence, warning messages are sent with higher priority and security compared to other messages.
- Cognitive radio and Wideband-RTS for spectrum access (CMV) [1][3]. Messages which require less time to be transmitted employ a different access mechanism compared to messages which will require more time for transmission. The concept CMV brings forth ensures resource sharing and maximum resource utilization.
- An In-band bitmap vector for knowledge of 1-hop and 2-hop neighbor's location and hence, organization of the VANET (VeSOMAC) [1][4]. The In-Band header bitmap vector introduced in VeSOMAC controls and coordinates the entire operation of the protocol. The bitmap contains information of neighboring nodes' slot information. Using the bitmap header, slot information is exchanged across the entire network. Collisions are detected in the network by acknowledgements in the bitmap.

Combining the above concepts and utilizing them in a single MAC scheme may produce efficient medium accessing methods. In the following section, we try to implement some of the concepts reviewed in unison to create an efficient MAC protocol. We try to analyze the protocol's ability to addresses major issues in VANETs such as efficient use of spectrum, minimization of packet delay, as well as authentication, security and prioritized delivery of safety messages.

## 3   Multiple MAC Implementation in VANETs

In this section, we try to introduce a new concept for multiple MAC implementations in VANETs using some ideas presented in the previously discussed MAC protocols.

### 3.1   Related Work

Huang, Jing and Raychaudhri [5] introduce a concept to implement MAC protocols for cognitive radio. They create a relationship between MAC protocols and cognitive radios and try to implement the same by proposing an Adaptive MAC protocol (AMAC) which could be used in wireless radio network environments. The concept presented is specifically applicable in VANETs due to dynamic network conditions, high radio node density and extreme service requirements of vehicular communications.

Cognet protocol [6] was used in describing and implementing the AMAC protocol. Cognet architecture consists of a global control plane concept which controls and exchanges information between cognitive radios in a network. To maintain such a communication, a MAC layer here would involve cross-layer parameters and tags to preserve the protocol consistency between radio devices or nodes sharing the same physical channel.

Global control plane (GCP) and data plane concepts presented by Jing and Ray-chaudhuri [6] calls for application of two different zones: one for control applications and the other dedicated solely for data transmission. The global control plane carries all control information while the data plane handles data transmission between nodes in the network. The concept is implemented using a low-cost control radio operating on a dedicated control channel which is in charge of all radio resource parameters. The GCP also helps with the initial loading of the network and its topology discovery. The data plane protocol stack on every node handles data transmission and the services associated between the wireless nodes. The GCP aids in establishing the operating PHY, MAC and routing parameters and hence, forming the control functions. Once the data path is established, the data is transmitted after negotiations take place utilizing resources of the GCP protocols. The actual MAC protocols which need to be switched to are present in the data plane. The AMAC protocol is implemented in the control plane and this enables the switching process between various MAC protocols in the data plane.

The AMAC protocol [5] is implemented using the GCP and data plane structure as explained previously. The main benefit of using cognitive radios is enhanced flexibility and accessibility. The flexibility to access various radio resources enables extreme wireless network capabilities. The AMAC protocol enables dynamic adaptation of MAC protocols which can be used to efficiently implement multiple MAC protocols in highly dynamic network like VANETs. The AMAC protocol establishes a scheme which starts with an initial MAC protocol and then switches to another MAC protocol based on the physical channel parameters. Initially, all nodes in the network begin a process of powering on, bootstrapping and network discovery. The PHY/MAC capabilities and current status are configured by the bootstrapping function in the PHY/MAC modules respectively.

A discovery protocol is run to determine the network and other parameters like shortest path for data transmission and end-to-end reachability. Data transmission is now initiated based on the exchanged control message. Once data transfer is initiated, a baseline MAC protocol is selected. Nodes access the PHY channel and communicate based on the MAC protocol while regularly monitoring the channel. In case the data transmission drops significantly, one of the main concerns in any network, the nodes start to observe the wireless channel. The nodes try to adapt to the PHY parameters such as operating channel frequency, power, rate, or modulation type. In case the PHY parameters are inadaptable, nodes may initiate for a switch to another apt MAC protocol using MAC switching schemes. A MAC switching scheme lays out a set of rules according to which nodes mutually convert to another MAC protocol. Huang et. al. [5], propose two different MAC switching schemes based on performance degradation threshold and predicted future traffic patterns. These schemes enable nodes to automatically switch MAC protocols depending on the nodal network environment. In this way, AMAC enables multiple implementations of MAC protocols.

In cases where the network dynamicity and nodal density is high, an automatic switching scheme may witness high delay, restrict the switching capabilities to a couple of MAC protocols, or use more resources to evaluate the suitable protocol. Instead, if there are geographical zones allocated by the CA in which particular MAC protocols need to be implemented, the switching process will be much simpler and will make use of significantly less resources. The information about the MAC protocol zones may be based on traffic density or previously evaluated performances. Computation for the most suitable MAC protocol can take place at a central RSU if present in the zone. Also, previously calculated information about the MAC protocol can be stored in the OBU by the CA. This information has to be periodically updated. The case of predetermined geographical zones for MAC protocols will reduce use of computational and radio resources, and decrease latency. This will enable faster switching and we use this idea in this particular paper.

### 3.2 The combined MAC protocol for VANETs

#### 3.2.1 System Setup

We determined some prerequisites for implementation of the protocol. In this section we outline those parameters. Let the condition at the start of network operations be called idle. While in Idle state, the hardware and software pre-requisites for each vehicular node are as follows.

Radio devices in the entire network will be assumed to be cognitive radio nodes. This implies that cognitive radio technology is implemented in the radio devices and hence, the node has capabilities of the cognitive radio family to dynamically select a wide variety of radio parameters and network protocol standards. This will enable it to adapt to detected or observed radio links and corresponding network conditions. The cognitive radio will be capable of searching and accessing spectrum white space from all bands to effectively use the spectrum with superior power control and modulation techniques. Moreover, at the network layer, the cognitive radio system will be capable of making runtime changes to the protocols used for routing, packet transmission and congestion control when the network topology is modified.

As described in Secure VANET MAC [2] and by the IEEE 802.11p draft [7], we assume that every vehicular node has an On–board-Unit (OBU) with a secure database. The OBU is completely defined and certified by a central Certification Authority (CA). Each OBU has a key vector described by the CA and has public key infrastructure information. The system also provides for an in-band bitmap vector as in the VeSOMAC protocol. All the above information is contained in every OBU and hence, every node in the vehicular network. These features ensure that the network is secure and adheres to the standards set by the IEEE.

#### 3.2.2 Architecture and Implementation Process

After all the initial parameters are met, let us consider the case where nodes are ready to form the network. Let us now assume that nodes have started making contact with each other and that a network has been constructed. We now implement the AMAC protocol to combine concepts from the previously described protocols for effective MAC scheme implementation.

Initially, all nodes in the network power up and turn on the bootstrapping and discovery process. The PHY/MAC capabilities, current status are configured. Data transmission is initiated after the discovery protocol initiates the network parameters. After initiation, a baseline MAC protocol is determined. Depending on the zone location, a predetermined MAC protocol is implemented. In this paper, we considered

VANET MAC protocols which either divided the 5.9 GHz band into CCH and SCHs (Frequency division) or MAC protocols which used TDMA in their implementation.

We first assume that in a particular zone, the baseline MAC protocol considered is MAC A. MAC A protocol performs medium access by dividing DSRC into CCH and SCHs. Each node in the network then chooses preferred transmission channels. Information about every node's transmission channels is stored in a bitmap vector. The idea of a bitmap vector was presented by the VeSOMAC protocol [5]. However, in this case the bitmap vector will be modified to store the SCHs information as shown in Figure 1. The bitmap vectors of nodes in the network are exchanged throughout the network and the vectors are updated accordingly. Bitmap vectors are compared at every node to evaluate the preferred SCHs of other nodes. Transmission takes place once the information is assessed. A transmitting node first sends a wideband RTS to the receiver. On receiving this Wideband-RTS signal, the receiver then chooses a channel which has a better RSS using wideband spectral sensing. The receiver then sends a CTS on the channel it selects and transmission of data takes place. Several nodes may be able to exchange data at a particular time in different channels. Once transmission takes place, bitmaps vectors with updated information are again exchanged. If the zone changes or AMAC automatically switches the MAC protocol, then let us assume that the MAC protocol to be implemented is MAC B. Here, nodes in the network choose a transmission time slot based on TDMA allocations. MAC B also employs a bitmap vector which has information of the times slots of every node in the network. Again, this bitmap vector information is exchanged by all neighboring nodes and hence, every node has information about its 1-hop and 2-hop neighboring nodes. This information enables transfer of data packets between nodes during the appropriate time slot. MAC B scheme is the same as VeSOMAC protocol and hence, advantages posted by VeSOMAC such as self-configuration, reorganization of the network and delay reduction present the same advantages in this case.

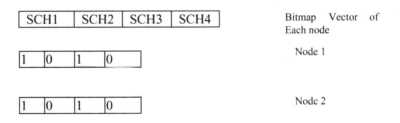

**Fig. 1.** Bitmap vectors in MAC A

In this manner, novel features presented in CMV, VeSOMAC and Secure VANET MAC can be combined to form robust and efficient MAC protocols to be used in VANETs. As cognitive radio is the next step for wireless network implementation, it is important to study the possibility of multiple MAC implementations in VANETs. In the following section we evaluate the above proposed Multiple MAC implementation scheme for VANETs.

## 4  Theoretical Scheme Analysis

The above proposed medium access scheme for VANETs employs cognitive radio technology for the effective implementation of the MAC layer protocols in VANETs. This theoretical study describes the necessity to implement cognitive radios in VANETs to mainly create a universal radio module which will be capable of adapting to any spectrum condition while used in across different parts of the world. Moreover, cognitive radio will be able to adapt to any new protocol or environment by the addition of softwares, and thus will save additional hardware costs which would be incurred otherwise. Hence, looking at practical implementation, using cognitive radios will mean reduced costs for the user and at the same time will provide for better radios with more data handling capacity.

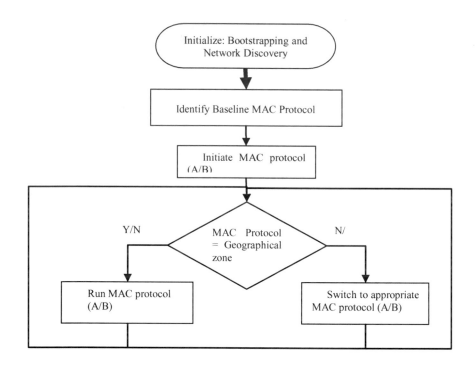

**Fig. 2.** Work Flow of the MAC Scheme using AMAC

Data Security in VANETs is prioritized by including a key vector allocated by a Certification Authority in data transmissions. The MAC scheme proposes the use of AMAC protocol [5] which enables switching between MAC protocols. Priority of safety messages is addressed by enabling safety message transmission in any channel of the DSRC. Employing a modified bitmap vector scheme allows for reduced utilization of network resources, and may successively reduce the latency of propagation of MAC messages. The concepts VeSOMAC brings forth are employed in the MAC scheme and this will ensure self-reorganization and collision detection in the network.

Although only two protocols have been mentioned in implementation of multiple MAC protocols in this paper, on utilizing the AMAC concept, this number could be increased. Hence, this scheme offers excellent flexibility and adaptability.

## 5 Conclusion and Future Work

In this paper, we reviewed three novel MAC protocols proposed exclusively for VANETs which were based on the DSRC band. We highlighted important features and novel concepts they proposed and try to utilize them in Unison to create a more efficient MAC protocol. By employing AMAC protocol, we present theoretical approaches to multiple MAC protocol implementations for VANETs. Aspects related to efficient use of spectrum, minimized packet delay, security and authentication have been addressed in the schemes presented.

To enhance this research work, further evaluation of the MAC schemes is required. It is essential to analyze the performances of MAC schemes which we named MAC A and MAC B in this paper. Further research related to the AMAC protocol may yield tips to enhance it further.

## References

[1] Yanamandram, S., Shahnasser, H.: Analysis of DSRC based MAC protocols for VANETs. In: International Conference on Ultra Modern Telecommunications & Workshops, ICUMT 2009 (2009)

[2] Chung, S.-c., Yoo, J., Kim, C.-k.: Cognitive MAC for VANET based on the WAVE systems. In: Proc. IEEE ICACT 2009, February 15-18, vol. 01, pp. 41–46 (2009)

[3] Qian, Y., Lu, K., Moayeri, N.: A Secure VANET MAC Protocol for DSRC Applications. In: Proceedings of IEEE Globecom 2008, New Orleans, LA, November 30 – December 4 (2008)

[4] Yu, F., Biswas, S.: A Self-Organizing MAC Protocol for DSRC based Vehicular Ad Hoc Networks,icdcsw. In: 27th International Conference on Distributed Computing Systems Workshops (ICDCSW 2007), p. 88 (2007)

[5] Huang, K.-C., Jing, X., Raychaudhuri, D.: MAC Protocol Adaptation in Cognitive Radio Networks: An Experimental Study. In: Proceedings of 18th International Conference on Computer Communications and Networks, ICCCN 2009 (2009)

[6] Jing, X., Raychaudhuri, D.: Global Control Plane Architecture for Cognitive Radio Networks. In: Proceedings of IEEE CogNets 2007 Workshop - Towards Cognition in Wireless Networks (in conjunction with IEEE ICC), June 24-28 (2007)

[7] Jiang, D., Delgrossi, L.: IEEE 802.11p: Towards an International Standard for Wireless Access in Vehicular Environments. In: Vehicular Technology Conference, VTC Spring 2008, pp. 2036–2040 (2008)

# A General Description of a New Character Recognition Process Based on Ontology

Hacene Belhadef, Aicha Eutamene, and Mohamed Khireddine Kholadi

{hacene_belhadef,aicha.eutamene,kholladi}@umc.edu.dz

**Abstract.** In this paper, we present a general description of a new character recognition process based on ontology, semantically annotated by a domain expert. Such process is based essentially on a matching step between two ontologies, the first represents a domain ontology, containing the typographical description of different characters represent an alphabet of a well definite language (Latin for example), the second ontology, describes the document in question in the form of concepts where each concept represents a grapheme located in a well-defined order in the document.

**Keywords:** character recognition, grapheme, matching, ontology, semantic annotation, typographical features.

## 1 Introduction

The general purpose of character recognition either printed or handwritten is transformed into a readable representation and exploited by a machine. The recognition process is not always easy as long as the contents of the documents may have multiple representations. In the case of printed documents, size, style (Bold, Italic... etc), and melting characters and other factors play a crucial role in such a process. As for handwritten documents, the conditions of safeguard are often not adequate. Today a large number of books and manuscripts are preserved in museums and archives and are at risk of disappearing due to several factors such as moisture, acidity .., which requires scanning these documents in order to preserve the heritage and exploit a more efficient manner. The digitization of documents is the most effective and fast for this problem, it is to convert a document in paper form into a digital image. Transcription is another solution, but it is less used and limited to manuscripts documents not-long.

The result image of such operation of digitization is used as raw material in the recognition process, to decorticate the content and extract the necessary primitives for the identification and characters recognition, also the entire contents of the document, to use it in a lot of area such as the restoration of national heritage or world, classification, indexing and archiving.

Whatever the rich content of the documents, but this wealth is still insufficient to help the process of character recognition. In this article we are aware that one step annotation document is required to add information further helping this process to accomplish its task.

V. Snasel, J. Platos, and E. El-Qawasmeh (Eds.): ICDIPC 2011, Part II, CCIS 189, pp. 538–546, 2011.
© Springer-Verlag Berlin Heidelberg 2011

The annotation of an image through the construction of ontology constitutes the main tool for associating semantics to an image and allows the use of research methods more powerful and able to answer complex queries.

The association between data and ontology then allows the software agents to take advantage of the knowledge represented in ontology to better use the images. There are several annotation types; Figure 1 shows our choice for semantic type annotation on an ontology created after a step of segmentation and feature extraction.

This article is organized as follows. In First, we present an overview on the two concepts strongly linked to our process, as the ontology and annotation. In the paragraphs that follow, we present a description of the stages of our process scanning until the last step is the post processing showing our contribution to enrich this process.

## 2  Ontology

The concept of ontology is a concept that is not always easy to characterize. Indeed, it is used in different contexts: philosophy, linguistics, intelligence (AI), and each one's have its particular definition. The most commonly accepted definition is that given by T. Gruber in 1993: "a specification of a conceptualization to help programs and humans to share knowledge "[1]. More specifically: "... the Ontology is an explicit formal specification of a shared conceptualization. » According to Gruber," a conceptualization is the result of modeling phenomena in the domain of interest. This model identifies concepts and relations describing these phenomena. "Explicit" means that the concepts and their relationships are typed, and constraints on the use of these types are clearly explained. "Formal" refers to the fact that ontology should be understandable by the machine. "Shared" reflects the idea that ontology should capture the knowledge commonly accepted by consensus of all community stakeholders in the field [2].

## 3  Semantic Annotation

The annotation is used to associate to documents a rich description (metadata) additional, complementary, describing their content, based on consensual vocabularies and independent of applications. It may be as text, structured, or semantic. it fills the poverty in the semantic level provided by a document.

There are many semantic annotation tools that can be distinguished by the nature of information resources annotated (text, image, video, etc...), the user annotation (Automatic, semi-automatic or manual) and the ontology reference used [3]. There are simple tools for annotation, like Flickr and ACDSee [18] Allowing the addition of descriptions textual content. Other tools, like [4] and [5] propose a more complex with a graph concepts and spatial ontology in RDF [19]. These tools allow annotations on the image, its areas, and spatial relationships between them ("A is the area right of the region B)...

The annotation on the content of manuscripts is to describe what's in an image, for example, objects and characters that appear on the image, relationships between character forming words and sentences. However the notation on the context is used for describing the image using these contextual elements. The date or the age and the conditions under which the document was written. In the field of digital cameras, a tool that is widely used for annotating contextual image archive EXIF (Exchangeable Image File) When taking a photo, most digital cameras add to the header image at EXIF description. This description has metadata on the photo (name, size, date) on the camera (model, maximum resolution) and the settings used to shoot (flash intensity, the aperture ) [6]. As for our annotation module (Figure 1), the reader may refer to section 4.5 for more information.

## 4   Description of Our System

In this section we describe the different steps of our proposed process, including the steps of annotation and mapping that distinguish between such process and another classic, located in the literature. Figure 1 shows these steps starting with digital acquisition and arriving at post-treatment through segmentation, extraction of features and other steps.

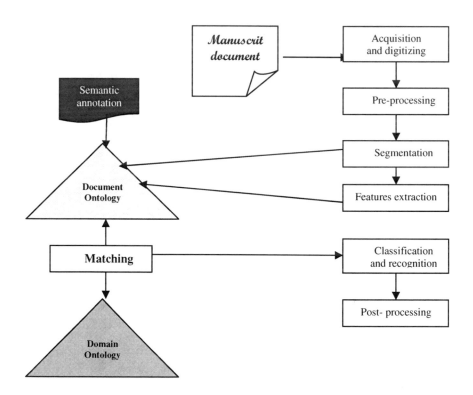

**Fig. 1.** Architecture of our system

## 4.1  Acquisition and Digitizing

The acquisition allows the conversion of paper document in the form of a digital image. This step is important because she cares about preparing documents to be seized, the choice and configuration of hardware input (scanner) and that the format for storing images [7].

Systems acquisition of the most common, are essentially linear scanners or cameras (CCD). The resolution of the scanned image influence the steps a subsequent recognition system. It is commonly accepted that the optimal resolution of an image depends on the thickness of the line of writing. Thus, for subsequent treatments can be applied correctly, it must the trait of writing has a minimum thickness of 3 pixels, an image resolution of between 100 and 300 points per inch (8 to 12 pixels / mm).

Current scanners have a maximum resolution is 300 dpi[1]. They allow image capture of text or binary or grayscale gray is the same color [8]. Convert a paper document into electronic document is the purpose of document recognition systems. This task is a necessity for access to a wider audience and offer new services such as preservation of ancient documents, consultation documents rare, Rapid duplication and economic structures, research information more efficient and finally the possibility of share knowledge, [9], [10] ... etc.

## 4.2  Pre-processing

The pre-processing included all preparatory operations image processing; its role is to prepare the image document for further process steps. It includes all functions performed by the segmentation and feature extraction to produce a version cleansed of the original image so that it can be used directly and effectively. This step is not specific to a given type of writing but it is part of any system pattern recognition to improve the quality of information for process steps that follow. So the pre-processing's are used to eliminate the defects associated with scanned image; these defects can be of two types: those related to the channel scan (tilt brightness, noise ...) or those related to quality intrinsic to the document (the wet spots, appearance of back, holes ...) [11].

## 4.3  Segmentation

Segmentation is an essential step in the recognition process. It conditions strongly its robustness and determines its approach to a priori recognition. There are therefore two approaches: the comprehensive and analytical approach. To avoid segmentation problem of drawing a word into letters, the overall approach does not use segmentation and therefore consider the layout of the word in its entirety as to recognize the shape. For cons, the analytical approach based on segmentation and seeks to isolate and then identify meaningful units of the path of a word priori to match letters that compose it.

Therefore good segmentation allows the present system to recognize characters in good conditions, cons improper segmentation, in turn, will lead falling rate of recognition [12] [13].

---

[1] dpi: dots par inch.

The segmentation process is generally subdivided into two main stages, the first step is to horizontal segmentation is to locate the entity to recognize this entity may be a paragraph, a line, word or group of characters, the second being cons vertical segmentation, it is to locate items that comprise the entity we want to recognize these elements can be words or characters.

### 4.4  Extraction of Features

The extraction of feature is a crucial and very important in the recognition process, because subsequent treatments will no longer manipulate the original image but the results provided by this step. Its role locates the letters in the word and spatial relationships between different lexical units indicating their limitations left and right. These characteristics are generally classified into two families: the structural characteristics (loops, concavities, overruns, extreme points of the route, intersections, etc ....) and the statistical characteristics that derived measures of spatial distribution of pixels (zoning, moment invariants, Fourier descriptors, density points, contours, etc.)...

The feature extraction of characters may carry on:

- The form itself
- It's skeleton
- By Design

### 4.5  Creation of Ontologies

This step is to create two ontologies: domain ontology and document ontology.

**Document ontology:** This ontology represents the contents of the document; it is created after an operation of segmentation and extraction of primitives, representing typographic forms of character of the processed document; where each concept of ontology represents a grapheme located in a well-defined order in the document.

Example of an excerpt from document ontology represents the word: LIRE

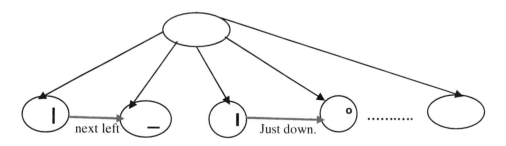

**Fig. 2.** Representation of the word "LIRE"

**Domain ontology:** This ontology contains typographical features of character of the Latin alphabet, which are represented in the figure below. Figure 3, presents this ontology created under protégé editor [20].

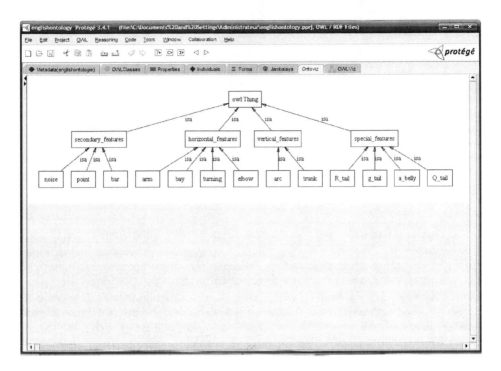

**Fig. 3.** Typographical features (grapheme)

## 4.6  Semantic Annotation

Before performing the step of annotation, one must first create the document ontology. This last, represents the different characteristics of contents processed document. The representation of documents has evolved classical representation is the representation of gross document to the structured representation. Representation Structured documents are usually described using the XML (Extensible Markup Language) are the presentation of XML schema or DTD (Document Type Definition).

Contrary to the conventional representation of a document that reflects only the text content and information is presented in a flat without any treatment, the structural presentation focuses on the presentation of structured content, and all information is associated with a label, be logical or physical.

The physical structure describes the organization of the document (Lines, Paragraphs, Images...) thus that the format of information (Center, Left, Right...) is the description of the appearance of document to the user. However the logical structure, presents the significance of this information (Title, Name_lauthor, Date...). [14]

In our case the annotation is performed on the ontology document written in OWL (Web Ontology Language) the purpose of this annotation is the enrichment of the ontology by semantic information that are not on the document and can query the ontology by and the inference mechanism to facilitate and accelerate the recognition process.

## 4.7  Matching

The process of matching is an algorithm that takes as input parameters: the schema Target (ontology document) and the destination schema (reference ontology). This process determines the values semantic similarities between elements and attributes patterns. The objective here is to find correspondences nodes of the source and target ontology, that's why the similarity measures should be used to estimate the similarity between the paired elements and the identification and recognition of characters represented by these nodes. This process can be used in the stage of recognition or in the stage of post-processing.

## 4.8  Classification and Recognition

Character recognition can decide on the identity of a character from a learning of its form. This step requires a prior step of parameterization of the form, defining data, measurements, or visual cues that underlie the recognition method. Depending on the nature of this information; there are several categories of methods: syntax (described by a grammar), structural (described by a graph) or statistical (descriptions by partitioning the space). These have by far the greatest interest with methods based on neural networks or stochastic model [7]. Recently several authors seek to extend recognition to the manuscripts recognition of words, sentences and entire texts. In [15] the author proposed an approach for recognition of characters and offers its adaptation for the recognition of handwriting, using a system based on a MRF modeling and programming dynamic 2D.

In [16] the author uses a General Markov bi-dimensional approach, for document recognition manuscripts (AMBER)-based programming Dynamic and inspired by the method of Knight. This approach has allowed the build script mail [17]. Proposes a system of recognition of handwritten words Arab isolated, belonging to a lexicon, based on a hybrid system based on Neural Networks and Models Hidden Markov (HMM) and segmented into graphemes [11].

## 4.9  Post-processing

A document consists of a set of characters. Therefore, recognition of these characters implies recognition of the full text. But it often happens, for multiple reasons, the system is wrong or does not identify certain character, which renders some words invalid. The main goal of this phase is to improve the recognition result by making corrections spelling or using morphological tools references such as dictionaries, thesauri, ontology Contextual, etc.... The identification of lexical units in the document does not only concern primary system of recognition. The majority of recognition methods are limited to the analysis of physical structure and recognition logic remains to develop, for which we propose in our system add other steps, such as checking and syntax semantic content of documents, by defining a grammar or a contextual ontology.

In the field of heritage restoration, especially the old documents that have been preserved in non-appropriate conditions, these documents may experience problems such as lack of significant portions or deleted words or paragraphs that constitute the document. One solution proposed to solve this problem is the use of ontologies by verifying the semantic of the lexical and syntactic token.

## 5 Conclusion

The field of recognition of handwritten documents is rather quite recent, the work is growing and several issues remain open, although an abundance of research about this area.

In this paper we have presented a new recognition process or rather new approach based on the creation of a ontology representing the contents of a handwritten document and a step of semantic annotation which tries to enrich this last ontology, then a step of matching with a domain ontology for character identification.

We also plan to create a global ontology that brings together all the Latin alphabet, and define the different spatial relationships between all typographical forms (grapheme) and defining appropriate similarity measures for the process of matching, and we plan in the step of post-processing, to use of an external resource such as WordNet for syntactical and grammatical checking .

## References

1. Studer, R., Benjamins, V., Fensel, D.: Knowledge Engineering: Principles and Methods. IEEE Transactions on Data and Knowledge Engineering 25(162), 161–197 (1998)
2. Gruber, R.: Towards Principles for the Design of Ontologies Used for Knowledge Sharing. In: International Workshop on Formal Ontology, Available as technical report KSL-93-04, Padova, Italy (1993)
3. Amardeilh, F.: Web Sémantique et Informatique Linguistique: Propositions Méthodologiques et Réalisation d'une Plateforme Logicielle. Doctoral Thesis, Univ. Paris X, pp. 223–253 (2007)
4. Lux, M., Klieber, W., Granitzer, M.: Caliph & Emir: Semantics in Multimedia Retrieval and Annotation. In: Proceedings of the 19th International CODATA Conference 2004: The Information Society: New Horizons for Science, Berlin, Allemane (2004)
5. Hollink, L., Nguyen, G., Schreiber, G., Wielemaker, J., Wielinga, B., Worring, M.: Adding Spatial Semantics to Image Annotations. In: Proceedings of the 4th International Workshop on Knowledge Markup and Semantic Annotation (2004)
6. Viana, W., Bringel, J., Gensel, J., Oliver, M.V., Hervé, M.: PhotoMap: Annotations Spatio-Temporelles Automatiques de Photos Personnelles pour les Utilisateurs Nomades. SAGEO (2007)
7. Belaïd A. : Reconnaissance Automatique de l'Ecriture et du Document LORIA (2010), http://www.colisciences.net/pdf/reconnaissance.pdf
8. Reconnaissance de l'Ecriture Arabe pour l'Informatique, http://rimbaccar.unblog.fr/
9. European Project DEBORA, http://debora.enssib.fr/
10. Lebourgeois, F., Trinh, E., Allier, B., Eglin, V., Empotz, H.: Document Images Analysis Solutions for Digital Libraries. In: 1st International Workshop on Document Image Analysis for Libraries, DIAL 2004, pp. 2–24. IEEE Computer Society, Los Alamitos (2004)

11. Ketata, D., Khemakhem, M.: Un survol sur l'Analyse et la Reconnaissance de Documents: Imprimé. In: Ancien et Manuscrit, Colloque International Francophone sur l'écrit et le document, CIFED (2010)
12. Casey, R.G., Lecolinet, E.: A Survey of Methods and Strategies in Character Segmentation. IEEE Transactions on Pattern Analysis and Machine Intelligence 18(7) (July 1996)
13. Lu, Y.: Machine Printed Character Segmentation-An Overview. Pattern Recognition 28(1) (1995)
14. BenMessaoud, I., ElAbed, H.: Vers un Système d'Annotation Automatique de Documents Historiques basé sur les Techniques des Modèles Markoviens. In: Colloque International Francophone sur l'écrit et le document, CIFED (2010)
15. Chevalier, S.: Reconnaissance d'Ecriture Manuscrite par des Techniques Markoviennes: une Approche Bidimensionnelle et Générique. Thèse de doctorat, Université René Descartes- Paris 5 (2004)
16. Lemaitre, M.: Approche Markovienne Bidimensionnelle d'Analyse et de Reconnaissance de Documents Manuscrits. Thèse de doctorat, Université de Paris 5 (2007)
17. Menasri, F.: Contributions à la Reconnaissance de l'Ecriture Arabe Manuscrite. Thèse de doctorat, Université paris Descartes (2008)
18. ACD Systems International Inc., http://www.acdsee.com
19. The World Wide Web Consortium (W3C), http://www.w3c.org
20. Official website of Protégé, http://protege.stanford.edu/

# Author Index